WRITING

A Journey

CANADIAN EDITION

WRITING

A Journey

CANADIAN EDITION

Lester Faigley
UNIVERSITY OF TEXAS AT AUSTIN

Melanie Rubens
SENECA COLLEGE

With contributions by

Rhonda Roth, Seneca College
Lynsay Ripley, Seneca College

Pearson Canada
Toronto

Library and Archives Canada Cataloguing in Publication

Faigley, Lester, 1947–
  Writing : a journey / Lester Faigley, Melanie Rubens. — Canadian ed.

U.S. ed. issued under title: Writing, a guide for college and beyond.
ISBN 978-0-321-55860-2

1. English language—Rhetoric. 2. Academic writing. 3. Critical thinking.
I. Rubens, Melanie, 1962– II. Title.

PE1408.F35 2010   808'.042   C2010-902145-2

ISBN 978-0-321-55860-2

Vice-President, Editorial Director: Gary Bennett
Editor-in-Chief: Ky Pruesse
Acquisitions Editor: David S. Le Gallais
Marketing Manager: Loula March
Senior Developmental Editor: Madhu Ranadive
Production Editor: Richard di Santo
Copy Editor: Nancy Mucklow
Proofreaders: Lisa Berland, Camille Isaacs
Production Coordinator: Avinash Chandra
Compositor: Nelson Gonzalez
Photo and Permissions Researcher: Sandy Cooke
Art Director: Julia Hall
Interior Designers: Stuart Jackman, Miguel Acevedo
Cover Designers: Stuart Jackman, Quinn Banting
Cover Images: Getty Images

For permission to reproduce copyrighted material, the publisher gratefully acknowledges the copyright holders listed on pages 642–643, which are considered an extension of this copyright page.

1 2 3 4 5   14 13 12 11 10

Printed and bound in the United States of America.

Brief Contents

PART 1
The Writer as Explorer

PART 2
The Writer as Guide

CONTENTS

CONTENTS

PART 3
The Writer as Researcher

PART 4
The Writer as Editor

Preface

It is sometimes difficult to convince students that good writing is a valuable skill to have. Many students associate learning how to write well with boring lectures, tedious assignments, and uninteresting textbooks. Unfortunately, students often feel disconnected from the process of writing because there is a lack of "personal relevance" for them. In the Canadian edition of *Writing: A Journey*, we have made currency and relevancy the guiding principles which will motivate and engage writers to find meaning in their work and will, hopefully, inspire them to further develop their own style. A textbook should be a catalyst for critical inquiry, provide global perspectives and be relevant to its users. This text offers instruction—both visually and textually—to encourage students to become better writers.

This book is written from these beliefs:

A guide to writing should be relevant to its readers.	The text should be relevant to a student writer's world, not a teacher's.
A guide to writing should be easy to use.	No matter where you open the book, the content on a particular page and the place of that content in the overall organization should be evident.
A guide to writing should show what readers and writers actually do.	Students learn best by seeing a process step-by-step, not by reading discussions of what they readers and writers do.
A guide to writing should be engaging.	Textbooks don't have to be dull. Furthermore, students learn faster and remember longer when a book is well designed.

Writing: A Journey is a Dorling Kindersley design. DK books are easy to use and handsome in presentation. Their visual format allows readers to find what they are looking for quickly and easily. They provide just the right amount of information in a stimulating format. In other words, DK books typically achieve what we, as writing teachers, hope our students might achieve—to produce high-quality and engaging writing.

DK books are accessible and inviting because they pay a great deal of attention to how words and images work together on the page. The designers at DK think hard about how design can improve learning. They are experts in taking something complicated and breaking it down into uncomplicated steps and elements. This expertise is essential to guide students through the complex processes of reading, writing, and researching in college and university.

Many writing teachers agree that the main goal of first year college and university writing courses is to engage in critical inquiry: thinking, reading, and writing.

It can be as simple as:

- What did you see? Read? (observation)
- What does it mean? (interpretation)
- Why is it important? (reflection)

Students should find, evaluate, analyze, and synthesize sources and integrate their ideas with those of others.

In addition, students should respond to different situations and the needs of different audiences, understand how genres shape reading and writing, and write in several genres through this type of critical inquiry.

While generating information through inquiry, students should develop flexible strategies for generating, revising, editing, and proofreading, and should understand how to collaborate effectively with others.

Students should learn the common formats for different kinds of texts, practise appropriate documentation, and control surface features of grammar, mechanics, and spelling.

Writing: A Journey helps students to achieve these goals by using a combination of concise, accessible instruction, visual explanations, plentiful examples, and appealing assignments and readings. Important concepts and processes are presented in concise, easy to navigate layouts, letting students see at a glance the key points they should master.

Key features in *Writing: A Journey*

Practical instruction on design and using visuals

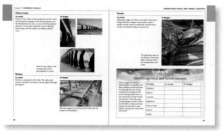

Concise chapters on design and using visuals are included in Part 1, which encourage students to think of design and images as relevant to the "end product" and offer practical advice for making design and visuals part of the composing process.

Process guides

When students internalize an overview of the process of writing, they are better able to monitor what they need to do to produce successful writing. The writing guides in each of the eight chapters in Part 2 are designed as "Process Maps" to give a visual organization. Students first see an overview of how to write in each of the eight major "aims," and then the process is presented in detail with specific strategies for invention, drafting and revising, all with reference to the process as a whole.

Writers at work

Even though strategies can guide the process of writing, the process is nevertheless messy, and working on any significant piece of writing nearly always involves going back and forth among activities. The "Writer at work" sections in Part 2 show examples of student writers working through the whole creative process of writing. These examples demonstrate how strategies of invention can produce the necessary raw material that leads to a manageable topic, and how strategies for revision can focus and develop a writer's ideas. "Staying on Track" boxes focus on common writing problems and give students concrete advice for how to avoid such problems.

Dynamic readings

The experience of stimulating reading inspires good writing. In this first Canadian edition, readings have been selected from a variety of media that include academic, professional, and personal sources. They vary in length, in type and in most certainly in subject matter. Some are controversial, but all are accessible and relevant to a Canadian audience. Most reading selections are designed to look like original publications (an editorial looks like a page from a newspaper, a Web article looks like a Web page), reminding students of the original context and the importance of design and visual elements.

Engaging writing projects

More and more, college and university students are expected to be able to write in different genres as well as for different purposes. Furthermore, it seems that students better grasp the conventions of the academic essay if they have opportunities to write in more than one genre. The "Projects" that conclude the eight aims chapters in Part 2 offer a variety of assignments, ranging from essays to a field observation paper, a profile, a film review, and a position argument. Eleven student papers, all with sources and citations and many with images, give students realistic, accurate models to learn from.

Guides for researching

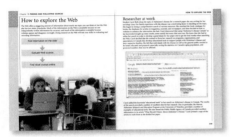

One of the more complex processes associated with student writing is the ability to accurately research and document external sources. Students often learn these skills by seeing concrete examples. In Part 3, the "Researcher at work" feature shows students complete assignments by using the strategies given in the chapters, including avoiding plagiarism, evaluating sources, and using the Internet as a research tool. Documentation guidelines for MLA and APA styles are provided in Chapters 20 and 21 as well as model research papers in both formats. These chapters feature several visual "source samples," which show students how to find the essential information needed to put together a citation.

Guides for style and editing

Part 4 offers guides for style and editing with summary checklists.

Resources for teachers and students

An *Instructor's Manual* will be available to instructors who have adopted this book. The *Instructor's Manual* offers detailed chapter-by-chapter suggestions to help both new and experienced instructors. For every chapter in the student text, this manual includes chapter goals and chapter challenges, suggestions for different ways to use the textbook's assignments and boxed tips, additional activities and resources, and more. Finally, the manual offers suggested syllabi and ideas for teaching students with different learning styles.

MyCanadianCompLab

(www.mycanadiancomplab.ca) is a state-of-the-art interactive and instructive solution designed to help students to meet the challenges of their writing courses and assist students in all their future writing. MyCanadianCompLab provides access to a wealth of resources all geared to meet your learning needs. See the opening pages of this text for details.

MyCanadianComp Lab will give you access to the Pearson eText. The eText gives students access to the text whenever and wherever they have access to the Internet. eText pages look exactly like the printed text, offering powerful new functionality for students and instructors. Users can create notes, highlight text in different colours, create bookmarks, zoom, click hyperlinked words and phrases to view definitions (where available), and view in single-page or two-page view.

A student access card for MyCanadianCompLab is packaged with every new copy of the text. Access codes can also be purchased through campus bookstores or through the website.

CourseSmart for Instructors

CourseSmart goes beyond traditional expectations—providing instant, online access to the textbooks and course materials you need at a lower cost for students. And even as students save money, you can save time and hassle with a digital eTextbook that allows you to search for the most relevant content at the very moment you need it. Whether it's evaluating textbooks or creating lecture notes to help students with difficult concepts, CourseSmart can make life a little easier. See how when you visit www.coursesmart.com/instructors.

CourseSmart for Students

CourseSmart goes beyond traditional expectations—providing instant, online access to the textbooks and course materials you need at an average savings of 50%. With instant access from any computer and the ability to search your text, you'll find the content you need quickly, no matter where you are. And with online tools like highlighting and note-taking, you can save time and study efficiently. See all the benefits at www.coursesmart.com/students.

Technology Specialists

Pearson's Technology Specialists work with faculty and campus course designers to ensure that Pearson technology products, assessment tools, and online course materials are tailored to meet your specific needs. This highly qualified team is dedicated to helping schools take full advantage of a wide range of educational resources, by assisting in the integration of a variety of instructional materials and media formats. Your local Pearson Education sales representative can provide you with more details on this service program.

Acknowledgments for the US Edition

It takes a village to create a book, and for this book the village was global, relying on daily collaboration with my co-creators in London, New York, New Jersey, Massachusetts, Maine, and here at home in Austin. The list of people to thank is long. I'll begin with Lynn Huddon, executive editor for Longman Publishers, with whom I have written seven previous books and editions and whom I have come to know as one of the best in her profession. Lynn is an extraordinarily talented editor, and this book results from those talents: her vision of taking a radical new approach to a guide for writing, her managerial ability in assembling and organizing a diverse group of people, and her editorial skills and attention to detail. I told her at the outset that I would not attempt to write this book with anyone else because it seemed way too ambitious for the time we allowed ourselves, but I knew that if she began the project, she would do everything necessary to make it happen. My development editor, Katharine Glynn, has been a delight to write with because she is not only highly competent but also makes the process fun. She has kept stress to a minimum in what could have been a highly stressful project. And she too is one of the best at what she does.

Others at Longman who contributed their wisdom and experience include Roth Wilkofsky, president; Tim Stookesberry, vice president of marketing; Joseph Opiela, editorial director; Megan Galvin-Fak, executive marketing manager; Sandra McGuire, senior marketing manager; Laura Coaty, market research director; Donna Campion, senior supplements editor; Jenna Egan, media supplements editor; Mary Ellen Curley, director of development for English; Wendy Ann Fredericks, cover design manager; Rona Tuccillo, photo researcher; Bob Ginsberg, production manager; Michael Greer, development editor; and Nicole Solano, editorial assistant. At Pre-Press, two other excellent people whom I have enjoyed working with in the past guided the book into print: Melissa Mattson, production manager, and copy editor Elsa van Bergen. Margery Niblock compiled the index.

The process of writing this book has been unlike anything I have ever done before because the book was designed in London at Dorling Kindersley at the same time it was written in Austin, with megabytes of pixels crossing the Atlantic day and night. The experience of working with Stuart Jackman, design director of DK Education, was nothing short of magical. While writing this book, my first act of the morning, even before coffee, was to see what creative gifts Stuart had sent me overnight. Even more than his artistry, Stuart taught me a great deal about using effective design for learning. Sophie Mitchell, publisher for DK Education, also made editorial contributions and helped to initiate and keep the DK collaboration running smoothly.

I also benefited from collaborators in Austin, especially Susan "George" Schorn, who contributed ideas and her prose in many places in the first three parts of the book and has written the Instructor's Manual. Grace Bernhardt and Kelly Kessler also helped in the early stages. Russell Cobb created resources to accompany the e-Book version of this text. I cannot say enough about how much I have learned over the years from colleagues and students at the University of Texas, a few of whom are represented by their writing here. Colleagues across the country have also given me advice and encouragement by reviewing chapters, testing chapters in their classes, and participating in focus group. And special thanks go to the students who participated in the class tests and contributed their thinking to the book.

Finally, without my wife Linda's deep reserves of patience in putting up with a husband who becomes distracted and grumpy when he is writing, the book would never have been written.

Lester Faigley
University of Texas at Austin

Acknowledgments for the Canadian Edition

Dedicated in loving memory of John Rubens.

Writing a book is not an individual project, but a collaborative one. I would like to thank the editorial and creative teams at Pearson for their invaluable input and professionalism and add a special thanks to Madhu Ranadive for her infinite patience and David Le Gallais for his support. Finally, a note of gratitude to Frances and Gaye for their perspectives and encouragement throughout this journey.

I would also like to acknowledge the following reviewers:

Sue Adams, *Sheridan Institute of Technology*; Trevor Arkell, *Humber College*; Kathryn Brillinger, *Conestoga College*; Greg Chan, *Kwantlen University College*; Brent Cotton, *Georgian College*; Chandra Hodgson, *Humber College*; Moira Langley, *Kwantlen University College*; Tatiana Mitchell, *Seneca College*; Patricia Morgan, *Humber College*; Cynthia Rowland, *Algonquin College*; and Marena Walkowiak, *George Brown College*.

Melanie Rubens
Seneca College

WRITING

A Journey

CANADIAN EDITION

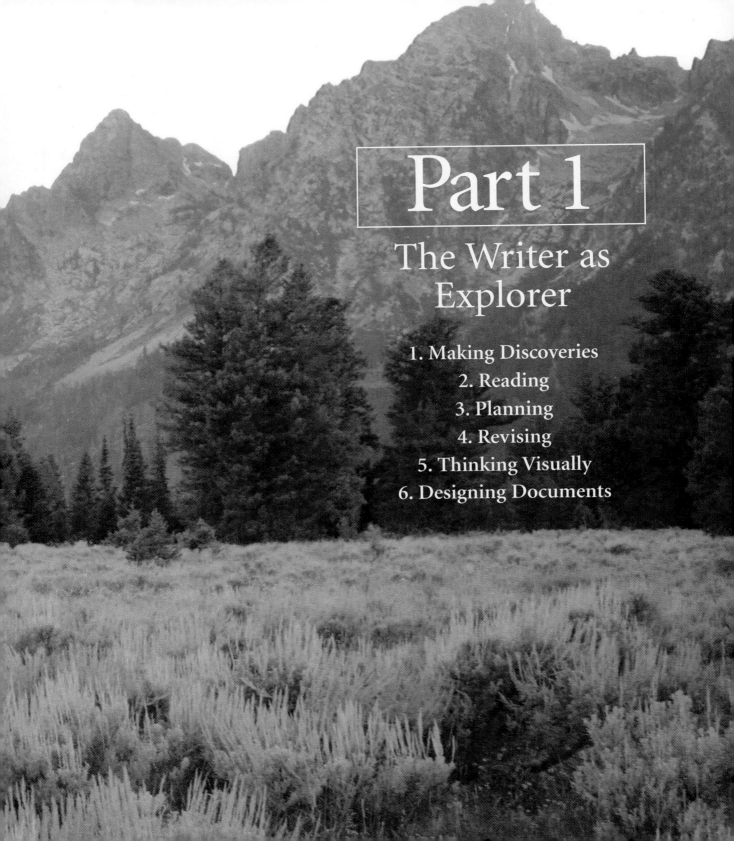

Part 1

The Writer as Explorer

1
Making Discoveries

Go outside. Don't plan where to go. Wander toward nothing in particular. Walk slowly. Pause often. Look up. Look down. Widen your field of vision. Shield your eyes with your hands and look as far as you can see in the distance. No matter how familiar you are with the place, you'll see something that you have never seen before.

Look with new eyes

Walk long enough so you forget about what is most pressing at the moment. Look for secrets that no one else sees. The dance of light in the canopy of a tree. A second-storey cornice on a building. The clarity of reflections in dark puddles. The faint outline of a chalk drawing on the sidewalk. The date stamped on a fire hydrant. The dark blue of a distant slope dotted with blue-green trees.

Take in the sounds. What can you hear besides human-made noises? Even in the middle of a city you may hear birds claiming territories. Listen to the sounds wind makes. Take in the smells. Close your eyes and focus. You can distinguish different smells. Feel the leaves on different plants. Touch the trunks of trees. The world is full of distinct textures.

Explore the world

Ralph Waldo Emerson observed that "the writer is an explorer. Every step is an advance into a new land." Walking in a strange city or hiking in a forest for the first time is exciting because each step reveals something new. But you can experience the same excitement in places you know well if you see them with new eyes.

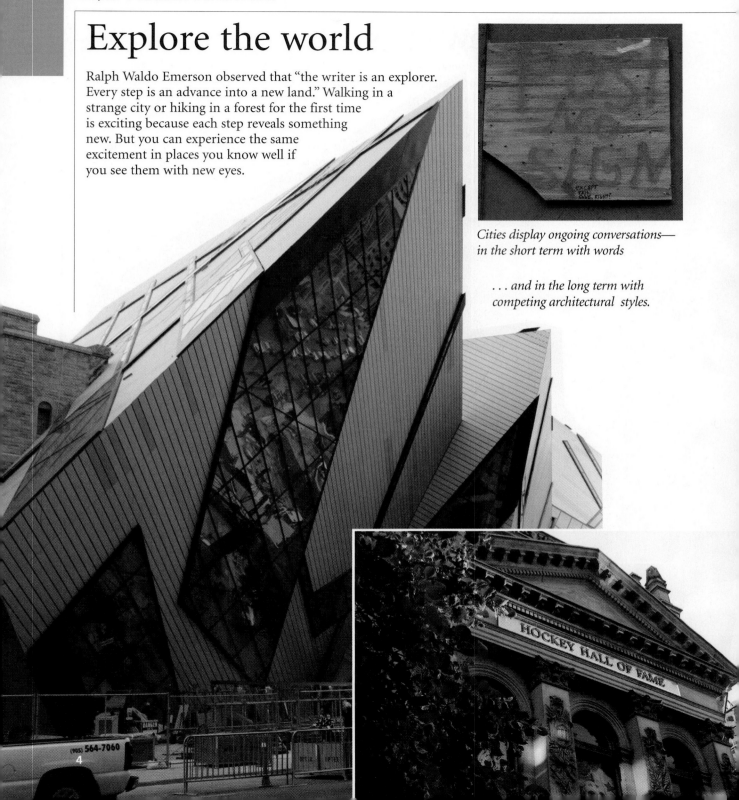

Cities display ongoing conversations—in the short term with words

. . . and in the long term with competing architectural styles.

Nearly forty million vehicles pass over the Golden Gate Bridge in California each year. But only those people who walk or bike across the bridge can appreciate many of its splendid details.

WRITE NOW

Discovering history

Go to the oldest part of your city or town. Take a notebook with you. Your assignment is to learn as much as you can about the history of particular buildings from observing. For some buildings with visible signs of their past, it will be easy to find their history. But for others you will have to dig deeper. Small details give clues. For example, between 1900 and 1950, experts believed that green paint had a calming effect. The interiors of hospitals, asylums, schools, government buildings, and even kitchens in houses were painted the same shade of light green. Look closely at the colours under peeling paint. (Remember that old paint is often lead-based and hazardous to small children.)

If your town has old railroad tracks, walk along them. Before the automobile became dominant, towns were organized around railroads. Look for evidence such as the concrete foundation of a loading dock torn down long ago. If you live in a newer suburban environment, take a close look at strip malls, which typically have a high turnover of businesses. Often you can find traces of earlier occupants.

Describe three details about three buildings (or about one building if you can identify separate details) or other manufactured structures as precisely as you can. Give their exact location. Then write what you can infer about the history of each building or object from the details.

Find a territory

Writers begin by exploring. When they start writing, exploration doesn't stop. Once they start, writers find things they could not have imagined. Where writers end up is often far away from where they thought they were going.

Most writing in college and university concerns exploration because academic disciplines seek to create new knowledge and to rethink what is known. Colleges and universities bring together people who ask interesting questions: How does recent archaeological evidence change our understanding of Homer's *Iliad* and *Odyssey*? Why does eyesight deteriorate with age? How do volcanoes affect the world climate? How do chameleons regenerate lost body parts? How do Rousseau's ideas about nature continue to shape notions about wilderness? How do electric eels generate voltage and not get shocked in the process? How can a poll of a thousand people represent 33 million Canadians with only a 4% margin of error?

Writers in colleges and universities respond to these questions and many others. They challenge old answers and contribute new answers. Readers of college writing expect to learn something when they read—new knowledge, a fresh interpretation, another point of view that they had not considered.

At first glance the expectations of college writing seem impossible. How can you as a student expect to contribute new knowledge? But just as there is a great deal that maps do not show, you can find many uncertainties, controversies, and unresolved problems in any field of study. You just have to ask the right questions.

Ask interesting questions

Good questions can take you to places that will interest you and your readers alike.

- Focus on an area you don't know and want to know more about.

- Find out where experts disagree. What exactly is the source of the disagreement? Why do they come to different conclusions using the same evidence?

- Analyze explanations of current trends and events. What possible causes might be left out?

- Examine proposals to solve problems. Does the solution fix the problem? Will people support the solution if it costs them effort or money?

- Compare what people claim and the reality. Often people (especially politicians) represent things and their role in making them as much better than they actually are.

Determine what do you want to accomplish

Writers, like explorers, start with what they think they want to accomplish. Often the assignment will contain key words such as *analyze, argue, describe, evaluate, propose, reflect,* and *report* that will assist you in determining what direction to take.

Analyze	Find connections among a set of facts, events, or readings and make them meaningful (see Chapters 12 and 13).
Argue	Convince others to accept or reject a particular position (see Chapters 15 and 16).
Describe	Observe details carefully and select details that create a dominant impression (see Chapter 9).
Evaluate	Argue that something is good, bad, best, or worst in its class according to criteria that you set out (see Chapter 14).

Propose	Identify a particular problem and explain why your solution is the best one (see Chapter 15).
Reflect	Narrate personal experience and personal insights (see Chapter 10).
Report	Organize and communicate information (see Chapter 11).

A specific audience might be mentioned in the assignment. If you are writing for a specific audience, what will those readers know about your topic? What will they likely have read about your topic? What attitudes are they likely to have about your topic?

Use strategies for finding a topic

Sometimes your instructor will assign a topic, but sometimes you will have to come up with your own topic. Look first at material from your course. You might find a topic to explore from the readings or from class discussion.

Start with what interests you. It's hard to write about topics that you care little about. If your assignment gives you a range of options, make more than one list.

Personal	1. History of anime in Japan 2. Cave exploration and conservation 3. Learning to windsurf
CAMPUS	1. Pros and cons of computer fees 2. Excessive litter on campus 3. Fellowships for study-abroad programs
COMMUNITY	1. Safe bicycle commuting 2. Bilingual education programs 3. Better public transportation
NATION/WORLD	1. Advertising aimed at preschool children 2. Censorship of the Internet 3. Genetically altered crops

WRITE NOW

Mapping your campus

Your campus likely has an information desk for students and visitors. Information centres typically will have several brochures with maps. Visit the information desk and collect everything that includes a map. Then compare the maps. Make a checklist for what the maps show and don't show (building names, streets, shuttle bus routes, bicycle routes, parking, landmarks, hotels, and more).

Create a map for new students on your campus that contains insider knowledge that would not appear on the maps your school produces. For example, where can you find the best burger on or close to campus? The best cup of coffee or cookies? A quiet place to study? A great place to meet friends? Make a list of places that need to be included on your map. Then draw the map.

Take inventory when you have a topic

A good way to begin writing about a subject is to take inventory of what you know about it. The classic reporters' questions can assist you in thinking about it.

1. *Who* is doing it?
2. *What* is happening or at issue?
3. *When* is it happening?
4. *Where* is it happening?
5. *How* is it happening?
6. *Why* is it happening?

If you don't know the answers to all the questions, you'll know where to start looking.

DECLINE OF FROGS AND TOADS

<u>WHO?</u> Frogs and toads populations worldwide

<u>WHAT?</u> Declined by 50% according to scientists

<u>WHERE?</u> Worldwide but especially in the Americas

<u>WHEN?</u> Since 1950

<u>HOW?</u> Deadly skin infection for tropical frogs and toads; pesticides and pollution worldwide

<u>WHY?</u> (1) Frogs and toads breathe partially through their skin, making them more vulnerable to disease, pollution, and toxic chemicals.

(2) A tropical fungus that causes disease in frogs has spread because of climate change due to global warming.

Brainstorm

There is more than one way to get ideas for a topic. One way to determine what you are looking for is to brainstorm a list. For example, opposite is a list of observations and questions on lyme disease.

- A friend had lyme disease for a year and went to many doctors before it was diagnosed.

- Why is lyme disease hard to diagnose?

- Overpopulation of deer spreads lyme disease.

- Are deer the only animals that spread the ticks that transmit lyme disease?

- What methods can control the deer population in suburbs?

- How can you control ticks in yards?

Freewrite

Another way to find out how much you know about a topic is to freewrite—write nonstop.

1. Put a tentative topic at the top of the page. Then write as fast as you can for five to ten minutes.

2. Don't stop to correct mistakes. Let your ideas flow wherever they take you, even if they take you well outside the boundaries of your topic. The idea is that the constant flow of words will generate ideas—some useful, and some not.

3. If you get stuck, write the same sentence over again, or write about how hungry you are or how hard it is to write. Thoughts will eventually start reappearing.

4. After you've finished, read what you have written and underline any key ideas.

5. Select one of the ideas and put it at the top of the page. Then write nonstop again for five to ten minutes.

Use guides

Writers can take advantage of guides developed by libraries or online academic resource sites. Your library's online subject catalogues often divide big subjects into smaller and more manageable ones. For example, if you type "nanotechnology" into the subject search window in your online catalogue, you likely will get results similar to those below.

A subject search for "nanotechnology" in a library's online catalogue generates a list of subtopics that may point to a manageable, specific topic.

Online subject directories including Google's search engine provide lists of links on particular subjects.

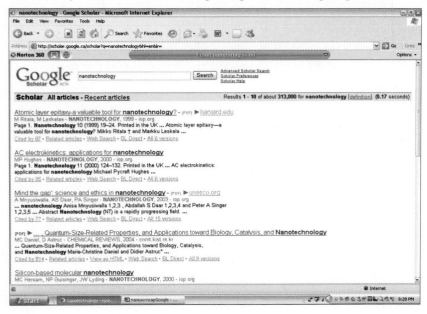

Google's search engine provides links to online sources for "nanotechnology." An additional tool of the search engine, Google Scholar provides a search of scholarly literature, including abstracts, academic journals, and articles for "nanotechnology."

Mind Mapping

First, start with the general subject you plan to write about. State it in a few words. Draw a box around it.

Obesity in children

Second, think about what can be said about this topic. At this point you don't want specifics but general categories.

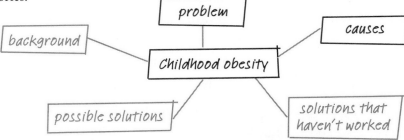

Third, generate topics about each category based on your assignment question.

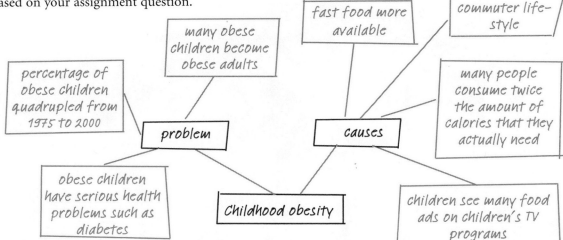

The process continues until the topics become specific.

When you finish the mind map, look at how it might be translated into writing. You probably don't want to include everything that is in the map. Get a coloured marker and put a line around the parts about which you intend to write.

2

Reading

Along with learning to write well, learning to think critically is the most important skill you will gain in college and university because your success in your professional and public life will depend on it. Becoming a better critical thinker will help you to become a better writer because you will understand subjects in greater complexity and you will be better able to evaluate, revise, and edit what you write.

Become a critical reader

Critical thinking begins with critical reading. For most of what you read, one time is not enough. Skim it once to get an overall idea of the point. Scan it again for more specific detail. Finally, read it through for comprehension. Write notes as you read. When you start asking questions about what you are reading, you are engaging in critical reading, which reading is a four-part process. First, begin by asking where a piece of writing came from and why it was written. Second, read the text carefully to find the author's central claim (thesis) and the major points. Third, decide if you can trust the author. Fourth, read the text again to understand how it works.

1. Where did it come from?

- Who wrote this material?
- Where and when did it first appear? In a book, newspaper, magazine, or online in a blog?
- What else has been written about the topic or issue?
- What do you expect after reading the title?

2. What does it say?

- What is the topic or issue?
- What is the writer's claim or main point?
- What reasons or evidence does the writer offer?
- Who is the intended audience? What does the writer assume the readers know and believe?

3. Can you trust the writer?

- Does the writer have the necessary knowledge and experience to write on this subject?
- Do you detect a bias in the writer's argument or position?
- Are the facts relevant to the writer's claims?
- Can you trust the writer's facts? Where did the facts come from?
- Does the writer acknowledge opposing views and unfavourable evidence? Does the writer deal fairly with opposing views?

4. How does it work?

- How is the piece of writing organized? How are the major points arranged?
- How does the writer conclude? Does the conclusion follow from the evidence the writer offers? What impression does the writer create?
- How would you characterize the style? Describe the language that the writer uses.
- How does the writer represent herself or himself?

WRITE NOW

Analyze information for students on your campus

No doubt your school mailed you a great deal of information when you were admitted. Schools continue to distribute information to students when they get to campus. You can find informative brochures and flyers at your school's student services building and in the health centre.

Pick one of the brochures or flyers to analyze. Remember that you are the intended audience.

Write a one-page evaluation of the effectiveness or ineffectiveness of the brochure or flyer for a prospective student audience. If it is ineffective, what changes need to be made to make it effective? If it works, what does it do well?

13

Look with a critical eye

Critical viewing, like critical reading, requires thinking about where the image or visual came from. Begin by asking the following:

- What kind of an image or visual is it?

- Who created this image (movie, advertisement, television program, and so on)?

- What is it about? What is portrayed in the image?

- Where did it first appear? Where do you usually find images like this one?

- When did it appear?

The Pharaoh Menkaure (Mycerinus) and his queen, Giza, Old Kingdom, 2548–2530 BCE. One of the finest statues from ancient Egypt depicts a royal couple. Compare the statue to formal portraits of famous couples today. Why does the queen have one arm around his waist and the other touching the king's arm? Do you think it depicts how they looked in real life? Or how they might have wanted to look in the afterlife? How do you think people in ancient Egypt might have viewed this statue?

The following questions are primarily for still images. For animations, movies, and television, you also have to ask questions about how the story is being told and what is being represented in the images you see.

- What attracts your eye first? If there is an attention-grabbing element, how does it connect with the rest of the image?

- What impression of the subject does the image create?

- How does the image appeal to the values of the audience? (For example, politicians love to be photographed with children because it makes them appear more like their constituents.)

- How does the image relate to what surrounds it?

- Was it intended to serve purposes besides art and entertainment?

- Have computer graphics been used to enhance or manipulate the image in a way that is unnatural?

Arthur Rothstein made this photograph of black clouds of dust rising over the Texas Panhandle in March 1936. Look closely at the photo. What attracts your eye first? Snapshots usually put the horizon line in the center. Why did Rothstein put the horizon at the bottom? What impression does this photo convey to you?

WORKING TOGETHER

Analyze ads

Ads are used to sell or promote something through the use of images and text. Often, ads include subliminal messages that are designed to appeal to a consumer on a subconscious level. Find an ad for a well-known product or cause and bring a hardcopy (or screen capture) to class.

Answer these questions:

1. What is the purpose of the ad? Is it explicit?

2. Who is the intended audience? How do you know this? (What elements of the ad identify the target audience?)

3. Are there people (or animals) in the ad? Describe their appearance. Consider factors such as age, sex, race, ethnicity, body shape and body language, clothes, occupation, and relationships.

4. What is going on in the advertisement? What significance does this action have?

5. What are the basic themes? What is the advertisement about? (For example, the plot may involve two women in the same outfit, and the theme may be competition.)

6. What symbols or signs appear in the ad? How do they relate to the product or cause being advertised? In other words, do they provoke emotions for the product or cause? How?

7. How is language used in the ad? What devices are used to elicit an emotional response? Metaphor? Repetition? Alliteration? Comparison? Innuendo?

8. What political, economic, social, and cultural attitudes are reflected in the ads? Sexism? Ageism? Lookism? Alienation? Altruism? Conflict? Desire? Elitism?

9. What information do you need to make sense of the ad? Does it suggest certain beliefs? Does it reflect a certain lifestyle? Does it assume prior knowledge on the part of a person looking at the advertisement?

Organize in groups of three or four students. Exchange the ads and answer the same questions for your group's ads.

When you are finished, compare your answers for each ad. Discuss differences in your answers.

Read actively

If you own what you are reading, read with a pencil in hand. Pens and highlighters don't erase, and often you don't remember why you highlighted a particular sentence. It is sometimes better to use a notebook or private blog to capture your thoughts. Writing in any form can help you remember what you are reading.

Annotate what you read

Using annotating strategies will make your effort more rewarding.

Mark major points and key concepts	Sometimes major points are indicated by headings, but often you will need to locate them.
Connect passages	Notice how ideas connect to each other. Draw lines and arrows. If an idea connects to something a few pages before, write a note in the margin with the page number.
Ask questions	Note anything that puzzles you. Look up definitions for words you don't know as you go along.

Annotate difficult readings

Much of what you read in college or university will deal with unfamiliar concepts, which are often defined by other concepts. Annotating a difficult reading will help you understand the relationship of concepts, and the annotations will be valuable in remembering key points when you come back to the reading later. In this passage from John Heskett's *Toothpicks and Logos, Design in Everyday Life*, the author defines function in terms of two other concepts.

A more inclusive definition of function is needed, which can be opened up by breaking the concept of function into a twofold division: the key concepts of utility and significance.

definition of function – utility and significance

definition of utility

Utility can be defined as the quality of appropriateness in use. This means it is concerned with how things work, of the degree to which designs serve practical purposes and provide affordances or capabilities.

affordances? *? odd word – author is British*

example – kitchen knife

A simple example is a professional kitchen knife used to prepare food: its primary utility value is as a cutting tool. In order for it to work effectively, the blade needs to possess material qualities enabling a sharp edge to be maintained and for it to remain stable in use.

definition of significance

Significance as a concept in design, explains how forms assume meaning in the ways they are used, or the roles and meaning assigned them, often becoming powerful symbols or icons in patterns of habit and ritual. In contrast to the emphasis on efficiency, significance has more to do with expression and meaning.

other examples: computer keyboard, pencil, traffic light

It is possible to find designs of many kinds defined solely in terms of utility or significance. Many examples of the former are products related to the performance of professional services, tools with highly specific purposes, such as a hand saw or a lathe, or medical equipment, such as an ultrasound machine. Where information has to perform a highly specific task, as in a railway timetable, the layout and type forms should be clean, simple, and directed wholly to imparting essential facts. A primary condition of utilitarian design is that it must effectively execute or support certain tasks. In contrast, a piece of jewellery, a porcelain figurine, or a frame for a family photograph has no such specific purpose—instead its purpose can be described in terms of contemplative pleasure or adornment.

examples of designs for utility

examples of designs for significance

Map what you read

Drawing a map of a text can help you to identify key points and understand the relationships of concepts.

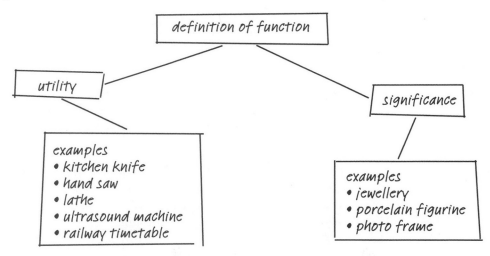

Make notes

Write down your thoughts as you read. Often you will find that something you read reminds you of something else. Jot that down. It might give you ideas for writing. Think about what impresses as you read. And think about what else you might read if you want to write about this subject.

Recognize fallacies

Reasoning depends less on proving a claim than it does on finding evidence for that claim that readers will accept as valid. Logical fallacies, or kinds of faulty reasoning patterns, reflect a failure to provide sufficient evidence for a claim made by the writer.

Fallacies of logic

Begging the question	*Politicians are inherently dishonest because no honest person would run for public office.* The fallacy of begging the question occurs when the claim is restated and passed off as evidence.
Either–or	*Either we eliminate the regulation of businesses or else profits will suffer.* The either–or fallacy suggests that there are only two choices in a complex situation. Rarely, if ever, is this the case. (In this example, the writer ignores the fact that Enron was unregulated and went bankrupt.)
Hasty generalization	*We have been in a drought for three years; that's a sure sign of climate change.* A hasty generalization is a broad claim made on the basis of a few occurrences. Climate cycles occur regularly over spans of a few years; climate trends must be observed over centuries.
Non sequitur	*A university that can raise a billion dollars from alumni should not have to raise tuition.* A *non sequitur* (which is a Latin term meaning "it does not follow") ties together two unrelated ideas. In this case, the argument fails to recognize that the money for capital campaigns is often donated for special purposes such as athletic facilities and is not part of a university's general revenue.
Oversimplification	*No one would run stop signs if we had a mandatory death penalty for doing it.* This claim may be true, but the argument would be unacceptable to most citizens. More complex, if less definitive, solutions are called for.
***Post hoc* fallacy**	*The stock market goes down when the AFC wins the Super Bowl in even years.* The *post hoc* fallacy (from the Latin *post hoc ergo hoc*, which means "after this, therefore this") assumes that things that follow in time have a causal relationship.
Rationalization	*I could have finished my paper on time if my printer had been working.* People frequently come up with excuses and weak explanations for their own and others' behaviour that often avoid actual causes.

Slippery slope	*If we decriminalize medical marijuana, then before long, everyone will be shooting up heroin on the street corners.* The slippery slope fallacy maintains that one thing inevitably causes something else (more serious) to happen.

Fallacies of emotion and language

Bandwagon appeals	*It doesn't matter if I copy a paper off the Web because everyone else does.* This argument suggests that everyone is doing it, so why shouldn't you? But on close examination, it may be that everyone really isn't doing it—and in any case, it may not be the right thing to do.
Name calling	Name calling is frequent in politics and among competing groups (*radical, terrorist, racist, fascist, separatist*). Unless these terms are carefully defined, they are meaningless.
Polarization	*All environmentalists are radicals.* Polarization, like name-calling, exaggerates positions and groups by representing them as extreme and divisive.
Straw man	*Environmentalists won't be satisfied until nobody is ever allowed to cut down a tree.* A straw man argument is a diversionary tactic that sets up another's position in a way that can be easily rejected. In fact, only a small percentage of environmentalists would make an argument even close to this one.

WRITE NOW

Analyze fallacies in opinion writing

Examine writing that expresses opinions: blogs, discussion boards, editorials, advocacy websites, letters to the editor, or editorial pages of a local/national newspaper. Critically examine the opinion and identify any possible fallacies.

Select the example that has the clearest fallacy. Explain (in writing) the cause of the fallacy.

Respond as a reader

Engage in a dialogue with what you read. Talk back to the author. Role-play with another student to get more ideas about what the writer is trying to say. If you are having trouble understanding a difficult section, read it aloud and listen to the author's voice. Hearing something read will sometimes help you to imagine being in a conversation with the author.

Make notes

As you read, write down your thoughts. Something you read may remind you of something else. Jot that down, too.

- Imagine that the author is with you. What points does the writer make that you would respond to in person?

- What questions would you have of the author? These indicate what you might need to look up.

- What ideas do you find that you might develop or interpret differently?

Write summaries

When you summarize, you state the major ideas of an entire source or part of a source in your own words. Most summaries are much shorter than the original because they include just the main points, not most of the examples and supporting material. The keys to writing a good summary are identify-ing the main points and then putting those points into your own words. If you use words from the source, you have to put those words in quotation marks. Provide a parenthetical (in-text) citation directly after the quoted material. See Chapters 20 and 21 for more information about citing sources.

John Heskett argues that the concept of function in design should be understood in terms of "utility" and "significance." He defines utility as the degree to which a design accomplishes its purpose, such as how well a knife cuts. Significance is defined as the degree to which an object is designed to give pleasure or create meaning. A piece of art is an example of something designed exclusively for significance.

Build on what you read

Keeping a reading journal is a good practice for a writer. You'll have a record of your thoughts as you read that you can return to later. Writing helps you comprehend difficult or lengthy readings with more clarity. Often you can connect different ideas from different readings. A reading journal is a great place to test ideas that you can later develop for a writing assignment.

Heskett says, "It is possible to find designs of many kinds defined solely in terms of utility and significance." I'll grant the distinction, but his examples suggest that most things have elements of both.

He uses tools as objects designed strictly for utility, but look at a tool catalogue and you'll see lots of bright colours and handsome cases. He uses a photograph frame as an example of significance. True enough that frames are often decorative, but a frame also has to fit the picture. The frame should use non-glare glass to reduce reflected light. A frame has to do more than just look good.

But a bigger point is that anything can have significance for a particular person. I have my grandfather's hammer. It is nearly worthless because the handle is so old and worn that it would snap if you swung it hard against a nail. I took the hammer to work one day to hang a picture, and shortly afterward it disappeared. I searched and couldn't find it. I forgot about it, but then I noticed it in a storeroom months later and recovered it.

3

Planning

How often do you find yourself lost in buildings on your campus? In some buildings, you feel comfortable and at ease right away. But in others you always feel disoriented, even after you memorize the route to your classroom. The rooms may be fine once you are in them. The problem is the layout or plan of the building.

A disorienting building lacks central spaces and signs. Directions are missing at intersections. All the hallways look alike.

Determine your direction

Poorly organized writing is like a poorly designed building. It takes too much effort to get to where you want to go. Effective writing keeps readers oriented. Writing that succeeds is organized around a central idea, much as successful buildings and even thriving neighbourhoods are.

Identify your centre

Often the challenge in writing is finding the centre that connects your sentences and paragraphs. Probably you have had the experience of driving around looking for a store or a house without having the address. Unless you were lucky, it was probably frustrating. Knowing your centre is like having an address. It makes the journey far easier.

Choosing a big topic, such as privacy, is like knowing only the general area of where something is located.

BROAD TOPIC:
privacy and surveillance

SPECIFIC TOPIC:
Which public spaces should be under constant surveillance with micro-devices invisible to the human eye?

Think about where you are headed

Writing is a dynamic activity that goes back and forth between your mind and the page. It involves many stages of thinking, writing, revising, and editing. Nevertheless, having an overall strategy will allow your thinking to evolve into writing that communicates with your readers.

Read your assignment again. Often the assignment will tell you in which direction to go.

Reflect

You will need to think about an idea or concept in terms of your own history and life experience (see Chapter 10).

Describe

Often you will need to visit a site, observe details, and make notes, which you will later use to write a description (see Chapter 9).

Inform

You will need to report information or explain a concept or idea (see Chapter 11).

Analyze

You will need to interpret a text or a set of data to find connections and reach conclusions (see Chapter 12).

Analyze causes

You will need to identify probable causes of a trend or phenomenon and give evidence for your analysis (see Chapter 13).

Evaluate

You will need to determine whether something is good or bad based on criteria that you identify (see Chapter 14).

Argue

You will need to take a position on an issue or propose a course of action (see Chapters 15 and 16).

Why write?

Writing is a tool that allows you to explore what you think and to communicate those ideas in a coherent, organized way. All writing has a purpose—for example, journals, blogs, and social networking sites can be forums to express personal opinion or examine personal experiences; narratives can provide entertainment; and even shopping lists serve a purpose by identifying needed items. Regardless of its form, writing is an important means of communication.

Write a thesis

Write a thesis statement

Central ideas in writing are often expressed in a thesis statement. This statement, traditionally found at the beginning of an academic paper, presents your argument (your position on a topic) in a clear, definitive way.

Thesis statements that simply announce your intention (e.g., "In my paper, I am going to discuss privacy") or just state a fact (e.g., "Privacy issues are invasions into someone's personal life") are not thesis statements.

Write a working thesis

Writing is a work in progress, meaning that as you research, write, and revise, your argument will evolve. As your content changes and your paper takes shape, you might need to refine your thesis. In addition, your thesis is also affected by the purpose of the assignment.

Describe

THESIS: An Amazon.ca account has a list of every book purchased dating back ten years, plus records of every item browsed but not bought. No wonder Amazon's recommendations of what a person likes are so uncannily accurate!

Analyze

THESIS: Understanding how the concept of privacy is legally defined is critical for strengthening privacy laws.

Inform

THESIS: Imagine an organization that compels its customers and clients to reveal vast amounts of personal data, including phone number, preferences, spouse's name, workplace, home address, personal assets, income level, and legal transactions—and then sells that data. This is exactly what many online companies today are doing.

Argue

THESIS: Unlike the government, online organizations and social networking sites have almost no restrictions on what information they collect or what they do with that information. Laws should be passed that make these organizations accountable for the misuse of personal information and allow people to have greater participation in how that information is used.

Evaluate

THESIS: Using personal consumer data to refuse service or offer inferior service to customers who likely will not spend much money is an example of the misuse of personal information.

Reflect

THESIS: Data profiling is the government's way of saying "We are watching you."

Analyze causes

THESIS: Many laws to protect privacy are on the books, but these laws are ineffective for the digital era because they were written to protect people from government spying and intrusion rather than from the collection and selling of personal information by companies.

Evaluate your working thesis

Ask yourself these questions about your working thesis.

1. Is it specific?
2. Is it manageable in terms of the assigned length and the amount of time you have?
3. Is it interesting to your intended readers?

Example 1

THESIS: Steroids are a problem in major league baseball.

- **Specific?** The thesis is too broad. What exactly is the problem? Is the problem the same now as it was a few years ago?
- **Manageable?** Because the thesis is not limited, it cannot be discussed adequately.
- **Interesting?** The topic is potentially interesting, but many people are aware that baseball players used steroids. How can you lead readers to think about the topic in a new way?

Example 1 revised

THESIS: Home run records from 1993 through 2004 should be placed in a special category because of the high use of steroids in major league baseball before testing began in 2004.

Example 2

THESIS: "Nanotechnology" refers to any technology that deals with particles measured in units of a nanometre, which is one billionth (10^{-9}) of a metre.

- **Specific?** The thesis is specific, but it is too narrow. It offers only a definition of nanotechnology.
- **Manageable?** The thesis states a fact.
- **Interesting?** Nanotechnology could be interesting if some of its potential effects are included.

Example 2 revised

THESIS: Nanotechnology may soon change concepts of social identity by making it possible for individuals to alter their physical appearances either through cosmetic surgery performed by nanorobots or changes in genetic sequences on chromosomes.

Plan your route

Experienced travellers have multiple strategies for getting to their destinations. Sometimes they have the route planned in advance and follow it exactly. In other cases, they know they have to be flexible, such as when you find traffic stopped and must take an alternate route. Experienced writers work in much the same way, using different strategies for different writing tasks.

Determine a plan

Get out your notes and all the information you have collected. You may find it helpful to write major points on sticky notes so you can move them around. If your topic is the effects of nanotechnology on the body, you might produce an organization plan similar to this one.

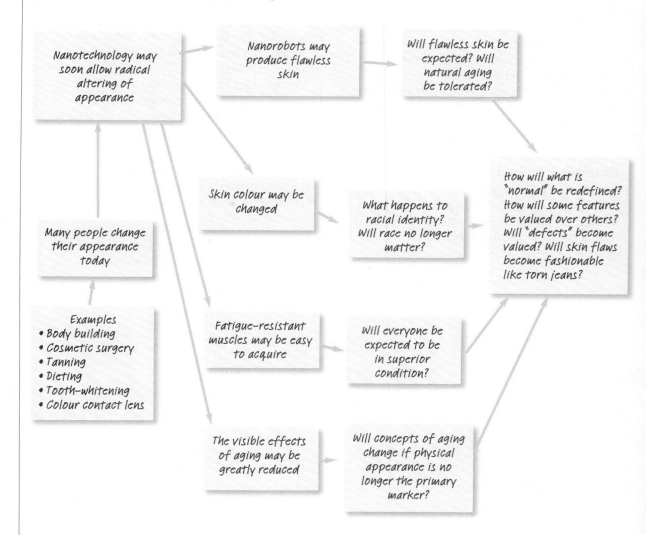

Make a writing plan

Writing plans often take the form of outlines, either formal outlines or working outlines.

A formal outline typically begins with the thesis statement, which anchors the entire outline.

THESIS: Nanotechnology may soon allow radical altering of the human body, which will have major social consequences.

I. Altering the appearance of the body has become common.
    A. Cosmetic surgery is now routine.
    B. Body building is popular.
    C. Most people are aware of diet and many attempt to control their weight.
    D. Tanning, changing eye colour, and tooth-whitening are common.

II. Nanotechnology may soon radically accelerate these trends.
    A. Nanorobots may produce flawless skin.
    B. Skin colour may be changed.
    C. Wrinkles and other signs of aging may be eliminated or reduced.
    D. Muscle tissue may be enhanced.

A working outline is a sketch of how you will arrange the major sections.

<u>Effects of nanotechnology on the body</u>

SECTION 1: Begin with how people change the appearance of their bodies today.

SECTION 2: Discuss how nanotechnology will accelerate these trends, giving people the potential for perfect skin, changing their skin colour, and reducing aging.

SECTION 3: Move to the questions these technologies raise, such as how aging will be perceived and how race will be understood.

SECTION 4: Raise the issue of how "normal" will be defined if people can choose how they look.

SECTION 5: Expand the idea of "normal" to who will control what is desirable and how social hierarchies might be changed or reinforced.

SECTION 6: End by connecting body issues to larger issues such as who gets to live for how long.

WRITE NOW

Make a plan

First, write a working thesis. Ask the questions on page 25.
- Is the thesis specific?
- Is it manageable?
- Is it interesting?

Revise your thesis if necessary.

Then use two of the three methods—a visual organization plan, a formal outline, or a working outline—to develop a plan for writing a paper based on the thesis. When you finish, compare the plans. Which will be easier to use for writing your paper?

4

Revising

When you return to a place after you have been away for some time, often you gain enough distance to "re-see" it in a totally different way. The same is true for writing. Skilled writers know that they have to revise several times to get the results they want. In order to revise effectively, they must "re-see," which, after all, is what revision means.

See again

Pretend you are someone who is either uninformed about your subject or else someone who is informed but is likely to disagree with you. If possible, think of an actual person and pretend to be that person. Read your draft aloud all the way through. Consider what that person might think of your arguments. When you read aloud, you often hear clunky phrases and catch errors, but do no more in this stage than put checks in the margins that you can return to later. You don't want to get bogged down with the little stuff. You want an overall sense of how well you accomplished what you set out to do. Finally, read the paragraphs in backwards order. This shows where the flow of ideas is disorganized or insufficiently developed.

Evaluate your first draft

Use these questions to evaluate your first draft. Note any places where you might make improvements.

Does your paper or project meet the assignment?

- Look again at your assignment and especially at the key words such as *analyze, define, evaluate,* and *propose.* Does your paper or project do what the assignment asks for? If not, how can you change it?
- Look again at the assignment for specific guidelines regarding length, format, and amount of research. Does your work meet these guidelines? If not, how can you change it?

Do you have a clear focus?

- Underline your thesis. Think how you might make it more precise.
- Underline the main idea of each paragraph. Does it occur at the beginning of the paragraph? Check how each paragraph connects to your thesis. Think about how you can strengthen the connections.

Are your main points adequately developed?

- Put parentheses around the reasons and evidence that support your main points.
- Can you find places to add more examples and details that would help to explain your main points?
- Have you integrated your quotations seamlessly into your work?

Is your organization effective?

- Make a quick outline of your draft if you have not done so already.
- Mark the places where you find abrupt shifts or gaps.
- Think about how you might rearrange sections or paragraphs to make your draft more effective.

Do you consider your potential readers' knowledge and points of view?

- Where do you give background if your readers are unfamiliar with your subject?
- Where do you acknowledge any opposing views your readers might have?

Do you represent yourself effectively?

- To the extent you can, forget for a moment that you wrote what you are reading. What impression do you have of you, the writer?
- Do you have an appropriate tone?
- Is your work visually effective? Have you selected an attractive and readable font? Used headings and illustrations where they are helpful?

When you finish, make a list of your goals in the revision. You may have to scrap some of the draft and start over, but you will have a better sense of your subject and your goals. Good writers sometimes prepare many drafts and revisions before they are satisfied with the final result.

Learn strategies for revising

Now it's time to go through your draft in detail. You should work on the goals you identify in your review. Also, look for other opportunities using this checklist.

1. Keep your audience in mind.	Reread each of your paragraphs' opening sentences and ask yourself whether they are engaging enough to keep your readers interested. Do they introduce the information discussed in the paragraph?
2. Sharpen your focus wherever possible.	You may have started out with a large topic but most of what you wrote concerns only one aspect. Do you need to revise your thesis and supporting paragraphs?
3. Check if key terms are adequately defined.	What are your key terms? Are they defined precisely enough to be meaningful?
4. Develop where necessary.	Do the key points and claims need more explanation and supporting evidence? Look for opportunities to add support without becoming redundant.
5. Check links between paragraphs.	Look for any place where you make abrupt shifts. Can you make the transitions better? Check if you have used transition words to signal the change from one paragraph to the next.
6. Consider your title.	Many writers don't think much about titles, but they are very important. A good title makes the reader want to read what you have written. Be as specific as you can in your title, and if possible, suggest your position.
7. Consider your introduction.	In the introduction, provide a strong and meaningful opening to establish a context for your argument and thesis.
8. Consider your conclusion.	Restating your thesis isn't the best way to finish; conclusions that offer only summary bore readers. The worst endings say something like "in my paper I've said this." Effective conclusions are interesting and provocative. While they conclude your argument, they also leave readers with something to think about.
9. Improve the visual aspects of your text.	Does the font you selected look attractive using your printer? Would headings and subheadings help to identify key sections? If you include statistical data, would charts be effective? Would illustrations help to establish key points?

Perform peer editing

Your instructor may ask you to respond to the drafts of your classmates. Responding to other people's writing requires the same careful attention you give to your own draft. To write a helpful response, you should go through the draft more than once.

First reading:
Read at your normal rate the first time through without stopping. When you finish you should have a clear sense of what the writer is trying to accomplish.

- Main idea: Write a sentence that summarizes what you think is the writer's main idea in the draft.
- Purpose: Write a sentence that summarizes what you think the writer was trying to accomplish in the draft.

Second reading:
In your second reading, you should be most concerned with the content, organization, and completeness of the draft. Make notes as you read.

- Introduction: Does the writer's first paragraph effectively introduce the topic and engage your interest?
- Thesis: Where exactly is the writer's thesis? Note in the margin where you think the thesis is located.
- Focus: Does the writer maintain focus on the thesis? Note any places where the writer seems to wander off to another topic.
- Organization: Are the sections and paragraphs ordered effectively? Do any paragraphs seem to be out of place? Do you note any abrupt shifts? Can you suggest a better order for the paragraphs?
- Completeness: Are there sections and paragraphs that lack key information or adequate development? Where do you want to know more?
- Sources: If the draft uses outside sources, are they cited accurately? If there are quotations, are they used correctly and worked into the fabric of the draft?
- Voice: Does the writer shift pronouns? "I" to "me" for example?

Third reading:
In your third reading, turn your attention to matters of audience, style, and tone.

- Audience: Who is the writer's intended audience? What does the writer assume the audience knows and believes?
- Style: Is the writer's style engaging? How would you describe the writer's voice?
- Tone: Is the tone appropriate for the writer's purpose and audience? Is the tone consistent throughout the draft? Are there places where another word or phrase might work better?

When you have finished the third reading, write a short paragraph on each bulleted item above, referring to specific paragraphs in the draft by number. Then end by answering these two questions:

1. **What does the writer do especially well in the draft?**

2. **What one or two things would most improve the draft in a revision?**

Pay attention to details

When you finish revising, you are ready for one final careful reading, keeping the goals of improving your style and eliminating errors in mind.

Edit for particular goals

1. Check the connections between sentences.	Notice how your sentences are connected. If you need to signal the relationship of one sentence to the next, use a transition word or phrase.
2. Check your sentences.	If you notice that a sentence doesn't sound right, think about how you might rephrase it. Often you will pick up problems by reading aloud. If a sentence seems too long, then you might break it into two or more sentences. If you notice a string of short sentences that sounds choppy, then you might combine them.
3. Check your paragraphs.	Review the first sentence of each paragraphs. Does it adequately present the main idea that follows? A topic sentence should clearly define the main point of the paragraph.
4. Eliminate wordiness.	Writers tend to introduce wordiness in drafts. Look for long expressions that can easily be shortened ("at this point in time" –> "now") and for unnecessary repetition. Remove unnecessary words like *very*, *really*, and *totally*.
5. Use active verbs.	Avoid forms of *be* (*is*, *are*, *was*, *were*) and verbs ending in *-ing*. Use strong verbs to make your style more lively. Sentences that begin with "This is" and "It is" often have better alternatives.

Proofread carefully

In your final pass through your text, eliminate errors and typos. To become an effective proofreader, you have to learn to slow down. Some writers find that moving from word to word with a pencil slows them down enough to find errors. Others read backwards to force concentration on each word.

1. Know what your spelling checker can and can't do.	Spelling checkers turn up many typos and misspellings that are hard to catch. But spelling checkers do not catch wrong words (e.g. "to much" should be "too much"), chopped endings ("three dog"), and similar errors.
2. Check for grammar and punctuation.	Nothing hurts your credibility more than leaving errors in what you write. Many job application letters get tossed in the reject pile because an applicant made a single, glaring error. Readers probably shouldn't make such harsh judgments when they find errors, but in real life they do.
3. Check for appropriate documentation.	Confirm that you have cited all material borrowed from external sources.

WRITE NOW

Write a helpful response

Read the following first draft and use the guidelines on page 31 to write a response that will help the writer revise the paper. Resist the urge to edit sentences and correct mechanical errors. The assignment asked the student to analyze an ad. The revised version of this paper is on pages 67–69.

Analysis of an Ad

In our modern world of today, we see thousands of advertisements every year, we buy many products because of ads. One of the products advertised a lot is milk. I chose an Andy Roddick ad for this assignment because he is my very favourite tennis player. There was another totally awesome milk ad with Stone Cold Steve Austin, but I couldn't find it.

I found the picture of Andy in Seventeen magazine. I don't read Seventeen any more, but my younger sister does, and I needed to find an ad. Andy looks totally cool in this photo. He was on the court with his tennis racquet. His milk mustache is visible to the eye.

I suppose the milk people wanted him because he is popular and good looking. The milk ads all have celebrities and sports stars. I read that the milk people were worried that younger people aren't drinking milk and they wanted young stars to pitch milk and praise it's benefits. I guess its working because the ad campaign has been around as long as I can remember. I've even heard copycats use slogans like "Got cookies?" "Got fish?" "Got fish?" "Got sports?" and even "Got Jesus?"

The Roddick ad probably works because Roddick is good looking. As I said before, the milk people like good looking stars. He has kind of a sexy pose too. He looks like a movie star.

In conclusion, the Andy Roddick ad is a good ad because young people like Andy Roddick. If they see Andy Roddick drinking milk, they want to drink milk to.

5
Thinking Visually

The principles of good design, like those of good writing, begin with your audience and what you are trying to accomplish.

Communicate with visuals and words

The word *writing* makes us think of words, yet in our daily experience reading newspapers, magazines, advertisements, posters, and signs, we find words combined with images and graphics. Similarly, the dominant visual media of our time—television and the Web—use words extensively. Think of the words in commercials or ads when you have the sound off and the running text across the bottom of the screen on news, sports, and financial programs. Understanding the relationships of words and visuals will make you a better writer.

What do visuals do best?

We've become accustomed to deciding whether we'll need to wear a sweater outside tomorrow by looking at the colours on a weather map. But even then, we depend on words to tell us whether the forecast is for today or tomorrow, and what each colour signifies. Visuals work well when they

- deliver spatial information, especially through maps, floor plans, and other graphic representations of space
- represent statistical relationships
- produce a strong immediate impact, even shock value
- emphasize a point made in words

What do words do best?

Words can do many things that images cannot. Written words work best when they

- communicate abstract ideas
- report information
- persuade using elaborated reasoning
- communicate online using minimal bandwidth

What can words and visuals do together?

Combining words and visuals allows writers to present very complex ideas, such as how atomic structure influences ionic bonding, and how the warming of oceans in the Arctic and Antarctic affects weather worldwide.

Understand visual and verbal concepts

We use many of the same terms to talk about texts with words and texts with visuals.

Emphasis

In words

Writers have many tools for creating emphasis, including headings, type size, boldfacing, italics, and other enhancements. Whatever comes at the beginning or the end receives more emphasis, whether it be a sentence, a paragraph, an essay, or a book.

In images

Emphasis is created by composition, by arranging elements so the attention goes where the designer wants it to go.

Balance

In words

People unconsciously expect balance, as when they move the knife to one side of the plate and the fork to the other. Balance in words can refer to parallelism, such as Caesar's famous words: *Veni, vidi, vici* (I came, I saw, I conquered). Balance can also mean that a writer presents more than one position on an issue.

In images

Balance in images is most often achieved by the placement of objects.

Contrast

In words

We often explain something unfamiliar by comparing and contrasting it to something more familiar. For example, a human's short-term memory is like a computer's random access memory in serving as an intermediate stop to long-term storage, but humans are far more limited than computers in capacity.

In images

Contrast is achieved with colour, size, shape, number, and position.

Repetition

In words

We expect certain elements to be repeated after they are announced in writing; for example, if there is a heading beginning with I, we expect to find a heading beginning with II later in the document.

In images

Architects use repetition to create visual patterns in buildings.

Point of view

In words

Point of view refers to the perspective of the writer: the first person singular *I*; the second person *you*; the third person *he, she, my cat*; or the first person plural *we*. It can also mean the writer is directly interacting with the subject or taking a distant view.

In images

Point of view refers to the vantage point of the photographer or artist.

Motion

In words

Motion is expressed with verbs. The train *sped, roared, whooshed, thundered, slowed, glided* through the station.

In images

Blurring suggests the motion of the train and the people on the platform.

Details

In words

Although images can show accurately what something looks like, images cannot tell us what it smells, sounds, tastes, or feels like. Furthermore, words can describe what we cannot see.

In images

The glistening moss on the shell of a red-eared slider indicates that it just emerged from the water.

WRITE NOW

Identifying visual and verbal concepts

Find a magazine article, a book chapter, or another text that contains several pictures. Go through the text to find examples of as many of the seven concepts listed here as you can locate in both words and pictures. Note the page and paragraph number where you find the concept and how exactly the concept is used. Which concepts are used most effectively?

Concept	In words	In images
Emphasis		
Balance		
Contrast		
Repetition		
Point of view		
Motion		
Details		

Know when to use images and graphics

Personal computers, digital cameras, scanners, printers, and the Web have made it easy to include images and graphics in what we write. But these technologies don't tell us when or how to use images and graphics.

Think about what an image or graphic communicates

- Think about your readers' expectations for the medium you are using. Most essays don't use images, but most websites and brochures do.

- Think about the purpose of an image or graphic. Does it illustrate a concept? Highlight an important point? Show something that is hard to explain in words alone? If you don't know the purpose, you may not need the image.

- Think about the placement of an image or graphic in your text. It should be as close as possible to a relevant point in your text.

- Think about the focus of an image. Will readers see the part that matters? If not, you may need to crop the image.

- Provide informative captions for the images and graphics you use and refer to them in your text. Photos without captions get lost in the text.

Format images for the medium you are using

Images that you want to print need to be of higher quality than those intended for the Web or the screen. Pay attention to the settings on your camera or scanner.

Digital cameras frequently make images with 72 dpi (dots per inch), which is the maximum you can display on the screen. Most printers use a resolution from 300 to 600 dpi. Use the high-quality setting on your camera for images you intend to print.

Scanners typically offer a range of resolution from 72 to 1600 dpi. The higher the number, the finer the image, but the file size becomes larger. Images on the Web or a screen display at 72 dpi, so higher resolutions do not improve the quality but do make the image slow to load.

Take pictures that aren't boring

No matter how easy it is now to take photographs, the great majority of pictures look the same. Why? It's because most people think pictures should look the same, taken at eye level with the subject in the centre.

The result is boring, boring, boring.

This kind of picture has been taken many, many times. How else might you see this subject?

Squat

Change the angle

Lie down

Find a new eye level

Climb a tree

Kneel

Most people never stop to experience the visual richness of the world. Look for detail. Be open to what you see.

Compose images

A common misperception is that photographs are a direct representation of reality. Nothing could be further from the truth. A photograph shows not so much *what* the photographer sees but rather *how* the photographer sees it. The key to becoming a good photographer is not to take pictures that show things exactly as they appear but to take pictures that convey meaning, organization, and an emotional response to the subject.

Eliminate nonessential elements
Most people include too much in their photographs. Decide what is essential and concentrate on getting those elements in the frame.

The horse, mud-spattered, with his head hanging low, shows his exhaustion.

Framing
If you are taking a portrait, usually the closer you can get to your subject, the better. If your camera has a zoom, use it.

Decide what you want in a frame. If your goal is to show the habitat of geese, you'll need a wide shot.

But if you want a portrait of a goose, get in tighter.

Create tables, charts, and graphs

Software makes it easy to create tables, charts, and graphs, which are often effective in conveying statistical information at a glance. Select the type of visual that best suits your purpose.

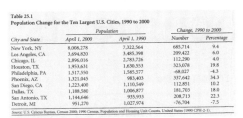

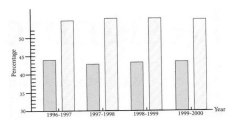

Tables

A table is used to display numerical data and similar types of information. It usually includes several items as well as variables for each item.

Bar Graphs

A bar graph compares the values of two or more items.

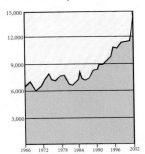

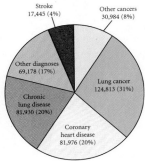

Line Graphs

A line graph shows change over time.

Pie Charts

A pie chart shows the parts making up a whole.

WORKING TOGETHER

Communicate with images and graphics

In a group of three or four students

Look at your textbooks for your other courses. Find one example where an image or graphic helps you to understand the material. Write briefly what exactly the image or graphic does that words alone could not. Find a second example where you think an image or graphic could be added. Write why an image or graphic would help.

Bring your examples to class and compare them with other group members. When do words work best? When is it more appropriate to communicate information through graphics and other visual media?

6

Designing Documents

We know at a glance who is telling the truth.

Start with your readers

Imagine yourself in the shoes of your reader. Pretend for a moment that someone else has written about your subject. What do you, the reader, want from the writer?

Tell your reader what you are writing about

An accurate and informative title is critical for readers to decide if they want to read what you have written. Furthermore, the title is critical to allow the reader to return to something read earlier.

Some genres require **abstracts**, which are short summaries of a document. Abstracts are required for scholarly articles in the sciences and social sciences as well as dissertations. Business reports and other reports often have executive summaries, which are similar to abstracts but often briefer.

Make your organization visible to readers

Most longer texts and many shorter ones include headings, which give readers an at-a-glance overview and make the text easier to follow and remember. Headings visually indicate the major and subordinate sections of a text.

Some genres have specific formats for organization, such as the APA-style report of research that is divided into four parts: introduction, method, results, and discussion. If you are writing in a genre that requires a specific format, follow it. Readers will be irritated if you don't.

Help your reader to navigate your text

Do the little things that help readers. Remember to include page numbers, which word processing software can insert for you. Make cross-references to other parts of your document when a subject is covered elsewhere. If you are citing sources, make sure they are all in your list of works cited.

Help your reader to understand the purposes for different parts of your text

A traditional way to add information without interrupting your running text is with footnotes. Today writers often use boxes or sidebars to supply extra information. If you use boxes or sidebars, indicate them with a different design or a different colour. The key is to make what is different look different.

You do research every day. If you compare prices online before you buy an airline ticket, or if you look up a detailed course description before registering for a class, you are doing research. If you want to settle an argument about the first Canadian woman to win an Olympic gold medal, you need to do research. In college and university, research means both investigating existing knowledge that is stored on computers and in libraries, and creating new knowledge through original analysis, surveys, experiments, and theorizing. When you start a research task in a college course, you need to understand the different kinds of possible research and to plan your strategy in advance.

If you have an assignment that requires research, look closely at what you are being asked to do.

If you have an assignment that requires research, look closely at what you are being asked to do. The assignment may ask you to review, compare, survey, analyze, evaluate, or prove that something is true or untrue. You may be writing for experts, for students like yourself, or for the general public. The purpose of your research and your potential audience will help guide your strategies for research.

Pull quotes are often set off from the body text with a larger font and a different colour.

Use headings and subheadings effectively

Readers increasingly expect you to divide what you write into sections and label those sections with headings. A system of consistent headings should map the overall organization.

Determine levels of headings

Determine the level of importance of each heading by making an outline to see what fits under what. Then make the headings conform to the different levels by choosing a font size and an effect such as bold-facing for each level. The type, the size, and the effect should signal the level of importance.

Phrase headings consistently

Headings should be similar in how they are worded. For example, if you are writing a heading for an informative brochure about a service, you might use the most frequently asked questions as your headings.

TITLE

Saepe et multum hoc mecum cogitavi, bonine an mali plus attulerit hominibus et civitatibus copia dicendi ac summum eloquentiae studium.

Major Heading

Ac me quidem diu cogitantem ratio ipsa in hanc potissi-mum sententiam ducit, ut existimem sapientiam sine eloquentia parum prodesse civitatibus, eloquentiam vero sine sapientia nimium obesse plerumque, prodesse numquam.

Level 2 heading Ac si volumus huius rei, quae vocatur eloquentia, sive artis sive studii sive exercitationis cuius-dam sive facultatis ab natura profectae considerare prin-cipium, reperiemus id ex honestissimis causis natum atque optimis rationibus profectum.

Be a Quitter! Join Quitters

Why quit smoking?
- You'll lower your risk for heart attack, stroke, and cancer.
- You'll look, feel, and smell a whole lot better.
- You'll have extra money to spend on things other than cigarettes.

How will the Quitters class help me?
- You'll find out your individual level of nicotine-dependence.
- You'll utilize a brand-switching technique.
- You'll explore the use of nicotine replacement therapies.

Headings function like gateways from one section to another.

Design pages

Word processing programs design pages for you with their default settings for margins, paragraph indentations, and justification. Even if you use the default settings, you still have a range of options. Thinking about design beforehand will lead to better decisions and a cleaner final product.

Choose the orientation, size of your page, and columns

You can usually use the defaults on your word processing program for academic essays (remember to select double-spacing for line spacing if the default is single-spaced). For other kinds of texts you may want a horizontal rather than a vertical orientation, a size other than a standard sheet of paper, and two columns or more rather than one.

Divide your text into units.

The paragraph is the basic unit of extended writing, but think also about when to use lists. This list is a bulleted list. You can also use a numbered list.

Use left-aligned text with a ragged right margin.

Fully justified text aligns the right margin, which gives a more formal look but can also leave unsightly rivers of extra white space running through the middle of your text.

Giddens 3

stay in the military after their commitment ends. Congress first gave the military the authority to retain soldiers after the Vietnam War when new volunteers were too few to replace departing soldiers. In November 2002 the Pentagon gave stop-loss orders for Reserve and National Guard units activated to fight terrorism (Robertson).

- This policy is neither forthcoming, safe, nor compassionate toward those most directly impacted—the soldiers and their families.
- As the United States became more and more entrenched in the conflict in Iraq, the military was stretched thinner and thinner.
- By 2004, approximately 40% of those serving in Iraq and Afghanistan came from the ranks of the part-time soldiers: the Reserves and the National Guard (Gerard).

While these individuals did know that their countries could call if they enlisted, they continue to bear an inordinate burden of actual combat time, and this new policy continues to create situations further removed from the job for which they had enlisted. Recruiters often pitch the military—including the Reserves and the Guard—to young, impressionable, and often underprivileged kids.

The Pitch

I have experienced this pitch firsthand and seen the eyes of my classmates as the recruiter promised them a better and richer tomorrow. Seeing a golden opportunity for self-respect and achievement, young men and women sign on the dotted line. Today, other young men and women are

Be conscious of white space.

White space can make your text more readable and set off more important elements. Headings stand out more with white space surrounding them. Leave room around graphics. You don't want words to crowd too close to graphics because both the words and the visuals will become hard to read.

Be aware of MLA and APA design specifications.

MLA and APA styles have specifications for margins, indentations, reference lists, and other things. See the sample papers in Chapters 20 and 21 if you are using MLA or APA style.

Understand typography

Just as people communicate with body languages, texts have a look and feel created by the layout, typefaces, type size, colour, density, and other elements.

Typography is the designer's term for letters and symbols that make up the print on the page. You are already using important aspects of typography when you use capital letters, italics, boldface, or different sizes of type to signal a new sentence, identify the title of a book, or distinguish a heading from the body text.

Word processing programs and personal computers now enable you to use dozens of different typefaces (fonts), bold and italic versions of these fonts, and a range of font sizes. Fortunately, you can rely on some simple design principles to make good typographic choices for your documents.

Choosing a font

A font family consists of the font in different sizes as well as in its boldface and italic forms. Although computers now make hundreds of font styles and sizes available to writers, you should avoid confusing readers with too many typographical features. Limit the fonts in a document to one or two font families. A common practice is to choose one font family for all titles and headings and another for the body text.

A font family

Arial Narrow

Arial Narrow Italic

Arial Regular

Arial Italic

Arial Bold

Arial Bold Italic

Arial Black

The font family Arial, shown above in 14 point, is composed of style variations on the Arial design that include a variety of weights.

Serif and sans serif typefaces

Typefaces are normally divided into two groups—serif and sans serif. Serif typefaces include horizontal lines—or serifs—on the major strokes of a letter or character. Sans serif typefaces, by contrast, do not have serifs. Notice the difference opposite.

The typical use and stylistic impact of the typefaces vary considerably. Serif typefaces are more traditional, conservative, and formal in appearance. By contrast, sans serif typefaces offer a more contemporary, progressive, and informal look. Serif is often used for longer pieces of writing, such as novels and textbooks. It is also the best bet for college and university papers. Check your professor's instructions to find out whether he or she requires a specific font for your work.

The difference between serif and sans serif fonts

The horizontal lines make serif easier to read because they guide the eye from left to right across the page.

This **SERIF** font is called Garamond

This **SANS SERIF** font is called Helvetica

Think about font style

Not all fonts are suitable for extended pieces of writing. Sentences and paragraphs printed in fonts that imitate calligraphy or handwriting are not only difficult to read but also informal in appearance. For most academic and business writing, you will probably want to choose a traditional font, such as **Times Roman**, that is easy to read and does not call attention to itself. This book is set in 10.5 point **Minion**.

Choosing the best font for the job

This piece of text is in a calligraphic font, and may be right for some special situations, but there is no doubt that every single reader will be aware of the struggle to decipher it.

This font is is **28 point Palace Script**

This piece of text is in a handwriting font, and although easier to read than the above, is still very difficult in large amounts.

This font is **17 point Feltpen**

This is about as normal a font as you can find. It is called Times Roman, for the simple reason that it was designed for use in the *London Times* newspaper, and so had to be as readable as possible.

This font is is **14 point Times Roman**

This font is also very readable and is very common as it is the default font on most computer software. It does however, require much more space than other fonts.

This font is **14 point Courier**

Think about font size

It's easy to change the size of a font when you write on a computer. For most types of writing in college and university, a 12-point font is the standard size for the main (body) text, with headings in a larger font.

Type sizes

8 point

12 point

18 point

36 point

48 point

Height can make a difference

To ensure that what you write can be read easily, you need to choose an appropriate size. Fonts differ by height, called the x–height, as well as point size. Fonts of the same point size can look different because of height. Effective size depends on the appearance of a font, not merely its point size.

To ensure that what you write can be read easily, you need to choose an appropriate size. Fonts differ by height, called the x-height, as well as point size. Fonts of the same point size can look different because of height. Effective size depends on the appearance of a font, not merely its point size.

Both texts are set the same "size" (12 point) but they appear different because of the x-heights. *Bembo*, left, looks much smaller and takes much less space than *Glypha*, right.

Type sizes for computer monitors

For webpages, you should consider using a larger font to compensate for the added difficulty of reading from a computer monitor. For overhead transparencies and computer-projected displays, you should use an even larger size (such as 32 point) to ensure that the text can be read from a distance.

Pixilation on the computer screen breaks up the font; thus the 12-point type in this example is too small.

You should consider enlarging to 18-point type as in this example.

When using an overhead projector or a computer-projected display, use 32-point font.

Checklist for evaluating document design

1. Audience	Who is the intended audience? Will the design be appealing to them? How does the design serve their needs?
2. Genre	What is the genre? Does the design meet the requirements of the genre? For example, a brochure should fit in your pocket.
3. Organization	Is the organization clear to readers? If headings are used, are they in the right places? If headings are used for more than one level, are these levels indicated consistently?
4. Readability	Is the typeface attractive and readable? Are the margins sufficient? Is any contrasting text, such as boldface, italics, or all caps, brief enough to be legible? If colour is used, does it direct emphasis to the right places?
5. Layout	Can the basic layout be made more effective? Is there adequate white space around headings, images, and graphics?

WRITE NOW

Analyze document design

Option 1
Collect samples of different pieces of writing (articles, editorials, ads) from a print source.

Option 2
Collect samples of different pieces of writing (personal or professional blogs, wikis, articles, ads) from a Web source.

Examine the design elements of each medium, focusing on the layout (how it looks on the page), readability, and organization of the text and images. Determine the target audience and genre. Finally, ask the following questions:

1. Is the layout effective? Does it help to make the piece of writing more accessible to the reader?
2. Does it contain the right combination of typeface features? Are there style conflicts (too much italicized text, for example) that impact the overall readability of the document?
3. Are headings used successfully to organize the information? Are they consistent throughout the document?
4. Does the document design meet the requirements of the genre?
5. How does the document design serve the target audience's needs?

Assess the overall differences between print and Web documents. How do the three main design elements (layout, readability, and organization) differ in print and on the Web?

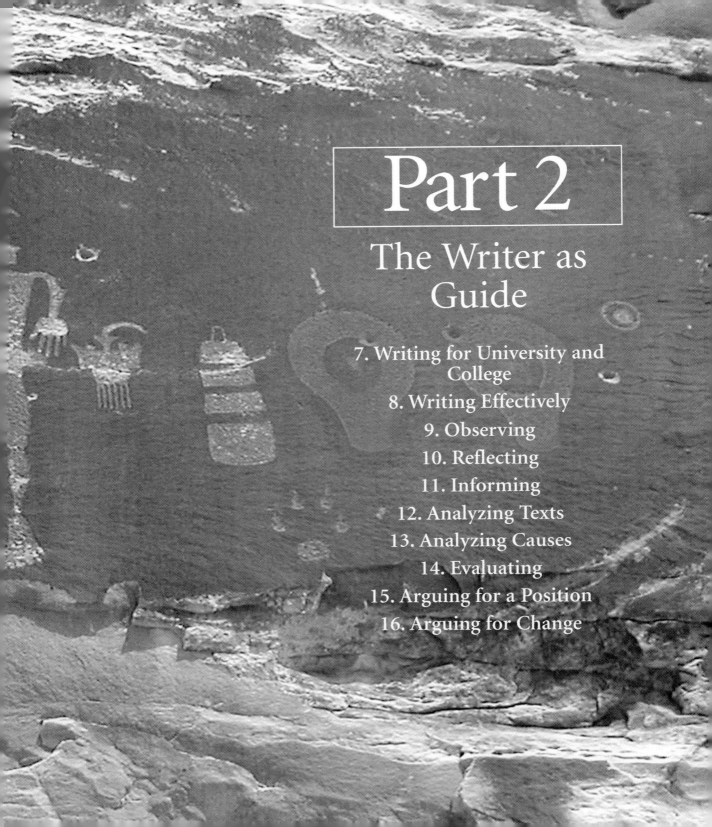

Part 2

The Writer as Guide

7

Writing for University and College

Writers today do many different kinds of writing for multiple purposes.

Understand the demands of writing in college and university

Post-secondary writing changes from course to course depending on the requirements of the course's discipline. What is expected in a philosophy course differs from what is expected in a biology course.

Nevertheless, there are some common expectations about post-secondary writing that extend across disciplines.

Post-secondary writing . . .	Writers are expected to . . .
States explicit claims	Make a claim that isn't obvious. The claim is often called a thesis statement.
Develops an argument	Support their claims with facts, evidence, reasons, and testimony from experts.
Analyzes with insight	Analyze in depth what they read and review.
Investigates complexity	Explore the complexity of a subject, challenging their readers by asking "Have you thought about this?" or "What if you discard the usual way of thinking about a subject and take the opposite point of view?"
Organizes with a hierarchical structure	Make the major parts evident to readers and indicate which parts are subordinate to others.
Signals with transitions	Indicate logical relationships clearly so readers can follow a pathway without getting lost.
Documents sources carefully	Provide the sources of information so readers can consult the same sources the writer used.

Think about your aim

What you want to accomplish guides your choices as a writer. You may want to reflect on your experience or the experiences of others. You may want to inform your readers about a subject. Or you may want to change your readers' attitudes about a subject or persuade them to take action. You will find out more about these aims for writing in the remaining chapters in Part 2.

AIM	FOCUS	EXAMPLES OF GENRES
Observing Chapter 9 page 70	Describing accurately and vividly to create a dominant impression	Ethnographies, travel accounts, case studies, photo essays, on-the-scene articles
Reflecting Chapter 10 page 120	Narrating personal experience and personal insights for a public audience	Journals, personal letters, blogs, memoirs, reflective essays, fiction, descriptions
Informing Chapter 11 page 174	Communicating information clearly in a form suited for the reader	Newspaper and magazine articles, academic articles, brochures, government reports, profiles, informational websites
Analyzing texts Chapter 12 page 224	Analyzing what makes a text effective or ineffective and why the author made particular choices	Rhetorical analysis, short story analysis, visual analysis, academic essays
Analyzing causes Chapter 13 page 288	Exploring why an event, phenomenon, or trend happened	Causal analysis, accident analysis, financial analysis, history, academic essays and reports
Evaluating Chapter 14 page 342	Assessing whether something is good or bad according to particular criteria	Reviews, evaluative essays, performance evaluations, product evaluations and discipline-specific evaluations
Arguing for a position Chapter 15 page 388	Convincing others through reasoned argument to accept or reject a position	Speeches, letters to the editor, op-ed columns, editorials, essays, analyses
Arguing for change Chapter 16 page 432	Convincing others through reasoned argument to take action	Speeches, business proposals, grant proposals, letters of application, advocacy websites, advertisements

Use your aim as a guide

In many cases, if you know your aim in advance, you have a good start toward how to structure your paper or project.

For example, you might want to evaluate a Shetland sheepdog (sheltie) as a breed. For an evaluation, you know that your thesis will take the form of _____ is a good/bad, better/best/worst _____ according to these criteria: _____, _____, _____. With this guide, you come up with the following: *The sheltie is one of the best breeds because shelties are highly intelligent, extremely loyal, responsive, and easy to train.*

Chapters 7 through 16 show you how to use your aim to guide the development of your paper or project.

WORKING TOGETHER

Use aims to create thesis statements

In a group of three or four students

Come up with a list of subjects that your group has some interest in and knows something about. They could be big subjects such as global warming or more limited subjects such as your school's parking problems.

As a group, brainstorm thesis statements for at least three aims. For example, on the subject of eating disorders, you might come up with something like the following:

Reflecting
My younger sister overcame her bulimia disorder during her last two years of high school when successes in school and in music improved her self-esteem.

Informing
Anorexia nervosa is diagnosed when patients weigh 15% under the normal body weight for their height and is characterized by starvation, excessive exercise, and sometimes forced vomiting.

Analyzing Causes
The causes of eating disorders are not a failure of will but medical illnesses that take on a life of their own.

Arguing for Change
Less money and effort should be spent to find drugs to treat eating disorders, and more effort should go toward teaching adolescents to deal with negative thoughts about their bodies and to develop a positive body image.

Think about your genre

Be aware of genre

Genre means a kind of writing or form of communication. When you walk into your video store, you find movies classified by genre: action, animation, comedy, documentary, drama, family, horror, sci-fi, and so on. The music industry classifies music by genre as well: alternative, blues, classical, country, electronic, folk, gospel, jazz, rap, reggae, rock, world, and so on.

Most of the time we recognize genre in writing immediately—junk mail, a letter of application, a novel, a lease for an apartment, an informative brochure. We know a great deal more than just the form. We know, for example, that junk mail is trying to sell something, and we know to be suspicious of any offers of free products. Likewise, we know that the person writing a letter of application wants to get a job or enter a selective program.

Be aware of how genre influences style

The genre has a strong influence on the style you will use. Compare the first paragraphs of a research report, a news article, and a blog on homosexuality and homophobia.

Research paper

Coming-out is the developmental process through which gays and lesbians recognize their sexual orientation and choose to integrate this knowledge into their personal and social lives (see Monteflores and Schultz, 1978). Although coming-out is an individual experience, there are commonalities. The goals of coming-out parallel three developmental tasks—developing self esteem, consolidating identity, and learning social skills related to the new identity. Closure in the coming-out process is achieved when a gay- or lesbian-positive feeling develops, when sexual orientation is appropriately placed in perspective relative to the individual's entire identity, and when contact with gay/lesbian peers and/or a gay/lesbian community is established (Ryan, 1999). Each person's sense of identity is made up of the picture others have of them, and their own perception of these characteristics. A "homosexual identity refers to a perception of self, as a homosexual in relation to a social setting" (Troiden, 1984). In essence, the process involved in the acquisition of a gay or lesbian identity is one of evolution in which a previously held negative image of one's sexual orientation is replaced progressively with a more neutral, and then hopefully, a positive one.

Ryan, B. *A New Look at Homophobia and Heterosexism in Canada*. The Canadian AIDS Society, 2003.

News article

Coming out of the closet is never easy. For some youth, it has been tremendously difficult, especially when staunch religious and cultural values are involved. Jen Blaser, 18, has experienced a lot of backlash for coming out. She has been a victim of an array of hate crimes that no teen should ever experience: Sexual assault, bullying, death threats, you name it, she's been through it.

Amy Chung, "'Coming out' not easy for gay kids; Religious and cultural values cause fear, anger— and backlash," *Toronto Sun,* June 25, 2008: 10

Blog

Have you or your friends said "that's so gay" when you really meant to say something is bad or stupid? You might laugh or think it's no big deal, but saying "that's so gay" is insulting to gay people and anyone who has gay relatives or just cares about gay people.

Can you imagine trying to come out when people are tossing this obnoxious phrase around? Coming out is tough, so why make it harder for GLBTQ people to be themselves by saying "that's so gay?" Just knock it off!

Sex etc Blog, "Think Before your Speak." October 10, 2008 (http://www.sexetc.org/blog/2008/10/10/think-before-you-speak/)

Even though each writer is writing about the same subject, notice what is different.

Sentence length	• The research paper has much longer sentences than the newspaper article or the blog.
Paragraph length	• The research paper has long paragraphs compared to the short paragraph of the newspaper article and the blog.
Word choice	• The research paper uses much more formal language than the blog. The newspaper language is neutral and easy to understand.
Relationship with the reader	• The research paper and newspaper writers are distant and objective. The blog writer is passionately involved with the issue.

WRITE NOW

Compare styles across genres

Find a newspaper article on a current social, economic, political, or scientific issue. Then find a scholarly article on the same subject using scholar.google.com/ or one of the databases on your library's website. Next, search blogs for the same subject using blogsearch.google.com.

Compare the styles of the scientific article, the newspaper article, and the blog using the following criteria: overall length, paragraph length, sentence length, word choice, relationship with the reader, and use of graphics and images. Write a summary of your analysis.

8

Writing Effectively

When people write for others, they become guides to show readers new places, point out new perspectives, and help them see old places with new eyes.

Understand the rhetorical situation

At the most basic level, communication involves the interaction of three things: the writer or speaker, the audience, and the subject. These three elements are often represented by a triangle.

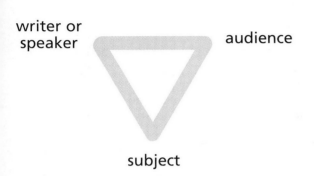

writer or
speaker

audience

subject

All three elements—speaker, subject, and audience—are necessary for an act of communication to occur. Think about all the times you talk and listen in a day. Who are the people you talk with regularly? What do you talk about? Even if you are talking to or writing to yourself, you still have an audience. And all three elements are in a dynamic relationship. Every one of us makes adjustments depending on our audience (think of how you talk to small children). Just as speakers adjust to audiences, audiences continually adjust to speakers (think of how your attitude toward a speaker changes for the better when that person can make you laugh).

Persuade others

The ancient Greeks recognized that the dynamic nature of the rhetorical triangle is the key to understanding how an audience is persuaded. Aristotle (384–323 BCE) defined *rhetoric* as the art of finding the best available means of persuasion in any situation. He set out three primary tactics of persuasion: appeals based on the trustworthiness of the speaker (ethos); appeals to the emotions and deepest-held values of the audience (pathos); and appeals to logic, reasoning, and evidence (logos).

These appeals likewise can be represented using the rhetorical triangle.

Aristotle's insight about how people can be persuaded remains relevant today. For example, imagine that you drive to work on a major highway every morning. Your drive coincides with a tremendous amount of truck traffic, and you have witnessed, first hand, two major fatal collisions involving speeding transport trucks. You want your city council to vote to reduce the speed limits for trucks on the regional highways to reduce the number of truck collisions. One approach would be to use logic and evidence, documenting that regional highways incur frequent and often fatal truck collisions because of excessive speed (logos). Another way would be to invite an expert on truck traffic safety to speak to the city council (ethos). A third way would be to appeal to the council about the unnecessary loss of life caused by the unsafe highway (pathos). Often, you will use all of these appeals to gain support of an audience.

Ethos
appeals based on the character and expertise of the writer or speaker

Pathos
appeals to the beliefs and values of the audience

Logos
appeals based on logic, reasoning, and evidence concerning the subject

Think about your audience

When you talk with someone face-to-face, you receive constant feedback from that person, even when you're doing all the talking. Your listener may nod in agreement, frown, act bored, or give you a variety of other signals.

Unless your listener is deliberately acting, you have a sense of how they are responding to what you are saying. If your listener looks puzzled, for example, you can try explaining again.

Imagine your readers

When you write, you rarely receive immediate response from readers. Most of the time you don't know exactly how readers will react to what you write. You have to think consciously about your readers and anticipate how they might respond.

Write for professors

College and university instructors expect more than what you can find out from a Google search or an online encyclopedia. Facts are easy to obtain from databases and print sources. Your instructors want to know how these facts are connected to your point of view.

Good college and university writing involves an element of surprise. If readers can predict exactly where a writer is going, even if they fully agree, they will either skim to the end or stop reading. Readers expect you to tell them something that they don't know already or present it in a way that leaves them thinking about it afterward.

WORKING TOGETHER

Analyze advertisement audiences

Magazines sell advertising by targeting themselves to specific readers. Bring to class a magazine that you read regularly or one that you find interesting. Organize in groups of three or four students and exchange magazines with each other. Look at the articles and the advertising in the magazine.

Analyze your classmate's magazine for these criteria.

1. What is the target age group?
2. What percentages of men and women are likely to read the magazine?
3. What income level is targeted?
4. Is a particular ethnicity being targeted?
5. What else is being assumed about the audience? For magazines that cover a specific subject or activity (for example, backpacking, beauty, snowboarding, parenting, fitness, cats, and so on), what other products and services do you find being advertised?

Share your analysis with other members of your group. Ask the person who brought the magazine you analyzed if he or she agrees with your description of the target audience.

STAYING ON TRACK

Know what professors and peer readers expect

Readers expect to be challenged.
Simple answers that can be easily looked up are not adequate.

OFF TRACK
The Kyoto Accord was signed in Kyoto, Japan on Dec. 11, 1997, by 180 countries. *(This fact is easily researched and does not provoke much debate.)*

ON TRACK
The Kyoto Accord, designed to help stabilize greenhouse gas concentrations, was not completely supported by the Canadian government, citing the potential for a recession should the country be forced to meet the Kyoto targets.

Readers expect claims to be backed up with reasons and evidence.
Simple explanations without support are not adequate.

OFF TRACK
Vancouver is a beautiful city, but I wouldn't move there because it rains too much. *(Does it rain more in Vancouver than anywhere else in Canada?)*

ON TRACK
According to Statistics Canada, Vancouver is fifth on the list of cities with the most rain days annually and, overall, receives less total precipitation than St. John's and Halifax.

Readers expect complex answers for complex problems.
Simple solutions for complex problems are not adequate.

OFF TRACK
We need posters urging students not to litter so much on campus. *(Are posters alone likely to solve the problem?)*

ON TRACK
Most of the litter on our campus is paper, bottles, and cans—all recyclable—yet there are almost no recycle containers on campus. Putting recycle containers in high-litter locations along with a "don't litter" campaign could go a long way toward making our campus cleaner.

Readers expect writers to be engaged.
Readers expect writers to be curious and genuinely concerned about their subjects.

OFF TRACK
Older people have to deal with too much bureaucracy to obtain health care. *(The statement rings true but doesn't motivate readers.)*

ON TRACK
After sitting with my 78-year-old aunt for several hours on hold, I became convinced that the prescription drug program is an aging Canadian's worst nightmare.

Think about your credibility

Some writers have credibility simply because of who they are. If you wonder what foods compose a balanced meal for your dog, you probably would listen carefully to the advice of a veterinarian. Most writers, however, have to convince their readers to keep reading by demonstrating knowledge of their subject and concern for their readers' needs.

Think about how you want your readers to see you

To get your readers to take you seriously, you must convince them that they can trust you. You need to get them to see you as someone with these traits:

Concerned

Readers want you to be committed to what you are writing about. They also expect you to be concerned with them as readers. After all, if you don't care about them, why should they read what you write?

Well informed

Many people ramble on about any subject without knowing anything about it. If they are family members, you have to suffer their opinions, but it is not always enjoyable. College and university writing requires that you do your homework on a subject.

Fair

Many writers look at only one side of an issue. But readers expect objectivity and an unbiased approach.

Ethical

Many writers use only the facts that support their positions, and may distort these facts and sources for their own purposes. Critical readers often notice what is being left out. Don't try to conceal what doesn't support your position. Acknowledging the other side can often strengthen your arguments.

STAYING ON TRACK

Build your credibility

Know what's at stake

What you are writing about should matter to your readers. If its importance is not evident, it's your job to explain why your readers should consider it important.

OFF TRACK

We should be concerned that two-thirds of Central and South America's 110 brightly coloured harlequin frog species have become extinct in the last twenty years. *(The loss of any species is unfortunate, but the writer gives us no other reason for concern.)*

ON TRACK

The rapid decline of amphibians worldwide due to global warming may be the advance warning of the loss of cold-weather species such as polar bears, penguins, and reindeer.

STAYING ON TRACK

Have your readers in mind
If you are writing about a specialized subject that your readers don't know much about, take the time to explain key concepts.

OFF TRACK
Reduction in the value of a debt security, especially a bond, results from a rise in interest rates. Conversely, a decline in interest rates results in an increase in the value of a debt security, especially bonds. *(The basic idea is here, but it is not expressed clearly, especially if the reader is not familiar with investing.)*

ON TRACK
Bond prices move inversely to interest rates. When interest rates go up, bond prices go down, and when interest rates go down, bond prices go up.

Think about alternative solutions and points of view.
Readers appreciate a writer's ability to see a subject from multiple perspectives.

OFF TRACK
We will reduce greenhouse gas and global warming only if we greatly increase wind-generated electricity. *(Wind power is an alternative energy source, but it is expensive, and many people don't want windmills in scenic areas. The writer also doesn't mention using energy more efficiently.)*

ON TRACK
If the world is serious about limiting carbon emissions to reduce global warming, then along with increasing efficient energy use, all non-carbon-emitting energy sources must be considered, including nuclear power. Nuclear power now produces about 15% of Canada's electricity with no emissions, but it comes with serious long-term disposal issues.

Write well
Nothing impresses readers more than graceful, fluent writing that is clear, direct, and forceful. Even if readers don't agree with you in the end, they still will appreciate your writing ability.

OFF TRACK
Nobody can live today without taking some risks, even very rich people. After all, we don't know what we're breathing in the air. A lot of food has chemicals and hormones in it. There's a big hole in the ozone, so more people will get skin cancer. And a lot of people have sexually transmitted diseases these days. *(The impact of the point is lost with unfocused writing.)*

ON TRACK
We live in a world of risks beyond our control, to the extent that it is difficult to think of anything that is risk free, down to the most basic human acts—sex in an era of AIDS, eating in an era of genetically altered food, walking outside in an ozone-depleted atmosphere, drinking water and breathing air laden with chemicals whose effects we do not understand.

Become an effective writer

Learning how to write well may be the most important part of your education. Many surveys that ask graduates what they most value about their education report that they rank writing and communication skills far above anything else they learned. You can be more confident and more successful in whatever you do knowing that you write well.

What makes college and university writing effective?

You can become a successful college writer if you do two things: write regularly, and learn what makes writing effective. Effective writing is judged by the following criteria:

On task
The paper or project does what the assignment asks for.

Focused
The paper or project has a clear thesis or main point, and all paragraphs are relevant to that main point.

Organized
The order of the major points and paragraphs is clear to the reader.

Developed
Major points are supported with reasons, evidence, and examples. If quotations are used, they support the main points.

Linked
Paragraphs and sentences have transitions that show relationships.

Stylistically fluent
The sentences are varied and energetic, and use active verbs.

Concise
The language is efficient without unnecessary words.

Correct
The final version is free from major structural and grammatical errors.

Well designed
The format is correct, the font readable, the headings consistent, and all photographs and charts clearly labelled.

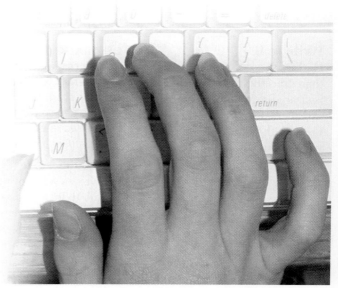

Effective writing

The qualities of effective writing are evident in Angela Yamashita's essay "Got Roddick?" Her assignment was to select an advertisement and analyze how it makes appeals to ethos, pathos, and logos.

Yamashita 1

Angela Yamashita

Dr. Sanchez

English 15

12 December 2010

Got Roddick?

Andy Roddick is one of the hottest professional athletes today. In 2003 he became the youngest American to finish ranked number one in the ATP rankings, and he's known not only for his excellent playing skills but also for his good looks and easygoing attitude. Ex-boyfriend to popular singer Mandy Moore, Roddick has been thrown into the spotlight and is now a teenage crush. It was his picture that stopped me while leafing through *Seventeen* and made me take a longer look. Roddick stands staring at the viewer, racquet over his shoulder, leaning against the net on the court. More prominent than his white pants, white tennis shirt, and white towel draped around his neck is the white milk mustache above his upper lip. The ad reads, "Now serving. I'm into power. So I drink milk. It packs 9 essential nutrients into every glass. Which comes in handy whether you're an athlete or an energetic fan." At the bottom of the page is the ad slogan (also in white) "Got Milk?"

The "Got Milk?" campaign has published numerous ads that try to convince adults to drink more milk. Everyone from rock groups to actors to athletes have participated in this campaign. In today's caffeine-obsessed society of coffee and soda drinkers, America's Dairy Farmers and Milk Processors (the association that sponsors the "Got Milk?" campaign) felt the need to reverse the decline in milk consumption by advertising milk in a new way. The catchy "Got Milk?" proved to be highly successful, and the campaign has been

The heading is in the correct MLA format. The paper is free of major errors.

The title plays off the theme of the ad and suggests the content.

The writer gets off to a fast start, introducing her subject in the first sentence.

The writer engages her subject.

Angela describes the ad with specifics.

Angela provides background information

Yamashita 2

"Got Milk?" ad featuring Andy Roddick

Angela includes the ad along with the caption.

mimicked by many others including "Got cookies?" "Got fish?" "Got sports?" and even "Got Jesus?" (Philpot). The Andy Roddick ad is typical of the "Got Milk?" series, urging people young and old to drink milk to remain healthy and strong. The Roddick ad primarily uses the appeals of ethos and pathos to persuade its audience. (The one gesture toward logos in the ad is the mention that milk has nine nutrients.)

Angela cites the source of her information.

Thesis of paper

To establish the ethos of their ads, America's Dairy Farmers and Milk Processors use celebrity endorsements. The "Got Milk?" campaign has enlisted a range of celebrities popular with young audiences from Kelly Clarkson to Sheryl Crow, Bebe Neuwirth to Ben Roethlisberger, T-Mac (Tracy McGrady) to Bernie Mac. Choosing Andy Roddick, the dominant young male player in American tennis, fits squarely in this lineup. Admired by a strong following of young adults (girls for his looks, boys for his athletic ability), Roddick is an ideal spokesman for establishing that milk is a healthy drink. Implicit in the ad is that milk will help you become a better athlete and better looking too.

Repeating "ethos" makes a smooth transition.

Angela explains why Andy Roddick was chosen as a spokesperson.

Yamashita 3

Pathos in the ad is conveyed not simply through Roddick's good looks. His pose is casual, almost slouching, yet his face is serious, one that suggests that he not only means business about playing tennis but also about his drink of choice. The words "I'm into power" don't mess around. They imply that you too can be more powerful by drinking milk. "Now serving" is also in your face, making a play on the word "serving" both as a tennis and a drink term.

The effectiveness of the "Got Milk?" campaign is demonstrated in gallons of milk sold. The campaign began in California in 1993 at a time when milk sales were rapidly eroding. A San Francisco ad agency developed the milk mustache idea, which is credited for stopping the downward trend in milk consumption in California. In 1995 the campaign went national. By 2000 national sales of milk remained consistent in contrast to annual declines in the early 1990s (Stamler). "Got Milk?" gave milk a brand identity that it had previously lacked, allowing it to compete with the well-established identities of Pepsi and Coca-Cola. Milk now has new challengers with more and more people going out to Starbucks and other breakfast bars. Nonetheless, the original formula of using celebrities like Andy Roddick who appeal to younger audiences continues to work. Milk isn't likely to go away soon as a popular beverage.

Angela analyzes the appeals to pathos.

Angela looks closely at the language the ad uses.

The history of the "Got Milk?" campaign is given briefly and the source is documented.

Angela's style is efficient and appropriate for college readers.

The ending provides new ideas for readers to think about rather than simply summarizing what has been said.

Yamashita 4

Works Cited

"Andy Rodick." *Got Milk?* 2003. Milk Processor Education Program,
    9 Oct. 2003. Web. 18 Nov. 2005.

Philpot, Robert. "Copycats Mimic 'Got Milk' Ads." *Milwaukee
    Journal Sentinel* 12 May 2002, final ed.: D3. Print.

Stamler, Bernard. "Got Sticking Power?" *New York Times* 30 July
    2001, late ed.: C11. Print.

Angela includes a list of works cited in the correct MLA format. If readers want to look at her sources, they should be able to find them easily.

9
Observing

Effective observations capture readers' attention through details that may be unfamiliar or surprising but always fresh and vivid.

Chapter contents

Writing observations

Observing is often the first step to understanding. In fields such as anthropology, sociology, and psychology, scientists observe people and processes and use their observations to answer questions: How is death regarded in Cree societies? What groups of people are most likely to visit an urban parkland? How do primates interact?

In everyday life, we use our observational skills to learn more about people and places we encounter. We learn about coffee-break protocol by watching how our co-workers tidy up the break room before they leave, and by listening to them complain about those who leave dirty cups and napkins behind. We learn how our neighbours feel about certain political issues by observing the signs they put up on their lawn. Businesses and governments also use observation to learn more about the people they serve. City officials might observe children playing on a public playground to see what kinds of equipment are used. They might also talk to the children's parents to learn why they bring their children to the playground at particular times of the day.

Observations begin with thorough research. Your firsthand impressions must be carefully recorded in as much detail as possible. These observations, often called field notes, provide your raw material. When you write as an observer, you place yourself in the background and give readers the clearest, most detailed view you can of your subject. What you see, what you hear, what you smell, taste, and feel as an observer can provide valuable information to your readers.

Components of observations

Where exactly is the place and who are the people?	**Identify your subject** Be specific about who or what you are observing. If it is a certain group of people, what sets them apart as a group? Do they share a common interest? Do they all use a particular space? Explain to readers how and why you limited your observations. If you are describing a place or event, what is special about the physical or chronological context?
What background do I need to provide? Do I need to explain why I chose this place or these people?	**Provide background on the subject** Readers need some idea of why your observations are significant. Is there a question that could be answered by your observations? Give readers the context they need to appreciate the picture you are about to present and to understand your motivation for observing.
How do I organize my observations?	**Assemble your observations** You may approach your observations chronologically, leading readers through your day-to-day or hour-by-hour experience as an observer. Or you may find other ways to organize that work better for your purposes: perhaps starting with the most surprising discovery you made while observing would interest readers, for example, and draw them into your writing.
What do my observations add up to?	**Place your observations in a larger context** Firsthand observation is a powerful tool for understanding, but it has its limits. What questions are left unanswered by your observations? How might your observations be atypical? Should they change the way people think or act? Give your readers a framework within which to understand your observations.

How many of my reactions and comments should I include?

Know when you are expected to be objective

Field observations in the sciences and social sciences keep the writer in the background, focusing instead on the subject. But essays often allow for personal reflection. Find out from your instructor what is expected.

Keys to observations

Photographs are valuable for providing concrete examples. For instance, Frank Lloyd Wright's attention to detail is evident in his 1905 design for the lobby of the Rookery Building in Chicago.

Build a strong sense of place

Help readers locate themselves along with you as you describe your observations. Tell them the date, time, and exact location of your observations, if possible. Give the names of the objects present.

Provide vivid, well-chosen details

Concrete imagery and descriptions of what you see, hear, smell, taste, and feel during your observations will ground your writing, helping readers "see" as if through your eyes.

Create an overall impression

Select your details to create an overall impression that grows out of the details. Think about which details will best build a coherent image for your readers.

Build trust with your audience by being precise and objective

Begin your observations with an open mind. The goal of observing is not to judge the people or your subjects but to learn as much about them as possible. Being precise about what you observe—not jumping to conclusions or relying on stereotypes—will heighten your objectivity. Precision will also enhance your credibility.

Provide visuals if needed

Photographs and other images can work in combination with words to enhance observations. Close attention to details is critical for both descriptive writing and descriptive visuals.

WORKING TOGETHER

Visit a place or event

In a group of three or four students

First make a visit individually to the same place or event, such as a museum, a parade or festival, or a political demonstration. Each group member should make notes about what he or she observes and write a one–two page synopsis of the visit. Then, as a group, read each other's synopses. How different was each person's experience? What, if anything, did they have in common?

Working together, draft a short introduction that summarizes the different perspectives your observations provide. What can an audience learn by reading multiple accounts of the same experience?

An effective observation

Effective observations rely on specific and relevant details to convey to readers a vivid sense of the subject or event.

A Homeless Past Stirs Pain
Evelyn Lau

Canadian poet and novelist Evelyn Lau has gained critical acclaim for her writing. Graphic depictions of life on the streets are one of the major themes of her work. In this poignant description, Lau examines the pain of her former existence.

Publish Date: February 19, 2009

It was a mild day, not raining, so I ventured out of my glass-and-concrete apartment building in Yaletown for a walk through the Downtown Eastside. A walk would put me in the mood—set the scene, so to speak—for the roundtable discussion I was scheduled to lead with two other writers at the Carnegie Centre that afternoon.

It had been years since I'd walked through this area, though of course I'd passed by on transit or in a car, peering like a tourist at the grey stream of misery around Main and Hastings, tamping down whatever emotion rose before it had an opportunity to overwhelm. It was so long ago, my time here, another life. Now I was the odd figure in the landscape, the one that didn't fit, among the prostitutes with their twisted faces stitching a jagged path down the sidewalk, the groups of dealers huddled in rank doorways. Perhaps I looked innocent, unblemished—no one offered to sell me drugs.

But the landmarks of my former life were still here, with their residues of memory. The Army & Navy, where I sought refuge as a

Lau introduces her topic and sets it, chronologically, in her past.

runaway, parting with a fistful of change for a hot dog or a soft-serve ice cream cone, eating it squatting in the fetid alley, the backpack that housed my most precious possession—reams of scrawled paper that would metamorphose into my first book—always within reach. A store called Model Express, where I bought my hooker clothes: cheap stretchy outfits in shiny gold and silver or hot pink, clothes that flashed and sparkled on the street corner. All the nights of degradation jumbled in my subconscious, inseparable from one another: crouched in the front seat of yet another car parked in an alley or by the docks, the fumbling of flesh under the sodium lights, the thundering of my pulse and the bite of bile in my throat.

Through vivid and explicit sensory detail, Lau provides a glimpse of her former life.

It wasn't until I passed a pawnshop that sadness slammed into me. The years peeled away and I was 14 again, it was Expo 86, and an essay I had written had won a contest in which the prize was a camera. I had immediately taken the camera to that pawnshop, where the man at the counter squinted at me suspiciously and asked for confirmation that I was of legal age, which I gave by lying and signing a document, and then he handed over… What? Twenty, 30 dollars? He already had too many cameras, he said, but sniffed my desperation, seeing before him an awkward adolescent in a Harley-Davidson T-shirt and an earring in the shape of a peace symbol, clutching a backpack that doubled as a pillow, trying to pretend that she was old enough for this life.

The yearning I felt now for that squandered prize! That chunky camera with its liquid lens, boxy and marvellous in my hands, abandoned to the grimy window of the pawnshop. Was that why I had never allowed myself to purchase a camera in all the years that followed? Why I could never look at the gleaming cases of photography equipment in drugstores without thinking of my precious writing prize, which I had had to sell for a fraction of its worth?

Lau describes her feelings about an incident in her past and how it resonated in her life.

It was ridiculous, the sadness, the maudlin self-pitying. I had work to do at the SFU–sponsored event, where writers would give advice on publishing to residents of the Downtown Eastside. There was the Carnegie Centre, on the crest of the hill, swarming with people. I was early, had walked faster than I had planned. "Hey, beautiful," a man called as I wriggled my way through the mass of loiterers on the corner, and I stifled a smile. This was a welcome change. In Yaletown, the yoga-toned passersby stared down their noses at me for not wearing the right clothes or carrying a designer handbag. Then a distant, automatic response leapt up: how much would he be willing to pay for a few minutes of my time? Somewhere along that walk, it was as if the present had fused with the past, as if in hurrying along Hastings Street, I had walked into the shadow of my former self.

Lau situates herself in the present, describing the same location.

I shook it off and went into the centre. More memories here: this was where I had come to turn hundreds of scribbled pages into neatly typewritten manuscripts that I sent off to literary magazines and contests. Had this place been such a hub of activity 20 years ago? I remembered the solitude of the typewriter room, how I was often the only person there, my fingers flying across the keyboard in a satisfying clatter. Now, in the lobby, a crowd swirled around me. A Native man hawked his cards and carvings; Chinese pensioners huddled over their mahjong tiles and foreign-language newspapers; women with canes made their heart-stopping progress down the warped marble stairs.

The volunteer for the Writers' Jamboree beckoned me over to join the other panellists, but I could hardly focus on their faces, their mobile mouths; everything seemed at a remove. Who was I? Where did I fit? I owned a condo in trendy Yaletown, was a published author of nine books of poetry and prose. This was true. It was also true that my suite overlooked the alley where stoned youth staggered to squabble and shoot up, true, too, that I earned poverty wages from sporadic freelance work, and sometimes lay awake at night worrying about being homeless again. Once in a while, I found myself peering into doorways and considering which coats and comforters would best keep out the cold. But now I found the press of other people overwhelming; the noise and bustle of public spaces sent me scurrying back to my lair. The accidental brush of a stranger's body in a crowd would spark a frantic rage that I wasn't always successful in smothering. How would I handle life on the streets if it came to that again?

Lau's struggles with her past are juxtaposed with her current life. This conflict is explicitly explored with strong imagery.

The hour of the workshop passed in a blur. For the first time ever, I had forgotten my notes—reaching into my purse minutes before the session began, my fingers grasped at air. Fortunately, we weren't expected to speak at length, and the round-table participants were a lively bunch. The applause that greeted each of the writers was deafening, a touching show of support and acceptance from the people who had received none growing up. It was a reminder of what had drawn me to this area, the relief of being in a place where no one was in a position to judge anyone else. This was a seductive lure, and I felt the tug of it again, sitting there around the dirty table while hands reached hungrily and unabashedly for stacks of cookies from the platter of refreshments.

In a subtle contrast to the rest of the piece, Lau highlights a positive incident that impacted her greatly.

An older woman at the workshop fixed me in her kind gaze and said she had appreciated my writing set in the Downtown Eastside but had been surprised when she'd come across an essay of mine describing quite a different neighbourhood, Yaletown. "It was still good, but it was so… different. I wonder, has having some success as a writer changed your material?"

I mumbled something about how as we get older and accumulate a variety of experiences, they influence and expand our work, but perhaps she felt I had turned away from this place, set out for greener pastures without looking back. Well, what was the result of looking back? A kind of swirling pain, a mounting wave of panic that had to be swallowed and anesthetized. It wasn't a good idea to look back, not even at the bright moments, the displays of compassion or generosity that sprang forth every day: the man who picked you up hitchhiking and didn't try to grope you in exchange for the free ride, the woman who gave you a bag of doughnuts because you reminded her of her daughter. I really didn't want to remember any of it. I took the bus back west, back to the land of Lululemon and purse-sized dogs, back to my condo where I looked out at the alley and fought for breath.

Source: http://www.straight.com/article-201936/homeless-past-stirs-pain

Carefully chosen adjectives and descriptive phrases allow the reader to experience Lau's journey.

How to read observations

Make notes as you read, either in the margins or on paper or a computer file. Circle any words or references that you don't know and look them up.

What is it?	• What kind of a text is it? An article? An essay? A website? Field notes? A photographic essay? What are your expectations for this kind of text? • What media are used? (Websites, for example, often combine images, words, and sounds.)
Where did it come from?	• Who wrote the observation? How authentic is the observation? • How and when were the observations made?
Who is the intended audience?	• What clues do you find about what readers the writer had in mind? • What does the writer assume that the readers already know about the subject? • What new knowledge is the writer providing?
What is the overall impression?	• Does the writer give precise, objective, concrete details? • Does the writer comment on the observations? • What sensory information is provided?
How are the observations organized?	• Chronologically? In order of perceived importance? Or some other way?
What is the larger context surrounding the writer's observations?	• For what purposes were the observations made?
How is it composed?	• How does the writer represent herself or himself? • How would you characterize the style? • How effective is the design? Is it easy to read? • If there are any photographs or other graphics, what information do they contribute?

Faces of Afghanistan

(PHOTO ESSAY)

Doug Schmidt

Doug Schmidt has been a reporter for the *Windsor Star* for 14 years. As a journalist, he has received the Governor General's Michener Citation as part of a team of investigators looking into the effects of air pollution. In 2007, he also received a National Newspaper Award nomination for an investigative report into a hospital murder. In his second tour in Afghanistan, Schmidt used his photographs and blogs to bring home the realities of Canada's military role in this war-torn nation. In this photo essay, Schmidt looks at the human side of the war, and explains in pictures why Canada fights.

Analyzing and Connecting

Return to these questions after you have finished looking at the images.

1. You can read about Schmidt's experience in his blog on page 150. In this photo essay, however, he relies on images to convey a certain message—one that may or may not be balanced. Assess his choices of images. Speculate on the purpose and the reasons these particular images were used.

2. Look closely at the images. What is the focus of all the pictures? What is absent? How does Schmidt represent the relationship of the people to their surroundings?

3. Overall, what is the dominant impression in all the images? Is it positive? Hopeful? Fearful? What emotions is he trying to convey?

4. Many of the portraits are of children or include children. Why would Schmidt focus on children in this portrayal?

SCHMIDT: FACES OF AFGHANISTAN

Capt. Tylere Couture greets neighbours

SCHMIDT: FACES OF AFGHANISTAN

Kandahar City

Afghan police head home after training

Girls of Naseran

Afghan boy with his pet bird

SCHMIDT: FACES OF AFGHANISTAN

Geoff Logue wins hearts and minds

New friends help pass the time at an army roadblock

Capt. Fraser Clark and the boys of Nasaran

Traditional women

A Small Place
(ESSAY)
Jamaica Kincaid

Jamaica Kincaid was born in Antigua in 1949, and she moved to New York City at age 18 to work as an au pair, taking care of rich people's children. She had planned to become a nurse, but while supporting herself with odd jobs, she began publishing her writing. She shortly gained wide acclaim for two works of fiction about life in Antigua, *At the Bottom of the River* (1983) and *Annie John* (1985). In 1988 she published *A Small Place,* a short, polemical nonfiction book about Antigua, from which the excerpt below is taken.

Analyzing and Connecting

Return to these questions after you have finished reading.

1. Kincaid describes Antigua, the place where she was born and grew up, from the perspective of a tourist just arriving on her island. Why does she describe Antigua from the point of view of the second-person "you"?

2. Examine places where Kincaid contrasts what a tourist sees and what the local sees. What causes the differences?

3. Kincaid writes, "A tourist is an ugly human being." Many readers have taken offence at her bitter tone; perhaps you will too. Why is she so deliberately provocative?

4. What is the alternative for an island like Antigua that offers little economic opportunity besides tourism? Is tourism necessarily bad? Should tourists be concerned about issues such as the sewage system of beach resorts?

If you go to Antigua as a tourist, this is what you will see. If you come by aeroplane, you will land at the V. C. Bird International Airport. Vere Cornwall (V. C.) Bird is the Prime Minister of Antigua. You may be the sort of tourist who would wonder why a Prime Minister would want an airport named after him—why not a school, why not a hospital, why not some great public monument? You are a tourist and you have not yet seen a school in Antigua, you have not yet seen the hospital in Antigua, you have not yet seen a public monument in Antigua. As your plane descends to land, you might say, What a beautiful island Antigua is—more beautiful than any of the other islands you have seen, and they were very beautiful, in their way, but they were much too green, much too lush with vegetation, which indicated to you, the tourist, that they got quite a bit of rainfall, and rain is the very thing that you, just now, do not want, for you are thinking of the hard and cold and dark and long days you spent working in North America (or, worse, Europe), earning some money so that you could stay in this place (Antigua) where the sun always shines and where the climate is deliciously hot and dry for the four to ten days you are going to be staying there; and since you are on your holiday, since you are a tourist, the thought of what it might be like for someone who had to live day in, day out in a place that suffers constantly from drought, and so has to watch carefully every drop of fresh water used (while at the same time surrounded by a sea and an ocean—the Caribbean Sea on one side, the Atlantic Ocean on the other), must never cross your mind.

You disembark from your plane. You go through customs. Since you are a tourist, a North American or European—to be frank, white—and not an Antiguan black returning to Antigua from Europe or North America with cardboard boxes of much needed cheap clothes and food for relatives, you move through customs swiftly, you move through customs with ease. Your bags are not searched. You emerge from customs into the hot, clean air: immediately you feel cleansed, immediately you feel blessed (which is to say special); you feel free. You see a man, a taxi driver; you ask him to take you to your destination; he quotes you a price. You immediately think that the price is in the local currency, for you are a tourist and you are familiar with these things (rates of exchange) and you feel even more free, for things seem so cheap, but then your driver ends by saying, "In U.S. currency." You may say, "Hmmmm, do you have a formal sheet that lists official prices and destinations?" Your driver obeys the law and shows you the sheet, and he apologises for the incredible mistake he has made in quoting you a price off the top of his head which is so vastly different (favoring him) from the one listed. You are driven to your hotel by this taxi driver in his taxi, a brand-new Japanese-made vehicle. The road on which you are traveling is a very bad road, very much in need of repair. You are feeling wonderful, so you say, "Oh, what a marvelous change these bad roads are from the splendid highways I am used to in North America." (Or, worse, Europe.) Your driver is reckless; he is a dangerous man who drives in the middle of the road when he thinks no other cars are coming in the opposite direction, passes other cars on blind curves that run uphill, drives at sixty miles an hour on narrow, curving roads when the road sign, a rusting, beat-up thing left over from colonial days, says 40 MPH. This might frighten you (you are on your holiday; you are a tourist); this might excite you (you are on your holiday; you are a tourist), though if you are from New York and take taxis you are used to this style of driving: most of the taxi drivers in New York are from places in the world like this.

Oh, but by now you are tired of all this looking, and you want to reach your destination—your hotel, your room. You long to refresh yourself; you long to eat some nice lobster, some nice local food. You take a bath, you brush your teeth. You get dressed again; as you get dressed, you look out the window. That water—have you ever seen anything like it? Far out, to the horizon, the color of the water is navy-blue; nearer, the water is the color of the North American sky. From there to the shore, the water is pale, silvery, clear, so clear that you can see its pinkish-white sand bottom. Oh, what beauty! Oh, what beauty! You have never seen anything like this. You are so excited. You breathe shallow. You breathe deep. You see a beautiful boy skimming the water, godlike, on a Windsurfer. You see an incredibly unattractive, fat, pastry-like-fleshed woman enjoying a walk on the beautiful sand, with a man, an incredibly unattractive, fat, pastrylike-fleshed man; you see the pleasure they're taking in their surroundings. Still standing, looking out the window, you see yourself lying on the beach, enjoying the amazing sun (a sun so powerful and yet so beautiful, the way it is always overhead as if on permanent guard, ready to stamp out any cloud that dares to darken and so empty rain on you and ruin your holiday; a sun that is your personal friend). You see yourself taking a walk on that beach, you see yourself meeting new people (only they are new in a very limited way, for they are people just like you). You see yourself eating some delicious, locally grown food. You see yourself, you see yourself . . . You must not wonder what exactly happened to the contents of your lavatory when you flushed it. You must not wonder where your bathwater went when you pulled out the stopper. You must not wonder what happened when you brushed your teeth. Oh, it might all end up in the water you are thinking of taking a swim in; the contents of your lavatory might, just might, graze gently against your ankle as you wade carefree in the water, for you see, in Antigua, there is no proper sewage-disposal system. But the Caribbean Sea is very big and the Atlantic Ocean is even bigger; it would amaze even you to know the number of black slaves this ocean has swallowed up. When you sit down to eat your delicious meal, it's better that you don't know that most of what you are eating came off a plane from Miami. And before it got on a plane in Miami, who knows where it came from? A good guess is that it came from a place like Antigua first, where it was grown dirt-cheap, went to Miami, and came back. There is a world of something in this, but I can't go into it right now.

The thing you have always suspected about yourself the minute you become a tourist is true: A tourist is an ugly human being. You are not an ugly person all the time; you are not an ugly person ordinarily; you are not an ugly person day to day. From day to day, you are a nice person. From day to day, all the people who are supposed to love you on the whole do. From day to day, as you walk down a busy street in the large and modern and prosperous city in which you work and live, dismayed, puzzled (a cliché, but only a cliché can explain you) at how alone you feel in this crowd, how awful it is to go unnoticed, how awful it is to go unloved, even as you are surrounded by more people than you could possibly get to know in a lifetime that lasted for millennia, and then out of the corner of your eye you see someone looking at you and absolute pleasure is written all over that person's face, and then you realize that you are not as revolting a presence as you think you are (for that look just told you so). And so, ordinarily, you are a nice person, an attractive person, a person capable of drawing to yourself the affection of other people (people just like you), a person at home in your own skin (sort of; I mean, in a way; I mean, your dismay and puzzlement are natural to you, because people like you just

seem to be like that, and so many of the things people like you find admirable about yourselves—the things you think about, the things you think really define you—seem rooted in these feelings): a person at home in your own house (and all its nice house things), with its nice back yard (and its nice back-yard things), at home on your street, your church, in community activities, your job, at home with your family, your relatives, your friends—you are a whole person. But one day, when you are sitting somewhere, alone in that crowd, and that awful feeling of displacedness comes over you, and really, as an ordinary person you are not well equipped to look too far inward and set yourself aright, because being ordinary is already so taxing, and being ordinary takes all you have out of you, and though the words "I must get away" do not actually pass across your lips, you make a leap from being that nice blob just sitting like a boob in your amniotic sac of the modern experience to being a person visiting heaps of death and ruin and feeling alive and inspired at the sight of it; to being a person lying on some faraway beach, your stilled body stinking and glistening in the sand, looking like something first forgotten, then remembered, then not important enough to go back for; to being a person marveling at the harmony (ordinarily, what you would say is the backwardness) and the union these other people (and they are other people) have with nature. And you look at the things they can do with a piece of ordinary cloth, the things they fashion out of cheap, vulgarly colored (to you) twine, the way they squat down over a hole they have made in the ground, the hole itself is something to marvel at, and since you are being an ugly person this ugly but joyful thought will swell inside you: their ancestors were not clever in the way yours were and not ruthless in the way yours were, for then would it not be you who would be in harmony with nature and backwards in that charming way? An ugly thing, that is what you are when you become a tourist, an ugly, empty thing, a stupid thing, a piece of rubbish pausing here and there to gaze at this and taste that, and it will never occur to you that the people who inhabit the place in which you have just paused cannot stand you, that behind their closed doors they laugh at your strangeness (you do not look the way they look); the physical sight of you does not please them; you have bad manners (it is their custom to eat their food with their hands; you try eating their way, you look silly; you try eating the way you always eat, you look silly); they do not like the way you speak (you have an accent); they collapse helpless from laughter, mimicking the way they imagine you must look as you carry out some everyday bodily function. They do not like you. *They do not like me!* That thought never actually occurs to you. Still, you feel a little uneasy. Still, you feel a little foolish. Still, you feel a little out of place. But the banality of your own life is very real to you; it drove you to this extreme, spending your days and your nights in the company of people who despise you, people you do not like really,

people you would not want to have as your actual neighbour. And so you must devote yourself to puzzling out how much of what you are told is really, really true (Is ground-up bottle glass in peanut sauce really a delicacy around here, or will it do just what you think ground-up bottle glass will do? Is this rare, multicolored, snout-mouthed fish really an aphrodisiac, or will it cause you to fall asleep permanently?). Oh, the hard work all of this is, and is it any wonder, then, that on your return home you feel the need of a long rest, so that you can recover from your life as a tourist?

That the native does not like the tourist is not hard to explain. For every native of every place is a potential tourist, and every tourist is a native of somewhere. Every native everywhere lives a life of overwhelming and crushing banality and boredom and desperation and depression, and every deed, good and bad, is an attempt to forget this. Every native would like to find a way out, every native would like a rest, every native would like a tour. But some natives—most natives in the world—cannot go anywhere. They are too poor to escape the reality of their lives; and they are too poor to live properly in the place where they live, which is the very place you, the tourist, want to go—so when the natives see you, the tourist, they envy you, they envy your ability to leave your own banality and boredom, they envy your ability to turn their own banality and boredom into a source of pleasure for yourself.

Low Wages, Strong Backs

(ARTICLE)

Tom Meagher and Suzanne Travers

Journalist Tom Meagher spent one month living and working as a low-wage day labourer in Passaic County, New Jersey. His story idea is not new. George Orwell wrote about his experiences of living among the desperately poor in the 1930s in *Down and Out in London and Paris,* and Barbara Ehrenreich has written recently about surviving on low-paying jobs in *Nickle and Dimed.* Nevertheless, Meagher describes vividly how difficult it is to start over with nothing in the bank. Meagher and cowriter Suzanne Travers reported his experience in a series of articles in 2005 for the *New Jersey Herald.*

Analyzing and Connecting

Return to these questions after you have finished reading.

1. Meagher takes an approach to reporting that is similar to the method that anthropologists call "ethnography." It requires living among the subjects you write about and learning firsthand about their world. What does Meagher learn about low-wage workers that he could not have found out by interviewing them?

2. The key to writing a live-the-experience article is to be believable. What strategies does Meagher use to convince his readers that he is telling the truth?

3. Another challenge in writing these articles is describing mind-numbing work. Look for specific description of jobs. What writing strategies do Meagher and Travers use?

4. How does Meagher's experience of living at the edge of homelessness differ from how politicians and the media represent poor people?

LOW WAGES, STRONG BACKS

Today I face the clock. Standing on an assembly line in a warehouse in Mount Olive, I wear safety goggles and stack boxes full of Euphoria perfume on a wooden pallet as they come off the conveyor belt. Women in white lab coats scurry around downstairs, pulling bottles randomly off the line to test them in the quality assurance room.

Folding or stacking or filling these boxes I am a cog in the production wheel, repeating motions that get my bit of the work done. Yesterday, it was open box, pull out bag, pull box from bag, pivot. Today it's fold, stack, slide. Everybody is interchangeable, especially temps like me.

My feet are tired from standing, but even worse is today's spot on the line: I'm directly in front of the clock. I don't think I can watch eight hours drag by, second by second. I keep my head down and force myself to fold 50 boxes before I look up again. When I do, it's only five minutes later. OK then, I'll do 100 boxes.

This job pays $8 an hour. That's nearly $3 more than I made last week stacking boxes of foam padding at a factory in Moonachie. This is temp work in the "light industrial" sector: warehouses and boxes and hours that stretch forever for dollars that don't.

Tom Meagher gets his evening call from his fiancée at a pay phone on Main Avenue in Passaic. KYE-RYUNG LEE/NEW JERSEY HERALD

I'm a newspaper reporter, though nobody in this warehouse knows it. I'm three weeks into a month-long project aimed at showing what life is like for people starting over in Passaic County: the thousands of new immigrants who arrive each year, or people who've lost jobs. What kind of work and housing exist for those who need both, fast? This is my assignment: Find a job and a place to live and write about the experience.

Last year, 85,069 Passaic County residents—17 percent of the county's population—lived below the federal poverty line, as compared with 722,300 —8.5 percent—statewide. Legal Services of New Jersey's Poverty Research Institute estimates that a single person living in

Passaic County needs to make $9.64 an hour to meet all his or her needs. Can I do that?

My experience won't be a perfect example of the temp life. I'm white, American-born, English-speaking and college-educated. I have health insurance through North Jersey Media Group, which owns the *Herald News*. I know if things get bad, I can go home. That's hardly the profile of most people in this situation. Still, I hope this project will illuminate the lives and challenges of those who come here, seeking a future, and those, born here, who struggle to live near the poverty line.

As a reporter, I make about $33,000. Like everyone I know, I work really hard just to scrape by. In the days before this assignment starts, I'm nervous and excited. I'm burnt out from months of cranking out stories, and I think that a few weeks at a no-stress job will be just what I need.

I begin on August 1, a Monday. I leave behind my checkbook, my ATM card, my credit card, my cell phone, my car keys, my fiancée and our apartment in Brooklyn. I've got $424 to get started, an amount based on a week's wages at the Poverty Research Institute's self-sufficiency level. I board a jitney shuttle bus in New York City and head for Paterson with a backpack full of clothes. Now I'm depressed to be alone and scared of what's ahead.

I get off on Main Street in South Paterson and go to the library to check the classifieds. There are rooms for rent in Haledon, Clifton and Passaic. I make calls at a payphone across the street. An agency in Fair Lawn will find me a room for a $100 fee, but that's almost a quarter of the money I have right now—not worth it.

Today is a scorcher, the beginning of a month of a dozen 90-plus-degree days. My backpack weighs about 40 pounds. I lug it down Main Avenue in Clifton. I don't want to waste money on sun-block, but I can feel my skin turning red. As the day goes by, my legs chafe against each other into a stinging rash. I make more calls. People want more money than I've got for a room: One place asks $165 a week, plus a $330 security deposit and $100 for the key.

I don't have a car to check out apartments, and every phone call or jitney ride chips away at my wad of cash. I check out a rooming house in the city of Passaic, then walk to another on Paulison Avenue. The house contains 11 of the 569 licensed rooming house units left in Passaic.

"You welfare? You work?" asks the landlady, Señora Maria Ortega. Work, I tell her. I don't have a job yet, but I'm going to get one.

She shows me a second-floor room. The house is a rambling Victorian. I can see a hint of its past in the bathroom's stained-glass windows. The room she

MEAGHER AND TRAVERS: LOW WAGES, STRONG BACKS

shows me is spacious, spare and worn. A patchwork of brown carpet pieces, woven and shag, covers the floor. There's a faint stench of mold and urine in the hallway, but it's tough to argue with $125 a week.

Señora Maria tells me I seem nice, but I can't have the room until tomorrow.

I take the jitney to see another place. No luck. It's 5 p.m., and I don't know where I'm going to sleep yet.

I start to panic.

I find a payphone and call my fiancée, Ginger, almost in tears. I'm scared and dejected. The heat has sucked the life out of me. I'm sore and sunburned and my legs are so chafed I can hardly walk. I spend $1.79 for dinner at White Castle and start calling hotels. The cheapest costs $70 a night, plus tax. I don't want to risk spending that much for one night when I still have to pay a security deposit.

In the end, I find a place to stay like most people do: through a friend. Ginger's friend's cousin's boyfriend lives in Jersey City and agrees to let me crash on his floor. The cousin picks me up, and I'm so relieved. I feel safe, and happy that I can relax, and so grateful I could cry.

The next day I am too spent to look for work. At 4 p.m., I move into Señora Maria's house. I have to give her two weeks' rent plus a $20 key deposit. In just two days, my $424 has dwindled to $110. It all adds up: jitney rides to look for apartments, phone cards to answer job ads. I eat a dinner of $2 cheeseburgers, unpack and go over every inch of the room. There's a flimsy wooden dresser and a plywood entertainment center where I stack my clothes. On the closet wall I later find a trace of who's been here before:

"Rainbow Lesbians Yelly n Jessie," someone has carved.

"2gether til eternity Was here 6/30/03 left 8/9/04"

I sleep with a hammer next to my pillow in case the door lock is as flimsy as it looks. I try to ignore the people outside, yelling and honking their car horns.

ON THE JOB

I spend the next two days looking for work. Up and down Main Avenue, through Clifton and Passaic, I fill out applications and stop at places with help-wanted signs. I use my real name, but I'm vague about my background. I try about 20 businesses, with little success. A taxi company needs drivers, but it takes four weeks to get a license. I've washed dishes for restaurants, but Venezia's needs only waiters. I stop by Brickforce Staffing, one of a few temporary employment agencies in the city of Passaic. A woman tells me to come in at 6 a.m. and ask for Nelson. I'm sick of walking everywhere. My employment opportunities would double if I had a bike. I see a few and am tempted to take one—why don't kids lock up their bikes? I call it a day and head home.

The next morning I'm up a few minutes after 5 a.m. It's still dark as I walk the mile downtown. At the Brickforce office, I sign a couple of forms and show my Social Security card. That's all it takes: I'm hired. The morning rush there is busy. People trickle in and, by 6 a.m., workers crowd around Nelson, the dispatcher, angling to be sent out on a job. Nelson takes calls from clients on a cell phone while juggling others on a speakerphone, all the while talking to jitney drivers over a Nextel walkie-talkie.

Later, I learn that Brickforce is well known, thanks to a word-of-mouth network. Brickforce acts as the middleman between warehouses and factories across North Jersey and a pool of laborers. The warehouses, or clients, use temps when regular workers are absent or when there's a big shipment coming in and not enough people to get the job done.

In economic terms, Brickforce supplies a product—workers—to its clients for a fee. The boxes we fold and move and stack are the clients' product, but I am Brickforce's product: a worker ready to work. Temporary agencies give the labor market flexibility to respond to demand: Their people can fill one factory's need one week, another factory's the next. At its best, it means flexibility for employees who may be between jobs or unable to take a full-time job. The light-industrial sector pays the lowest wages in the temp industry: between $5.15 and $9 an hour at Brickforce.

I pile into a jitney with about 20 other temps. There are no seat belts, and the bus rattles like a dishwasher—we shake back and forth like we're on Mr. Toad's Wild Ride. Brickforce subcontracts with a jitney service as an essential part of business. Because the agency transports us to the warehouses, it can promise on-time delivery of the necessary number of workers each day. Some temp agencies expect workers to get to the work site themselves, a problem for clients and agencies if workers show up late or not at all.

FINE PRINT
While Brickforce sells clients this competitive advantage, it charges employees for the ride. The rationale is that if Brickforce didn't shuttle us to warehouses, we'd have to pay to get there ourselves. I don't have a car and public transportation could take hours. Brickforce subtracts between $4 and $7 a day from my wages to pay for the rides to and from work. No one tells me this directly, but the arrangement is explained in a section of the application I signed on my first day.

Still, the deduction doesn't register until I get my first paycheck. The company jitney costs less than if I had to ride New Jersey Transit to Secaucus, where my first assignment is. But the jitney also means getting up at 5 a.m., in the dark, so I can walk to Brickforce. There I wait up to 30 minutes for the ride, then spend an hour or so onboard—sometimes standing in the aisle—as the driver drops off a few workers at one factory, a few more at another. Some afternoons I wait 90 minutes after my shift ends—all off the clock—to get picked up.

My co-worker Priyank says he doesn't mind the jitney, except when the driver forgets to pick him up. He's had to walk more than three miles home from a factory in Wood-Ridge to the city of Passaic.

Almost all the other temp workers speak Spanish and little English. I'm assigned to work with one man, and we develop a kind of sign language. I'm raring to go and working quickly, but it's only 8 a.m. My partner gestures with his hands, and the message is clear: Ease up a little. It turns out to be an unspoken rule of temping. Don't work too hard or too fast. The day is long and the work exhausting. No one pays you enough to wear yourself out. As it is, I can't pay my second week's rent. I make a deal with Señora Maria to pay her installments until I get a full paycheck.

I spend my first full week at a warehouse near Teterboro airport. It's ridiculously hot. We're assigned busy work while we wait more than a week for a truck carrying 1,000 boxes to arrive from California. When the driver gets in, Steve, my supervisor, tells him the delay has cost him $2,000 a day. Now there's work to do. Steve and I stand deep inside the trailer loading boxes onto pallets. We work through the afternoon break. My arms are sore and I'm soaked with sweat, but the action, the constant scooping, tossing, turning, feels exhilarating. When we're done I'm almost a little sad to see it end. We finish in two hours, for which I earn $14, before taxes.

LIFE OUT OF REACH

Another temp named Julio and I sort the 1,000 boxes, then assemble them in smaller stacks and label them. The radio blares commercials that advertise a life out of reach: Take your family to Dorney Park; buy a computer; invest in real estate. I put on gloves and grab a 2-foot-long roll of shrinkwrap. I tuck one end under the corner of a box and run around the stack in circles, wrapping it for transport. By the time I'm done, I'm dizzy.

Everything that comes through the warehouse—mostly women's clothes, shoes, handbags—is made in other countries. Basically, we take large shipments and repackage them into smaller ones that go out to discount clothing stores.

We break when the lunch truck arrives. I buy a slice of pizza. Julio eats his box lunch quickly and then sleeps. He sleeps on breaks, on the jitney, every moment he can. I pull out a Spanish phrase book and tell Julio I am trying to learn Spanish; he says he needs to learn English and we begin to talk. He's from Peru, where he used to be an accountant. He had a business and rented out apartments, but Peru's sour economy left him unable to find work to put his son through medical school. He came here last year on a tourist visa and started working at Brickforce.

SHEER EXHAUSTION

Julio, who does not use his real name for fear of deportation, lives with his aunt and her husband in Passaic. At 49, he's left behind his wife and children in Peru, but exhaustion keeps him from feeling lonely. He sleeps only four hours a night. "I work and work," he tells me.

He works at Brickforce from 6 a.m. to 4 p.m., then at McDonald's from 5 to 11 p.m., except on weekends, when he works the overnight shift. He takes home $375 a week for 78 hours of work. He pays no rent, so most of his paycheck goes back to his family in Peru, nearly $1,300 a month.

Julio's plan is to work in the U.S. for five years. He wants to work here legally, but he has no time to find out how to get the proper documents. He took a year preparing his family for his departure. They didn't want him to go. "That's a father's sacrifice," he says. You want your children to have a better life.

He calls home every Sunday. He misses his wife so much. Every time they talk, they cry. He carries photos of his wife, parents, sisters and children in a knapsack, wherever he goes. In some, they're smiling because it's Christmas, or they're relaxing with friends. Two pictures show Julio with his family at the airport the day he left Lima. Their faces have a stony, blank look of worry and disbelief.

AT HOME

Tenants in my rooming house have no kitchen access, and we aren't allowed appliances in our rooms. (The rules say no microwaves, no air conditioning.) My first paycheck, for the first day I worked, comes to $35.16 after taxes and the jitney fee. My second paycheck, for a full week's work, comes to $196.46. After paying $125 a week in rent, I'll have $5 a day to live on. I skip breakfast and decide to ration my money between lunch and dinner.

Fast-food dollar menus and value meals are a salvation, and I'm grateful for cheap slices of pizza. At the grocery store, two days of food money buys enough bread, peanut butter and jelly for 10 sandwiches—a couple days' worth. One payday, I treat myself to a two-piece fried chicken combo from KFC for $5.29. I think about food all the time.

In the evenings it's hot in my room, and I'm lonely. I've got a standing phone date with my girlfriend, Ginger. In the beginning I buy $5 phone cards so I can call her. They're supposed to charge 10 cents a minute, but there's a 90-cent surcharge every time I use the card at a payphone, so I can only make three or four calls per card. I miss her an almost unhealthy amount, even though she comes to visit every week or so. The fact that I can't call her when I want to is making our separation painful. I think of Julio. I can't imagine what it would be like to leave her behind and go to another country.

AN ODDITY

I've been at Brickforce a couple of weeks when Nelson tells me I'm a good worker. I get the sense that "good" means mostly that I'm on time. Nelson says he doesn't want me to be bounced between $8-an-hour jobs and $5-an-hour ones. He'll try to get me $8 an hour from now on.

Turns out the best-paying job is at the perfume factory in Mount Olive. After a few days, the regimentation there reminds me of high school. We're transported in buses, profanity's not allowed, we keep our bags in lockers, and the women constantly leave the assembly line in pairs to go to the bathroom. At day's end, everyone stops, waits for the end-of-shift buzzer and runs for the front door.

When he announced the job, Nelson said he needed five men and 10 women. Nobody questions this division of labor, and there are more women than men.

Later, I learn this segregation may be discrimination, banned by state and federal law. Last week, when I asked the company to comment on this story, it said, "Brickforce Staffing complies with all federal and state laws pertaining to hiring practices, wage and hour guidelines and any other applicable regulation and/or statute."

There also seems to be a hierarchy based on language. To work here, you're supposed to know English. I don't think Julio was even considered for this job for that reason. Most line workers are Spanish speakers with only basic English: hello, yes, no, thank you. The line supervisors are bilingual Latinos; the managers speak English only.

This makes me an oddity on the line. I'm the only white guy, and the only native English speaker, on the Brickforce jitney in the morning. Nobody talks to me. I imagine people assume I've just gotten out of jail. In the warehouses, though, I get a few questions.

"Why are you working for the agency?" asks one of the regulars at one warehouse. "It doesn't pay anything."

"Are you Polish? From Polonia?" someone else asks.

I've got dirty blond hair and a pink complexion, but a Latino co-worker asks me: "Are you white?"

The questions puzzle me until I realize what's behind them. It's rare to see white people in the Brickforce temp world. In downtown Passaic, someone with blond hair is probably from Poland. White Americans don't work these jobs; Caucasians who do are usually immigrants from Eastern Europe. My co-workers are trying to fit me into the categories that define their lives and this work. I think about the guy who asked if I'm white and marvel. The segregation of class along racial lines is so strong it's made him question what he can see before his eyes.

WINDING DOWN

By the two-week mark, I can't wait for this project to end. I begin to count down: two days until the weekend, one week until an overnight trip to Baltimore for my grandfather's memorial service; a few days more and I'll be done. I wake up every day, go to work, come home to shower, go to the library, then wait for Ginger's call.

Finally, it's August 31. I tell Nelson it's my last day and tell the rooming-house super I'm moving out on Sept. 1. The super says if I'm ever back in town I can stay there. I pack my things, take the jitney to Paterson and walk up Grand Street. I trudge onto New Street, over Interstate 80, to the *Herald News* office.

I kept a job and a roof over my head and my belly mostly full—a life of minimalist survival. I couldn't have supported a child or taken a vacation, a day off or a sick day. To do better, I'd need to do what so many, like Julio, do: work a second job. An illness or work slowdown could have plunged me into homelessness.

At the office, I put my bags down and hug my colleagues. In the weeks ahead, I'll find I'm still scraping by at the paper, but it's different than temping in Passaic. I can eat when I want to, see my girlfriend and friends, talk to my co-workers instead of laboring in silence. I feel connected to the world, and that makes a huge difference.

I'm relieved it's over. In a second, I step out of one life and back into my own.

How to write an observation

These steps for the process of writing an observation may not progress as neatly as this chart might suggest. Writing is not an assembly-line process. As you write, you are constantly reading what you have written and rethinking.

Writing may help you to remember details about what you have observed.

1 CHOOSE A SUBJECT

- Analyze the assignment.
- Identify your goals.
- Choose a person or people.
- Choose a place.
- Plan your observations.

2 MAKE OBSERVATIONS AND ANALYZE THEM

- Make observations.
- Analyze the observations.
- Analyze patterns and draw implications.
- Be a "participant observer."

Analyze your potential readers

- *What do your readers likely know about the place?*
- *What are your readers' expectations of the genre?*

3 WRITE A DRAFT

- Determine your thesis or the overall impression you want to convey.
- Determine your point of view.
- Determine an organizational strategy.
- Select details.
- Grab readers at the beginning, and leave them with something to think about.

4 REVISE, REVISE, REVISE

- Check that your paper or project fulfills the assignment.
- Make sure that you have a focused thesis or a clear overall impression.
- Revise your introduction, if needed, to draw readers in.
- Examine the organization.
- Add details to make the description more concrete.
- Check that the conclusion gives a sense of significance of the observations.
- Review the visual presentation.
- Proofread carefully.

5 SUBMITTED VERSION

- Make sure your finished writing meets all formatting requirements.

1: Choose a subject or place to observe

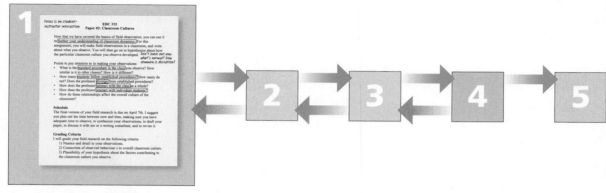

Analyze the assignment

- Read your assignment slowly and carefully. Look for the key words *observe, field research,* or *field observation*. These key words tell you that you are writing about your firsthand observations.
- Note any specifics about what you should observe.

Identify your goals

- Different kinds of observing have different goals. What makes an observation effective for this assignment?
- Think about what categories of subjects or places would fit the assignment.

Choose people or subjects in nature

- If your assignment asks you to observe people, think about whom you might observe—a supervisor, a front-desk person, an athlete on and off the court or field, players of video games or other games, viewers of television or performances, or people exercising.
- Consider how each person interacts with others or how a group maintains its identity.
- If your assignment asks you to observe a subject in nature, determine what you might observe—an animal in a natural setting or a natural phenomenon like a thunderstorm.

| **Choose a place** | • If your assignment asks you to observe a place, think about where you might observe—a park, a downtown street, a market, a mall, a restaurant, a factory, a bowling alley, or a game room. |
| | • Consider what recurring activities happen at the place you observe. |

Plan your observations	• Allow a considerable amount of time for making your observations.
	• Determine at what times you will need to visit and what will be going on.
	• Determine the logistics: How will you get there? What will you need to take with you?

| **Analyze your potential readers and genre expectations** | • What do your readers likely know about the place? |
| | • What are your readers' expectations of the genre? If you are doing observations in the sciences or social sciences, your readers will expect you to be objective and not to concentrate on your reactions. |

WRITE NOW

Find a place

Think about possible places that might work for your assignment. Divide a sheet of paper into four columns and label them *place, people, activi-* *ties,* and *times*. List your places in the first column. Then list the people who go there, their behaviour, and the times they are present.

PLACE	PEOPLE	ACTIVITIES	TIMES
Common room in student residence.	Some of the same people everyday.	They view particular programs but also talk and play cards or video games.	Busiest around late afternoon.

When you have at least five possible places, select the one you feel will work best.

Writer at work

Megan Garza was asked to write a micro-ethnography for her Curriculum and Instruction class. She made notes on and highlighted important parts of her assignment sheet.

Megan began by circling key words in the assignment.

Focus is on student-instructor interaction

EDC 332
Paper #2: Classroom Cultures

Now that we have covered the basics of field observation, you can use it to further your understanding of classroom dynamics. For this assignment, you will make field observations in a classroom, and write about what you observe. You will then go on to hypothesize about how the particular classroom culture you observe developed. *Don't leave out any: what's normal? How common is deviation?*

She also made notes to herself about important aspects of the assignment.

Points to pay attention to in making your observations:

- What is the standard procedure in the class you observe? How similar is it to other classes? How is it different?
- How many students follow established procedures? How many do not? Does the professor diverge from established procedures?
- How does the professor interact with the class as a whole?
- How does the professor interact with individual students?
- How do these relationships affect the overall culture of the classroom?

Schedule

The final version of your field research is due on April 7th. I suggest you plan out the time between now and then, making sure you have adequate time to observe, to synthesize your observations, to draft your paper, to discuss it with me or a writing consultant, and to revise it.

Grading Criteria

I will grade your field research on the following criteria:
1) Nuance and detail in your observations.
2) Connection of observed behaviours to overall classroom culture.
3) Plausibility of your hypothesis about the factors contributing to the classroom culture you observe.

After she felt she understood the assignment, Megan made a list of classes she was taking, and chose the one she thought would yield the best results.

English	<u>Advantage</u> Lots of interaction—conversation
	<u>Disadvantage</u> I talk a lot—would be hard to take good notes and still pay attention.
EDS	<u>Advantage</u> Would be interesting to look at Dr. Anzalone's interaction with us.
	<u>Disadvantage</u> Everyone in the class will want to do this.
*Chemistry	<u>Advantage</u> Lots to observe—chaotic atmosphere would be interesting to hypothesize about.
	<u>Disadvantage</u> Will be hard to observe and keep up with notes for class.
Math	<u>Advantage</u> Smaller class size would allow more observation of professor's interaction with individual students.
	<u>Disadvantage</u> I really need to focus exclusively on math when I'm in there.

<u>*Best choice. Ask Chris to help review notes if necessary.</u>

2: Make observations and analyze them

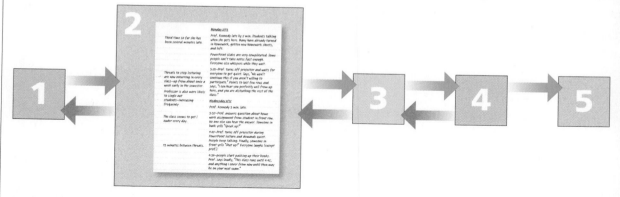

Make observations

- Take notes that record what you observe in detail.
- Write on the right side of your notebook only, saving the left side for observation and commentary after your observations are complete.
- Pay attention to all your senses—smell, taste, touch, and hearing as well as sight. Take photos if possible, or make recordings of sounds.

Be a "participant observer"

- Talk to the people you observe. Ask them questions about their activities, opinions, and feelings. If you are polite and unobtrusive, you will learn a great deal more than if you keep silent.
- Keep your own language distinct, in your notes, from the language of your subjects.

Analyze the observations

- How many different activities were going on during your observations?
- Which activities were particular to this place?
- Were there significant differences among the subjects you observed? Were these differences behavioural or of some other type?
- Did anything unusual happen?
- Why were the subjects there?

Analyze patterns and draw implications

- What patterns can you identify?
- What implications can you draw from these patterns?

Writer at work

Megan spent several weeks making observations of her class. Once a week, she would go back over her observations and makes comments on them, or note links between various days' observations. Here is a page from her notebook:

<u>Monday 2/13</u>

Third time so far she has been several minutes late.

Prof. Kennedy late by 5 min. Students talking when she gets here. Many have already turned in homework, gotten new homework sheets, and left.

PowerPoint slides are very complicated. Some people can't take notes fast enough. Everyone else whispers while they wait.

Threats to stop lecturing are now occurring in every class—up from about once a week early in the semester.

Professor is also more likely to single out students—increasing frequency

3:52—Prof. turns off projector and waits for everyone to get quiet. Says, "We won't continue this if you aren't willing to participate." Points to last few rows and says, "I can hear you perfectly well from up here, and you are disturbing the rest of the class."

<u>Wednesday 2/15</u>

Prof. Kennedy 3 min. late.

The class seems to get louder every day.

3:35—Prof. answers question about homework assignment from student in front row. No one else can hear the answer. Someone in back yells "Speak up!"

4:05—Prof. turns off projector during PowerPoint lecture and demands quiet. People keep talking. Finally, someone in front yells "Shut up!" Everyone laughs (except prof.).

13 minutes between threats.

4:30—people start packing up their books. Prof. says loudly, "This class runs until 4:45, and anything I cover from now until then may be on your next exam."

3: Write a draft

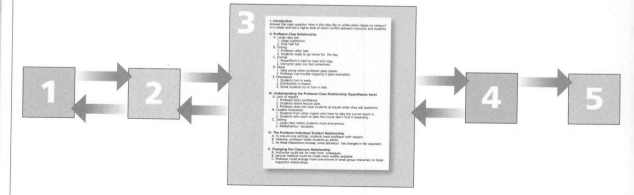

Determine your thesis or the overall impression you want to convey

- If your assignment asks you to observe for particular purpose, likely you will need to provide a clear, significant thesis early on.
- If you are writing a travel account or describing a place, you may not have an explicit thesis, but you will want to convey an overall impression through the details you select.

Determine your point of view

- If you are observing for a science or social science class, focus on when and what you observed.
- If you are writing a travel account or describing a place, you may want to foreground yourself as a participant—why you went there and how you responded to the place and people.

Determine an organization

- You might organize by chronology or by special location.
- You may need to classify your observations into subtopics and organize accordingly.

Select details

- Give accurate, specific information about the place and, if present, the people.
- Include short quotations if you record conversations, and attribute them accurately.

Grab readers at the beginning, and leave them with something to think about

- Choose an appropriate title that will immediately get readers' attention.
- Conclude by leaving your readers with a sense of why your observations matter. Press beyond the superficial.

STAYING ON TRACK

Work for precise description

Show, not tell

OFF TRACK
Hiking cross-country in the Arctic National Wildlife Refuge is very difficult.

ON TRACK
Every centimetre of ground in the Arctic National Wildlife Refuge challenges human walking: meadows of waist-high muskeg brush, quicksand beside the streams and slick rocks in them, loose shale on the hillsides, and uneven tundra hillocks on flat sections that offer no good way to negotiate—plant your foot on them and they collapse sideways, step between them and you sink to your calf.

Provide exact details

OFF TRACK
Grizzly bears and black bears look different.

ON TRACK
Rely on body shape rather than size and colour to distinguish grizzly bears from black bears. Grizzlies have a hump above their front shoulders; black bears lack this hump. In profile, grizzlies have a depression between their eyes and nose, while black bears have a "Roman" profile with a straight line between the forehead and nose.

Give names where possible

OFF TRACK
Many Canadian streets are named after Terry Fox.

ON TRACK
Streets named after Terry Fox can be found in many Canadian cities: Ottawa, Kingston, Mississauga, Thunder Bay, Vancouver, Saint-Eustache, Mascouche, Brighton, Brampton, and Sault Ste. Marie.

Writer at work

Megan realized that the format of her assignment would require her to re-organize her chronological observations. She decided to divide her observations into two main categories, following each one with a section of interpretation. Megan made a brief outline of the section headings she planned to use, and then filled in information from her observations pertaining to each section.

<u>Professor-class relationship</u>

- Large lecture—impersonal
- Professor lectures with PowerPoint, which students copy
- Students talk during class, annoying professor
- Strategies for getting students to be quiet are not effective
- Homework procedure disruptive to class

<u>Professor-individual student relationship</u>

- Students more respectful in one-on-one interactions
- Professor more patient in one-on-one interactions
- Some carryover of mutual respect to lectures for certain students

<u>Interpretation</u>

- Lack of mutual respect—neither students nor professor want to be there
- Required course for nonmajors
- Large lecture format makes the class impersonal

<u>Interpretation</u>

- Situation would be better if class were small
- Changing homework procedure and posting PowerPoints to website would help

I. Introduction
Answer the main question: How is this class like or unlike other classes on campus? It is noisier and has a higher level of direct conflict between instructor and students.

II. Professor–Class Relationship
A. Large class size
   1. The class is held in a large auditorium.
   2. The auditorium is only half full.
B. Timing
   1. Professor is often late.
   2. Students are ready to go home for the day.
C. Format
   1. PowerPoint is hard to read and copy.
   2. Instructor goes too fast sometimes.
D. Noise
   1. Noise gets worse when professor goes slower.
   2. Professor has trouble stopping it (give examples).
E. Homework
   1. Students turn in early.
   2. Distribution is chaotic.
   3. Some students try to turn in late.

III. Understanding the Professor–Class Relationship (hypothesize here)
A. Lack of respect
   1. Professor lacks confidence.
   2. Students resent lecture style.
   3. Professor does not treat students as equals when they ask questions.
B. Student motivation
   1. Students from other majors who have to take the course resent it.
   2. Students who want to take the course don't find it rewarding.
C. Setting
   1. Large class makes students more anonymous.
   2. Misbehaviour escalates.

IV. The Professor–Individual Student Relationship
A. In one-on-one settings, students treat professor with respect.
B. Likewise, professor treats students as adults.
C. As these interactions increase, some behaviour has changed in the classroom.

V. Changing the Classroom Relationship
A. Instructor could ask for help from colleagues.
B. Lecture material could be made more readily available.
C. Professor could arrange more one-on-one or small group interaction to foster respectful relationships.

4: Revise, revise, revise

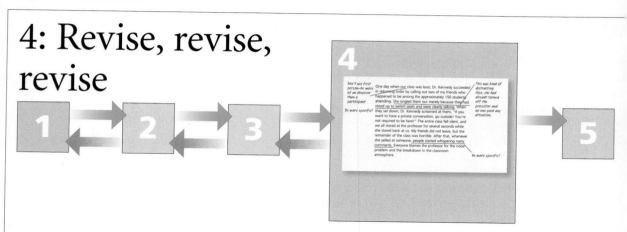

Skilled writers know that the secret to writing well is rewriting. Even the best writers often have to revise several times to get the result they want. You also must have effective strategies for revising if you're going to be successful. The biggest trap you can fall into is starting off with the little stuff first. Leave the small stuff for last.

Does your paper or project meet the assignment?	• Look again at the assignment for specific guidelines, including length, format, and amount of research. Does your work meet these guidelines?
Do you have a focused thesis or a clear overall impression?	• Is it clear to readers what is most important about your observations?
Is your introduction effective?	• Will your title grab people's attention? • Does your introduction draw readers in?
Is your organization effective?	• Is the order the best for your purpose? Possibly you may need to shift the order of some of your paragraphs.
Do you provide vivid, well-chosen details?	• Can you add details to increase interest and paint a clearer picture?
Is your conclusion effective?	• Do you place your observations in a larger overall context? • Do you leave readers with the feeling that they have learned something valuable?
Is the writing project visually effective?	• Is the font attractive and readable? • Are the headings and visuals effective?
Save the editing for last	• When you have finished revising, edit and proofread carefully.

A peer review guide is on page 31.

Writer at work

Megan took a draft of her paper to her instructor's office hours and talked with him about it. She made notes during their conversation and used his comments to guide her revisions. Here, she noted a passage with an overly personal and emotional tone:

Don't use first person—be more of an observer than a participant.

Be more specific?

One day when our class was loud, Dr. Kennedy succeeded in returning order by calling out two of my friends who happened to be among the approximately 150 students attending. She singled them out merely because they had stood up to switch seats and were clearly talking. When they sat down, Dr. Kennedy screamed at them, "If you want to have a private conversation, go outside! You're not required to be here!" The entire class fell silent, and we all stared at the professor for several seconds while she stared back at us. My friends did not leave, but the remainder of the class was horrible. After that, whenever she yelled at someone, people started whispering nasty comments. Everyone blames the professor for the noise problem and the breakdown in the classroom atmosphere.

This was kind of distracting. Also, she had already turned off the projector and no one paid any attention.

Be more specific?

Here is how Megan revised the passage:

On one occasion when the class was loud and ignored her initial attempt to quiet them by turning off the projector, Dr. Kennedy succeeded in returning order by calling out two young men among the approximately 150 students attending. These men were singled out because they had stood up to switch seats and were clearly talking. When they sat down, Dr. Kennedy screamed at them, "If you want to have a private conversation, go outside! You're not required to be here!" The entire class fell silent, and the students and professor stared at each other for several seconds. The young men did not leave, and the remainder of the class was tense. Similar incidents are frequent, and the students react with hostility and complaints. They blame the professor for the noise problem and the breakdown in the classroom atmosphere.

5: Print a version to submit

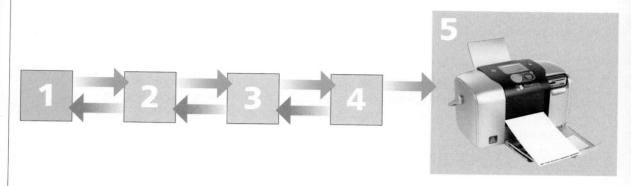

Garza 1

Megan Garza
Professor Anzalone
EDC 332
April 3, 2011

Chemistry 105:
An Analysis of Classroom Dynamics in a Large Lecture Course

Classroom student behaviour on our campus is similar from one class to the next. Most classes establish routines early, and students follow them obediently. Dr. Kennedy's Chemistry for Non-majors, CH 105, is like many other classes with standard procedures, but unlike most other classes, students often don't follow the procedures. The differences between CH 105 and other classes stem directly from the ways the students and the professor interact. Analyzing the professor–class relationship and the professor–individual student relationship suggests why students behave differently in CH 105.

The Professor–Class Relationship

The professor–class relationship sets the tone for the classroom environment and the professor's lecture style. The classroom is a large auditorium, and during most classes it is only half full. Students have plenty of room to spread out, and they relax and talk before class begins. Dr. Kennedy usually arrives a few minutes late, contributing to the students' restlessness, already at a high level because the class begins at 3:30 p.m. when students are ready for the school day to be over.

When the lecture begins, students often do not stop talking. The format of the lectures also contributes to the noise. Dr. Kennedy stands behind a podium with PowerPoint slides projected on a screen behind her. The majority of students find it necessary to copy the points on the slides verbatim. Dr. Kennedy often appears nervous and speaks rapidly, moving to the next slide before students are finished copying the previous one. When she moves too quickly, students howl in protest. Often she becomes impatient and continues anyway, causing resentment. But if she waits for everyone to finish writing, she encounters another problem: noise.

Student talking is the source of most of the conflicts during class. When Dr. Kennedy waits for slower writers to finish copying, the noise begins to build. In turn, the professor becomes annoyed and her patience wears thin. Her most frequent methods are to

1. turn off the projector,
2. stare impatiently,
3. threaten not to lecture,
4. make angry demands for order,
5. single out a loud group and denounce them.

Often she will combine methods if her first attempt is not successful.

On one occasion when the class was loud and ignored her initial attempt to quiet them by turning off the projector, Dr. Kennedy succeeded in returning order by calling out two young men among the approximately 150 students attending. These men were singled out because they had stood up to switch seats and were clearly talking. When they sat down, Dr. Kennedy screamed at them, "If you want to have a private conversation, go outside! You're not required to be here!" The entire class fell silent, and the students and professor stared at each other for several seconds. The young men did not leave, and the remainder of the class was tense. Similar incidents are frequent, and the students react with hostility and complaints. They blame the professor for the noise problem and the breakdown in the classroom atmosphere.

Another source of conflict is the homework procedure. The teaching assistants (TAs) for the class distribute homework assignments each Monday, which are due on the following Monday. The TAs sit on stage before class with stacks of homework assignments. Students often do not wait for the assignments to be passed out but instead rush the stage, collect the new assignment, and submit the completed assignment. Many then leave. The harried TAs rush up and down the aisles passing out assignments, continually interrupted with questions and latecomers. The chaotic procedure prompts Dr. Kennedy to ask repeatedly to get the assignments distributed and collected.

After the TAs have finished walking up and down the aisles, homework is no longer collected. Late students rush up to the stage in an attempt to get Dr. Kennedy to accept their work. At the beginning of the semester, she allowed work to be turned in after the class has started, but she shortly began to refuse because of the delays the late work was causing. Students who come late and are unable to submit their work grow angry and walk away from the stage with looks of disgust. Nevertheless, Monday's classes are always late getting started, with the professor agitated.

Understanding the Professor–Class Relationship

The keys to understanding the professor–class relationship lie in the degree of mutual respect, the reason students are enrolled, and the impersonal nature of a large lecture hall.

Mutual respect is critical for a successful class. Students do not take courses seriously if they believe that the material has no value and the professor is not competent. Many students use the excuse of an inexperienced or ineffective teacher to let their work suffer. Likewise, a professor does not give her best effort if she dislikes the class and finds the students lacking in intelligence. In this case, both the professor and the students have contributed to the generally hostile atmosphere. Dr. Kennedy's lecture method causes many problems because students insist on copying her slides and because many students resent the procedure. She evidently finds the lecture method necessary because of all the chemical equations and examples she must provide.

The professor's attitudes toward the students and the material are reflected in her lectures. The course is a simplified introduction to chemistry for non-science majors with no background in chemistry. In particular, when students ask questions, her response is often taken as condescending. Her tone of voice changes, and she often oversimplifies answers. If she considers the answer obvious, she will talk very slowly, as if she were responding to a small child.

An additional difficulty is the reason students are taking the course. Required courses outside of a student's major are rarely popular. Nevertheless, students do have options in fulfilling the science requirement, and many students in the class want to learn more about chemistry. The class is unrewarding for these students because it seems to be aimed at the lowest level possible, rendering it dull for professor and student alike.

Finally, the large lecture hall makes students anonymous. In a large group students are more likely to behave disrespectfully toward the professor and to flaunt Dr. Kennedy's weak authority. Students often mock her and call her rude names, behaviour that would be unlikely to occur in a small class.

The Professor–Individual Student Relationship

The professor relates to individual students more successfully than to the class as a whole. When students meet with the professor one-on-one or in groups of three or four, the atmosphere is one of mutual respect. Students call the professor Dr. Kennedy instead of the rude names they use in class, and Dr. Kennedy in turn speaks to them in a normal tone of voice and gives detailed answers to questions. She recognizes that the students are intelligent, even if they are novices at chemistry, and the students understand that she is genuinely concerned about their learning.

Some of this change in attitude has carried over to the classroom. Dr. Kennedy has begun to recognize individually some of the students in the class. Their questions are answered first and with a friendly tone. Dr. Kennedy is more likely to slow down when these students make a request. In turn, the students refrain from talking and behave politely.

Changing the Classroom Relationship

The causes of the breakdown of the student–professor classroom relationship in CH 105 are no doubt complex. Why an inexperienced professor was assigned to a potentially difficult class lies beyond the scope of this paper, but it is a contributing factor. The professor could use the advice of experienced colleagues on the basics of classroom management such as an improved procedure for distributing and collecting homework assignments. The content of PowerPoint slides should be made available to students on the class website. Certainly these changes would lead to immediate improvement.

The immediate cause of the poor classroom atmosphere is the lack of mutual respect. Both students and the professor are capable of respecting each other and communicating effectively in small-group interactions. But in the large lecture hall, the mutual respect breaks down. More small-group interactions could help students and the professor to get to know each other and consequently gain the respect of the other.

Projects

Observations span a wide range of writing, from objective scientific reports to highly personal descriptions of places. Accurate, detailed description is valued in all kinds of observations.

These projects are frequently written kinds of observations.

DESCRIPTION OF A PLACE

For an example of a description of a place, see pages 86–90.

Write an essay describing a place. Select one of these options:

Visit an urban neighbourhood that is not familiar to you. Pay close attention to what distinguishes this neighbourhood from other neighbourhoods in the city.

or

Visit a small town near you, preferably one that is not on a major highway. Likely you will find that many of the businesses that once thrived on Main Street or on the courthouse square are gone. Pay close attention to signs and other things that give indications to what goes on in the town.

Visit some stores, a local coffee shop, and other places where you can talk to people. Ask them about their neighbourhood or their town. Then reconstruct conversations in your notebook. Include some dialogue in your paper. If you go with someone else from your class, walk around independently. You should not come up with the same observations and conversations.

PEARSON
mycanadiancomplab

Go to **www.mycanadiancomplab.ca** to practise your grammar, punctuation, and mechanics skills. Go to the "Resources" tab within MyCanadianCompLab and then click on "Grammar." You will have access to a variety of exercises as well as direct instruction that will help you improve your basic skills and get a better grade in your course.

 **NATURAL OBSERVATION**

For an example of a natural observation, see pages 74–78.

 **FIELD OBSERVATION**

For an example of a field observation, see pages 91–99.

Find a setting in which you can observe animals or natural phenomena such as tides, weather patterns, or erosion. In a large city, you might watch pigeons interacting with people in a park, observe feeding time at a zoo, or watch how insects behave during a rainstorm.

Use your observations to generate a list of questions that would help you fill in any gaps in what you observed. Can you explain the behaviour of any animals you observed? If not, how could you determine the causes of their behaviour ? Can your localized observation of a spring-fed pool uncover the causes of the heavy algae growth there, or do you need to look further to find an explanation?

Write a brief description about what you observed, including the questions your observation raised, and any answers you found.

Observe people in a public setting you frequent, such as your student union, a library, a coffee shop, a residence lounge, a gym, a basketball court, or a bus route. Think of one or more questions that field observation might answer. For example, students who use your campus library go there for multiple reasons: to study, to find books, to find journal articles, to use a computer, to watch movies on DVD, to meet their friends, and others.

Collect field notes by observing. Take a notebook and write only on the right-hand pages. Use the left-hand pages later to analyze your data. Plan to spend at least three hours a week at your site for two weeks. You should gather at least ten pages of notes per week. Listen carefully to conversations and record direct quotations. After you leave the site, make comments on your notes on the left-hand page.

Analyze your notes after two weeks of observations. What constitutes abnormal behaviour? How do people learn the normal behaviour for that setting? What happens when the norm is violated by someone?

Write a detailed field observation that includes concrete details and quotations from people at your site. Make your paper interesting to readers by showing them something about the setting they didn't already know, or had never noticed.

10
Reflecting

A successful reflection engages readers and allows them to see an event, person, or thing through your eyes; but more important, by thinking about your reflections, readers often find out something about themselves.

Chapter contents

Writing reflections

When we reflect, we consider an idea or experience in order to come to a greater understanding of its significance. Unless we are writing in a private diary or journal, we use reflective writing to share our experience and its significance with others. Reflecting is also a way of understanding ourselves. By connecting memories of the past to our knowledge in the present, we learn about who we were and who we have become.

Reflective essays can address deeply emotional issues like family relationships, personal failings, and dramatic crises. But reflection does not always involve personal topics. In some cases, being too personal or confessional can limit a writer's ability to connect to his or her audience.

The goal of reflection should not be simply to vent pent-up emotions or to expose secrets (although when done well, these techniques can be effective). Instead, it should allow the audience to share a discovery of significance with the writer. A reflection on an important event in the history of a family should do more than focus on the writer's feelings; it should explore how each family member changed as a result.

Components of reflections

What people, places, and events stand out in my memory?	**Find a reflective topic** Listing is one way to identify possible topics for reflective writing. You might list people, events, or places that have been significant in your life, then look back over your list and check the items that seem especially vivid to you.
Will my readers be interested?	**Consider your readers** How interesting will this topic be to your readers? Will they want to share in your experience?
What is my purpose?	**Identify a purpose** A clear purpose makes the reflection coherent. Your purpose is not to teach a lesson about life but rather to convey the significance of the experience—why it is important or memorable and why it is worth writing and reading about.
What key details communicate the significance of my reflection?	**Provide concrete details** Concrete details stimulate readers' imagination and make your reflection come alive. Use factual details such as dates to provide background information. Augment visual details with your other senses: smells, sounds, tastes, and feelings. **Use dialogue when possible** Convey interaction between people with their words.
How do I organize my reflection?	**Think about your organization** Telling what happened in chronological order is the simplest organization for writers to use, but it is not the only one possible. Conceptual order explores different points and links them together. For example, you might reflect on a photograph, examining details one by one and discussing how they relate to your family's past.

What is the most engaging way to begin?

Start immediately
The beginning of a reflection must clearly establish the writer's involvement and gain the reader's interest.

Finish strong
Effective conclusions invite readers to reflect further. Ending with a question or an issue to think about is usually better than trying to sum up with a moral lesson.

Keys to reflections

Snapshots freeze important moments in people's lives.

Tell a good story
Readers have to be interested in your story to understand the significance. Often reflections gain and keep readers' interest by presenting a conflict or a difficult decision that must be resolved.

Let the details convey the significance
Select details carefully to communicate meaning. Identify people by more than how they look. Think about mannerisms, gestures, and habits to suggest their character.

Be honest
Telling the truth about your thoughts and actions can build a strong rapport with your audience, but beware of becoming sentimental. Too much emotion may turn readers off.

Focus on the little things in life
A reflection need not reveal earth-shattering secrets or teach crucial life lessons. It may be as simple as describing something that makes you happy. Remember that small moments of significance can be just as rewarding for readers as great events.

For a reflection on an image or object, let the reflection grow out of the details
Your close reading of details and your explanation of the significance of the experience is critical.

WORKING TOGETHER
Reflecting on photographs

In a group of three or four students
- Look at a selection of photographs from newspapers, magazines, or a photo Web log such as **www.chromasia.com.**
- Have each person work with two or three photos, making a list of the people each image reminds you of, the things the image makes you think about, and the places you associate with the image. Write a brief narrative for each image.
- Share your memories and narratives with the group. Which ones strike you as the most engaging and interesting? How would you develop or change the narratives of other students?

An effective reflection

Effective reflective writing can only come after honest examination of memories, perceptions, and meanings.

The Tale of One Refugee
Eva Kende

Eva Kende was born in Hungary, but at the age of 15, she left her homeland with her mother when the Soviet tanks entered Budapest on November 4, 1956. In this true story, she recalls the terrifying flight from her country and describes with great fondness the people she met along the way.

The Tale of One Refugee
By Eva Kende

In the wake of 9-11-01, there has been a lot of talk about refugees. I thought that perhaps people might like a glimpse into the heart of one, to understand the depth of the refugees' feelings towards their host country.

My mother and I arrived in Canada as refugees 45 years ago. Our sudden journey to the unfamiliar began with a trip to a luggage shop to buy two small bags that would hold our most prized worldly possessions. The Hungarian revolution of 1956 that had started with so much hope was quashed; Budapest was in ruins and bleeding. Mother yearned for the support and comfort of her brother, who had been living in Spain since the end of the Spanish Civil War there. It made her set aside all her fears and phobias about being away from home for more than an hour or two, and she declared that we were going. I was fifteen years old. No father, no siblings, just the two of us to face the great unknown.

She did not make her decision lightly. The great migration started soon after the Russian tanks ended all hope on November 4th, 1956. Now it was mid-December. We had spent the evenings of the past month glued to the radio, listening to Radio Free Europe broadcasting messages from friends and relatives who had safely made it to Austria. Mother's best friend, Mariska, who was a decisive leader, her husband, Odon and daughter Jutka were leaving, which gave mother the courage to join in this trek to the unknown.

It was decided that the five of us would have to rent a hotel room near the railroad station the night before so as not to be conspicuous in our neighbourhood leaving in the early morning carrying our satchels. We packed these small bags, over and over again. Mother's heavy stocking repair machine had to go in first. After all she had to make a living somehow, she rationalised. The doll my deceased father had given me for my first birthday, my constant companion and confidante during the war and throughout my childhood was also a must. Next came the family jewellery, part heirlooms, part items my father had collected "in case" we needed to sell something for essentials. The photo albums were declared essential and I couldn't part with my new burgundy sandals and navy blue suit, the fruit of my first job as a summer student at the Horticultural College, no matter how unpractical they were. Of course, I couldn't leave behind either the new pale blue silk blouse the clever fingers of my beloved great-aunt Nene had so lovingly made from strips of remnants. Two miniature paintings, to sell if the need arose, fitted inside nicely. As we had a little bit more room yet, mother opened the linen cupboard to look for small pieces of embroidery and lace that might be sellable as well. She couldn't bear to part with the beautiful pink embroidered bedding that she had commissioned when she gave birth to me, so we packed it too. We paraded up and down our apartment testing the weight of the satchels and decided that we could handle carrying them for hours.[1]

Outside events are the background for this family's personal chronology. Kende shows vividly the impact of the Hungarian Revolution on her mother's decision to leave.

Details about her personal possessions contrast with the seriousness of her family's situation

[1] I recently donated one of those bags, the pink bedding, a photo of my doll, and the ship's passenger list to Pier 21, an exhibition hall in Halifax dedicated to immigrants and refugees who were processed into Canada through the Pier 21 immigration facilities. http://pier21.ns.ca/index.html

KENDE: THE TALE OF ONE REFUGEE

My mother's cousin gave us a large sum of cash so that we could pay for the "guides" who led people across the border. We packed a string-bag with food and we were ready. We met Mariska and her family in the seedy hotel in the early evening. Our mood swung from sadness to nervous laughter and all ranges of emotion in between. We hardly slept. At about six in the morning of December 19th, 1956, before the city awakened, our ragtag team walked along the wide, empty avenue to the railway station.

For the first couple of hours, the trip to the industrial town of Gyor, halfway between the border and Budapest, was uneventful. I stared out the window, wondering if I would ever see this land again. But new regulations declared that you had to have a pass — which of course we didn't have—to travel into the border zone, which was a hundred kilometres long, established as an emergency measure by the Hungarian government. So, after Gyor, our troop, now swollen to about fifteen people, some of them total strangers, had to move into the baggage car to keep out of sight. I was lucky. I had a sled to sit on, but the Christmas tree behind me was prickly. At each station, when the border police came to inspect, all fifteen of us had to cram into the single toilet compartment of the car to hide. The largest person sat down on the fixture and the rest of us piled on top of her. This was repeated four or five times until we reached our destination, a small border village, at dusk. We marched to an outlying farmhouse where, crammed into the front room, was another small troop ready for the crossing. Suddenly, the door flew open and a very young uniformed border guard burst into the room. "You are all under arrest!" he shouted. "We are shipping you back to Budapest immediately. Anyone attempting to escape will be shot." Silence fell. He left the room and we heard some shots ring out in the yard. When he returned, people began to beg the guard to let us go and ply him with watches, money, and jewellery. He was stony-faced, but accepted the items. He assembled us and we started to march to what we thought surely was prison. There was no sign of our paid "guides." The direction we were going seemed to be wrong to me, but I imagined it could have been the deep dark of the night. Mother was ready to throw away her satchel as she stumbled from fear and exhaustion among the column of fearful humanity. I grabbed her bag and marched like a robot in silence. I didn't know what to think. Hours later it seemed, although I suspect it was less than half an hour, the guard called us to halt. He pointed into the inky darkness ahead of us and said: "There is the border and I am going to turn my back on you." It wasn't until a few metres later when mother tripped on a low wire that I started to believe him. We—by now there must have been about 30 of us—marched in silence for about an hour across muddy, evenly spaced ruts in the fields—it must have been recently ploughed—that sucked the shoes off our feet and wrenched our ankles. There was even a blind woman in the group with a seeing-eye dog. The lovely "sturdy" walking shoes a neighbour had given me for the trip were ruined. The soles separated from the uppers in several places.

I lugged the satchels while looking out for my mother stumbling along. About an hour into this walk across the fields, an apparition seemed to float in the sky.

A small town lit in bluish lights, with a prominent church spire—all the street lights in Hungary were yellow—appeared outlined in mid-air. Our relief was palpable. People started to break their self-imposed silence. Odon remarked that we must be close to Budapest by now, because the church spire looked familiar to him. We had been walking for a long time and it felt as if we had turned around and walked all the way back to Budapest. Everyone laughed at this feeble attempt at humour. The satchels got a little lighter and it seemed that the ruts became a little shallower. As we progressed, it became clear that the apparition was an Austrian village perched on a plateau. It was the prettiest sight! We marched into the town, finding it hard to temper our happiness and relief at having arrived. All the pent-up tensions of our uncertain day and night bubbled out in

Kende uses dialogue to recount a significant event in her flight from Hungary, one that resonated with her for many years.

KENDE: THE TALE OF ONE REFUGEE

noisy, uncontrollable chatter. A few windows opened, begging us to be quieter. The good burghers of the small town of Deutschkreutz had had very little sleep for the past month, as groups of Hungarians reached their village each night.

In the centre of the town, we were led to the firehall, which was empty save for a thick layer of clean straw topped by a layer of humans of every age, sex, and clad in every kind of garb that one could imagine. About three hundred people curled up in the space normally occupied by several fire-trucks. In the foyer, a huge pot of sweet tea with lemon was boiling away, and several women volunteers were spreading jam on slices of bread as fast as their arms could go. Someone begged me to take some, but all I could get down was some of the hot tea. The knot in my stomach was still too tight for me to eat. I had to quickly dismiss the thought of bedding down somewhere in a free patch of straw. Our friends were arranging for a taxi to go to Vienna, where they had some friends waiting. They were just US$11 short of what was needed to secure transportation for all of us. Mother and I had no currency. The forints my mother's cousin had sent us were reserved for guides; besides, forints were useless anyway, since the cabs accepted only western currencies. It was suggested that we stay and our friends would get some money in Vienna and send for us. Mother became upset. Never an independent soul, the thought of being left behind alone with me was more than she could handle. An argument ensued and I couldn't take any more. My facade crumbled and I sat on the spiky wrought iron fence of the church in the Town Square, in the middle of the night, and cried like a three-year-old.

My mother stood close by, still arguing with our friends, ignoring my childish outburst. Two young Hungarian men, obviously also new arrivals from across the border, came to ask what the problem was and I told them. They reached into their pockets and handed my mother two dollar bills to cover the shortfall of the taxi fare for all of us. She tried to repay them with some trin-

Expressions of hope and relief are evident in this reminiscence of the first part of her journey.

In spite of setbacks, Kende remembers the kindness of strangers and how it helped her (in a tangible way) to continue.

ket from our bags, but they just waved her off and disappeared into the night.

In Vienna, it became painfully clear that my shoes were wrecked. Slush and snow covering the streets kept my feet continually cold and wet. There were several relief agencies set up to help the refugees. For instance, one organisation gave everyone a green bag emblazoned with Unitarian Service Committee containing essential hygiene products. Another society gave out huge blocks of American processed cheese and powdered milk. We had cheese and reconstituted milk warmed on the radiator for supper for a month. Depots of used clothing were set up all over the city. The refugees gave tips to each other about where to go to get stuff. After several unsuccessful attempts, I finally landed a good pair of emerald-green leather shoes that fit well, although they didn't go with anything I wore. It didn't matter. All the refugees were clad in similarly mismatched garb. At this point, nobody cared, as long as they were warm and safe. All refugees walked the streets for hours admiring the well-stocked shop windows. Mother and I often bumped into friends and acquaintances. We exchanged news about mutual friends and where each one was heading to in this exodus.

Mother got in touch with her brother in Spain, but he discouraged us from trying to go there. Women couldn't make a living and he was not doing well enough to consider taking responsibility for us. He suggested we try to go to Canada or the USA. He sent us a little money to supplement the freebies. The larger problem was for us to get a visa for one of those countries. The US quota on refugees was closed. Only sponsored people were considered. We did not have a sponsor. The same situation faced us at the Canadian Embassy, where several refugees milled around in the square in front. Up to early December, the Embassy had handed out, on slips of paper, nameless appointments for processing into Canada, to all who asked. But if people succeeded in getting into the US, or decided to wait for other family

KENDE: THE TALE OF ONE REFUGEE

members, they didn't need these slips and gave them to others who needed them.

We milled about the square for about half an hour, until we found a man who had an extra slip. After a cursory medical exam, we were told to show up at the railroad station in a few days to be transported to the Canadian refugee camp in Wiener Neustadt where we would be gathered, processed and assigned transportation to Canada.

The Canadian camp at Wiener Neustadt was rumoured to be a former Nazi concentration camp. Some of the kids already in the camp would even take the newcomers to the ruins they claimed were the crematorium—I never tracked down whether this rumour was true. With nothing to do, the camp was always rife with rumours[2]—The camp certainly was not a pleasant place. The barrack-like structure had unheated bathrooms with rows of 20 sinks and toilets. It was so cold that water had frozen in most of the sinks. We were assigned cots in the middle room of a group of three, each containing metal beds with straw mattresses for

> Details about the beaureaucratic process reinforces the problems faced by many displaced persons.

---

[2] Because the memories of those days were too painful, it's only recently, more than 40 years after the fact, that I could face them and write about them. Previously, if asked about my experiences, I would answer as briefly as possible, closing the door on the memories as quickly as good manners allowed. I never tracked down what our camp was originally. I was afraid of the answers. Just recently, I found out, thanks to the extensive research conducted by Mr. Maurice Servranckx, that it's highly unlikely that these rumours were true. There were several German factories using prisoners as forced labourers from the concentration camp of Mauthausen, but there were no extermination camps in Wiener Neustadt. Judging by the rows of toilets and sinks, I would guess the brick buildings were formerly used as an army barracks, as a hospital, or possibly a residential school. Badly damaged during the war, the buildings were never repaired before being pressed into emergency service to organise the collection of refugees bound for Canada. Because our stay was short, a matter of 3-4 days, none of the refugees ever resented this inconvenience.

ten to twelve people. Children, adults, couples, singles, strangers and families were all heaped together. There was a pot-bellied stove in one corner valiantly trying to emit some comfort. Those near the stove roasted while those in the next row froze. The windows leaked so badly we put extra straw mattresses against them to try to keep out the cold. Luckily, we only stayed 3 days. Nevertheless, the food, although basic, was plentiful, hot, and we enjoyed the luxury of having meat daily. The mess hall, well heated, doubled as a classroom for English lessons between meals. I attended as many classes as offered, in preparation for our new life in Canada.

At dawn on January 24th, we were bussed to the train that was to take us to the port city of Bremenhaven in Germany to sail for Canada. One picture is engraved in my memory. I was shivering in the early dawn, waiting for the bus, when I saw in the well-lit doorway of the barracks the outline of a figure holding a fencing sword in one hand and a helmet tucked under the other arm. The picture was so incongruous that I stifled a giggle. I later found out that he was a young fencing champion, holding the items he treasured most. The train trip took all day and the next night. As we neared Bremenhaven, mother could hardly contain herself. Her brother, who she hadn't seen for 20 years, had promised to try to meet us at the ship. I was looking forward to seeing my larger-than-life uncle for the first time. As the train pulled into the station, grey with drizzle, there was no one to be seen. Then suddenly a lone figure came into view, mother shrieked, and I knew that it must be my Uncle Robert.

He accompanied us onto the ship, bought me a coke—my very first—in the bar and gave us warm scarves and a big box of dates and figs for snacking on the voyage. The visit was over in a couple of hours, and we sailed for Canada. Almost as soon as we passed the marvellous white cliffs of Dover, the sea turned mean and we spent most of our time being seasick. Whenever possible, we made it to the after-dinner dance which was great fun. There were a number of young German and Yugoslavian immigrants aboard, in addition to our

Details about the Canadian Camp are written in positive language, reinforcing the sense of hopefulness of the refugees.

KENDE: THE TALE OF ONE REFUGEE

group of Hungarian refugees, meaning plenty of dance partners, even for a fifteen-year-old. The immigrants were dressed in their most elegant duds, while the refugees sported the mismatched hand-me-downs they had collected from the relief agencies.

We arrived in Halifax on the afternoon of February fourth. The day was overcast and drizzly as we crowded the decks to get our first glimpse of Canada. We spent the night on the ship in harbour and in the morning we were led to a great hall for processing and from there onto our train for Winnipeg. Since most of the refugees knew little or nothing about Canada, had they been given a choice, they would have wanted to go to Montreal or Toronto, the only two places they had heard about from former immigrants. It would have been hard for those cities to provide such a large number of newcomers with jobs and temporary accommodations. Immigration decided to send each boat or planeload to a different city in Canada to even out the burden.[3]

The train was fabulous. We had never seen anything like it. It sported luxurious plush seats, friendly black porters in crisp uniforms, shiny brass fittings, polished wood everywhere, and boxes of Kellogg's Corn Flakes in every nook and cranny. We had never seen corn flakes before and never had dry cereal for breakfast. After tasting the freebie, we decided it was the Canadian equivalent to potato chips and snacked on it dry during the whole trip. As we left Halifax, we could see an occasional house here or there, but the sparseness of the population was odd to us mostly city folks. Even odder were the bright pastel colours of the houses. As the wheels

Kende provides a clear, early distinction between the types of people she encountered on her journey to Canada.

---

[3] I became something of a hero on this trip. My geography teacher was an exceptional lady who poured huge quantities of information into our reluctant heads. As a result, I knew a little about Winnipeg and could cite some of the information learned about industry, transportation and agriculture. I also managed to have a vocabulary of 20 words of English, so I was used as an "interpreter" communicating with the porters.

clicked away the miles, day and night, with plenty of time to think and talk, a few people had panic attacks now that they were nearing our unfamiliar destination. The enormity of what had happened to us in the last few months, and the scary prospect of having to start a new life in a strange land, having to speak a language few of the refugees knew, struck the weak, while the stronger ones continued to plot and plan to conquer adversity, and soar to great success now that they were truly free. Others relieved their tension with jokes and wisecracks, to the merriment of the group. I often wonder how a psychologist would have evaluated the mood swings of our group.[4]

In Montreal, a few of our sponsored compatriots, as well as a few adventurous ones, decided to stay behind even though they were told that they would not get help in getting settled from the Immigration Department if they didn't continue to our assigned destination, Winnipeg. From Montreal to Winnipeg, crossing the Canadian Shield, we hardly saw any populated areas. The sun shone brightly as frozen lakes followed forests and vice versa.

On February 8th, we arrived in Winnipeg. On the platform, a contingent of middle-aged ladies, wearing silk dresses, straw hats, and fur jackets, waited to welcome us, to minister to us and help ease our way into becoming Canadian. Our ragtag group, emerging from the train, suppressed a collective giggle at their elegance that clashed with our own dilapidated clothes. Nevertheless, the intentions of the ladies soon proved to be very genuine, even if their understanding of our plight was

Again, Kende shows the hopefulness of the refugees even though they faced many challenges.

---

[4] The long trip, and having to face the same problems together, built a special relationship among the people who shared this trek into the unknown. We became a very special "family," in which you could understand feelings. For instance, the young fencer and I were the only two Hungarian refugees, in different faculties, among 7000 students at the University of Manitoba. We relied heavily on that mutual support during our first two years.

somewhat deficient. The ladies spoke no Hungarian and we spoke no English. We communicated with hands and smiles.

With their kind help and that of countless others, we started our long and often arduous trek into becoming Canadians.

* * *

Being a refugee is like being an adopted child, with all the ambivalent feelings and loyalties. Love for the birth parent—or in this case the homeland—is embedded like the genes of an adopted child, but the loyalty for the adoptive country, born from gratitude, is usually so strong as to always cause conflict within the refugee's heart.

For instance, one favourite question among refugee groups is: "Who do you root for during the Olympics?" which usually elicits a lively debate that clearly shows the confusion of divided loyalties refugees feel for the rest of their lives.

For example: In hockey, I root for Canada. I learned to love this sport here from my stepfather. My loyalty is definitely with the Canadian team when it comes to swimming, because I was an official of the Canadian Amateur Swimming Association when my son was a competitive swimmer and back then I personally knew all the swimmers. However, I will root for the Hungarian competitor if no Canadian is entered in the event, because I remember the impromptu parade in my neighbourhood in 1952 when the champion swimmers were carried home on the crowd's shoulders. The various skiing events cause no problem. Living in the Rocky Mountains, my skiing loyalty definitely belongs to Canada, or more specifically to the Bow Valley athletes. In other events, I choose the individual or team, from my two homelands, that seems to be more accomplished in the particular sport. Luckily, there has not been an instance when a Hungarian athlete was competing head-to-head against a

In this final recollection, Kende talks about her growing respect and love for her adopted country.

Canadian at any Olympics. I would have been in big trouble then!

There is a subtle and often blurry difference between immigrants and refugees. An immigrant has consciously planned to leave his or her home and settle in a different country. There was time to choose, read up and familiarize oneself with the country, its culture and language. The refugees, on the other hand, were uprooted suddenly and thrust into a strange land, usually following some dramatic, stressful events in their birth-land. Each refugee has a story to tell about his or her path and arrival to Canada. The details may differ, but the message is usually the same.

The majority of refugees are the greatest flag-waving patriots in Canada. We came to this country in the wake of turmoil and danger in our homeland; penniless, destitute, still in mourning and in shock of having lost our home, friends and relatives in the span of a few turbulent weeks. We were confused, scared of our future, and found our dignity in tatters.

We arrived in Canada to find caring people, helping hands and a warm welcome. Through the years, we tried to achieve the success we dreamed of, succeeding at times and failing at others, but we knew that this great country, Canada, gave us the freedom to try again, in any way we desired. Here, we could keep our culture and pride of ethnic origin, yet become Canadian and raise our family in guaranteed peace. Show me another country that provides all that and asks nothing in return for its hospitality.

If you see a former refugee stand a little taller or have shiny eyes during the singing of O Canada, don't be surprised. That is our way of saying: "Thank You Canada! We love you!"

In a final note, Kende offers the thanks of many refugees who now call Canada home.

How to read reflections

Make notes as you read, either in the margins or on paper or a computer file. Circle any words or references that you don't know and look them up.

What is it?	• What kind of a text is it? A memoir? A letter? A diary? An essay? A short story? A photographic essay? What are your expectations for this kind of text? • What media are used? (Websites, for example, often combine images, words, and sounds.)
Where did it come from?	• Who wrote the reflection? • What do you know about the writer's background that might have influenced the reflection?
Who is the intended audience?	• What clues about the intended audience did you find? • What does the writer assume that the readers already know about the subject? • What new knowledge is the writer providing?
What is the significance of the reflection?	• Does the writer give precise, objective, concrete details? • Does the writer comment on the reflections? • What did you learn or come to understand differently after reading the reflection?
How is the reflection organized?	• Is the reflection ordered chronologically? In order of perceived importance? Or some other way?
How is it composed?	• How does the writer represent herself or himself? • How would you characterize the style? • How effective is the design? Is it easy to read? • If there are any photographs or other graphics, what information do they contribute?

Canadian Health Care Crisis Is about Values, Not Money

(COMMENTARY)

Nuala Kenny

Dr. Nuala Kenny is Professor of Bioethics at Dalhousie University and the former Deputy Minister of Health for the province of Nova Scotia. This excerpt was taken from her book *What Good is Health Care? Reflections on the Canadian Experience.*

Analyzing and Connecting

Return to these questions after you have finished reading.

1. What does Kenny reveal or explain in this commentary that is new to you? How does her reflection on the meaning of health and health care in Canada change or add to your feelings about the issue?

2. How is the focus of her reflection revealed in the commentary's title?

3. Kenny is an obvious choice to author a piece on health care in Canada. Why would Kenny choose to critique a system she had been part of in such a direct way? How do her personal experiences contribute to the authenticity of this piece of writing?

4. Overall, what is the tone of Kenny's message? What details help to support this tone?

CANADIAN HEALTH CARE CRISIS IS ABOUT VALUES, NOT MONEY

By Nuala Kenny

As reports over the last year from the Kirby Senate Committee and the Romanow Commission attest, our Canadian Health Care System is in crisis. But this is not just a Canadian problem. All health care systems in the world are in crisis. The same forces and issues creating the crisis in Canada are operating elsewhere. In Europe, there is fear health costs could spiral out of control, even in countries that have not experienced much of an increase in health's share of the GDP. Most European countries with two-tier health care, along with Australia and New Zealand, are experiencing erosion in the public portions of their systems along with escalating costs of private health insurance. That bastion of the free market—the United States—is in more turmoil than most. There the blame is on managed care but the crises are the same. While there are global social and economic forces at work here, each country will respond in its own way. The question for Canadians is what path will we choose?

The immediate crisis in our health care system is not just about money or inefficiencies. It is symptomatic of poorly articulated values regarding the meaning of health and health care, the place of health in society and the role of government in health and health care. The issues at stake in goal setting are not simply about creating new options for obtaining more money for health care. There are fundamental issues at stake regarding our core values—how we envision the relationship between health and human happiness, what we mean by health and what we imagine to be fair. In a sense, the pressing issues in health care are the issues about a just and caring society, not only in the here and now but for future generations as well.

The issues creating crises in modern health care cannot be addressed by simply throwing money at them. Our policy decisions are moral decisions. They are issues of justice, care and responsible citizenship. In a particular way, they relate to the troubling phenomena of the medicalization of life, the commercialization of care and of the power of the market to dominate the health care agenda.

How we frame the issues determines in large part our response. If health care is in crisis, what kind of crisis is it? We have defined the health care crisis as a resource allocation issue. Once the problem is cast in these terms the main questions revolve around funding. It's an all too familiar litany: the cost of health care is more than the provinces can afford, there are unacceptable waits for access to technology, costly new drugs are not being provided for all who might benefit, and there aren't enough hospital beds to meet demand. This way of thinking directs policy toward winners and losers in a grand allocation game. Because of the pervasiveness of technology and the almost unlimited potential benefit from medical science, framing the issue this way leads naturally to options that will increase the money available for these resources through private arrangements.

We need to reflect on deeper questions: What are the goals of health care and are the goals unlimited health benefits to all citizens? What kind of a *good* is health care? Is health care a private commodity to be purchased by those who can afford it or is it, in some way, symbolic of community itself? Is the sustainability of any health care system in a very real sense a test of the commitment to community? And if so, how do we test this commitment? What language do we use? What public spaces do we develop and nurture? How do we deal with the profound and often irreconcilable value differences such as a foray into public discourse will generate? What concepts of justice or citizenship do we embrace? Or has the commercialization of health and health care been so complete in this global world that the hoped-for public debate on these matters is only some idealistic—perhaps romantic—and nostalgic dream? Have the values of the market overrun those of justice and care?

The Canadian health care crisis is not primarily about resource allocation but rather about the future of health care as a good held in common and the possibility of just and compassionate decision making by citizens in a global world. The challenge is to develop new ways and debate in which citizens can act together to clarify the values at stake in the choices for our community.

A Blizzard Under Blue Sky

(SHORT STORY)

Pam Houston

Pam Houston is a teacher and writer who has also worked as a hunting and raft guide in the American West and Alaska. She often writes about the relationships women have with animals, in particular horses and dogs. In this story from her first collection, *Cowboys Are My Weakness* (1992), she addresses the personal topic of depression with humour.

Analyzing and Connecting

Return to these questions after you have finished reading.

1. Houston uses "dialogue" between herself and her dogs to enliven her reflection. Apart from humour, what do these "conversations" contribute to readers' understanding of the events she describes?

2. Note all the different sensory details Houston provides. See if you can find descriptions of sights, sounds, smells, tastes, and feelings. Which does Houston use most? Which ones stand out the most to you?

3. "I wish I could tell you I dropped right off to sleep," the narrator says. Why does Houston call attention to the contrast between real and ideal here? Why does she wish the truth were shaped differently? Why does she feel she "can't" tell readers she fell asleep?

4. Houston alerts readers to the revelation in her reflection at the very end. "I was five miles down the trail before I realized what had happened," she says. What exactly did happen? What changed for Houston during her camping trip? Does she adequately communicate this change to the reader? What might the reader learn from Houston's experience?

A Blizzard Under Blue Sky

The doctor said I was clinically depressed. It was February, the month in which depression runs rampant in the inversion-cloaked Salt Lake Valley and the city dwellers escape to Park City, where the snow is fresh and the sun is shining and everybody is happy, except me. In truth, my life was on the verge of more spectacular and satisfying discoveries than I had ever imagined, but of course I couldn't see that far ahead. What I saw was work that wasn't getting done, bills that weren't getting paid, and a man I'd given my heart to weekending in the desert with his ex.

The doctor said, "I can give you drugs."

I said, "No way."

She said, "The machine that drives you is broken. You need something to help you get it fixed."

I said, "Winter camping."

She said, "Whatever floats your boat."

One of the things I love the most about the natural world is the way it gives you what's good for you even if you don't know it at the time. I had never been winter camping before, at least not in the high country, and the weekend I chose to try and fix my machine was the same weekend the air mass they called the Alaska Clipper showed up. It was thirty-two degrees below zero in town on the night I spent in my snow cave. I don't know how cold it was out on Beaver Creek. I had listened to the weather forecast, and to the advice of my housemate, Alex, who was an experienced winter camper.

"I don't know what you think you're going to prove by freezing to death," Alex said, "but if you've got to go, take my bivvy sack; it's warmer than anything you have."

"Thanks," I said.

"If you mix Kool-Aid with your water it won't freeze up," he said, "and don't forget lighting paste for your stove."

"Okay," I said.

"I hope it turns out to be worth it," he said, "because you are going to freeze your butt."

When everything in your life is uncertain, there's nothing quite like the clarity and precision of fresh snow and blue sky. That was the first thought I had on Saturday morning as I stepped away from the warmth of my truck and let my skis slap the snow in front of me. There was no wind and no clouds that morning, just still air and cold sunshine. The hair in my nostrils froze almost immediately. When I took a deep breath, my lungs only filled up halfway.

I opened the tailgate to excited whines and whimpers. I never go skiing without Jackson and Hailey: my two best friends, my yin and yang of dogs. Some of you might know Jackson. He's the oversized sheepdog-and-something-else with the great big nose and the bark that will shatter glass. He gets out and about more than I do. People I've never seen before come by my house daily and call him by name. He's all grace, and he's tireless; he won't go skiing with me unless I let him lead. Hailey is not so graceful, and her body seems in constant indecision when she runs. When we ski she stays behind me, and on the downhills she tries to sneak rides on my skis.

The dogs ran circles in the chest-high snow while I inventoried my backpack one more time to make sure I had everything I needed. My sleeping bag, my Thermarest, my stove, Alex's bivvy sack, matches, lighting paste, flashlight, knife. I brought three pairs of long underwear— tops and bottoms—so I could change once before I went to bed, and once again in the morning, so I wouldn't get chilled by my own sweat. I brought paper and pen, and Kool-Aid to mix with my water. I brought Mountain House chicken stew and some freeze-dried green peas, some peanut butter and honey, lots of dried apricots, coffee and Carnation instant breakfast for morning.

Jackson stood very still while I adjusted his backpack. He carries the dog food and enough water for all of us. He takes himself very seriously when he's got his pack on. He won't step off the trail for any reason, not even to chase rabbits, and he gets nervous and angry if I do. That morning he was impatient with me. "Miles to go, Mom," he said over his shoulder. I snapped my boots into my skis and we were off.

There are not too many good things you can say about temperatures that dip past twenty below zero, except this: They turn the landscape into a crystal palace and they turn your vision into Superman's. In the cold thin morning air the trees and mountains, even the twigs and shadows, seemed to leap out of the background like a 3-D movie, only it was better than 3-D because I could feel the sharpness of the air.

I have a friend in Moab who swears that Utah is the center of the fourth dimension, and although I know he has in mind something much different and more complicated than subzero weather, it was there, on that ice-edged morning, that I felt on the verge of seeing something more than depth perception in the brutal clarity of the morning sun.

As I kicked along the first couple of miles, I noticed the sun crawling higher in the sky and yet the day wasn't really warming, and I wondered if I should have brought another vest, another layer to put between me and the cold night ahead.

It was utterly quiet out there, and what minimal noise we made intruded on the morning like a brass band: the squeaking of my bindings, the slosh of the water in Jackson's pack, the whoosh of nylon, the jangle of dog tags. It was the bass line and percussion to some primal song, and I kept wanting to sing to it, but I didn't know the words.

Jackson and I crested the top of a hill and stopped to wait for Hailey. The trail stretched out as far as we could see into the meadow below us and beyond, a double track and pole plants carving though softer trails of rabbit and deer.

"Nice place," I said to Jackson, and his tail thumped the snow underneath him without sound.

We stopped for lunch near something that looked like it could be a lake in its other life, or maybe just a womb-shaped meadow. I made peanut butter and honey sandwiches for all of us, and we opened the apricots.

"It's fabulous here," I told the dogs. "But so far it's not working."

There had never been anything wrong with my life that a few good days in the wilderness wouldn't cure, but there I sat in the middle of all those crystal-coated trees, all that diamond-studded sunshine, and I didn't feel any better. Apparently clinical depression was not like having a bad day, it wasn't even like having a lot of bad days, it was more like a house of mirrors, it was like being in a room full of one-way glass.

"Come on, Mom," Jackson said. "Ski harder, go faster, climb higher."

Hailey turned her belly to the sun and groaned.

"He's right," I told her. "It's all we can do."

After lunch the sun had moved behind our backs, throwing a whole different light on the path ahead of us. The snow we moved through stopped being simply white and became translucent, hinting at other colors, reflections of blues and purples and grays. I thought of *Moby Dick*, you know, the whiteness of the whale, where white is really the absence of all color, and whiteness equals truth, and Ahab's search is finally futile, as he finds nothing but his own reflection.

"Put your mind where your skis are," Jackson said, and we made considerably better time after that.

The sun was getting quite low in the sky when I asked Jackson if he thought we should stop to build the snow cave, and he said he'd look for the next good bank. About one hundred yards down the trail we found it, a gentle slope with eastern exposure that didn't look like it would cave in under any circumstances. Jackson started to dig first.

Let me make one thing clear. I knew only slightly more about building snow caves than Jackson, having never built one, and all my knowledge coming from disaster tales of winter camping fatalities. I knew several things *not* to do when building a snow cave, but I was having a hard time knowing what exactly to do. But Jackson helped, and Hailey supervised, and before too long we had a little cave built, just big enough for three. We ate dinner quite pleased with our accomplishments and set the bivvy sack up inside the cave just as the sun slipped away and dusk came over Beaver Creek.

The temperature, which hadn't exactly soared during the day, dropped twenty degrees in as many minutes, and suddenly it didn't seem like such a great idea to change my long underwear. The original plan was to sleep with the dogs inside the bivvy sack but outside the sleeping bag, which was okay with Jackson the super-metabolizer, but not so with Hailey, the couch potato. She whined and wriggled and managed to stuff her entire fat body down inside my mummy bag, and Jackson stretched out full-length on top.

One of the unfortunate things about winter camping is that it has to happen when the days are so short. Fourteen hours is a long time to lie in a snow cave under the most perfect of circumstances. And when it's thirty-two below, or forty, fourteen hours seems like weeks.

I wish I could tell you I dropped right off to sleep. In truth, fear crept into my spine with the cold and I never closed my eyes. Cuddled there, amid my dogs and water bottles, I spent half of the night chastising myself for thinking I was Wonder Woman, not only risking my own life but the lives of my dogs, and the other half trying to keep the numbness in my feet from crawling up to my knees. When I did doze off, which was actually more like blacking out than dozing off, I'd come back to my senses wondering if I had frozen to death, but the alternating pain and numbness that started in my extremities and worked its way into my bones convinced me I must still be alive.

It was a clear night, and every now and again I would poke my head out of its nest of down and nylon to watch the progress of the moon across the sky. There is no doubt that it was the longest and most uncomfortable night of my life.

HOUSTON: A BLIZZARD UNDER BLUE SKY

But then the sky began to get gray, and then it began to get pink, and before too long the sun was on my bivvy sack, not warm, exactly, but holding the promise of warmth later in the day. And I ate apricots and drank Kool-Aid-flavored coffee and celebrated the rebirth of my fingers and toes, and the survival of many more important parts of my body. I sang "Rocky Mountain High" and "If I Had a Hammer," and yodeled and whistled, and even danced the two-step with Jackson and let him lick my face. And when Hailey finally emerged from the sleeping bag a full hour after I did, we shared a peanut butter and honey sandwich and she said nothing ever tasted so good.

We broke camp and packed up and kicked in the snow cave with something resembling glee.

I was five miles down the trail before I realized what had happened. Not once in that fourteen-hour night did I think about deadlines, or bills, or the man in the desert. For the first time in many months I was happy to see a day beginning. The morning sunshine was like a present from the gods. What really happened, of course, is that I remembered about joy.

I know that one night out at thirty-two below doesn't sound like much to those of you who have climbed Everest or run the Iditarod or kayaked to Antarctica, and I won't try to convince you that my life was like the movies where depression goes away in one weekend, and all of life's problems vanish with a moment's clear sight. The simple truth of the matter is this: On Sunday I had a glimpse outside of the house of mirrors, on Saturday I couldn't have seen my way out of a paper bag. And while I was skiing back toward the truck that morning, a wind came up behind us and swirled the snow around our bodies like a blizzard under blue sky. And I was struck by the simple perfection of the snowflakes, and startled by the hopefulness of sun on frozen trees.

Let It Snow

(ESSAY)

David Sedaris

David Sedaris is a writer, playwright, and radio commentator whose work often has an autobiographical focus. He became famous for *The Santaland Diaries,* a play about his job as a Christmas elf in Macy's department store. In this essay, from his collection *Dress Your Family in Corduroy and Denim,* he recalls a single day from his childhood in North Carolina.

Analyzing and Connecting

Return to these questions after you have finished reading.

1. On the surface, this story centres around a snowstorm, and children playing in it. Underlying these events are the much darker issues of the narrator's mother, her drinking, and her treatment of her children. How exactly does the snowstorm focus Sedaris's investigation of his family's past?

2. The narrator, as a Grade 5 student, thinks that having his sister get hit by a car would be "the perfect solution" to their problem. What do you believe the adult narrator thinks of this "solution"? Are there any other clues that the narrator feels differently now?

3. The humour turns a potentially sad story into a ridiculous one. Think about how this essay might have been written without the humour. Could it be as effective?

4. Although this story deals with intensely personal issues, the tone is quite ironic and detached. Given the tone, what do you make of the story's ending, with the children surrounding their mother "tightly on all sides," finally going back to their house?

Let It Snow

In Binghamton, New York, winter meant snow, and though I was young when we left, I was able to recall great heaps of it, and use that memory as evidence that North Carolina was, at best, a third-rate institution. What little snow there was would usually melt an hour or two after hitting the ground, and there you'd be in your windbreaker and unconvincing mittens, forming a lumpy figure made mostly of mud. Snow Negroes, we called them.

The winter I was in the fifth grade we got lucky. Snow fell, and for the first time in years, it accumulated. School was canceled and two days later we got lucky again. There were eight inches on the ground, and rather than melting, it froze. On the fifth day of our vacation my mother had a little breakdown. Our presence had disrupted the secret life she led while we were at school, and when she could no longer take it she threw us out. It wasn't a gentle request, but something closer to an eviction. "Get the hell out of my house," she said.

We reminded her that it was our house, too, and she opened the front door and shoved us into the carport. "And stay out!" she shouted.

My sisters and I went down the hill and sledded with other children from the neighborhood. A few hours later we returned home, surprised to find that the door was still locked. "Oh, come on," we said. I rang the bell and when no one answered we went to the window and saw our mother in the kitchen, watching television. Normally she waited until five o'clock to have a drink, but for the past few days she'd been making an exception. Drinking didn't count if you followed a glass of wine with a cup of coffee, and so she had both a goblet and a mug positioned before her on the countertop.

"Hey!" we yelled. "Open the door. It's us." We knocked on the pane, and without looking in our direction, she refilled her goblet and left the room.

"That bitch," my sister Lisa said. We pounded again and again, and when our mother failed to answer we went around back and threw snowballs at her bedroom window. "You are going to be in so much trouble when Dad gets home!" we shouted, and in response my mother pulled the drapes. Dusk approached, and as it grew colder it occurred to us that we could possibly die. It happened, surely. Selfish mothers wanted the house to themselves, and their children were discovered years later, frozen like mastodons in blocks of ice.

My sister Gretchen suggested that we call our father, but none of us knew his number, and he probably wouldn't have done anything anyway. He'd gone to work specifically to escape our mother, and between the weather and her mood, it could be hours or even days before he returned home.

"One of us should get hit by a car," I said. "That would teach the both of them." I pictured Gretchen, her life hanging by a thread as my parents paced the halls of Rex Hospital, wishing they had been more attentive. It was really the perfect solution. With her out of the way, the rest of us would be more valuable and have a bit more room to spread out. "Gretchen, go lie in the street."

"Make Amy do it," she said.

Amy, in turn, pushed it off onto Tiffany, who was the youngest and had no concept of death. "It's like sleeping," we told her. "Only you get a canopy bed."

Poor Tiffany. She'd do just about anything in return for a little affection. All you had to do was call her Tiff and whatever you wanted was yours: her allowance money, her dinner, the contents of her Easter basket. Her eagerness to please was absolute and naked. When we asked her to lie in the middle of the street, her only question was "Where?"

We chose a quiet dip between two hills, a spot where drivers were almost required to skid out of control. She took her place, this six-year-old in a butter-colored coat, and we gathered on the curb to watch. The first car to happen by belonged to a neighbor, a fellow Yankee who had outfitted his tires with chains and stopped a few feet from our sister's body. "Is that a person?" he asked.

"Well, sort of," Lisa said. She explained that we'd been locked out of our house and though the man appeared to accept it as a reasonable explanation, I'm pretty sure it was him who told on us. Another car passed and then we saw our mother, this puffy figure awkwardly negotiating the crest of the hill. She did not own a pair of pants, and her legs were buried to the calves in snow. We wanted to send her home, to kick her out of nature just as she had kicked us out of the house, but it was hard to stay angry at someone that pitiful-looking.

"Are you wearing your *loafers*?" Lisa asked, and in response our mother raised her bare foot. "I was wearing loafers," she said. "I mean, really, it was there a second ago."

This was how things went. One moment she was locking us out of our own house and the next we were rooting around in the snow, looking for her left shoe. "Oh, forget about it," she said. "It'll turn up in a few days." Gretchen fitted her cap over my mother's foot. Lisa secured it with her scarf, and surrounding her tightly on all sides, we made our way back home.

Why We Fight

(BLOG)

Doug Schmidt

Doug Schmidt spent six month in Afghanistan with Canadian troops, writing about their day-to-day lives, sharing their fears, and trying to come to terms with the very real dangers that confront them on a daily basis. The entries for July and November honour their mission.

Analyzing and Connecting

Return to these questions after you have finished reading.

1. Acts of compassion and kindness are interspersed between descriptions of death and violence in both entries. What is the significance of offsetting positive and negative actions?

2. "Death follows you everywhere at all times no matter what you do in Afghanistan." What point is Schmidt trying to make with this statement?

3. "I feel very alienated from my fellow Canadians ... this is a valuable mission ... for what Canadians believe they stand for." How do you interpret the meaning of this statement, especially the second phrase, *"for what Canadians believe they stand for"*?

4. How does Schmidt personalize these entries? What strategies does he use to make the people come alive?

07-02-2008

KANDAHAR, Afghanistan—Maureen Eykelenboom's son was a medic with the Canadian Forces in Afghanistan who saw things most Canadians couldn't fathom let alone would ever come close to having to experience. Andrew, known to his friends as Boomer, once plugged the severed legs of an interpreter, hit by a rocket, from bleeding out, thus saving his life. He and a fellow soldier did this while a battle raged on around them. Another time, the corporal scooped together into a body bag the pieces of a blown-apart comrade.

Boomer, 23, was packing his bags and getting ready for vacation when he volunteered on one last convoy to the volatile border town of Spin Boldak. His armoured G-Wagon was spotted and targeted by a suicide bomber, and Boomer, like dozens of other Canadian soldiers serving in Afghanistan since 2002, was himself blasted to death on August 11, 2006.

His mother, sporting the shiny Silver Cross on her lapel that next-of-kin get when their children, husbands, or wives die while serving their country, made an emotional trip back to Kandahar for Canada Day, when she addressed Canadian soldiers on the current Roto, telling the mostly young volunteers that they don't have to die to become heroes, but that they are heroes just by willing to sacrifice themselves in the service of others. It's a message she and others here wonder whether others back home really understand.

"We are here in Afghanistan to help a people who asked for our help. My son said, 'Mom, people in the village I was just in have nothing—even our street people in Canada have more.'"

The most worthwhile thing Boomer told his mother he did while on his tour was putting smiles on children's faces while committing small acts of kindness. He and his comrades would pass out food, pencils, and whatever else they could get their hands on, and they were soon asking their folks back home to send them care packages of educational supplies, clothing, medical equipment, and other necessities to hand out.

During my six-week visit to Kandahar, embedded with the Canadian military, more international soldiers were killed in Afghanistan than in the ongoing conflict in Iraq. Two Canadian captains died, while a Canadian major lost his legs. An American colonel was killed with three of his men on Ambush Alley, and the flags were flying at half-mast more often than not whenever I was at Kandahar Airfield. Death follows you everywhere at all times no matter what you do in Afghanistan.

And yet, I was left with the impression that Canada's soldiers remain focused and determined and convinced that what they are doing is right and that they are making a difference in the lives of a very downtrodden people.

"These soldiers see things and do things that we can't comprehend," said Maureen, who set up "Boomer's Legacy" after her son's death to raise funds back home so that other soldiers serving in Afghanistan could continue those kinds of personalized efforts. The military lawyers said it wouldn't be acceptable for civilians to raise money and partner soldiers to carry out humanitarian assistance, but just-retired Chief of Defense Staff Gen. Rick Hillier told them to make it happen anyway. The Assistance to Afghanistan Trust Fund was established in 2006, and part of it is made up of donations from the Boomer's Legacy Fund created a year ago. This week, Maureen Eykelenboom presented the latest $80,000 cheque to Canada's Joint Task Force Kandahar.

The money goes to projects, causes, and immediate needs identified by the front-line soldiers themselves in the field; there is little bureaucracy, and every cent of every donated dollar is used for the intended purpose. Much of the funds go towards children in need of urgent medical treatment they would otherwise never get. I was at a district council meeting of Afghan village elders last week when a payment was announced to a local shepherd who lost 24 of his sheep in June when their combined weight was enough to set off a roadside bomb intended to kill passing soldiers. The Canadian visitors at that meeting made a point of telling the local leaders that it was regular folks back home, and not their government or the military, that was compensating the shepherd, and doing so even though insurgents were to blame. I was later told there were Taliban among those elders attending.

"Maybe that suicide bomber may have had a better choice if he'd had an education," Maureen said of the individual who blew himself up with Boomer.

As important as raising money to assist Afghans, Maureen Eykelenboom said her group is also about raising awareness back home.

"Canadians need to wake up and realize who they have in their military," she said. The soldiers she meets "feel they can make a difference, and they are making a difference, and we need to show them that respect, and as a country we need to support them in their missions."

In addition to the funds, her group has also collected 52,000 homemade Boomer Caps, more than half of which have been distributed to children in other countries where there is a need to keep small heads warm.

Around her neck, Maureen wears a medallion with a depiction of her son on one side and the words "Just Freedom" on the other. "In Canada, we have it and we don't even think about it—here, they don't have it."

Afghanistan and the military took her son, but Maureen Eykelenboom is a big supporter of both. Canada is here, she said, so girls can go to school and women can be educated, and so "they're allowed to make choices for themselves."

Afghanistan is still a place where being a woman predominantly means remaining illiterate, being cloistered in a high-walled family compound, and only being allowed in public under the heavy cloak of a burqa and in the accompaniment of a close male relative.

When the Afghans find out, probably through education, that you're nowhere as a society when half your population is locked away with the livestock, then our mission of helping Afghanistan is well on its way to being accomplished.

11-10-2008

Remembrance Day is about remembering, but in so doing, it's also about honouring and thanking.

One group of largely unsung Canadian heroes I met this summer in the Afghan badlands were the so-called POMLETS, soldiers who began in the fall of 2007 deploying with and trying to whip into shape the widely despised Afghan National Police, who were, for the most part, removed in name only from the regular criminal elements that make that country such a wild and crazy place.

It's a dangerous mission.

"Three-quarters of the Canadian task force would be petrified to do what we do," Captain Sheldon Maerz told me during a visit this summer to a group of soldiers tasked with mentoring the Afghan police in the Panjwaii district west of Kandahar city.

"Nobody does what we do ... there's a lotta risk," said Maerz. This was the self-described Saskatchewan farmboy's second tour to Talibanland. In 2006, the Afghan cops were "thugs, they were armed gangs," he said, recalling one incident in which an Afghan cop was caught red-handed calling in insurgent mortar fire on Canadian positions.

"We have a huge way to go," said Maerz. As if to underline that, the day after we met, some of his ANP charges were shot up on a village visit by, go figure, a member of another ANP crew. The week I visited their heavily armed and fortified compound in the village of Bazar-i-Panjwaii, the POMLETs were without a cook—he was killed a few weeks earlier after ignoring warnings to stay away from the Canadians.

The main thing being taught the local police, Maerz said, is "survivability"—staying alive. In Kandahar Province, where 1,000 ANP were killed in 2007, it's Gary Cooper in High Noon every single day. Only the cops here, said Sgt. Todd MacLeod of Centreville, New Brunswick, don't go anywhere in smaller numbers than a squad of six.

A cop's job is serving people, and that means meeting people, and that's where the job of the POMLETs gets hairiest. Mingling with the locals in Bazar-i-Panjwaii means also mingling with the Taliban, and it also means the Canadian mentors must rely on their ANP charges to do what they've been taught, or risk getting a bunch of them killed.

As I joined them on one morning patrol, I was told some of the people we'd be meeting were the people determined to kill them.

"When we go out there, people think, wow, they've got balls," said Sgt. Tim Seeley, a Winnipeg reservist who helped oversee—by participating in such foot patrols—reconstruction efforts in the area. As the soldiers go prancing down the main drag of the village, with its colourful and busy bumper-to-bumper array of shops, they know they're drawing attention from everyone, and they know there are many enemies taking mental note ... they keep a special eye open for anyone who might be reaching for their cellphone.

The area's Pashtun, with their codes of honour and warrior tradition, respect courage, and as the patrol leaves the main drag to begin winding its way through the narrow mudwall-lined side alleys, locals pop out, cast furtive glances in every direction for spies, and then approach the ANP and Canadians to pass on words of encouragement and information on insurgents.

"If you control the cruelty, it would be good—God will be happy with you," one elder says through a Pashto interpreter. Another points to a nearby compound and whispers it's the home of a local mullah who supports the Taliban and whose sons openly wander the alleys at night toting AK-47s. The patrol takes notes and promises a greater future street presence as more and more police recruits undergo training.

Something that angers and frustrates the Canadian POMLETs I talk with is the way their Afghan charges are sometimes dealt with by other task force members. "The way Canadians treat these guys ... it's one of my big piss-offs ... these guys risk their lives," one POMLET told me. Most Canadian soldiers don't interact directly with their Afghan counterparts, but POMLETs not only train and patrol with them but share close quarters and get to know them on a personal level.

Maerz feels that same kind of frustration when he goes home: "I feel very alienated from my fellow Canadians," says the captain, adding: "This is a valuable mission ... for what Canadians believe they stand for."

Safely back home now, I remember almost daily one or another of the troops I shared time with in Kandahar and who helped keep me alive so I could tell their stories to the folks back home, many of whom take their freedom for granted.

I don't, and for that, thanks.

How to write a reflection

These steps for the process of writing a reflection may not progress as neatly as this chart might suggest. Writing is not an assembly-line process. Writing about a remembered event, place, or person is, in itself, a powerful way to reflect. Be open to uncovering insights and understanding more broadly the significance.

1 CHOOSE A SUBJECT

- Analyze the assignment.
- Explore possible topics.
- Remember places and objects.
- Consider the significance.

2 DEVELOP A RESPONSE

- Generate details.
- Make people come alive.
- Think about the context.
- Relate your experience to the experiences of others.

Analyze your potential readers

- *What do your readers likely know about the subject?*
- *How can you engage readers?*
- *What will they gain from reading your reflection?*

3 WRITE A DRAFT

- Select vivid details and dialogue.
- Decide on an organization.
- Craft a strong beginning.
- Conclude by inviting further reflection.
- Consider your voice and tone.
- Choose a title that will interest readers.

4 REVISE, REVISE, REVISE

- Check that your paper or project fulfills the assignment.
- Make sure that the subject is focused.
- Add details, description, or dialogue.
- Make sure your voice and tone will engage readers.
- Examine your organization and think of possible better ways to organize.
- Review the visual presentation.
- Proofread carefully.

5 SUBMITTED VERSION

- Make sure your finished writing meets all formatting requirements.

1: Find a reflective topic and a focus for writing about it

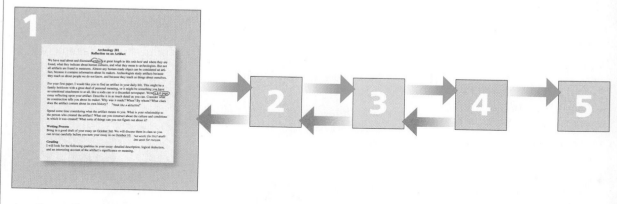

Analyze the assignment

- Read your assignment slowly and carefully. Look for key words like *reflect, consider,* or *contemplate.* These key words tell you that you are writing a reflective essay.

- Identify any information about the length specified, date due, formatting, and other requirements. You can attend to this information later. At this point you want to give your attention to your topic and the focus of your reflection.

Explore possible topics

- Think about your family. What memories stand out about your parents? Your brothers and sisters? Your own child or children? Your grandparents and other close relatives? Your pets? Your shared family experiences including vacations and holidays? Make a list of events and situations associated with your family.

- Think about work experience. What was your first job? Did you ever have a great boss or a horrible boss? Do any other workers stand out? What important learning experiences did you have on the job? Make a list of events and situations associated with work.

- Think about your school experience. What school memories stand out? Did a teacher have a strong influence on you? Did a coach make a difference in your life? What were the social groups in your school? Make a list of events and situations associated with school.

- Think about friends and social relationships. What memories stand out about your friends? About people you've met? About people you've dated? Make a list of events and situations associated with friends and social relationships.

- Review all of your lists and put a check beside any items that look like interesting possibilities for writing.

Remember places and objects	• Is a particular place important? Why is it critical? For example, how did you gain an understanding of your mother's attitudes when you visited the place where she grew up?
	• Is a particular object important? For example, can you describe the locket that belonged to your great-grandmother and was passed down to you?
Consider the significance	• Ask yourself, "Why is this person, event, place, or object significant to me?"
	• Think about why the person, place, event, or object seems more important now than in your initial experience. How did your view change?
	• How did you change as a result of being around this person, event, place, or object?
Analyze your potential readers	• What do your readers likely know about the subject?
	• What might you need to tell readers about your background?
	• How can you engage readers?
	• What will they gain from reading your reflection?

WRITE NOW

Explore memories

- Select one of the items that you have checked on your lists.
- Freewrite for five minutes to explore the event, situation, place, or object. What was your initial reaction? Who else was there? Did you share your reaction at the time?
- Freewrite for five minutes to explore your current perspective. How did an experience change you? Why do you remember this person, event, place, or object so well? Looking back, what do you see now that you didn't recognize at the time?
- Stop and read what you have written. Do you see possibilities for writing at length about this person, event, or situation? If you do, then begin generating more content using any of the outlining techniques from Chapter 3. If the idea seems limited, try freewriting about another person, event, place, or object.

Writer at work

Janine Carter received the following assignment in her Introduction to Archeology class. She made notes on her assignment sheet as the class discussed the assignment.

Archeology 201
Reflection on an Artifact

We have read about and discussed artifacts at great length in this unit—how and where they are found, what they indicate about human cultures, and what they mean to archeologists. But not all artifacts are found in museums. Almost any human-made object can be considered an artifact, because it contains information about its makers. Archeologists study artifacts because they teach us about people we do not know, and because they teach us things about ourselves.

For your first paper, I would like you to find an artifact in your daily life. This might be a family heirloom with a great deal of personal meaning, or it might be something you have no emotional attachment to at all, like a pop can or a discarded newspaper. Write a 4-6 page essay reflecting upon your artifact. Describe it in as much detail as you can. Consider what its construction tells you about its maker. Why was it made? When? By whom? What clues does the artifact contain about its own history?   *"Think like a detective"*

Use lots of detail

Spend some time considering what the artifact means to you. What is your relationship to the person who created the artifact? What can you construct about the culture and conditions in which it was created? What sorts of things can you not figure out about it?

Writing Process
Bring in a good draft of your essay on October 3. We will discuss them in class so you can revise carefully before you turn your essay in on October 10.   *Two weeks for first draft*
One week for revision

Grading
I will look for the following qualities in your essay: detailed description, logical deduction, and an interesting account of the artifact's significance or meaning.

Then Janine made a list of possible objects to write about.

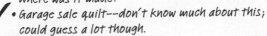

<u>HEIRLOOMS/EMOTIONAL CONNECTION</u>
- Aunt Marie's tulip quilt--shows my connection to a long line of quilters
- ~~Sea shells from Girl Scout camp~~—NOT HUMAN-MADE
- Bracelet from graduation
- Terry's photo
- Stuffed elephant—shows how much I have grown up. Where was it made?
✓ - Garage sale quilt--don't know much about this; could guess a lot though.
- Diploma

<u>LESS IMPORTANT OBJECTS</u>
- Cereal box--ingredients show lack of nutrition. Pictures show how kids are bombarded with cartoons and colourful images. Expiration date and other clues to where it was made.
- Desk in residence room--Must have been used by dozens of people like me (?)
- Old calendar
- Old cookbook
- A floppy disk--Could talk about how fast technology is changing. Do I have one?

2: Develop a response

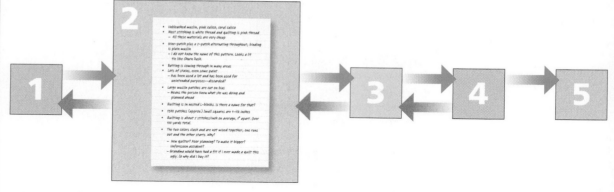

Generate details

- Write down all the sights, sounds, smells, tastes, and tactile sensations you associate with your topic.
- If you are using a photograph or other object, write a detailed description of it.
- If you are remembering a past event, write down everything that happened: what people said and did, how you felt as things happened, and anything else you remember or feel is significant.

Make people come alive

- Use dialogue to let readers hear people talk, which reveals much about character.
- Record the little mannerisms, gestures, clothing, and personal habits that distinguish people.
- Don't forget to make yourself come alive. If you are reflecting on an incident from your childhood, how old were you? What do you remember about yourself at that age?

Think about the context

- How does your memory compare with similar experiences you have read or heard about from others?
- Does your memory connect to any larger trends or events going on at the time?

Relate your experience to the experiences of others

- The very fact that you find the topic memorable means there is something there you can share with others. Think about how to make it obvious to them.
- How is your subject particular to you? What do you notice as you reflect that other people might not notice? This is the "added value" that will make your reflection more than a mere description or memory.

Writer at work

Janine Carter sat down with her garage-sale quilt and a pen and paper. She observed it carefully and made a list of detailed observations about its physical appearance. Then she added her conclusions and guesses about the quilt, its history, and its maker, based on these clues.

Janine thought about her relationship to the quilt. She jotted down, in no particular order, what she remembered about buying the quilt, conversations she had had with her grandmother about quilting, and ideas that occurred to her.

- Unbleached muslin, pink calico, coral calico
- Most stitching is white thread and quilting is pink thread
  - All these materials are very cheap

- Nine-patch plus a 5-patch alternating throughout; binding is plain muslin
  - I do not know the name of this pattern. Looks a little like Churn Dash.

- Batting is coming through in many areas
- Lots of stains, even some paint
  - Has been used a lot and has been used for unintended purposes—discarded?

- Large muslin patches are cut on bias
  - Means the person knew what she was doing and planned ahead

- Quilting is in nested L-blocks. Is there a name for that?

- 1372 patches (approx.) Small squares are 1-1/2 inches

- Quilting is about 5 stitches/inch on average, 1" apart. Over 100 yards total.

- The two colours clash and are not mixed together; one runs out and the other starts. Why?

  - New quilter? Poor planning? To make it bigger? Unforeseen accident?
  - Grandma would have had a fit if I ever made a quilt this ugly. So why did I buy it?

3: Write a draft

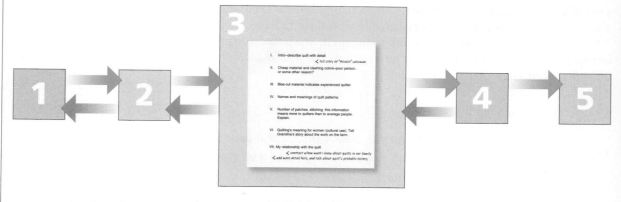

Select vivid details and dialogue

- Don't rely solely on visual memory. Include sounds, smells, tastes, and tactile feelings.
- Describe people's mannerisms, gestures, and voices.
- Use dialogue to reveal character.

Decide on an organization

- Use chronological order to help readers re-live events with you.
- Use conceptual order to show connections and links between ideas.

Craft a strong beginning

- Start with an incident or a place that is the focus.

Conclude by inviting further reflection

- Have you discovered anything new in the process of writing the reflection to share in your conclusion?
- A conclusion can sometimes change the entire tone of a reflection. Do you want to surprise your readers?
- Above all, your conclusion should help readers make sense of your reflection.

Consider your voice and tone

- Who are you writing for? How do you want your audience to feel upon reading your reflection?
- How interested will your readers be in your reflection? Can you add details or something else to draw them in?

Choose a title that will interest readers in your essay

- Your title should suggest the direction or the significance of your reflection.

Writer at work

Janine Carter tried organizing her essay in several different ways. Because she knew so little about the quilt's history, she did not feel chronological organization would be a good strategy. However, as she worked through her draft she realized that readers would appreciate a first-hand account of her purchase. She decided to include this story near the beginning of her essay, after describing the quilt. She organized the rest of her essay around the questions that occurred to her as she considered the quilt's appearance. As she worked, she referred back to her assignment frequently to make sure she was fulfilling all its terms. She decided to cut one section, about the names of various quilt patterns, because it was too general and distracted from the main focus of her essay. Here is the original outline Janine began working from, along with revisions she made.

I.   Intro—describe quilt with detail
                              < *tell story of "Miracle" salesman*

II. Cheap material and clashing colours–poor
     person, or some other reason?

III. Bias-cut material indicates experienced quilter

IV. ~~Names and meanings of quilt patterns.~~

V.   Number of patches, stitching: this information
     means more to quilters than to average people.
     Explain.

VI. Quilting's meaning for women (cultural use). Tell
     Grandma's story about the work on the farm.

VII. My relationship with the quilt
                    < *contrast w/how much I know about quilts in our family*
              < *add more detail here, and talk about quilt's probable history*

4: Revise, revise, revise

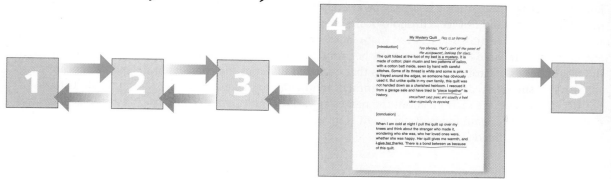

Skilled writers know that the secret to writing well is revising. Even the best writers often have to revise several times to get the result they want. You also must have effective strategies for revising if you're going to be successful. The biggest trap you can fall into is starting off with correcting errors. Focusing on grammatical or structural errors may distract you from looking at bigger problems of content analysis.

Does your paper or project meet the assignment?	• Look again at the assignment for specific guidelines, including length, format, and amount of research. Does your work meet these guidelines?
Is the subject focused?	• Will readers find your subject early on? • Is the significance evident?
Can you add dialogue, description, and other details?	• Can you make events and memories from the past more concrete?
Is your tone engaging?	• Will readers sympathize and identify with you, or will they find your tone too negative, angry, inflammatory, or personal? • Does your tone fit your topic? Some intensely personal topics may not be suited to humorous treatment.
Is your organization effective?	• Are links between concepts and ideas clear? • Are there any places where you find abrupt shifts or gaps? • Are there sections or paragraphs that could be rearranged to make your draft more effective?
Is the writing project visually effective?	• Is the font attractive and readable? • Are the headings and visuals effective? • If you have included an image associated with your reflection, where should it be placed for maximum impact?
Save the editing for last	• When you have finished revising, edit and proofread carefully.

A peer review guide is on page 31.

Writer at work

Janine Carter was not satisfied with her opening paragraph or her title. After talking to an advisor at her campus writing centre, she worked on ending her opening paragraph with a surprising twist that would engage readers. She also realized that she could draw out the concept of "miracles" to tie the beginning and end together. Here are the first drafts of Janine's opening and concluding paragraphs, with her notes.

My Mystery Quilt   *This is so boring!*

[introduction]   *Too obvious. That's sort of the point of the assignment, looking for clues.*

The quilt folded at the foot of my bed is a mystery. It is made of cotton: plain muslin and two patterns of calico, with a cotton batting inside, sewn by hand with careful stitches. Some of its thread is white and some is pink. It is frayed around the edges, so someone has obviously used it. But unlike quilts in my own family, this quilt was not handed down as a cherished heirloom. I rescued it from a garage sale and have tried to "piece together" its history.

advisor says puns are usually a bad idea—especially in opening

[conclusion]

When I am cold at night I pull the quilt up over my knees and think about the stranger who made it, wondering who she was, who her loved ones were, whether she was happy. Her quilt gives me warmth, and I give her thanks. There is a bond between us because of this quilt.

This is boring/obvious. Can I make it more special?

5: Print a version to submit

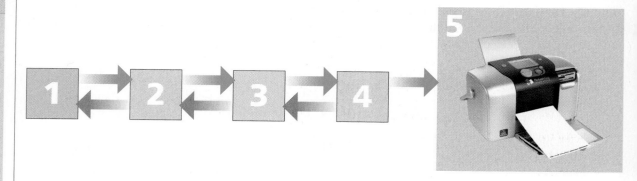

Carter 1

Janine Carter
Dr. Shapiro
Archaeology 201
10 October 2011

The Miracle Quilt

The quilt folded at the foot of my bed has a long history. It is made of cotton: plain muslin and two patterns of calico, with cotton batting inside, sewn by hand with careful stitches. Some of its thread is white and some is pink. It is frayed around the edges and has obviously lived a long, useful life. It is steeped in memories. Unfortunately, I don't know what any of them are.

I found the quilt at a city-wide garage sale. At the end of the auditorium, taking up half of the bleachers, was a vendor's booth called "Miracles by the Pound." The gentleman who ran the booth went around buying up vintage fabrics in bad condition. He would dump huge piles of them on the bleachers for people to pick through. When you had found what you wanted, he would weigh it on a scale and tell you how much it cost. Everything was five dollars per pound. As he weighed your purchase, he would call out the price so everyone at the garage sale could hear what a good deal you were getting. My quilt weighed three pounds. "Fifteen dollar miracle!" the vendor sang out as I opened my purse.

My quilt had already been dug out of the pile and discarded by another woman at the garage sale, who had two or three other vintage quilts in her

Fig. 1. Detail of the miracle quilt.

arms. She told me she bought old, damaged quilts and cut them up to make sofa pillows. My quilt didn't interest her because it wasn't in very good shape, and the blocks were the wrong size for the pillow forms she used. I come from a family of quilters, so when I saw the quilt I felt it needed a good home. I didn't like the idea of someone using it to wrap around furniture in a moving van, or even cutting it up for pillows. I took it home and washed it, and put it on my bed, and took a good look at it.

The quilt was probably made by someone poor, or at least very frugal, I decided. The muslin, which provides the background, is the cheapest unbleached kind. Even the binding around the edges, which in most quilts is a bright, contrasting colour, is plain muslin. Whoever pieced the quilt—and it was almost certainly a woman, because quilting has always been women's work—started out using a coral-toned calico. But before she finished, she ran out and had to switch to a rose-coloured calico. The effect is jarring, as the colours do not complement each other. The coral marches two-thirds of the way across the quilt, and then stumbles into rose. I do not know why the quiltmaker did not work the two colours evenly throughout the quilt; this is what my own grandmother taught me to do when I didn't have enough of one colour. Perhaps she was inexperienced; perhaps this was her first quilt, or perhaps she hadn't intended to make the quilt as large as it is. The coral would have been sufficient to cover a single bed; maybe, I think to myself, someone proposed to her while she was making it, and she ended up enlarging it to fit a double bed after she got married.

But there are other clues that suggest experience and planning. The octagon-shaped patches of muslin that centre the five-patch blocks are cut so that the lines of quilting cross them on the bias—that is, diagonally across the up-and-down and side-to-side warp and woof threads of the fabric. Fabric is more flexible on the bias (this, my grandmother once explained to me, is why clothing cut on the bias fits and looks better, and is more expensive). A needle slips in and out between the threads more easily, so a quilter is wise to arrange pieces so as to maximize bias quilting. The quilting itself (that is the stitching through all the layers of the quilt) is respectable enough, about five stitches per inch. No fancy 12-stitch-per-inch quilting like the ones you would see in a showpiece quilt, but quite firm and straight, in neat pink rows spaced an inch apart. The quilting pattern is in L-shaped blocks, which I have never seen before. There must be over one hundred yards of quilting all together; the length of a football field, taken one stitch at a time.

The quilt's pattern looks like a variation of wagon tracks, but it uses an octagonal block like a "churn-dash" pattern that sets it apart from a more straightforward Irish chain. Nine-patch and five-patch blocks alternate across it. By my count it contains 1,372 separate pieces, all cut, sewn, and quilted by hand. The nine-patch blocks use 1-1/2-inch patches. These may seem like insignificant details to most people, but to quilters they are important. They tell you how much work went into the quilt. The first nine-patch quilt I made with my grandmother contained a grand total of 675 patches, and I thought it would take forever to sew it (even using a sewing machine!). I remember asking my grandmother how she ever made her more complicated quilts: the flower garden with its thousands of tiny hexagons; the Dutchman's puzzle that was so mesmerizing you could hardly stop your eyes from running over it, trying to pick out the "real" pattern. "Doesn't quilting drive you crazy sometimes?" I asked her. She thought that was pretty funny. "Quilting was how we used to keep from going crazy," she told me.

When she first married my grandfather and moved to a farm in the Brazos River bottom over sixty years ago, there was no television and no neighbours for miles. In the spring, rain would turn the roads to thick clay mud, and no one could get off their property for days at a time. Quilting was the way women dealt with the isolation. "That is what the pioneer women did too," she told me. Stuck out alone on the prairies and in the mountains, they kept their sanity by cutting and arranging hundreds of pieces of cloth in different patterns, methodically assembling quilts to bring some order into their own bleak lives.

"It looks like hard work to you now," my grandmother explained, "but for us it was like a vacation. So much of women's work was never done, but you could sit down after dinner in the evening and finish a quilt block and feel like you had done something that would last. You might have spent the whole day dirtying and washing the same set of dishes three times, feeding the same chickens and milking the same cows twice, and you knew you'd have to get up in the morning and do the same things all over again, from top to bottom. But quilt blocks added up to something. Nobody was going to take your finished quilt block and sit down at the breakfast table and pick it apart, and expect you to sew it back together again before lunch. It was done, and it stayed done. There wasn't much else you could say that about, on a farm."

In my family, quilts are heirlooms and are handed down with stories about who made them, who owned them, what they were used for, and what events they had been part of. Some were wedding presents, others were made for relatives when they were first born. I don't know the stories that go with my miracle quilt. It has had a hard life; that is easy to see. Most of the binding has frayed off and there are some spots where the quilt has holes worn straight through it—top, batting, and backing. There are stains that suggest coffee or tea or perhaps medicines from a sickbed spilled on it. There are some spots of dried paint. Evidently at some point it was used as a drop-cloth. But at least, I tell myself, it has found a home with someone who appreciates the work that went into it, and can guess at some of its history.

When I am cold at night I pull the quilt up over my knees and think about the stranger who made it, wondering who she was, who her loved ones were, whether she was happy. Her quilt gives me warmth, and I give her thanks. Though we will never meet, or even know each other's identity, there is a bond between us because of this quilt. And so it seems that the man who sold me this quilt was right: it is a sort of miracle.

Projects

Reflections focus on people, places, events, and things—past and present—that have significance in the writer's life. Successful reflections engage readers in their subjects and convey the importance of the person, event, or place.

These projects are frequently written kinds of reflections.

REFLECTION ON THE PAST

For an example of a reflective essay, see pages 147–149.

List people, events, or places that have been significant in your life or in some way changed you. Many reflections focus on a conflict of some kind and how it was resolved. Look back over your list and check the items that seem especially vivid to you.

Take a few minutes to write first about the person, event, or place as you remember it, and then write about how you regard it today. What was your initial reaction? Did your initial reaction change over time? Why do you feel differently now? Refer to page 162 for more details.

Think about the significance of the person, event, or place in your life. What details best convey that significance? If conversations were involved, remember what was said and create dialogue. Refer to page 162 for more details.

Organize your essay around the focus. Capture your reader's attention with a strong vivid introduction. If there is a conflict in your reflection, begin with it!

Show the significance through descriptions, vivid details, and dialogue. Make the characters and the places come to life.

FAMILY PHOTOGRAPH

For an example of a reflection on a family, see pages 147–149.

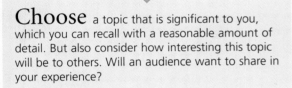

Family photographs and cherished objects can be subjects for reflection. Try carefully observing (or picturing in your mind) an object or photograph that has special meaning for you. Write down all the details you can. What memories does each observation evoke? Do you find that different aspects of the photograph make you feel different ways?

Choose a topic that is significant to you, which you can recall with a reasonable amount of detail. But also consider how interesting this topic will be to others. Will an audience want to share in your experience?

Write a reflective essay about the photo you chose. What does the photograph convey that other similar snapshots do not? What does it hide or not show? What does it say about your family?

REFLECTION ON THE PRESENT

For an example of a reflection on the present, see pages 150–155.

Not all reflective writing is about the past. You can visit a place or go to an event and focus on your interaction with it instead of the place or event itself. How do you feel when you walk through a local cemetery? What do you think about? What do you notice about the grounds, headstones, and grave decorations? Do you come away from the experience with any interesting realizations about yourself and your life?

Connect the place or event with your life. You are "reading" it in terms of your own experiences. These connections should be the centre of your writing.

Identify a focus. Then write the most vivid introduction you can that will highlight it. Select your strongest observations and reactions, and elaborate on that material.

Describe the experience in an essay. Use specific, vivid details to express your feelings.

11
Informing

Good informative writing begins with what the reader needs to know and then presents that information effectively.

Chapter contents

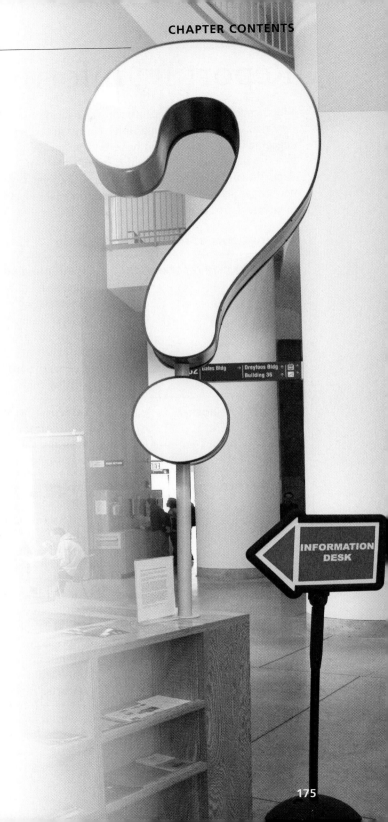

Reporting information

Whether reading the news, following a recipe, hooking up a new computer, deciding which course to take, or engaging in a multitude of other events in our daily lives, we depend on reliable and clear information. Reporting information takes many forms, ranging from newspaper articles and reports of experimental research to tables, charts, and simple lists of information.

In one sense, most kinds of writing, including writing to reflect and writing to persuade, also report information. The main difference is that the focus of a report and other informative kinds of writing is on the subject, not on the writer's reflections or on changing the readers' minds or on getting them to take action.

Components of informative writing

Where do I find information?	**Find information** Research is necessary for many types of informative writing. Scientists make observations in the field and conduct experiments to create new knowledge. Journalists interview people for the information to include in articles. Social workers assemble observation notes in order to write case studies. Knowing where to find information and knowing how much you need is critical for writing reports.
What does it mean?	**Interpret information** Writers not only report what they read and observe. They construct meaning through selecting what and what not to include and in organizing that information.
How can I explain it?	**Explain information** Often what you know well is difficult to explain to others. In order to do so effectively, you will need to break down a process into steps that you can describe. Explaining a process sometimes requires you to think about something familiar in a new way.
What are the implications?	**Explore questions and problems** Not all informative writing is about topics with which you are familiar or ones that you can bring to closure. Often post-secondary writing involves issues or problems that perplex us and for which we cannot come to a definitive conclusion. The goal in such writing is not the ending but the journey. Difficult issues often leave you conflicted; readers appreciate writers who deal honestly with those conflicts.
Where does the information come from?	All writers must acknowledge the original source(s) of their research. Informative writing often relies on external sources for evidence, facts, and support. Recognize the contributions of these resources through accurate documentation.

Keys to informative writing

Narrow the topic

A central difficulty in writing to inform is knowing where to stop. For any large subject, a lifetime may be insufficient. The key to success is limiting your topic to one you can cover adequately in the space you have.

Start quickly

The title and introduction should entice readers to want to read the rest. Dull, generic titles and vague, general introductory paragraphs discourage further reading. Offer a new viewpoint that challenges the usual, commonplace one.

Keep readers interested

Readers become bored quickly if they have heard it all before. Once you have made your readers curious to know more about your subject, don't disappoint them.

Define key terms

Writers should define clearly any key terms and concepts that might be unfamiliar.

Provide relevant examples, illustrations, and details

The examples, illustrations, and details are essentials elements of informative writing, whether it is a news article, a report, a paper, or even a set of instructions or a cookbook. Select them carefully.

Remain objective

Writers whose purpose is to inform usually stay in the background, taking the stance of an impartial, objective observer. An objective tone and the absence of bias helps readers to believe the information is accurate and that the writer is trustworthy.

Provide accurate information

Informative writing frequently draws on outside sources of information, including library research, Web research, interviews, surveys, and observations. Even if writers are familiar with a subject, they find out what experts have to say about it to remain current and informed.

Document the sources of information

If you use sources in a college assignment, you will be expected to document those sources. Lakshmi Kotra's essay at the end of this chapter (see pages 214–221) follows an academic format for citing sources.

Conclude with strength

Besides a sudden stop, a plain summary is the weakest possible conclusion. Leave your readers with something to think about—a memorable example, an anecdote that illustrates a key point, implications of the information you have provided, a quotation that expresses a main point vividly, or a projection into the future.

Satellite photography helped the world to understand the damage caused by the tsunami that struck Indonesia on December 28, 2004.

Explain with charts and graphs

Charts and graphs show facts and relationships that are often difficult to communicate using words alone. A good chart makes the significance of the data clear at a glance.

Explain with images

Pictures don't always tell a thousand words; indeed, we need words to understand what is represented in pictures. Nevertheless, photographs, drawings, maps, and other graphics can provide concrete evidence to support what is being explained in words.

WORKING TOGETHER

Explain a concept or activity

In a group of three or four students

First select a concept or activity that you know a great deal about (through your courses, your work experience, or your personal interests) but your classmates likely do not. Subjects might range from the second law of thermodynamics and postmodern architecture to video gaming, dancing, and growing your own herbs. In your group give each person five minutes to explain the concept or activity.

Listen carefully to each classmate, and when each finishes, stop for a minute to note

- what you knew already
- what you found engaging
- what you wanted to know more about
- what you didn't understand

After the last person finishes, share your notes with the group. You'll have an immediate audience response to your explanation.

Effective informative writing

Informative writing succeeds when readers can connect new facts and concepts to what they already know.

Rates of Return

Joseph Berger and Andrew Parkin

June 2009

This document, excerpted from *The Price of Knowledge, Access and Student Finance in Canada,* was prepared for the Millennium Scholarship Foundation and presents information about the value of post-secondary credentials in terms of earning potential and employment. This chapter focuses on the "rates of return" or the comparison of educational investment and financial success.

RATES OF RETURN (PART III-CHAPTER 1)

17

Chapter 1

III. Rates of Return

Higher education has not only become increasingly central to individual and societal wealth and quality of life, it has also become more expensive. Since the 1990s, there has been a significant increase in tuition and the additional costs almost all students face, including ancillary fees, accommodation, books and equipment, food and transit.[4] An understanding of the benefits of a post-secondary degree must take both these trends into account. The rate of return allows for the assessment of the value of education as if it were an investment. It represents the net worth of education once costs are considered, including upfront costs like tuition and books as well as costs such as forgone income. The rate of return acts as a de facto interest rate that is equivalent to the proportion of the total cost returned to the individual as a benefit, in the form of earnings. Expressed as a percentage, the rate of return allows for the comparison of investments in education to financial products.

Canadian researchers have confirmed that the returns to post-secondary education have risen over the past decades:

* According to Emery's survey of the literature in Canada (2005), rates of return increased steadily from the 1960s to the early 1990s, where they peaked at 16 percent (women) and 12 percent (men) before dropping off only slightly.

* Belzil and Hansen (2006) examined rates of return using census data, finding an increase during the 1990s, from 9 percent in 1991 to 11 percent in 2001, although they tend to vary by discipline, gender and region. Notably, the authors demonstrated that the rate of return to post-secondary education increased significantly despite the large tuition increases of the 1990s.

* Similarly, Jorgen Hansen (2007), using census data from 1991, 1996 and 2001, finds that the rate of return increased during the 1990s for most fields of study. Hansen reports increases in the rates of return for females in the humanities, social sciences, business and commerce, agricultural/biological/nutritional/food sciences, health and mathematics/computer/physical sciences. He found no change in educational/recreational/counselling services and engineering and a small decline in the fine and applied arts. Rates of return for males increased in every field except educational/recreational/counselling services (which did not change) and fine and applied arts (which declined).

* Demers (2008) uses 2006 census data to examine the returns to education in Quebec. He finds that the amount of taxes paid increases with educational attainment in the province. Additionally, he identifies a rate of return to individuals who receive a bachelor's degree of 10.6 percent, as well as a public rate of return of 8.5 percent. Demers also describes how unemployment levels decrease with educational attainment.

While much of the literature is focused on the benefits of a university education, there is some evidence that similar trends occur at the college level. As mentioned above, Boothby and Drewes (2006) report that the college earnings premium increased between 1980 and 2000. Ferrer and Riddell (2002) also identify a small earnings premium to non-university post-secondary education (compared to those with a high school education). While college graduates enjoy a more modest earnings premium than university graduates, they still benefit from a substantial rate of return for two reasons. First, college is typically cheaper than university in Canada. Also, college programs tend to be shorter,

The opening statements of this section introduces the issue—that post–secondary education has become expensive.

Berger and Parkin point out a way to evaluate the investment of an education.

The researchers provide extensive evidence from external sources to support work.

4.   These figures will be presented in Chapter 4.

reducing the opportunity cost (the forgone income the individual would otherwise earn).

This analysis of the benefits of post-secondary education focusing on the returns to individuals is inevitably incomplete. There are significant societal benefits that underpin the argument for increased educational attainment. As Figure 1.III.1 demonstrates, post-secondary graduates pay the lion's share of taxes in Canada and receive a relatively small portion of government transfers.

Beyond government revenues and expenditure, educational attainment is associated with a number of positive characteristics. Riddell (2006) offers a summary of the four areas that are discussed in the literature on returns to schooling. The first concerns intergenerational effects. Higher levels of parental education are associated with lower levels of teenage pregnancy, child abuse and neglect and reduced crime in children. The second area is health. Riddell points to a pair of studies that find a causal relationship—not mere correlation—between education and health. In particular, there is evidence to suggest that even when controlling for levels of health knowledge, individuals with higher levels of education use that knowledge more efficiently. Studies by Lleras-Muney (2005) and Lleras-Muney and Lichtenberg (2002) reveal strong correlations between levels of education and mortality, as well as the use of more recently

approved prescription drugs. Third, evidence from the United States suggests that increasing educational attainment can reduce arrests, incarcerations and self-reported crime. Fourth, higher levels of educational attainment are associated with greater civic participation, particularly voting. As the U.S.-based Institute for Higher Education Policy (1998) has noted, greater levels of post-secondary education within the population lead to increased productivity, consumption and charitable giving.

Of course, by definition, examining earnings premiums and rates of return focuses on the average experience of post-secondary graduates. A recent Statistics Canada project commissioned by the Canada Millennium Scholarship Foundation and the Higher Education Quality Council of Ontario examines the situation of highly educated young Canadian workers with below-average earnings. Specifically, the study examines the characteristics of these graduates and then explores their shifting experience within the labour market.

Compared to other OECD countries, Canada has the highest proportion of post-secondary graduates earning less than half the median income. Among those aged 25 to 64, almost 18 percent of university graduates and 23 percent of college graduates earned less than half the median income ($16,917) in 2006. On the surface, this suggests that the earnings benefits of post-secondary

> Considerations other than financial gain are highlighted here.

Figure 1.III.1 — Percentage of the Population and Share of Income Tax Paid and of Government Transfers Received by Level of Education among Canadians Aged 25 to 64 in 2006

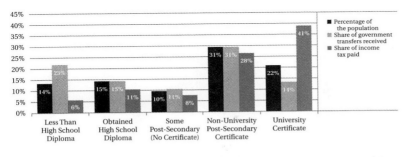

Source: Statistics Canada, Survey of Labour and Income Dynamics, custom tabulation.

> Statistics in the form of a chart are used to "show" specific information.

RATES OF RETURN (PART III-CHAPTER 1)

education are not as robust as the literature claims. In fact, as the Statistics Canada report explains, few Canadians with a post-secondary education who fully participate in the labour market find themselves with relatively low wages. Among university graduates with very low earnings, 43 percent reported doing something other than working as their main activity for the year in question; 24 per cent reported being self-employed (and therefore had an incentive to report low earnings in the tax files that form the basis for the SLID data) and five percent reported both. On the college side, one-third reported something other than working as their main activity; 27 percent were self-employed; and five percent reported both. Leaving aside those who were self-employed or were not working as their major activity in 2006, only five percent of Canada's university-educated population and eight percent of its college-educated population earned less than half the median. The Statistics Canada report explains how this phenomenon is more common among women and among those who studied arts and communications technologies or parks, recreation and fitness. Furthermore, post-secondary-educated individuals in Newfoundland and Labrador, Prince Edward Island and New Brunswick were more likely than those in other provinces to earn less than half the national median.

In short, though a small minority of Canadians who have completed university or college studies earn relatively low wages, their situation is more easily explained by the nature of their participation in the labour market and by the regional variations in the Canadian economy than by the outcomes of their post-secondary studies. For the vast majority of Canadians, higher education pays.

The final statement clearly identifies the position presented in the chapter.

How to read informative writing

Make notes as you read, either in the margins, if it is your copy, or on paper or a computer file. Circle any words or references that you don't know and look them up.

What is it?	• What kind of a text is it? An article? An essay? A report? A set of instructions? A chart? A brochure? A website? An executive summary? What are your expectations for this kind of text? • What media are used? (Websites, for example, often combine images, words, and sounds.)
Where did it come from?	• Who wrote this material? • Where did it first appear? In a book, newspaper, magazine, online, in a company, or in an organization?
What is the writer's thesis or main idea?	• Where is the thesis or main idea located? • If you cannot find a specific claim, what is the main focus? • What are the key ideas or concepts that the writer considers? • What are the key terms? Are they defined?
Who is the intended audience?	• What clues do you find about whom the writer had in mind as the readers? • What does the writer assume that the readers already know about the subject? • What new knowledge is the writer providing?
How is the piece of writing organized?	• Look for the main idea in each paragraph or section. It helps to write them down. Then examine how each part connects to the others. • Where are the details and examples located? Do they support the main points?
What kinds of sources are cited?	• Are they from books, newspapers, periodicals, or the Web? • Are they completely documented?
How is it composed?	• How does the writer represent herself or himself? • How would you characterize the style? • How effective is the design? Is it easy to read? • If there are any photographs, charts, or other graphics, what information do they contribute?

Hacking Social Networks

(ARTICLE)

Lynn Greiner

Lynn Greiner is a Toronto-based writer who analyzes the business of technology. In this article, she presents one of the many problems affecting social networking sites.

Analyzing and Connecting

Return to these questions after you have finished reading.

1. At end of the first paragraph, Greiner makes a statement about "a fundamental human need." What purpose does it serve?

2. Greiner uses a lot of jargon (specialized vocabulary and idioms of a particular group) throughout this piece. How does this impact the reading? The audience? The point? Does it make the piece more credible?

3. Reflect on the content of this article. Are you surprised by the information presented? Does it change your perspective on online communities at all?

4. How would you describe the tone of this article? What clues helped you to reach this decision?

BUSINESS:
THE 8TH
LAYER

HACKING SOCIAL NETWORKS

By Lynn Greiner

The more users trust the community the more they risk having their trust compromised.

If you're a gregarious creature, chances are you indulge that tendency on one or more social networking websites. Whether it's Facebook, MySpace, Xing, Orkut, Friendster, LinkedIn, or even Twitter, such services provide the answer to a fundamental human need: belonging.

However, these online communities are composed of the same mix of interests as their physical counterparts. There are village idiots and smart alecks, jerks and nice people, good guys and, alas, bad guys.

According to researchers at Moscow-based anti-malware vendor Kaspersky Lab, the bad guys are having a field day dreaming up nefarious and lucrative ways to exploit the trust people have in their online networks. Senior malware analyst and social network specialist Sergey Golovanov says he's been seeing increased buzz on hacker forums, with bad guys sharing ways to compromise social-networking sites.

Last January, CNN reported, Facebook user Bryan Rutberg's status update suddenly became a plea for assistance, and one of his online friends received a direct message saying that Rutberg was visiting the U.K., had been robbed, and needed funds to get home. That friend wired $1,143 to Rutberg's London address, to help his buddy.

There's one thing wrong with this heartwarming picture of friend helping friend; the whole time, Rutberg was sitting safely at home in Seattle, unaware of the goings-on. His Facebook account had been hacked, and the $1,143 is now in the pockets of person or persons unknown.

Hacking social network user accounts can be disturbingly easy, Golovanov says, because of our innate tendency to trust our friends. If someone you know posts a message on your Facebook wall, telling you that embarrassing pictures of you are posted at a particular location, you're apt to click the link to find out how embarrassing the photos really are (and possibly figure out how to get even with the person who posted them).

Malware authors take advantage of that trust to compromise accounts. Consider, for example, the malware called Koobface. Infesting both Facebook and MySpace in recent months, it

HACKING SOCIAL NETWORKS

BUSINESS: THE 8TH LAYER

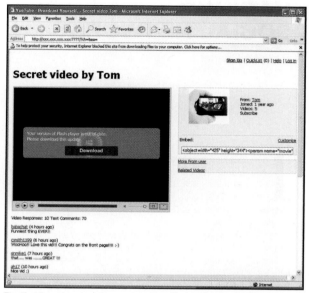

The Koobface virus prompts users to update Flash with a (bogus) file.

masquerades as a message from a friend and directs victims to a supposedly funny video. That link pops up an alert that a Flash Player update is required for viewing while kindly pointing you to the necessary file.

That file is not, however, a Flash update but a Trojan that promptly installs a proxy and a backdoor, preparing the victim's machine for future mischief. Oh, and it also takes advantage of the user's logged-on state to blast out its phony message to all of his or her contacts, starting yet another infection cycle.

Members of a 20 million strong Russian social network similar to Facebook, Vkontakte.ru, were

hit last October with a scam that combines several media. According to Golovanov's colleague Denis Maslennikov, who monitors mobile malware, members receive a message, again supposedly from a friend, saying they can get a credit to their mobile-phone account by installing an application. The link they click installs a program that actually sends an SMS message to a premium number, netting the crook the usage fee. Multiply even a few dollars per victim by a user base of that size, and you're talking big money.

Compromised accounts are bought and sold online, much like stolen credit card numbers (they can be purchased by the hundred,

if you know where to look), providing cyber-crooks an unending supply of potential nodes for their botnets, along with victims for their scams. In fact, if you want to acquire a particular "friend," such access can be had too, for a price.

Social networks have to pay their bills like everyone else, so enterprising malware purveyors have yet another venue for profit—advertising. No, they don't buy ads. What they do buy are tools that let them hack legitimate banner ads based on Adobe Flash, enabling them to install malware when clicked.

Other hacks aren't so high-tech but can be equally destructive. Social engineering on social networking sites need not involve malware—only trusting victims and people who, for whatever reason, want to take advantage of them.

Take, for example, the story (again from CNN) of the 18-year-old Wisconsin student who created a female persona on Facebook to persuade his teenage classmates to send "her" pictures of themselves in the nude. He then allegedly used the photos to blackmail the young men into performing sex acts with him. The only malware involved here was inside the perpetrator's head; he has since been arrested and faces a dozen charges ranging from possession of child pornography to sexual assault of a child under 16.

He's not the first, nor will he be the last, to pretend to be someone else online for some sort of profit. MySpace has reportedly found and removed 90,000 known sex offend-

BUSINESS: THE 8TH LAYER

ers from its rolls over the past couple of years.

Perhaps sadder was the case of the Missouri mother who pretended to be a 16-year-old boy on MySpace to, she later claimed, discover what a former friend was saying about her teenage daughter. Again, no tech was involved, aside from the social network itself. The victim, a 13-year-old girl struggling with depression and self-esteem problems, was completely taken in by this apparently nice "guy" and his interest in her, and

Parents." It teaches the basics, as well as ways for parents to protect their kids.

There may be times, however, when you really do want to hack a social network, so to speak. I use "hack" in a very broad sense here, but sometimes you need to influence how, and how often, you show up in searches. LinkedIn, a predominantly business-oriented social network, actually scores your profile and advises you on ways to improve your chances of being found when you want to be.

tions that it makes burglars drool and sharpen their crowbars. And all age groups forget that not just pals will see those naughty pictures from last week's party; the boss (or a potential boss) might be online too.

Yet there's something about social networking that's liberating to many; that's what makes it so hackable. Average folks wouldn't think of dancing naked down Main Street, but that's effectively what they do online, posting their deepest thoughts and fears (not to men-

COMPROMISED ACCOUNTS ARE ACTUALLY BOUGHT AND SOLD ONLINE, MUCH LIKE STOLEN CREDIT CARD NUMBERS (YOU CAN PURCHASE THEM BY THE HUNDRED, IF YOU KNOW WHERE TO LOOK), PROVIDING CYBER-CROOKS WITH AN UNENDING SUPPLY OF POTENTIAL NODES FOR THEIR BOTNETS, ALONG WITH VICTIMS FOR THEIR SCAMS.

when the "boy" dumped her and then posted insulting, publicly viewable comments about her, she hanged herself in her bedroom and died the next day.

Parents with more responsible motives are actually the fastest-growing demographic on Facebook. Whether they want to keep an eye on their offspring or simply catch up with their own old friends, enough members in the over-35 set have become social networkers that Stanford University is offering a four-part lecture series called "Facebook for

Post a photo, it says. Complete your profile. Get people to recommend you. And recommend other people to create cross-links between profiles.

For those with a nefarious goal, the more information about yourself you post online, the more attractive you are. Young people often, sometimes inadvertently, give away their location, the name of their school, and enough other information to put themselves at risk from predators. Adults who should know better post enough information about upcoming vaca-

tion that funny but compromising cellphone photo), while trusting their friends to do them no evil. It's what being part of a community is all about.

Which makes hackers very happy, and sometimes very rich. ◄

Lynn Greiner (lynng@ca.inter.net) analyzes the business of technology from Toronto.

DOI: 10.1145/1516035.1516038
© 2009 ACM 1091-3556/09/0300 $5.00

Sustainability within a Generation: A New Vision for Canada

(EXECUTIVE SUMMARY)

David R. Boyd

Sustainability within a Generation: A New Vision for Canada was issued in 2004 by the David Suzuki Foundation. This executive summary is based on the full 62-page report that examines Canada's environmental performance to date and recommends changes that will improve this country's environmental record.

Analyzing and Connecting

Return to these questions after you have finished reading.

1. Any executive summary usually makes its main point quickly and clearly, condensing the bulk of the report into a more manageable length. Where is the main point of this summary expressed, and what is it?

2. Note specific details included in this summary. Do any of the statistics cited seem particularly significant? Which ones, and why? Do you get the sense that the data is reliable? Do you think the conclusions are justified, based on this summary? Why or why not?

3. Review the nine critical challenges indentified in this summary. What do they add to your understanding of the issue? Would further details make the information more relevant? Or redundant?

4. Reflect on the findings reported in this summary. Do they surprise you at al l, or change your perspective?

5. An executive summary is, of course, only a summary. It leaves out much of the detailed information found in the rest of the report. Think about what this summary does and does not tell the reader. What questions does it leave unanswered? What gaps does it leave in your knowledge of the issue? What kinds of follow-up would you like to see in the report? What more would you like to find out about the issue? The David Suzuki Foundation?

The full report can be downloaded for free at **http://www.davidsuzuki.org/files/WOL/DSF-GG-En-Final.pdf.** You can explore the rest of the report and see how well it answers your questions.

Canadians are the among the most staunchly pro-environment citizens on the planet. According to Statistics Canada, nine out of ten Canadians rate the environment as one of their top concerns. However, despite our strong values and extraordinary natural assets, Canada is struggling environmentally. We finished 28th out of the 29 developed nations in an extensive Organisation for Economic Co-operation and Development (OECD) study that examined 25 key indicators in categories including air, water, energy, waste, climate change, ozone depletion, agriculture, transportation, and biological diversity.

There is a disturbing gap between our environmental values and poor environmental record. To close this gap, Canada needs to develop and implement an ambitious new environmental, economic, and social agenda.

The goal of this new agenda is to make Canada a world leader in sustainability by 2030. Sustainability is neither a lofty ideal nor an academic concept, but an urgent imperative for humanity. Sustainability means living within the Earth's limits. In a sustainable future, no Canadian would think twice about going outside for a walk or drinking a glass of tap water. Food would be free from pesticide residues, antibiotics, and growth hormones. Air, water, and soil would be uncontaminated by toxic substances. In a sustainable future, it would be safe to swim in every Canadian river and lake; safe to eat fish wherever they were caught. Clean, renewable energy would be generated by harnessing the sun, the wind, water, and heat of the Earth.

A sustainable future would mean a global climate undisturbed by human impacts. Canadians would no longer fear sunburn or cancer caused by damage to the ozone layer. No one would worry about nature's extraordinary diversity diminishing at human hands. Endangered ecosystems and species would recover and thrive. Canadians would be confident that future generations would enjoy the same spectacular natural heritage and quality of life that we enjoy today. Canada should strive to be the world's most environmentally friendly nation, making waste, pollution, and ecosystem destruction remnants of the past.

Moving Forward: Critical Challenges

In order to move towards a prosperous, just and sustainable future, Canada must concentrate its efforts on nine critical challenges:

- GENERATING GENUINE WEALTH: Supplementing the narrow goal of economic growth with the objective of genuine wealth

SUSTAINABILITY WITHIN A GENERATION: A NEW VISION FOR CANADA

- IMPROVING EFFICIENCY: Increasing the efficiency of energy and resource use by a factor of four to 10 times

- SHIFTING TO CLEAN ENERGY: Replacing fossil fuels with clean, low-impact renewable sources of energy

- REDUCING WASTE AND POLLUTION: Moving from a linear "throw-away" economy to a cyclical "reduce, re-use, and recycle" economy

- PROTECTING AND CONSERVING WATER: Recognizing and respecting the value of water in our laws, policies, and actions

- PRODUCING HEALTHY FOOD: Ensuring Canadian food is healthy, and produced in ways that do not compromise our land, water, or biodiversity

- CONSERVING, PROTECTING, AND RESTORING CANADIAN NATURE: Taking effective steps to stop the decline of biodiversity and revive the health of ecosystems

- BUILDING SUSTAINABLE CITIES: Avoiding urban sprawl in order to protect agricultural land and wild places, and improve our quality of life

- PROMOTING GLOBAL SUSTAINABILITY: Increasing Canada's contribution to sustainable development in poor countries

Conclusion

To succeed in achieving these goals, Canadians must demand a renewed commitment from all levels of government. We can no longer accept talk when action is required or voluntary programs where standards are necessary.

The overall thrust of this vision is to ensure that our quality of life improves in the years and decades ahead. Major changes are required to fulfill the vision of achieving sustainability and generating genuine wealth. These changes require Canadians to summon unprecedented ingenuity, wisdom, and compassion. Yet our successful track record of innovation on issues such as protecting the ozone layer and banning land mines inspires confidence that we can achieve our goal of a prosperous, sustainable future.

Whale Watching Guidelines

(INFORMATIONAL WEBSITE)

OceanSounds and WWF, 2008

Whale Watching is a page on the OceanSounds website, written in collaboration with the World Wildlife Foundation (WWF). It offers important information about how to safely view the whale's delicate marine ecosystem.

Analyzing and Connecting

Return to these questions after you have finished reading.

1. The webpage is designed to help potential whale watchers view whale activity safely. Notice that the site contains specific information on whale behaviour, research, and generic safety information. Why did the site's designers choose to combine different types of information here?

2. This page contains a number of striking photographs and graphics. Apart from showing the whales in their natural environment, what purpose do the images serve in context of this site?

3. Consider the tone of this webpage. While the designers are concerned about warning people of the potential dangers of whale watching, they also do not want to discourage people from enjoying this experience. Are they successful in striking a balance between these two goals?

4. This site demonstrates how important informational writing can be. Many people are unaware of how sensitive the whale's environment actually is and how a human presence can affect it. How much of the information in this site were you previously aware of? Would this information make you more or less likely to go whale watching?

WHALE WATCHING GUIDELINES

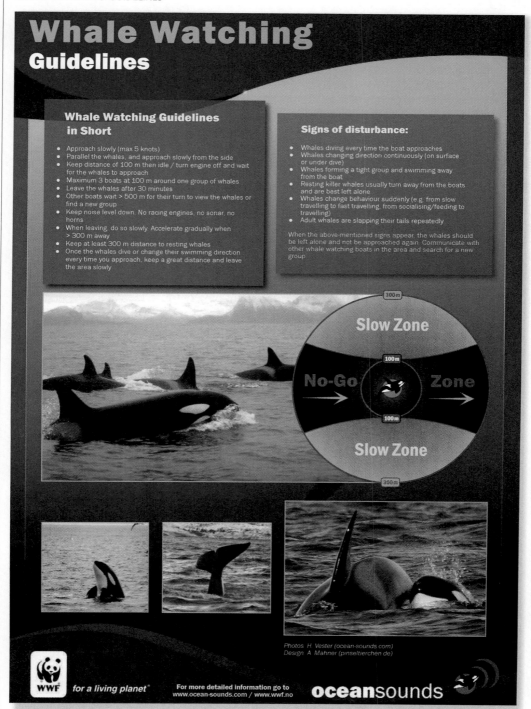

Guidelines for Killer Whale Safaris in Norway

Learning about the killer whales' behaviour will minimise impact & disturbance of the whales as well as enhancing your guests' experience. That is why we ask you to make use of the following information when going on whale watching trips. If you are a skipper, please inform your crew members about these guidelines.

The following guidelines are based on existing guidelines for killer whale watching, and have been supplemented by information from other places, e.g. the USA & Canada, where whale watching has a long tradition. These guidelines are supplemented with experiences we have gathered ourselves through our long-term research project.

Killer whales coming close to land in Northern Norway during winter enter a critical time and habitat, they come to feed and to breed (to give birth and nurture their newborns). We therefore need to pay close attention to the behaviour of the whales in order to minimise disturbance. Only then can we have a sustainable whale watching business. Make sure you learn to understand the behaviour of the whales before you go on whale watching tours.

These guidelines are voluntary, but of course we hope that most whale watching operators will support them. They are written specifically for encounters with killer whales (orcinus orca), but they will also apply for most other whales and seals.

Killer Whale Behaviour

Whales are more approachable during some behavioural states than others. Therefore you need to learn the basics of killer whale behaviour.

Feeding
Killer whales have a variety of prey (from fish to marine mammals) and seem to specialise if nutritious prey is available. In Norway, killer whales feed mostly on herring, but they have been seen feeding on birds and seals, too. They have developed different strategies to capture herring.

- Carousel feeding:
  Whales herd herring into tight ball close to surface and stun them with tail slaps. Fish jumping and scales, pieces of fish, and stunned herring can be observed on the surface.
- Subsurface feeding:
  Whales swim back and forth in a limited area. Activity of animals on surface, such as porpoising and some tail slaps.
- Travel feeding:
  During travelling in a line in loose formations, they stop occasionally to feed individually.
- Seine fishing feeding:
  Killer whales also follow fishing boats seining for herring and feed on the discarded fish of these operations.
  This behaviour occurred and increased during the last years, due to an increase in herring catch quotas.

Travelling
Whales moving forward, with all animals in the group facing the same direction, either in a line or in groups.

Socialising
Whales are engaged in a variety of physical interactions and aerial behaviours such as breaching, spy hopping, headstands, lobtailing and flipper slaps, rolling around, chasing each other, and sexual behaviour.

Resting
Whales floating motionless at the surface for a few minutes, or swimming slowly in tight groups, diving and surfacing in a regular pattern.

When feeding or socialising, they are often more tolerant to boats. Travelling whales can be followed slowly (adjust boat speed to the speed of the whales) in a parallel course. Leave at signs of disturbance. Whales that are disturbed during travelling may be prevented from reaching places that may be important for activities such as feeding, resting or socialising. Needless to say, these behaviours are to a different extent critical for the survival of the killer whales.

What to do when you spot whales:

- Slow down at >300 m from the nearest animals and observe their behaviour for a few minutes before approaching.
  After you have assessed the whales' behaviour, direction, and speed, approach them at maximum 5 knots. Whales typically travel at 3-4 knots, which means that you will catch up to them easily if you travel at 5 knots. Driving faster will increase disturbance and may invoke avoidance behaviour. This, in turn, will affect your costumers' experience with the whales negatively.

- Be considerate of other whale watchers, so that all have a chance to view without disturbance. Maintain radio communication with other boats in the area. The best approach is to take turns viewing the whales. Rotate every 30 minutes to view whales. After a viewing time of 30 minutes the boats should leave the whales and search for a new group. They should not return to the same group afterwards.
  Maximum number of boats (regardless of their size) around one group of killer whales is three (3). Boats approaching later must wait at a distance of at least 500 m from the whales and wait for their turn or find another group of whales. The waiting boats should be clustered together at one place to minimise disturbance (idling or engines shut off).

How to approach whales

- Approach no closer than 100 m and parallel the whales (i.e. go their direction without alteration of course) at their current speed, or shift your engine into neutral (idle) or shut it off.

- Approach killer whales from the side, never directly from behind or head-on. If whales head towards you, put the engine in neutral or shut it off, then wait. The whales must be given a chance to choose whether to pass by or to avoid the boat.
  Boats should not "leap frog", i.e. repeatedly rush to position themselves in front of the whales. This will only invoke avoidance behaviour and will affect your business negatively. It is far better to be patient and wait for the whales to approach you.

WHALE WATCHING GUIDELINES

When close to the whales

If the whales are:

Feeding
Keep a distance of 100 m from the feeding action at all times. If the feeding is moving closer to your boat, move away from it. You should be careful NOT to be in the whales' way! DO NOT drop snorkellers over the herring. However, if you lie still with your engine turned off: do not move, but let the whales simply pass by you. By starting your engine you will just cause unnecessary noise and disturbance.

Seine feeding
When whales feed from a fishing boat, keep a distance of 200 m from the fishing boat and stop your boat at one position. Don't move back and forth; you may disturb the fishermen's fishing activities as well as the feeding whales.

Socialising
This is the best time to view whales! Nevertheless, approach them carefully, make yourself aware of their whereabouts, especially if they show up behind your boat, close to the pro-pellers. Then you should slowly put your engine into neutral. THIS is the best time to introduce snorkellers!

Travelling
Go parallel to whales, adjust to their speed, and move with them at a 100 m distance. Do not trap them between land and your boat.

Resting
Resting whales should be left alone, keep a distance of 300 m, turn off your engine. DO NOT introduce snorkellers.

Mating
Keep a distance of 100 m and turn off your engine. DO NOT introduce snorkellers.

Breeding/calving
If you witness a birth, leave the animals alone or keep a distance of >300 m. Turn off your engine! DO NOT introduce snorkellers.

How long can you stay with the whales?

- The time spent with the whales should be limited to 30 minutes when within 100 m from the whales.

- Leave whales slowly! When leaving the group: start your engine only after the whales are more than 200 m away from you. Depart slowly, gradually accelerating when more than 300 m away.

Keep noise down / at a minimum

- Keep noise levels down. Avoid horns, whistles, or racing engines. Turn off your fish finder signals / sonar signals. When observing feeding killer whales, the skippers must remember that the killer whales in Norwegian waters feed on herring very close to the surface, and that herring react to engine noise. Motoring close to feeding killer whale may result in fish swimming away from the boat and away from the killer whales. Essentially, it may result is disturbing the whole feeding. The best strategy for observing feeding killer whales is to idle or turn off the engine, and to enjoy the view.

- Killer whales, like all other whales and dolphins, live in a world of sounds where vocalizations and hearing play an important role in all aspects of their lives (social behaviour, feeding, navigating, etc.). Therefore the noise level in the sea should be kept low.

Boats that are very noisy should not be used for whale watching. If used nevertheless, they should keep a greater distance (> 500 m) to the whales and reduce their speed, even stopping their engines and approach the whales with smaller less noisy boats.

- It is important that all vessels restrict their movements to the greatest extent possible and avoid surrounding the whales. When whales are travelling close to shore, avoid herding them near shore or in between your boat and the shore (do not trap them between your boat and the shoreline). Necessary course alterations should be kept small and made slowly.

Guidelines for snorkelling and diving

Although no incidents have been reported of killer whales hurting a swimmer in Norwegian waters, this is not a safety guarantee. Killer whales in Norway are known to feed on seals and birds as well as on herring, they are top predators, and in Canada snorkelling with the whales is strictly forbidden. Should you take the risk of viewing whales underwater, it can be a great experience. But this type of whale watching puts especially high demands on both the operators and the pas-sengers. Only physically fit and experienced people should be taken on such trips. Way too often boats with divers approach too fast and too close to the whales, believing that this is the best way of getting a "close view" of the whales. In practice this sort of boat behaviour only disturbs the whales and scares them off.

The most limiting factor for this activity is the weather condi-tion. In windy situations snorkellers are not permitted in the water because they can drift away too easily. Otherwise, the same guidelines of approaching, staying with, and departing from the whales apply for boats with snorkellers as for those without.
The divers should be released into the water in a distance from the whales, not midst into action (e.g. feeding). Let the whales decide whether they want to approach the people or not. Divers should swim slowly, best is to just lie on the water surface calmly and watch. The best time to view whales "underwater" is when they are socialising, then you often have whales curiously approaching the snorkellers. Snorkel-lers should not be introduced into the water when whales are resting, mating, and breeding/giving birth or show signs of disturbance.

It is also extremely important to be aware of the presence of other vessels, and to not let divers into the water in situations where other boats might have difficulties in spotting them. Keep a diving flag in a highly visible position on your boat at all times!

Only a maximum of 4 divers should be released into the water at the same time, to minimise noise and disturbance through movements, and to maximise the divers' safety. One additional safety diver should be in the water with the snorkellers at all times.

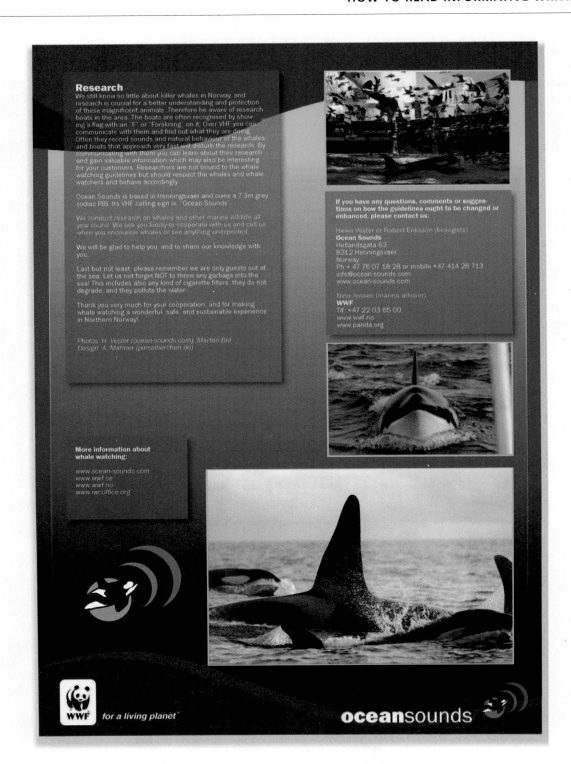

Research

We still know so little about killer whales in Norway, and research is crucial for a better understanding and protection of these magnificent animals. Therefore be aware of research boats in the area. The boats are often recognised by showing a flag with an "F" or "Forskning" on it. Over VHF you can communicate with them and find out what they are doing. Often they record sounds and natural behaviour of the whales, and boats that approach very fast will disturb the research. By communicating with them you can learn about their research and gain valuable information which may also be interesting for your customers. Researchers are not bound to the whale watching guidelines but should respect the whales and whale watchers and behave accordingly.

Ocean Sounds is based in Henningsvaer and owns a 7.3m grey zodiac RIB. Its VHF calling sign is "Ocean Sounds".

We conduct research on whales and other marine wildlife all year round. We ask you kindly to cooperate with us and call us when you encounter whales or see anything unexpected.

We will be glad to help you, and to share our knowledge with you.

Last but not least, please remember we are only guests out at the sea. Let us not forget NOT to throw any garbage into the sea! This includes also any kind of cigarette filters; they do not degrade, and they pollute the water.

Thank you very much for your cooperation, and for making whale watching a wonderful, safe, and sustainable experience in Northern Norway!

Photos: H. Vester (ocean-sounds.com), Marten Bril
Design: A. Mahner (pinseltierchen.de)

If you have any questions, comments or suggestions on how the guidelines ought to be changed or enhanced, please contact us:

Heike Vester or Robert Eriksson (biologists)
Ocean Sounds
Hellandsgata 63
8312 Henningsvaer
Norway
Ph + 47 76 07 18 28 or mobile +47 414 26 713
info@ocean-sounds.com
www.ocean-sounds.com

Nina Jensen (marine adviser)
WWF
Tlf: +47 22 03 65 00
www.wwf.no
www.panda.org

More information about whale watching:

www.ocean-sounds.com
www.wwf.se
www.wwf.no
www.iwcoffice.org

WWF *for a living planet*

oceansounds

How to write to inform

These steps for the process of informative writing may not progress as neatly as this chart might suggest. Writing is not an assembly-line process. As you write, you are constantly reading what you have written and rethinking.

Keep your readers in mind while you are writing, and if you don't know who your readers might be, imagine someone. What questions might that person have? Where would they appreciate a more detailed explanation?

1 ASSESS THE WRITING TASK & BEGIN RESEARCH

- Read the assignment, carefully noting key words.

- Determine what kind of writing is required. Who are the potential readers?

- Find the limits of your topic. What do you not need to cover? How far do you need to go in breaking down your explanations?

- Review class notes and textbooks; talk to instructor and peers.

Welcome to the Encyclopedia of Astronomy and Astrophysics

This unique resource covers the entire field of astronomy and astrophysics and this online version includes the full text of over 2,750 online articles, plus sophisticated search and retrieval functionality, links to the primary literature, and is frequently updated with new material. An active editorial team, headed by the Encyclopedia's editor-in-chief, Paul Murdin, oversees the continual commissioning, reviewing and loading of new and revised content.

Subjects	Recent articles	Forthcoming articles
Cosmology	Variable stars: observing eruptive variables by amateurs Taichi Kato	Dark Matter : Its Nature Georg Raffelt
Galaxies		Nobel Prize Winners in Astronomy Patick Moore
Interstellar Medium	Nebulae: observing by amateurs Owen Brazell	Giacconi, Riccardo Paul Murdin
Stars		
Solar System	Astronomical photography by amateurs with telescopes Nik Szymanek	European Southern Observatory Catherine Cesarsky
Sun		
Earth		Observatory De Haute

Do background research

Search library subject indexes and catalogues, periodicals, indexes, and online indexes.

2 CHOOSE A TOPIC & WRITE A THESIS

- Within the scope of the assignment, explore what interests you.

- Ask yourself, "Who else will be interested in this topic?"

- Make a list of issues, questions, or problems associated with the topic area.

- Make idea maps about possible topics.

- Discuss possible choices with your peers, co-workers, or instructor.

- Ask questions:

  What happened? What do people need to know?

  Who is my audience?

  How can I connect with them on this topic?

- Narrow your topic. When you learn more about your topic, you should be able to identify one aspect or concept that you can cover thoroughly.

- Write a working thesis that describes what you plan to report or explain.

- If you are unsure if you can follow through with your thesis, do additional research and revise your thesis.

3 WRITE A DRAFT

- Write your revised thesis and main points.
- Think about how you will organize your main points.
- Draft an introduction that will make readers interested in your subject.
- Build the organization by identifying the topic of each paragraph.
- Draft a conclusion that does more than summarize.
- Write an engaging title.

4 REVISE, REVISE, REVISE

- Reorganize your ideas for clarity.
- Add detail or further explanation where needed.
- Cut material that distracts from your thesis.
- Check that all key terms are defined.
- Frame your report with an introduction that interests readers and a conclusion that makes a point or raises an interesting question.
- Check that any sources are appropriately quoted or summarized and that they are documented correctly.
- Revise the title to be more accurate and to make readers more interested.
- Review the visual presentation of your report for readability and maximum impact.
- Proofread carefully.

5 PRINT A VERSION TO SUBMIT

- Make sure your finished writing meets all formatting requirements.

1: Assess the writing task and begin research

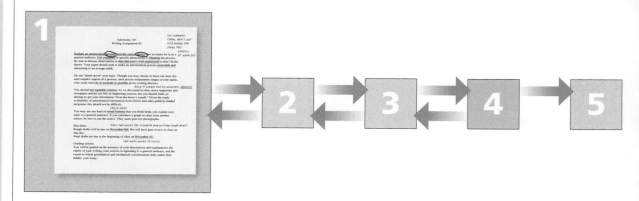

Analyze the assignment	Read your assignment slowly and carefully. Mark off any information about the length specified, date due, formatting, and other requirements. You can attend to this information later. At this point you want to zero in on the subject you will write about and how you will approach that subject.
What kind of writing is required?	Look for key words such as *compare and contrast, define, discuss,* or *explain*. Often these key words will help you in determining what direction to take. Highlight key words in all questions and commands.

Compare and contrast
Examine how two or more things are alike and how they differ.

Define
Make a claim about how something should be defined, according to features that you set out.

Discuss
Summarize what is known about a particular subject or issue, including research findings.

Explain
Go into detail about how something works or make an unfamiliar subject comprehensible.

Is the audience specified?	If the audience is mentioned in the assignment, how much will they know about your subject? How much background will you need to provide? What attitudes are they likely to have about your subject?
Find a topic	Sometimes you know immediately what you want to write about, but most often, it takes some time to find the right topic. Think first about what is most interesting to you. Give yourself some time to identify the right topic for you. See Chapter 1.
What do you know about the general topic?	A good first step is to make an inventory of what you know. Make a list of possible ideas. After you write down as many ideas as you can, go back through the list and place a star beside the ideas that seem most promising. See Chapter 3.
What ideas can you find in your course notes, class discussions, and your textbooks?	Often you need to look no further than your course materials for possible topics. Think about subjects raised in lectures, in class discussions, or in your textbooks for potential ideas.
What might you find in a print or online library?	Subject directories in your library's online catalogue are a valuable source of potential topics. See Chapter 18.
What might you find on the Web?	Google searches and other search engines often turn up promising ideas to pursue. Yahoo has a subject directory that breaks down large topics into subtopics. See Chapter 18.
What might you find doing field research?	Sometimes the information you need cannot be found in libraries or on the Web, and you have to collect the information firsthand through interviews, surveys, or observations. See Chapter 9.

WRITE NOW

Explore possible topics

1. Make a list of concepts in your courses. Textbooks usually highlight key concepts, so use them and your course notes to develop your list.
2. Put a check beside the concepts that look most interesting to write about or the ones that mean the most to you.
3. Put a question mark beside the concepts that you don't know much about. If you choose one of these concepts, you will probably have to do in-depth research—by talking to people, using the Internet, or going to the library.
4. Select a possible concept. Freewrite for five minutes about why this concept is interesting to you and how it affects you and other people.

Writer at work

Astronomy 101
Writing Assignment #2

Use examples (Show, don't just tell) Galaxy 999 shows this

Explain an astronomical (process,) and the current (theory) that accounts for it, to a general audience. Use examples of specific phenomena to illustrate the process. Be sure to discuss observations or data that aren't well understood or don't fit the theory. Your paper should seek to make an astronomical process accessible and interesting to an average adult.

process at work, b/c

Do not "dumb down" your topic. Though you may choose to leave out more dry and complex aspects of a process, such as precise temperature ranges or time spans, your essay must be as accurate as possible given existing theories.

Keep it simple but be accurate. Interest

You should use reputable sources. As we discussed in class, newsmagazines and newspaper articles are fine as supporting sources, but you should make an attempt to get your information "from the horse's mouth." Given the ready availability of astronomical information from NASA and other publicly funded programs, this should not be difficult.

Check NASA

You may use any kind of visual features that you think helps you explain your topic to a general audience. If you reproduce a graph or chart from another source, be sure to cite the source. The same goes for photographs.

Due dates   *Have two weeks for research and writing rough draft*

Rough drafts will be due on April 22. We will have peer review in class on that day.

Final drafts are due at the beginning of class on May 6.

Two more weeks to revise

Grading criteria

You will be graded on the accuracy of your descriptions and explanations, the clarity of your writing, your success in appealing to a general audience, and the extent to which grammatical and mechanical considerations help, rather than hinder, your essay.

Assess the assignment

Lakshmi Kotra wrote a report in response to this assignment in her Introduction to Astronomy course. She made the following notes and observations to help determine what her essay needed to accomplish, and to explore how she might find a good topic.

Highlight key words

Lakshmi began by highlighting the words in the assignment that gave her specific information about the writing tasks she was to perform.

Identify goals

Then, she made notes on the assignment sheet to specify what she needed to do.

Note time frame

She also made notes about the time frame she has to work in.

Plan strategy

Lakshmi made notes about possible sources for her paper. Then she sketched out a brief timeline to follow.

<u>SOURCES</u>

- Go back over lecture notes—Unit 3 was easiest for me to understand so may be best for a general audience?
- Review theories—what makes an idea a theory; who decides what is the accepted theory?
- See book also, esp. Table of contents, for topic ideas.
- Library subject index
- Online subject index
- Check NASA archives online for good pictures. Maybe categories there would help too.
- Ask Dr. Jenson if we can do something we haven't covered in class yet.

***Get to the library by <u>Friday</u> so topic is ready over the weekend. See if Karen wants to go too. Check reference librarian hours first, just in case.

- Outline over the weekend so I have next week to ask Dr. Jenson for help with the rough draft, if I need it.
- Visuals will help make the essay interesting and appealing to a general audience, and also can help explain. So maybe pick two or three topics and then look at NASA images and other visuals to see what is available. This should help narrow down my choices.

2: Choose a topic and write a thesis

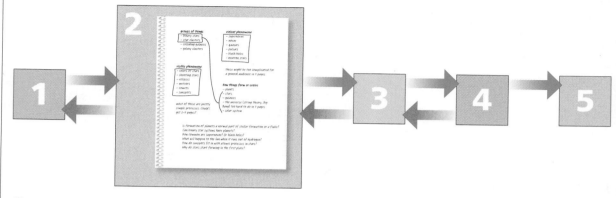

Connect your ideas

After you have done preliminary research and collected ideas, it's time to list possible topics and begin making connections. Circle the most interesting possibilities.

Choose a topic you will enjoy writing about

Writing is fun when you discover new things along the way. Choose a topic you want to explore. If your topic isn't interesting for you, it likely won't be for your readers either.

Choose a topic that your readers will enjoy reading about

Readers may ask, "Why are you telling me this?" Your subject should be interesting to your readers. If the subject isn't one that is immediately interesting, think about ways you can make it so.

Choose a topic that either you know something about or for which you can find the information you need

A central difficulty with writing to inform is determining where to stop. The key to success is to limit the topic. Choose a topic for which you can find the information you need and which you can cover thoroughly in the space you have. If you choose an unfamiliar topic, you must be strongly committed to learning much about it in a short time.

Narrow your topic and write a thesis

Look for ways of dividing large topics into smaller categories, and select one that is promising.

1. What is your topic exactly? (Try to state your answer in specific terms.)

2. What points do you want to make about your topic?

3. What exactly is your purpose in this project? To inform? Explain? Compare?

4. Develop a working thesis that draws on your answers to questions 1 and 2 and that reflects the purpose you described in your answer to question 3.

STAYING ON TRACK

Evaluate your thesis

Your thesis should fulfill the assignment

If your assignment is informative, your purpose is not to argue, judge, or persuade.

OFF TRACK
"Sometimes an MPP introduces a private member's bill to embarrass the government."
(evaluates rather than informs)

ON TRACK
"A private member's bill, a piece of legislation introduced by an MPP, serves two purposes: to change an existing law or create a new one."

Your thesis should be interesting

A strong, well-worded thesis clearly identifies the direction your paper is going to take. Challenge your readers with a specific point of view. Vague or generic theses will not encourage the audience to continue reading.

OFF TRACK
"There are many steps involved before a bill becomes a law."
(vague, bland)

ON TRACK
"Only a tiny fraction of the public bills proposed to Cabinet will ever become laws, and of those, most will accrue so many bizarre amendments and riders that they will barely resemble the original document."

Your thesis should be focused

You cannot cover a large, broad subject in five pages. Narrow your thesis to a topic you can treat in-depth.

OFF TRACK
"Many new products were developed in the 1950s to support the boom in housing construction."
(possibly interesting if particular products are described)

ON TRACK
"The rush to create new housing for returning WWII veterans in the 1950s resulted in many houses that are now extremely hazardous to live in."

Writer at work

groups of things
- binary stars
- star clusters
- colliding galaxies
- galaxy clusters

violent phenomena
- supernovae
- novae
- quasars
- pulsars
- black holes
- neutron stars

these might be too complicated for
a general audience in 7 pages

visible phenomena
- colours of stars
- shooting stars
- eclipses
- meteors
- comets
- sunspots

most of these are pretty
simple processes. Could I
get 5-7 pages?

How things form or evolve
- plants
- stars
- galaxies
- the universe (string theory, Big
Bang) too hard to do in 7 pages
- solar system

Is formation of planets a normal part of stellar formation or a fluke?
Can binary star systems have planets?
How common are supernovae? Or black holes?
What will happen to the Sun when it runs out of hydrogen?
How do sunspots fit in with atomic processes in stars?
Why do stars start forming in the first place?

Map possible topics

Lakshmi Kotra began by reviewing her class notes and her textbooks. She also looked in the library's online catalogue subject index and an online subject index. She listed all the possible topics she came across in these sources. Then she made an idea map of the topics that appealed to her, clustering types of theories, and adding new ones as they occurred to her. She made a few notes on some of her topic areas, describing how well they would meet the needs of her assignment. And she jotted down questions she had about some topics as well.

Narrow the search

Lakshmi narrowed her search by considering how complicated a topic she wanted to take on. Since she had to explain the theory to a general audience, she ruled out topics like black holes and string theory. She noticed that stellar processes showed up several times in her lists of interesting topics.

Identify the topic

Lakshmi settled on stellar formation as a theory that interested her and which she felt confident she could explain in lay person's terms. Her preliminary research also indicated there was a wealth of observational data and photos that she could use in her report.

Find images and get source information

Lakshmi wanted to include photographs of star formation, and she located images that she could use legally on NASA's website. She carefully recorded all the information she would need to find the images again and to document the images in her paper.

GRIN
GREAT IMAGES IN NASA

Browse by Subject
Browse by Center
Search by Keywords
Frequent Questions
How to Use GRIN
Copyright Information

National Aeronautics and Space Administration

NASA Center: Hubble Space Telescope Center
Image # : PR95-44A
Date : 04/01/1995

Title
The Eagle Nebula

Full Description
These eerie, dark pillar-like structures are columns of cool interstellar hydrogen gas and dust that are also incubators for new stars. The pillars protrude from the interior wall of a dark molecular cloud like stalagmites from the floor of a cavern. They are part of the "Eagle Nebula" (also called M16 -- the 16th object in Charles Messier's 18th century catalog of "fuzzy" objects that aren't comets), a nearby star-forming region 7,000 light-years away in the constellation Serpens. Ultraviolet light is responsible for illuminating the convoluted surfaces of the columns and the ghostly streamers of gas boiling away from their surfaces, producing the dramatic visual effects that highlight the three dimensional nature of the clouds. The tallest pillar (left) is about a light-year long from base to tip. As the pillars themselves are slowly eroded away by the ultraviolet light, small globules of even denser gas buried within the pillars are uncovered. These globules have been dubbed "EGGs." EGGs is an acronym for "Evaporating Gaseous Globules," but it is also a word that describes what these objects are. Forming inside at least some of the EGGs are embryonic stars, stars that abruptly stop growing when the EGGs are uncovered and they are separated from the larger reservoir of gas from which they were drawing mass. Eventually, the stars themselves emerge from the EGGs as the EGGs themselves succumb to photoevaporation. The picture was taken on April 1, 1995 with the Hubble Space Telescope Wide Field and Planetary Camera 2. The color image is constructed from three separate images taken in the light of emission from different types of atoms. Red shows emission from singly-ionized sulfur atoms. Green shows emission from hydrogen. Blue shows light emitted by doubly- ionized oxygen atoms.

AUTHOR: U.S. National Aeronautics and Space Administration

DATE: April 1, 1995

PAGE TITLE: The Eagle nebula.

SITE TITLE: Great Images in NASA

DATE OF RETRIEVAL: April 5, 2005

URL: http://grin.hq.nasa.gov/ABSTRACTS/GPN-000987.html

3: Write a draft

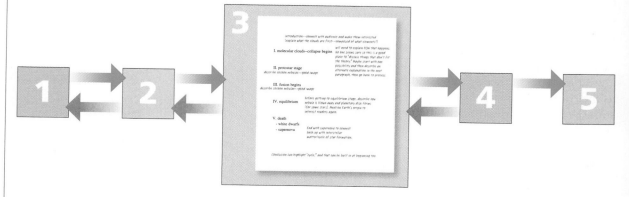

Organize your information

Gather your notes and other materials. Think about how you want to convey the information to your readers.

- If your subject matter occurs over time, you might want to use a chronological order.
- If you need to discuss several aspects, you likely will need to identify key concepts and think about how they relate to each other. An idea map can help you to determine these relationships.
- If you are comparing two or more things, you will want to think about how these things are similar and how they are different.

Make a working outline

A working outline is a tool that you can use as you write your first draft. The more detailed it is, the better. (If you would prefer to write a complete, formal outline before drafting your essay, by all means do so.) To make your outline, follow these steps:

1. List the sections of your essay, in the order that you expect them to appear.
2. Write two or three complete sentences describing the content and purpose of each section.
3. Now, review your outline. Does the project as you have described it here achieve the purpose you intend it to?

Think about a title

An effective title motivates your readers to want to read what you have written. Be as specific as you can.

Consider the use of visuals

Would a table or chart be helpful? Photographs? A map? Do you need headings and subheadings?

STAYING ON TRACK

Write an effective introduction and conclusion

Write an effective introduction

Get off to a strong start. Don't pad the beginning with generalizations or empty sentences.

OFF TRACK

"Because we all live such busy, hectic lives in these modern times, everyone wants to know why we must wait for hours and hours at the airport before boarding a flight."
(boring, predictable beginning—a signal that the paper will be dull)

ON TRACK

"It's a traveller's worst nightmare: the long line of people at the security gate, snaking back and forth across the waiting area. What exactly goes on in an airport screening area, and how does it help to keep us safe?"

Write an effective conclusion

Remember that a summary of what you have just written is the weakest way to conclude. Think of something interesting for your reader to take away, such as an unexpected implication or a provocative example.

OFF TRACK

"In conclusion, we have seen how peer-to-peer file sharing works."
(ineffective; says only that the paper is finished)

ON TRACK

"The peer-to-peer file sharing process is relatively simple. Unfortunately, in many cases it is also illegal. It is ironic that a technology intended to help people has resulted in turning many of them into *de facto* criminals."
(ends with a significant point, which helps readers remember the paper)

Writer at work

Lakshmi Kotra began with the following rough outline of the process she planned to write about.

Introduction—connect with audience and make them interested
(explain what the clouds are first—composed of what elements?)

I. molecular clouds—collapse begins

will need to explain HOW that happens. No one seems sure so this is a good place to "discuss things that don't fit the theory." Maybe start with one possibility and then describe an alternate explanation in the next paragraph, then go back to process.

II. protostar stage

describe cocoon nebulae—good image

III. fusion begins

will need to explain fusion process

IV. equilibrium

Before getting to equilibrium stage, describe how nebula is blown away and planetary disk forms (for some stars). Mention Earth's origin to interest readers again.

V. death
- white dwarfs
- supernova

End with supernova to connect back up with interstellar matter/cycle of star formation.

Conclusion can highlight "cycle," and that can be built in at beginning too.

Think about organization

Lakshmi recognized that the process she was describing naturally lent itself to chronological, or time-order, organization, because one thing has to happen after another for a star to form. However, she found that she had to "break out" from the simple timeline of stellar formation at some points, to explain in more detail or to trace multiple possibilities.

Make notes on how to develop the subject

She made notes on her outline indicating where she would step away from the chronological pattern to do this explaining. As she considered how she wanted to end her essay, she realized the idea of a "life cycle" for stars could point back toward the essay's beginning. This strategy helped her focus her thesis.

Connect with readers

Lakshmi realized that stellar formation would probably seem like a distant and forbidding topic to a general audience, so she thought carefully about making a connection with her readers. She began by trying out some different ways to introduce her essay. Here are some of her initial attempts and the comments she made on them. Lakshmi decided to work with the last of these openings and see how well she could integrate it with the rest of her essay.

Stars have a complex and fascinating life cycle. Saying it's fascinating doesn't make it fascinating to readers.

Have you ever looked up at the stars at night and wondered why they are there? Vague. Kind of sounds like I'm going to talk about religious or spiritual issues.

Astronomers have spent many years studying the life cycle of stars. So? Anyway, I just want to talk about what they've found, not how long it took them.

If "sunshine on your shoulders" makes you happy, you will be even happier to know that the sun will keep shining for at least another 8 billion years. Too corny. Does anyone even remember that song? Anyway, "happy" isn't the way I want readers to feel. But using a familiar phrase might be good.

"Twinkle, twinkle little star. How I wonder what you are." Good—more personal than "Have you ever looked up at the stars and wondered . . ." Astronomers wonder too. That could be the connection between them and scientists' work. More familiar song, also.

4: Revise, revise, revise

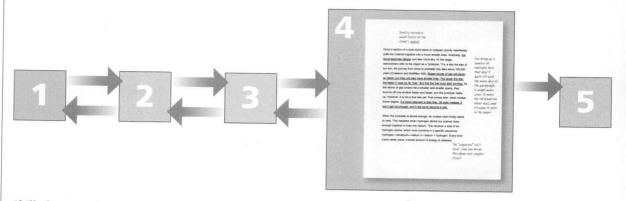

Skilled writers know that the secret to writing well is revising. Even the best writers often have to revise several times to get the result they want. You also must have effective strategies for revising if you're going to be successful. The biggest trap you can fall into is starting off with the little stuff first (for example, grammar mistakes). Leave the small stuff for last.

Does your paper or project meet the assignment?	• Look again at your assignment. Does your paper or project do what the assignment asks?
	• Look again at the assignment for specific guidelines, including length, format, and amount of research. Does your work meet these guidelines?
Is your title specific?	• Vague titles suggest a dull treatment of the topic. Can you make your title more accurate?
Does your writing have a clear focus?	• Does your project have an explicitly stated thesis? If not, is your thesis clearly implied?
	• Is each paragraph related to your thesis?
	• Do you get off track at any point by introducing other topics?
	• Are your main points adequately developed?
	• Do you support your main points with reasons and evidence?
	• Can you add more examples and details that would help to explain your main points?
Is your organization effective?	• Is the order of your main points clear to your reader?
	• Are there any places where you find abrupt shifts or gaps?
	• Are there sections or paragraphs that could be rearranged to make your draft more effective?
Is your introduction effective?	• Do you have any general statements that you might cut to get off to a faster start?

- Can you think of a vivid example that might draw in readers?
- Can you use a striking fact to get readers interested?
- Does your introduction make clear where you are headed?

Is your conclusion effective?	• Conclusions that only summarize tend to bore readers. Does your conclusion add anything new to what you've said already? • Can you use the conclusion to discuss further implications? • Have you left your audience with a final provocative idea that might invite further discussion?
Do you represent yourself effectively?	• To the extent you can, forget for a moment that you wrote what you are reading. What impression do you have of you, the writer? • Does "the writer" create an appropriate tone? • Has "the writer" done his or her homework?
Is the writing project visually effective?	• Is the font attractive and readable? • Are the headings and visuals effective?
Save the editing for last	When you have finished revising, edit and proofread carefully.

STAYING ON TRACK

Reviewing your draft

Give yourself plenty of time for reviewing your draft. For detailed information on how to participate in a peer review, how to review it yourself, and how to respond to comments from your classmates, your instructor, or a campus writing advisor, see pages 28–32.

Some good questions to ask yourself when reviewing informative writing	• Are the explanations in the essay easy to follow? • Are there gaps or places where you feel you need more information? • Are any unusual or discipline-specific words defined for readers? Have these definitions been cited appropriately? • Can the reader construct a clear picture of what the essay describes? • Is the essay interesting enough to catch readers' attention and keep them engaged?

Writer at work

Density increases much faster at the cloud's <u>centre</u>

Once a section of a dust cloud starts to collapse, gravity relentlessly pulls the material together into a much smaller area. Gradually, <u>the cloud becomes denser</u> and less cloudlike. At this stage, astronomers refer to the object as a "protostar." For a star the size of our sun, the journey from cloud to protostar may take about 100,000 years (Chaisson and McMillan 429). <u>Bigger clouds of gas will develop faster—but they will also have shorter lives. The larger the star, the faster it uses up its "fuel." But first the fuel must start burning.</u> As the atoms of gas crowd into a smaller and smaller space, they bounce off one another faster and faster, and the protostar heats up. However, it is not a true star yet. That comes later, when nuclear <u>fusion begins. If a cloud segment is less than .08 solar masses, it won't get hot enough, and it will never become a star.</u>

When the protostar is dense enough, its nuclear heart finally starts to beat. This happens when hydrogen atoms are pushed close enough together to fuse into helium. This requires a total of six hydrogen atoms, which must combine in a specific sequence: hydrogen—deuterium—helium 3—helium + hydrogen. Every time fusion takes place, a small amount of energy is released.

You bring up a number of concepts here that don''t quite fit with the main idea of the paragraph. It might make sense to move the information about mass and lifespan to later in the paper

The "sequence" isn't clear. Can you break this down into simpler steps?

Read carefully your instructor's comments
Lakshmi Kotra gave a copy of her first draft to her instructor for feedback. She used his comments to guide her revision of the essay.

Determine a plan for revision in light of your instructor's comments
Based on her instructor's comments, Lakshmi decided to shift some information on the rates at which stars burn nuclear fuel from an earlier section of the paper to her later discussion of the fates of stars with different masses. This strategy also allowed her to flesh out the description of "brown dwarfs"—starlike objects that do not develop into stars.

Act on specific comments
She also took her instructor's advice about simplifying her explanation of hydrogen fusion.

Read your paper aloud to catch mistakes and awkward phrasing
Lakshmi also read her essay aloud to help identify spelling errors and missing or poorly chosen words.

Visit your writing centre
Finally, Lakshmi visited her school's writing centre. She asked for specific help in making the paper accessible for an audience without a scientific background. Working with an advisor, she recognized the need to define scientific terms, like *nebulae, protostar,* and *equilibrium,* that might not be familiar to a general audience.

5: Print a version to submit

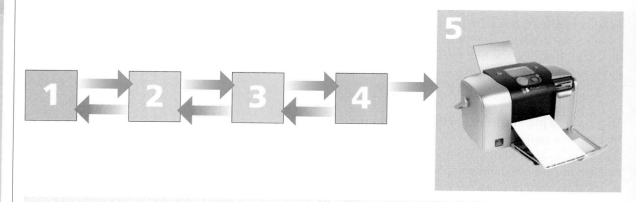

Kotra 1

Lakshmi Kotra
Professor Jenson
Astronomy 101
6 May 2011

The Life Cycle of Stars

"Twinkle, twinkle, little star; how I wonder what you are." This old nursery rhyme may not seem profound, but it echoes some of the biggest questions astronomers puzzle over: What are stars made of? How do they form? How are they born and how do they die? Current theories of star formation answer some of these questions, but not all of them. We do know that, even though stars are separated from one another by vast amounts of space, their life cycles are intertwined.

Twinkling stars are born in dark, cold clouds of dust and gas called nebulae. These clouds consist mainly of hydrogen, and may be as cold as 10 degrees Kelvin (Chaisson and McMillan 427). Nebulae are very dense compared to the near-vacuum of interstellar space. But something must concentrate this dust and gas even more if a star is to form. This first part of the star-forming process is not fully understood. Some force has to cause a portion of the nebula to begin collapsing. Magnetism and rotation are two forces already at work in most clouds, but astronomers have long thought that these forces are more likely to counteract the collapsing force of gravity (Chaisson and McMillan 427). However, new research may have found a solution to this problem. In some clouds, magnetic fields may cancel out some or all of the rotational force. This reorganization would allow gravity to begin collapsing the star (Farivar).

Another theory is that a shock wave from some outside event or object might trigger the collapse of a cloud. The Eagle Nebula provides a good illustration of this theory. Ultraviolet radiation from super-hot stars in the nebula has been observed bombarding the surrounding dust and gas. The radiation has stripped away a lot of dust but left dense columns of cloud where stars are believed to be forming. The impact of this "stellar wind" may have also triggered the star formation. Smaller clumps of denser gas are contracting within the columns, taking their first step on the journey to stardom (see fig. 1).

Once a section of a dust cloud starts to collapse, gravity relentlessly pulls the material together into a much smaller area. Gradually, the centre of the cloud becomes denser and less cloudlike. At this stage, astronomers refer to the object as a "protostar." For a star the size of our sun, the journey from cloud to protostar may take about 100,000 years (Chaisson and McMillan 429). As the atoms of gas crowd into a smaller and smaller space, they bounce off one

Fig. 1. Eagle Nebula
The columns of interstellar gas in the Eagle Nebula are incubators for new stars (US, NASA, "Eagle").

another faster and faster, and the protostar heats up. However, it is not a true star yet. That comes later, when nuclear fusion begins. For now, the developing protostar is still surrounded by a shroud of dust that hides it from view. This dust mantle is called a cocoon nebula. Some protostars can be detected by the infrared glow of their cocoon nebulae (Chaisson and McMillan 435-36).

Over millions of years, the protostar continues to grow and change, like a butterfly in its cocoon. Gravity keeps compacting it, making it smaller in size and denser. When the protostar is dense enough, its nuclear heart finally starts to beat. This happens when hydrogen atoms are pushed close enough together to fuse into helium. The fusion process involves several steps. First, two hydrogen atoms will fuse to form an atom of deuterium, or heavy hydrogen. When a third hydrogen atom joins the deuterium atom, an isotope called helium 3 results. Finally, when two helium 3 atoms fuse together, an atom of regular helium plus two of hydrogen are created. But the crucial part of this process is that, every time fusion takes place, a small amount of energy is released. The radiation emitted from the fusion of hydrogen into helium is what makes the majority of stars shine. Fusion radiation from the Sun lights our planet in the daytime, makes the moon shine at night—and gives you sunburn.

During the intense heating at the end of the protostar stage, and when hydrogen fusion is beginning, intense radiation streams off the young star. The dust and gas that have surrounded the protostar are swept away by this energy bombardment, and the star emerges from its cocoon. This phenomenon can be observed visually in NGC 4214. Young stars in this nebula are pouring out radiation that has created "bubbles" in the surrounding gas. Brighter and older stars have pushed away more of the dust and gas. The bubbles around these stars are bigger than those around younger or cooler stars in the nebula (see fig. 2).

Sometimes, not all of a protostar's dust cocoon blows away. According to one theory, you can look around our own solar system and see the remnants of the dust that once surrounded our Sun. In fact, you are standing on some of it. The Earth and the rest of the planets in our solar system are believed to have formed from a disk of dust and gas left over after the sun formed. The reasons this happens are not entirely clear, but astronomers now think that many stellar systems have planetary disks around them. The Orion Nebula provides some confirmation of this theory. There, astronomers have observed many

Fig. 2. Star Formation
Clusters of new stars form from interstellar gas and dust in galaxy NGC 4214 (US, NASA, "Star").

glowing disks of dust, called "proplyds." They think these disks are actually young stars surrounded by material that will eventually form a system of orbiting planets (see fig. 3).

The size of the original dust cloud a star is born from will also determine how it dies. Some protostars don't quite have what it takes to become a star. Clumps of dust and gas that are smaller than .08 solar masses never get hot enough to begin fusing hydrogen (Chaisson and McMillan 433). These "brown dwarfs" produce infrared radiation, but they never shine visibly.

True stars burn through their nuclear fuel at different rates. The larger the star, the faster its fuel is fused. Smaller stars, like our Sun,

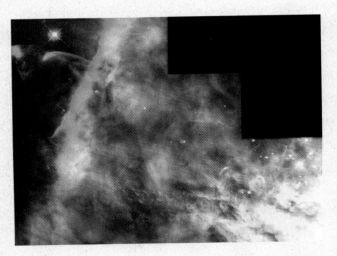

Fig. 3. Orion Nebula
This composite photo of the Orion nebula assembled from images taken by the Hubble Space Telescope shows the beginnings of new solar systems surrounding young stars (US, NASA, "Orion").

are called "dwarf stars." If they began life with less than eight times the mass of our Sun, they will quietly burn hydrogen for perhaps ten billion years. Toward the end of their lives, as they begin to run out of fuel, they will swell briefly into red giant stars, fusing their helium into carbon, and cooling substantially. Finally, they will subside into "white dwarf" stars, about the size of the planet earth. Provided they do not have nearby neighbouring stars that might interact with them, white dwarfs gradually dim and cool, until they go dark altogether (Chaisson and McMillan 459). This cooling process is what astronomers predict will some day happen to our Sun.

A star of more than about eight solar masses has a shorter but much more spectacular life. It will fuse all its available fuel in well under one billion years—perhaps in as little as one million years. When a giant star has run through all its available nuclear fuel, it develops a core of iron atoms, which cannot be fused into anything else. When this core has grown to about 1.4 solar masses, the star will explode in a supernova. All that will be left of the original star is a dark neutron star or black hole (Chaisson and McMillan 475). But the shock wave from the supernova may go on to trigger new star formation in dust clouds nearby. In this way, dying stars contribute to the birth of new ones, and the life cycle of stars continues.

Works Cited

Chaisson, Eric, and Steve McMillan. *Astronomy Today*. 3rd ed.
Upper Saddle River: Prentice, 1997. Print.

Farivar, Cyrus. "Galactic Map Aids Stellar Formation Theory." *The Daily Californian*. The Daily Californian, 23 Jan. 2002. Web. 8 Apr. 2005.

United States. National Aeronautics and Space Administration.
"The Eagle Nebula." *Great Images in NASA*. NASA, 1 Apr. 1995. Web. 5 Apr. 2005.

- - -. - - -. "Fireworks of Star Formation Light Up a Galaxy." *Great Images in NASA*. NASA, 6 Jan. 2000. Web. 5 Apr. 2005.

- - -. - - -. "The Orion Nebula." *Great Images in NASA*. NASA, 20 Nov. 1995. Web. 5 Apr. 2005.

Projects

No matter how diverse its forms, successful informative writing begins with the basics.

- What do readers already know about a subject?
- What do readers need to know about a subject?
- What kind of writing is best suited for particular readers? A website? A brochure? An article? Or something else?

You'll do many kinds of informative writing in your life after college or university. The following projects are common informative writing tasks.

INSTRUCTIONS

For an example, see pages 191–195.

Be aware that informational documents with instructions are much harder to write than most people expect. They usually require a lot of detail, but should be carefully balanced between giving important information and simply "telling" people what to do.

Think of a fairly comon activity you have learned to do.

Imagine someone who wants to learn to do the same activity. What information would you provide and how could you simply and accurately instruct him or her?

Write a document that includes information and instructions explaining how to perform a task like setting up new software on a computer or creating a playlist on an iPod. When you are finished, have a volunteer "test" the accuracy of your information? Did it work?

PEARSON
mycanadiancomplab

Go to **www.mycanadiancomplab.ca** to practise your grammar, punctuation, and mechanics skills. Go to the "Resources" tab within MyCanadianCompLab and then click on "Grammar." You will have access to a variety of exercises as well as direct instruction that will help you improve your basic skills and get a better grade in your course.

EXECUTIVE SUMMARY
For an example, see pages 188–190

REPORT
For an example, see pages 179–182.

Consider the purpose of an executive summary. How does it differ from other types of formal documents? How is the information organized?

Read several samples of executive summaries from various sources. Are they all written for the same audience? How does the information in each summary vary depending on audience?

Think carefully about the content of an executive summary. What information is present and what is missing? Why is this important?

Think of a subject you know a great deal about but on which most other people are either uninformed or misinformed, especially those who are your intended readers.

Your subject might come from your life experience
- What's it like to grow up on a family farm?
- What's it like to be an immigrant to Canada?

Your hobbies
- What's the best way to train for a marathon?
- How can you avoid injuries in sports by stretching?

Your personal interests
- Why should everyone over age 20 pay attention to cholesterol?

A place that you have found fascinating, or a subject you have studied in school
- Is the nature of conceptual art misunderstood?
- What breakthroughs in nanotechnology can we expect in the near future?

Consider what will likely be most interesting about your subject to your readers.

Engage your readers with a provocative title and a thesis that will challenge them to think about your subject in new ways.

Aim for a report of 700–1000 words or about 3–5 double-spaced pages.

12
Analyzing Texts

Every piece of writing, every painting, every building, every movie, every new product, every advertisement, is a response to what came before it.

Chapter contents

Writing to analyze

Critical reading and viewing are essential skills for all kinds of writing. Analysis is a more specific aim where those critical reading and viewing skills are applied to particular subjects. Analysis involves dividing a whole into parts that can be studied both as individual entities and as parts of the whole.

Rhetorical analysis is a kind of analysis that divides a whole into parts to understand how speaking or writing conveys meaning. Thus the goal of a rhetorical analysis is to understand how a particular act of writing or speaking influenced particular people at a particular time.

Visual analysis is closely related to rhetorical analysis. It applies the tools of rhetorical analysis to understanding how other human creations make meaning, including art, buildings, photographs, dance, memorials, advertisements—any kind of symbolic communication.

Literary analysis takes into account elements of literature such as plot, character, and setting, paying particular attention to language and metaphor. The goal of literary analysis is to interpret a literary text and support that interpretation with evidence or, more simply, to make a discovery about a text that you share with your readers.

Text and context

A rhetorical, visual, or literary analysis may be concerned with either text or context, but often it examines both. Textual analysis focuses on the features of a text—the words and evidence in a speech, the images and patterns in a picture, and so on. For a textual analysis, ask

- What is the subject?

- What is the author's claim or what are the main ideas?

- What is the medium of the text? A newspaper? A website? A scholarly journal? A photograph? A short story?

- What appeals are used? What are the author's credentials, and how does she represent herself? What facts or evidence does she present? What values does she share with you and the rest of her audience? What emotions does she try to evoke?

- How is the text organized?

- What kind of style does the author use? Formal or informal, satirical or humorous? Are any metaphors used?

Contextual analysis reconstructs the cultural environment, or context, that existed when a particular rhetorical event took place, and then depends on that re-creation to produce clues about persuasive tactics and appeals. For a contextual analysis, ask

- Who is the author? What else has she written or said on this subject? Who does she borrow from or quote? What motivated her to address this issue?

- Who is the audience? What are the occasion and forum for writing? Would the argument have been constructed differently if it had been presented in a different medium? What motivated the newspaper, magazine, or other medium to publish it?

- What is the larger conversation? When did the text appear? Why did it appear at that particular moment? Who or what might this text be responding to?

The statue of Castor stands at the entrance of the Piazza del Campidoglio in Rome. A textual analysis focuses on the statue itself. The size and realism of the statue makes it a masterpiece of classical Roman sculpture.

A contextual analysis focuses on the surroundings and the history of the statue. Legend has Castor and his twin brother Pollux, the mythical sons of Leda, assisting Romans in an early battle. Romans built a large temple in the Forum to honour them. The statues of Castor and Pollux were uncovered in sixteenth-century excavations and brought in 1583 to stand at the top of the Cordonata, a staircase designed by Michelangelo as part of a renovation of the Piazza del Campidoglio commissioned by Pope Paul III Farnese in 1536.

WORKING TOGETHER

Analyze text and context

In a group of three or four students

Find several examples of verbal and visual texts. These might be ads you have seen on television or heard on the radio, photos or editorials in the student newspaper, or websites.

- What is the context in which this text was produced?
- How was the creator of the text attempting to influence or persuade the audience? What appeals are made?
- In the visual texts, what connections or associations is the reader invited to create?
- In the verbal texts, what claims and reasons are explicitly stated?

Writing a rhetorical analysis

People often use the term *rhetoric* to describe empty language. "The Governor-General's speech was just a bunch of rhetoric," you might say, meaning that the Governor-General offered noble-sounding words but no real ideas. But rhetoric originated with a much more positive meaning. According to Aristotle, rhetoric is "the art of finding in any given case the available means of persuasion." Rhetoric is concerned with producing effective pieces of communication.

Rhetoric can also be used to interpret or analyze. Students of rhetoric know not only how to produce effective communication, but also how to understand communication. The two skills complement each other: Becoming a better writer makes you a better analyst, and becoming a better analyst makes you a better writer. For an example of rhetorical analysis, see pages 234–238.

Components of a rhetorical analysis

What is the author's purpose?	**Identify the purpose** Some texts have an obvious purpose; for example, an ad wants you to buy something. But texts can have more than one purpose. A politician who accuses an opponent of being corrupt may also be making a case for her own honesty.
Who is the audience?	**Examine the audience** The most effective texts are ones that are tailored specifically for an audience. What can you determine about the actual audience's values, attitudes, and beliefs? How does the author create an audience in the text by making assumptions about what the audience believes?
Who is the author of my text?	**Examine the author** How did the author come to this subject? Is the author an expert or an outsider?
What is the background of my text?	**Examine the context** What else has been said or written on this topic? What was going on at the time that influenced this text?
Which rhetorical appeals are used in my text?	**Analyze rhetorical appeals** Aristotle set out three primary tactics of argument: appeals to the emotions and deepest held values of the audience (pathos), appeals based on the trustworthiness of the speaker (ethos), and appeals to good reasons (logos).
How does the language and style contribute to the purpose?	**Examine the language and style** Is the style formal? Informal? Academic? Does the writer or speaker use humour or satire? What metaphors are used?

Keys to rhetorical analysis

Choose a text that you care about

Your paper will require close multiple readings of the text. Your interest (or lack of interest) in your text will come through in your paper.

Write a descriptive title
The title of your essay should indicate the focus of your analysis.

Check your thesis
Make sure your thesis is sensible and realistic as well as being supported by evidence and examples in the text.

Interrogate evidence
Look closely at the evidence supporting the writer's claims. Is it convincing? Are there gaps? Can it be interpreted in a different way? Is counterevidence acknowledged?

Examine underlying values, attitudes, and beliefs
When a writer or speaker neglects the audience's values, attitudes, and beliefs, the text is rarely persuasive.

Identify fallacies
Be aware when only one side of the story is being presented, when claims and accusations are grossly exaggerated, and when complex issues are oversimplified. See pages 18–19.

Identify relationships
An effective rhetorical analysis makes connections, showing how strategies in the text are responses to other texts and the larger context.

Recognize complexity
Many texts cannot be reduced to a sound bite. Successful rhetorical analyses often read between the lines to explain why a statement may be ironic or what is not being said. Readers appreciate being shown something they may not otherwise have noticed.

Writing a visual analysis

We are bombarded by images on a daily basis. They compete for our attention, urge us to buy things, and guide us on our way home from work. These visual texts frequently attempt to persuade us, to make us think, feel, or act a certain way. Yet we rarely stop to consider how they do their work.

Visual texts leave room for the audience to interpret to a greater degree than many verbal texts, which make them particularly rich subjects for analysis. For an example of visual analysis, see pages 67–69.

Components of a visual analysis

What kind of visual is it?	**Describe what you see** Is it a single image, part of a series, a sign, a building, or something else? What are the conventions for this kind of visual?
What is the image about?	**Consider the subject** What does the image depict? What is the setting? What is the purpose? Are words connected with the image?
How is the image arranged?	**Analyze the composition** What elements are most prominent? Which are repeated? Which are balanced or in contrast to each other? Which details are important? What is missing?
What is the context?	**Examine the context** Who created the image? When and where did it first appear? Can you determine why it was created?
What visuals are like it?	**Look for connections** What is the genre? What kind of visual is it? What elements have you seen before? Which remind you of other visuals?

Keys to visual analysis

Choose a visual text that you care about
If an image or other visual text means something to you, you will find it easier to analyze.

Pay close attention to details
Identify the key details that keep the viewer's attention and convey meaning. Also, examine the point of view—the viewer's perspective of the subject.

Provide a frame for understanding
You will need to provide a context for understanding a visual text, giving a sense of how it is a response to events and trends going on at the time and how it was initially understood.

Go beyond the obvious
A successful visual analysis gets readers to make connections and see aspects that they otherwise would not have noticed.

Writing a literary analysis

A literary analysis takes different forms. One form is to analyze patterns, such as how the repetition of particular images and even words contributes to the meaning. Another form is to pose a problem, such as why a particular character behaves in an odd way or why the narrator leaves out key information. Another approach is to use comparison and contrast to provide an analysis of two characters, two works of literature, or any pairs that help readers gain insight into a work. Finally, you can use one or more critical strategies as your approach. By using biographical criticism, for example, you might show how the life and times of the author shaped the literary work you are studying.

For an example of literary analysis, see pages 255–267.

Components of a literary analysis

What is my purpose?	**State an arguable thesis** Your purpose is to give your readers an arguable thesis and support-able interpretation that demonstrates you have closely read the text.
How do I support my thesis and interpretation?	**Provide as much relevant evidence as possible** You must show that your thesis and interpretation are supported by evidence from the text. Cite precise passages from the work and refer to specific details. Your instructor may ask you to use second-ary sources in addition to the text.
What components should I look for?	**Use literary concepts to support your ideas** Take into account literary concepts such as character, setting, theme, motif, symbol, point of view, and imagery to express your ideas. Your analysis will likely answer such questions as who are the characters, what is the setting and what role does it play, what are themes or motifs in the text, from what point of view is the work told, what language choices are made, and what is the significance of the title?
Should I give a plot summary?	**Avoid plot summaries** Assume your readers are familiar with the literary work. Do not give plot summaries unless the summary relates directly to your thesis. Remember a plot summary is not an interpretation nor is it an arguable thesis.

Keys to literary analysis

Choose a topic that you care about
Your paper will require close multiple readings of the text. Make sure you are interested in your topic and feel that you have something to say about it.

Become familiar with your text
Convince your readers that you have closely read the work and that you have carefully annotated the work with pencil in hand as you read.

Write a descriptive title
The title of your analysis should provide clues as to your overall topic and thesis.

Evaluate and revise your thesis
Make sure your thesis is specific and significant. If you identify a pattern but say nothing about why it is important, your reader will ask "So what?" What does the pattern contribute to an overall interpretation?

Select your evidence and examples with an eye on your thesis
Make sure your evidence and examples are relevant to your thesis. Explain the significance of the evidence for your thesis.

Use the present tense
In writing about literature, refer to events in the present tense.

Document carefully
You will be quoting from the literary text and perhaps using secondary sources as well. Be sure to carefully document your sources using MLA format.

An effective analysis

A successful analysis can be generally textual or contextual in nature. But the two approaches are not mutually exclusive—in fact, most analysts consider the details of the text, but also attend to the particulars of context as well.

theguardian **Straight from the Heart**
Tim Collins

On July 11, 2005, a woman named Marie Fatayi-Williams made an immensely moving speech in London at the site where her son Anthony had been killed in a terrorist bombing four days earlier. Her speech was reported in numerous media outlets. *The Guardian*, a British newspaper, printed Fatayi-Williams's speech on July 13, with an analysis and commentary by Tim Collins. Collins considers the factors that make Fatayi-Williams's speech so powerful, and places it in a larger context of responses to terrorism.

Caught in the spotlight of history, set on the stage of a very public event, Marie Fatayi-Williams, the mother of Anthony Fatayi-Williams, 26 and missing since Thursday, appeals for news of her son. Her words are a mixture of stirring rhetoric, heartfelt appeal and a stateswoman-like vision, and so speak on many levels to the nation and the world. Her appeal is a simple one—where is my son? If he has been killed, then why? Who has gained?

Marie has found herself, as I did on the eve of the invasion of Iraq, an unwitting voice, speaking amid momentous events. Her appeal, delivered on Monday not far from Tavistock Square, where she fears her son died in the bomb attack on the number 30 bus, gives a verbal form to the whirlpool of emotions that have engulfed society as the result of last week's bombings. I suspect Marie, like myself, had no idea that her words would find such wide recognition, have fed such an acute hunger for explanation, have slaked such a thirst for expression of the sheer horror of Thursday's events.

This kind of speech is normally the preserve of the great orators, statesmen and playwrights, of Shakespeare, Churchill or Lincoln. It is often a single speech, a soliloquy or address from the steps of the gallows, that explains, inspires, exhorts and challenges. But always such addresses are crafted for effect and consciously intended to sway and influence, and often, as in the case of Shakespeare's Henry V, they are set in the mouth

Collins points out the appeal to pathos—the beliefs and values of the audience—that lies at the heart of Fatayi-Williams's speech.

Collins identifies the genre of the speech, which is usually crafted for a specific occasion. Marie's speech is remarkable because it is spontaneous.

of a long dead hero or delivered by wordsmiths who are masters of their craft. It is rare in history that such oratory is the genuine article, springing from the heart and bursting forth to an unwitting audience. In Marie's case, her speech gains its power as a vehicle of grief and loss, and of the angst of a mother who yearns for her beloved son. In my case it was the opposite emotion from which I drew inspiration—an appeal to understand, to empathize, to give courage and purpose. I was motivated by a need to warn and teach as well as to encourage. Marie's motivation is a reflection on loss and that most powerful of all emotions, a mother's love.

The form the address takes is as poignant as the language used. There is an initial explanation of the extraordinary circumstances of the loss, a cri de coeur for the innocent blood lost, a rejection of the act by its comparison to the great liberators, and the assertion that her loss is all our loss in the family of humanity. It ends with her personal grief for her flesh and blood, her hopes and pride. The language echoes verses of the Bible as well as from the Koran. It has raw passion as well as heart-rending pathos.

> Several rhetorical techniques used in the speech connect it to a larger historical tradition.

With only a photograph of her son and a sheet of paper as a prompt, Marie's words burst out with as much emotion as anger. Her speech stands in stark contrast to the pronounce-ments of politicians, prepared by aides and delivered from copious notes. It is indeed the raw originality and authentic angst that give the delivery such impact, the plea such effect. No knighted veteran of the Royal Shakespeare Company could deliver such an address without hours or even days of rehearsal. I know from my own experience that only momen-tous events can provoke such a moment, only raw emotion can inspire such a spontaneous plea. I am often asked how long it took me to write my speech, delivered to my regi-ment, the Royal Irish, on the eve of the invasion of Iraq on March 19, 2003, at Fort Blair Mayne camp in the Kuwaiti desert. My answer is simple—not one moment. There was no plan; I spoke without notes. For me there was only the loom-ing specter of actual warfare and the certainty of loss and killing, and I was speaking to myself as well as to my men. I suspect for Marie there was only the yawning black void of loss, the cavern left behind in her life caused by the loss of a son who can never be replaced.

> Collins's own experience informs his understanding of what Fatayi-Williams might have been feeling. This helps assure his audience that he is qualified to comment on the meaning of her speech.

What, then, can we take from this? Marie's appeal is as important as it is momentous. Her words are as free from hatred as they are free from self-interest; it is clear that no man can give her her heart's desire—her son. I was also struck by the quiet dignity of her words, the clarity of her view and the weight of her convictions. She does not condemn, she appeals; her words act as an indictment of all war and violence, not just acts of terror but also the unnecessary aggression of nation states. Her message is simple: here is a human who only wanted to give, to succeed and to make his mother proud. Where is the victory in his death? Where is the progress in his destruction? In her own words: "What inspiration can senseless slaughter provide?"

Collins examines how Marie creates her ethos, which convinces her audience of her sincerity and lack of malice.

I am certain that Marie's appeal will go down as one of the great speeches of our new century. It will give comfort to the families and friends of the dead and injured, both of this act and no doubt, regrettably, of events still to come. It should act as a caution to statesmen and leaders, a focus for public grief and, ultimately, as a challenge to, as well as a condemnation of, the perpetrators.

Collins sees Fatayi-Williams's directness as perhaps the most important aspect of her speech. She responds to historic events in a way that personalizes them and shows their human cost.

Marie is already an icon of the loss of Thursday July 7. Having travelled from Africa to find a better life, Anthony Fatayi-Williams carried the hopes and pride of his family. Now, as his mother has travelled to London, arguably one of the most cosmopolitan and integrated cities in the world, and standing nearby a wrecked icon of that city, a red double-decker bus, she has made an appeal which is as haunting as it is relevant, as poignant as it is appealing. It is a fact that such oratory as both Marie and I produced is born of momentous events, and inspired by hope and fears in equal measure.

But Marie's appeal is also important on another level. I have long urged soldiers in conflict zones to keep communicating with the population in order to be seen as people—it is easier to kill uniforms than it is to kill people. On July 7 the suicide bombers attacked icons of a society that they hated more than they loved life, the red London bus and the tube. Marie's speech has stressed the real victims' identities. They are all of us.

Marie's speech

This is Anthony, Anthony Fatayi-Williams, 26 years old, he's missing and we fear that he was in the bus explosion . . . on Thursday. We don't know. We do know from the witnesses that he left the Northern line in Euston. We know he made a call to his office at Amec at 9.41 from the NW1 area to say he could not make [it] by the tube but he would find alternative means to work.

Marie Fatayi-Williams

Since then he has not made any contact with any single person. Not New York, not Madrid, not London. There has been widespread slaughter of innocent people. There have been streams of tears, innocent tears. There have been rivers of blood, innocent blood. Death in the morning, people going to find their livelihood, death in the noontime on the highways and streets.

They are not warriors. Which cause has been served? Certainly not the cause of God, not the cause of Allah because God Almighty only gives life and is full of mercy. Anyone who has been misled, or is being misled to believe that by killing innocent people he or she is serving God should think again because it's not true. Terrorism is not the way, terrorism is not the way. It doesn't beget peace. We can't deliver peace by terrorism, never can we deliver peace by killing people. Throughout history, those people who have changed the world have done so without violence, they have won people to their cause through peaceful protest. Nelson Mandela, Martin Luther King, Mahatma Gandhi, their discipline, their self-sacrifice, their conviction made people turn towards them, to follow them. What inspiration can senseless slaughter provide? Death and destruction of young people in their prime as well as old and helpless can never be the foundations for building society.

My son Anthony is my first son, my only son, the head of my family. In African society, we hold on to sons. He has dreams and hopes and I, his mother, must fight to protect them. This is now the fifth day, five days on, and we are waiting to know what happened to him and I, his mother, I need to know what happened to Anthony. His young sisters need to know what happened, his uncles and aunties need to know what happened to Anthony, his father needs to know what happened to Anthony. Millions of my friends back home in Nigeria need to know what happened to Anthony. His friends surrounding me here, who have put this together, need to know what has happened to Anthony. I need to know, I want to protect him. I'm his mother, I will fight till I die to protect him. To protect his values and to protect his memory.

Innocent blood will always cry to God Almighty for reparation. How much blood must be spilled? How many tears shall we cry? How many mothers' hearts must be maimed? My heart is maimed. I pray I will see my son, Anthony. Why? I need to know, Anthony needs to know, Anthony needs to know, so do many other unaccounted for innocent victims, they need to know.

It's time to stop and think. We cannot live in fear because we are surrounded by hatred. Look around us today. Anthony is a Nigerian, born in London, worked in London, he is a world citizen. Here today we have Christians, Muslims, Jews, Sikhs, Hindus, all of us united in love for Anthony. Hatred begets only hatred. It is time to stop this vicious cycle of killing. We must all stand together, for our common humanity. I need to know what happened to my Anthony. He's the love of my life. My first son, my first son, 26. He tells me one day, "Mummy, I don't want to die, I don't want to die. I want to live, I want to take care of you, I will do great things for you, I will look after you, you will see what I will achieve for you. I will make you happy." And he was making me happy. I am proud of him, I am still very proud of him but I need to now where he is, I need to know what happened to him. I grieve, I am sad, I am distraught, I am destroyed.

He didn't do anything to anybody, he loved everybody so much. If what I hear is true, even when he came out of the underground he was directing people to take buses, to be sure that they were OK. Then he called his office at the same time to tell them he was running late. He was a multi-purpose person, trying to save people, trying to call his office, trying to meet his appointments. What did he then do to deserve this? Where is he, someone tell me, where is he?

How to read analyses

Make notes as you read, either in the margins, if it is your own copy, or on paper or a computer file. Circle any words or references that you don't know and look them up.

What kind of analysis is it?	• Is it a rhetorical analysis? A literary analysis? An analysis of a visual? An analysis of an object?
Where did it come from?	• Who wrote the analysis? • What do you know about the writer's background that might have influenced the analysis?
Who is the intended audience?	• What clues do you find about whom the writer had in mind as the readers? • What does the writer assume that the readers already know about the subject? • What new knowledge is the writer providing?
What is the focus of the analysis?	• What does the writer have to say about the context or background? • What does the writer have to say about how the text or object is composed?
What is the significance of the analysis?	• Does the writer make specific claims? • What did you learn or come to understand differently by reading the analysis?
How is it composed?	• How does the writer represent herself or himself? • How would you characterize the style? • If there are any photographs or other graphics, what information do they contribute?

Dude, Where's My Job?

(EDITORIAL)

Lianne George

MACLEAN'S   Lianne George is co-author of *The Ego Boom: Why the World Really Does Revolve Around You* and blogs regularly for Macleans.ca, Canada's national weekly current affairs magazine.

Analyzing and Connecting

Return to these questions after you have finished reading.

1. George's editorial is an analysis that concludes with, "I always mention the birthday thing because it's so simple, but Gen Y does believe that the most important holiday of the year is their birthday because it's the one they don't have to share." First, from your experience, do you agree with George's assertion about young people? If you agree, does this apparent selfish perspective mean that young people are only interested in themselves?

2. According to George, who is responsible for Generation Y's sense of entitlement?

3. *Schadenfreude* (delight in another person's misfortune) is the possible reaction to the failure of the millennial cohort to get what they think they deserve. What does this reaction say about the general public's opinion of Generation Y? Is it fair? Is it accurate?

4. In the second-last paragraph, George points out a surprising benefit to the challenges that the Gen Y cohort will face in the economic downturn. In your own words, explain the upside of this challenge. How realistic is George's solution to the problem?

Dude, where's my job?

Jan 14, 2009 by Lianne George

It was only 18 months ago that the *Wall Street Journal* ran an article outlining the lavish demands of a new generation of workers, known collectively as Gen Y or Millennials or Net Gen. At the time, the thinking was that this group—ages 30 and under—had employers over a barrel. For one thing, there were relatively few of them, and employers, facing an imminent wave of boomer retirements, would be competing for the best of this young cohort. Also, since this is the Internet generation, they were believed to possess magical and mysterious tech skills that would prove invaluable in the workplace of the future.

Emboldened by these dual advantages, Millennials set their expectations high. Not only did they want fun, fulfilling work, with flexible hours, good salaries, and ample vacation, they wanted to be celebrated, too. Literally, feted. Savvy employers had taken to embracing measures like prize packages for a job well done, "public displays of appreciation," and, in the case of one manufacturer in Texas, retaining a "celebration assistant" in charge of helium balloons and confetti. This was smart business, according to 30-year-old Jason Ryan Dorsey, a self-appointed Gen Y expert—who consults with companies like Kraft and Four Seasons Hotels and Resorts about the peculiarities and preferences of his generation. "Marking milestones is major," he told *Forbes* magazine. "No birthday should go uncelebrated, and the first day on the job should be unforgettable." Which is great, except for one thing: what happens when the most entitled generation in history slams into the worst job market in 30 years?

At the turn of 2009, in the midst of massive layoffs and hiring freezes, not to mention cut-rate Christmas parties where punch just wasn't in the budget, these demands seem cringe-worthy—even more so than they did before. If ever there

GEORGE: DUDE, WHERE'S MY JOB?

was a sign that the era of the sellers' employment market is over, it came last month when Google—the Santa Claus of corporate perk-giving—instituted a hiring freeze and, among other things, cancelled its New York office's decidedly Millennial-friendly tradition of afternoon tea. Almost as soon as they began for this cohort, it would appear its halcyon days are over.

In November alone, 71,000 Canadians lost their jobs—27 per cent of the newly unemployed are people aged 24 and under—and economists predict this is only a bellwether of worse to come. Suddenly, many of those retiring boomers can't afford to retire. Making matters worse, Millennials are saddled with more debt than any previous generation (an average of $5,631 per year in student debt alone, not to mention the load sitting on their credit cards, and what they're doling out in car payments). This recession is not what they signed up for.

"They were absolutely told that 'You're part of a blessed generation and you are going to be in control of your own destiny,'" says Winnipeg native Steven Rothberg, owner of CollegeRecruiter.com, a company that recruits college graduates mostly in the U.S. "The spring 2008 grads have had to do some major adjusting. They graduated with the expectation that it was going to be a sellers' market, that they were going to have multiple offers, step into an upper management role and have significant strategic impact on a Fortune 500 company, and that's just not the reality." Until last year, he said, university and college students in their senior year, even the mediocre ones, could expect job offers as early as Oct. 1 of their final year. Now, employers are waiting until the spring to make hiring decisions, waiting to see how the economy shakes out, and leaving more students graduating into uncertainty.

There will be *schadenfreude* from those who see Millennial entitlement as a moral failing. "I hear people say this a lot," says Dorsey of his boomer executive clients. "They say, 'Your generation just needs one good recession and then they'll appreciate their jobs.' " But this is too simplistic an assessment of why "kids today" are the way they are. They're not genetically lazy or spoiled, any more than children of the Depression are inherently thrifty. Whatever overblown expectations this generation has are the product of decades of conditioning, and not only by overzealous boomer parents. Well-intentioned attempts to make this generation feel good about itself have, in fact, left them poorly prepared to weather a tough economic storm.

Consider that this is the first cohort to come of age in a time of institutionalized self-esteem. Beginning in the seventies, programs designed to boost children's self-esteem were installed in schools and at home, in the form of books and TV shows like *Mister Rogers' Neighborhood.* Throughout the eighties, according to the research of Jean Twenge, a professor of psychology at San Diego State University, the number of studies published on the benefits of self-esteem programs doubled, and in the nineties, it doubled again. Then came the elimination of competition, harsh red marking pens, and the arrival of books with titles like *Celebrate Yourself: Six Steps to Building Your Self-Esteem.* "Generation Me's expectations are highly optimistic," Twenge wrote in her 2006 book on the narcissistic tendencies of this group. "They expect to go to college, to make lots of money, and perhaps even to be famous." Unfortunately, there's a fine line between optimism and confidence, and irrational entitlement.

But it wasn't just indulgent teachers and coddling parents that formed this generation's world view. The self-esteem revolution happened to dovetail with a consumer shift toward an ever-greater focus on the individual. Marketers trained their sights on young people more intently than ever before, piggybacking on the self-esteem movement to offer youth heaps of affirmation in the form of a countless array of products—just for them! They realized that parents, flush with credit and disposable income, were inordinately concerned with their kids' opinions, even when it came to grown-up purchasing decisions (from cars to family vacations). Tweens spend about $2.9 billion a year and influence purchases worth another $20 billion. From the age of eight, Millennials saw themselves reflected everywhere: in ads for tween shampoos, designer fashions, and fragrances. By the time they got to university, credit card companies were handing out application forms along with student orientation packages. The message, as always: if you want it, you should have it.

It only makes sense that the environment in which they were raised would inform what they expected from a job—namely, flexibility, authority, instant respect and continuous affirmation. (This is a generation, after all, in which seven out of 10 rank themselves "above average" in academic ability.) "They're not going to put up with the 'paying your dues' and being in the mailroom for the first three years," says Rothberg. "In their mind it's, 'I graduated. I've always succeeded. I've always got a trophy for everything I've done. All of my friends and everyone I know is above average, so when I go into a place of work, I'm either going to set that place on fire or they're not good enough for me and I'm out of there.' "

But there is a surprising upside to this attitude that may wind up benefiting both the young workers and the companies that employ them. Ironically, the Millennials' addiction to affirmation may also turn out to be their saving grace. "What is interesting about this generation," says Max Valiquette, president of Toronto-based youth marketing firm Youthography, "is that a lot of the carrots and perks they're asking for have nothing to do with money, and almost everything to do with how they work." Very few of them have had hard experience scrimping to make rent. (In fact, in 2006, 44 per cent of Canadian adults ages 20 to 29 were living with mom and dad). Instead, Dorsey says, the incentives they crave involve self-determination, being recognized for good work, and regular feedback—things that cost no money at all. In other words, to some degree employers may be able to substitute applause for hard currency and still keep young employees perfectly happy, a potential boon in a cash-strapped economy.

For those young workers fortunate enough to find or keep work in the midst of the storm, life is about to provide some eye-opening lessons, and the same might be said for the companies trying to balance their need for young ambitious workers with their immediate need to keep costs down. "Smart companies are going to see this as an unparalleled opportunity to build Gen Y loyalty," says Dorsey. "I always mention the birthday thing because it's so simple, but Gen Y really does believe that the most important holiday of the year is their birthday because it's the one they don't have to share." If this turns out to be true, expect to be eating a lot of cake in 2009.

Contemplating Inuit Presence in Literature
(COMMENTARY)
Zebedee Nungak

Inuit writer and satirist Zebedee Nungak explores the difficulties of "making public" the literature of a traditional oral culture. In his commentary, he suggests that there is only selective interest in authentic Inuit life, but that Inuit literature has a great potential to go mainstream with the right support.

Analyzing and Connecting
Return to these questions after you have finished reading.

1. Nungak's commentary describes a deep cultural tradition of storytelling—mentally archiving historical accounts and legends and then passing them on orally. Given what is generally not known about Inuit culture, why do you suppose Nungak chose to preface his commentary with this amount of cultural background?

2. Note each example Nungak uses to show the importance of transitioning oral culture to a written one. What types of examples does he use? Does he provide enough evidence to convince you that his point of view is valid?

3. Consider Nungak's statement in the second last paragraph, "there's not much ready assistance for Inuit with aspirations and talent in the field of writing." How is this statement significant in the context of the overall commentary?

One of the strongest traditions of Inuit has been the preservation of culture and identity through *unikkaat* (stories) and *unikkaatuat* (legends). A mere generation ago, most Inuit adults were greatly skilled storytellers, who retained impressive volumes of historical accounts and legends in their memory. Story telling, central to the Inuit identity, served throughout the oft-mentioned "time immemorial" to faithfully retain the record of happenings important to Inuit collective culture. Amazingly, the human memory served as an archive for these.

Another feature of Inuit daily life was the "daily narrative." The family would re-group at day's end, and recount the events and happenings of the day. A natural extension of this forum was the reciting of legends and stories by the more elderly members of the family. Here would be told the stories of Kaujjajuq, the mistreated orphan boy who suddenly grew in size and wreaked revenge on his tormentors. "Never mistreat orphans" was the moral of this story.

Then there was Atungaq, who journeyed around the world with his wife, encountering many different types of people, who all rated their own physical and cultural descriptions. The baby daughter whom they had left behind at the start of their circumnavigation was an old woman by the time of their return. But Atungaq and his wife had not aged at all during their trip. Such were the stories that Inuit youngsters were entertained with, and fell asleep by, on the way to becoming "librarians" for the following generation, to perpetuate this knowledge.

Through such methods, the vast wealth of Inuit cultural knowledge survived millennia. Thereafter, anthropologists and social scientists collected and recorded them by modern means, to preserve them for history, and future generations. Here comes to mind Danish-Greenlandic explorer Knud Rasmussen, whose name is synonymous the world over with the collection and transmission of Inuit culture. Inuit culture was destined to end up residing in the written word, and other mediums, which could not have been imagined long ago.

Qallunaat have often been amazed at the accuracy of Inuit accounts of historical events. Generation to generation oral transmission kept alive accurate stories of Inuit contacts with Martin Frobisher in 1576-78, and with Henry Hudson's mutinous crew in 1611. The dates may not be specified in the Inuit versions, but the events, in their detail, have

NUNGAK: CONTEMPLATING INUIT PRESENCE IN LITERATURE

survived to be verified hundreds of years later with the written accounts of them recorded by Qallunaat.

Since Inuit traditions are oral and not literary, Inuit have had to process through a transition to find a suitable "zone of comfort" in the field of written literature. In past times, writing seemed to be something for "others" to do, and was not at all a pre-occupation of Inuit. For a long time, it seemed that Inuit were neither meant, nor expected to be, writers. That is, in the way that Qallunaat have been authors, poets, and producers of written works for centuries.

From the late 1950s onward, Inuit have proven themselves more than capable as writers ever since magazines, newsletters, and other publications have been available to them across the Arctic. But for the most part, Inuit writing has yet to make its presence noticeable in the world of mainstream literature. Several Inuit have pioneered the literary trail as published authors, but these are still far too few. Inuit writers have yet to attain such "firsts" as making the bestseller lists, or winning mainline literary prizes for written works.

Over the years, I've encountered more than a few Inuit who were seriously into writing. One of them was a friend from school days in "the great land of the Qallunaat," who had maintained a daily journal for many years. He was about to develop his manuscript into a book when he had the great misfortune to lose his journals. Somehow, sharing the pain of his loss planted a seed of determination within me to start compiling my own recollections of those years in writing.

Then there was a young woman who had kept a pile of her deceased grandfather's diaries, who wanted to know if I knew how to turn them into published works. Not having a clue about who to approach, and how to go about even making inquiries, I was not able to provide her with any guidance, and felt terribly useless. These were writings by a traditional Inuk, written entirely in Inuktitut, surely valuable and deserving to be in print.

During a field trip to Nunavik communities many years ago, a man brought us a manuscript written entirely in Inuktitut syllabics. Its tidy order, in titled chapters, and its style of being written in verses, like in the Bible, was uniquely impressive. It was a book detailing a way of life that is quickly fading into distant memory. Properly edited and illustrated, it could have easily made a run in mainstream literature as a textbook for the study of Inuit culture.

The tragedy thus far is that nobody is actively searching out the Inuit world for such material. Journals, diaries, and manuscripts gather dust in many an obscure shelf, never to be brought to the attention of people who can cause such works by Inuit writers to eventually become published. Worse yet, stories lay unwritten by potential writers, never to bloom beyond the gleam in their writer's eye. This great, untapped resource has to become the primary pre-occupation of people who can generate interest in it, and plug for its development.

Now, there's readily available support and funding for Inuit who are carvers, artists, print-makers, throat chanters, drum dancers, musicians, and hunting, fishing and travel guides. I've discovered since taking up writing that there's not much ready assistance for Inuit with aspirations and talent in the field of writing.

Inuit writers should start agitating just enough to force this deficiency to be given serious attention. Ways and means have to be found for Inuit writers to attain a presence in the world of letters and literature.

Federal Express Logo
(CORPORATE LOGO)
Landor Associates

Federal Express, founded in 1973, created a new market for rapid delivery of packages and documents. By 1993 the company had greatly expanded and operated around the world. Federal Express hired the design firm Landor Associates to create a new logo. By this time Federal Express had become universally known as FedEx, which Landor chose to use for the new logo. The FedEx logo quickly became one of the most recognizable in the world.

Analyzing and Connecting
Return to these questions after you have finished looking at the logos.

1. Make a list of all the logos you can think of. What makes these logos memorable?

2. Logos were originally designed to distinguish products and companies. Notice how many now look similar. Why do you think so many logos look alike?

3. Which logos suggest what a company actually does?

4. Your school probably has a logo. How frequently do you see the logo? What message does the logo convey about your school?

Have you noticed the solid white arrow in the FedEx logo?

Volkswagen Beetle

(PRODUCT DESIGN)

The Volkswagen Type 1, better known as the Beetle or Bug, is the most produced car in history. From 1938 until the last original Beetle came off an assembly line in Puebla, Mexico, over twenty-one million were built. The Beetle began in Nazi Germany, when Adolf Hitler commissioned Ferdinand Porsche to produce a car for common people. Only a handful were produced before World War II started in 1939. Volkswagen was soon back in production after the war, and by 1954, the number of Beetles passed a million. Volkswagen began shipping cars to North America at a time when cars here were big and boxy. The VW Beetle was just the opposite—small and rounded, inexpensive, and three times as fuel-efficient. Beetles dominated the small-car market until Japanese imports showed up in large numbers in the mid-1970s.

More than the story of a car, however, the Beetle demonstrates how what we buy reflects cultural attitudes and values.

Analyzing and Connecting

Return to these questions after you have finished reading.

1. Volkswagen ads in North America in the 1960s appealed to simplicity—simple shape, simple technology—which grew out of long-standing values of honesty, economy, and lack of pretense. Look at automobile ads today, both in print and on television. What values do they appeal to?

2. Your campus may have a building that is better known by a nickname than its official name. Is the building liked or disliked by students? How does the nickname change the image of the building? For example, is it more friendly or less friendly?

3. Look up the word *bug* in the *Oxford English Dictionary*, which traces the histories of words. Your library has the print OED and may allow access through the library's website. How has the meaning of *bug* changed over time? Think about how *bug* is used today. For example, a common saying among computer programmers is, "It's not a bug, it's a feature." Identify examples of other words such as *pimp* that have changed meanings in recent years.

4. Think of other products that we find cute and loveable. What makes them cute and loveable? Does advertising promote these associations?

When Adolf Hitler became Chancellor of Germany in 1933, he declared that a centrepiece of Nazism would be the motorization of the country. He asked Ferdinand Porsche to design a car that would be affordable for everyone.

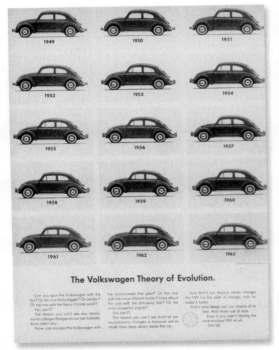

Clever advertising helped make the Beetle a hit in the 1960s. The American advertising firm Doyle Dane Bernbach (DDB) began a campaign in 1959 that emphasized the differences between the Beetle and bulky American cars that changed designs yearly.

VOLKSWAGEN BEETLE

In 1968, Walt Disney's *The Love Bug* created a new generation of Beetle fans and led to a series of *Herbie* sequels.

Beetles became part of the counterculture of the 1960s. Many were hand-painted and customized in various ways, even adding fins that mocked American cars.

Misery has enough company.
Dare to be happy.

In 1998 Volkswagen launched the New Beetle, which benefited from the loveable image of the original Beetle.

Everyday Use
(SHORT STORY)
Alice Walker

Alice Walker was born in Eatonville, Georgia, in 1944, and won a scholarship in 1961 to Spelman College in Atlanta. Her third novel, *The Color Purple*, published in 1982, became a bestseller, won a Pulitzer Prize, and established her reputation as one of the finest living writers in the United States. "Everyday Use" is one of her best-loved short stories.

Analyzing and Connecting
Return to these questions after you have finished reading.

1. Who is the narrator in the story? How does the point of view of the narrator affect the information we are given in the story?

2. Describe each of the main characters in the story. Use specific evidence from the text to support your descriptions. Which character do you find the most sympathetic? Explain.

3. The idea of heritage plays a big role in the story. Compare and contrast the meaning of heritage from each of the main characters' points of view.

4. Another important theme in the story is the idea of intergenerational conflict. Read the story paying particular attention to examples of this conflict and describe the conflict in a few sentences.

5. Explain the symbolic meaning the quilts serve in the story.

6. Why do you think the story is titled "Everyday Use"?

Note: See page 264 for a student's analysis of the use of symbolism in "Everyday Use."

Everyday Use

For your grandmama

I will wait for her in the yard that Maggie and I made so clean and wavy yesterday afternoon. A yard like this is more comfortable than most people know. It is not just a yard. It is like an extended living room. When the hard clay is swept clean as a floor and the fine sand around the edges lined with tiny, irregular grooves anyone can come and sit and look up into the elm tree and wait for the breezes that never come inside the house.

Maggie will be nervous until after her sister goes: she will stand hopelessly in corners, homely and ashamed of the burn scars down her arms and legs, eyeing her sister with a mixture of envy and awe. She thinks her sister has held life always in the palm of one hand, that "no" is a word the world never learned to say to her.

You've no doubt seen those TV shows where the child who has "made it" is confronted, as a surprise, by her own mother and father, tottering in weakly from backstage. (A pleasant surprise, of course: What would they do if parent and child came on the show only to curse out and insult each other?) On TV mother and child embrace and smile into each other's faces. Sometimes the mother and father weep, the child wraps them in her arms and leans across the table to tell how she would not have made it without their help. I have seen these programs.

Sometimes I dream a dream in which Dee and I are suddenly brought together on a TV program of this sort. Out of a dark and soft-seated limousine I am ushered into a bright room filled with many people. There I meet a smiling, gray, sporty man like Johnny Carson who shakes my hand and tells me what a fine girl I have. Then we are on the stage and Dee is embracing me with tears in her eyes. She pins on my dress a large orchid, even though she has told me once that she thinks orchids are tacky flowers.

In real life I am a large, big-boned woman with rough, man-working hands. In the winter I wear flannel nightgowns to bed and overalls during the day. I can kill and clean a hog as mercilessly as a man. My fat keeps me hot in zero weather. I can work outside all day, breaking ice to get water for washing. I can eat pork liver cooked over the open fire minutes after it comes steaming from the hog. One winter I knocked a bull calf straight in the brain between the eyes with a sledge hammer and had the meat hung up to chill before nightfall. But of course all this does not show on television. I am the way my daughter would want me to be: a hundred pounds lighter, my skin like an uncooked barley pancake. My hair glistens in the hot bright lights. Johnny Carson has much to do to keep up with my quick and witty tongue.

But that is a mistake. I know even before I wake up. Who ever knew a Johnson with a quick tongue? Who can even imagine me looking a strange white man in the eye? It seems to me I have talked to them always with one foot raised in flight, with my head turned in whichever way is farthest from them. Dee, though. She would always look anyone in the eye. Hesitation was no part of her nature.

"How do I look, Mama?" Maggie says, showing just enough of her thin body enveloped in pink skirt and red blouse for me to know she's there, almost hidden by the door.

"Come out into the yard," I say.

Have you ever seen a lame animal, perhaps a dog run over by some careless person rich enough to own a car, sidle up to someone who is ignorant enough to be kind to him? That is the way my Maggie walks. She has been like this, chin on chest, eyes on ground, feet in shuffle, ever since the fire that burned the other house to the ground.

Dee is lighter than Maggie, with nicer hair and a fuller figure. She's a woman now, though sometimes I forget. How long ago was it that the other house burned? Ten, twelve years? Sometimes I can still hear the flames and feel Maggie's arms sticking to me, her hair smoking and her dress falling off her in little black papery flakes. Her eyes seemed stretched open, blazed open by the flames reflected in them. And Dee. I see her standing off under the sweet gum tree she used to dig gum out of; a look of concentration on her face as she watched the last dingy gray board of the house fall in toward the red-hot brick chimney. Why don't you do a dance around the ashes? I'd wanted to ask her. She had hated the house that much.

I used to think she hated Maggie, too. But that was before we raised the money, the church and me, to send her to Augusta to school. She used to read to us without pity; forcing words, lies, other folks' habits, whole lives upon us two, sitting trapped and ignorant underneath her voice. She washed us in a river of make-believe, burned us with a lot of knowledge we didn't necessarily need to know. Pressed us to her with the serious way she read, to shove us away at just the moment, like dimwits, we seemed about to understand.

Dee wanted nice things. A yellow organdy dress to wear to her graduation from high school; black pumps to match a green suit she'd made from an old suit somebody gave me. She was determined to stare down any disaster in her efforts. Her eyelids would not flicker for minutes at a time. Often I fought off the temptation to shake her. At sixteen she had a style of her own: and knew what style was.

I never had an education myself. After second grade the school was closed down. Don't ask me why: in 1927 colored asked fewer questions than they do now. Sometimes Maggie reads to me. She stumbles along good-naturedly but can't see well. She knows she is not bright. Like good looks and money, quickness passed her by. She will marry John Thomas (who has mossy teeth in an earnest face) and then I'll be free to sit here and I guess just sing church songs to myself. Although I never was a good singer. Never could carry a tune. I was a ways better at a man's job. I used to love to milk till I was hoofed in the side in '49. Cows are soothing and slow and don't bother you, unless you try to milk them the wrong way.

I have deliberately turned my back on the house. It is three rooms, just like the one that burned, except the roof is tin; they don't make shingle roofs any more. There are no real windows, just some holes cut in the sides, like the portholes in a ship, but not round and not square, with rawhide holding the shutters up on the outside. This house is in a pasture, too, like the other one. No doubt when Dee sees it she will want to tear it down. She wrote me once that no matter where we "choose" to live, she will manage to come see us. But she will never bring her friends. Maggie and I thought about this and Maggie asked me, "Mama, when did Dee ever *have* any friends?"

She had a few. Furtive boys in pink shirts hanging about on washday after school. Nervous girls who never laughed. Impressed with her they worshiped the well-turned phrase, the cute shape, the scalding humor that erupted like bubbles in lye. She read to them.

When she was courting Jimmy T she didn't have much time to pay to us, but turned all her faultfinding power on him. He *flew* to marry a cheap city girl from a family of ignorant flashy people. She hardly had time to recompose herself.

When she comes I will meet—but there they are!

Maggie attempts to make a dash for the house, in her shuffling way, but I stay her with my hand. "Come back here," I say. And she stops and tries to dig a well in the sand with her toe.

It is hard to see them clearly through the strong sun. But even the first glimpse of leg out of the car tells me it is Dee. Her feet were always neat-looking, as if God himself had shaped them with a certain style. From the other side of the car comes a short, stocky man. Hair is all over his head a foot long and hanging from his chin like a kinky mule tail. I hear Maggie suck in her breath. "Uhnnnh," is what it sounds like. Like when you see the wriggling end of a snake just in front of your foot on the road. "Uhnnnh."

Dee next. A dress down to the ground, in this hot weather. A dress so loud hurts my eyes. There are yellows and oranges enough to throw back the light of the sun. I feel my whole face warming from the heat waves it throws out. Earrings, too, gold and hanging down to her shoulders. Bracelets dangling and making noises when she moves her arm up to shake the folds of the dress out of her armpits. The dress is loose and flows, and as she walks closer, I like it. I hear Maggie go "Uhnnnh" again. It is her sister's hair. It stands straight up like the wool on a sheep. It is black as night and around the edges are two long pigtails that rope about like small lizards disappearing behind her ears.

"Wa-su-zo-Tean-o!" she says, coming on in that gliding way the dress makes her move. The short stocky fellow with the hair to his navel is all grinning and he follows up with "Asalamalakim, my mother and sister!" He moves to hug Maggie but she falls back, right up against the back of my chair. I feel her trembling there and when I look up I see the perspiration falling off her chin.

"Don't get up," says Dee. Since I am stout it takes something of a push. You can see me trying to move a second or two before I make it. She turns, showing white heels through her sandals, and goes back to the car. Out she peeks next with a Polaroid. She stoops down quickly and lines up picture after picture of me sitting there in front of the house with Maggie cowering behind me. She never takes a shot without making sure the house is included. When a cow comes nibbling around the edge of the yard she snaps it and me and Maggie *and* the house. Then she puts the Polaroid in the back seat of the car, and comes up and kisses me on the forehead.

Meanwhile Asalamalakim is going through the motions with Maggie's hand. Maggie's hand is as limp as a fish, and probably as cold, despite the sweat, and she keeps trying to pull it back. It looks like Asalamalakim wants to shake hands but wants to do it fancy. Or maybe he don't know how people shake hands. Anyhow, he soon gives up on Maggie.

"Well," I say. "Dee."

"No, Mama," she says. "Not 'Dee,' Wangero Leewanika Kemanjo!"

"What happened to 'Dee'?" I wanted to know.

"She's dead," Wangero said. "I couldn't bear it any longer, being named after the people who oppress me."

"You know as well as me you was named after your aunt Dicie," I said. Dicie is my sister. She named Dee. We called her "Big Dee" after Dee was born.

"But who was *she* named after?" asked Wangero.

"I guess after Grandma Dee," I said.

"And who was she named after?" asked Wangero.

"Her mother," I said, and saw Wangero was getting tired. "That's about as far back as I can trace it," I said. Though, in fact, I probably could have carried it back beyond the Civil War through the branches.

"Well," said Asalamalakim, "there you are."

"Uhnnnh," I heard Maggie say.

"There I was not," I said, "before 'Dicie' cropped up in our family, so why should I try to trace it that far back?"

He just stood there grinning, looking down on me like somebody inspecting a Model A car. Every once in a while he and Wangero sent eye signals over my head.

"How do you pronounce this name?" I asked.

"You don't have to call me by it if you don't want to," said Wangero.

"Why shouldn't I?" I asked. "If that's what you want us to call you, we'll call you."

"I know it might sound awkward at first," said Wangero.

"I'll get used to it," I said. "Ream it out again."

Well, soon we got the name out of the way. Asalamalakim had a name twice as long and three times as hard. After I tripped over it two or three times he told me to just call him Hakim-a-barber. I wanted to ask him was he a barber, but I didn't really think he was, so I didn't ask.

"You must belong to those beef-cattle peoples down the road," I said. They said "Asalamalakim" when they met you, too, but they didn't shake hands. Always too busy: feeding the cattle, fixing the fences, putting up salt-lick shelters, throwing down hay. When the white folks poisoned some of the herd the men stayed up all night with rifles in their hands. I walked a mile and a half just to see the sight.

Hakim-a-barber said, "I accept some of their doctrines, but farming and raising cattle is not my style." (They didn't tell me, and I didn't ask, whether Wangero (Dee) had really gone and married him.)

We sat down to eat and right away he said he didn't eat collards and pork was unclean. Wangero, though, went on through the chitlins and corn bread, the greens and everything else. She talked a blue streak over the sweet potatoes. Everything delighted her. Even the fact that we still used the benches her daddy made for the table when we couldn't afford to buy chairs.

"Oh, Mama!" she cried. Then turned to Hakim-a-barber. "I never knew how lovely these benches are. You can feel the rump prints," she said, running her hands underneath her and along the bench. Then she gave a sigh and her hand closed over Grandma Dee's butter dish. "That's it!" she said. "I knew there was something I wanted to ask you if I could have." She jumped up from the table and went over in the corner where the churn stood, the milk in it clabber by now. She looked at the churn and looked at it.

"This churn top is what I need," she said. "Didn't Uncle Buddy whittle it out of a tree you all used to have?"

"Yes," I said.

"Uh huh," she said happily. "And I want the dasher, too."

"Uncle Buddy whittle that, too?" asked the barber.

Dee (Wangero) looked up at me.

"Aunt Dee's first husband whittled the dash," said Maggie so low you almost couldn't hear her. "His name was Henry, but they called him Stash."

"Maggie's brain is like an elephant's," Wangero said, laughing. "I can use the churn top as a centerpiece for the alcove table," she said, sliding a plate over the churn, "and I'll think of something artistic to do with the dasher."

When she finished wrapping the dasher the handle stuck out. I took it for a moment in my hands. You didn't even have to look close to see where hands pushing the dasher up and down to make butter had left a kind of sink on the wood. In fact, there were a lot of small sinks; you could see where thumbs and fingers had sunk into the wood. It was beautiful light yellow wood, from a tree that grew in the yard where Big Dee and Stash had lived.

After dinner Dee (Wangero) went to the trunk at the foot of my bed and started rifling through it. Maggie hung back in the kitchen over the dishpan. Out came Wangero with two quilts. They had been pieced by Grandma Dee and then Big Dee and me had hung them on the quilt frames on the front porch and quilted them. One was in the Lone Star pattern. The other was Walk Around the Mountain. In both of them were scraps of dresses Grandma Dee had worn fifty and more years ago. Bits and pieces of Grandpa Jarrell's paisley shirts. And one teeny faded blue piece, about the size of a penny matchbox, that was from Great Grandpa Ezra's uniform that he wore in the Civil War.

"Mama," Wangero said sweet as a bird. "Can I have these old quilts?"

I heard something fall in the kitchen, and a minute later the kitchen door slammed.

"Why don't you take one or two of the others?" I asked. "These old things was just done by me and Big Dee from some tops your grandma pieced before she died."

"No," said Wangero. "I don't want those. They are stitched around the borders by machine."

"That'll make them last better," I said.

"That's not the point," said Wangero. "These are all pieces of dresses Grandma used to wear. She did all this stitching by hand. Imagine!" She held the quilts securely in her arms, stroking them.

"Some of the pieces, like those lavender ones, come from old clothes her mother handed down to her," I said, moving up to touch the quilts. Dee (Wangero) moved back just enough so that I couldn't reach the quilts. They already belonged to her.

"Imagine!" she breathed again, clutching them closely to her bosom.

"The truth is," I said, "I promised to give them quilts to Maggie, for when she marries John Thomas."

She gasped like a bee had stung her.

"Maggie can't appreciate these quilts!" she said. "She'd probably be backward enough to put them to everyday use."

"I reckon she would," I said. "God knows I been saving 'em for long enough with nobody using 'em. I hope she will!" I didn't want to bring up how I had offered Dee (Wangero) a quilt when she went away to college. Then she had told me they were old-fashioned, out of style.

"But they're *priceless*!" she was saying now, furiously; for she has a temper. "Maggie would put them on the bed and in five years they'd be in rags. Less than that!"

"She can always make some more," I said. "Maggie knows how to quilt."

Dee (Wangero) looked at me with hatred. "You just will not understand. The point is these quilts, *these* quilts!"

"Well," I said, stumped. "What would *you* do with them!"

"Hang them," she said. As if that was the only thing you *could* do with quilts.

Maggie by now was standing in the door. I could almost hear the sound her feet made as they scraped over each other.

"She can have them, Mama," she said, like somebody used to never winning anything, or having anything reserved for her. "I can 'member Grandma Dee without the quilts."

I looked at her hard. She had filled her bottom lip with checkerberry snuff and it gave her face a kind of dopey, hangdog look. It was Grandma Dee and Big Dee who taught her how to quilt herself. She stood there with her scarred hands hidden in the folds of her skirt. She looked at her sister with something like fear but she wasn't mad at her. This was Maggie's portion. This was the way she knew God to work.

When I looked at her like that something hit me in the top of my head and ran down to the soles of my feet. Just like when I'm in church and the spirit of God touches me and I get happy and shout. I did something I never had done before: hugged Maggie to me, then dragged her on into the room, snatched the quilts out of Miss Wangero's hands and dumped them into Maggie's lap. Maggie just sat there on my bed with her mouth open.

"Take one or two of the others," I said to Dee.

But she turned without a word and went out to Hakim-a-barber.

"You just don't understand," she said, as Maggie and I came out to the car.

"What don't I understand?" I wanted to know.

"Your heritage," she said. And then she turned to Maggie, kissed her, and said, "You ought to try to make something of yourself, too, Maggie. It's really a new day for us. But from the way you and Mama still live you'd never know it."

She put on some sunglasses that hid everything above the tip of her nose and her chin.

Maggie smiled; maybe at the sunglasses. But a real smile, not scared. After we watched the car dust settle I asked Maggie to bring me a dip of snuff. And then the two of us sat there just enjoying, until it was time to go in the house and go to bed.

LITERARY ANALYSIS

Shaunte Huff

Dr. Logan

Introduction to Literature

5 May 2011

"Make Something of Yourself": Symbolism in Alice Walker's "Everyday Use"

In her short story "Everyday Use," Alice Walker uses symbolism to give readers a fuller understanding of the narrator's relationship with her two daughters. Household objects, clothing, and fire all work together in the story to depict the narrator's complicated feelings toward her older daughter Dee and her younger daughter Maggie. In some ways the two daughters represent the past and the future, and the narrator's complex attitude toward the two of them reflects her own position between her past heritage and the "new day" Dee talks about.

Although the narrator of the story clearly loves both her daughters, she is honest enough to admit that she has always been a little awed by Dee, the older sister. Dee has gone to school and moved away from home. Maggie, who has stayed at home with her mother, is an object of pity. She acts like "a lame animal" (257). Her mother sometimes forgets that she is not a child anymore. The dress that burned off of Maggie "in little black papery flakes" during the house fire (257) has left her scarred and vulnerable. Dee, on the other hand, comes back to visit wrapped in a bright, voluminous new dress that "throws out heat waves" of its own. Maggie and Dee's dresses are important symbols because they remind us of the dresses and other clothes used in the quilts Dee wants to take with her. The fabric of the quilts is a link to history—the dresses worn by Dee's grandmother, for whom she is named, older fabrics passed down from older relatives, and even a piece of a Union Army uniform from the Civil War. Dee's new dress is probably an African dashiki; she has appropriated it from a heritage so distant none of her family can remember it. And yet, the narrator admits, "as she walks closer, I like it" (259).

The narrator associates Dee with fire and burning. The old house that Dee hated burned down, and while Maggie was burned in the fire, Dee was unharmed. In fact, the way the narrator describes Dee staring at the burning house—"a look of concentration on her face as she watched the last dingy gray board of the house fall in toward the red-hot brick chimney"—leaves us wondering if perhaps Dee somehow caused the house to burn down, through sheer hatred. In high school, Dee read to her mother and Maggie and, according to the narrator, "burned us with a lot of knowledge we didn't necessarily need to know" (257). Dee's wit is a "scalding humor that erupted like bubbles in lye" (258).

Now that Dee has returned home for a visit, she seems to have changed. Instead of wanting to tear down the new house, as her mother fears, Dee takes picture after picture of it. Instead of scorning the old quilts that her mother had offered to her when she went off to college, now Dee wants to take them with her. But we soon see that Dee's new interest in the past consumes her family's history in much the same way a fire would. She takes away the cover and dasher from her mother's churn, even though the churn is full of milk ready to be made into butter. The narrator lets Dee have them, even though she won't be able to make butter without them. They are treasured family heirlooms and it is clear she will miss them from the way she considers the dasher carefully before handing it over to Dee:

> I took it for a moment in my hands. You didn't even have to look close to see where hands pushing the dasher up and down to make butter had left a kind of sink in the wood. In fact, there were a lot of small sinks; you could see where thumbs and fingers had sunk into the wood. It was a beautiful light yellow wood, from a tree that grew in the yard where Big Dee and Stash had lived. (261)

The family's history is physically imprinted on their possessions, through long years of everyday use. Dee wants to take these possessions away and enshrine them, but not touch or use them. Dee disassembles a very useful churn into knick-knacks for her house, saying she will "think of something artistic to do with the dasher" (261). Maggie and her mother live in the midst of their heritage, and use it, and leave their own imprint on it, while Dee relegates it to alcoves and corners.

Dee's disconnect with her history is evident in her own lack of memory. She "never knew" about the grooves in the benches until she sits in them after returning home (261). She doesn't remember that she wants the churn cover and dash until she sees and touches

LITERARY ANALYSIS

the butter dish. She doesn't remember who carved the dasher. She doesn't know why she is named Dee. She has to take photographs of everything, including her family. She does this even before she kisses her mother hello. She needs tangible things to stand in for her past as she moves forward. She sheds her family name and takes another, African one. She is moving back toward a more distant past that she has no real connection with.

Maggie, on the other hand, says. "I can 'member Grandma Dee without the quilts" (262). Maggie is truly attached to the quilts; she is upset that Dee wants them (she drops something in the kitchen and the door slams when Dee asks for them), but she does not need them in order to establish a connection to the past. Maggie knows how to quilt because she learned from her grandmother. "Maggie's brain is like an elephant's" says Dee (261), and she does not seem to mean it as a compliment.

Maggie can make quilts, but Dee is a quilt. She is a pastiche of names, dresses, tastes, loyalties, and desires. Ever since high school she has been re-making herself from the outside—demanding and getting a yellow organdy dress, making over a green suit handed down from someone else. Dee never learned to make quilts because she was too busy re-making herself. She has given up part of her past and wants to put it into a museum, whereas Maggie has kept the past alive. Maggie is all of one piece.

In the end, Walker seems to be saying that neither sister is "right" or "wrong" in living the way they do. Dee's selfish attempts to connect with her past on her own terms are part of her ongoing struggle to better herself, and live her life fearlessly—a trait her mother clearly admires in her. "Who can even imagine me looking a strange white man in the eye? . . . Dee, though. She would always look anyone in the eye" (257). But Maggie's stay-at-home, shy ways, which obviously irritate her mother sometimes, are unimportant when compared to Maggie's memory of her family, her ability to quilt, and her humility. The narrator's moment of inspiration in the story comes when she looks hard at Maggie, whose face has "a kind of dopey, hangdog look," … "with her scarred hands hidden in the folds of her skirt" (263). Maggie, she realizes, has always assumed that Dee was better than her, more deserving of her. She is half afraid of her sister but she still loves her. It is at this moment that the narrator is able to see Maggie's worth clearly, in relation to Dee.

At the beginning of the story, the narrator says that Maggie "thinks her sister had held life always in the palm of one hand, that 'no' is a word the world never learned to say to her" (256). It is when Dee tries to take the quilts promised to Maggie that the world, in the form of the narrator, finally says "no" to Dee—or rather, "yes" to Maggie—by dumping the quilts in her lap.

How to write a rhetorical analysis

These steps for the process of writing a rhetorical analysis may not progress as neatly as this chart might suggest. Writing is not an assembly-line process.

As you write, be open to new insights about the subject you are analyzing. Writing often generates new ideas that you can use to strengthen your analysis.

1 SELECT A TEXT TO ANALYZE

- Examine the assignment.
- Find a text or texts.
- Make an analytical claim.
- Research the context.
- Research the author and audience.

2 ANALYZE CONTEXT AND TEXT

- Consider the medium and genre.
- Identify the main claim or claims.
- Consider the evidence.
- Analyze the appeals.
- Situate the text in its context.
- Consider the style and tone.

3 WRITE A DRAFT

- Select vivid details and dialogue.
- Decide on an organization.
- Craft a strong beginning.
- Conclude by inviting further reflection.
- Consider your voice and tone.
- Choose a title that will interest readers.

4 REVISE, REVISE, REVISE

- Check that your paper or project fulfills the assignment.
- Make sure that the subject is focused.
- Add details, description, or dialogue.
- Make sure your voice and tone will engage readers.
- Examine your organization and think of possible better ways to organize.
- Review the visual presentation.
- Proofread carefully.

5 PRINT A VERSION TO SUBMIT

- Make sure your finished writing meets all formatting requirements.

1: Select a text to analyze

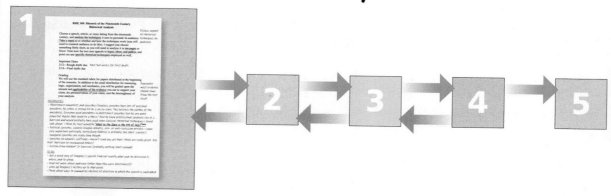

Examine the assignment	• Read your assignment slowly and carefully. Look for the key words *analyze* or *critique*. These key words tell you that you are writing an analysis. • Make a note of any information about the length specified, date due, formatting, and other requirements. You can attend to this information later. At this point you want to zero in on the subject and your analytical claim.
Find a text to analyze	• Look for a text or image that offers an argument or opinion—one that tries to influence the thoughts, feelings, or actions of its audience. • Newspaper editorials, activist websites, speeches, art, and advertisements are all good sources of texts for analysis.
Make an analytical claim	• Ask: What will my analysis reveal for readers that they might not otherwise have realized about the text? • Think about the evidence you will need to support your claim. It may come from the text itself, or from your research into the piece's context.
Research the context	• What else was being written and said about this subject at the time the text was written? • What events were taking place that might have influenced the author?
Research the author and audience	• Who is the author or creator? What else has he or she said on this subject? What motivated him or her to produce this text? • Who is the audience? Where did the text first appear (or, why was this image made or created)? Why did it appear at that particular moment?

Find a verbal text to analyze

Find at least three examples of verbal texts that intend to persuade you in some way. They may ask you to do something specific such as buy a product or vote for a candidate or else they may aim at changing your attitude. Note what makes each text interesting and make a tentative claim.

Text	Deadspin.com blog
What makes it interesting	Takes a humorous look at sports, exposing the pretensions and lack of honesty among sports figures.
Claim	Deadspin.com represents the spirit of many blogs in going for the truth underneath layers of hype and having fun along the way.

Find a visual text to analyze

Identify at least three visual texts for possible analysis. Look for a visual text that in some way attempts to influence the viewer—an advertisement, a public building, a statue, a controversial work of art, a dramatic photograph, a television commercial, or a corporate logo. Note what makes it interesting and make a tentative claim.

Text	Logos of competing political candidates
What makes it interesting	Candidate X's logo appears much better than candidate Y's logo among people I have asked, but they cannot explain why.
Claim	Candidate X has a better logo than candidate Y because the typeface and colours of X's logo express strength, energy, and movement while those on Y's logo suggest indecision and weakness.

Writer at work

Katya Browoski was asked to write an analysis for her Canadian Literature class. Upon receiving the assignment, she made the following notes and observations.

Can 451: National Identity and Literary Themes: A Correlation

Katya began high-
lighting key words
in the assignment
and noting specifics
about the length,
due date, and for-
matting for the
essay.

While Canadian literature shares universal themes with other national literatures, there are some unique features and attitudes of the writing from this country that clearly help to define the Canadian "identity" and its symbiotic relationship to the history and culture of the nation. Analyze one of the "unique" Canadian themes listed below, drawing conclusions from the readings in an attempt to gain insight into our national identity.

Choose 2 or more texts that you feel relate to the themes, and analyze their contents in relation to the question above. Point out the specific relationship to Canadian culture/identity.

Make sure there is a clear relationship to cultural or national identity.

Important dates:
Feb 14: Rough drafts due
Mar 1: final draft due

Grading:
We will use the standard rubric for formal papers distributed at the beginning of the semester. In addition to the usual distribu-tion for analysis, logic, organization, and mechanics, you will be graded on the applicability of the textual evidence you use to support your argument, the clarity of your argument and the thoroughness of your analysis

Remember...most evidence should come from the texts themselves...

She made some comments about some of the readings that might support her assignment

→ POSSIBILITIES:

Of the four themes (survival, manhood/masculinity, cultural schizophrenia, generational conflict) – survival has most relevance to me
Anthology – lots of different historical texts/short stories that could be used; pathos and ethos
Non-fiction support – well-known Can. writers who have identified specific themes in Can lit (e.g., Atwood and Frye)...tie into national character...
Use typical symbols (weather)...good options to show relationship of theme (survival) and identity

→ Fiction: Sinclair Ross (Field of Wheat); Catherine Traill (The Old Doctor) and Thomas Raddall (The Wedding Gift)
Non-Fiction: Survival (Atwood); Frye

After some preliminary reading, she chose several texts to analyze and made a list of research she would need to do

TO DO:
Look for commonalities amongst the short stories
Find/establish relationship to theme of survival – looking up other main symbols of Can lit might help, but may dilute analysis
Think about ways to tie in fiction/nonfiction

2: Analyze context and text

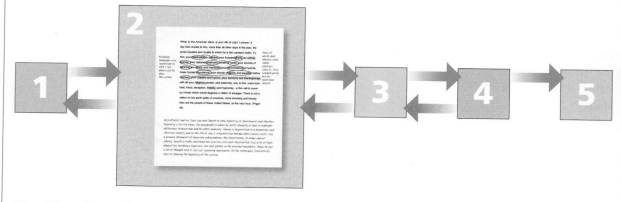

Consider the medium and genre	• What is the medium? • What is the genre of the piece? Is it an editorial? A short story? An advertisement?
Consider the main claim or claims	• Summarize the point, or describe the subject.
Consider the evidence	• Note all the reasons and evidence given to support the claim.
Analyze the appeals	• How is the author presented? As a credible, trustworthy person? • How logical are the arguments? Are there any logical fallacies? • What emotions, if any, does the author appeal to? • How effective is each one of these appeals and techniques? How effective are they all together? Why are they effective or not effective?
Situate the text in its context	• Where do you find evidence that this text was responding to other texts and events? • What does this text contribute to the ongoing conversation of which it is part?
Consider the style and tone	• How would you characterize the style? Is the style formal? Informal? Academic? • How would you characterize the tone? Does the writer or speaker use humour or satire? • How is language used to influence the audience? Repetition? Contrast? Particular word choices? What metaphors are used?

Writer at work

Katya read her chosen texts carefully several times, making notes in the margins about the relationships she saw emerging from the readings. She then wrote an abstract of her findings and used it to help construct an overall approach to her analysis.

Survival—a central symbol in Canadian literature that has both a physical and cultural significance. In early literary examples, it meant "staying alive" in the face of hostile elements (from nature or other people). In other examples, it could refer to surviving a crisis or disaster (often related to climate). Culturally, survival could suggest the "hanging on" as a people, retaining religion, language, and traditions under an alien government. Evident in French Canadian as well as Aboriginal literature, this type of survival can also be applied to the immigrant experience, where new Canadians attempt to invoke the sustaining traditions of the old while adapting to the new.

With Atwood's and Frye's support, the relationship of physical survival, climate, and a cultural identity starts to surface as the main focus of the three readings.

3: Write a draft

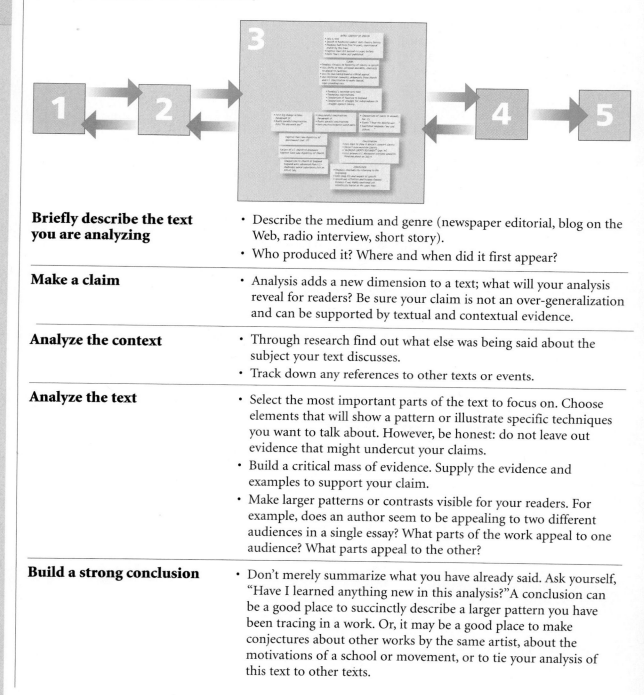

Briefly describe the text you are analyzing

- Describe the medium and genre (newspaper editorial, blog on the Web, radio interview, short story).
- Who produced it? Where and when did it first appear?

Make a claim

- Analysis adds a new dimension to a text; what will your analysis reveal for readers? Be sure your claim is not an over-generalization and can be supported by textual and contextual evidence.

Analyze the context

- Through research find out what else was being said about the subject your text discusses.
- Track down any references to other texts or events.

Analyze the text

- Select the most important parts of the text to focus on. Choose elements that will show a pattern or illustrate specific techniques you want to talk about. However, be honest: do not leave out evidence that might undercut your claims.
- Build a critical mass of evidence. Supply the evidence and examples to support your claim.
- Make larger patterns or contrasts visible for your readers. For example, does an author seem to be appealing to two different audiences in a single essay? What parts of the work appeal to one audience? What parts appeal to the other?

Build a strong conclusion

- Don't merely summarize what you have already said. Ask yourself, "Have I learned anything new in this analysis?" A conclusion can be a good place to succinctly describe a larger pattern you have been tracing in a work. Or, it may be a good place to make conjectures about other works by the same artist, about the motivations of a school or movement, or to tie your analysis of this text to other texts.

Writer at work

Katya Browoski used note cards
to determine an organization for
her paper.

INTRO:
- Start with quote from Atwood about Nature
- Establish context – survival as an "identifier" of Can. culture
- Provide current and past images to show continuity of theme

POINT?
Physical survival, climate, and cultural identity related in Can fiction – survival remains a defining theme of national character

Part I
Environmental harshness affects outcome

Part II
Climate affects relationships of main characters

Part III
Relationship of characters to the land they love/hate

Introduction of Frye's theory to solidify argument

Atwood referenced as support to solidify position

4: Revise, revise, revise

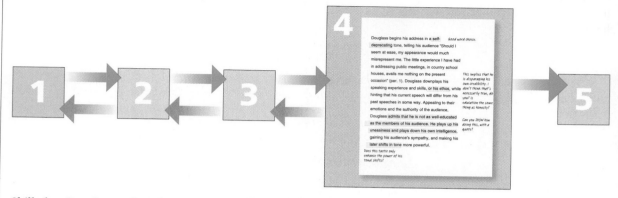

Skilled writers know that the secret to writing well is rewriting. Leave correcting errors for last.

Does your paper or project meet the assignment?

- Look again at your assignment. Does your paper or project do what the assignment asks?
- Check the assignment for specific guidelines, including length, format, and amount of research. Does your work meet these guidelines?

Does your analysis have a clear purpose?

- Does it tell readers something they would not have otherwise noticed?
- Do you make some kind of claim about the work you are analyzing? Is it a debatable claim?

Do you support your analysis with evidence?

- Do you provide a background, intended audience, and the larger conversation surrounding the text(s) you are analyzing?
- Can you provide additional analysis to support your claims?

Is your organization effective?

- Is the order of your main points clear to your reader?
- Are there any places where you find abrupt shifts or gaps?
- Are there sections or paragraphs that could be rearranged to make your draft more effective?

Is the writing project visually effective?

- Is the font attractive and readable?
- Are the headings and visuals effective?

Save the editing for last

- When you have finished revising, edit and proofread carefully.

A peer review guide is on page 31.

Writer at work

Katya received comments from her instructor on her rough draft. She used his comments in conjunction with a visit to the writing centre to revise her draft

Katya received specific feedback on the introduction of her paper, where she establishes the connection between theme and culture.

To see how she responded to the comments, see the submitted paper on page 280.

Katya found several other gaps in her paper, which she fixed by adding more textual references that clearly showed her position. She edited the paper carefully, eliminating redundant quotations, revising syntax, and editing for grammar and spelling.

Is this really what the paper is about?

Not sure why this quotation is relevant...

"The Hostile Canadian Environment"

"Canadian literature is not equivalent to Canadian content" (Atwood 281) Margaret Atwood, believes the theme of survival is an important piece of history in Canadian literature. The hostile Canadian environment has played an important role in Canadian culture and identity since the initial establishment of the "Great White North" as an independent nation. The harsh climate and overwhelmingly vast land is even the main aspect of Canadian living that other cultures use to identify Canada. The hardships associated with this physical struggle in the environment were more significant in earlier years, when resources were scarce and day-to-day life was deeply impacted by the conflict with nature. Naturally, surviving the impingement of the harsh Canadian elements became the norm for early settlers who exerted much of their physical energy into assuring they were able to stay alive and provide for their families. This burdening reality reflected literature of the time and continued to provide an important theme relative to Canadian life in modern literature. Though the theme broadened in ideas over the years and branched out to include other sub genres of survival, the core idea relates back to surviving hostile elements in rough Canadian terrain. Many of the ideas expressed by writers of Canadian literature help support the theme of physical survival within a hostile environment. The Canadian short stories "The Wedding Gift," by Thomas Raddall, "A Field of Wheat," by Sinclair Ross and "The Old Doctor" by Catharine Parr Traill help illustrate key points that support relative themes and portray how hostile environments have an impact on the outcome of the story, how this impact affects the characters and their relationships, and conclusively, how the characters express their own feelings for the great harshness of their surrounding natural environment. Each of these intriguing examples gives the reader a greater understanding of the deep connection between the hostile Canadian environment and its overall impact on Canadian literature whether portrayed in a positive or negative undertone.

Some vague references here...check wording...

What does this exactly mean?

5: Print a version to submit

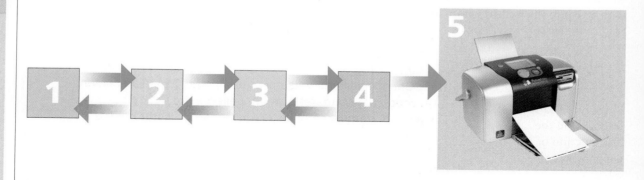

Browoski 1

Katya Browoski
Prof. M. J. Johns
CAN 451
01/03/2011

Survival and Climate:
National Identity in Canadian Literature

"Canadian writers as a whole do not trust Nature, they are always suspecting some dirty trick. An often encountered sentiment is that Nature has betrayed expectation. It was supposed to be different" (Atwood 49). Margaret Atwood, one of Canada's most famous writers, believes that "survival" is an important theme in Canadian literature. Applied to the physical, the challenges created by a difficult climate have played an important role in forming Canadian "character" and identity since the initial founding of the "Great White North" as an independent nation. The harsh climate and overwhelmingly immense land have even become the main attributes of Canadian living that other cultures use to identify this nation. The hardships associated with a physical struggle in the environment were more significant in years of early nationhood, when resources were scarce and day-to-day life was deeply impacted by the conflict with nature.

Naturally, surviving the harsh Canadian elements became the norm for early settlers who exerted much of their physical energy into staying alive and being able to provide for their families. This burdening reality reflected literature of the time and continued to provide an important theme relative to Canadian life in modern literature. Though the theme broadened over the years and branched out to include other sub-genres of survival, the core concept relates back to surviving hostile elements in rough Canadian terrain.

The theme of physical survival within a hostile environment is expressed by many Canadian writers. The short stories "The Wedding Gift," by Thomas Raddall; "A Field of Wheat," by Sinclair Ross; and "The Old Doctor," by Catharine Parr Traill illustrate key points that support survival as a theme and portray how hostile environments have an impact on the outcome of the story, how this impact affects the characters and their relationships, and conclusively, and how the characters express their own feelings for the great harshness of their natural environment. Each of these examples provides a deeper understanding of the profound connection between the hostile Canadian environment and its overall impact on Canadian literature and cultural identity.

Hostile climates have quite a significant impact on the outcome of the story. In the "The Wedding Gift," the harsh conditions offer the young protagonist Kezia "a way out" of an arranged marriage. The freezing temperatures and threatening storm give Kezia a valid reason to bundle up with the priest, for the sake of surviving the night in the harsh climate. "A delicious warmth crept over them. They relaxed in each other's arms. Outside, the storm hissed…" (Raddall 91). The impact of weather was a blessing for Kezia, who used the hostile conditions to her advantage in order secure her own fate, instead of the one that had been dictated to her. In contrast, the challenging climate provides a more negative outcome in the story "A Field of Wheat." The family in this story suffers complete destruction of crops; their home and barn are ravaged as a result of a storm's impact. "This winter they wouldn't have so much as an onion or potato" (Ross 105). This story clearly identifies the hardships Canadian farmers faced because of the unsympathetic weather. In the story "The Old Doctor," there is no major storm that affects the outcome of the story. Deviating slightly, this story is more of a generalized narration that depicts the day-to-day challenges Canadians faced as a result of the stressful environmental conditions. The Old Doctor narrates adversities associated with illness, over-consumption of natural resources, and survival of the fittest:

He had been settled many years in the Province and had seen a great deal of
the ups and downs of life in Canada. The hardships and toils of a
Backwoodsman's life he knew from his constant acquaintance with settlers of
all sorts and conditions. (Parr Traill 20)

Similarly, the harsh Canadian conditions also directly shape the characters and their
relationships. In "The Wedding Gift," each character is affected differently as a result of the
storm. For Mr. Barclay and Mr. Hathaway, the storm has a counteractive effect from that
which they desired, as it allowed Kezia to deceive them as well as the priest in order to
escape the planned marriage. In contrast, the storm provides a positive outcome for Kezia
and begins her new relationship with the priest. "Rolled in the furs once more, their arms
went about each other instinctively, and the young man's face found the comfortable nook
against Kezia's soft throat" (Raddall 93). The hostile elements present the greatest impact
on the relationship between Kezia and the young priest because the storm is the most significant factor that brought them together. To the contrary, the story "A Field of Wheat"
depicts how the unfavourable conditions have similar impact on all of the characters. In
particular, this story illustrates the strained relationship between a husband and wife as a
result of the damaging effects of the storm. "They'd be brave, go on again, forget about
the crop. Go on, go on—next year and the next … But she'd had enough. This time he'd
go on alone (Ross 104). The couple in this story are deeply emotionally and financially
affected as a result of the heartless storm. Their relationship suffers from the stress and
physical threat they experience due to the conditions in which they live. Alternately, "The
Old Doctor" uses people's ability to thrive and flourish in the naturally coarse environment
as a way to judge their character, ethics, and morals. He is apathetic to those who are
inert and wasteful: "Mere bookworms will starve in Canada. Idle hands make no head"
(Parr Traill 21). He builds relationships only with those who work diligently and avoid overuse of natural resources. He has great respect for the environment and relates his personal message to his patients in hopes it will provide them with more knowledge to successfully survive and prosper in their difficult habitat

Although the overall theme of surviving the hostile climate is relatively similar among the
stories, the characters each possess their own feelings and thoughts relative to their living

conditions. Often, the personal views of characters vary greatly between love and respect for the land and fear and loathing of it. In the story "The Wedding Gift," Kezia feels hopeful anticipation that the storm will provide conditions too difficult for her to complete her journey to marry Mr. Hathaway. "Winter. Snow on the ground … But not enough, not nearly enough snow for Miss Kezia Barnes, who was going to Bristol Creek to marry Mr. Hathaway" (Raddall 83). There is no fear of the harsh conditions. In fact, Kezia connects with the great storm as something that will help her avoid her pre-determined fate and takes solace in the face of the dangerous conditions. In contrast, the characters in the story "A Field of Wheat" do not find any comfort in the harsh conditions. The family feels bitterness, rage, and desperation as a result of the impeding weather that threatens to completely destroy their livelihood. In seconds, the heartless conditions shatter the family's life and work. "She tried to face the kitchen to get the floor dried and the broken lamps swept up. But it was not the kitchen; it was tomorrow, next week, next year. The going on, the waste of life, the hopelessness" (Ross 104). The characters only experience the negative side effects of their environment. Similar to Kezia's feelings about the weather, "The Old Doctor" displays no uneasy emotions regarding the natural rough environment. In fact, The Doctor is the only character who expresses complete respect and admiration for the natural beauty and its challenging conditions. He criticizes others for complaining about the difficulties associated with early Canadian life. In his opinion, the climate is "naturally fine" (Parr Traill 19), and it is the actions of humans that damage nature and not the other way around:

> It roused his furious indignation when he beheld the natural beauties of a place
> disfigured, and spots that seemed by nature fitted for man's recreation
> despoiled of trees and turf and crowded with buildings. (Parr Traill 20)

The history of Canadian literature is strongly connected to the theme of physical survival. Over the years, many notable authors analyzed the significance of this theme in relation to identifying Canadian writing. Northrop Frye, a respected Canadian writer and historian, created the term "garrison mentality" to identify the theme of a feared natural environment. Margaret Atwood later revised this idea to specifically include the theme of survival within the Canadian culture and how it directly relates to the relationship between people and the land (Patton 63). "The Wedding Gift," "A Field of Wheat," and "The Old Doctor" represent this important theme in past and contemporary Canadian literature, identifying how physical survival in the harsh elements affected character representations, emotions, and plots. "Reading Canadian literature thus becomes a search for embattled settlers, explorers, families, artists, and ecosystems variously surviving, or not, brute indifferent nature" (Patton 64).

Works Cited

Atwood, Margaret. *Survival: A Thematic Guide to Canadian Literature.* Toronto: McClelland, 1972. Print.

Parr Traill, Catherine. "The Old Doctor: A Backwoods Sketch." *Canadian Short Stories.* Eds. Russell Brown and Donna Bennett. Toronto: Pearson, 2005. 17-22. Print.

Patton, Christopher. "The Garrison Revisited." *Northern Poetry Review.* 2006. 28 July. Web. 10 Jan 2009.

Raddall, Thomas. *The Wedding Gift and Other Stories.* Toronto: McClelland, 1947. Print.

Ross, Sinclair. "A Field of Wheat." *Canadian Short Stories.* Eds. Russell Brown and Donna Bennett. Toronto: Pearson, 2005. 97-105. Print.

Projects

Analyzing is valuable for clarifying and developing your own thinking as well as for giving your readers a broader understanding.

These projects are frequently written kinds of analyses.

RHETORICAL ANALYSIS

For an example of a rhetorical analysis, see pages 234–238.

Select a text to analyze—a speech, a sermon, an editorial, a persuasive letter, an essay, a website, a pamphlet, a brochure, or another kind of text.

Explain briefly what kind of text it is, when and where it was first published or spoken, and its main argument.

Make a claim about the text, which you support with close analysis.

Analyze the context. Is the text part of a larger debate? What other texts or events does it respond to? Who is the author? What motivated the author to write this text? What can you infer about the intended audience?

Analyze the appeals. What appeals to values and emotions are used? What appeals to logic are used? Do you find any logical fallacies (see pages 18–19)? Do you trust the writer?

Analyze the organization and style. What are the major parts and how are they arranged? Is the style formal, informal, satirical, or something else? Are any metaphors used?

VISUAL ANALYSIS

For an example of a visual analysis, see pages 250–251.

Find a visual text to analyze. You might analyze a popular consumer product, a public building, advertising, art, or a map.

Make a claim about the visual text. Support your claim with close analysis. Describe key features.

Analyze the context. Where and when was the visual created? What was the purpose? Who created it? What can you infer about the intended audience?

Analyze the visual text. What kind of visual is it? What is the medium? How is it arranged? How would you characterize the style? Are any words connected?

CRITICAL LITERARY ANALYSIS

For an example of a critical literary analysis, see pages 264–267.

Read carefully a short story or other literary text. Map out the plot. What is the conflict and how is it resolved?

Examine the characterization, including the major and minor characters. Characters are not real people, but instead they are constructed for a purpose. What role does each character perform? The setting, too, is a character. What role does the setting play in the story?

Consider the point of view. Does a character tell the story? Or is the narrator an all-knowing observer? Describe the language, style, and tone of the story. Identify any important images, symbols, and metaphors.

Identify the story's central theme. How does the title of the story relate to the theme?

Write an arguable thesis that connects one or more elements—characters, setting, language, metaphors, and so on—to the overall theme. A paper that begins with an engaging thesis arouses the reader's interest. Support your thesis with evidence from the text. A successful paper shares a discovery with the reader.

13

Analyzing Causes

An effective causal analysis moves beyond the obvious to examine complex underlying causes.

Chapter contents

Writing to analyze causes

Have you ever wondered why your car is hard to start on a cold morning? Why all the shoppers in the supermarket seem to converge on the checkout stands at the same time? Why a company's stock price rises when it announces hundreds of layoffs?

Questions of causation confront us all the time. We spend much of our daily lives puzzling over them—trying to start the car, pick the best time to visit the supermarket, or buy the most valuable stock. Causal investigation also drives scientists, as they search for cures to diseases, try to explain certain behaviours in people and animals, and attempt to predict the weather. In your professional life, you will have to make many detailed causal analyses. You may need to find out why consumers have stopped buying your product suddenly, or why a particular sector of a factory is much more productive than others.

Answering these kinds of questions requires a causal analysis, which typically takes the form "SOMETHING causes (or does not cause) SOMETHING ELSE." The causal claim is at the centre of a causal analysis. Therefore, to get started on a causal analysis, you need to propose one or more causes.

Methods of analyzing causes

Causal analyses can be challenging to write because any topic worth writing about is likely to be complex. Causes can be hard to identify, and there may be more than one cause behind any given phenomenon. The philosopher John Stuart Mill (1806–1873) developed four different methods for finding causes.

1 The Common Factor Method

If you look at all the cases of a phenomenon, and find a single factor that is common to all of them, that common factor is probably the cause. For example, if a number of people in your dormitory all develop symptoms of food poisoning, and it turns out they all ate the potato salad from the cafeteria salad bar the night before, the potato salad is probably the cause of their illness.

2 The Single Difference Method

This method is useful when you have two similar situations, with only one leading to an effect. Look for something that was present in one case and not the other. It is commonly used in scientific experiments under controlled conditions. You might grow a group of identical soybean plants, for example, giving them all equal amounts of light and water, but only feeding fertilizer to half of them. If the fertilized plants grow faster, the fertilizer is probably the cause.

3 Concomitant Variation

This method is also frequently used by scientists, especially when they cannot completely control the conditions they are observing. Investigators look for a similar pattern of variation between a possible cause and a possible effect. If you give different amounts of fertilizer to each soybean plant in the example, and the plants getting the most fertilizer grow the tallest, while the ones getting the least stay the smallest, a causal relationship between fertilizer and accelerated growth is likely.

4 The Process of Elimination

The more complex the set of causes behind a phenomenon, the more likely you are to use the process of elimination. Let's return to the soybean plants from the earlier example. You are fairly certain that adding fertilizer to the plants causes them to grow faster. Yet you notice that some plants have developed spots on their leaves. Some of the spotted plants get a lot of fertilizer, and some only get a little, but they all have a similar number of leaf spots, so the fertilizer is probably not the cause. Upon further investigation, you find that an absentminded professor has been emptying the remains of his diet cola into the spotted plants' pots every evening. Even though conditions among the spotted plants are not identical, it is reasonable to infer that the cola is causing the spotting. It is the only factor "left over" after you have accounted for all the others' impact on the plants.

Which method should I use?

You can use more than one of Mill's methods to evaluate possible causes. For example, the common factor and single difference methods are often combined: If everyone in your dorm who got sick had eaten the potato salad and the fruit cocktail, you would have to find someone who ate the fruit cocktail, but not the potato salad, to determine which food was the cause of illness. If anyone who ate fruit cocktail stayed healthy, you can eliminate it as a possible cause and focus on the potato salad.

Keys to causal analysis

Pay attention to effects

It's not enough to simply identify causes. In order for a causal analysis to matter, you must make clear why the effects are important. Otherwise, readers are apt to ask, "So what?". We often look for causes so that we can prevent something bad from happening, or facilitate something good. You may make the case that the film versions of *101 Dalmatians* led to an increase in the popularity of Dalmation dogs, but your analysis gains more stature if you further explore that effect: many of the puppies bred and sold to people who saw the movie ended up in animal shelters because their new owners were not prepared for such high-energy pets.

Identify what is at stake

Because a strong causal claim may inspire people to change policies or behaviours or take other action, you will find that some members of your audience hold different stakes in the outcome of your analysis. Their stakes can influence the ways and the degree to which they oppose your claim. For example, although the causal link between cigarette smoke and cancer was widely accepted in scientific circles for many years, tobacco companies argued vociferously that no such link existed. Their stake was financial: if their product was shown to cause a serious disease, they stood to lose customers and money.

Move beyond the obvious to identify underlying causes

When people are involved, you can expect causes to be complex. Perhaps the cause you are seeking to link to an effect is only one of several causes. You'll need to address all the contributing causes, not just the one you are focusing on. You should also consider whether one cause arises from another. For example, lower life expectancies among poor people are usually attributable to a number of factors, such as poor nutrition, and dangerous jobs. But some factors that affect life expectancy are indirectly linked to poverty: education level, for example, determines the type of job you can get—and poverty usually makes it much harder to get a good education. A well-thought-out causal analysis will trace multiple causes and consider their cumulative effect.

Avoid mistaking correlation for causation

A common pitfall of causal analysis is confusing causation with correlation. Events can be correlated, or mutually related in some way, without one being the cause of the other. Deaths by drowning and baseball games are correlated. But does one cause the other? Or is it because both occur most frequently in the summer?

Consider a visual explanation of causation

Investigators of accidents often use causal charts to identify the factors that lead to accidents. Accidents almost never happen from a single cause. Most often a combination of factors leads to accidents.

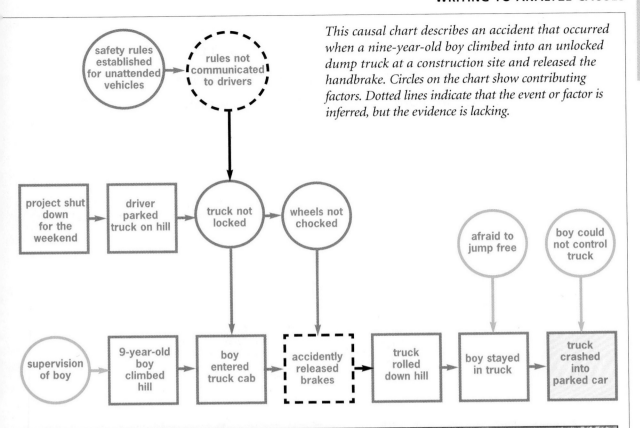

This causal chart describes an accident that occurred when a nine-year-old boy climbed into an unlocked dump truck at a construction site and released the handbrake. Circles on the chart show contributing factors. Dotted lines indicate that the event or factor is inferred, but the evidence is lacking.

WORKING TOGETHER

Find causes

In a group of three or four students

Brainstorm to create a list of "Why?" questions about causes. You list might include questions such as "Why is the sky blue?" or "Why do music CDs cost $15 when DVDs of entire films, with director's cuts, outtakes, and other extras, only cost $19?" Try to come up with at least ten or fifteen questions.

Working together, come up with as many possible causes for each phenomenon as you can. Use your imagination, but stay within the realm of possibility. You might want to arrange your responses from the most plausible to the least plausible.

An effective causal analysis

Effective causal analyses examine the significance of cause-and-effect relationships.

Pesticides, Parasite May Cause Frog Deformities
Stentor Danielson

Over the past ten to fifteen years, more and more frogs have been discovered with deformed, missing, or extra hind legs. Concerned about these abnormalities, scientists worldwide have been searching for the cause. In this *National Geographic News* article from July 2002, science journalist Stentor Danielson looks at a careful study of the interplay between two potential causes: a waterborne parasite and common pesticides.

Pesticides, Parasite May Cause Frog Deformities

Frogs with extra legs or missing legs have been showing up with greater frequency over the past decade, and scientists have been baffled by the cause.

Some researchers have concluded that pesticide runoff from farms is to blame; others say a common parasite is the culprit. Now, a new study suggests that both these factors in combination have disturbed normal development in many frogs, leading to the abnormalities.

The study, published today in the *Proceedings of the National Academy of Sciences*, was based on tests in both the laboratory and the field that were designed to examine the interaction of parasites and pesticides. The research team, led by Joseph Kiesecker, found that only frogs infected by the larvae of a parasite, the trematode worm, developed deformities, but infected frogs exposed to pesticide runoff experienced much higher levels of deformities.

Danielson begins by briefly laying out the problem and by explaining how his article will add to previous discussions: new research indicates that two potential causes need to be considered together in order to get a clear picture of what is happening.

"It is not uncommon now for 20 to 30 percent of the frogs at many locations to have limb deformities," said Kiesecker, an assistant professor of biology at Penn State University.

Abnormalities have been documented in 52 species of amphibians, mainly frogs, in 46 U.S. states and four Canadian provinces, according to the U.S. Geological Survey. Reports of deformed frogs have been particularly common in New England and the Upper Midwest and on the Pacific coast.

Although there is some disagreement about what levels of deformities occur naturally in frog populations, most researchers agree that current levels are above normal.

Kiesecker and other researchers have warned that the physiological problems seen in frogs may foreshadow similar effects on humans.

Infected by Trematodes

During its life cycle, the parasitic trematode depends on several hosts, including pond snails. Tadpoles in ponds with snails pick up trematode larvae, called cercariae. In some cases the cercariae develop into hard cysts, which interfere with the tadpole's metamorphosis into a frog. When the cysts occur in tissue that later develops into legs, the cysts disrupt the animal's normal development and cause duplicate or missing legs.

The trematode also affects people—although not so dramatically as in developing frogs. It's the same parasite that causes "swimmer's itch," a common ailment in people who swim in ponds and lakes. Eventually, the human immune system defeats the cercariae, leaving the victim with just a rash.

Pesticides, Parasite May Cause Frog Deformities

In tropical climates trematodes cause schistosomiasis, a disease that kills millions of people. The World Health Organization estimates that 120 million people worldwide suffer from schistosomiasis.

Kiesecker's team took tadpoles from Centre County, Pennsylvania, and placed them in six local ponds—three affected by pesticide runoff and three pesticide-free. In each

Statistics provide a sense of the scope of the phenomenon. Notice the use of a government source for this information— sources which are usually credible and respected by readers.

At the end of this introductory section, Danielson places an important point about the issue: it could directly affect humans.

Details about one of the causes are explained step-by-step.

pond, the tadpoles were separated into two groups. One group was placed inside a fine mesh that kept out cercariae.

Only the tadpoles that were exposed to cercariae developed deformities. "We learned from the first field experiment that tadpoles have to be exposed to trematode infection for limb deformities to develop," Kiesecker said.

Pesticide Problems

Kiesecker's team then compared the rate of infection between trematode-exposed tadpoles in the different ponds. The team discovered that rates of infection were much higher in the ponds that received pesticide runoff.

This result parallels the finding of a study in 2000 in which frogs from the same pond—that is, those experiencing the same environmental conditions—were found to have similar deformities.

To examine the effects of pesticides on cercariae development, the team conducted lab experiments on four groups of tadpoles—three groups exposed to three common pesticides and a control group. The pesticides were Atrazine, the most commonly used pesticide in North America; Malathion, a common household pesticide that also is used to control insect pests in agricultural fields; and Esfenvalerate, a synthetic pyrethroid pesticide. The tadpoles were all exposed to cercariae.

When they counted the number of cysts that formed in the tadpoles, the researchers found much higher levels in the tadpoles exposed to pesticides. The team also took blood samples before and after the experiments to determine whether the tadpoles' white blood cell count—a measure of immune system health—was affected.

"The tadpoles that we exposed to pesticides had fewer of this particular kind of white blood cell compared to the tadpoles that we did not expose to pesticides, suggesting that pesticides make these animals more susceptible to parasitic infections," Kiesecker said.

Danielson explains how an experiment was designed to isolate possible causes of the limb mutations. The careful control of conditions led to a "single difference" method: the only difference between affected and unaffected frogs was their exposure to cercariae.

The additional variable of exposure to pesticides shows concomitant variation. The rate of malformation among affected frogs fluctuated in direct relation to the amount of exposure to pesticides.

Scientists repeated the pond test under controlled laboratory conditions and got similar results, with more detailed findings. In scientific causal analysis, repeatability of results strengthens the case for causality.

Pesticides have been found to have additional harmful effects on frogs. A study published in April in the *Proceedings of the National Academy of Sciences* found that Atrazine interfered with the sexual development of male frogs in the Midwest, reducing their levels of testosterone to below the levels found in female frogs.

"Atrazine-exposed frogs don't have normal reproductive systems," said Tyrone Hayes, the leader of a team from the University of California at Berkeley. "The males have ovaries in their testes and much smaller vocal organs."

Additional tests give scientists more information about the possible causal chain between pesticides and malformation.

Human Impacts?

Kiesecker said society can learn a lot from the experiments because "amphibians are particularly sensitive to environmental changes that appear to be associated with the recent emergence of new diseases and resurgence of old diseases that infect humans."

Especially disturbing, he added, is that the concentrations of two of the pesticides that caused the deformities in frogs, Esfenvalerate and Atrazine, were low enough for the water to be considered safe for human consumption under Environmental Protection Agency standards.

"Frogs may be a sentinel species that is warning us about the interplay between human-caused environmental change and disease susceptibility," he said, adding: "Hopefully, people will listen."

In other recent research on this problem, a study published in the July 1 issue of *Environmental Science & Technology* indicates that frog deformities may also occur as a result of exposure to ultraviolet (UV) radiation. At levels close to 60 percent of normal sunlight, frogs experienced deformities.

A survey of ponds in the Duluth, Minnesota, area showed that frogs in only three of 26 ponds were at risk of UV-induced deformities, because wetlands absorb a significant portion of the radiation. However, Steve Diamond of the Environmental Protection Agency's Duluth office and leader of the UV study said there may be cause for concern if human activities cause UV levels to rise.

Danielson closes by reminding readers of the possibility that the cause-and-effect relationship at work in frogs might have parallels for humans.

How to read causal analyses

Make notes as you read, either in the margins, if it is your copy, or on paper or a computer file. Circle any words or references that you don't know and look them up.

What is it?	• What kind of a text is it? An article? An essay? A chart? A scientific report? A website? An executive summary? What are your expectations for this kind of text? • What media are used? (Websites, for example, often combine images, words, and sounds.)
Where did it come from?	• Who wrote the analysis? • Where did it first appear? In a book, newspaper, magazine, online, in a company, or in an organization?
What is the writer's thesis or main idea?	• What is the writer's topic? What effect is he or she trying to determine the cause of? • Why is this topic important? • What are the key ideas or concepts that the writer considers? • What are the key terms? How does the writer define those terms?
Who is the intended audience?	• What clues do you find about whom the writer had in mind as the readers? • What does the writer assume that the readers already know about the subject? • What new knowledge is the writer providing?
How are causes analyzed?	• What methods does the writer use to determine causation? • Does the writer consider multiple causes? • How complex is the analysis? Does the writer examine relationships between causes, or look at how one cause may arise from another? • Can you think of other causes that the writer doesn't consider?
What kinds of evidence are given?	• Is the evidence from books, newspapers, periodicals, the Web, or field research? • Is the evidence convincing that the causes given are the actual causes?
How is it composed?	• How does the writer represent herself or himself? • How would you characterize the style? • How effective is the design? Is it easy to read? • If there are any photographs, charts, or other graphics, what information do they contribute?

Canadian Women on Their Own Are the Poorest of the Poor

(EDITORIAL)

Monica Townson

Analyzing and Connecting

Return to these questions after you have finished reading.

1. Through statistics, Townson paints a very stark picture of the plight of women in Canada. Why does she use this strategy at the beginning of this piece? What purpose does it serve?

2. What cause[s] does Townson identify as the root of women's poverty? Can you speculate on what other variables could be considered contributing factors?

3. What other arguments have you previously encountered about poverty in Canada? Who made these arguments? Which were most convincing?

4. According to the conclusion, what is the overriding cause of women's poverty? How does this change the point of the editorial?

Canadian Women on Their Own Are Poorest of the Poor

by Monica Townson
September 8, 2009

Only 9% of all Canadians were considered poor in 2007. It was the lowest rate of low income in 30 years. But that was before the recession hit last fall. We don't yet have income data for 2008, but, if past experience is anything to go by, poverty rates will go up again as declining economic growth shows up in the numbers. And that's bad news for women whose high rates of poverty remain unaddressed.

Women on their own are the poorest of the poor, especially women raising children in lone-parent families, who are almost five times more likely to be poor than those in two-parent families. Yet their plight has been virtually ignored by the policy-makers. Older women on their own are also 13 times more likely to be poor than seniors living in families, with more than 14% of them having had low incomes in 2007. That these two groups of women had such high rates of poverty, at a time when poverty rates for others had dropped to relatively low levels, must surely be a cause for serious concern.

Women are also among the poorest of the poor within Canada's most vulnerable populations: Aboriginal people, people from racialized communities, recent immigrants (many of whom are also from racialized communities), and persons with disabilities. As one report puts it, "Gender creates a cleavage of vulnerability that cuts across all other groups."

The roots of women's poverty can be found in the way they are treated when they are in paid employment, and the situation in which they find themselves if they are not. Women who work full-time year-round earn only 71% of the average earnings of men working full-time. Wage gaps between women and men are even higher when hourly wage rates are compared. Most women don't have pension plans at work, nor do most men, but women's low wages make it almost impossible for them to save for retirement.

Public pension plans such as Old Age Security and the Canada Pension Plan provide only a basic income for seniors. Retirement pensions from the CPP, for example, are intended to replace earnings. But women's low earnings during their working life are reflected in the retirement pensions they get from the CPP. In a year when the maximum CPP retirement pension is $908.75 a month, the average monthly retirement pension being paid to women who retired in May 2009 was only $391.29, compared with an average of $564.23 a month for retired men.

In many provinces, attempts to reduce poverty have focused on getting people off welfare and into jobs. But paid work for women coming off welfare may simply mean they are joining the ranks of the working poor. Women's jobs are much more likely to be part-time, contract work, working through a temporary help agency, or working on their own. And lack of affordable child care also limits women's choices of paid employment. Almost 40% of women's jobs, compared with 30% of men's jobs, are poorly paid, with little job security and no benefits such as pensions.

Women account for 60% of minimum-wage workers, but minimum wages in all provinces are less than $10 an hour, making it virtually impossible for these workers to earn a decent living. Women are unlikely to get EI benefits when they are out of work: only 39% of unemployed women compared with 45% of unemployed men are receiving benefits.

Single-parent mothers on welfare have seen their incomes fall sharply when inflation is taken into account. In Ontario, for example, the income of a lone parent with one child dropped by over $5,900 between 1994 and 2006.

A key objective of policies to deal with the recession must surely be to protect those who are most vulnerable. That's why the issue of women's equality must be put back on the policy agenda. We can't use the current economic recession as an excuse to postpone taking action on the continuing poverty in which many women find themselves. In these uncertain times, our commitment to protect those who are most vulnerable matters more than ever.

If You Build It, They Will Come—on Foot

(ESSAY)

Jay Walljasper

Jay Walljasper was the editor of *Utne Magazine* for ten years and has written frequently about positive social and political initiatives for newspapers and magazines. He is now the Executive Editor of *Ode Magazine*, where this essay first appeared in 2005.

Analyzing and Connecting

Return to these questions after you have finished reading.

1. Notice how Walljaspar piles up examples beginning with Copenhagen. Why does he use this strategy? At what point do you know his thesis?

2. The trend of creating new public spaces runs counter to the trends of people spending more time in front of computers and watching television. How does Walljaspar explain the causes of this trend?

3. Architect Jan Gehl makes the claim that people anywhere will gather in public if you give them a good place to do it. Is a "good place" the only factor in getting people to gather? Why then have so many attempts at pedestrian malls and other public spaces been unsuccessful?

4. Visit a public space in your city or town. How new is it? Are people using it frequently? What kinds of activities do they do in this space?

If You Build It, They Will Come—on Foot

It's a dark and wintry night in Copenhagen, and the streets are bustling. The temperature stands above freezing, but winds blow hard enough to knock down a good share of the bicycles parked all around. Scandinavians are notorious for their stolid reserve, but it's all smiles and animated conversation here as people of many ages and affiliations stroll through the city center on a Thursday evening.

A knot of teenage boys, each outfitted with a slice of pizza, swagger down the main pedestrian street. Older women discreetly inspect shop windows for the coming spring fashions. An accomplished balalaika player draws a small crowd in a square as he jams with a very amateur guitarist. Earnest young people collect money for UNICEF relief efforts. A surprising number of babies in strollers are out for a breath of fresh January air. Two African men pass by, pushing a piano. Several stylishly dressed women sit at the edge of a waterless fountain, talking on mobile phones. Candlelit restaurants and cafes beckon everyone inside.

"Cultures and climates differ all over the world," notes architect Jan Gehl, "but people are the same. They will gather in public if you give them a good place to do it." Gehl, an urban design professor at the Danish Royal Academy of Fine Arts and international consultant, has charted the progress of Copenhagen's central pedestri-

an district since it opened in 1962. At that time cars were overrunning the city, and the pedestrian zone was conceived as a way to bring vitality back to the declining urban center. "Shopkeepers protested vehemently that it would kill their businesses," he recalls, "but everyone was happy with it once it started. Some now even claim it was their idea."

The pedestrian zone has been expanded a bit each year ever since, with parking spaces gradually removed and biking and transit facilities improved. Cafes, once thought to be an exclusively Mediterranean institution, have become the center of Copenhagen's social life. Gehl documents that people's use of the area has more than tripled over the past 40 years. The pedestrian district is now the thriving heart of a reinvigorated city.

Copenhagen's comeback gives hope to growing numbers of citizens around the world who want to make sure that lively public places don't disappear in this era of rampant traffic, proliferating malls, heightened security measures, overpowering commercialization, and the general indifference of many who think the internet and their own families can provide all the social interaction they need.

While only a century ago streets almost everywhere were crowded with people, many are now nearly empty—especially in the fast-growing suburbs sprouting all over the globe, but in some

WALLJASPER: IF YOU BUILD IT, THEY WILL COME—ON FOOT

Bryant Park in midtown Manhattan was neglected for much of the twentieth century and became the turf of drug dealers through the early 1980s. Today it is one of the most popular public spaces in New York City.

older towns and cities, too. Walking through the center of certain North American communities can be a profoundly alienating experience, as if the whole place had been evacuated for an emergency that no one told you about.

Even in the crowded urban quarters of Asia and Africa, public spaces are suffering under the onslaught of increasing traffic and misguided development plans imported from the West. The decline of public places represents a loss far deeper than simple nostalgia for the quiet, comfortable ways of the past. "The street, the square, the park, the market, the playground are the river of life," explains Kathleen Madden, one of the directors of the New York-based Project for Public Spaces, which works with citizens around the world to improve their communities.

Public spaces are favorite places to meet, talk, sit, look, relax, play, stroll, flirt, eat, drink, smoke, peoplewatch, read, soak in sunshine and feel part of a broader whole. They are the starting point for all community, commerce and democracy. Indeed, on an evolutionary level, the future of the human race depends on public spaces. It's where young women meet and court with young men—an essential act for the propagation of the species.

Numerous studies in fields ranging from social psychology to magazine cover design have proved that nothing grabs people's attention more than other people, especially other people's faces. We are hard-wired with a desire for congenial places to gather. That's why it's particularly surprising how much we overlook the importance of public places today.

"If you asked people 20 years ago why they went to central Copenhagen, they would have said it was to shop," observes Jan Gehl, sitting in the former navy barracks that houses his "urban quality" consulting firm Gehl + Associates. "But if you asked them today, they would say it was because they wanted to go to town." That small change of phrase represents the best hope for the future of public spaces. Historically, Gehl explains, public spaces were central to everyone's lives. It's how people traveled about town, where they shopped and socialized.

Living in cramped homes, often with no yards, and certainly no cars or refrigerators, they had little choice but to use public spaces. Walking was most people's way to get around. Urban families depended on markets and shopping districts for the day's food. Parks were the only place for kids to play or see nature. Squares and churches and taverns were the few spots to meet friends.

But all that changed during the 20th century. Cars took over the streets in industrialized nations (and in wide swaths of the developing world too), putting many more places within easy reach but making walking and biking dangerous. Towns and cities spread out, with many merchants moving to outlying shopping malls. Telephones, refrigerators, television, computers, and suburban homes with big yards transformed our daily lives. People withdrew from the public realm.

No longer essential, public spaces were neglected. Many newly constructed communities simply forgot about sidewalks, parks, downtowns, transit, playgrounds, and people's pleasure in taking a walk after dinner and bumping into their neighbors. Today, many folks wonder if public spaces serve any real purpose anymore. "Some places have gone down the drain and become completely deserted," Gehl notes, brandishing a photo to prove his point. "See this, it's a health club in Atlanta, in America. It's built on top of seven stories of parking. People there don't go out on the streets. They even drive their cars to the health club to walk and get exercise.

"But other places have decided to do something about it—they fight back," he adds, pointing to another photo, a street scene in Norway, where dozens of people are enjoying themselves at an outdoor cafe alongside a sidewalk filled with people. Gehl ticks off a list of places that have revitalized themselves by creating great public places: Copenhagen; Barcelona, Spain; Lyon, France; Bogota, Colombia;

Vancouver, Canada; the American city of Portland, Ore.; and the small Danish city of Vejle. His definitive book *New City Spaces* (2000, Danish Architectural Press), written with partner Lars Gemzoe, includes more success stories from Cordoba, Argentina; Melbourne, Australia; Curitiba, Brazil; Freiburg, Germany; and Strasbourg, France.

Melbourne made great efforts to keep its streets pedestrian-friendly by widening sidewalks and adding attractive features that ignited a spectacular increase in people going out in public. Cordoba turned its riverfront into a series of popular parks. Curitiba pioneered an innovative bus rapid transit system that prevented traffic from overwhelming the fast-growing city.

Portland put curbs on suburban sprawl and transformed a ho-hum downtown into a bustling urban magnet, starting by demolishing a parking garage to build a town square. Barcelona and Lyon best illustrate the power of public spaces. Once thought of as dull industrial centers, both are now widely celebrated as sophisticated, glamorous places that attract international attention and instill local residents with a sense of pride.

Barcelona is now mentioned in the same breath as Paris and Rome as the epitome of a great European city. The heart of Barcelona—and of Barcelona's revival—is Las Ramblas, a pedestrian promenade so popular it has spawned a new Spanish word: Ramblistas, meaning the folks who hang out in the area. In the spirit of liberation following the end of the Franco dictatorship, during which time public assembly was severely discouraged, local citizens and officials created new squares and public spaces all across the city and suburbs to celebrate the return of democracy and heal the scars of political and civic repression. Some of them fit so well with the urban fabric of the old city that visitors often assume they are centuries old.

Creating popular public places yields substantial economic return in the form of business investment, strengthened local economies and tourism, while enhancing the quality of existing public spaces can bring rewards to an already prosperous area. Take New York's Bryant Park, which was off-limits to most citizens in the early 1980s due to non-stop drug dealing. A renovation of the park, which tore out the shrubbery that gave drug dealers a sense of privacy and added ample seating to invite everyone else back, has transformed the place into one of New York's most beloved gathering spots.

The key to restoring life to our public places—and our communities as a whole—is understanding that most people today have more options than in the past. A trip downtown or to the farmer's market or the local library is now recreational as much as it is practical—the chance to have fun, hang out with other folks, and enjoy the surroundings. "People are not out in public spaces because they have to but because they love to," Gehl explains.

If the idea of a new movement rising up to change the face of communities all around the planet strikes you as far-fetched, consider the Crossroads mall in Bellevue, Washington. A standard-issue, auto-dominated suburb east of Seattle, Bellevue seems way off-the-radar of any upsurge to promote lively public spaces. Especially Crossroads, a '70s-era enclosed mall surrounded by acres of parking a mile south of Microsoft's sprawling campus.

But look again. Whimsical public art dots the parking lot, and cafe tables and sidewalk merchandise displays flank the entrances—just like in a classic downtown. An impressively well-stocked newsstand greets you in the hall of the main entrance, right next to a used bookstore. Wandering through the mall you find the local public library, a police station and a branch of city hall, where I am told "you can do nearly everything they do at the main office." There are even comfy chairs stationed right outside the bathrooms and a giant-sized chess board where kids can push around pawns and bishops almost as big as they are.

Some of the usual franchise suspects are here: Bed, Bath and Beyond; a JoAnn fabrics superstore; a Pier One home furnishings store, but you'll find locally owned businesses too, like a wine shop and a ceramics studio. The food court—where you can choose among Indian, Russian, Thai, Mexican, Korean, Greek, barbecue, Vietnamese, Italian, a juice bar or a burger joint—features local restaurateurs. Breakfast, lunch or dinner arrive on a ceramic plate with metal (not plastic!) cutlery.

Many of the tables face a stage, where on this particular Thursday Black History Month is being observed with an impressive program of music, theatre and dance—all of it first rate. The audience is multiethnic, reflecting the changing demographics of American suburbia. The loudest applause comes from a delegation of preschoolers visiting from a nearby daycare center.

Ron Sher, who transformed Crossroads from a failing mall into a spirited gathering place, sits down with me for lunch and, in between greeting customers and conducting mini-meetings with shop owners, outlines the next phase of his vision. "I want a mix of upscale and affordable housing built on a part of the parking lot, so this could become a true town square that some people walk to." I pinch myself to make sure this is all real, that I am actually talking to a shopping center developer who is telling me, "I want to get people together with the city to discuss how to step this up to be even more of a community center."

Now, of course, I would prefer to hang out in Copenhagen, or Barcelona, or the famous Pike Place market in downtown Seattle. So would many of the people in Bellevue. But the fact is they live in Bellevue, and it's a great thing they have a mall where they can take care of their errands, meet their neighbors and have some fun. If a lively public place can take root here, it can happen anywhere.

Why Should I Be Nice To You? Coffee Shops and the Politics of Good Service
(ESSAY)

Emily Raine

Emily Raine recently received a Master's degree in Communication Studies at McGill University in Montreal. She also writes about graffiti and street art. This essay appeared in the online journal *Bad Subjects* in 2005.

Analyzing and Connecting

Return to these questions after you have finished reading.

1. What exactly is Raine's causal argument about why work in coffee chains is worse than in other kinds of service jobs?

2. Raine mixes technical terms with informal language. For example, she says "café labor is heavily grounded in the rationalism of Fordist manufacturing principles," which is the technical term for the method of assembly-line production developed by Henry Ford. But she says she "felt like an aproned Coke machine." Look for other examples of technical and informal language. Why does she mix them?

3. Why is it important from the employer's perspective that coffee shop employees not act like individuals?

4. Have you ever worked in a restaurant, coffee shop, retail store, or another service industry? If so, how was your experience similar to or different from Raine's? If not, think about your experiences as a customer in coffee shops and similar businesses. How did the employees behave?

5. Look at the last paragraph. Raine makes a new claim that rudeness allows workers to retain their individuality. Why does she put this claim in the conclusion? Does it lead to a strong conclusion?

eserver » bad home » bad editorials » 2006 » raza/race: why support immigrants?

Bad Subjects

home   about   articles   authors   books   contact us   **editorials**   links   news   reviews

Why Should I Be Nice To You?
Coffee Shops and the Politics of Good Service

"There is no more precious commodity than the relationship of trust and confidence a company has with its employees."

–Starbucks Coffee Company
Chairman Howard Schultz

I actually like to serve. I'm not sure if this comes from some innate inclination to mother and fuss over strangers, or if it's because the movement and sociability of service work provides a much-needed antidote to the solitude of academic research, but I've always found something about service industry work satisfying. I've done the gamut of service jobs, from fine dining to cocktail waitressing to hip euro-bistro counter work, and the only job where I've ever felt truly whipped was working as a barista at one of the now-ubiquitous specialty coffee chains, those bastions of jazz and public solitude that have spread through urban landscapes over the last ten years or so. The pay was poor, the shifts long and oddly dispersed, the work boring and monotonous, the managers demanding, and the customers regularly displayed that unique spleen that emerges in even the most pleasant people before they've had the morning's first coffee. I often felt like an aproned Coke machine, such was the effect my sparkling personality had on the clientele. And yet, some combination of service professionalism, fear of termination and an imperative to be "nice" allowed me to suck it up, smile and continue to

Bad Subjects

home   about   articles   authors   books   contact us   **editorials**   links   news   reviews

provide that intangible trait that the industry holds above all else; good service.

Good service in coffee shops doesn't amount to much. Unlike table service, where interaction with customers spans a minimum of half an hour, the average contact with a café customer lasts less than ten seconds. Consider how specialty cafés are laid out: the customer service counter is arranged in a long line that clients move along to "use" the café. The linear coffee bar resembles an assembly line, and indeed, café labor is heavily grounded in the rationalism of Fordist manufacturing principles, which had already been tested for use in hospitality services by fast food chains. Each of the café workers is assigned a specific stage in the service process to perform exclusively, such as taking orders, using the cash registers, or handing clients cups of brewed coffee.

The specialization of tasks increases the speed of transactions and limits the duration of any one employee's interaction with the clientele. This means that in a given visit a customer might order from one worker, receive food from the next, then brewed coffee or tea from yet another, then pay a cashier before proceeding down the line of the counter, finishing the trip at the espresso machine which is always situated at its end. Ultimately, each of the café's products is processed and served by a different employee, who repeats the same preparation task for hours and attends to each customer only as they receive that one product.

Needless to say, the productive work in cafés is dreary and repetitive. Further, this style of service severely curtails interaction with the clientele, and the very brevity of each transaction precludes much chance for authentic friendliness or conversation—even asking about someone's day would slow the entire operation. The one aspect of service work that can be unpredictable—people—becomes redundant, and interaction with customers is reduced to a fatiguing eight hour long smile and the repetition of sentiments that allude to good service, such as injunctions to enjoy their purchases or to have a nice day. Rather than friendly exchanges with customers, barista workers' good

Bad Subjects

home   about   articles   authors   books   contact us   **editorials**   links   news   reviews

service is reduced to a quick rictus in the customer's direction between a great deal of friendly interaction with the espresso machine.

As the hospitality industry really took off in the sixties, good service became one of the trademarks of its advertising claims, a way for brands to distinguish themselves from the rest of the pack. One needn't think too hard to come up with a litany of service slogans that holler the good graces of their personnel—at Starbucks where the baristas make the magic, at PSA where smiles aren't just painted on, or at McDonald's where smiles are free. Employee friendliness emerged as one of the chief distinguishing brand features of personal services, which means that the workers themselves become an aspect of the product for sale.

Our notions of good service revolve around a series of platitudes about professionalism—we're at your service, with a smile, where the customer's always right—each bragging the centrality of the customer to everything "we" do. Such claims imply an easy and equal exchange between two parties: the "we" that gladly serves and the "you" that happily receives. There is, however, always a third party involved in the service exchange, and that's whoever has hired the server, the body that ultimately decides just what the dimensions of good service will be.

Like most employees, a service worker sells labor to an employer at a set rate, often minimum wage, and the employer sells the product of that labor, the service itself, at market values. In many hospitality services, where gratuities make up the majority of employment revenue, the worker directly benefits from giving good service, which of course translates to good tips. But for the vast majority of service staff, and particularly those employed in venues yielding little or no gratuities—fast food outlets, café chains, cleaning and maintenance operations—this promises many workers little more than a unilateral imperative to be perpetually bright and amenable.

The vast majority of service personnel do not spontaneously produce an unaffected display of cheer and good will continuously for the duration of a

Bad **Subjects**

shift. When a company markets its products on servers' friendliness, they must then monitor and control employees' friendliness, so good service is defined and enforced from above. Particularly in chains, which are premised upon their consistent reproduction of the same experience in numerous locations, organizations are obliged to impose systems to manage employees' interaction their customers. In some chains, namely the fast food giants such as McDonald's and Burger King, employee banter is scripted into cash registers, so that as soon as a customer orders, workers are cued to offer, "would you like a dessert with that?" (an offer of dubious benefit to the customer) and to wish them a nice day. Ultimately, this has allowed corporations to be able to assimilate "good service"—or, friendly workers— into their overall brand image.

While cafés genuflect toward the notion of good service, their layouts and management styles preclude much possibility of creating the warmth that this would entail. Good service is, of course, important, but not if it interferes with throughput. What's more, these cafés have been at the forefront of a new wave of organizations that not only market themselves on service quality but also describe employees' job satisfaction as the seed from which this flowers.

Perhaps the most glaring example of this is Starbucks, where cheerful young workers are displayed behind elevated counters as they banter back and forth, calling out fancy Italian drink names and creating theatre out of their productive labour. Starbucks' corporate literature gushes not only about the good service its customers will receive, but about the great joy that its "partners" take in providing it, given the company's unique ability to "provide a great work environment and treat each other with respect and dignity," and where its partners are "emotionally and intellectually committed to Starbucks success." In the epigraph to this essay, Starbucks' chairman even describes the company's relationship with its workers as a commodity. Not only does Starbucks offer good service, but it attempts to guarantee something even better: good service provided by employees that are genuinely happy to give it.

eserver » bad home » bad editorials » 2006 » raza/race: why support immigrants?

Bad Subjects

home   about   articles   authors   books   contact us   **editorials**   links   news   reviews

Starbucks has branded a new kind of worker, the happy, wholesome, perfume-free barista. The company offers unusual benefits for service workers, including stock options, health insurance, dental plans and other perks such as product discounts and giveaways. Further, they do so very, very publicly, and the company's promotional materials are filled with moving accounts of workers who never dreamed that corporate America could care so much. With the other hand, though, the company has smashed unionization drives in New York, Vancouver and at its Seattle roaster; it schedules workers at oddly timed shifts that never quite add up to full-time hours; the company pays only nominally more than minimum wage, and their staffs are still unable to subsist schlepping lattes alone.

Starbucks is not alone in marketing itself as an enlightened employer. When General Motors introduced its Saturn line, the new brand was promoted almost entirely on the company's good relations with its staff. The company's advertising spots often featured pictures of and quotes from the union contract, describing their unique partnership between manufacturer, workers and union, which allowed blue-collar personnel to have a say in everything from automobile designs to what would be served for lunch. The company rightly guessed that this strategy would go over well with liberal consumers concerned about the ethics of their purchases. Better yet, Saturn could market its cars based on workers' happiness whether personnel were satisfied or not, because very few consumers would ever have the chance to interact with them.

At the specialty coffee chains, however, consumers have to talk to employees, yet nobody ever really asks. The café service counter runs like a smooth piece of machinery, and I found that most people preferred to pretend that they were interacting with an appliance. In such short transactions, it is exceedingly difficult for customers to remember the humanity of each of the four to seven people they might interact with to get their coffees. Even fast food counters have one server who processes each customer's order, yet in cafés the workers just become another gadget in the well-oiled café machine. This is a definite downside for the employees—clients are much ruder to café

Bad Subjects

home   about   articles   authors   books   contact us   **editorials**   links   news   reviews

staff than in any other sector of the industry I ever worked in. I found that people were more likely to be annoyed than touched by any reference to my having a personality, and it took no small amount of thought on my part to realize why.

Barista workers are hired to represent an abstract category of worker, not to act as individuals. Because of the service system marked by short customer interaction periods and a homogenous staff, the services rendered are linked in the consumer imagination to the company and not to any one individual worker. Workers' assimilation into the company image makes employees in chain service as branded as the products they serve. The chain gang, the workers who hold these eminently collegiate after-school jobs, are proscribed sales scripts and drilled on customer service scenarios to standardize interactions with customers. The company issues protocols for hair length, color and maintenance, visible piercings and tattoos as well as personal hygiene and acceptable odorific products. Workers are made more interchangeable by the use of uniforms, which, of course, serve to make the staff just that. The organization is a constant intermediary in every transaction, interjecting its presence in every detail of the service experience, and this standardization amounts to an absorption of individuals' personalities into the corporate image.

Many of the measures that chains take to secure the homogeneity of their employees do not strike us as particularly alarming, likely because similar restrictions have been in place for several hundred years. Good service today has inherited many of the trappings of the good servant of yore, including prohibitions against eating, drinking, sitting or relaxing in front the served, entering and exiting through back doors and wearing uniforms to visually mark workers' status. These measures almost completely efface the social identities of staff during work hours, providing few clues to workers' status in their free time. Contact between service workers and their customers is thus limited to purely functional relations, so that the public only see them as workers, as makers of quality coffee, and never as possible peers.

Bad Subjects

home   about   articles   authors   books   contact us   **editorials**   links   news   reviews

Maintaining such divisions is integral to good service because this display of class distinctions ultimately underlies our notions of service quality. Good service means not only serving well, but also allowing customers to feel justified in issuing orders, to feel okay about being served—which, in turn, requires demonstrations of class difference and the smiles that suggest servers' comfort with having a subordinate role in the service exchange.

Unlike the penguin-suited household servant staffs whose class status was clearly defined, service industry workers today often have much more in common from a class perspective with those that they serve. This not only creates an imperative for them to wear their class otherness on their sleeves, as it were, but also to accept their subordinate role to those they serve by being unshakably tractable and polite.

Faith Popcorn has rather famously referred to the four-dollar latte as a "small indulgence," noting that while this is a lot to pay for a glass of hot milk, it is quite inexpensive for the feeling of luxury that can accompany it. In this service climate, the class status of the server and the served—anyone who can justify spending this much on a coffee—is blurry, indeed. Coffee shops that market themselves on employee satisfaction assert the same happy servant that allows politically conscientious consumers who are in many cases the workers' own age and class peers, to feel justified in receiving good service. Good service—as both an apparent affirmation of subordinate classes' desire to serve and as an enforced one-sided politeness—reproduces the class distinctions that have historically characterized servant-served relationships so that these are perpetuated within the contemporary service market.

The specialty coffee companies are large corporations, and for the twenty-somethings who stock their counters, barista work is too temporary to bother fighting the system. Mostly, people simply quit. Dissatisfied workers are stuck with engaging in tactics that will change nothing but allow them to make the best of their lot. These include minor infractions such as taking liberties with the uniforms or grabbing little bits of company time for their own pleasure, what Michel de Certeau calls *la perruque* and the companies themselves call

Bad Subjects

"time theft." As my time in the chain gang wore on, I developed my own tactic, the only one I found that jostled the customers out of their complacency and allowed me to be a barista and a person.

There is no easy way to serve without being a servant, and I have always found that the best way to do so is to show my actual emotions rather than affecting a smooth display of interminable patience and good will. For café customers, bettering baristas' lots can be as simple as asking about their day, addressing them by name—any little gesture to show that you noticed the person behind the service that they can provide. My tactic as a worker is equally simple, but it is simultaneously an assertion of individual identity at work, a refusal of the class distinctions that characterize the service environment and a rebuttal to the companies that would promote my satisfaction with their system: be rude. Not arbitrarily rude, of course—customers are people, too, and nobody gains anything by spreading bad will. But on those occasions when customer or management behavior warranted a zinging comeback, I would give it.

Rudeness, when it is demanded, undermines companies' claims on workers' personal warmth and allows them to retain their individuality by expressing genuine rather than affected feelings in at-work interpersonal exchanges. It is a refusal of the class distinctions that underlie consumers' unilateral prerogative of rudeness and servers' unilateral imperative to be nice. It runs contrary to everything that we have been taught, not only about service but about interrelating with others. But this seems to be the only method of asserting one's person-hood in the service environment, where workers' personalities are all too easily reduced to a space-time, conflated with the drinks they serve. Baristas of the world, if you want to avoid becoming a green-aproned coffee dispensary, you're just going to have to tell people off about it.

I'm So Tired: What Your Brain Might Be Trying to Tell You

(WEB ARTICLE)

Catherine Pratt

In this article, Catherine Pratt, a self-confidence specialist, looks at the possible causes of a very common complaint.

Analyzing and Connecting

Return to these questions after you have finished reading.

1. Pratt's analysis traces a plausible chain of causation, but her argument is far from conclusive. How do her claims stand up to the various methods of determining causation outlined in this chapter?

2. What is noticeably absent in this article is supporting evidence from outside sources. In what ways does this impact the validity of her analysis?

3. Examine the tone and structure of this piece. Who is the intended audience? What elements from the writing helped you to form this position?

4. The article concludes with a very simplistic solution. Why was it written this way? What purpose would it serve?

I'm So Tired: What Your Brain Might Be Trying to Tell You

by Catherine Pratt
www.Life-With-Confidence.com

"I'm so tired today"

How many times during the day do you hear people say this? Often just hearing someone say those four words will suddenly make you feel tired too even if you weren't just a few minutes before. The thought of being so tired has now entered your mind. One way to prevent this it to just become aware of what's influencing you. In this case, you could counteract it with the thought of "I feel full of energy today."

Thoughts like the one above can influence how you feel but your brain may also be trying to tell you something. If you're not listening, the mind may try to make you slow down or even stop what you're doing by making you feel more and more tired. If you feel exhausted all the time, it makes it really tough to feel confident about yourself and to do the activities that increase your self esteem. It's important to figure out why you're feeling the way you do.

Here are some reasons why you might be feeling so tired:

Are you bored?

If you're bored with your job or your personal life, you're going to feel tired. It's amazing how much your attitude towards life will affect how you feel.

Here's an example: you come home from work and just collapse on the couch because you're so tired. You have no desire to move and don't want to do anything. The phone rings. It's your best friend, and he's just won backstage tickets to a band that you love. How do you feel now? Five minutes ago you were dead tired. Now that you're getting the chance to do something exciting and new, you're full of

energy again. You don't even think about being tired anymore. The difference is that you have something exciting and fun to look forwards to now.

So, take a good look at what's happening in your life. Do you feel like you're trapped doing the same thing every day with no hope for escape? I used to feel like my whole life was "get up, go to work, come home, make dinner, do a few chores, go to bed, repeat again tomorrow." When I came home I would just be so tired. Once I realized what was happening and changed it, it was absolutely amazing how much energy I suddenly had. Life is way too short to spend it bored out of your mind. So, what's happening in your life? Is it time to look for a new job? Do you need to try something new?

Are you frustrated?

Just like the previous point, if you're frustrated with what's happening in your life or with the world in general, you can end up feeling tired all the time. Especially, if you're at the point where you feel like you don't have any options. You feel like you're a victim and that there's nothing you can do. The truth is that you always have options and different choices you can make. You just need to figure out what they are. Ask yourself, what are you feeling and why?

Are there medical issues? (thyroid, etc.)

Sometimes there really could be a medical reason as to why you're not functioning at full potential. Could be a good opportunity just to get checked out by your physician.

Do you have SAD (Seasonal Affective Disorder)?

SAD is estimated to affect 6 out of every 100 people in North America during the winter months. If you're feeling constantly tired and are craving carbohydrates and sweet foods, you might have SAD which is caused by a lack of sunlight. . . .

Are you eating well?

Sugar and caffeine can give us a temporary feeling of energy but you'll find that you're even more tired a few hours later. Plus, the next day you're also going to be tired from what you ate the day before. . . .

Are you doing too much, staying up too late?

We all need some downtime but today's society runs at full speed 24 hours a day, seven days a week and it's very easy to get caught up in it. Also, I know all the best TV shows seem to be on way past my bedtime. Burning yourself out from doing too much or not getting enough sleep is eventually going to catch up with you.

Are you around negative people?

Negative people can be like black holes which just suck all your energy out of you because they're emotionally draining to be around. Be careful of allowing negative people to steal your energy. . . .

I'm So Tired Summary

Feeling tired is one of the most common complaints that physicians hear. It's also not an easy one to diagnose as it could be caused by so many different ailments. The suggestions above are just a few reasons of why you might be feeling so tired. The important thing is that if you are feeling tired all the time, take the time to listen and see if your mind and body are trying to tell you something. There could be a quick and easy fix to your situation and it could also end up changing your life.

How to write a causal analysis

These steps for the process of writing a causal analysis may not progress as neatly as this chart might suggest. Writing is not an assembly-line process. As you write, you are constantly reading what you have written, rethinking, and revising.

Continue thinking about causation as you write and revise. The process of writing may lead you to additional causal relationships.

1 MAKE A CAUSAL CLAIM

- Examine a social trend, law, or policy.
- Analyze problems in your neighbourhood or at your school.
- Investigate natural phenomena.
- Investigate the impact of human activity on the environment.
- Put your claim in the form "_____ causes (or does not cause) _____."

2 THINK ABOUT THE POSSIBLE CAUSES

- What are the obvious causes?
- What are the underlying causes?
- What causes might be hidden?
- What are the causes that most people have not recognized before?

Think about what is at stake

- What could or should change once the cause is known? What could people do differently in the future?
- If the cause is obvious to everyone, then it probably isn't worth writing about.

Analyze your potential readers

- Who are your readers? Do they have a stake in your analysis?
- How familiar will they be with the trend, event, or phenomenon you are writing about?
- What are they likely to know and not know?
- How likely are they to accept your causal explanation?

3 WRITE A DRAFT

- Describe the trend, event, or phenomenon.
- Give the background your readers will need.
- If the trend or event you are analyzing is unfamiliar to your readers, explain the cause or the chain of causation.
- Another way to organize the body of your analysis is to set out the causes that have already been offered and reject them one by one. Then you can present the cause or causes that you think are the right ones.
- A third method is to look at a series of causes one by one, analyzing the importance of each.
- Do more than simply summarize in your conclusion. You might consider additional effects beyond those you have previously noted, or explain to readers any action you think should be taken based on your conclusions.
- Choose a title that will interest readers in your essay.
- Include any necessary images or tables.

4 REVISE, REVISE, REVISE

- Check that your causal analysis fulfills the assignment.
- Make sure that your claim is clear and that you have sufficient evidence to convince readers.
- Look at additional potential causes, if necessary.
- Reconsider how multiple causes might interact.
- Go further back in the causal chain, if necessary, showing how the causes you examine have their roots in other events.
- Examine the organization of your analysis and think of possible better ways to organize.
- Review the visual presentation of your analysis for readability and maximum impact.
- Proofread carefully.

5 PRINT A VERSION TO SUBMIT

- Make sure your finished writing meets all formatting requirements.

1: Make a causal claim

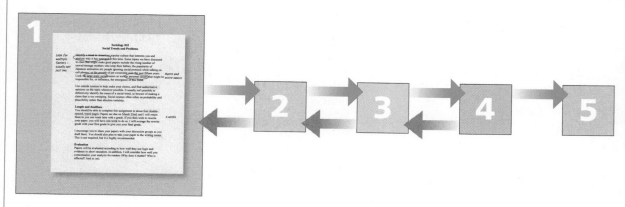

Analyze the assignment

- Read your assignment slowly and carefully. Look for key words like *causes, effect, result, consequences, repercussions, impact, why,* and *influence.* These key words tell you that you are writing a causal analysis.

- Highlight any information about the length specified, date due, formatting, and other requirements. You can attend to this information later. At this point you want to give your attention to the topic and criteria you will use in your analysis.

Explore possible topics

- Make a list of significant trade and industry events that have changed the national economic landscape. Make notes about the causes of these events and how people have been affected by them.

- Make a list of social trends including music, television shows, movies, sports, exercising, childrearing, and leisure. Look at your list and think about where and why a particular trend originates. Make notes about the origins of trends on your list.

- Make a list of important historical events or discoveries that changed the course of civilization. Make notes about what led to these events or discoveries and how people's lives were changed by them.

Think about what's at stake

- Remember that people often have a stake in the outcome of a causal claim. Ask: Who will agree with me? Who will disagree, and why?

- Think about why your analysis matters. If people accept your causal claim, will anything change?

STAYING ON TRACK

Make a claim that matters

Make an arguable claim

Easy answers generally make bad arguments. If all the sources you consult agree about the cause of the effect you are interested in, there is probably no need for you to make another argument saying the same thing. Look for a phenomenon that hasn't been explained to everyone's satisfaction.

OFF TRACK

Cigarette smoke is a leading cause of lung cancer.

ON TRACK

New research indicates that childhood asthma may be linked to exposure to cockroaches.

Explain why it matters

Readers need to know why this cause-and-effect relationship is important. If we determine the cause of this phenomenon, what will change? What can we do? What might happen?

OFF TRACK

This paper will investigate the most common causes of foundation failure in subsidized housing.

ON TRACK

Foundation failure, especially cracked slabs, can cost anywhere from a few thousand to tens of thousands of dollars to repair. Determining the primary causes of foundation failure can help homeowners and insurers protect themselves against economic loss and inconvenience.

WRITE NOW

Think about causal factors

1. Consider trends or problems you are familiar with—in your daily life, or in the larger world.
2. List these trends and problems on the right side of a piece of paper. On the left side, write down what you think some of the causes of the problems might be. Underline the causes that you are confident about.
3. Look over your two lists. Which topics seem most interesting to you? If an entry has many underlined causes or effects, it may be too obvious to write about.

Writer at work

Sean Booker was asked to write a paper analyzing the causes of a current trend in popular culture for a course in Social Trends and Problems. He made the following notes on his assignment sheet while his class was discussing the assignment.

Sociology 032
Social Trends and Problems

Look for multiple factors – usually not just one

Identify a trend in popular culture that interests you and analyze why it has emerged at this time. Some topics we have discussed in class that might make good papers include the rising number of unwed teenage mothers who keep their babies; the popularity of Japanese anime or manga; people ignoring social protocol while talking on cell phones; or the growth of pet ownership over the past fifteen years. Look for large-scale social causes as well as personal causes that might be responsible for, or influence, the emergence of this trend.

Macro and micro causes

Use outside sources to help make your claims, and find authoritative opinions on the topic whenever possible. It usually isn't possible to definitively identify the cause of a social trend, so beware of making a claim that is too sweeping. Social science often relies on probability and plausibility rather than absolute certainty.

Length and deadlines
You should be able to complete this assignment in about four double-spaced, typed pages. Papers are due on Aug. 18, and I will return them to you one week later with a grade. If you then wish to rewrite your paper, you will have one week to do so. I will average the rewrite grade with your first grade to give you your final grade.

2 weeks

I encourage you to share your papers with your discussion groups as you draft them. You should also plan to take your paper to the writing centre. This is not required, but it is highly recommended.

Evaluation
Papers will be evaluated according to how well they use logic and evidence to show causation. In addition, I will consider how well you contextualize your analysis for readers (Why does it matter? Who is affected? And so on).

Read the assignment closely
Sean Booker began by circling the words and phrases that indicated his analytical task. Then he highlighted information about dates and processes for the project.

Choose a topic
Sean Booker made a list of trends he might write about. After each item on his list, he made notes about why the topic would matter, and to whom. He also made preliminary observations about where he might find "authoritative opinions" on each topic, wrote down any possible causes that occurred to him at the time, and noted any other observations or questions he had about that topic. Finally, he chose one trend for further research.

POPULARITY OF ANIME
- Is it more popular with certain age groups or other demographic groups?
- Is there any scholarly/authoritative research on it? Maybe in Art History?
- I've seen tons of magazines devoted to it at the bookstore.
- Could interview Graham about the collection he has.

POPULARITY OF RAP/HIPHOP MUSIC   **** Best research**
(especially among white teenagers) **possibilities****

- What percentage of sales of rap music are to white kids?
- Is it any different from white teenagers liking rock n' roll in the 50s?
- Because it annoys parents?
- Does it indicate racial tolerance?
- I know there has been research on this from an economic viewpoint.

SUV SALES
- Why do people want to drive "off-roading" cars to work every day?
- Are sales declining with rising gas prices?
- Is this even a trend any more? People are buying VWs and Mini Coopers now.

"ILLEGAL" FILE SHARING
- Why do so many people do it if it is "illegal"? (Because you get something for free.)
- What are the arguments saying that it is or isn't illegal?
- Easy answer: people are willing to "steal" in this case because there is still significant disagreement over whether it is really stealing.

2: Think about possible causes

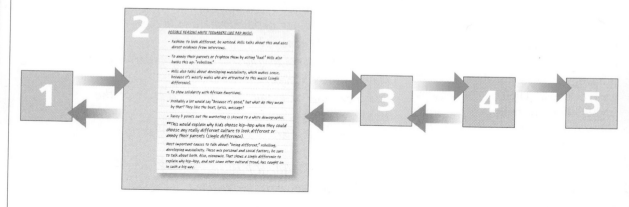

Find the obvious causes, and then dig deeper

- **What causal factors might be hidden from the general observer, and why?** Use your imagination; hidden causes require new thinking if they are to be uncovered.

- **How do various causal factors interact?** Several causes together might contribute to an effect, rather than any single cause being the determining factor.

- **What "causes the cause" that you have identified?** What prior conditions does each cause arise from? If poor attendance is a factor in drop-out rates, what causes some students to have poor attendance in the first place?

Analyze your audience

- **Think about who is affected by the phenomenon you are investigating.** Who is in a position to react to your claims, and make changes?

- **If you don't know who your audience is, do some research to find out who is interested in your topic.** Who has offered opinions or responded to previous causal claims on this topic?

Research your analysis

- **Look for some disagreement among your sources.** If they all agree on the cause, your analysis won't matter much.

- **When your sources disagree, ask why.** Does one give more weight to some pieces of evidence than to others? Do they draw different conclusions from the same evidence? Do they use Mill's methods of determining causation in different ways?

- **Be on the lookout for new potential causes, or new findings that could help you rule out potential causes.**

Writer at work

Sean Booker began his analysis by brainstorming for all the possible causes he could think of. Then, he researched the topic to find information on the causes he had listed and also to learn about other potential causes that had been put forward.

Sean Booker thought about his own experience with the trend to help define his audience. He also noted the types of audiences his sources appeared to be writing for. Finally, Sean Booker identified what he thought were the most likely causes of rap's popularity with white teenagers. He did this analysis by applying Mill's methods of determining causation and by weighing the opinions of the authoritative sources he had read.

POSSIBLE REASONS WHITE TEENAGERS LIKE RAP MUSIC:

- Fashion: to look different, be noticed. Mills talks about this and uses direct evidence from interviews. Davis talks about "branding" urban Black culture.
- To annoy their parents or frighten them by acting "bad." Mills also backs this up: "rebellion." Deviant behaviour is also mentioned by Miranda & Claes.
- Mills also talks about developing masculinity, which makes sense, because it's mostly males who are attracted to this music (single difference).
- Probably a lot would say "Because it's good," but what do they mean by that? They like the beat, lyrics, message?
- Davey D points out the marketing is skewed to a white demographic.

**Explain why kids choose hip-hop when they could choose any really different culture to look different or annoy their parents (single difference).

Most important causes to talk about: "being different," rebelling, developing masculinity. These mix personal and social factors; be sure to talk about both. Also, economic. That shows a single difference to explain why hip-hop, and not some other cultural trend, has caught on in such a big way.

3: Write a draft

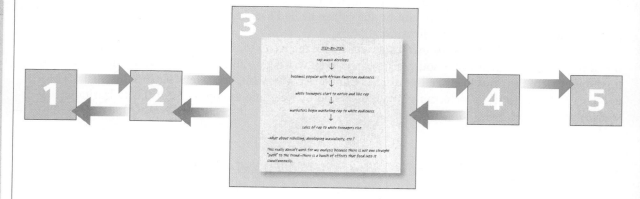

Introduce what you will be analyzing

- Describe the trend, event, or phenomenon you will be analyzing.
- Give your readers any background information they will need.
- Explain why it is important to determine the cause of this phenomenon.

Describe the causal relationship

- Explain how the chain of causation works to produce the effect in question. Break down each step so readers can follow the process.
- Alternatively, set out the causes offered by other people and show how they can be ruled out. Then, introduce your own claim and demonstrate why it is superior to others'.
- A third method is to look at a series of possible causes one at a time, analyzing each and making a claim about its relative impact on a phenomenon.

Anticipate and address opposing viewpoints

- Acknowledge other stakeholders in the analysis, and consider their claims.
- Demonstrate why your claim is preferable.

Conclude by doing more than summarizing

- Spell out the importance of the analysis, if you haven't already done so.
- Consider additional effects you haven't previously discussed.
- Explain any action you think needs to be taken based on your conclusion.

STAYING ON TRACK

Make a claim that matters

Don't confuse correlation with causation

Mill's method of concomitant variation might lead you to conclude that any mutual relationship between two events is causal. Remember that concomitant variation only determines cause when all other variables are accounted for.

OFF TRACK
The lives of many lower-income Canadians have been steadily improving for a decade or more, due to many factors.

ON TRACK
Welfare reforms have affected poverty in Canada. The policies of three get-tough provinces—British Columbia, Alberta, and Ontario—have helped to increase the percentage of Canadians who work, and to reduce the numbers who live below the poverty line by making it much harder for employable people to stay on the dole.

Identify the stakeholders in your analysis

Be especially alert for opinions about your topic from people who would be adversely affected by a different causal outcome.

OFF TRACK
Can mega-doses of vitamin C prevent colds, flu, and other illnesses? Good health is important to everyone, so we should all be interested in the news that vitamin C has many important health benefits.

ON TRACK
Can mega-doses of vitamin C prevent colds, flu, and other illnesses? The supplements industry has spent millions of dollars to convince consumers that this is the case. The industry stands to make hundreds of millions more if people believe them. But evidence from independent researchers casts some doubt on the effectiveness of mega-doses of vitamin C in preventing illness.

Writer at work

Sean Booker tested three organizational patterns for his analysis. First he looked at how describing a chain of causation could illuminate his analysis. Next, he considered examining causes one by one and eliminating them before describing the cause he thought was correct. Finally, he structured his analysis as an examination of possible causes, one by one, with accompanying discussion of each cause's relative contribution to the overall effect. This seemed to Sean Booker like the best method for making his analysis, so he used it to write his draft.

STEP-BY-STEP:

rap music develops

↓

becomes popular with North American suburban audiences

↓

white teenagers start to notice and like rap

↓

marketers begin marketing rap to white audiences

↓

sales of rap to white teenagers rise

—What about rebelling, developing masculinity, etc.?

This really doesn't work for my analysis because there is not one straight "path" to the trend—there is a bunch of effects that feed into it simultaneously.

<u>DISPROVING ALTERNATE CAUSES:</u>

White kids like rap just because "it is good" and they are colourblind about music.
  - Actually, they are acutely aware of the racial difference between themselves and the performers; that's part of why they like it.

White kids like rap because they feel sympathy with Black urban culture.

  - I'm the only person who even thought of this reason. A lot of people I know who listen to rap know next to nothing about Black culture, so this is pretty clearly wrong. But what good does it do to bring it up and refute it if no one else would have even considered it as a possibility?

I guess the problem here is that there isn't a big controversy over which causes are "right." That kind of controversy would work better with this structure. It's more a question of how many different causes there might be, and how they might work together.

<u>ONE CAUSE AT A TIME:</u>

- Appeal of the fashion and style is one possible cause. Explain how it fills a need for white teenagers.
- Rebellion against social expectations. Explain why white kids need to do this.
- Developing masculinity. Explain how social pressures lead white male teenagers to think rap's message makes them more masculine.
- Marketing. Look at how rap is marketed to white kids, amplifying all the causes above.

This strategy is the best approach because it lets me look at all the possible causes in detail and finish with the one that sort of gathers up and amplifies the first three.

4: Revise, revise, revise

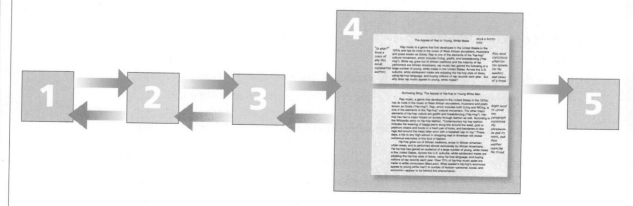

Skilled writers know that the secret to writing well is rewriting. Even the best writers often have to revise several times to get the result they want. You also must have effective strategies for revising if you're going to be successful. The biggest trap you can fall into is starting off with the little stuff first. Leave the small stuff for last.

Does your paper or project meet the assignment?	• Look again at your assignment. Does your paper or project do what the assignment asks?
	• Look again at the assignment for specific guidelines, including length, format, and amount of research. Does your work meet these guidelines?
Is your causal claim arguable?	• Do enough people disagree with you to make the evaluation worthwhile?
	• Who cares about this topic? Do you explain to readers why it is important?
Do you use logical means of determining causation?	• Do you examine common factors, single differences, and concomitant variations?
	• Do you use more than one method whenever possible?
	• Do you avoid confusing correlation with causation?
Is your evidence authoritative and convincing?	• Have you found the most accurate information about your topic available?
	• Have you identified stakeholders in your analysis?
	• Have you carefully examined the analysis and conclusions of people who have already expressed an opinion on this topic?

Do you address opposing views?	• Have you acknowledged the opinions of people who disagree with your claim? • Have you shown how your causal claim is preferable?
Is the writing project visually effective?	• Is the font attractive and readable? • Are the headings and visuals effective? • If you use images or tables as part of your analysis, are they legible and appropriately placed?
Save the editing for last	When you have finished revising, edit and proofread carefully.

Writer at work

Sean Booker talked with his peer group about his analysis, and took his draft to the writing centre for a consultation. He wrote notes on the draft to help him revise, and then he made some changes to the draft. His peers particularly urged him to focus his introduction. Here is the draft of Sean Booker's introduction as he originally wrote it, with notes he made, and as he revised it for his final draft.

The Appeal of Rap to Young, White Males

Need a better title

"So what?" Need a sense of why this needs explanation or why it matters

Rap music is a genre that first developed in the United States in the 1970s and has its roots in the music of West African storytellers, musicians and poets known as Griots. Rap is one of the elements of the "hip-hop" cultural movement, which includes DJing, graffiti, and breakdancing ("Hip-Hop"). While rap grew out of African traditions and the majority of rap performers are Black, rap music has gained the following of a large number of young, white males in North America. Across the suburbs, white adolescent males are adopting the hip-hop style of dress, using hip-hop language, and buying millions of rap records each year. But why does rap music appeal to young, white males?

Also, need statistics/ authoritative opinion for the numbers and claims of a trend.

Borrowing Bling: The Appeal of Hip-Hop to Young, White Men

Rap music, a genre that developed in the United States in the 1970s, has its roots in the music of West African storytellers, musicians, and poets known as Griots ("Hip-Hop"). Rap, which includes both DJing and MCing, is one of the elements of hip-hop cultural movement. The other major elements of hip-hop culture are graffiti and breakdancing ("Hip Hop"). Hip-hop has had a major impact on society through fashion as well: "Contemporary hip-hop fashion includes the wearing of baggy jeans slung low around the waist, gold or platinum chains and boots or a fresh pair of kicks, and bandannas or doo rags tied around the head often worn with a baseball cap on top" ("Hip Hop Music"). These days, a trip to any high school or shopping mall in North America will reveal numerous examples of this kind of fashion.

Hip-hop grew out of African traditions, arose in Black urban areas, and is performed almost exclusively by Black artists. Yet hip-hop has gained an audience of a large number of young, white suburban males. White adolescent males are adapting the "hip-hop aesthetic" (Davis)—appropriating a hip-hop style of dress, using hip-hop language, and buying millions of rap records every year. Over 70 percent of hip-hop music sales are made to white consumers (MacLean). What explains hip-hop's enormous appeal to young white males? A number of factors—personal, social, and economic—appear to be behind this phenomenon.

STAYING ON TRACK

Reviewing your draft

Give yourself plenty of time for reviewing your draft. For detailed information on how to participate in a peer review, how to review it yourself, and how to respond to comments from your classmates, your instructor, or a campus writing consultant, see pages 31–32.

Some good questions to ask yourself when reviewing causal analysis

- Is my causal claim clear? Have I avoided oversimplifying?
- Will my audience understand why this issue is important?
- Have I accounted for the various stakeholders in this analysis?
- Have I considered all possible causes? Have I used sound logic to evaluate them?
- Have I provided evidence to support my claim?

5: Print a version to submit

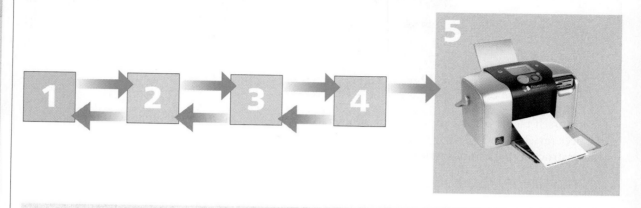

Sean Booker

Professor Martinez

SOC 032

18 August 2010

Borrowing Bling: The Appeal of Hip-Hop to Young, White Men

Rap music, a genre that developed in the United States in the 1970s, has its roots in the music of West African storytellers, musicians, and poets known as Griots ("Hip-Hop"). Rap, which includes both DJing and MCing, is one of the elements of the hip-hop cultural movement. The other major elements of hip-hop culture are graffiti and breakdancing ("Hip Hop"). Hip-hop has had a major impact on society through fashion as well: "Contemporary hip-hop fashion includes the wearing a baggy jeans slung low around the waist, gold or platinum chains and boots or a fresh pair of kicks, and bandannas or doo rags tied around the head often worn with a baseball cap on top" ("Hip Hop Music"). These days, a trip to any high school or shopping mall in North America will reveal numerous examples of this kind of fashion.

Hip-hop grew out of African traditions, arose in Black urban areas, and is performed almost exclusively by Black artists. Yet, hip-hop has gained an audience of a large number of young, white suburban males. White adolescent males are adapting the "hip-hop aesthetic" (Davis)—appropriating a hip-hop style of dress, using hip-hop language, and buying millions of rap records every year. Over 70 percent of hip-hop

Booker 2

music sales are made to white consumers (MacLean). What explains hip-hop's enormous appeal to young, white men? A number of factors—personal, social, and economic—appear to be behind this phenomenon.

On a personal level, hip-hop appeals to young, white males because it allows them to escape from the constraints of white society and experience the world of the rapper. Many white youth "rebelled against the suburban rules and opted for . . . a more relaxed or 'chill' lifestyle" (Davis). Rap music details urban Black culture, sometimes describing a violent and gritty life on the street, or alternately, a life filled with the glamour of flashy jewellery, nice cars, women, and money. Both of these worldviews differ vastly from the often insulated predictable world of the young, white adolescent. Prof. Fiona Mills interviewed young, white rap listeners for her essay "Rap and Young, White Males: Masculinity, Masking and Denial." She found that young, white men are drawn to the escapist and exotic aspects of rap.

But hip-hop is more than an outlet for personal fantasy. It can also provide a highly defined alternative culture that appeals to the young, white man who may have trouble finding himself within white culture (Hydro033) and who may consciously reject white culture: "In North America, there is a tradition of whites being attracted to the stereotypes of Black music—to its danger, its looseness, often as a rejection of their [own] social norms" (Dunlevy). The fact that hip-hop especially appeals to young men at a time in their lives when they are seeking to define themselves supports this theory. For a white teenager trying desperately to establish himself as a unique person, hip-hop style may appeal because it is something he can easily recognize and emulate, and something that then sets him apart from his white peers. It is a means for situating himself in society.

Additionally, Mills explains that rap music, with its focus on sex, money, drugs and violence, builds a "hyper masculine aura." White males are drawn to because it gives them a model for establishing their masculinity. As Mills revealed in her study, white males often begin listening to music, around age 12 or 13, just as they are entering adolescence and beginning to establish their masculine identities. In contrast, Mills found that Black males reported listening to rap music from a very young age. Mills suggests that the white adolescents she interviewed saw rap music, "as a way of asserting their manhood by associating themselves with an overtly masculine culture—one in which femininity had no place."

Rap music also appeals to young, white men because it is a way to rebel against their parents and white society in general (WhiteClef). By associating themselves with a musical culture that involves heavy use of profane language and often centres on violence and drugs, white males establish their rebellion against societal standards. This musical subculture often conveys "messages and values that are considered antisocial" (Miranda and Claes), and many like rap for the simple fact that their parents do not approve of its foul language, portrayal of violence, and treatment of women ("Death of a Teenager").

These factors all help to explain why young, white men might be drawn to hip-hop and rap music and what they might gain from adopting its cultural markers, but do these factors alone explain hip-hop's enormous popularity with white consumers? There are many other types of music and culture that might appeal to white adolescents on the same grounds as hip-hop. Why has hip-hop become such a huge cultural phenomenon?

Marketing may well be the answer: "No other music is being marketed like hip-hop" (Dunlevy). Hip-hop historian and journalist Davey D has chronicled the economic pressures that led to hip-hop being marketed directly to white audiences. Historically, advertisers and record companies have cared little about young Black consumers, who typically have less disposable income than white consumers (Davis). Young white males, on the other hand are a key demographic that all marketers pursue. As Davey D puts it, "as major corporations saw lots of white kids getting down with hip-hop, they decided to do whatever it took to appeal to what is considered a lucrative demographic . . . what this all boils down to was there was a premium placed on white/more affluent listeners." To attract a white clientele, Davey D argues, record companies and promoters began putting out hip-hop acts that fed white stereotypes about Black culture. As a result, "you have a genre of music that was born in the harshest ghettos outselling any other music, and now attracting the desired Holy Grail for corporate advertisers—white folks 18 to 34 [translation: Generation X.]."

If Davey D's argument is correct, then the popularity of hip-hop among young white men is cause for concern. While cultural crossover is in many ways a good thing and can help promote understanding among people, some feel that hip-hop is being used to manipulate consumers and even promote racial stereotypes: "This commercial exploitation of gansta-rap stereotypes amounts to media violence that feeds into negative images of racialized ethnicities" (Pieters). If true, this would be a sad statement about today's white hip-hop fans. Like white audiences at the 1920s vaudeville show, they could be exposed to a parody of Black culture and think it was the real thing.

Works Cited

D, Davey. "Hip Hop's Ultimate Battle: Race and the Politics of Divide and Conquer." *Davey D's Hip Hop Dailey News*. N.p., 10 Jan. 2003. Web. 10 July 2009.

Dunlevy, T'Cha. "Scrambling the Colour Code in Music: As White Music Fans Embrace Black Culture, Things Get Touchy." *Ottawa Citizen* 27 May 2000: J3. Print

"Hip Hop Music." *Wikipedia.* Wikipedia, 31 July 2009. Web. 3 Aug. 2009.

Hydro033. "Rap Music Fuels Racism?" *TheChez.net.* N.p., 10 June 2009. Web. 4 Aug. 2009.

Maclean, Natalie. "Bring on the Bling: Rappers Give Cristal and Hennessy Street Cred." *San Francisco Chronicle*. Hearst Communications, 16 Dec. 2004. Web. 15 July 2009.

Mills, Fiona. "Rap and Young, White Males: Masculinity, Masking and Denial." *Journal of American Popular Culture*. Americana: The Institute for the Study of American Popular Culture, Dec. 2001. Web. 31 July 2009.

Miranda, Dave, and Michel Claes. "Rap Music Genres and Deviant Behaviors in French-Canadian Adolescents." *Journal of Youth and Adolescence*. 33.2 (2004): 113–22. Print.

Pieters, Gary. "Hip Hop Culture's Identify Crisis." *Toronto Star*. Toronto Star, 17 May 2007. Web. 14 July, 2009.

WhiteClef. "Hip Hop Caters to Whites?" *24hourhiphop.com*. 24hiphop.com, 22 Dec 2008. Web. 10 July 2009.

Projects

A causal analysis answers the question, "How did something get that way?" It first has to identify what that something is: an event, an object, a phenomenon, or a trend. Once it hass identified the **what,** then it moves to the **how** and **why**.

Causal analyses have several different purposes. Sometimes we are just curious about why something happened. In some cases, we may want to repeat something, such as the successful sales of a product. In other cases, we may want to prevent potentially bad effects from occurring. And in still other cases, we might want to forecast the future.

The following projects give you a range of opportunities for causal analysis.

CAUSAL ANALYSIS
For an example of analyzing, see pages 317–319.

 Identify a significant change in human behaviour over a period of months or years. Why have mega-churches grown rapidly in the U.S.? Why has reality television become popular? Why has the wealthiest one percent of Canadians grown significantly richer over the past twenty years? Why have homicide rates dropped to levels not seen since the 1960s? Why are children increasingly obese?

 Determine the time span of the trend. When did it start? When did it stop? Is it still going on? You likely will need to do research.

Analyze the possible causes of the trend, arguing for the ones you think are most likely the true causes. Look for underlying and hidden causes.

 Remember that providing facts is not the same thing as establishing causes, even though facts can help support your causal analysis.

PEARSON
mycanadiancomplab

Go to **www.mycanadiancomplab.ca** to practise your grammar, punctuation, and mechanics skills. Go to the "Resources" tab within MyCanadianCompLab and then click on "Grammar." You will have access to a variety of exercises as well as direct instruction that will help you improve your basic skills and help you get a better grade in your course.

ANALYZING CLAIMS AND STAKEHOLDERS

For an example of analyzing claims and stakeholders, see pages 302–307.

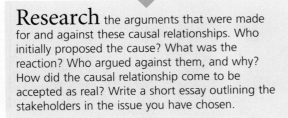

Identify a causal relationship that is now generally accepted but was once in doubt, such as Galileo's explanation of the phases of the moon, the link between DDT and the decline of bald eagle populations, or the effects of vitamin B12 on developing fetuses.

Research the arguments that were made for and against these causal relationships. Who initially proposed the cause? What was the reaction? Who argued against them, and why? How did the causal relationship come to be accepted as real? Write a short essay outlining the stakeholders in the issue you have chosen.

Explain the arguments made for and against the now-accepted cause, and the evidence presented. Which of Mill's methods of determining causation did each party use (see pages 290–291)? Why were the arguments of the now-accepted cause more effective?

CAUSAL ANALYSIS OF A HUMAN-INFLUENCED NATURAL PHENOMENON

For an example of analyzing a human-influenced natural phenomenon, see pages 294–297.

Find a natural phenomenon or trend that is (or may be) the result of human activity. Is global warming the result of human activity? Why are more and more bacteria developing resistance to antibiotics? Choose a topic that interests you and which you feel is important. If you think the topic is important, it will be easier to convince your audience that your analysis is important.

Research the possible causes of the phenomenon, focusing on the ones you think are most likely the true causes. Remember to look at underlying and hidden causes.

Think about possible alternative causes. Do you need to incorporate them? If you don't think they are valid causes, then you need to refute them.

Recognize that causal relationships between humans and the natural world are complex and play out on such a large scale, and that it is often difficult to prove them definitively. Don't oversimplify or make sweeping claims that can't be proven.

14

Evaluating

Convincing evaluations rely on selecting criteria
and supporting a claim with reasons and evidence.

Chapter contents

Writing to evaluate

You make evaluations every day. You choose a favourite CD, a favourite restaurant, a favourite ring tone on your cell phone. Newspapers and websites feature "best of" polls that let people vote for the restaurant, movie, television show, or band they think is the "best." To some extent, these judgments are a matter of personal taste. Yet, if you look into the reasons people give for their preferences, you often find that different people use similar criteria to make evaluations.

For example, think about a restaurant you like. What are your reasons for feeling this way? Is it clean? The food fresh? The prices low? Is it convenient to your home or campus? Do you like the atmosphere? These are criteria that most people will use to judge a restaurant. That's why some restaurants are always crowded, while many others quickly go out of business.

Goals of evaluation

When you write an evaluation, your goal is usually to convince readers to agree with your judgment or, at the very least, recognize your point of view. Convincing other people that your judgment is sound depends on the validity of the criteria you will use to make your evaluation. Will the criteria you're using as the basis of your evaluation be convincing to other people? You may think a movie is good because it has exceptional cinematography, but an action-movie fan is less likely to go see a movie just because it is visually beautiful. Sometimes you must argue for the validity of your criteria before readers will accept them. If they don't accept your criteria, they won't agree with your conclusions.

An evaluative claim

An evaluation can be stated in the form "SOMETHING is good (or bad, the best or the worst) if measured by these criteria." Usually, the most important task when writing an evaluation is to determine the kind of criteria to use.

Suppose you want to convince your student Speakers' Committee to host a talk by a well-known filmmaker who you believe would be a better choice than other potential speakers. You could argue that, because she is famous, the filmmaker will draw many students to her talk, thus raising the profile of the Speakers' Program, and generating more money in ticket sales. You could also argue that the filmmaker's talk would be a culturally enriching experience for students because she has made many critically acclaimed movies. You might argue that a large number of students on campus have expressed their desire to hear the filmmaker, and that the Speakers' Committee has an obligation to provide speakers the students want to hear.

Criteria for evaluation

Each of these arguments uses different kinds of criteria. An argument that the filmmaker will draw students and make money is based on **practical criteria.** An argument that her artistic achievement makes her a worthwhile speaker is based on **aesthetic criteria.** An argument that the committee is bound to consider the wishes of students is based on **ethical criteria.** These are the three basic categories of criteria for all evaluative arguments.

Things are usually judged to be good (or bad) either because they work well (practicality), because they are beautiful (aesthetics), or because they are morally fair or just (ethics). An evaluative argument may use any or all of these types of criteria and can emphasize them in different ways. For example, if you want to convince your roommate to go to an expensive sushi restaurant, you would probably emphasize the aesthetic experience of enjoying fresh sushi in a fashionable atmosphere. You would want to downplay practical criteria like cost, especially if your roommate's budget requires that he usually dine on Ramen noodles instead of sushi.

Components of evaluations

What will make a good subject to evaluate?	**Find something to evaluate** Listing is one way to identify possible subjects for evaluation. You might list restaurants, buildings, cars, computers, and other objects. You might evaluate a film, a book, a TV show, a political speech, or certain policies or courses at your school.
What is my working thesis?	**Write a working thesis** Your thesis should argue that something is good/better/best or bad/worst, successful or unsuccessful on the basis of criteria that you name.
What values are most important for my readers?	**Consider your readers** How interesting will this topic be to your readers? What criteria will be most convincing to them?
What are the appropriate criteria for my subject?	**Choose the appropriate criteria** **Practical criteria** will demand that the subject being evaluated work efficiently or lead to good outcomes (profits, satisfied customers, improved conditions, lower costs, and so on). **Aesthetic criteria** hinge on the importance and value of beauty, image, or tradition. **Ethical criteria** are used to evaluate whether something is morally right and consistent with the law and with rules of fair play.
Who would disagree with me?	**Consider other views** Has anyone evaluated your subject before? What criteria did they use? For example, you might hate horror movies because they give you bad dreams, but many other people love them. You should consider why they have such a strong following.
What is the most engaging way to begin?	**Start quickly** You may have to give some background but get quickly to your subject.
What is the most effective way to end?	**Finish strong** If you have not announced your stance, then you can make your summary evaluation. If your readers know where you stand, you might end with a compelling example.

Keys to evaluations

Briefly describe your subject

Your readers may be unfamiliar with what you are evaluating. Give your readers a brief description.

Explain your criteria

The importance of many criteria may not be evident to your readers. You may need to state explicitly each criterion you use and explain why it is relevant.

Be fair

Be honest about the strengths and weaknesses of what you are evaluating. Rarely is anything perfectly good or absolutely bad. Your credibility will increase if you give a balanced view.

Support your judgments with evidence

Back up your claims with specific evidence. If you write that a restaurant serves inedible food, describe examples in detail.

Define criteria for visual evaluations

Criteria for visual evaluations may require additional work to define and explain.

The Sharp Centre for Design at the Ontario College of Art and Design in Toronto remains controversial on aesthetic criteria. Some people find it a worthy example of innovative architecture that adds to the character of the city; others object to it because they find it out of scale with the surrounding neighbourhood.

WORKING TOGETHER
What makes an effective review?

In a group of three or four students

- Look at a selection of short, amateur online reviews, such as customer book reviews at Amazon.com, consumer reviews on a site like Epinions.com, or user comments on a film at www.imdb.com.

- Select several examples of reviews that you think are persuasive and several that are not (see if you can find some persuasive reviews that you don't necessarily agree with).

- As a group, discuss the following: What criteria do reviewers of similar products share? What types of criteria do the persuasive reviews use? What types do the less persuasive reviews use? Do you see any patterns that make reviews persuasive?

An effective evaluation

A successful evaluation makes a claim about the value of something. It supports its main claim with criteria that the audience will agree are important.

The Value of Solitude
Robert Kull

Robert Kull is the author of *Solitude: Seeking Wisdom in Extremes.* A radical adventurer and spiritual seeker, he has spent 45 years exploring the wild edges of North and South America and the risky depths of his inner world. In this article, he explains the benefits of being alone.

THE VALUE OF SOLITUDE

Robert Kull

ALTHOUGH MANY CULTURES have long recognized solitude as an opportunity to look inward, in our culture we sometimes think that spending time alone is unhealthy. Some psychologists even argue that since we're social beings, meaning is found only through relationship with other people. But we are more profoundly relational than that. To be fully human we need relationships with other people, with the non-human world, and with our own inner depths. In solitude we have the opportunity to explore all these domains of relationship. We are also spiritual beings and may feel called into solitude to seek communion with a numinous Presence we can directly experience, but not clearly define.

The author first acknowledges the traditional position that people need other people to be fulfilled.

347

Solitude offers an opportunity to explore the sense of alienation many of us live with and to realize that being alone is not the same as feeling isolated or lonely. I've been exploring solitude—sometimes during months alone in the wilderness—for forty years, and I've learned that the core of my loneliness is not separation from other people, but feeling disconnected from myself. Solitude provides a respite from the demands of social life and creates a space for personal healing. Paradoxically, spending time alone can soften our sense of alienation from others.

Spending time in wilderness solitude is a fascinating adventure. We have carried specialization to such an extreme in the service of efficient productivity that daily life can seem boringly repetitious. Activities we used to enjoy when young are lost to the demands of adulthood. Living alone in the wilderness requires that we learn to do everything required for survival. The satisfaction of such self-reliance is deeply rewarding.

Not everyone agrees, and there has been a long and sometimes acrimonious argument about the value of solitude. Perhaps the most common objection is that withdrawing from social engagement is self-indulgent and irresponsible. But to say a solitary person is shirking responsibility is to claim complete understanding of the world. We can never really know what contribution we're making; we can only be true to our deepest calling and trust that we're doing what we're meant to do. I've found that my desire to contribute to the lives of others deepens in solitude.

We each have a social identity, a persona held in place by our interactions with other people. In solitude this persona begins to lose solidity and dissolve. The process is sometimes terrifying and there are few easy escapes. Solitude challenges us to face our inner dark-

Kull offers the traditional view and counters with an alternate position on being alone.

Kull now challenges the idea that withdrawing from the world is selfish by showing how solitude deepens social connections.

ness and to discover that we're not identical to the conception we often have of ourselves.

For me, deep wilderness solitude is profoundly meaningful, but I don't actually recommend it to others. It can be painful and dangerous. We must be called to it from within, and if we require external encouragement, we're not yet ready. But I do think many of us can benefit from stepping out of our hectic daily activities to spend time alone. Often when asked how we are, we reply, "Busy." This seems to refer to an on-going state of stress as well as to constant physical and mental activity. We live with the sense that we don't have enough time to do what we believe we must do.

Kull builds the credibility of his position by identifying the common challenges of people.

We tend to value activity above everything else, but all beings need to rest and recuperate. The widespread occurrence of depression in our culture may be linked to our refusal to allow ourselves quiet time. Feeling the need to be constantly busy can prevent us from turning inward. When we are out of balance, our activity doesn't arise from a place of stillness and wisdom. Much of our activity is ecologically destructive, and frequently our efforts to fix the problems we have caused only deepen the wounds. If, though, we can relax our demands for material goods, the Earth might be able to heal herself. Perhaps we can find fulfillment in non-material terms and learn that what we seek we already have.

He returns to his argument about the recuperative power of solitude.

We are sometimes so focused on progress that we don't experience our lives as they are here and now. Yet the world will always be exactly as it is in each moment—no matter how much time and energy we expend denying this simple fact. If our plans for the future are not grounded in joy in this moment, our lives go unlived.

We frequently don't perceive ourselves to be biological beings in a living world. Theoretically, we know we depend on the physical systems of Earth, but experientially we are alienated from those systems. We treat the Earth as a stranger we should protect for pragmatic or ethical reasons, but until we begin to actually experience non-human creatures as family and the Earth as our home, we are unlikely to make the changes necessary for our survival.

Solitude has the power to catalyze shifts in perception. The felt experience of belonging to the ecosphere is psychologically and spiritually healing and may have profound implications for changing our patterns of behaviour. Along with economic and legislative solutions, we need inner transformation. Solitude evokes the spacious wonder of living in a sacred world.

He then provides a more abstract position, connecting the physical and metaphysical in support of solitude.

He ends with a strong commentary about the physical, emotional, and spiritual relationships between people and the world.

How to read evaluations

Make notes as you read, either in the margins, if it is your own copy, or on paper or a computer file. Circle any words or references that you don't know and look them up.

What is it?	• What kind of a text is it? A review? An essay? A blog? An editorial? What are your expectations for this kind of text? • What media are used? (Websites, for example, often combine images, words, and sounds.)
Where did it come from?	• Who wrote the evaluation? • What do you know about the writer's background that might have influenced the evaluation?
What is the writer's thesis or main idea?	• What is the writer's topic? What effect is he or she trying to determine the cause of ? • Why is this topic important? • What are the key ideas or concepts that the writer considers? • What are the key terms? How does the writer define those terms?
Who is the intended audience?	• What clues do you find about whom the writer had in mind as the readers? • What does the writer assume that the readers already know about the subject? • What new knowledge is the writer providing?
Does the writer make a clear evaluative claim?	• What exactly is the writer's evaluative claim?
What are the criteria used in the evaluation?	• Does the writer use practical criteria? Aesthetic criteria? Ethical criteria? (See page 344.) • Does the writer argue for how these criteria apply to the subject? • Does the writer acknowledge opposing views?
How is it composed?	• How does the writer represent herself or himself? • How would you characterize the style? • If there are any photographs or other graphics, what information do they contribute?

Learning to Love PowerPoint
(ARTICLE)
David Byrne

Musician, author, artist, and producer David Byrne has worked in multiple media, often challenging his audience to inspect or question convention. In this article, published in *Wired* magazine in 2003, he shares his discoveries about the potential artistic uses of PowerPoint software.

Analyzing and Connecting
Return to these questions after you have finished reading.

1. Byrne's evaluation of PowerPoint is based largely on aesthetic criteria. Notice, however, that he does not claim PowerPoint necessarily makes beautiful images (though he says it is possible to do so). What exactly does Byrne feel makes PowerPoint aesthetically valuable?

2. What is Byrne's assessment of PowerPoint's practical value? Why do you think he discusses this aspect of the software early in the essay?

3. Byrne provides several still examples of his work in PowerPoint to demonstrate the potential he sees in the program. How do these images help him make his case? Do you find them helpful in understanding the value Byrne sees in PowerPoint?

Learning to Love PowerPoint

A while ago, I decided to base the book-tour readings from my pseudoreligious tract *The New Sins* on sales presentations. I was going for a fair dose of irony and satire, and what could be better than using PowerPoint and a projector, the same tools that every sales and marketing person relies on?

Having never used the program before, I found it limiting, inflexible, and biased, like most software. On top of that, PowerPoint makes hilariously bad-looking visuals. But that's a small price to pay for ease and utility. We live in a world where convenience beats quality every time. It was, for my purposes, perfect.

I began to see PowerPoint as a metaprogram, one that organizes and presents stuff created in other applications. Initially, I made presentations about presentations; they were almost completely without content. The content, I learned, was in the medium itself. I discovered that I could attach my photographs, short videos, scanned images, and music. What's more, the application can be made to run by itself—no one even needs to be at the

podium. How fantastic!

Although I began by making fun of the medium, I soon realized I could actually create things that were beautiful. I could bend the program to my own whim and use it as an artistic agent. The pieces became like short films: Some were sweet, some were scary, and some were *mysterioso*. I discovered that even without text, I could make works that were "about" something, something beyond themselves, and that they could even have emotional resonance. What had I stumbled upon? Surely some techie or computer artist was already using this dumb program as an artistic medium. I couldn't really have this territory all to myself—or could I?

In thinking about graphic design, industrial design, and what might really

* David Byrne. "Learning to Love PowerPoint."
Written by David Byrne, artist and musician.
Originally written for and published by *Wired*.
Reprinted by permission.

be the cutting-edge of design, I realized it would have to be genetic engineering. Dolly* (God rest her soul) represents the latest in design, but it is, in her case, design we cannot see. Dolly looks like any other sheep, which is precisely the point. The dogma of some graphic designers is that their work be invisible. This perfection has been achieved with Dolly.

I began this project making fun of the iconography of PowerPoint, which wasn't hard to do, but soon realized that the pieces were taking on lives of their own. This whirlwind of arrows, pointing everywhere and nowhere—each one color-coded to represent God knows what aspects of growth, market share, or regional trends—ends up capturing the excitement and pleasant confusion of the marketplace, the everyday street, personal relationships, and the simultaneity of multitasking. Does it really do all that? If you imagine you are inside there it does.

This is Dan Rather's profile. Expanded to the nth degree. Taken to infinity. Overlayed on the back of Patrick Stewart's head. It's recombinant phrenology. The elements of phrenology recombined in ways that follow the rules of irrational logic, a rigorous

methodology that follows nonrational rules. It is a structure for following your intuition and your obsessions. It is the hyperfocused scribblings of the mad and the gifted. The order and structure give it the appearance of rationality and scientific rigor. This appearance is easy to emulate.

Phrenology sought to reveal criminal propensities—and those of potential leaders and geniuses—in the shapes and bumps of the head and face. Nowadays we see it as a scientific justification for racist and cultural biases. A dangerous pseudoscience. But if phrenology was the genetic profiling of a previous era, what will supplant genetic profiling when that too appears as ridiculous as phrenology does to us now? Nonrational logic will not go away.

---

* Dolly, a sheep born in 1996, became famous as the first mammal to be cloned from an adult cell.

PowerPoint Is Evil

(OPINION)

Edward Tufte

Edward Tufte, professor emeritus of political science, computer science and statistics, and graphic design at Yale University, is well-known as a proponent of simpler, clearer graphical information. His publishing company, Graphics Press, has produced many books on the importance of good graphic design and ways to achieve it. The following essay appeared in response to David Byrne's article on PowerPoint, in the same 2003 issue of *Wired* magazine.

Analyzing and Connecting

Return to these questions after you have finished reading.

1. Tufte and Byrne come to different conclusions on the value of PowerPoint. What criteria does each writer use to evaluate the software? Are these criteria the cause of their disagreement? Or do they have different opinions about how well PowerPoint meets their criteria?

2. Tufte's essay is a good example of how aesthetic, practical, and ethical criteria can overlap. Ugly charts, he argues, do not communicate information well, and therefore fail practically as well as aesthetically. Respect for one's audience, an ethical consideration, also has practical implications: If your audience feels insulted, they will not listen to you. If you were writing this essay, would you weigh the ethical, practical, and aesthetic criteria the same way Tufte does? Why or why not?

3. Tufte's argument centres on the responsibilities of the presenter to his or her audience, while Byrne's piece focuses on the creative possibilities PowerPoint offers to the presenter. What kind of audience is more likely to be persuaded by Tufte's piece? What kind of audience is more likely to appreciate Byrne's?

4. After reading both essays, consider your own experiences with PowerPoint. Are you more inclined to agree with Byrne or with Tufte? Can you see ways in which their essays share some common ground? Have the two writers left out any points that you think are important?

TUFTE: POWERPOINT IS EVIL

IMAGINE a widely used and expensive prescription drug that promised to make us beautiful but didn't. Instead the drug had frequent, serious side effects: It induced stupidity, turned everyone into bores, wasted time, and degraded the quality and credibility of communication. These side effects would rightly lead to a worldwide product recall.

Yet slideware—computer programs for presentations—is everywhere: in corporate America, in government bureaucracies, even in our schools. Several hundred million copies of Microsoft PowerPoint are churning out trillions of slides each year. Slideware may help speakers outline their talks, but convenience for the speaker can be punishing to both content and audience. The standard PowerPoint presentation elevates format over content, betraying an attitude of commercialism that turns everything into a sales pitch.

Of course, data-driven meetings are nothing new. Years before today's slideware, presentations at companies such as IBM and in the military used bullet lists shown by overhead projectors. But the format has become ubiquitous under PowerPoint, which was created in 1984 and later acquired by Microsoft. PowerPoint's pushy style seeks to set up a speaker's dominance over the audience. The speaker, after all, is making power points with bullets to followers. Could any metaphor be worse? Voicemail menu systems? Billboards? Television? Stalin?

Particularly disturbing is the adoption of the PowerPoint cognitive style in our schools. Rather than learning to write a report using sentences, children are being taught how to formulate client pitches and infomercials. Elementary school PowerPoint exercises (as seen in teacher guides and in student work posted on the Internet) typically consist of 10 to 20 words and a piece of clip art on each slide in a presentation of three to six slides—a total of perhaps 80 words (15 seconds of silent reading) for a week of work. Students would be better off if the schools simply closed down on those days and everyone went to the Exploratorium or wrote an illustrated essay explaining something.

In a business setting, a PowerPoint slide typically shows 40 words, which is about eight seconds' worth of silent reading material. With so little information per slide, many, many slides are needed. Audiences consequently endure a relentless sequentiality, one damn slide after another. When information is stacked in time, it is difficult to understand context and evaluate relationships. Visual reasoning usually works more effectively when relevant information is shown side by side. Often, the more intense the detail, the greater the clarity and understanding. This is especially so for statistical data, where the fundamental analytical act is to make comparisons.

Consider an important and intriguing table of survival rates for those with cancer relative to those without cancer for the same time

Estimates of relative survival rates, by cancer site[12]

	% survival rates and their standard errors			
	5 year	10 year	15 year	20 year
Prostate	98.8 0.4	95.2 0.9	87.1 1.7	81.1 3.0
Thyroid	96.0 0.8	95.8 1.2	94.0 1.6	95.4 2.1
Testis	94.7 1.1	94.0 1.3	91.1 1.8	88.2 2.3
Melanomas	89.0 0.8	86.7 1.1	83.5 1.5	82.8 1.9
Breast	86.4 0.4	78.3 0.6	71.3 0.7	65.0 1.0
Hodgkin's disease	85.1 1.7	79.8 2.0	73.8 2.4	67.1 2.8
Corpus uteri, uterus	84.3 1.0	83.2 1.3	80.8 1.7	79.2 2.0
Urinary, bladder	82.1 1.0	76.2 1.4	70.3 1.9	67.9 2.4
Cervix, uteri	70.5 1.6	64.1 1.8	62.8 2.1	60.0 2.4

GOOD
A traditional table: rich, informative, clear.

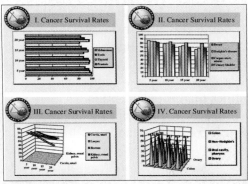

BAD
PowerPoint chartjunk: smarmy, chaotic, incoherent.

period. Some 196 numbers and 57 words describe survival rates and their standard errors for 24 cancers.

Applying the PowerPoint templates to this nice, straightforward table yields an analytical disaster. The data explodes into six separate chaotic slides, consuming 2.9 times the area of the table. Everything is wrong with these smarmy, incoherent graphs: the encoded legends, the meaningless color, the logo-type branding. They are uncomparative, indifferent to content and evidence, and so data-starved as to be almost pointless. Chartjunk is a clear sign of statistical stupidity. Poking a finger into the eye of thought, these data graphics would turn into a nasty travesty if used for a serious purpose, such as helping cancer patients assess their survival chances. To sell a product that messes up data with such systematic intensity, Microsoft abandons any pretense of statistical integrity and reasoning.

Presentations largely stand or fall on the quality, relevance, and integrity of the content. If your numbers are boring, then you've got the wrong numbers. If your words or images are not on point, making them dance in color won't make them relevant. Audience boredom is usually a content failure, not a decoration failure.

At a minimum, a presentation format should do no harm. Yet the PowerPoint style routinely disrupts, dominates, and trivializes content. Thus PowerPoint presentations too often resemble a school play—very loud, very slow, and very simple.

The practical conclusions are clear. PowerPoint is a competent slide manager and projector. But rather than supplementing a presentation, it has become a substitute for it. Such misuse ignores the most important rule of speaking: Respect your audience.

Junk Food That's Good for You?

(EDITORIAL)

Cathy Gulli

MACLEAN'S   In response to criticism, the Canadian government has proposed that the food industry be given discretionary authority to fortify junk food. Gulli looks at the controversy sparked by this proposal.

Analyzing and Connecting

Return to these questions after you have finished reading.

1. Why is the idea of fortified "junk food" so contradictory? Will this change affect consumers' opinions of junk food? Will it increase the number of people eating junk?

2. Practical considerations like increased trade are used to counter the argument that fortifying junk food is problematic. What other societal issues have been treated this same way? Note how in many instances, the human cost is countered with an economic one.

3. Who benefits in debates such as these? Think of other health issues (butter vs. margarine; bottled water vs. tap) and try to determine each stakeholder's purpose.

Junk Food That's Good for You?
May 15, 2009 by Cathy Gulli

If you think that "nutritious chocolate bar" sounds like an oxymoron, you may be surprised to learn of a controversial proposal Health Canada is reviewing that would give the food industry "discretionary" authority to fortify junk food with vitamins and minerals such as iron and calcium.

In its latest issue, the *Canadian Medical Association Journal* describes the debate. On the one hand, critics say that this is a cheap way of making junk food seem healthy. They worry that it will encourage consumption and further aggravate Canada's rising obesity problem. Supporters, on the other hand, argue that if people are going to eat junk food anyway then it might as well contain nutrients.

Wise to the dicey situation, Health Minister Leona Aglukak apparently intercepted changes to the Food and Drugs Regulations before they appeared in the Canada Gazette on Mar. 31, so that they could be further considered. A Health Canada spokesperson told the CMAJ she "balked at the prospect of being labelled the Fortified Junk Food Queen."

Fortification has been going on for decades in Canada. But historically it's only occurred when there has been a clear and widespread deficiency of a nutrient throughout the greater population. Vitamin D has been added to milk since the 1970s to alleviate the incidence of rickets in children; white flour for bread has long been enriched to replace the nutrients lost during processing.

Junk food fortification, however, is misguided, says Dr Yoni Freedhoff, a weight expert in Ottawa, because it won't address a specific deficiency crisis. If anything, he told the CMAJ, these changes will improve things for processed food companies more than for Canadian consumers. "With the fortification, the food industry will have ample ammunition with which to advertise how helpful their food has now become."

What's more, some dissidents are concerned that junk food fortification could put Canadians at risk of consuming dangerously high levels of certain nutrients when these products are eaten in excess or in combination with other nutrient-rich or fortified products, including multivitamin supplements. That's why Health Canada has so far controlled fortification strictly.

But Health Canada told the CMAJ that "stakeholders" have repeatedly complained that the current regulations are too strict and actually stunt the development of new products that could be beneficial to Canadians. These proponents point to other countries, including the U.S., where fortification of foods is more open and available to consumers. That means that fortified junk food could lead to more commercial trade of goods.

And Canadians themselves may be in favour of such a move. Focus group testing by Health Canada revealed that people who already consumed junk food said they'd eat fortified versions if the price and taste were the same. "But they did not indicate they would consume more," a Health Canada spokesperson pointed out to the CMAJ.

Of course, the absence of such a statement by focus group participants doesn't mean it wouldn't happen.

The Nitpicking Nation
(ARTICLE)
Stephanie Rosenbloom

The New York Times | In addition to being a journalist for the *New York Times*, 1997 Colgate University graduate Stephanie Rosenbloom began acting at a young age and has directed plays since she was a senior in high school. She writes articles about real estate and about how people adapt new technologies for their own purposes. "The Nitpicking Nation" appeared in the *New York Times* in May 2006.

Analyzing and Connecting
Return to these questions after you have finished reading.

1. In one way "The Nitpicking Nation" is not a classic evaluation but rather a look at how people make evaluations on Craigslist. But it also indirectly evaluates Craigslist. What positive and negative aspects of Craigslist are given?

2. Visit Craigslist.org, and compare housing and roommate ads for a city in the United States with those in a city in another country. Make a list of what is desirable and undesirable in roommates or house-sharing partners for both cities. Which criteria are the same on both lists? Which are different?

3. What criteria do you use to evaluate roommates? What makes an ideal roommate in your view?

4. Think of a product that you already own or would like to own. Enter the name of the product on Google followed by the word *review*. If you don't find many reviews, try consumersearch.com. Read several reviews and make a list of the criteria most frequently used to evaluate the product.

THE NITPICKING NATION

THEY are single, gay, straight, biracial, conservative, liberal and tattooed—and they have as many preferences for a potential roommate as an online dater has for a potential lover. They are bankers, fetishists, self-declared nerds and drug users. They have old wounds and new hopes, and are willing to barter their cooking and sexual expertise for free or discounted rent.

They are all seeking and selling housing on Craigslist.org, the electronic listing service with sites in all 50 states and more than 200 worldwide. And because users pay nothing (for now) and are able to go on at length about who they are and what they want, their postings provide a sociological window into housing trends and desires across the country, from the neon cityscape of the Las Vegas Strip to the wheat fields of Wichita, Kan.

Myriad other sites provide roommate-matching services, but in the last decade Craigslist has emerged as the gold standard. It is easy to navigate, has an extensive number of listings and does not require people to complete an online sign-up sheet to view postings in their entirety. And the intimate and sometimes politically incorrect nature of Craigslist postings can make them fun to read—amusing, frank and even kinky.

Perhaps the most eyebrow-raising thing about the housing listings is the abundance of users—even young, savvy residents of anything-goes metropolises like Los Angeles and Miami—who want mellow, nonpartying roommates. Las Vegas sounds more like Snore City if you judge it by its housing listings. And New Yorkers can come off sounding square. "No parties" and "no drama" are common refrains.

There are exceptions, but even club-hopping Paris Hilton hopefuls seem to have their limits. As four women (ages 19 to 22) seeking a fifth roommate in Boston wrote, "We want a partier, not a puker."

People in their 20s often list their alma maters and request a roommate in their own age group. Cleanliness is a must, or at least "clean-ish," "decently clean" or "clean in public spaces." And spending life with a "professional" appears to be just as important to users of Craigslist's housing listings as it is to users of Match.com.

Some listings have stirred up trouble, however, and the Chicago Lawyers' Committee for Civil Rights Under Law, a nonprofit group, has filed a lawsuit in federal court against Craigslist for "publishing housing advertisements which exclude prospective tenants on the basis of race, gender, family status, marital status, national origin and religion."

A news release issued by the organization said that the Craigslist postings contained such language as "no minorities," "African-Americans and Arabians tend to clash with me so that won't work out," "ladies, please rent from me," "requirements: clean godly Christian male," "will allow only single occupancy," and "no children."

The suit is addressed on Craigslist: "Although in all likelihood this suit will be dismissed on the grounds that Internet sites cannot legally be held liable for content posted by users, Craigslist has no need to hide behind this well-established immunity."

The statement also says that Craigslist respects constitutionally protected free speech rights and that "discriminatory postings are

ROSENBLOOM: THE NITPICKING NATION

exceedingly uncommon, and those few that do reach the site are typically removed quickly by our users through the flagging system that accompanies each ad."

Craig Newmark, the founder of Craigslist, said that its "culture of trust" inspires users to be straightforward. In fact, some users do not even feel compelled to embellish the descriptions of their spaces, as housing advertisements commonly do. Rather, they take a certain pride in the gritty crudeness of their offerings. A small room for rent in the East Village is described as "definitely a young person's apartment" with "two small junky TV's that we have cheap antennas on, but we get the normal channels, and that is enough for us."

"There is no window," the listing says, "but you have a full-sized door."

And where else do you find housing listings that include candid photographs of the owner or leaseholder instead of the property they are advertising? (A man in Fort Lauderdale, Fla., compromised and included images of his bare room and his bare chest.)

Indeed, Craigslist is where sex and real estate can truly merge. Near Dallas, a married couple are looking for a female roommate "with benefits." A listing for Astoria, Queens, reads: "I am offering a free room for up to three months for any females who are ticklish." A single man in Los Angeles is offering foot massages and free rent to women with comely feet.

Those are some of the tamer overtures, though the majority of roommate listings are not suggestive.

But just who are the most desirable roommates?

Many people prefer women to men. There are women who feel more comfortable sharing a home with someone of the same sex, men who say they get along better with female housemates, and a few cyberspace Casanovas who want to take a shot at turning a roommate into a bedmate. Interns are also desirable, apparently because they are thought to be hard-working, responsible and willing to pay good money for cramped rooms.

But couples are sometimes lumped into a list of the unacceptable, like cigarette smoking. Overall, Democrats are more vocal than Republicans in expressing a desire not to live with the opposing party, though two "hip professional guys" found elusive harmony on Capitol Hill: "One guy is straight, and one is gay. One is a Republican, and the other is a Democrat," they wrote in a listing for a third roommate. "We appreciate and welcome diversity."

Users in the San Francisco Bay Area appear to be among the least interested in rooming with a pet. This area had the highest percentage of "no pets" listings during a key-word search last Thursday (slightly more than 16 percent of 32,295 housing listings). In Boston, about 14 percent of 45,880 listings said "no pets."

Dallas, Wyoming and Birmingham, Ala., seemed quite pet-friendly by comparison: only about 1 percent of the housing listings in each location said "no pets." But Wichita, Kan., emerged as one of the most accepting places, with less than 1 percent of the listings snubbing pets.

In some parts of the country Craigslist housing postings are an essential part of the real estate biosphere. New York is by far the leader in this regard (it had some 180,245 housing listings last Thursday).

Mr. Newmark said there were two reasons for that. "New York real estate is kind of a blood sport," he said, "and also, because our site is free, brokers tend to post a lot of redundant ads."

He said he hoped to address that problem in a matter of weeks by beginning to charge a fee.

Although Mr. Newmark has not studied how the number of housing listings fluctuates day to day, he believes they remain fairly steady on weekdays and drop off on weekends.

Boston had 45,880 housing listings last Thursday, and the San Francisco Bay Area had 32,295. In other places like Montana and Louisville, Ky., there were just a few hundred postings, and North Dakota had fewer than 100.

The New York listings include some of the most expensive, precarious sleeping arrangements in the country. A sofa bed in the living room/kitchen of a one-bedroom apartment on 55th Street between Eighth and Ninth Avenues is $683 a month. You could get a 780-square-foot one-bedroom cottage in Savannah, Ga., for $665 a month. A couch on the West Coast, in a Los Angeles apartment belonging to three actors, is merely $400 a month and includes utilities, cable, Netflix membership, Starbucks wireless membership and wireless Internet, as well as household staples like toothpaste and shampoo.

New Yorkers are also adept at constructing what the military calls a zone of separation. A woman with an apartment at Union Square posted a photograph, not of the bedroom she wanted to rent out for $1,150 a month, but of a large divider she planned to use to create the bedroom from part of her living room.

Near Columbus Circle, a "very small, but cozy space enclosed by tall bookshelves and bamboo screens" is listed for $1,700 a month.

Potential occupants are advised that they must be older than 30 and cannot wear shoes inside the apartment, smoke, consume alcohol, invite guests over or have "sleepovers."

A plethora of "no smokers" statements in the New York housing listings make it appear that the public smoking ban has infiltrated private spaces, too.

But while cigarettes are a deal breaker for some, a number of Craigslist users across the country (Denver and Boulder, Colo.; San Francisco; Boston; and Portland, Ore., to name but a few) say that they are "420 friendly," slang for marijuana use. References to 420 were nonexistent in other cities, including Little Rock, Ark.; Santa Fe, N.M.; and Boise, Idaho.

There are also myriad references to amenities, everything from the use of old record collections and video games to a trapeze suspended in a Brooklyn loft. A posting for a room for rent in Detroit lacks images of the property, though there is a photograph of the L.C.D. television.

And if nothing else, Craigslist housing postings in the United States confirm the zaniness of the hunt and provide a taste of the free-spirited, random connections that have always been part of the experience.

A posting in Asheville, N.C., says that two 21-year-old women are planning to drive almost 20 hours to Austin, Tex., this summer, where they will rent a two-bedroom apartment for $550 a month. "We are looking for one or two (yeah, you can bring a buddy) cool people to ride out there and split an apartment with us," the listing reads. "Are you up for being spontaneous?"

Would-be Jack Kerouacs, take note: they hit the road at the end of the month.

How to write an evaluation

These steps for the process of writing an evaluation may not progress as neatly as this chart might suggest. Writing is not an assembly-line process.

As you write and revise, think about how you might sharpen your criteria and better explain how they apply to what you are evaluating. Your instructor and fellow students may give you comments that help you to rethink your argument from the beginning.

1 CHOOSE A SUBJECT

- Analyze the assignment.
- Explore possible subjects by making lists.
- Analyze a subject.

2 THINK ABOUT YOUR CRITERIA

- Find the obvious criteria, then dig deeper.
- Research your argument by finding evidence and reliable sources.

Think about what is at stake

- Who will agree with you?
- Who will disagree? Why?
- Why does your evaluation matter?

Analyze your readers

- How familiar will your readers be with your topic? How much background information will they need?
- Which of your criteria are most likely to appeal to your audience? Which criteria might they find unconvincing or unimportant?

3 WRITE A DRAFT

- Introduce the issue and give the necessary background.
- Describe your criteria and offer evidence.
- Anticipate and address opposing viewpoints.
- Conclude with either your position, a compelling example, or who is affected.
- Choose a title that will interest readers in your essay.

4 REVISE, REVISE, REVISE

- Check that your paper or project fulfills the assignment.
- Is your evaluative claim arguable?
- Are your criteria reasonable, and will your audience accept them?
- Is your evidence convincing and sufficient?
- Do you address opposing views?
- Review the visual presentation of your paper or project.
- Proofread carefully.

5 PRINT A VERSION TO SUBMIT

- Make sure your finished writing meets all formatting requirements.

1: Choose a subject

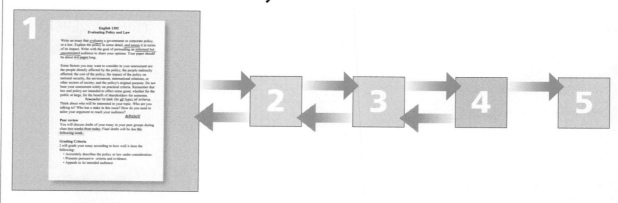

Analyze the assignment	• Read your assignment slowly and carefully. Look for key words like *evaluate, rank, review,* and *assess.* These key words tell you that you are writing an evaluative essay.
	• Mark off any information about the length specified, date due, formatting, and other requirements. You can attend to this information later.
Explore possible subjects by making lists	• Make a list of goods and services you consume; sports, entertainment, or hobbies you enjoy; books you have read recently; films you have seen; speeches you have heard; or policies and laws that affect you or concern you.
	• Consider which items on your list you might evaluate. Which are interesting to you? Which would likely interest your readers? Put checkmarks by these items.
	• Choose something to evaluate that people can disagree on. You will learn the most, and interest readers most, if you build a strong evaluation that persuades your opponents to re-think their position.
Analyze a subject	• What does your subject attempt to achieve? What do other similar subjects attempt to achieve? (For example, a mountain bike is designed to climb and descend trails, but a good mountain bike will be lightweight, durable, and have good suspension.)
	• Who is the audience for your subject? (Mountain bikes appeal to people who prefer to ride on trails rather than pavement.)
Think about what's at stake	• Who will agree with you? Who will disagree, and why?
	• Think about why your evaluation matters.

Make an arguable claim

A claim that is too obvious or too general will not produce an interesting evaluation.

Don't waste your time—or your readers'.

OFF TRACK
Wayne Gretzky was a great hockey player.
ON TRACK
Bobby Orr was the most influencial defenceman in professional hockey.

OFF TRACK
Running is great exercise and a great way to lose weight.
ON TRACK
If you start running to lose weight, be aware of the risks: your body running exerts eight times its weight on your feet, ankles, legs, hips, and lower back, often causing injury to your joints. Swimming, biking, or exercise machines might be the better choice.

Finding a subject to evaluate

1. Make a list of possible subjects to evaluate, and select the one that appears most promising.
2. Freewrite for five minutes about what you like and dislike about this particular subject.
3. Freewrite for five minutes about what you like and dislike about things in the same category (Mexican restaurants, world leaders, horror movies, mountain bikes, and so on).
4. Freewrite for five minutes about what people in general like and dislike about things in this category.
5. Underline the likes and dislikes in all three freewrites. You should gain a sense of how your evaluation stacks up against those of others. You may discover a way you can write against the grain, showing others a good or bad aspect of this subject that they may not have observed.

Writer at work

Kim Tong began by circling words and phrases that indicated her evaluative task and highlighted information about dates and processes for the project. She then made notes and a list of possible subjects. She chose online communities, which she knew about firsthand as she was taking several online subjects.

CUL 2250—Virtual Worlds

Write an essay that evaluates "life on the internet." Explain in detail how virtual identities and alternate ways of being are by-products of the internet age and how emerging from the virtual medium is a growing community with shared cultural rules and norms that exists only in cyberspace.

Synthesize (put together) various points of view in an explanation of "cyber" communities and their cultural impact, with the goal of persuading an informed audience to share your opinion. Your paper should be 4–6 pages long.

The following are some factors you might want to consider in your assessment: people who are constantly involved with the internet; the people who use the internet only for a specific purpose; the societal cost of virtual environments; the advantages of virtual communities over traditional f2f dialogue; and other criteria that could impact your assessment.
Remember to look for all types of criteria.
Think about your audience. Who would be interested in this topic? Who are you talking to? Who are the stakeholders? How do you need to tailor your argument to reach your audience?
AUDIENCE

Peer review
You will discuss drafts of your essay in your peer groups during class two weeks from today. Final drafts will be due the following week.

Grading Criteria
I will grade your essay according to how well it does the following:
- Accurately describes the virtual world phenomenon
- Presents persuasive criteria and evidence
- Appeals to its intended audience

CLAIMS COULD BE:

1. The current social networking fad is destroying relationships
2. Virtual worlds provide a valuable alternate "way of being"
3. YouTube is the ultimate invasion of privacy
4. Online communities are a haven for the maladjusted

FREEWRITE:

I remember my first online class...it was interesting to read about people as they [seemed] really honest with their points of views. It took some time to switch identities – from face to face to "virtual," but the online community that was created allowed us to express ourselves in ways that we would never do in a traditional discussion. Anyway, it seemed that the virtual experience opened up opportunities for debate, discussion, investigation, and even argument without having to leave the house.

2: Think about your criteria and your audience

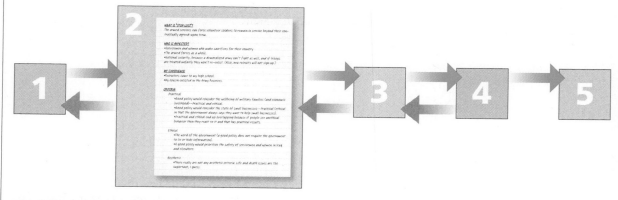

Find the obvious criteria, and then dig deeper

- Write down the criteria you already know you will use in your evaluation. For example, a good study location is quiet, well-lit, safe, and easy to get to.

- Consider other criteria you might not be aware you're using to judge by. Perhaps you gravitate toward the student union rather than the library because you are allowed to drink coffee there. Maybe you began avoiding the library when its poor lighting started to hurt your eyes.

- Think about whether these criteria are practical, aesthetic, or ethical. It isn't that important for you to classify each criterion exactly because there is often overlap between these categories. But you may run into trouble with your audience if you rely too much on one type of criteria, such as aesthetics, and neglect others, like practicality, such as a beautiful chair that hurts your back.

Research your argument

- Find evidence to show how the thing you are evaluating meets or doesn't meet your criteria. If you claim that a symphony has a compelling melodic theme in the first movement, describe the passage in detail.

- Go to reliable sources to find out how others have evaluated the same thing. Do other reviewers tend to agree or disagree with you? Do they use criteria that you don't? Are they addressing the same audience you are?

Analyze your audience

- Consider which of your criteria are most likely to appeal to your audience. Which criteria might they find unconvincing or unimportant?

- How familiar will readers be with your topic? How much background information will they need?

STAYING ON TRACK

Specify and argue for your criteria

Specify your criteria
Show exactly how your criteria apply to what you are evaluating.

OFF TRACK
Border collies make the best pets because they are smart, friendly, and easy to train. *[Vague; many pets are smart, friendly, and easy to train.]*

ON TRACK
Border collies are ideal family pets because their intelligence and trainability enable them to fit into almost any household, no matter how crowded.

Support your criteria
Give evidence to demonstrate why your criteria are valid.

OFF TRACK
Swimming is better exercise than running because you get a better workout. *[How so?]*

ON TRACK
Health professionals maintain that for those who have access to pools or lakes, swimming is the best workout because it exercises all major muscle groups and it's not prone to causing injuries.

Don't assume your audience shares your criteria
It's easy to forget that other people have different concerns and priorities. Your challenge as a writer is finding common ground with people who think differently.

OFF TRACK
Coach X is a bad coach who should be fired because he has lost to our rival school three years in a row. *[For some fans beating the big rival is the only criterion, but not all fans.]*

ON TRACK
While coach X hasn't beaten our big rival in three years, he has succeeded in increasing attendance by 50%, adding a new sports complex built by donations, and raising the players' graduation rate to 80%.

Writer at work

Kim Tong made the following notes about her evaluative claim:

WHAT IS AN ONLINE COMMUNITY?

Defined as a group of people who share a particular purpose or goal and who come together in a virtual space to interact

WHO IS AFFECTED?

Any person who engages in online discourse belongs to a "community" though not all people participate at the same level of interest.

MY EXPERIENCE

- Several opportunities through online learning
- Member of several social networking sites

CRITERIA

Practical

- Creates a forum for a bigger exchange of ideas
- Allows for great research opportunities
- Could help develop sub set of new skills
- Supports socially awkward people to become more involved

Ethical

- Free flow of opinion would not be censored or suppressed
- Hidden social issues could find a forum for discussion without censure

Aesthetic

- Other than the site, there aren't really any aesthetic criteria

<u>AUDIENCE</u>

Who benefits from these types of communities? What do they know about it? How should I appeal to them?

Students
- Feel direct connection with each other and the content
- Need to see the value of participation

Introverts
- Can feel less awkward — will be able to "hide" self without hiding point of view.
- Will be better able to participate in social situations — may transfer skills to real life?

<u>BACKGROUND</u>

Most people are familiar with the internet, but may not realize how "involved" they can get...may need a little information about "communities" like FB or worlds like Second Life. However, probably more important to explain the value of virtual exchange of ideas...

<u>TO RESEARCH</u>

- Need to find out about different forms (e.g. blogs)
- Research who has written on the topic (don't need many, but need some external voices to back up claim)

3: Write a draft

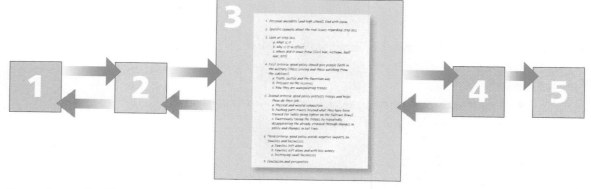

Introduce the issue

- Give your readers any background information they will need.
- State your stance up front, if you wish. Some evaluations work better if the writer's judgment is issued at the beginning; sometimes, it is more effective to build up a mass of evidence and then issue your verdict at the end.

Describe your criteria and offer evidence

- Organize the criteria you present to be as effective as possible. Do you want to start with the most important one, or build up to it? Try both ways, and see which seems more convincing.
- Explain each criterion and give reasons to support its use, if readers are unlikely to automatically accept it.
- Analyze how well the thing you are evaluating meets each criterion. Provide specific examples.

Anticipate and address opposing viewpoints

- Acknowledge why others may have a different opinion from yours.
- Demonstrate why your evaluation is better by pointing out either why your criteria are better or why you have better evidence and reasons.

Conclude with strength

- State your position at the end of your argument if you haven't done so previously.
- Offer a compelling example or analogy to end your essay.
- State explicitly what is at stake in your evaluation, especially if you are evaluating a policy or issue that affects many people.

Choose a title that will interest readers in your essay

- A bland, generic title like "An Evaluation of X" gives little incentive to read the paper.

Writer at work

Based on her preliminary research, Kim created a working outline for her essay.

1. Online communities are changing the way we define and view the concept of a community.
   a. The internet allows us to network with millions of people around the world, and it is being used to encourage and create online communities more than ever.
      i. The internet provides something for everyone.
   b. Being online allows those who are generally shy to feel more comfortable expressing their thoughts.
   c. Online communities allow members to have a freedom of speech with limited to no restrictions, creating a safe place for heated discussions.
   d. Online communities provide a library of information, available at your fingertips.
   e. The cyber world has become the equivalent to a secondary society for many people, and the impact of online communities is something that affects millions of people around the world.

2. The internet offers something for everyone.
   a. All users are accepted and encouraged to get involved in creating online forums that suit their needs and interests.
      i. The internet provides a world where you choose your own destiny.
      ii. Allowing users to create their own forums ensures that everyone can find their own place in cyber world.
   b. The internet creates a huge arena for many different online cultures, where people from all around the world who have a common goal can come together in one connected place.

3. Online communities are formed with the intention of creating a society where everyone can feel comfortable.
   a. The internet is a safe haven for many people who consider themselves to be anti-social or are uncomfortable in public places.
      i. Being online allows these people to express their thoughts and voice their opinions without feeling the pressure that they would normally feel in public.
      ii. Members are able to enter a world where no one can judge them based on physical appearance.
   b. Online interaction is a step up from the expectations of a traditional society.
   c. There is no pressure and all members can be confident in expressing their views on certain topics.

4. Online communities allow participants to have freedom of speech, with limited to no restrictions.
   a. Joining online forums allows members to freely voice their opinions on certain topics. There are however certain rules that users must abide by.
      i. These rules are dictated by both the users and creators of online communities.
   b. Online discussions where one party doesn't agree with the other will always become heated, but being online gives you the reassurance that your views on certain political topics and issues will not be met with retaliation.
   c. Debating over certain issues online can ensure that a normally violent protest in a traditional community stays peaceful online as no one could be physically hurt for expressing their feelings.

5. Being online opens up a world of information for all those who use it, and navigating through online communities is a very informative experience.
   a. The education and insight offered through online forums are usually vast and infinite.
   b. In traditional communities people have to physically leave their homes to go to libraries to research topics that they are unsure of.
      i. Online communities can be very large so you can get insight from hundreds of different people.
      ii. Being a part of an online community allows you to do your own research, discuss your topics with others and get their insight or opinions—all from the comfort of your own home.

6. The cyber society proves to be a secondary world for many people.
   a. The development of online communities encourages users from all around the world, who share a common goal, to come together to share their thoughts and ideas.
   b. The impact of online communities is that the physical boundaries are removed.
      i. What remains is a world where people can network with each other with the click of a button.
      ii. The violence that is common in our communities today is removed when people are able to interact with each other online.
      iii. The cyber world is web of information created and edited by its millions of users.
   c. Unlike traditional communities, the online world is an informative society that is boundless and conveniently provides the resources and tools people need to accomplish whatever it is they set out to do.

4: Revise, revise, revise

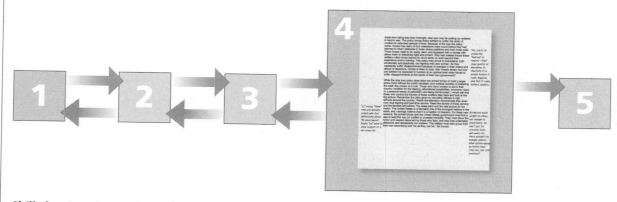

Skilled writers know that the secret to writing well is revising. Leave correcting errors for last.

Does your paper or project meet the assignment?	• Look again at your assignment. Does your paper or project do what the assignment asks? • Look again at the assignment for specific guidelines, including length, format, and amount of research. Does your work meet these guidelines?
Is your evaluative claim arguable?	• Do enough people disagree with you to make the evaluation worthwhile? • Does anyone but you care about this topic?
Are your criteria reasonable, and will your audience accept them?	• Do you provide compelling reasons for readers to accept your criteria for evaluation, if they weren't predisposed to do so? • Do you weight criteria appropriately, balancing aesthetic, ethical, and practical considerations in a way likely to appeal to your audience?
Is your evidence convincing and sufficient?	• Will readers believe what you say about the thing you are evaluating? What proof do you offer that it does or doesn't meet your criteria? • Are your descriptions clear and accurate? • Is the assignment documented correctly?
Do you address opposing views?	• Have you acknowledged the opinions of people who disagree with you? • Where do you show why your evaluation is better?
Is the writing project visually effective?	• Is the font attractive and readable? • Are the headings and visuals effective? • If you use images or tables as part of your evaluation, are they legible and appropriately placed?
Save the editing for last	When you have finished revising, edit and proofread carefully.

A peer review guide is on page 31.

Writer at work

Working with a group of her fellow students, Kim made comments on her rough draft and used them to help produce a final version of her essay.

May not be true...need to adjust this statement.

Online communities are the best way for people to participate in the 21st century. Online communities give people voices where they never had them before. As Amy Bruckman discusses in "Finding One's Own Space in Cyberspace," the internet allows us to network with millions of people around the world, and the internet is being used to encourage and create online communities more than ever before. The internet is for everyone! As opposed to traditional communities, being online provides a different world where those who are generally shy or introverted can feel more comfortable expressing their thoughts and feelings. Online communities allow participants to have freedom of speech with limited to no restrictions, creating a safe place for debates or other heated discussions. Another important observation is that online communities provide a library of information right at your fingertips. The cyber world is affecting millions of people around the world.

Sounds a bit like propaganda...may not appeal to this audience...need to tone it down..

Finishes abruptly...needs a little more context to set up this topic...this final statement does not actually contribute to my point

5: Print a version to submit

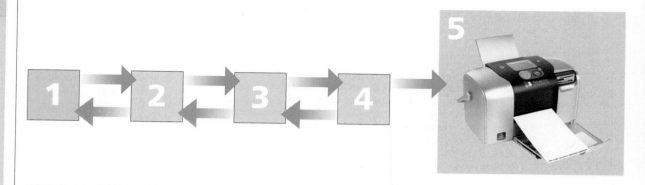

Tong 1

Kim G. Tong
CUL 2250
Dr. G. Murphy
10 April 2011

Virtual Communities: An Alternate Way of Being

Friendwise. LinkedIn. Bebo. Facebook. Twitter. Orkut. Unfamiliar not so many years ago, these names now represent the most popular social networking sites available online. As cyber communities, they are changing the way society defines and views "community," with its own norms and values. The internet "is filled with millions of individuals who are looking to meet other people" (Social Networking) and, as such, offers everyone the opportunity to participate in a safe and, if necessary, anonymous setting without fear of censure. Compared to traditional communities, virtual communities provide worlds where the introverted or terminally shy can express their thoughts and feelings. Virtual communities also permit freedom of speech or expression with few restrictions, creating a forum for heated discussions. Another advantage of the virtual community is access to an infinite amount of information. With a click of a mouse, a member can find, interact, discuss, or even argue about current events or ancient history without ever

Tong 2

leaving the comfort of their homes. Their potential is limited only by its membership, so as an alternative to the usual face-to-face experience, the virtual community has become the latest meeting place.

As Amy Bruckman discusses in "Finding One's Own Space in Cyberspace," virtual communities allow millions of people around the world to network, and the internet is being used to encourage and create online communities more than ever before (128). All users are accepted and encouraged to get involved in creating or joining online forums. Members who share common interests can access worlds where they choose their own destinies: "Selective advertising can help a community achieve a desired ambiance" (Bruckman 133). Enabling users to create their own forums ultimately ensures that everyone can find their own place in cyber world—a place where they feel they would most fit in. A virtual community benefits its members by making the world more accessible, where people from all around the world who have a common goal can come together in one connected place.

Online communities are formed by members who want to "regularly engage in sharing and learning, based on their common interests" (Tremblay 3) and who want to create a society where everyone can feel comfortable. The way people interact with each other is being significantly affected by the increased popularity of virtual communities. "The idea that some people might be excluded from a community ruffles a lot of feathers" (Bruckman 132), so being online allows individuals to express their thoughts and voice their opinions without feeling the pressure that they would normally feel in public. "Blogs are becoming an important component of the internet landscape, providing authors and readers with an avenue for unedited expression, reaction, and connection . . . ("7 Things"). Members are able to enter a world where no one can see or judge them based on their appearance or other physical attributes. This type of online interaction is a step up from the expectations of traditional society—there is no pressure and all members can be confident in expressing their views on certain topics.

In spite of the perceived freedom of belonging to a virtual community, members must still follow and abide by certain rules, which are dictated by both the users and creators of the sites. "The personality of the community's founder can have a great influence on what sort of place it becomes" (Bruckman 131). This ensures that all online forums have some form of leadership: "The existence of a moderator to filter postings often makes for a more focused and civil discussion" (Bruckman 133). In discussions where disagreements become heated or malicious, being online gives the reassurance that views on controversial topics and issues will not be met with physical retaliation. Debating certain issues online can guarantee that a normally violent reaction in a traditional community stays peaceful online, in that members are not physically hurt for expressing their thoughts and feelings.

Many people join online communities with the intention of learning from other people, as well as exchanging and sharing information and knowledge (Tremblay 6). The education and insight that is offered through online forums is vast and infinite: "... blogs are an increasingly accepted instructional technology tool" ("7 Things"). In traditional communities, people must physically leave their homes to find the information they are seeking. Access can be limited and frustrating, and feedback is confined to a few people in the participants' physical world. Online communities, on the other hand, are very large, and insight from hundreds of different people is always available. When interacting online, "Students often learn as much from each other as from instructors or textbooks ..." ("7 Things"). Being a part of an online community allows for personal and meaningful research, discussions about relevant topics with others, and extensive insight or opinions from an international community—all from a home computer.

The virtual community proves to be an alternate social world for many people. Online communities encourage users from all around the world, who share a common goal, to come together to share their thoughts and ideas (Social Networking). Online, physical boundaries are removed, and what remains is a world where people can network with others at the click of a button. Aggression and/or hostility, which can define communities today, is removed when people are able to interact with each other online instead. Many people can, therefore, effectively get their opinions across without retribution. The virtual world is a network of information created and edited by millions of users. Unlike traditional communities, the online world is an informative society that is boundless and conveniently provides the resources and tools people need to accomplish whatever it is they set out to do.

Works Cited

Bruckman, A. "Finding One's Own Space in Cyberspace." *The Mercury Reader: A Custom Publication.* Comp. M. Rubens. Toronto: Pearson, 2006. 128–38. Print.

"7 Things You Should Know About . . . Blogs." *EDUCAUSE Learning Initiative.* 2007. Web. 21 Aug., 2009

Tremblay, Diane-Gabrielle. "Virtual Communities of Practice: Towards New Modes of Learning and Knowledge Creation." Université du Québec. 2004. Web. 21 Aug. 2009.

"What Is Social Networking?" *Social Networking.* WhatIsSocialNetworking.com, 2008. Web. 30 Mar, 2008.

Projects

You likely have a great deal of experience making consumer evaluations, and when you have time to do your homework to compare features, quality, and price, probably you will make a good decision. For other evaluations, however, the criteria may not be obvious. Often the keys are finding the right criteria and convincing your readers that these criteria are the best ones to use.

These projects are frequently written kinds of evaluations.

Go to **www.mycanadiancomplab.ca** to practise your grammar, punctuation, and mechanics skills. Go to the "Resources" tab within MyCanadianCompLab and then click on "Grammar." You will have access to a variety of exercises as well as direct instruction that will help you improve your basic skills and get a better grade in your course.

EVALUATE A NON-TRADITIONAL SUBJECT

For an example of an evaluation of a nontraditional subject, see pages 347–350.

Think of controversial subjects on your campus or in your community for which you can find recent articles in your campus or local newspaper. For example, is your mayor or city manager an effective leader? Is your campus recreational sports facility adequate? Is a new condominium complex built on city land that was used as a park good or bad?

Identify what is at stake in the evaluation. Who thinks it is good or effective? Who thinks it is bad or ineffective? Why does it matter?

List the criteria that make something or someone good or bad. Which criteria are the most important? Which will you have to argue for?

Analyze your potential readers. How familiar will they be with what you are evaluating? Which criteria will they likely accept and which might they disagree with?

Write a draft. Introduce your subject and give the necessary background. Make your evaluative claim either at the beginning or as your conclusion. Describe each criterion and evaluate your subject on each criterion. Be sure to address opposing viewpoints by acknowledging how their evaluations might be different.

EVALUATE AN ARTICLE

For an example of an article, see pages 352–354.

Find a current article from the local or campus newspaper that affects you. Examples include issues related to post-secondary tuition, the environment, local politics, or any other topic that you feel strongly about.

Consider your target audience. Who else is affected by this issue? Who is responsible for the problem? How did the problem originate?

Determine the criteria for your evaluation. Which criteria will be most important for others who are affected by the same issue?

Take a clear position on the issue. Is the problem being dealt with fairly, effectively, and efficiently? Sometimes good intentions lead to bad results. If you think the proposed solutions are fair or effective, explain why according to the criteria you set out. If you don't, then provide reasons and examples to support your position.

MACLEAN'S FILM REVIEW

For an example of a review, see pages 359–361.

Select a film to review. Choose a specific magazine, newspaper, or online publication as the place where you would publish the review. Read some reviews in that publication and notice the criteria that they use. You will need to keep the audience in mind.

Watch the film more than once and take notes. Analyze the film's genre. What makes a good horror movie? A good action-adventure movie? A good documentary? A good comedy? These will be your criteria for evaluation.

Find information on the film. The Internet Movie Database (**www.imdb.com**) is a good place to start. Look at the director's credits to find other films that he or she has done. Look at the information about the actors and locations.

Write a thesis that makes an evaluative claim: the film is a successful or unsuccessful example of its genre. Go beyond the obvious in selecting criteria. A comedy is supposed to make you laugh, but movies that are only gags tend to wear thin. Comedies that have engaging characters keep your interest. Acting often makes the difference between a good movie and a great movie. Use evidence from the film to support your claim.

15
Arguing for a Position

Position arguments aim to change readers' attitudes and beliefs or at least get them to consider a view different from their own.

Chapter contents

Writing a position argument

Many people think of the term *argument* as a synonym for *debate* or *disagreement*. College and university courses and professional careers, however, require a different kind of argument—one that, most of the time, is cooler in emotion and more elaborate in detail than oral debate. At first glance an argument in writing doesn't seem to have much in common with debate. But the basic elements and ways of reasoning used in written arguments are similar to those we use in everyday conversations. Let's look at an example of an informal discussion.

SEAN: I think students should not pay tuition to go to college and university.

CARMEN: Cool idea, but why should students not pay?

SEAN: Because you don't have pay to go to high school.

CARMEN: Yeah, but that's different. The law says that everyone has to go to high school, at least to age 16. Everyone doesn't have to go to college.

SEAN: Well, in some other countries like the United Kingdom, students don't have to pay tuition.

CARMEN: Their system of education is different. Plus you're wrong. Students started paying tuition at British universities in the fall of 1998.

SEAN: OK, maybe the United Kingdom isn't a good example. But students should have a right to go to college or university, just like they have the right to drive on the highway.

CARMEN: Why? What evidence do you have that things would be better if everyone went to college or university? It would put an enormous drain on the economy. People would have to pay a lot more in taxes.

In this discussion Sean starts out by making a claim that students should not have to pay tuition. Carmen immediately asks him why students should not have to pay tuition. She wants a reason to accept his claim. Scholars who study argument maintain that *an argument must have a claim and one or more reasons to support that claim.* Something less might be persuasive, but it isn't an argument.

If Sean's assertion were a bumper sticker, it might read "MAKE POST-SECONDARY EDUCATION FREE FOR ALL." The assertion is a claim but it is not an argument, because it lacks a reason. Many reasons are possible for arguing for free tuition:

- College and university should be free for all because everyone is entitled to a good education.

- College and university should be free for all because the economy will benefit.

- College and university should be free for all because a democracy requires educated citizens.

When a claim has a reason attached, then it becomes an argument.

A reason is typically offered in a **because-clause,** a statement that begins with the word *because* and that provides a supporting reason for the claim. Sean's first attempt is to argue that students shouldn't have to pay to go to college or university because they don't have to pay to go to high school.

The word *because* signals a **link** between the reason and the claim. Just having a reason for a claim, however, doesn't mean that the audience will be convinced. When Sean tells Carmen that students don't have to pay to go to public high schools, Carmen does not accept the link. Carmen asks **"So what?"** every time Sean presents a new reason. Carmen will accept Sean's claim only if she accepts that his reason supports his claim. Carmen challenges Sean's links and keeps asking "So what?". For her, Sean's reasons are not good reasons.

It is not hard to think of reasons. What is difficult is to convince your audience that your reasons are *good reasons*. In a conversation, you get immediate feedback that tells you whether your listener agrees or disagrees. When you are writing, there usually is not someone who can give you immediate feedback. Consequently, if you are going to convince someone who doesn't agree with you or know what you know already, you have to be more specific about what you are claiming, you have to connect with the values you hold in common with your readers, and you have to anticipate what questions and objections your readers might have.

Components of position arguments

What exactly is my issue?	**Define the issue** Your subject should be clear to your readers. If readers are unfamiliar with the issue, you should give enough examples so they understand the issue in concrete terms.
What exactly is my stand on the issue?	**State your position** You may want to state your thesis in the opening paragraph to let readers know your position immediately. If your issue is unfamiliar, you may want to find out more before you state your position. In any case, you should take a definite position on the issue.
What are the reasons for my position?	**Find one or more reasons** You need to give one or more reasons for your position. Write as many because-clauses as you can think of. Use the ones that are most convincing.
Where can I find evidence?	**Provide evidence** In support of your reasons, provide evidence—in the form of examples, statistics, and testimony of experts—that the reasons are valid. When the issue is unfamiliar, more evidence than usual is required.
Who disagrees with my position?	**Acknowledge opposing views and limitations of the claim** If everybody thinks the same way, then there is no need to write a position argument. Anticipate what objections might be made to your position. You can answer possible objections in two ways: that the objections are not valid or that the objections have some validity but your argument is stronger.

Keys to position arguments

Understand your goal	A well-written and well-reasoned position argument may not change minds entirely, but it can convince readers that a reasonable person can hold this point of view. Position arguments do not necessarily have winners and losers. Your goal is to invite a response that creates a dialogue.
Be sensitive to the context	Even position arguments that have become classics and in a sense "timeless" frequently were written in response to a historical event; for example, Martin Luther King, Jr. wrote his powerful argument for civil disobedience, "Letter from Birmingham Jail," in response to a published statement by eight Birmingham clergymen. A careful analysis of a recent or historical event often provides your argument with a sense of immediacy.
Rely on careful definitions	What exactly does *freedom of speech* mean? What exactly does *privacy* mean? What exactly does *animal rights* mean? Getting readers to accept a definition is often the key to a position argument. For example, torturing animals is against the law. Animal rights activists argue that raising and slaughtering animals for food is torture and thus would extend the definition. If you can get readers to accept your definition, then they will agree with your position.
Use quality sources	Find the highest-quality sources for citing evidence. Recent sources are critical for current topics, such as the relationship of certain diets to disease. But don't discount older sources. They can provide historical context.
Create credibility	You have probably noticed that many times in the course of reading, you get a strong sense of the writer's character, even if you know nothing about the person. Be honest about strengths and weaknesses and about what you don't know, and avoid easy labels. If readers trust you are sincere, they will take you seriously.
Cultivate a sense of humour and a distinctive voice	A reasonable voice doesn't have to be a dull one. Humour is a legitimate tool of argument, especially when the stakes are high and tempers are flaring.
Argue responsibly	When you begin an argument by stating "in my opinion," you are not arguing responsibly. Readers assume that if you make a claim in writing, you believe that claim. More importantly, it is rarely just your opinion. Most beliefs and assumptions are shared by many people. When other members of your community share your opinion, your readers should consider your position seriously.

Provide visuals if needed   Images can supply relevant examples for some issues. If you have statistical data to present, consider including a table or chart.

If you choose to argue that graffiti should be considered art, you will need to provide images as examples.

WORKING TOGETHER

Identify reasons that support conflicting claims

In a group of three or four students   Select a controversial issue for which there are multiple points of view. You can find a list of issues at **www.dir.yahoo.com/ Society_and_Culture/Issues_and_Causes/.** Explore the links for one of the issues to get a sense of the range of opinion. Then decide which websites will give your group a range of views on the issue.

Each member of your group will analyze two websites. Write down the following for each site.

- What is the main claim of the website?

- What reason or reasons are given?

- What evidence (facts, examples, statistics, and the testimony of authorities) is offered?

Bring your answers to class and compare them with other members of your group. How do the reasons differ for opposing claims? What assumptions underlie the reasons? How does the evidence differ?

An effective position argument

Position arguments succeed when readers consider the writer's position as one to take seriously.

Enhanced Driver's Licences Too Smart for Their Own Good

Stuart Trew and Roch Tassé

Roch Tassé is the coordinator of the International Civil Liberties Monitoring Group, and Stuart Trew is the Council of Canadians' trade campaigner. This article was in *The Toronto Star* in June 2009.

Personal information readily accessible to anyone with simple card-reading technology

Stuart Trew and Roch Tassé

A common refrain coming out of Homeland Security chief Janet Napolitano's visit to Ottawa and Detroit last week was that the Canada-U.S. border is getting thicker and stickier even as Canadian officials work overtime to implement measures that are meant to get us across that border more efficiently and securely.

One of those measures—"enhanced" drivers licences (EDLs) now available in Ontario, Quebec, B.C. and Manitoba—has been rushed into production to meet today's implementation date of the Western Hemisphere Travel Initiative. This unilateral U.S. law requires all travellers entering the United States to show a valid passport or other form of secure identification when crossing the border.

But as privacy and civil liberties groups have been saying for a while, the EDL card poses its own thick and sticky questions that have not been satisfactorily answered by either the federal government, which has jurisdiction over privacy and citizenship matters, or the provincial ministries issuing the new "enhanced" licences.

For example, why introduce a new citizenship document specific to the Canada-U.S. border when the internationally recognized passport will do the trick?

Or, as even the smart-card industry wonders, why include technology used for monitoring the movement of livestock and other commodities in a citizenship document?

More crucially, why ignore calls from Canada's federal and provincial privacy commissioners, as well as groups like the civil liberty groups, to put a freeze on "enhanced" licences until they can be adequately debated and assessed by Parliament? It's not as if there's nothing to talk about.

First, the radio frequency identification devices (RFID) that will be used to transmit the personal ID number in your EDL to border officials contain no security or authentication features, cannot be turned off, and are designed to be read at distances of more than 10 metres using inexpensive and commercially available technology.

This creates a significant threat of "surreptitious location tracking," according to Canada's privacy commissioners. The protective sleeve proposed by several provincial governments is demonstrably unreliable at blocking the RFID signal and constitutes an unacceptable privacy risk.

Facial recognition screening of all card applicants, as proposed in Ontario and B.C. to reduce fraud, has a shaky success rate at best, creating a significant and unacceptable risk of false positive matches, which could increase wait times as even more people are pulled aside for questioning.

Trew and Tassé announce their concerns in the first three paragraphs. They suggest possible problems with the new enhanced driver's licences.

They follow up with questions about the way the new EDL's have been pushed through.

The writers now begin to show the faults in the technology and the possible repercussions if used.

TREW AND TASSÉ: ENHANCED DRIVER'S LICENCES TOO SMART FOR THEIR OWN GOOD

Recently, a journalist for *La Presse* demonstrated just how insecure Quebec's EDLs are by successfully reading the number of a colleague's card and cloning that card with a different but similar photograph. It might explain why, when announcing Quebec's EDL card this year, Premier Jean Charest could point only to hypothetical benefits.

Furthermore, the range of personal information collected through EDL programs, once shared with U.S. authorities, can be circulated excessively among a whole range of agencies under the authority of the Department of Homeland Security. It's important to note that Canada's privacy laws do not hold once that information crosses the border.

So while the border may appear to be getting thicker for some, it is becoming increasingly permeable to flows of personal information on Canadian citizens to U.S. security and immigration databases, where it can be used to mine for what the DHS considers risky behaviour.

A final warning about how Canadian private information may be used by U.S. security agencies.

Some provincial governments have taken these concerns seriously. Based on the high costs involved with a new identity document, the lack of clear benefits to travellers, the significant privacy risks, and the lack of prior public consultation, the Saskatchewan government suspended its own proposed EDL project this year. The New Brunswick and Prince Edward Island governments, citing excessive costs, have also abandoned theirs.

The Harper government owes it to Canadians to freeze the EDL program now and hold a parliamentary hearing into the new technology, its alleged benefits and the stated privacy risks.

The writers provide a solution to the problem—freeze the program until more is learned about the new technology.

Napolitano has repeatedly said that from now on Canadians must treat the U.S. border as any other international checkpoint. It might feel like an inconvenience for some who are used to crossing into the U.S. without a passport, but the costs—real and in terms of privacy—of these provincial EDL projects will be much higher.

What the writers want the readers to learn: that the potential loss of privacy may be too high a price for a secure border.

How to read position arguments

Make notes as you read, either in the margins or on paper or a computer file. Circle any words or references that you don't know and look them up.

What is it?	• What kind of a text is it? An article? An essay? A chart? A scientific report? A website? An executive summary? What are your expectations for this kind of text?
	• What media are used? (Websites, for example, often combine images, words, and sounds.)
Where did it come from?	• Who wrote the analysis?
	• Where did it first appear? In a book, newspaper, magazine, online, in a company, or in an organization?
What is the writer's thesis or main idea?	• What is the writer's topic? What effect is he or she trying to determine the cause of?
	• Why is this topic important?
	• What are the key ideas or concepts that the writer considers?
	• What are the key terms? How does the writer define those terms?
Who is the intended audience?	• What clues do you find about whom the writer had in mind as readers?
	• What does the writer assume that the readers already know about the subject?
	• What new knowledge is the writer providing?
What are the reasons that support the claim?	• Is there one primary reason?
	• Are multiple reasons given?
	• Do you find any fallacies in the reasons (see pages 18–19)?
What kinds of evidence are given?	• Is the evidence from books, newspapers, periodicals, the Web, or field research?
	• Is the evidence convincing that the causes given are the actual causes?
How is it composed?	• How does the writer represent himself or herself?
	• How would you characterize the style?
	• How effective is the design? Is it easy to read?
	• If there are any photographs, charts, or other graphics, what information do they contribute?

The Color of Mayhem
(ARTICLE)
Michael Marriott

The New York Times Michael Marriott writes on technology and its impact for the *New York Times*. In this article, he examines evidence of racial and ethnic stereotyping in some of the most popular video games currently on the market.

Analyzing and Connecting
Return to these questions after you have finished reading.

1. Marriott uses a straightforward reporting style in this article, primarily allowing other people to express their opinions but not expressing one himself. Instead, he arranges the various voices of people he has interviewed to provide the semblance of a back-and-forth argument. How would this piece change if Marriott wrote it instead as an editorial, taking a stand of his own and backing it with quotes from his interviewees?

2. Marriott also supplies evidence to clarify the issue. How compelling do you find the facts he presents? How credible do you feel his sources are? Were some more credible than others?

3. How many different claims can you find in this article? Who are the parties making each claim What reasons do they use to support their arguments? And how do the various parties in the debate respond to one another's claims?

The Color of Mayhem

by Michael Marriott

THE SCREEN CRACKLES WITH CRIMINALITY as a gang of urban predators itch for a kill. The scene erupts into automatic-weapons fire in a drive-by nightmare of screaming car engines, senseless death and destruction set to a thumping rap soundtrack.

The action is not part of a new film, but of a video game in development—the latest permutation of *Grand Theft Auto,* one of the most popular game series ever. Partly set in a city resembling gang-ridden stretches of Los Angeles of the 1990s, it features a digital cast of African-American and Hispanic men, some wearing braided hair and scarves over their faces and aiming Uzis from low-riding cars.

The sense of place, peril and pigmentation evident in previews of the game, *Grand Theft Auto: San Andreas,* underscores what some critics consider a disturbing trend: popular video games that play on racial stereotypes, including images of black youths committing and reveling in violent street crime.

"They are nothing more than pixilated minstrel shows," said Joe Morgan, a telecommunications executive in Manhattan who is black and is helping rear his girlfriend's 7-year-old son, who plays video games. Mr. Morgan argues that games like the *Grand Theft Auto* sequel, which was described glowingly and at length in a game magazine the boy recently brought home, are dangerously reinforcing stereotypes.

"A lot of young people are unable to discern between reality and satirical depictions," he said. "It makes them very vulnerable."

His complaint echoes a concern that many civil rights and other groups, including the National Association for the Advancement of Colored People, have long raised about stereotyping in movies, and the detrimental impact it may have on racial understanding and relations.

The issue, critics say, is not that the games' representation of racial and ethnic minorities is as blatantly threatening as the sort found at hate sites on the Web, where players are asked to gun down virtual black or Jewish characters. Rather, the racial and ethnic depictions and story lines are more subtle, and therefore, some say, more insidious.

"It's not just the kinds of stereotyping people generally think of," said Eileen Espejo, a senior associate at Children Now, an advocacy group in Oakland, Calif., that has studied video games. "It is the kind of limiting what characters of color can do and cannot do in the games that sends a message to kids."

Video game developers counter that no offense is intended. They say their games are simply parodies, or a reflection of a sort of "browning" of popular culture that transcends race and sells to all in a marketplace captivated by hip-hop styles, themes and attitude.

Several games scheduled for wide release this fall or early next year are notable for their portrayal of urban black culture:

Def Jam Fight for NY, from Electronic Arts, a sort of "MTV Raps" meets "W.W.E. SmackDown!" in which mostly hip-hop-style characters (one with the voice of the rapper Snoop Dogg) slap, kick and pummel one another in locations like a 125th Street train station in Harlem.

25 to Life, from Eidos Interactive, an "urban action game" set to a hip-hop soundtrack that allows gamers to play as police officers or criminals, and includes lots of images of young gun-toting black gangsters.

Notorious: Die to Drive, described by its developer, Ubisoft, as featuring "gangsta-style car combat" with players seeking to "rule the streets of four West Coast neighborhoods." Ubisoft's Web site describes the payoff succinctly: "High-priced honeys, the finest bling, and millionaire cribs are just some of the rewards for the notorious few who can survive this most dangerous game. Once you go *Notorious,* there's no going back."

The prominence of black characters in those story lines is all the more striking because of the narrow range of video games in which blacks have been present, if present at all, over the years. A 2001 study by Children Now, for example, found that of 1,500 video-game characters surveyed, 288 were African-American males—and 83 percent of those were represented as athletes.

The portrayal of blacks as athletes has taken on a new wrinkle in *NBA Ballers,* released in April by Midway Games (with an "all ages" rating). It not only pits stars of the National Basketball Association, most of them black, in fierce one-on-one matches, but also encourages players to experience a millionaire lifestyle off the court—accumulating virtual cash that can buy mansions, Cadillac Escalades, yachts and attractive "friends." The style of play emphasizes a street-edged aggression, sizzling with swagger and showboating moves on the court.

John Vignocchi, a lead designer with Midway who worked on *NBA Ballers,* contends that the world portrayed in such games is one that gamers take for granted. "Hip-hop culture has kind of crossed over," said Mr. Vignocchi, who is white. "Look at what everyone is wearing, at what everyone is listening to." Racial stereotyping, he insisted, is "not the intention of the game."

Leon E. Wynter, a cultural critic and author of *American Skin: Big Business, Pop Culture, and the End of White America* (Crown, 2002), said that the infusion of popular aspects of black youth culture into the mainstream American media was a double-edged sword. On one hand, Mr. Wynter said, the game characters bristle with aspects "solidly associated with nonwhite people."

"The bad news is that the larger aspects of the humanity of people who happen to be nonwhite are not always transferred," he noted. "This is an extension and reflection of what we're seeing in other forms of entertainment, especially filmed entertainment aimed particularly at predominantly young male audiences."

As video games extend their prominence as a mainstream form of entertainment—the *Grand Theft Auto* series alone has sold more than 30 million games since 1998—their share of consumer dollars rivals Hollywood box-office revenues.

Video game sales in the United States reached $7 billion last year, according to the Entertainment Software Association. Game hardware, including consoles, added more than $3 billion to that total, industry analysts estimate. But with Hollywood-scale success have come Hollywood-style pressures, including the need for games to "open big" and achieve enough success to sustain lucrative sequels.

"Games are attempting to drive market share beyond the traditional 8- to 14-year-old male player," said Michael Gartenberg, research director for Jupiter Research, an Internet consulting firm. Part of that drive, he suggested, involves having video games reflect what has proved to work in popular films. And as in Hollywood, that may mean subject matter that drives sales even as it draws criticism for gratuitous violence, sexual exploitation or racial insensitivity.

In any case, limiting content to realistic, multidimensional portrayals of racial minorities may be unfair to game developers, Mr. Gartenberg suggested. "Video games are fantasies," he said, "and are not attempting to mirror any reality whatsoever."

But Esther Iverem, editor and film critic for www.seeingblack.com, a Washington-based website offering black opinion on cultural and political matters, said she worried about the effects of games like earlier versions of *Grand Theft Auto* on black youngsters, including her 11-year-old son. "These games don't teach them anything about respect, tolerance, and responsibility," Ms. Iverem said, but are instead "validating a much-too-accepted stereotype, an accepted caricature."

Others, like the cultural critic Michael Eric Dyson, point out that racial stereotypes conveyed through video games have an effect not only on the self-image of minority youths but also on perceptions among whites. Dr. Dyson, a professor of religious studies and African studies at the University of Pennsylvania, describes some video games as addictive "video crack."

"They are pervasive, and their influence profound," he said.

Def Jam's co-founder, Russell Simmons, said the images of hip-hop culture, even those played out in video games, had been good for the country. "The most important thing for race relations in America in the last I don't know how many years is hip-hop."

"Now Eminem and 50 Cent think they are the same people," Mr. Simmons said, comparing a popular white rapper with a popular black rapper. "They're faced with the same struggle, and they recognize their common thread of poverty."

Mr. Morgan, the telecommunications executive, rejects that argument. In fact, he limits the 7-year-old gamer in his household, Elijah Wilson, to the cartoonish games for Nintendo Game Boy to avoid exposure to content he finds objectionable.

"They ingest these images," Mr. Morgan said of racial stereotypes he had found in games like *NBA Ballers*. "The result is a self-fulfilling prophecy, something straight out of central casting."

"It won't," Mr. Morgan added emphatically, "happen in my house."

Canadians Are Creative
(LETTER TO THE EDITOR)
Norm Bolen

Norm Bolen, president and CEO of the Canadian Film and Television Production Association, writes about the unique needs of the Canadian film, television, and interactive media industry in June 2009.

Analyzing and Connecting
Return to these questions after you have finished reading.

1. Position arguments are sometimes written as rebuttals to the position arguments of others. What exactly does Bolen find wrong with the original argument?

2. How credible is Bolen's rebuttal?

3. Bolen gives a number of reasons to justify his claim that Canadian media needs continuous public financial support. Which are most convincing? Can you think of any others?

4. How might the defenders of the original position react to Bolen's position? What type of reasons or evidence would they need to produce a counter-argument?

Re: Broadcast-TV Profitability In Teamwork, Report Says, May 27.

This article focuses on a new report by DBRS Ltd. that suggests lower advertising revenues for conventional TV broadcasters have brought the sector to a "fork in the road." But the suggestion by the report's author that the CRTC should consider reducing Canadian programming requirements for private conventional television broadcasters is not a fork in the road; it is a cultural U-turn that would make broadcasters, such as CTV and Canwest, little more than repeat stations for the American networks.

The report suggests the fees collected to support Canadian television production over the years "have created a dependency rather than an innovative and growing industry."

This assertion is just plain wrong. The Canadian film, television, and interactive media production industry is recognized around the world for its creativity, innovation, and business acumen. Canadian content producers have earned an enviable international reputation for creating content with excellent commercial potential and high production values.

Canadian audiences are increasingly watching television shows that are "made-in-Canada." But so are Americans, Europeans, and viewers from all corners of the world. It is no coincidence that there will soon be numerous Canadian-produced television programs, such as Flashpoint, The Listener, and The Bridge, broadcast in prime time on major U.S. networks such as NBC and CBS, not to mention the Canadian programs airing on smaller U.S. networks and specialty channels.

The Canadian market is too small to fully finance the high cost of producing high-quality Canadian content that can compete for audiences with the immense spillover of U.S. content available in Canada. That's why Canadian content production requires public and industry financial support.

The Canadian content production industry is no more "dependent" than the Canadian auto, aerospace, or farming sectors. The fact is Canadian content producers contribute far more to Canada's creative economy every year than they receive in support. Hundreds of small- and medium-sized production companies do business in every region of the country and generate about $2.3-billion in Canadian film and television content production activity annually. This includes $231-million in exports and close to 60,000 Canadian jobs every year.

The Canadian production sector believes diluting conventional broadcasters' Canadian content obligations will not solve its economic woes. Moreover, any reduction would erode the very strong foundation that Canada's film, television, and interactive media sector has built in the creative economy—an economy with a proven track record and strong growth potential in global markets.

The economy will recover soon enough. But the damage caused by eroding this foundation could send a generation of creative Canadians to the U.S., or elsewhere, in search of work.

The Death of English (LOL)
(ARTICLE)
Lily Huang

The impact of texting on language is an issue that is often debated. In this article, writer Lily Huang looks at some of the positive outcomes of this controversial argument.

Analyzing and Connecting
Return to these questions after you have finished reading.

1. Huang positions her primary claim as a question. Why would she do this? Would the impact of the piece change if she were to take a definitive stand at the beginning?

2. The statistics and references to texts in this piece are readily available. How does this type of factual information add to the validity of the argument?

3. How would this piece change if it were written from personal experience only? How would it affect its credibility?

4. What aspects of Huang's position are most likely to provoke criticism? Why?

The Death of English (LOL)

In an experiment, the more adept children were at text messaging, the better they did in spelling and writing.

Lily Huang
NEWSWEEK
Aug 11, 2008

The most hotly contested controversy sparked by the text-messaging phenomenon of the past eight years is over truant letters. "Textese," a nascent dialect of English that subverts letters and numbers to produce ultra-concise words and sentiments, is horrifying language loyalists and pedagogues. And their fears are stoked by some staggering numbers: this year the world is on track to produce 2.3 trillion messages—a nearly 20 percent increase from 2007 and almost 150 percent from 2000. The accompanying revenue for telephone companies is growing nearly as fast—to an estimated $60 billion this year. In the English-speaking world, Britain alone generates well over 6 billion messages every month. People are communicating more and faster than ever, but some worry that, as textese drops consonants, vowels and punctuation and makes no distinction between letters and numbers, people will no longer know how we're really supposed to communicate. Will text messaging produce generations of illiterates? Could this—OMG— be the death of the English language?

Those raising the alarm aren't linguists. They're teachers who have had to red-pen some ridiculous practices in high-school papers and concerned citizens who believe it their moral duty to write grammar books. The latter can be quite prominent, like John Humphrys, a television broadcaster and household name in Britain, for whom texting is "vandalism," and Lynne Truss, author of "Eats, Shoots and Leaves," who actually enjoys texting so much she never abbreviates. Britain, one of the first countries where texting became a national habit, has also produced some of the most bitter anti-texting vitriol; "textese," wrote John Sutherland in The Guardian, "masks dyslexia." But linguists, if anyone is paying attention, have kept quiet on this score—until now. In a new book, Britain's most prolific linguist finally sets a few things straight.

David Crystal's "Txtng: The Gr8 Db8" (Oxford) makes two general points: that the language of texting is hardly as deviant as people think, and that texting actually makes young people better communicators, not worse. Crystal spells out the first point by marshalling real linguistic evidence. He breaks down the distinctive elements of texting language—pictograms; initialisms, or acronyms; contractions, and others—and points out similar examples in linguistic practice from the ancient Egyptians to 20th-century broadcasting. Shakespeare freely used elisions, novel syntax, and several thousand made-up words (his own name was signed in six different ways). Even some common conventions are relatively newfangled: rules for using the oft-abused apostrophe were set only in the middle of the 19th century. The point is that tailored text predates the text message, so we might as well accept that ours is a language of vandals. Who even knows what p.m. stands for? ("Post meridiem," Latin for "after midday," first recorded by a lazy delinquent in 1666.)

Where the naysayers see destruction, Crystal sees growth. He believes in the same theory of evolution for language as some evolutionary biologists do for life: change isn't gradual. Monumental developments interrupt periods of stasis, always as a result of crucial external developments. The American Revolution had much greater consequences for the English language than texting has had thus far. The resulting differences between American and British English, Crystal says, are more pronounced than the differences between, say, the language of newspapers and text messages. (Interestingly, there are hardly any differences between American and British texting.)

As soon as linguists began to peer into the uproar over texting, researchers examined the effects of texting experimentally. The results disproved conventional wisdom: in one British experiment last year, children who texted—and who wielded plenty of abbreviations—scored higher on reading and vocabulary tests. In fact, the more adept they were at abbreviating, the better they did in spelling and writing. Far from being a means to getting around literacy, texting seems to give literacy a boost. The effect is similar to what happens when parents yak away to infants or read to toddlers: the more exposure children get to language, by whatever means, the more verbally skilled they become.

"Before you can write abbreviated forms effectively and play with them, you need to have a sense of how the sounds of your language relate to the letters," says Crystal. The same study also found the children with the highest scores to be the first to have gotten their own cell phones.

Which doesn't let the teenager who LOLs in a term paper off the hook—but that's not so much a question of language ability as of judgment. It, too, should go the way of all slang ever inappropriately used in a classroom—rebuked with a red pen, not seized upon as a symptom of generational decline. Even if electronic communication engenders its own kind of carelessness, it's no worse than the carelessness of academic jargon or journalistic shorthand. It certainly doesn't engender stupidity. One look at the winners of text-poetry contests in Britain proves that the force behind texting is a penchant for innovation, not linguistic laziness. Electronic communication, Crystal says, "has introduced that kind of creative spirit into spelling once again." That heathen Shakespeare would have been onboard.

How to write a position argument

These steps for the process of writing a position argument may not progress as neatly as this chart might suggest. Writing is not an assembly-line process.

As you write and revise you may think of additional reasons to support your position. Your instructor and fellow students may give you comments that help you to rethink your argument. Use their comments to work through your paper or project again, strengthening your content and making your writing better organized and more readable.

1 FIND AN ISSUE

- Make a list of possible issues.
- Select a possible issue.
- Read about your issue.

Analyze your potential readers

- *What do your readers likely know about the issue?*
- *What views do your readers likely have about the issue?*
- *Do your readers likely agree or disagree with your position? If they disagree, why exactly do they disagree?*

2 DEVELOP REASONS AND WRITE A WORKING THESIS

- Take a definite position.
- Develop reasons by considering whether you can argue from a definition, compare or contrast, consider good and bad effects, or refute objections.
- Support your reasons by making observations and finding facts, statistics, and statements from authorities.
- Write a working thesis.

3 WRITE A DRAFT

- Introduce the issue and give the necessary background.
- Think about how readers will view you, the writer.
- If you argue from a definition, set out the criteria.
- Avoid fallacies.
- Address opposing views.
- Make counterarguments if necessary.
- Conclude with strength.
- Choose a title that will interest readers.

4 REVISE, REVISE, REVISE

- Check that your position argument fulfills the assignment.
- Make sure that your claim is arguable and focused.
- Check your reasons and add more if you can.
- Add additional evidence where reasons need more support.
- Examine the organization.
- Review the visual presentation.
- Proofread carefully.

5 PRINT A VERSION TO SUBMIT

- Make sure your finished writing meets all formatting requirements.

1: Find an issue

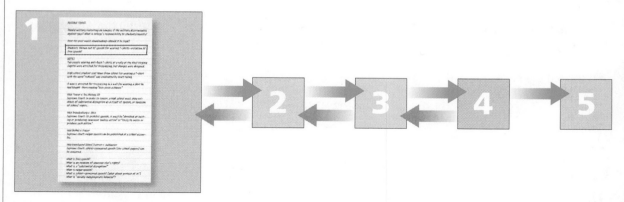

Analyze the assignment

- Read your assignment slowly and carefully. Look for key words like *argue for, take a stand,* and *write on a controversial issue.* These key words tell you that you are writing a position argument.
- Mark off any information about the length specified, date due, formatting, and other requirements. You can attend to this information later. At this point you want to give your attention to finding an issue if one is not specified.

Make a list of possible campus issues

Think about issues that are debated on your campus such as these:

- Should smoking be banned on campus?
- Should university athletes get paid for playing sports that bring in revenue?
- Should admissions decisions be based exclusively on academic achievement?
- Should knowledge of a foreign language be required for all degree plans?
- Should fraternities be banned from campuses if they are caught encouraging alcohol abuse?

Make a list of possible community issues

Think about issues that are debated in your community such as these:

- Should adults who ride bicycles be required to wear helmets?
- Should high schools be allowed to search students for drugs at any time?
- Should bilingual education programs be expanded?
- Should bike lanes be built throughout your community to encourage more people to ride bicycles?
- Should more tax dollars be shifted from building highways to public transportation?

Make a list of possible national and international issues

Think about national and international issues such as these:

- Should advertising be banned on television shows aimed at preschool children?
- Should the Internet be censored?
- Should the government be allowed to monitor all phone calls and all email to combat terrorism?
- Should handguns be outlawed?
- Should people who are terminally ill be allowed to end their lives?
- Should the United Nations punish nations with poor human rights records?

Read about your issue

- What are the major points of view on your issue?
- Who are the experts on this issue? What do they have to say?
- What major claims are being offered?
- What reasons are given to support the claims?
- What kinds of evidence are used to support the reasons?

Analyze your potential readers

- For whom does this issue matter? Whose interests are at stake?
- What attitudes and beliefs will your readers likely have about this issue?
- What key terms will you need to define or explain?
- What assumptions do you have in common with your readers?
- Where will your readers most likely disagree with you?

WRITE NOW

Choose an issue that you care about

1. Make a list of issues that fulfill your assignment.
2. Put a checkmark beside the issues that look most interesting to write about or the ones that mean the most to you.
3. Put a question mark beside the issues that you don't know very much about. If you choose one of these issues, you will probably have to do in-depth research—by talking to people, by using the Internet, or by going to the library.
4. Select a possible issue. What is your stand on this issue? Write nonstop for five minutes about why this issue is important and how it affects you.

Writer at work

Chris Nguyen received a writing assignment in her government class and made the following notes on her assignment sheet.

GOV 322—Issues in Contemporary Society
Paper 3: Arguing for a Position

"We should or shouldn't do X" is one possible thesis.

Choose a current public controversy that has affected you or your friends in some way. Investigate the issues at stake and then write a 4–6 page essay that takes a stand: defending an action or policy, condemning it, recommending it, or making some other claim about the controversy. The bulk of your paper should be concerned with supporting your claim, using facts and reasons.

Use outside sources to back up your opinion, and find the most authoritative sources possible. Do not simply cite the opinions of people who agree with you. Respect your readers by showing them the full spectrum of opinion on your issue, not just one or two sides.

Deadlines

2 weeks

Papers are due on March 24, and I will return them to you one week later with a grade. If you then wish to rewrite your paper, you will have one week to do so. I will average the rewrite grade with your first grade to give you your final grade.

I encourage you to share your papers with your discussion groups as you draft them. You should also plan to take your paper to the writing centre. This is not required, but it is highly recommended.

Evaluation

Papers will be evaluated according to how thoroughly they assess all the angles of a controversy. A strong paper will look closely at more than one or two "sides" of an issue, and will use credible sources that carry significant weight in the public debate over the issue in question.

Read the assignment closely

Chris Nguyen began by marking information about due dates and requirements. She noted her instructor's suggestion that students might phrase their thesis in a particular way. She also wrote down her teacher's advice to avoid oversimplifying the controversy.

POSSIBLE TOPICS

Should credit card companies be allowed on campus to sign students up for credit cards that they may not really need?

Peer to peer music downloading – should it be legal?

Students face criminal charges for their stance on abortion – violation of free speech?

Choose a topic

Chris made a list of potential topics for her paper. She began by thinking of controversies she and her friends had talked about in the recent past. She chose to write about a recent event on campus, in which a number of students at a university were charged with criminal trespass for expressing their opinion.

Explore the issue

Chris looked for news articles about similar events, and court proceedings that followed. As she researched, she made a list of events she wanted to compare to the event at the university. She also referenced other articles on similar topics.

NOTES

Students at a middle school criticized for supporting gay rights.

Canadian Border Agency in trouble over allowing derogatory t-shirts to cross the border

A man is arrested for trespassing in a mall for wearing a shirt he had just bought reading "Give peace a chance".

Charter of Human Rights – section 2 – Freedom of Expression guarantee

Canadian Constitution Foundation – trespassing on public institutions

Identify key terms

Chris compiled a list of key terms to help her think about her issue.

What is free speech?
What is a violation of someone's rights?
What is a "substantial disruption"?
What is socially acceptable bevaviour?

2: Develop reasons and write a working thesis

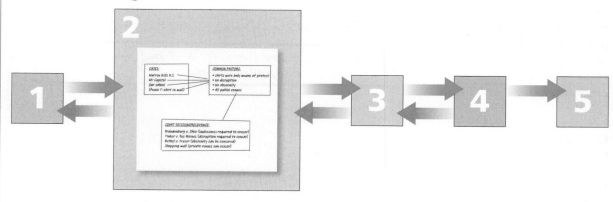

Take a definite position

- Why do you take this position? Write down the first things you think of that form your thinking on this issue.

Develop reasons

- Can you argue from a definition? Is _____ a _____? Are cheerleaders athletes? Are zoos guilty of cruelty to animals?
- Can you compare and contrast? Is _____ like or unlike _____? Should health care in Canada be more like health care in the United States? Is the war in Afghanistan like the Vietnam War?
- Can you argue that good things will result from your position or bad things can be avoided? Is ecotourism the long-term answer to preserving endangered rain forests?
- Can you refute objections to your position?

Support your reasons

- Can you support your reasons by going to a site and making observations?
- Can you find facts to support your reasons?
- Can you find statistics to support your reasons?
- Can you find statements from authorities to support your reasons?

Write a working thesis

- Is your thesis arguable? Statements of fact are not arguable unless the facts are disputed.
  NOT ARGUABLE: The Canadian university system expanded during the 1960s and 1970s to accommodate the large baby boomer cohort.
  ARGUABLE: The expansion of Canadian universities for the large baby boomer cohort of the 1960s and 1970s forced them to lower their entrance standards for subsequent cohorts in order to keep their classrooms full.

ARGUABLE: The increase in the number of visas to foreign workers in technology industries is the major cause of unemployment in those industries.

- Is your thesis specific? A thesis may be arguable but too broad to be treated adequately in a short paper.

ARGUABLE, BUT TOO BROAD: We should take action to resolve the serious traffic problem in our city.

ARGUABLE AND FOCUSED: The existing freight railway that runs through the centre of the city should be converted to a passenger railway because it is the cheapest and most quickly implemented way to decrease traffic congestion downtown.

STAYING ON TRACK

Evaluate your thesis

Once you have a working thesis, ask these questions:

1. Is it arguable?
2. Is it specific?
3. Is it manageable in the length and time you have?
4. Is it interesting to your intended readers?

OFF TRACK	
Many young Canadians play video games on a regular basis.	**ARGUABLE?** The thesis states a commonly acknowledged fact.
	SPECIFIC? The thesis is a bland general statement.
	MANAGEABLE? A known fact is stated in the thesis, so there is little to research. Several surveys report this finding.
	INTERESTING? Video games are interesting as a cultural trend, but nearly everyone is aware of the trend.

ON TRACK	
Video games are valuable because they improve children's visual attention skills, literacy skills, and computer literacy skills.	**ARGUABLE?** The thesis takes a position contrary to the usual view of video games.
	SPECIFIC? The thesis gives specific reasons for the claim.
	MANAGEABLE? The thesis is manageable if research can be located and observations of game playing included.
	INTERESTING? The topic is interesting because it challenges conventional wisdom.

Writer at work

I believe the University of Calgary was wrong to censure the students for expressing their opinion.

HOW TO ARGUE?????

Chris Nguyen knew how she felt, but she didn't know at first how to make a convincing case. She read more about events similar to the one that happened on the UofC campus, and she became convinced that the univesity had acted improperly, and perhaps illegally. She examined the cases she had researched and drew an idea map.

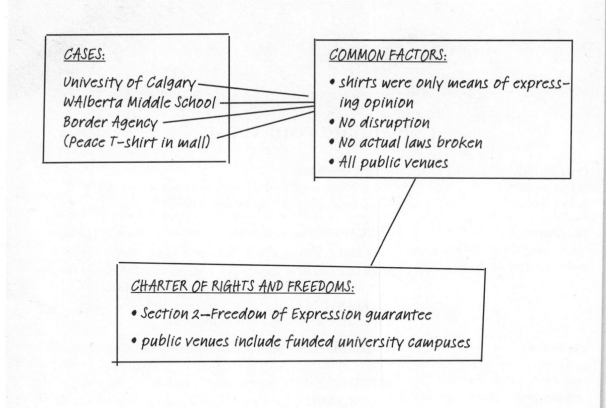

CASES:
Univesity of Calgary
WAlberta Middle School
Border Agency
(Peace T-shirt in mall)

COMMON FACTORS:
• shirts were only means of expressing opinion
• No disruption
• No actual laws broken
• All public venues

CHARTER OF RIGHTS AND FREEDOMS:
• Section 2—Freedom of Expression guarantee
• public venues include funded university campuses

Chris used the idea map to define the conditions in which speech can be restricted.

CRITERIA FOR FREE SPEECH
• Cannot incite violence
• Cannot threaten violence
• Cannot be obscene (although what exactly is obscene isn't clear)
• Only on public property
• Only for adults

Censuring students would be justified if
• The students were doing something "directed to and likely to incite imminent lawless action" NO
• They used vulgar or obscene language NO
• They were in a private venue NO
• They were minors NO

WORKING THESIS
FREE SPEECH, a cornerstone of democracy is a guaranteed right in Canada and the United States.

Chris's research supported a more specific claim than the one she initially made: that the repression of free speech can be justified only under very specific circumstances. She revised her thesis to focus on this stronger and, she thought, more interesting claim. Here is the final working thesis Chris used to begin drafting her essay:

The right to freedom of expression in North America is guaranteed. To express your opinion publicly within limits is protected by law providing that the opinion does not incite imminent lawless action.

3: Write a draft

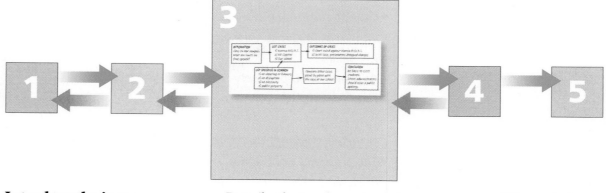

Introduce the issue	• Describe the trend, event, or phenomenon you will be analyzing. • Give your readers any background information they will need.
Think about how readers will view you, the writer	• What group or groups will readers consider you a part of? At the very least, they will consider you as a college or university student. What assumptions will they have about you? • Think about how you can connect with your readers as you write by appealing to their sense of fairness, their core beliefs, and their sense of logic.
If you argue from a definition, set out the criteria	• Which criteria are necessary for _____ to be a _____? • Which are not necessary? • Which are most important? • Does your case in point meet all the necessary criteria?
Avoid fallacies	• Fallacies generally arise from a lack of evidence or faulty evidence. • You can find a list of fallacies on pages 18–19.
Anticipate and address opposing viewpoints	• Acknowledge other stakeholders for the issue, and consider their positions. • Explain why your position is preferable.
Make counterarguments if necessary	• Examine the facts on which a competing claim is based. Are the facts accurate, current, and a representative sample? Are sources treated fairly or taken out of context? • Examine the primary assumption of a claim that you are rejecting. Is the assumption flawed? What other assumptions are involved?

Conclude with strength

- Avoid summarizing what you have just said.
- Spell out the importance of the analysis, if you haven't already done so.
- Consider additional effects you haven't previously discussed.
- Explain any action you think needs to be taken based on your conclusion.

Choose a title that will interest readers

- Make your title specific.
- Engage your readers with the issue.

STAYING ON TRACK

Facts vs. your opinion

Distinguish facts from opinions

Find facts to support what you think. You may be surprised to find that the facts are not what you anticipated.

OFF TRACK
I believe that Canadians have the best medical care in the world.

ON TRACK
On one of the most trusted indicators of health—life expectancy at birth—in 2008 Canada ranks 8th behind Japan, Singapore, Hong Kong, and even small countries like Macau and Andorra.

OFF TRACK
It is obvious from watching television news that youth crime is on the rise.

ON TRACK
While violent crime remains the staple of local news, Statistics Canada states that youth crime rates dropped 6% and youth violent crime rates dropped 2% between 1995 and 2004.

Writer at work

Chris mapped the ideas she would need to include in her paper.

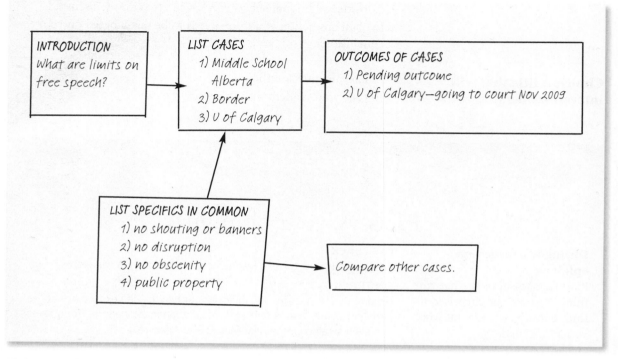

Chris began by writing the common factors in the cases because they would be the core of her paper. She would build the rest of the paper around these four factors.

These are the factors the three cases have in common:

1) In each case, no other action took place; only opinions on t-shirts or banners were visible.

2) None of the events were disrupted by the messages.

3) All took place in government-funded venues: a public school, a government agency, and a university.

Chris next made a working outline, which she used to write her paper.

1) describe limits on free speech

2) introduce the three cases; end with claim that censoring freedom of expression was unconstitutional

3) list factors that the cases have in common

4) introduce standard of lawless action for restricting free speech

5) discuss the Alberta Middle School case

6) discuss Border Agency case

7) discuss U of Calgary case

8) make the distinction between public and private venues

9) point out that all cases were at public venues

10) raise the issue of minors and point out that college students are of legal age

11) conclude with a call for upholding right to free speech

4: Revise, revise, revise

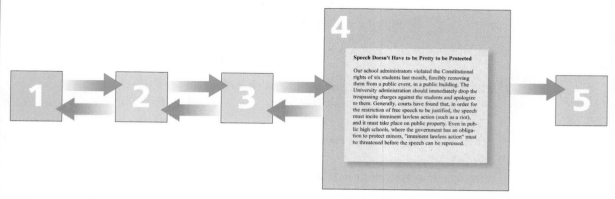

Skilled writers know that the secret to writing well is revision. Even the best writers often have to revise several times to get the result they want. You also must have effective strategies for revising if you're going to be successful. The biggest trap you can fall into is starting off with the little stuff first. Leave the small stuff for last.

Does your position argument fulfill the assignment?	• Look again at your assignment. Does your paper or project do what the assignment asks? • Look again at the assignment for specific guidelines, including length, format, and amount of research. Does your work meet these guidelines?
Is your claim arguable and focused?	• Is your position arguable? Statements of fact and statements of religious belief are not arguable. • Can you make your claim more specific to avoid ambiguous language and situations where your claim may not apply?
Are your reasons adequate?	• Are your reasons clear to your readers? • Can you add additional reasons to strengthen your argument? • Have you acknowledged the views of people who disagree with your position? • Have you shown how your position is preferable?
Are your reasons supported with evidence?	• Have you found the most accurate information available about your issue? • Can you find additional evidence in the form of examples, quotations from experts, statistics, comparisons, and on-site observations? • Have you documented all your sources accurately?

Is your organization effective?	• Are your reasons in the best possible order?
	• Do you get off to a fast start with your title and introduction? Can you do more to gain and keep the reader's interest?
	• Is your conclusion only a summary of what you have said? If so, can you think of an implication or an example that gets at the heart of the issue?
Is the writing project visually effective?	• Is the font attractive and readable?
	• Are the headings and visuals effective?
	• If you use images or tables as part of your analysis, are they legible and appropriately placed? Do you have captions for each?
Save the editing for last	When you have finished revising, edit and proofread carefully.

A peer review guide is on page 31.

Writer at work

Chris Nguyen took her first draft of the essay to her school's writing centre. In particular, she asked to discuss the paper's opening, which she felt was too abrupt. The consultant at the writing centre suggested that one possible strategy was to adjust the thesis and not focus specifically on one case but instead, to use that case as evidence for a sharper position of free speech rights. Chris found this change worked well for her essay, giving her claim more weight.

Chris had her thesis in the second sentence in her first draft. Moving it to the end of the introductory section allowed her to explain the issue of restricting free speech before announcing her position. Her revised paper is on the next page.

Speech Doesn't Have to Be Pretty to Be Protected

University of Calgary violated the rights of six students last month, charging them with trespassing on a publicly funded property. The University administration should immediately drop the trespassing charges against the students and apologize to them. Generally, courts have found that, in order for the restriction of free speech to be justified, the speech must incite imminent lawless action (such as a riot), and it must take place on public property. Even in public high schools, where the government has an obligation to protect minors, "imminent lawless action" must be threatened before the speech can be repressed.

5: Print a version to submit

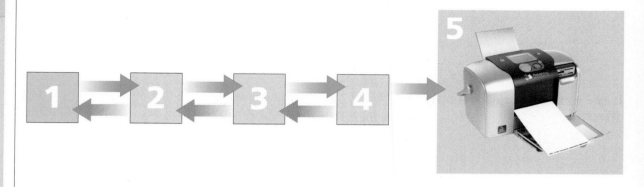

Nguyen 1

Chris Nguyen
Professor Conley
GOV 322
24 March 2011

Speech Doesn't Have to be Pretty to Be Protected

The Canadian Charter of Rights and Freedoms guarantees the right to freedom of expression. This important right is the one of the foundations of democracy. Yet many people do not understand what the right to free speech really means. Free speech is the right to say what you think—within limits. It is not the right cause mayhem, or to threaten violence, or to incite others to violence. Authority figures also need to understand the limits on free speech. Generally, courts have found that in order for the restriction of free speech to be justified, the speech or message must incite imminent lawless action (such as a riot), and it must take place on public property. Even in public high schools, where the government has an obligation to protect minors, "imminent lawless action" must be threatened before the speech can be repressed.

Nguyen 2

Clearly, it's not always easy to tell when restriction of free speech is justified. Consider these recent controversies over free speech:

- Students in a rural Alberta middle school were reprimanded for wearing T-shirts that featured the phrase "Homophobia is Gay" (Ferguson).
- The Canadian Border Services Agency was censured for allowing into Canada a T-shirt bearing slogans that used profanity and racist slang to defame most ethnic groups (Crawford).
- Several university students from the University of Calgary were charged with trespassing for expressing their opinions and beliefs as part of the campus Pro-life club ("Free Speech").

In the first two cases, it's been established that authorities did not have the right to curtail the speech of, or messages expressed by, the people involved: the first case was challenged by parents, and the Border Agency was cleared of any wrongdoing in the second case as no actual law had been broken (Crawford). By examining the similarities and differences among these three cases, it becomes clear that in the third case, the administration's prosecution of its fee-paying students did in fact contravene the Charter of Human Rights.

These are the factors the three cases have in common:

1. In each of these cases, there was no public disruption or reaction as a result of the language and/or imagery worn.
2. All took place in government-funded venues: a public high school, a government agency, and a government-funded university.

The similarities are important because they show how, in each case, each person or group acted within their constitutionally protected right to free expression.

The first factor shows how each of the cases fails to meet the standard of intent to incite others to action (Crawford). It was ruled that in order to ban forms of expression, the government has to prove the expression was directed to and likely to incite "lawless" action. If the act of expression did not seem likely to cause a riot, for example, it could not be restricted. Simply making people angry or uncomfortable is not justification for censorship.

In the first case, the only people who objected to the "Homophobia" T-shirt were school officials, who claim the phrase "homophobia is gay" was offensive and violated the school's dress code restrictions ("School Deserves Dressing Down"). However, it is clear that the school failed to prove that the shirt might threaten to incite a riot and furthermore failed to prove that it violated any of the particular real "provisions" of their dress code policy.

In the second case, the Canadian border services agency was cleared of any wrongdoing when it was decided that allowing the offensive T-shirt into Canada didn't actually violate Canadian hate laws as there was no intent to incite others to action. Opponents argue that these T-shirts were in fact "hateful," and violated community standards, but they had to agree that the T-shirts were not actually illegal according to Canadian law.

None of the cases met the test for vulgar or obscene language. Vulgar or obscene language can be regulated to some extent without violating the freedom of speech or the First Amendment in the US constitution. In one US case, the Supreme Court ruled that public school officials could prohibit vulgar speech at a school assembly. The court said that "the undoubted freedom to advocate unpopular and controversial views in schools and classrooms must be balanced against the societies countervailing interest in teaching students the boundaries of socially appropriate behaviour." In the middle school case, the vice-principal was one of the few officials who thought "homophobia is gay" was offensive, and the fact that the phrase is used constantly on television and other media shows it is not considered obscene by society at large.

In Border Services Agency case, the T-shirts were singled out for their discriminatory content. They carried a message that would clearly offend members of many ethnic minorities, but according to Canadian law, they did not meet the exact criteria of "public incitement of hatred."

Finally, public vs. private venue is an important factor in the protection of free speech. The Charter of Human Rights guarantees that the government will not infringe on the right to free expression. However, private entities are free to do so. For example, protesters can be thrown out of a private meeting of club members. Restaurants and clubs can deny entry to anyone who does not meet the dress code. Of course, anyone with private property also has to consider the economic impact of limiting speech. Recently an American shopping mall owner had police arrest a man wearing a "give peace a chance" T-shirt ("Man Arrested") that he had just bought in the mall. Not surprisingly, the mall owner received a great deal of bad publicity about his decision. Concerned citizens who felt this action was extreme approached the police, who arrested the man. The trespassing charges against him were dropped. This incident illustrates how free speech is negotiated in the marketplace.

In the case at the University of Calgary, the Pro Life members will go to trial in November of 2009 on charges of trespassing ("Free Speech"). Even though the message being expressed by the Pro-Life club at the university is protected under section 2—the Freedom of Expression guarantee in the Canadian Charter of Rights and Freedoms—it defied the university's internal policy on censorship. How can tuition-paying students be trespassing on a taxpayer-funded university campus?

The middle school case should be decided in favour of the students even though the expression took place in a public school. It is generally felt that schools can take special steps to protect minors: vulgar or obscene speech can be censored, and school-sponsored forms of expression, like newspapers, can be censored. But these actions are justified because the students are minors. Presumably, they need more guidance as they learn about the boundaries of socially acceptable behaviour. But at a university, most, if not all, students are legal adults, so it does not make sense to say that any post-secondary institution was "teaching students the boundaries of socially appropriate behaviour" by censoring their messages at a public event (Breakenridge). It is not the job of a college or university administration to censor the right to free speech.

Voltaire said, "I disapprove of what you say, but I will defend to the death your right to say it." Freedom of expression is a fundamental right in Canada, and is protected by the Canadian Charter of Rights and Freedoms. Some personal expressions will certainly offend the sensibilities of some citizens, but if there was no indication whatsoever that inciting others to action was the direct result of the message, then the students and institutions in these cases were clearly exercising their constitutional rights to free speech.

Works Cited

Breakenridge, Rob. "The 'War on Offensiveness' Is Basically Unwinnable." *Calgary Herald.* CanWest MediaWorks Publications, 17 Feb. 2009. Web. 31 Mar. 2009.

Canada. *Canadian Charter of Rights and Freedoms.* Ottawa: 1993. Print.

Crawford, Trish. "The Shock Value of Profane T-Shirts." *TheStar.com.* Toronto Star, 24 Jan. 2005. Web. 10 Apr. 2009.

Ferguson, Amanda. "'Gay' T-shirt Raises Eyebrows, Offends Some." *Ctvedmonton.ca.* CTV News, 28 Aug. 2008. Web. 31 Mar. 2009.

"Free Speech on Campus." *Canadian Constitution Foundation.* CCF, 12 July 2009. Web. 1 Apr. 2009.

"Man Arrested for 'Peace' T-shirt." *Reuters.* CNN, 4 Mar. 2003. Web. 25 Mar. 2009.

"School Deserves Dressing Down over Dress Code Decision." *Calgary Herald.* Can West MediaWorks Publications, 29 May 2008. Web. 10 Mar. 2009.

Projects

Much of what passes for position arguments on television talk shows and on talk radio is little more than shouted assertions and name calling. Arguments in writing are different in character. They are not merely statements of someone's opinion, but are reasoned arguments backed by evidence. They aim not to get in the last word but rather to advance the discussion on an issue so that all benefit from hearing different points of view. These projects frequently are written kinds of position arguments.

𝕿𝖍𝖊 𝕹𝖊𝖜 𝖄𝖔𝖗𝖐 𝕿𝖎𝖒𝖊𝖘 **POSITION ARGUMENT**
For an example of a position argument, see pages 398–401.

Make a position claim on a controversial issue. See pages 410–411 for help on identifying an issue.

Think about what's at stake. Would everyone agree with you? Then your claim probably isn't interesting or important. If you can think of people who would disagree, then something is at stake.

Identify the key term. Often position arguments depend on the definition of the key term. What criteria are necessary for something to meet this definition? How would others benefit from a different definition?

Analyze your potential readers. How does the claim you are making affect them? How familiar are they with the issue? How likely will they be to accept your claim or the definition that underlies your claim?

Write an essay on a controversial issue that takes a stand supported by developed reasons.

PEARSON
mycanadiancomp**lab**

Go to **www.mycanadiancomplab.ca** to practise your grammar, punctuation, and mechanics skills. Go to the "Resources" tab within MyCanadianCompLab and then click on "Grammar." You will have access to a variety of exercises as well as direct instruction that will help you improve your basic skills and get a better grade in your course.

REBUTTAL ARGUMENT

For an example of a rebuttal argument, see pages 402–404.

Identify a position argument to argue against. What is its main claim or claims? A fair summary of your opponent's position should be included in your finished rebuttal.

Examine the facts on which the claim is based. Are the facts accurate? Are the facts current? Can the statistics be interpreted differently? How reliable are the author's sources?

Analyze the assumptions on which the claim is based. What is the primary assumption of the claim you are rejecting? What are the secondary assumptions? How are these assumptions flawed? What fallacies does the author commit (see pages 18–19)?

Consider your readers. To what extent do your potential readers support the claim you are rejecting? If they strongly support that claim, then how do you get them to change their minds? What beliefs and assumptions do you share with them?

Write a rebuttal. Make your aim clear in your thesis statement. Identify the issue you are writing about and give background information if the issue is likely to be unfamiliar to your readers. Question the evidence and show the flaws in the argument you are rejecting. Conclude on a strong note with your counterargument or counterproposal.

NARRATIVE POSITION ARGUMENT

Think about an experience you have had that makes an implicit causal argument. Have you ever experienced being stereotyped? Have you ever had to jump through many unnecessary bureaucratic hoops? Have you ever been treated differently because of your perceived level of income? Have you ever experienced unfair application of laws and law enforcement?

How common is your experience? If other people have similar experiences, probably what happened to you will ring true.

Describe the experience in detail. When did it happen? How old were you? Why were you there? Who else was there? Where did it happen? If the place is important, describe what it looked like.

Reflect on the significance of the event. How did you feel about the experience when it happened? How do you feel about the experience now? What long-term effects has it had on your life?

Write an essay. You might need to give some background, but if the story is compelling, often it is best to jump right in. Let the story do most of the work. Avoid drawing a simple moral lesson. Your readers should feel the same way you do if you tell your story well.

16
Arguing for Change

Arguments for change begin with questioning. We can make many changes in our lives if we convince ourselves that the effort is worth it. Convincing others to take action for change is always harder.

Chapter contents

Making an argument for change

Every day we hear and read arguments that some action should be taken. We even make these arguments to ourselves: We should exercise more; we should change our work habits. We can make many changes in our lives if we convince ourselves that the effort is worth it.

Convincing others to take action for change is always harder. Other people might not see the same problem that you see or they might not think that the problem is important. And even if they do see the same problem and think it is important, they may not want to commit the time and resources to do something about it. In the short term, at least, doing nothing is the easy choice. Nevertheless, most people aren't satisfied with doing nothing about a problem they think is important. We are impatient when we believe something is wrong or something could be improved. We expect things to change; indeed, we have even designed our political system to guarantee an election at least every four years. The problem we face in persuading others is not so much that people are resistant to change but that the change we propose is the right one and worthy of their effort to make it happen.

Every major construction project, every large-scale product, every major scientific endeavour starts with an argument for change—an argument to do something that we are not currently doing and to take action. Arguments for change can even involve changing an entire government. These kinds of arguments are called proposal arguments, and they take the classic form: *We should (or should not) do SOMETHING.*

Components of proposal arguments

What exactly is the problem?	**Identify the problem** Sometimes, problems are evident to your intended readers. If your city is constantly tearing up the streets and then leaving them for months without doing anything to repair them, then you shouldn't have much trouble convincing the citizens of your city that streets should be repaired more quickly. But if you raise a problem that will be unfamiliar to most of your readers, you will first have to argue that the problem exists and it is in their interest that something should be done about it.
What is my solution?	**State your proposed solution** You need to have a clear, definite statement of exactly what you are proposing. Say exactly what you want others to do. You might want to place this statement near the beginning of your argument, or later, after you have considered and rejected other possible solutions. VAGUE: Our city should encourage all citizens to conserve water. SPECIFIC: Our city should provide incentives to conserve water, including offering rain barrels for the minimal cost of $10, replacing at no cost old toilets with water-efficient toilets, and providing rebates up to $500 dollars to those who replace grass with plants that require little water.

Will my solution work?	**Convince your readers that your solution will work** When your readers agree that a problem exists and a solution should be found, your next task is to convince them that your solution is the best one to resolve the problem. Many college and university campuses suffer from transportation and parking problems. If your campus is one of them, then your readers likely will agree that the problems exist. The question is what to do about them. One possible solution is to add a light-rail line to campus from your city's planned light-rail system. If you argue for adding a light-rail line, you must project how many people will ride it and how many car trips will be reduced as a result.
Why is my solution better than others?	**Show why your solution is better than other possible solutions** An obvious solution to a lack of parking is to build a parking garage. But parking garages also cost money, and they might even encourage more people to drive, further aggravating the traffic problem. Another solution is to provide more buses, which would not require building a light-rail line and likely would be cheaper. You must think why rail would be preferable. You might argue that students would be more likely to use light rail and that light rail encourages people and businesses to locate close to stations.
Will people be willing to implement my solution?	**Demonstrate that your solution is feasible** Your solution not only has to work; it must have a realistic chance of being implemented. Can we afford it? Will it take too long to do? Will people accept it? What else might not get done? A light-rail link might be ideal for getting students to and from campus, but it would cost a great deal of money to construct. The rail proposal is feasible only if you have a concrete proposal for how it would be funded. If the money is to come partly from students, you must argue that students would be willing to pay for the convenience.
How can I convince my readers?	**Focus on the audience** All effective writing attends to the audience, but in no form of writing is the audience more important than in arguments for change. Readers have to be convinced that "we really have a problem, and we need to do something about it." It's not enough just to get readers to agree that the problem exists. They have to believe that the problem is worth solving. Arguments for change must appeal to the heart as well as the mind.
Keys to proposal arguments	**Convince readers that you can be trusted** To gain the trust of your readers, you first must convince them that you are well informed. You also must convince them that you are fair and sincere and that your heart is in the right place. Readers think favourably of good writers. Poor writers lose readers on all counts, even with the same ideas as a good writer.

Convince your readers that you have their best interests in mind

At the outset many readers may not have much interest in the problem you identify. If you are proposing adding bike lanes to streets in your city, you likely will need the support of people who will never use them. Indeed, they may be initially opposed to converting vehicle lanes to bike lanes. You have to think about the problem from their perspective. You could argue that if more people rode bicycles, there would be more parking places for those who drive and less air pollution for everyone.

Convince your readers with evidence

You may need a great deal of evidence for a problem that is unfamiliar to your readers. A problem well known to other students may be unknown to faculty, staff, and other members of the community. Statistics are often helpful in establishing that a problem affects many people. Likewise, you will need evidence that your solution will work and that it can be accomplished. Most actions require money. Often you will need evidence about how much what you propose will cost and where the money will come from.

Emphasize what you have in common with your readers and be honest about differences

You may not share the assumptions and beliefs of your audience. Think about what may separate you from your audience and what you have in common. When you can establish common ground with your readers because you live in the same community, have similar goals, or share experiences, then you can be frank about any differences you might have. Readers appreciate honesty.

Show exactly how your proposal will have good consequences and possibly reduce bad consequences

Predicting the future is never easy. Think about how your proposal can make good things happen or reduce bad things. Has a solution similar to the one that you are proposing been tried elsewhere? Can you connect to other good consequences? For example, saving water also saves the energy required to run a water treatment plant and to pump it to a home or business.

End with strength

Remember that you want your readers to take action. If you have a powerful example, use it in the conclusion. Inspire your readers to want something better than the status quo. Leave them with a strong impression.

WARNING: Second-hand smoke contains carbon monoxide, ammonia, formaldehyde, benzo[a]pyrene and nitrosamines. These chemicals can harm your children.

Health Canada

Campaigns against smoking frequently use images of children.

Use visuals for supporting evidence

Pictures alone don't make arguments for change. But they often provide vivid evidence for arguments for change. For example, photographs of children working in factories and mines helped to get child labour laws adopted in the early 1900s.

Charts, graphs, and maps also can be important as supporting evidence for arguments for change. They should be clearly labelled, and a caption should explain their significance and connection to the argument.

WORKING TOGETHER

Make a list of problems to solve

In a group of three or four students

First make a list of all the things you can think of that are problems: your library closes too early for late-night study, there is too little work-study aid on your campus, your roommate is a slob, the weather stays too hot or too cold for too long, store clerks are rude, and on and on. Share your list with the group. Then discuss the following.

• Which items turned up on more than one list?

• Which problems are the most important?

• Which are possible to solve?

• Which problems are the most interesting to your group?

• Which problems are the least interesting to your group?

An effective argument for change

Readers have to be motivated to take action to solve a problem.

The Universal Declaration of Human Rights
United Nations

On December 10, 1948, the General Assembly of the United Nations adopted and proclaimed the Universal Declaration of Human Rights, the full text of which appears in the following pages. Following this historic act, the Assembly called upon all Member countries to publicize the text of the Declaration and "to cause it to be disseminated, displayed, read and expounded principally in schools and other educational institutions, without distinction based on the political status of countries or territories."

The Universal Declaration of Human Rights

PREAMBLE

Whereas recognition of the inherent dignity and of the equal and inalienable rights of all members of the human family is the foundation of freedom, justice and peace in the world,

Whereas disregard and contempt for human rights have resulted in barbarous acts which have outraged the conscience of mankind, and the advent of a world in which human beings shall enjoy freedom of speech and belief and freedom from fear and want has been proclaimed as the highest aspiration of the common people,

The basic premise for the Declaration

Whereas it is essential, if man is not to be compelled to have recourse, as a last resort, to rebellion against tyranny and oppression, that human rights should be protected by the rule of law,

Whereas it is essential to promote the development of friendly relations between nations,

Whereas the peoples of the United Nations have in the Charter reaffirmed their faith in fundamental human rights, in the dignity and worth of the human person and in the equal rights of men and women and have determined to promote social progress and better standards of life in larger freedom,

Whereas Member States have pledged themselves to achieve, in co-operation with the United Nations, the promotion of universal respect for and observance of human rights and fundamental freedoms,

Whereas a common understanding of these rights and freedoms is of the greatest importance for the full realization of this pledge,

The rationale for the Declaration

Now, Therefore **THE GENERAL ASSEMBLY proclaims THIS UNIVERSAL DECLARATION OF HUMAN RIGHTS** as a common standard of achievement for all peoples and all nations, to the end that every individual and every organ of society, keeping this Declaration constantly in mind, shall strive by teaching and education to promote respect for these rights and freedoms and by progressive measures, national and international, to secure their universal and effective recognition and observance, both among the peoples of Member States themselves and among the peoples of territories under their jurisdiction.

As a result, a solution that will protect the rights of all peoples

Article 1.

- All human beings are born free and equal in dignity and rights. They are endowed with reason and conscience and should act towards one another in a spirit of brotherhood.

Article 2.

- Everyone is entitled to all the rights and freedoms set forth in this Declaration, without distinction of any kind, such as race, colour, sex, language, religion, political or other opinion, national or social origin, property, birth or other status. Furthermore, no distinction shall be made on the basis of the political, jurisdictional or international status of the country or territory to which a person belongs, whether it be independent, trust, non-self-governing or under any other limitation of sovereignty.

Article 3.

- Everyone has the right to life, liberty and security of person.

Article 4.

- No one shall be held in slavery or servitude; slavery and the slave trade shall be prohibited in all their forms.

Article 5.

- No one shall be subjected to torture or to cruel, inhuman or degrading treatment or punishment.

Article 6.

- Everyone has the right to recognition everywhere as a person before the law.

Article 7.

- All are equal before the law and are entitled without any discrimination to equal protection of the law. All are entitled to equal protection against any discrimination in violation of this Declaration and against any incitement to such discrimination.

The first articles talk about basic human rights.

Article 8.

- Everyone has the right to an effective remedy by the competent national tribunals for acts violating the fundamental rights granted him by the constitution or by law.

Article 9.

- No one shall be subjected to arbitrary arrest, detention or exile.

Article 10.

- Everyone is entitled in full equality to a fair and public hearing by an independent and impartial tribunal, in the

It then talks about personal rights and freedoms

determination of his rights and obligations and of any criminal charge against him.

Article 11.

- (1) Everyone charged with a penal offence has the right to be presumed innocent until proved guilty according to law in a public trial at which he has had all the guarantees necessary for his defence.

- (2) No one shall be held guilty of any penal offence on account of any act or omission which did not constitute a penal offence, under national or international law, at the time when it was committed. Nor shall a heavier penalty be imposed than the one that was applicable at the time the penal offence was committed.

Article 12.

- No one shall be subjected to arbitrary interference with his privacy, family, home or correspondence, nor to attacks upon his honour and reputation. Everyone has the right to the protection of the law against such interference or attacks.

Article 13.

- (1) Everyone has the right to freedom of movement and residence within the borders of each state.

- (2) Everyone has the right to leave any country, including his own, and to return to his country.

Article 14.

- (1) Everyone has the right to seek and to enjoy in other countries asylum from persecution.

- (2) This right may not be invoked in the case of prosecutions genuinely arising from non-political crimes or from acts contrary to the purposes and principles of the United Nations.

Article 15.

- (1) Everyone has the right to a nationality.

- (2) No one shall be arbitrarily deprived of his nationality nor denied the right to change his nationality.

Article 16.

- (1) Men and women of full age, without any limitation due to race, nationality or religion, have the right to marry and to found a family. They are entitled to equal rights as to marriage, during marriage and at its dissolution.

- (2) Marriage shall be entered into only with the free and full consent of the intending spouses.

- (3) The family is the natural and fundamental group unit of society and is entitled to protection by society and the State.

Article 17.

- (1) Everyone has the right to own property alone as well as in association with others.

- (2) No one shall be arbitrarily deprived of his property.

Article 18.

- Everyone has the right to freedom of thought, conscience and religion; this right includes freedom to change his religion or belief, and freedom, either alone or in community with others and in public or private, to manifest his religion or belief in teaching, practice, worship and observance.

Article 19.

- Everyone has the right to freedom of opinion and expression; this right includes freedom to hold opinions without interference and to seek, receive and impart information and ideas through any media and regardless of frontiers.

Article 20.

- (1) Everyone has the right to freedom of peaceful assembly and association.

- (2) No one may be compelled to belong to an association.

Article 21.

- (1) Everyone has the right to take part in the government of his country, directly or through freely chosen representatives.

- (2) Everyone has the right of equal access to public service in his country.

- (3) The will of the people shall be the basis of the authority of government; this will shall be expressed in periodic and genuine elections which shall be by universal and equal suffrage and shall be held by secret vote or by equivalent free voting procedures.

Article 22.

- Everyone, as a member of society, has the right to social security and is entitled to realization, through national effort and international co-operation and in accordance with the organization and resources of each State, of the economic, social and cultural rights indispensable for his dignity and the free development of his personality.

Article 23.

- (1) Everyone has the right to work, to free choice of employment, to just and favourable conditions of work and to protection against unemployment.

- (2) Everyone, without any discrimination, has the right to equal pay for equal work.

- (3) Everyone who works has the right to just and favourable remuneration ensuring for himself and his family an existence worthy of human dignity, and supplemented, if necessary, by other means of social protection.

- (4) Everyone has the right to form and to join trade unions for the protection of his interests.

Article 24.

- Everyone has the right to rest and leisure, including reasonable limitation of working hours and periodic holidays with pay.

Article 25.

- (1) Everyone has the right to a standard of living adequate for the health and well-being of himself and of his family, including food, clothing, housing and medical care and necessary social services, and the right to security in the event of unemployment, sickness, disability, widowhood, old age or other lack of livelihood in circumstances beyond his control.

- (2) Motherhood and childhood are entitled to special care and assistance. All children, whether born in or out of wedlock, shall enjoy the same social protection.

Article 26.

- (1) Everyone has the right to education. Education shall be free, at least in the elementary and fundamental stages. Elementary education shall be compulsory. Technical and professional education shall be made generally available and higher education shall be equally accessible to all on the basis of merit.

- (2) Education shall be directed to the full development of the human personality and to the strengthening of respect for human rights and fundamental freedoms. It shall promote understanding, tolerance and friendship among all nations, racial or religious groups, and shall further the activities of the United Nations for the maintenance of peace.

- (3) Parents have a prior right to choose the kind of education that shall be given to their children.

Article 27.

- (1) Everyone has the right freely to participate in the cultural life of the community, to enjoy the arts and to share in scientific advancement and its benefits.

- (2) Everyone has the right to the protection of the moral and material interests resulting from any scientific, literary or artistic production of which he is the author.

Article 28.

- Everyone is entitled to a social and international order in which the rights and freedoms set forth in this Declaration can be fully realized.

Article 29.

- (1) Everyone has duties to the community in which alone the free and full development of his personality is possible.

- (2) In the exercise of his rights and freedoms, everyone shall be subject only to such limitations as are determined by law solely for the purpose of securing due recognition and respect for the rights and freedoms of others and of meeting the just requirements of morality, public order and the general welfare in a democratic society.

- (3) These rights and freedoms may in no case be exercised contrary to the purposes and principles of the United Nations.

Article 30.

- Nothing in this Declaration may be interpreted as implying for any State, group or person any right to engage in any activity or to perform any act aimed at the destruction of any of the rights and freedoms set forth herein.

The final article reiterates its original position that all persons are entitled to and deserve universal rights and freedoms.

How to read arguments for change

Make notes as you read, either in the margins or on paper or a computer file. Circle any words or references that you don't know and look them up.

What is it?	• What kind of a text is it? An editorial? An essay? An advertisement? A grant proposal? A website? A business proposal? What are your expectations for this kind of text?
	• What media are used? (Websites, for example, often combine images, words, and sounds.)
Where did it come from?	• Who wrote this material?
	• Where did it first appear? In a book, newspaper, magazine, online, in a company, or in an organization?
What is the problem?	• Where is the evidence for the problem? Does this evidence establish that the problem exists?
	• How important is the problem?
	• Whom does the problem affect? (These people are called the stakeholders.)
	• What else has been written about the problem?
What is the solution?	• What exactly is the solution that the writer proposes?
	• Where is the evidence for the proposed solution? Does this evidence convince you that the proposal will solve the problem?
	• What kinds of sources are cited? Are they from books, newspapers, periodicals, or the Web? Are they completely documented?
How feasible is the proposed solution?	• Does the writer make a case that this is practical, and will people support the solution?
	• If the solution costs money, where does the money come from?
How is it composed?	• How is the piece of writing organized?
	• How does the writer represent herself or himself?
	• How would you characterize the style?
	• How effective is the design? Is it easy to read?
	• If there are any photographs, charts, or other graphics, what information do they contribute?

A Trail of DNA and Data
(ESSAY)
Paul Saffo

The Washington Post   Paul Saffo writes frequently about the long-term impacts of technological change on business and society. His essays have appeared in *Fortune, Harvard Business Review,* the *Los Angeles Times, Newsweek,* the *New York Times,* and the *Washington Post*, where this argument appeared in April 2005.

Analyzing and Connecting
Return to these questions after you have finished reading.

1. Saffo does not give specific proposals at the end of this essay but rather makes a general proposal. Would specific proposals make the essay stronger? Why or why not?

2. How might Saffo answer a critic who might say, "You can't outlaw technology; the technology will get out there anyway"?

3. Saffo gives a negative scenario for identification technology. Can you think of a positive scenario? For example, the miniaturization of computers can be used for cell imaging and therapeutics for treating cancer. Is Saffo's essay weaker because he doesn't offer a positive scenario?

4. Many facilities that store money, weapons, nuclear materials, biohazards, or other restricted materials now use digital face recognition systems to authenticate everyone who walks in the door, which nearly everyone agrees is a good idea. But using face recognition systems in public places has created controversy. For example, the city of Tampa deployed a face-recognition system in the nightlife district of Ybor City in an effort to catch criminals. The people who attended clubs and restaurants were unaware their images were being entered into databases. Should the practice be allowed? What are the risks of false identifications? What policy would you recommend that would catch criminals without invading the privacy of every visitor?

5. If you shop online, you must enable "cookies," which keep track of what you put into your shopping cart and allow the online store to recognize you when you return. But the cookies also can be used to monitor what other websites you visit, and your email address can be used to disclose your identity, even if you give no credit-card information. This information can be and often is sold to other companies without your knowledge. Propose improvements to Canada's privacy laws.

A Trail of DNA and Data

If you're worried about privacy and identity theft, imagine this:

The scene: Somewhere in Washington.

The date: April 3, 2020.

You sit steaming while the officer hops off his electric cycle and walks up to the car window. "You realize that you ran that red light again, don't you, Mr. Witherspoon?" It's no surprise that he knows your name; the intersection camera scanned your license plate and your guilty face, and matched both in the DMV database. The cop had the full scoop before you rolled to a stop.

"I know, I know, but the sun was in my eyes," you plead as you fumble for your driver's license.

"Oh, don't bother with that," the officer replies, waving off the license while squinting at his hand-held scanner. Of course. Even though the old state licensing system had been revamped back in 2014 into a "secure" national program, the new licenses had been so compromised that the street price of a phony card in Tijuana had plummeted to five euros. In frustration, law enforcement was turning to pure biometrics.

"Could you lick this please?" the officer asks, passing you a nanofiber blotter. You comply and then slide the blotter into the palm-sized gizmo he is holding, which reads your DNA and runs a match against a national genomic database maintained by a consortium of drug companies and credit agencies. It also checks

half a dozen metabolic fractions looking for everything from drugs and alcohol to lack of sleep.

The officer looks at the screen, and frowns, "Okay. I'll let you off with a warning, but you really need more sleep. I also see that your retinal implants are past warranty, and your car tells me that you are six months overdue on its navigation firmware upgrade. You really need to take care of both or next time it's a ticket."

This creepy scenario is all too plausible. The technologies described are already being developed for industrial and medical applications, and the steadily dropping cost and size of such systems will make them affordable and practical police tools well before 2020. The resulting intrusiveness would make today's system of search warrants and wiretaps quaint anachronisms.

Some people find this future alluring and believe that it holds out the promise of using sophisticated ID techniques to catch everyone from careless drivers to bomb-toting terrorists in a biometric dragnet. We have already seen places such as Truro, Mass., Baton Rouge, La. and Miami ask hundreds or thousands of citizens to submit to DNA mass-testing to catch killers. Biometric devices sensing for SARS symptoms are omnipresent in Asian airports. And the first prototypes of systems that test in real time for SARS, HIV and bird flu have been deployed abroad.

The ubiquitous collection and use of biometric information may be inevitable, but the notion that it can deliver reliable, theft-proof evidence of identity is pure science fiction. Consider that oldest of biometric identifiers—fingerprints. Long the exclusive domain of government databases and FBI agents who dust for prints at crime scenes, fingerprints are now being used by electronic print readers on everything from ATMs to laptops. Sticking your finger on a sensor beats having to remember a password or toting an easily lost smart card.

But be careful what you touch, because you are leaving your identity behind every time you take a drink. A Japanese cryptographer has demonstrated how, with a bit of gummi bear gelatin, some cyanoacrylic glue, a digital camera and a bit of digital fiddling, he can easily capture a print off a glass and confect an artificial finger that foils fingerprint readers with an 80 percent success rate. Frightening as this is, at least the stunt is far less grisly than the tale, perhaps aprocryphal, of some South African crooks who snipped the finger off an elderly retiree, rushed her still-warm digit down to a government ATM, stuck it on the print reader and collected the victim's pension payment. (Scanners there now gauge a finger's temperature, too.)

Today's biometric advances are the stuff of tomorrow's hackers and clever crooks, and anything that can be detected eventually will be counterfeited. Iris scanners are gaining in popularity in the corporate world, exploiting the fact that human iris patterns are apparently as unique as fingerprints. And unlike prints, iris images aren't left behind every time someone gets a latte at Starbucks. But hide something valuable enough behind a door protected by an iris scanner, and I guarantee that someone will

figure out how to capture an iris image and transfer it to a contact lens good enough to fool the readers. And capturing your iris may not even require sticking a digital camera in your face—after all, verification requires that the representation of your iris exist as a cloud of binary bits of data somewhere in cyberspace, open to being hacked, copied, stolen and downloaded. The more complex the system, the greater the likelihood that there are flaws that crooks can exploit.

DNA is the gold standard of biometrics, but even DNA starts to look like fool's gold under close inspection. With a bit of discipline, one can keep a card sale or a PIN secret, but if your DNA becomes your identity, you are sharing your secret with the world every time you sneeze or touch something. The novelist Scott Turow has already written about a hapless sap framed for a murder by an angry spouse who spreads his DNA at the scene of a killing.

The potential for DNA identity theft is enough to make us all wear a gauze mask and keep our hands in our pockets. DNA can of course be easily copied—after all, its architecture is designed for duplication—but that is the least of its problems. Unlike a credit card number, DNA can't be retired and swapped for a new sequence if it falls into the hands of crooks or snoops. Once your DNA identity is stolen, you live with the consequences forever.

This hasn't stopped innovators from using DNA as an indicator of authenticity. The artist Thomas Kinkade signs his most valuable paintings with an ink containing a bit of his DNA. (He calls it a "forgeryproof DNA Matrix signature.") We don't know how much of Tom is really in his paintings, but perhaps it's enough for forgers to duplicate the ink, as well as the distinctive brush strokes.

The biggest problem with DNA is that it says so much more about us than an arbitrary serial number does. Give up your Social Security number and a stranger can inspect your credit rating. But surrender your DNA and a snoop can discover your innermost genetic secrets—your ancestry, genetic defects and predispositions to certain diseases. Of course we will have strong genetic privacy laws, but those laws will allow consumers to "voluntarily" surrender their information in the course of applying for work or pleading for health care. A genetic market-place not unlike today's consumer information business will emerge, swarming with health insurers attempting to prune out risky individuals, drug companies seeking customers and employers managing potential worker injury liability.

Faced with this prospect, any sensible privacy maven would conclude that DNA is too dangerous to collect, much less use for a task as unimportant as turning on a laptop or working a cash machine. But society will not be able to resist its use. The pharmaceutical industry will need our DNA to concoct customized wonder drugs that will fix everything from high cholesterol to halitosis. And crime fighters will make giving DNA information part of our civic duty and national security. Once they start collecting, the temptation to use it for other purposes will be too great.

Moreover, snoops won't even need a bit of actual DNA to invade our privacy because it will be so much easier to access its digital representation on any number of databanks off in cyberspace. Our Mr. Witherspoon will get junk mail about obscure medical conditions that he's never heard of because some direct marketing firm "bot" will inspect his digital DNA and discover that he has a latent disease or condition that his doctor didn't notice at his annual checkup.

It is tempting to conclude that Americans will rise up in revolt, but experience suggests otherwise. Americans profess a concern for privacy, but they happily reveal their deepest financial and personal secrets for a free magazine subscription or cheesy electronic trinket. So they probably will eagerly surrender their biometric identities as well, trading fingerprint IDs for frequent shopper privileges at the local supermarket and genetic data to find out how to have the cholesterol count of a teenager.

Biometric identity systems are inevitable, but they are no silver bullet when it comes to identity protection. The solution to identity protection lies in the hard work of implementing system-wide and nationwide technical and policy changes. Without those changes, the deployment of biometric sensors will merely increase the opportunities for snoops and thieves—and escalate the cost to ordinary citizens.

It's time to fix the problems in our current systems and try to anticipate the unique challenges that will accompany the expanded use of biometrics. It's the only way to keep tomorrow's crooks from stealing your fingers and face and, with them, your entire identity.

Tuition Fees in Canada 2008–2009
(ARTICLE)
Canadian Federation of Students

This article is a clear warning about the negative impact of prohibitive tuition fees for Canadian college and university students.

Analyzing and Connecting
Return to these questions after you have finished reading.

1. The first two sentences of the introduction provide a strong commentary on the impact of high tuition fees. How does this information set the tone?

2. The CFS provides an historical overview of tuition fees in Canada. In what ways does this "retrospective" help to solidify the main position? What purpose does it serve?

3. What is the effect of comparing the Canadian situation to the international evidence? Why is a global perspective important to this discussion?

4. "Financial reasons" are identified as the most significant barrier to post-secondary education, especially for students from low- to middle-income families. Speculate on the short-term and long-term consequences of the tuition fees barrier.

INTRODUCTION

In the past fifteen years, tuition fees in Canada have grown to become the single largest expense for most university and college students. Rapidly increasing tuition fees have caused post-secondary education to become unaffordable for many low- and middle-income Canadians. The dramatic tuition fee increases during this period were the direct result of cuts to public funding for post-secondary education by the federal government and, to a somewhat lesser extent, provincial governments. Public funding currently accounts for an average of approximately 57% of university and college operating funding, down from 84% just two decades ago. During the same period tuition fees have grown from 14% of operating funding to over 34%.[1] This constitutes a rapid re-orientation of Canada's post-secondary education system away from a publicly funded model and towards a privitised user fee system.

HISTORICAL OVERVIEW: TUITION FEES IN CANADA

Pre-WWII (1867 to 1938)

Prior to the Second World War, very little public funding was provided to Canada's universities (community colleges had not yet been established). University funding relied almost exclusively on private donations and substantial tuition fees. Many universities' academic programs were tied to denominational churches of the Christian faith, and relied heavily on church funding. Only a small portion of the Canadian population attended university, and the vast majority of students came from Canada's wealthiest families.

Post-War (1946 to 1980)

Following the war, the federal government made grants to attend university widely available to returning soldiers as part of a veterans re-integration program. The federal government also began directly funding universities during this time, and continued to do so after most of the veterans had graduated. As well, most provincial governments began providing funding for post-secondary education institutions.

By the mid-1960s, nearly all funding for Canada's universities was provided by the federal and provincial governments. This allowed for tuition fees to be reduced to a token amount. Not surprisingly, post-secondary education enrolment exploded, with Canadians from all backgrounds gaining access to higher education for the first time.

Starting in the mid- to late-1960s, provincial college systems were established in most provinces. Because of public investment, tuition fees at most colleges were either token or nil. This era represented a time when Canadian governments not only recognised the social and economic value of mass post-secondary education, they also invested public funds to reflect that commitment. For a period at the end of the 1960s, Newfoundland & Labrador abolished tuition fees altogether.

By the early 1970s, most of the discussions about post-secondary education began to focus on the elimination of tuition fees. In 1976, the Canadian government signed on to the United Nations' Covenant on Economic, Social, and Cultural Rights promising to gradually introduce free education at all levels.

1980s

In the early 1980s, a value shift began to take root in governments in Canada and most other western countries, as most jurisdictions began cutting funding for public programs. Post-secondary education was an easy target for these funding cuts. Because universities and colleges are funded through a combination of both federal and provincial grants plus user fees, governments were able to cut funding by forcing students and their families to subsidise the difference. For various reasons, this option was not available for governments looking to cut public investment in health-care or primary and secondary education. Between the early 1980s and the early 1990s, average tuition fees at Canadian universities more than doubled. Average tuition fees at colleges, excluding those in Québec, more than tripled.

1994 to 2000

In 1995, the federal Liberal government announced a further cut of $7 billion in public funding to provincial programs, including post-secondary education, health-care, housing, and social assistance. These post-secondary education cuts were directly passed on to students, resulting in the largest tuition fee increases in Canadian history.

2000 to the present

As access to university and college became increasingly restricted and students were forced to suffer greater debt loads in order to afford higher education, the Canadian Federation of Students was able to successfully turn the tide in several provinces. Since 2000, every province in Canada has responded to pressure from students by introducing tuition fee freezes and increasing provincial funding for post-secondary education. Tuition fees were actually reduced in British Columbia (2001), Manitoba (2000), Newfoundland and Labrador (2002, 2003, and 2004), Prince Edward Island (2007) and Nova Scotia (2008 and 2009).

Québec was unique among the provinces because it resisted passing the cost of federal funding cuts on to students. Before the government increased tuition fees in 2007, they had been frozen for 35 of the last 40 years. Currently they are increasing by $100 per year, a smaller amount than most other provinces. Despite indications from the governing political party that they may introduce fees, college remains free in Québec.

At the beginning of the 1990s, average undergraduate tuition fees in Canada were $1,464. Today, these fees have risen more than three-fold to $4,917. While inflation declined by 0.8% this past year, tuition fees increased 3.6%.[2]

CANADIAN FEDERATION OF STUDENTS: TUITION FEES IN CANADA 2008–2009

Other compulsory fees, commonly referred to as "ancillary fees", have also increased rapidly. In fall 2009, average ancillary fees in Canada reached $749, up 6.8% from 2008.

GRADUATE, PROFESSIONAL, AND INTERNATIONAL STUDENTS

Master's, PhD, international students, and students in professional programs have faced the steepest increases in tuition fees. Unlike most undergraduate students, graduate students are enrolled year-round, and therefore have to pay tuition fees during the summer months. Thus, not only do graduate students pay higher fees, they also pay them for four months more than undergraduate students on the typical fall and winter academic schedule.

The higher fees for graduate and professional students are often justified by arguing that those with advanced degrees earn more during their lifetimes in the workforce. However, the increased earnings of professionals has been notoriously exaggerated by university and college presidents in their campaign for higher fees. Recent research has found that a PhD graduate only nets an average of $4,000 more per year over a masters graduate, despite requiring several additional years of school. In addition, advocates for higher fees also ignore the fact that those who earn higher incomes as a result of post-secondary education also pay higher income taxes that pay for the cost of their post-secondary education. Finally, the earnings-potential argument for higher fees does not address the up-front impact of high tuition fees on entry to these programs.

Students studying in Canada from other countries probably fare the worst of all, since tuition fee regulation has rarely applied to international students. Tuition fees for these students are typically triple those of Canadian students. Undergraduate international students are also currently facing higher increases than those from Canada. Tuition fees increased by 7.1% in fall 2009 – almost double the rise in domestic fees.

WHAT IS THE IMPACT OF HIGH FEES?

Recent studies reveal the effects of high tuition fees on access to post-secondary education for students from low- and middle-income backgrounds. Statistics Canada reports that students from low-income families are less than half as likely to participate in university than those from high-income families.[3]

Statistics Canada's Youth in Transition Survey tallied the reasons cited by high school graduates who did not participate in post-secondary education. By an overwhelming margin, the most frequently reported barrier to university and college for these students was "financial reasons".[4]

University of British Columbia researcher Lori McElroy found that students with little or no debt were more than twice as likely to finish their degree than students with high levels of debt. The completion rate for students with under $1000 of debt was 71%, while the completion rate for those with over $10,000 was 34%.[5]

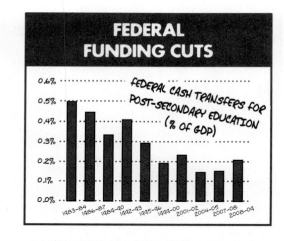

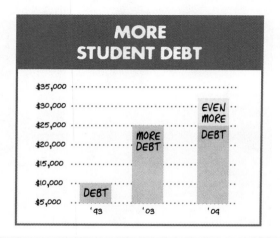

TUITION FEES IN CANADA

Similar results were found in the United States. Researchers at the University of California, Los Angeles (UCLA) found that for every $1,000 increase in tuition fees, enrolment rates dropped by 15%. The study demonstrated that the decrease in enrolment was composed "almost exclusively from minority and low-income students".[6]

The Canadian Association of University Teachers recently analysed the long-term trend of tuition fees as a proportion of after-tax family income in Canada. They found that the burden of rising tuition fees has weighed far more heavily on the budgets of the poorest Canadians.[7]

TUITION FEES: THE INTERNATIONAL EVIDENCE

New Zealand

In 1992, the New Zealand government stopped regulating tuition fees and implemented income-contingent repayment for student loans.[8] By 1999 tuition fees had nearly tripled. Today, total student debt in this country of only 4.2 million people is over $6 billion NZD (approximately $4.3 billion CAD).

The New Zealand Educational Institute has calculated that it takes women in New Zealand an average of 28 years to pay for three years of tertiary study, twice as long as it takes men.[9] It also estimates that a teacher with a $30,000 student loan would take 16 years to repay it, and would have to pay over $23,538 in interest. The Institute also notes that a non-supervisory Early Childhood Teacher with the same debt ($30,000) will likely never pay off her loan, but she will pay $69,000 in interest over 40 years.

United States of America

According to the National Center for Education Statistics, between 1988 and 1998, cuts in state funding were the primary factor in tuition fee increases at public four-year institutions. Moreover, despite record tuition fee increases since the 1999-2000 year, the U.S. post-secondary education system is still suffering a quality crisis. Even in the face of a 14% tuition fee hike in 2003—the highest tuition fee increase in more than a decade—U.S. public institutions have reported program cuts, faculty reductions, and staff layoffs. Tuition fees at U.S. public institutions have now reached approximately 70% of the annual income of poor families.

United Kingdom

Under the auspices of increasing revenue and quality at British universities, the government imposed post-secondary tuition fees for the first time in British history in 1998. Yet, in 2001, the Guardian newspaper released a study demonstrating that the operating budgets of universities did not increase after tuition fees were imposed.

This occurred because once the costs were downloaded onto students and their families, the government proceeded to cut post-secondary education funding. In fact, public funding for universities fell each consecutive year after tuition fees were introduced. Total per student funding, both public funding from the government and tuition fees, was lower in 2002-2003 than in 1996-1997, the year before tuition fees were introduced. After only five short years cumulative student loan debt in Britain now stands at £33.4 billion with no improvement in quality or access on the horizon.

CONCLUSION

Post-secondary education is a necessity for individuals and society at large. A better educated population is correlated with a reduced crime rate, decreased health care expenditures and greater civic engagement. A university or college education is virtually a pre- requisite for meaningful participation in today's economy. By increasing the financial barriers to post-secondary education, policy-makers are taking great risks with the future prosperity of Canadians.

The proponents of higher tuition fees in the countries described above have campaigned on the notion that the overall level of funding resulting from higher tuition fees will lead to better quality education. The lesson from the UK, US and New Zealand has been that higher tuition fees are consistently offset by cuts in public funding, reduced access to higher education, massive student debt burdens, and no quality improvements. There is a lesson to be learned from these experiences for Canadian policy-makers.

1. Canadian Association of University Teachers. CAUT Almanac of Post-Secondary Education in Canada - 2009. Ottawa, 2009.

2. Statistics Canada. University Tuition Fees – 2009. The Daily. October 20, 2009.

3. Statistics Canada, "Participation in postsecondary education and family income," The Daily. Friday, December 7, 2001.

4. Statistics Canada and Human Resources and Skills Development Canada, "At a Crossroads: First Results for the 18 to 20-Year-old Cohort of the Youth in Transition Survey", January 2002.

5. McElroy, Lori. Student Aid and University Persistence: Does Debt Matter? Montreal: Canada Millennium Scholarship Foundation, 2005.

6. Kane, Thomas. "The Price of Admission: Rethinking How Americans Pay for College". University of California Press, November 1999.

7. Canadian Association of University Teachers. "The Economics of Access: The Fiscal Reality of PSE Costs for Low-Income Families." CAUT Education Review 8.2 (2006).

8. Income contingent repayment (ICR) for student loans extends debt repayment for most students, guaranteeing greater overall indebtedness. Income contingent repayment schemes were vigourously resisted by students in Canada during the mid-1990s, and more recently in Ontario where former Premier Bob Rae recommended their implementation. Student resistance in Canada has kept ICR from being implemented.

9. New Zealand Educational Institute. "Submission on Student Support in New Zealand". Wellington: New Zealand Educational Institute, 2003:4.

NEDIC
(WEBSITE)

Established in 1985, the National Eating Disorder Information Centre (NEDIC) is a Canadian non-profit organization that provides information and resources on eating disorders and weight preoccupation.

Analyzing and Connecting
Return to these questions after you have finished reading.

1. The website's focus is "to inform the public about eating disorders and related issues." Has it achieved its purpose? What did you learn that was new?

2. Its mandate is also prevention. What strategies are used in the site to promote positive body image?

3. Under "Give & Get Help," the site offers several personal stories. What is the effect of these testimonials? What impact do you think they are intended to have on the audience?

4. How do the images and graphics contribute to the overall message? How important are the links?

nedic

Home | Login | Contact Us | Feedback

information on eating disorders and weight preoccupation

Know the Facts | Give & Get Help | Get Involved | What's New | Resource Library | Store | About NEDIC

SEARCH

Toll Free 1-866-NEDIC-20 (1-866-633-4220) Toronto 416-340-4156

Overview

You are here: home > about nedic > overview

The National Eating Disorder Information Centre (NEDIC) is a non-profit organization founded in 1985 to provide information and resources on eating disorders and food and weight preoccupation. One of our main goals is to inform the public about eating disorders and related issues.

The Mental Health Programs and Services division of the Ontario Ministry of Health and Long Term Care has mandated NEDIC to provide information about issues related to eating disorders, including up-to-date information on what treatment is available.

NEDIC is a program of the University Health Network in Toronto, Canada.

What does NEDIC do?

- **Develops and disseminates information and resources on eating disorders and food and weight preoccupation.**
- **Staffs a telephone helpline** that provides information on treatment or support. Our phones - 416-340-4156 in Toronto/GTA, or 1-866-NEDIC-20 (1-866-63342-20) across Canada - are staffed from 9 am to 5 pm Monday through Friday (Eastern Standard Time). We return messages as quickly as possible.
- **Provides displays** on eating disorders at local community events. NEDIC may be available to staff these displays.
- **Runs prevention & awareness campaigns** like Eating Disorder Awareness Week (first full week in February annually) and International No Diet Day (May 6). For more information, see Prevention & Health Promotion.
- **Assists communities** by helping organizations develop information materials, by providing support and advice, by connecting organizations and individuals working in the area of food and weight preoccupation, and by sharing information and resources.
- **Runs workshops and presentations** for schools, community groups and professional bodies on the prevention of disordered eating, promotion of positive body image, and healthy lifestyles.

NEDIC

Home | Login | Contact Us | Feedback

information on eating disorders and weight preoccupation

Know the Facts | Give & Get Help | Get Involved | What's New | Resource Library | Store | About NEDIC

SEARCH

Toll Free 1-866-NEDIC-20 (1-866-633-4220)   Toronto 416-340-4156

Social, Cultural & Biological Influences

You are here: <u>home</u> > <u>know the facts</u> > social, cultural & biological influences

The societies we live in have strong beliefs and attitudes toward just about everything. Different groups within a given society adapt these beliefs, attitudes and behaviours. Our beliefs and attitudes toward our selves and our bodies are shaped in some way by these cultural influences. Our physical make-up and health also affect our feelings and behaviour.

The following information looks at positive and negative socio-cultural and physical influences, and how we can make healthy choices.

Q. Does the media cause eating disorders?

A. The media doesn't cause eating disorders but they send out the clear message that you should be thin. They keep showing or telling us certain lies about women, such as:

- Everyone can be thin.
- Only thin women's bodies are beautiful and sexually desirable.
- If you're thin you will be confident, successful, healthy and happy.
- You can't and shouldn't be happy with yourself unless your body looks exactly like the thin ideal.

The "beauty" and diet industries make more than $45 billion every year. They encourage us not to like our bodies or ourselves. Their profit depends on it.

When we believe that there is a real link between being thin, over-controlled about food and weight and being happy and successful, we are more likely to develop disordered eating.

As consumers, we need to look critically at the media and act. Just blaming the media is not the answer.

Related Links

- <u>Mind on the Media</u>
- <u>Media Awareness</u>

nedic

Home | Login | Contact Us | Feedback

information on eating disorders and weight preoccupation

Know the Facts | Give & Get Help | Get Involved | What's New | Resource Library | Store | About NEDIC

SEARCH

Toll Free 1-866-NEDIC-20 (1-866-633-4220)   Toronto 416-340-4156

Personal Stories

You are here: home > give & get help > personal stories

A great way of understanding what others have gone through is by reading personal essays and stories by those who have struggled with disordered eating and those who have supported someone in their recovery process. It's important to know that you are not alone and it's also a good way to find out what has worked for others.

Do you have a story you'd like to share? Please submit your story by e-mailing us a Microsoft Word document of no more than 1,500 words. Note: Not all stories submitted will be posted.

Battling Bulimia

Eating Disorders and Depression: a story of survival

Inside the Experience

Life is too short to obsess

Self-Esteem Lost and Found

Kelly's Story

Celebrating our Natural Sizes

Mirror, Mirror on the Wall . . . Are Muscular Men the Best of All?
(MAGAZINE ARTICLE)
Nancy Clark

Nancy Clark is a nutrition consultant for both casual exercisers and competitive athletes. She published this article in *American Fitness,* a magazine published by Aerobics and Fitness Association of America, the largest organization of the fitness professionals.

Analyzing and Connecting
Return to these questions after you have finished reading.

1. In paragraph 2, the author, Nancy Clark, cites a study that concludes young men are highly influenced by media images. In your experience do you believe that the media has that much influence? Think of examples pro and con.

2. Other writers have argued that Barbie's thin waist, thin thighs, and long legs remain the ideal body image for women, reinforced by models on television and magazine covers and a multitude of media images. Less than 2 percent of women, however, have the genes to achieve this image. It seems most women don't like what they see in the mirror. Do body issues differ with gender?

3. The solution proposed is media education. If media images are the problem, then how effectively can media be the solution?

4. How does the fact that Americans are some of the most obese people on the planet correlate with the fitness obsession? Are these facts two sides of the same coin? Explain.

Mirror, mirror on the wall ...are muscular men the best of all?

The hidden turmoil of muscle dysmorphia – Nutrition

BY NANCY CLARK

MUSCLE DYSMORPHIA IS A NEW SYNDROME EMERGING BEHIND GYM DOORS. You might notice it in your gym's weight room. Some weightlifters pathologically believe their muscles are too small. They have poor body image (i.e., are ashamed of, embarrassed by and unhappy with their bodies) and a passionate desire to not only build muscle, but also avoid gaining fat. This preoccupation with building muscles manifests itself in excessive weightlifting (e.g., spending four or more hours per day at the gym), attention to diet (e.g., consuming protein shakes on a rigid schedule), time spent "body-checking" (e.g., looking in mirrors, CDs, window reflections, etc.), excessively weighing themselves (i.e., 10 to 20 times per day), too little time spent with family

and friends and, not uncommonly, anabolic steroid use.

Is this overconcern with body size a new obsession? Perhaps. In the past few years, we have been increasingly exposed to half-naked, muscular male bodies (e.g., Calvin Klein underwear ads). Evidently, even brief exposure to these images can affect a man's view of his body. In a study of the media's effect on male body image, a group of college men viewed advertisements featuring muscular men, while another group viewed neutral advertisements without partially naked male bodies. Then, the men (unaware of the hypothesis being tested) were given a body image assessment. Those exposed to the muscular images showed a significantly greater

Chapter 16 **ARGUING FOR CHANGE**

CLARK: MIRROR, MIRROR ON THE WALL . . . ARE MUSCULAR MEN THE BEST OF ALL?

discrepancy between the body they ideally want to have and their current body size (Leit, Gray and Pope 2002). Another study suggests up to a third of teenage boys are trying to gain weight to be stronger, fitter, attain a better body image and perform better in sports (O'Dea and Rawstone 2001).

The irony is while college-age men believe a larger physique is more attractive to the opposite sex, women report desiring a normal-sized body. In a study of men from the United States, Austria and France, the subjects were shown a spectrum of body images and asked to choose:

- the body they felt represented their own
- the body they would ideally like to have
- the body of an average man their age and
- the male body they felt women preferred.

The men chose an ideal male body that was about 28 pounds more muscular than their current bodies. They also reported believing women prefer a male body with 30 pounds more muscle than they currently possessed. Yet, an accompanying study indicated women actually preferred an ordinary male body without added muscle (Pope 2000).

At the 2003 Massachusetts Eating Disorders Association's (MEDA) annual conference, Dr. Roberto Olivardia shared his research on adolescent boys' body image. Olivardia is a psychology instructor at Harvard Medical School and co-author of *The Adonis Complex: The Secret Crisis of Male Body Obsession* (Free Press, 2000). The title alludes to Adonis, the Greek god who exemplifies ideal masculine beauty and desire of all women. Olivardia

explained that adolescence is a time for exploring "Who am I?" Without a doubt, so much of who a teen is, is defined by his body. Because today's boys have been exposed from day one to GI Joe action figures, Hulk Hogan and Nintendo's Duke Nukem, they have relentlessly received strong messages that muscular bodies are desirable. Those at risk for muscle dysmorphia include adolescent boys who were teased as children about being too fat or short. Individuals at highest risk are those who base their self-esteem solely on their appearance.

In our society, muscularity is commonly associated with masculinity. According to Olivardia, compared to ordinary men, muscular men tend to command more respect and are deemed more powerful, threatening and sexually virile. Muscular men perceive others as "backing off" and "taking them seriously." Not surprisingly, men's desire for muscles has manifested itself in a dramatic increase in muscle (and penile) implants.

Olivardia expressed concern the "bigger is better" mindset can often lead to anabolic steroid use. He cited statistics from a study with 3,400 high school male seniors: 6.6 percent reported having used steroids; more than two-thirds of that group started before age 16 (Buckley et al. 1988). Olivardia regrets males commonly use steroids in secrecy and shame. "Men will tell someone they use cocaine before they admit to using 'juice.'" This commonly keeps them from seeking help.

Steroids carry with them serious medical concerns: breast enlargement, impotence, acne, mood swings, risk of heart disease, prostate cancer, liver damage and AIDS (from sharing needles)—not to mention sudden death, although it may occur 20 years from current use. "Roid rage," the fierce temper that contributes to brutal murders and violence against women, is an immediate danger.

What's the solution? According to Olivardia, young men need education about realistic body size to correct the distorted thought "if some muscle is good, then more must be better." They might also need treatment for obsessive-compulsive disorder. Sadly, most men believe they are the only ones with this problem and, thereby, take a long time to admit needing therapy. When they do, too few programs exist to help them explore the function this obsession serves in their lives—a sense of control. They mistakenly believe control over their bodies equates to control over their lives.

If you are a male struggling with dysmorphia, read *The Adonis Complex: The Secret Crisis of Male Body Obsession* and other books available at **www.gurze.com**. A Web search on "muscle dysmorphia" can also yield hundreds of articles with helpful information. Most importantly, know you are not alone—seek help and find peace.

REFERENCES

Buckley, W.E., et al. "Estimated prevalence of anabolic steroid use in high school seniors." *JAMA,* 260 (1988): 3441–5.

Leit, R.A., Gray, J.J. and Pope, H.G. "The media's representation of the ideal male body: A cause for muscle dysmorphia?" *Int'l. J. Eating Disorders,* 31 (April 2002): 334–8.

O'Dea, J.A. and Rawstone, P. "Male adolescents identify their weight gain practices, reasons for desired weight gain, and source of weight gain information." *J. Am. Diel. Assoc.* 101, no. 1 (January 2001): 105–7.

Pope, H.J., et al. "Body image perception among men in three countries." *Am. J. Psychiatry,* 157 (August 2000): 1297–301.

How to write an argument for change

These steps for the process of writing an argument for change may not progress as neatly as this chart might suggest. Writing is not an assembly-line process.

As you write and revise, imagine that you are in a conversation with an audience that contains people who both agree and disagree with you. Think about what you would say to both and speak to these diverse readers.

1 IDENTIFY THE PROBLEM

- Identify the problem, what causes it, and whom it affects.

- Describe what has been done or not done to address the problem.

- Make a claim advocating a specific change or course of action. Put the claim in this form: We should (or should not) do _____ .

2 PRESENT YOUR PROPOSAL

- State your solution as specifically as you can.

- Consider other solutions and describe why your solution is better.

- Examine if the solution will have enough money and support to be implemented.

Do background research

- *What has been written about the problem?*

- *What other solutions have been proposed?*

- *Where have other solutions been effective or ineffective?*

Analyze your potential readers

- *Whom are you writing for?*

- *How interested will your readers be in this problem?*

- *How would your solution benefit them directly and indirectly?*

3 WRITE A DRAFT

- Define the problem. Give the background your readers will need.

- Discuss other possible solutions.

- Present your solution.

- Argue that your proposal will work.

- Conclude with a call for action.

- Write a title that will interest readers.

- Include any neccessary images, tables, or graphics.

- *Participate in peer review, meet with your instructor, or visit your writing centre.*

4 REVISE, REVISE, REVISE

- Recheck that your proposal fulfills the assignment.

- Make sure that your proposal claim is clear and focused.

- Add detail or further explanation about the problem.

- Add detail or further explanation about how your solution addresses the problem.

- Make sure you have considered other solutions and explain why yours is better.

- Examine your organization and think of possible better ways to organize.

- Review the visual presentation of your report for readability and maximum impact.

- Proofread carefully.

5 PRINT A VERSION TO SUBMIT

- Make sure your finished writing meets all formatting requirements.

1: Identify the problem

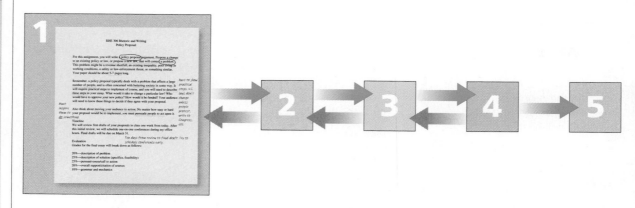

Analyze the assignment	• Read your assignment slowly and carefully. Look for the key words *propose* or *problem* and *solution*. These key words tell you that you are writing a proposal.
	• Highlight any information about the length specified, date due, formatting, and other requirements. You can attend to this information later. At this point you want to zero in on the subject and your proposal claim.
Identify the problem	• What exactly is the problem?
	• Who is most affected by the problem?
	• What causes the problem?
	• Has anyone tried to do anything about it? If so, why haven't they succeeded?
	• What is likely to happen in the future if the problem isn't solved?
Do background research in online and print library sources, Web sources, government documents, experts in the field, and possibly field research such as a survey	• What has been written about the problem?
	• What other solutions have been proposed?
	• Where have other solutions been effective?
	• Where have other solutions failed?
Make a proposal claim	• Proposal claims advocate a specific change or course of action. Put the claim in this form: We should (or should not) do _____.

Make an idea map

When you have a number of ideas and facts about a topic, write them on sticky notes. Then post the sticky notes and move them around, so you can begin to see how they might fit together. When you find an organization that suits your subject, make a working outline from your sticky notes.

PROPOSAL
Eliminate the Olympic
Games

WHO WOULD SUPPORT?
Anti –poverty activists
Taxpayers?

REASONS WHY
Excessive costs to host city
Corruption
Political involvement
Corporate agenda

WHO WOULD OPPOSE?
Governments
Business/sponsors
Athletes

COUNTERARGUMENTS
Increase business
    opportunities to the
    host
Global exposure –
    increase of tourism
Employment benefits

WOULD IT WORK?
Unlikely...not enough
    support from
    government/business
Pressure from general
    public could affect
    some changes

Writer at work

Tanvir Tagheziakan was asked to create a proposal argument for his writing class. Upon receiving the assignment, he made the following notes and observations.

EAC954CS

For this assignment, you will present a position in the form of a proposal. Propose a change to an existing idea or concept that continues to be an accepted part of society. Choose something like raising the age of majority, creating universal day care, or instituting standardized testing at the post-secondary level. Your paper should be 5–8 pages long.

Remember: a proposal for change typically deals with an issue that affects a large number of people and is often concerned with bettering society in some way. It requires specific and detailed reasons for addressing this issue, and clear identification of the benefits. Your audience will need to know these things to decide if they agree with your proposal.

Also, think about convincing your audience. No matter how unpopular your proposal would seem, you must persuade people to at least see the value of the proposed change.

Timeline

We will review first drafts of your proposals in class one week from today. After this initial review, we will schedule one-on-one conferences during my office hours. Final drafts will be due on April 10.

Evaluation

Grades for the final essay will break down as follows:

20%—description of the problem
25%—description of the solution (specifics)
45%—persuasiveness/overall support/citation/documentation
10%—grammar and mechanics

Read the assignment closely

Tanvir began by highlighting key words in the assignment and noting specifics about the length and due date.

Choose a topic

Tanvir listed possible topics and then considered the strengths and weaknesses of each. He chose one that could be developed adequately and could motivate his audience.

Plan research strategies

Tanvir made a list of possible sources of information to begin his research.

POSSIBLE TOPICS

– Create a standardized form of testing for steroid use in all team sports (professional, educational, recreational).

> Might be too broad. Also, the science involved might be hard to explain in 5–8 pages

– Move the capital of NB to St. John.

> Too regional?

– Eliminate the Olympic games as an unnecessary and costly expense.

An issue of high interest.
Good for capturing audience.

> Could give lots of specific steps (funding, building plans, tourist info).

– Reformulate the means by which the CBC receives federal funds.

> Would be very dry, though popular T.V. shows could be used to provoke interest/make people want to act.

To Do:
– Search Internet for current discussion on this topic.
– Search periodicals for discussions of this topic.
– Search academic and sports journals for more sophisticated discussions.
– Any books???
– What groups (political, sociological) are discussing this right now?

2: Present your proposal

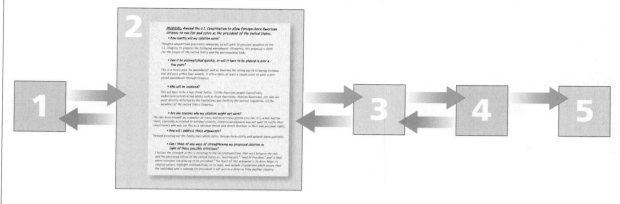

State your proposal as specifically as you can

- What exactly do you want to achieve?
- Can it be accomplished quickly or at all?
- Has anything like it been tried before?
- Who will be involved?
- Can you think of any reasons why it might not work?
- How will you address those arguments?
- Can you think of any ways of strengthening your proposal in light of those possible criticisms?

Consider other options

- What else has been proposed for this problem, including doing nothing?
- What are the advantages and disadvantages of those other options?

Examine the feasibility of your proposal

- How easy is your proposal to implement?
- Will the people who will be most affected be willing to go along with it? (For example, lots of things can be accomplished if enough people volunteer, but groups often have difficulty getting enough volunteers to work without pay.)
- If it costs money, how do you propose paying for it?
- Who is most likely to reject your proposal because it is not practical enough?
- How can you convince your readers that your proposal can be achieved?

Analyze your potential readers

- Whom are you writing for?
- How interested will your readers be in this problem?
- How much does this problem affect them?
- How would your proposal benefit them directly and indirectly?

STAYING ON TRACK

Acknowledging other points of view

Write for readers who may disagree with you

Arguments that ignore other points of view and other possible solutions tend to convince only those who agree with you before you start writing. Your goal is to convince those who haven't thought about the problem and those who might disagree at the outset but can be persuaded. Think about why readers might disagree.

- Are they misinformed about the problem? If so, you will need to provide accurate information.
- Do they have different assumptions about the problem? If so, can you show them that your assumptions are better?
- Do they share your goals but think your solution is not the right one? If so, you will need to explain why your solution is better.

You might have to do some research to find out the views of others. If you are writing about a local problem, you may need to talk to people.

Deal fairly with other solutions and other points of view

OFF TRACK

Free tuition for all high school graduates who attend community colleges is an idea too ridiculous to consider.
(No reason is given for rejecting an alternative solution, and those who propose it are insulted.)

ON TRACK

Free tuition for all high school graduates is a desirable solution to get more students to attend college, but is not likely to be implemented because of the cost. A solution targeted to low-income or at-risk students similar to the Millennium Project, which is funded by the MEI, could be implemented in our province.
(The author offers a reason for rejecting an alternative solution and proposes a solution that has some common ground with the alternative.)

Writer at work

Tanvir began by laying out his proposal as specifically as possible. He used the following list of questions to guide his argument.

<u>PROPOSAL:</u> Eliminate the Olympic Games since they are no longer necessary or cost-effective.

- **How exactly will my proposal work?**

Through detailed descriptions and presentations of corruption, financial irresponsibility, and political hidden agendas, I will hopefully convince readers that the Games are not viable anymore.

- **Can it be accomplished quickly or all?**

It is unlikely that the general public will have the power to stop the Games, but it could convince more people not to support them (buying merchandise etc.), allowing them to express their disapproval in a tangible way.

- **Who will be involved?**

People who are affected by the Games (displaced by the venues, for example) or host city taxpayers who have been burdened with debt.

- **Are there any reasons why my proposal won't work?**

Many...too much corporate and government investment

- **How will I address those arguments?**

By providing details about the societal/economical benefits of eliminating the Games

<u>FEASIBILITY</u>

- **How easy is this to implement?**

Not easy at all...but the point is that it might open up dialogue about the validity of the Games

- **Will the people most affected be willing to support it?**

Probably

• Who is likely to reject it?

Any group with an investment (government, big business, athletes)

<u>POTENTIAL READERS</u>
• For whom am I writing?

General public

• How interested will the readers be in this proposal?

It comes up each Olympic year, and hopefully, making it more personally relevant (ie. The cost of the Vancouver Games) will peak interest.

• How would this proposal benefit the readers?

Directly, it would speak to the interests of the host city's population; indirectly,
it brings to the forefront a national concern.

3: Write a draft

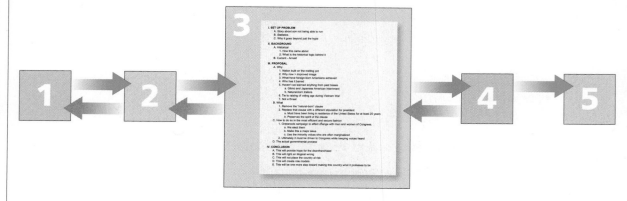

Define the problem

- Set out the issue or problem. You might need to argue for the seriousness of the problem, and you might have to give some background on how it came about.

Present your solution

- Make clear the goals of your proposal.
- Describe in detail the specific reasons for this proposal and how it will solve the problem you have identified. You can impress your readers by the care with which you have thought through this problem.
- Explain the positive consequences that will follow from your proposal. What good things will happen and what bad things will be avoided if your proposal is implemented?
- If necessary, describe other solutions that have been attempted and others that are possible. Explain why other solutions either don't solve the problem or are unrealistic.

Argue that your solution can be done

- Your proposal for solving the problem is a truly good idea only if it can be put into practice. If people have to change the ways they are doing things now, explain why they would want to change. If your proposal costs money, you need to identify exactly where the money would come from.

Conclude with a call for action

- Make a call for action. You should put your readers in a position such that if they agree with you, they will take action if possible. You might restate and emphasize what exactly they need to do.

Writer at work

Here is the outline Tanvir used to build the first draft of his proposal.

I. ESTABLISH CONTEXT
    A. Change in purpose of the Games
    B. Demonstration of athleticism becomes secondary to other agendas

II. BACKGROUND
    A. Historical
        1. Purpose of the Ancient Games
        2. Importance of the early Games

III. PROPOSAL
    A. Why
        1. Politics
            a) Used as a platform for mass exposure of ideology
            b) Cold War sports
        2. Costs
            a) Taxpayer responsibility to cover the cost
            b) Displaced people
        3. Scandals and corruption
            a) Cheating
            b) Bribery
            c) Money laundering

IV. CONCLUSION
    A. Original purpose no longer applicable
    B. Lack of integrity makes the Games fraudulent
    C. Eliminating Games will relieve huge unnecessary burden

4: Revise, revise, revise

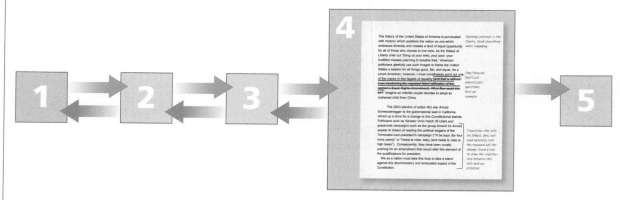

Take a break from your writing and come back to it with "fresh eyes." When you return, imagine you are someone who has never seen your proposal before. Read the proposal out loud. When you are done, ask yourself: Do I understand the problem? Does it really seem like a problem that must be dealt with? Is the proposal clear? Does it seem like it is worth the trouble? Do I think it will really work? How much will it cost in money, effort, or inconvenience? The biggest trap you can fall into is starting off with the little stuff first. Leave the small stuff for last.

Does your paper or project meet the assignment?	• Look again at your assignment. Does your paper or project do what the assignment asks? • Look again at the assignment for specific guidelines, including length, format, and amount of research. Does your work meet these guidelines?
Is the proposal claim clear and focused?	• Does the proposal claim address the problem? • Does the proposal claim provoke a reaction?
Do you identify the problem adequately?	• Do you need more evidence that the problem exists and is a serious concern? • Will your readers find credible any sources you include? Can you think of other sources that might be more persuasive?
Is it clear how your proposal will address a problem?	• Can you find more evidence that your proposal will resolve the problem? • Do you address potential objections to your proposal? • Do you provide evidence that your solution is feasible? For example, if your solution requires money, where will the money come from?

Do you consider alternative solutions?	• Do you explain why your solution is better than the alternatives?
Is your organization effective?	• Is the order of your main points clear to your reader? • Are there any places where you find abrupt shifts or gaps? • Are there sections or paragraphs that could be rearranged to make your draft more effective?
Is your introduction effective?	• Can you get off to a faster start, perhaps with a striking example? • Can you think of a better way to engage your readers to be interested in the problem you identify? • Does your introduction give your readers a sense of why the problem is important?
Is your conclusion effective?	• Does your conclusion have a call for action? • Do you make it clear exactly what you want your readers to do?
Do you represent yourself effectively?	• To the extent you can, forget for a moment that you wrote what you are reading. What impression do you have of you, the writer? • Does "the writer" create an appropriate tone? • Has "the writer" done his or her homework?
Is the writing project visually effective?	• Is the font attractive and readable? • Is the overall layout attractive and readable? • If headings are used, do they make clear what comes under each of them? • Is each photograph, chart, graph, map, or table clearly labelled? Does each visual have a caption?
Save the editing for last	When you have finished revising, edit and proofread carefully.

A peer review guide is on page 31.

Writer at work

During peer review of his paper, and in his meeting with his instructor, Tanvir made notes on his first draft. He used the comments to guide his revision.

The Olympic Games originated in Ancient Greece— *Need more for context...* since 776 BCE, the games have had a turbulent and violent history, being turned over from civilization to civilization ("Brief History"). Towards the start of the Common Era, the games were banned for 1500 years until revived by Pierre de Fredy in the late 1800s/early 1900s—whose main goal of the modern games was to train French soldiers, so they can get into shape and create unity and peace throughout the world ("Olympic History"). However, as the Games evolved to encompass women and different cultures, the main intention, to demonstrate the feats of athletes, began to turn political, while people associated with the Olympics were found to be corrupt and costs were skyrocketing. In essence, the Olympic Games have become so convoluted with the agendas of other parties (e.g. politicians, businesses, etc.) that it has lost its original meaning of exhibiting great athleticism—thus, the Olympic Games have become unnecessary. They have become astronomically expensive to hold, while being plagued with decades of scandals and corruption, and finally, the true goals of the Olympics have diminished to serve other purposes.

Stay focused...is this statement really important to the point?

This info needs to be rearranged to better match ideas in outline...maybe stronger words ??

Look for ways to focus

Tanvir responded to suggestions from his teacher and his peers to make his introduction less wordy and better focused on the main point. He removed material that did not obviously inform readers about the problem.

Check transitions

He also worked on strengthening transitions between paragraphs.

Read your paper aloud

Finally, Tanvir read his essay aloud to check for misspelled words, awkward phrasing, and other mechanical problems.

STAYING ON TRACK

Reviewing your draft

Give yourself plenty of time for reviewing your draft. For detailed information on how to participate in a peer review, how to review it yourself, and how to respond to comments from your classmates, your instructor, or a campus writing consultant, see pages 29–32.

Some good questions to ask yourself when reviewing an argument for change

- Do you connect the problem to your readers? Even if the problem doesn't affect them directly, at the very least you should appeal to their sense of fairness.

- Can you explain more specifically how your proposal will work?

- Does your conclusion connect with the attitudes and values of your readers in addition to making clear what you want them to do? Can you add an additional point? Can you sharpen your call to action?

5: Print a version to submit

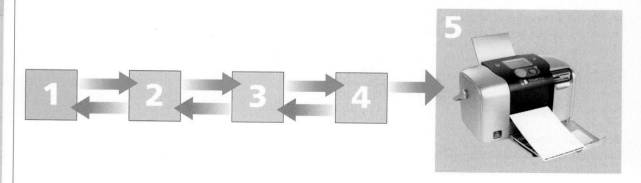

Tanvir Tagheziakan

Professor Rubens

EAC954CS

10 April 2011

The Olympics: An Obscene Waste of Money

The Olympic Games originated in Ancient Greece, and since 776 BCE, the Games have had a turbulent and violent history, being turned over from civilization to civilization ("Brief History"). Towards the start of the Common Era, the games were banned for 1500 years until revived by Pierre de Fredy in the late 1800s. His main goal of the modern games was to train French soldiers, so they could get into shape and create unity and peace throughout the world ("Olympic History"). However, as the Games evolved, the main intention—to demonstrate the feats of athletes—began to turn political, while people associated with the Olympics became corrupt and costs skyrocketed. In essence, the Olympic Games have become so convoluted with the agendas of other parties (e.g., politicians, businesses, etc.) that they have lost their original meaning of exhibiting great athleticism. Thus, the Olympic Games have become an unnecessary burden. They have become overtly political, astronomically expensive to host, and plagued with decades of scandals and corruption; the true goals of the Olympics have slowly disappeared to serve other purposes.

For centuries, Greece held the Olympic Games in the highest regard. The Olympic Games of the past were tied to religion, culture, national identity and of course, unity (Pattakos). However, what makes the Games of the past so unique, compared to the modern-day Games, is the peace that was recognized during times of war. Of course, the Olympics were held every four years, but even during the most horrifying of wars, the Greeks and their enemies all observed peace to appease the gods for the few weeks of Olympic gaming. The Olympic Games were banned by Christian Byzantine Emperor Theodosius I, and the ban held for 1500 years, until Pierre de Fredy decided to revive the games; and with his vision of creating a world of peace and friendly athletic competition (Pattakos), he helped to create the International Olympic Committee, which would hold the games every four years, just as the Greeks did in the past.

Given the historical roots of the game, it is evident that the hope for the modern-day Olympic Games was to create the atmosphere of peace—where violence and politics would have no forum. However, the Games veered away from this ideology. Instead, they went down an ugly path of fierce nationalism, and nations would use the Games for their own political agenda. For example, during the 1972 Summer Olympics, tragic events unfolded as a terrorist group claimed the lives of 11 Israeli athletes and a German police officer ("Olympic Team Murder"). The reason for the massacre in Munich was to spread the terrorists' political message, and the entire world would be witness to their struggle. It is apparent that the terrorists used the Olympics because of their mass forum—thousands upon thousands of athletes and fans would witness the heinous acts committed. To grab attention, they used what was supposed to be something peaceful and turned it deadly, thus scarring the Olympics forever. During that same year, the US and Soviet Union basketball teams were to face off in the final round of amateur basketball—the game was not immune to the politics of the Cold War and the fierce rivalry between the United States and

Soviet Union. When the United States team lost, it was a loss for the entire country and to some, a direct blow to democracy (Saraceno). People believed the bout between the two nations signified a battle between good and evil; communism versus democracy. America's pride took a hit when the team lost—the idea of the "Reds" beating the glorious boys of the United States was too much to bear for many citizens—something impossible to recuperate from, since many felt the Soviet Union were not competitors but enemies. It seems the Olympic Games were rife with political agendas; rather than promoting peace and unity, many nations decided to use the Games as a forum for their political message. A game between two rivalling nations could not be viewed as a friendly, competitive match—instead, it was a match between good and evil. By manipulating the games like this, the primary principle of peace, or athletes exhibiting great skills, as during the Ancient Olympic Games, would slowly fade away and be abandoned for the more contentious option of politics, presented in the guise of competitive sport.

As politics continue to sully the international sporting event, businesses and large corporations continue to find ways of reaping monetary rewards, no matter the cost. Many cities, such as Vancouver and Beijing, did not think of the consequences of hosting the Olympic Games in their city. The city or government councils of the respective cities certainly did not ask themselves whether or not it was even feasible to hold the Games, especially during tough economic times. Instead, the cities opted to the hold the Games for their own motives—Beijing, to represent China as a country that is open and friendly (as opposed to the current image of being closed), while Vancouver wanted to hold the Game for the prestige—not to support athletes, or to bring world peace, but for the prestige. Of course, holding an event like the Olympics can be expensive, so it should be given to those cities that find it financially possible. However, Vancouver has already racked up a bill of nearly six billion dollars (Braham), which of course, citizens across Canada will be paying for, or at least most of it. In addition to this, the Olympics have done little to stir employment or create economic growth too; for example, during the Olympics in the state of Utah, job growth went down 37% compared to before the Olympics (Abbs). The benefits, if any, of hosting the Olympics certainly do not outweigh the costs, which have done more to damage cities than improve them. City councillors need to start asking themselves whether or not the Games are even worth hosting, considering the myriad other problems a city might be facing—for example, homelessness rampant in Vancouver is being swept under the rug by city officials to make the city look cleaner (Abbs). Of course, construction companies would enjoy being in a city hosting the Olympics—business goes up. Cities will do anything to look good for the Olympics, and as the construction of the new venues or infrastructure get underway (e.g., new transit system), land value increases, and the citizens become victims of excessive costs. They are often "displaced"—kicked out or evicted because of increasing rent (Abbs). Corporate greed and prestige have become the two main values of the Olympic Games currently, and rather than spend money on pressing issues and bigger concerns, aesthetics are pushed to the forefront. Making things *look* better, as opposed to *making* them better, becomes the mantra. Cities are not taking care of the welfare of the citizens whenever the Olympics come into town, but instead mount debts and marginalize citizens. In fact, there is little transparency when it comes to spending for the Olympics, and this can worry citizens (e.g., will their taxes be higher the next time they look at their pay stub?). The Olympic Games have become totally unnecessary in locations where gross human violations have occurred or lack of care for citizens is evident—they only serve to help the wealthy, keep businesses booming and give cities huge makeovers, when money could easily be put towards infrastructure, health care or education. As this continues to pose a problem for many nations across the world, the other concerns surrounding the games include rampant corruption.

Apart from skyrocketing costs and the greed of capitalism, the other problem the Olympic Games face is the gross number of scandals year after year. It could be someone cheating or an official being bribed—whatever the case, most of these scandals scar the Olympics for good. In fact, corruption heightened when a man named Juan Antonio Samaranch took reign as president of the International Olympic Committee. During his presidency until his retirement, the Olympics were plagued with scandals, including knowing and ignoring bribery between judges and hosting cities, lack of proper drug testing for athletes, and getting paid huge salaries compared to the competing athletes, most of whom, lived below the poverty line ("Corruption in Sports"). The list goes on—the fact that such scandals plagued the Olympics for nearly twenty years certainly signals that integrity has been lost and cannot easily be recovered. If these unethical acts occurred, there should have been a neutral regulatory body to investigate them. Also, since taxpayers foot a majority of the bill for hosting the Olympics, the accounting books, which were alleged to have evidence of money laundering ("Corruption in Sports"), should have been transparent—simply through pressure on hosting cities. People would like to know how their money is spent, and for twenty years, the IOC took advantage of its position and was simply corrupted by power. This in turn left a black eye in the prestigious international sporting event that is the Olympics.

In essence, there is no need for the Olympics anymore. Their original purpose, to demonstrate the feats of amateur and professional athletes alike, diminished long ago. Nations now use the Olympics, not for friendly competition but for their own political agendas, creating national unity for all the wrong reasons. Cities hosting the Olympics face the arduous task of gathering the funds to make the city look better, while businesses greedily take the opportunity to drive up land value. Finally, corruption has left the Olympics with a black eye—their integrity has been reduced to nothing thanks to the International Olympic Committee. The Olympic Games are definitely a burden for most average citizens of the host city. They will just create bigger debts for cities, more political conflict and be a forum for corruption, leaving those in power (e.g., IOC) richer while the athletes and fans are short-changed. Over the years, it has become less about athletic competition and more of just an "act" about who puts on the best light show. .

Tagheziakan 6

Works Cited

Abbs, Maryann. "Massacres and Profits: A Brief History of the Olympics." *No Vancouver 2010 Winter Olympics On Stolen Native Land.* N.p., 13 Mar. 2007. Web. 24 Mar. 2009.

Braham, Daphne. "Olympics Bill tops $6 Billion So Far." *Vancouver Sun.* CanWest Publishing, 23 Jan. 2009. Web. 24 Mar. 2009.

"Brief History." *Nostos: Hellenic Information Society (UK).* N.p., 2000. Web. 23 Mar. 2009.

"Corruption in Sports." *Blackboard Academic Suite.* Blackboard Academic Suite. 24 Mar. 2009. <http://bbol.embanet.com/courses/1/SE-EAC954/content/_491188_1/dir_unit11.zip/index.html>.

"Olympic History." *CTV Olympics.* CTVglobemedia, 30 Jan. 2009. Web. 23 Mar. 2009.

"Olympic Team Murder." *Palestine Facts.* palestinefacts.org, n.d. Web. 24 Mar. 2009.

Pattakos, Alex. "Original Meaning of the Olympic Games." *Huffington Post.* HuffingtonPost.com, 12 Aug. 2008. Web. 23 Mar. 2009.

Saraceno, Frank. "Classic 1972 USA vs. USSR Basketball Game." *ESPN.* ESPN.com, 6 Aug. 2004. Web. 24 Mar. 2009.

Projects

If you want to persuade your readers to do something, you must convince them that a problem exists and that something needs to be done about it. You'll likely make the best argument for change if the problem matters to you. Most groups and organizations are faced with problems. You'll be able to argue with conviction, and you might even bring about change.

The following projects will give you experience in the kinds of proposals frequent in the workplace and in public life.

A PROPOSAL

For an example of a proposal, see pages 448–451

Write a proposal of 1000–1250 words (about five to seven double-spaced pages) that would solve a problem that you identify.

Choose a problem with which you have personal experience, but you should also think about how many other people this problem affects. Your proposal should take them into account as part of your audience.

Find out who would be in a position to enact your proposal. How can you make your proposal seem like a good idea to these people?

Propose your options as specifically as you can. What exactly do you want to achieve? How exactly will your solution work? Has anything like it been tried elsewhere? Who will be involved?

Consider other options that have been or might be proposed for this problem, including doing nothing. What are the advantages and disadvantages of those options?

Examine how easy your proposal is to implement. Will the people most affected be willing to go along with it? Lots of things can be accomplished if enough people volunteer, but groups often have difficulty getting enough volunteers to work without pay. If it costs money, how do you propose paying for it?

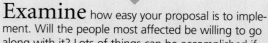

PEARSON

mycanadiancomplab

Go to **www.mycanadiancomplab.ca** to practise your grammar, punctuation, and mechanics skills. Go to the "Resources" tab within MyCanadianCompLab and then click on "Grammar." You will have access to a variety of exercises as well as direct instruction that will help you improve your basic skills and get a better grade in your course.

FORMAL PROPOSAL

For an example proposal,
see pages 452–455.

TEAMWORK: PROBLEM–SOLUTION

For an example of an alternative
proposal, see pages 460–463.

You may not have a lot of experience writing proposals. Nevertheless, proposals have had a profound impact on your life. Almost every program, law, policy, or business that affects you had to be proposed before it became a reality.

Find a proposal argument that you and three or four classmates are interested in. This might be a proposal to widen a road in your town, to pass a law making English the official language of your provincial government, or something similar.

Think of some things in your life that were proposed by people: the building where you attended high school, for example. At some point, that building was proposed as a way of solving a certain problem—perhaps your town had one old, overflowing high school, and your building was proposed to solve the overcrowding. Its location was probably chosen carefully, to avoid causing more problems with traffic, and to ensure that it was easy for students to reach.

As a group discuss the four components of the proposal as outlined in this chapter: What is the problem being addressed? What is the solution? Is it workable and fair? Is it feasible?

Then have each person in the group construct a one- or two-page counterproposal. Your counterproposals should address the same problem as the original proposal, but should offer different solutions. Your analysis of the workability, fairness, and feasibility of the original proposal will help you shape your counterproposals. Is there a way to solve the problem that is cheaper? Less disruptive? More fair? Less risky?

Choose something you are familiar with that went through a proposal process. Try to reconstruct the four components of the original proposal. What problem do you think people were trying to solve? How did concerns about fairness and feasibility shape the program, building, or policy?

Outline your re-created proposal in a page or two.

Present your counterproposals to the rest of your group, and discuss which is the most appealing. You may find that a combination of elements of the different proposals ends up being the best.

Ask yourself if this policy, program, or business truly solved the problem it was intended to solve? Clearly, the proposal itself was successful, for the school was built, the law was passed, or the business was started. But how successful was the proposed solution in reality?

Part 3

The Writer as Researcher

17

Planning Research

When you begin doing research, you need to understand the requirements of your assignment, identify the different sources of information available, and plan your strategy well in advance.

Analyze the research task

If you have an assignment that requires research, look closely at what you are being asked to do. The assignment may ask you to review, compare, survey, analyze, evaluate, or prove that something is true or untrue. You may be writing for experts, for students like yourself, or for the general public. The purpose of your research and your potential audience will help guide your strategies for research. The key is understanding what is expected of you. You are being asked to

1. Determine the type of assignment.
2. Choose and define a subject.
3. Ask a question about the subject.
4. Find out what has been said about this subject.
5. Make a contribution to the discussion about this subject.

Determine the type of assignment

Often your assignment will tell you how to get started. Look for keywords:

- An *analysis* or *examination* requires you to look at an issue in detail, explaining how it has evolved, whom or what it affects, and what is at stake.
- A *survey* requires you to gather opinions about a particular issue, either by a questionnaire or by interviews.
- An *evaluation* requires you to make critical judgments.
- An *argument* requires you to assemble evidence in support of a claim you make.

Ask your instructor for guidance if you remain unsure what is expected.

Find a subject that interests you

When you ask meaningful questions, your research will be enjoyable. Your course work may give you some ideas about questions to ask. Personal experience is often a good source of questions related to your research topic: What was the cause of something that happened to you? Was your experience typical or atypical? How can you solve a problem you have? What do experts think about the issues that concern you? Working with a topic that has already aroused your curiosity makes it more likely that your findings will interest others.

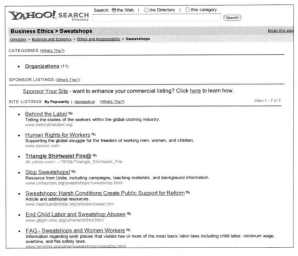

A good way to begin is by browsing a subject directory available through your library or on the Web. Subject directories can show you many different aspects of a single topic.

491

Ask a question

Often you'll be surprised by the amount of information your initial browsing uncovers. Your next task will be to identify in that mass of information a question for your research assignment. This question will be the focus of the remainder of your research and ultimately of your paper. Browsing sources on the topic of solid waste recycling might lead you to a researchable question such as

- Do cities save or lose money on recycling programs?
- Why can't all plastics be recycled?
- Are Canadians being persuaded to recycle more paper, aluminum, and plastic?

Focus your research question

Think about how to make your research question specific enough so that you can treat it thoroughly in a paper. Reading about your subject will help you to focus your research question.

- Would privatizing recycling save money?
- Should our province mandate the use of degradable plastics that decay along with kitchen and yard waste in compost heaps?
- Besides paper bags that deplete forests, what are the alternatives to plastic bags that contaminate soil in landfills and sabotage the recycling system by jamming the machinery that sorts bottles and cans?

Determine what kind of research you need to do

Once you have formulated a research question, begin thinking about what kind of research you will need to do to address the question.

Primary research

Much of the research done in university creates new information through **primary research**: experiments, data-gathering surveys and interviews, detailed observations, and the examination of historical documents. Although some undergraduates do not do primary research, sometimes you may be researching a question that requires you to gather first-hand information. For example, if you are researching a campus issue such as the impact of a new library fee on students' budgets, you may need to conduct interviews, make observations, or take a survey.

Secondary research

Most researchers rely partly or exclusively on the work of others as a source of information. Research based on the work of others is called **secondary research**. In the past this information was contained almost exclusively in collections of print materials housed in libraries, but today an enormous amount of information is available electronically through library databases and the World Wide Web (see Chapter 18).

Determine what you need

Is the scope of your issue ...	Then research might include ...
Local? (Inadequate bike lanes, local noise ordinances, school policies)	• interviews and observations • local newspapers • other local media: television, radio
Regional? (Provincial taxes, highway construction, watershed protection)	• some of the sources above • provincial government offices • regional organizations, clubs, or associations, e.g., the Better Business Bureau of Mainland British Columbia, Greater Frederickton Area Mothers Against Drunk Driving
National? (Federal agricultural subsidies, immigration, daycare policies)	• some of the sources above • federal government offices • national organizations, clubs, or associations, e.g., the Canadian Automobile Association • national network news on television and radio • national newspapers or magazines, e.g., the *Globe and Mail* or *Maclean's*
International? (Trade imbalances, military conflicts, global climate change)	• some of the sources above • federal government offices • international agencies such as UNICEF • international news outlets such as Canada News-Wire • foreign newspapers or magazines like *Le Monde* and *der Spiegel*

You can also find sources you need by thinking about people affected by your issue. Where is your issue being discussed?

Who is interested in this issue?	**Where would they read, write, talk, or hear about it?**	**In what different media might the information appear?**
scientists teachers voters minors senior citizens policy makers stock brokers	scientific journals political journals scholarly journals newspapers magazines books Web forums government documents	online television radio print film/DVD

Set a Schedule

Use your assignment, your personal schedule, and your knowledge of the sources you'll need to schedule your research. Allow yourself some large blocks of uninterrupted time, especially during the browsing stage.

Assignment: Research paper for a government course, analyzing a recent financial fraud

Days until first draft is due: 17

Days 1–3:
PRELIMINARY research, one hour each evening

Days 4–6:
IN-DEPTH library research—Schedule appointment with reference librarian for assistance in how to access different sources of information

Days 7–9:
Go over collected material, think about research question/hypothesis

Days 10–12:
Begin drafting

Days 13–14:
Revise rough draft for clarity, organization, and ideas

Days 15–16:
Follow-up research or verify questionable sources as needed

Day 17:
Fine-tune draft

Assignment: Paper utilising field research for an introduction to social research course

Weeks until project due: 7

Week 1:
Research and brainstorm topics; discuss short list of possible topics/methods with professor; make final decision

Week 2:
Research survey/interview methods; design appropriate method

Week 3:
Conduct field research

Week 4:
Analyze data and do follow-up if necessary

Week 5:
Draft paper—go back to library if necessary

Week 6:
Take draft to writing centre; revise

Week 7:
Proofread, fine tune, and make sure all charts and images print correctly

Draft a working thesis

Once you have done some preliminary research into your question, you need to craft a working thesis. Perhaps you have found a lot of interesting material on the development of Pablum by three Canadian doctors at the Hospital for Sick Children in the 1930s. You have discovered that the scientific management of everything from food to behaviour increased the role and authority of physicians in child-care issues. As you research the question of why physicians' role in child rearing changed, a working thesis begins to emerge.

Write your topic, research question, and working thesis on a note card or sheet of paper. Keep your working thesis handy. You may need to revise it several times until the wording is precise. As you research, ask yourself, does this information tend to support my thesis? Information that does not support your thesis may still be important! It may lead you to adjust your thesis, or even abandon it altogether. You may need to find another source or reason that shows your thesis is still valid.

TOPIC:

The development of Pablum in the 1930s by Canadian doctors at the Hospital for Sick Children.

RESEARCH QUESTION:

How did the development of Pablum in the 1930s reflect the changing role of physicians in child-care issues?

WORKING THESIS:

Canadian society welcomed the scientific approach to infant feeding and food products. This was manifested by the great acceptance of Pablum, developed by three Canadian doctors in the 1930s at Sick Kids Hospital. The scientific management of everything from food to behaviour advice increased the professional role and authority of physicians in child-care issues.

WORKING TOGETHER

Determine what information you need

Select one of the possible topics below or identify a topic that will work for your assignment. Write a brief list or paragraph describing the types of research that might be used to investigate the question. What kinds of information would you need? Where would you look for it?

1. How much does an average Canadian couple spend to adopt a child from overseas?
2. How have budget cuts in colleges affected students at your institution?
3. How did the building of the Trans-Canadian Railroad affect Confederation in Canada?
4. How does Canada Post raise money for the Foundation for Mental Health?

How to plan research

When you receive a research assignment, your first instinct might be to start gathering information right away. If you take a little time to set goals, explore your subject, narrow your subject, and determine what you need, you will be more efficient in searching and you will obtain better results.

Determine the type of assignment

Choose and find a subject that interests you

Browse sources for background information, e.g., encyclopedias

Browse books and articles

Browse a subject directory, e.g., Yahoo

Determine what specific kinds of information you need

Set a schedule

Draft a working thesis

Researcher at work

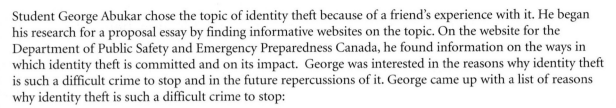

Identity Theft

What Is Identity Theft?

What is Phishing?

What are the Most Common Ways to Commit Identity Theft?

What is the Department of Public Safety and Emergency Preparedness doing about identity theft?

   What Should I Do to Avoid Becoming a Victim of Identity Theft?

   What Should I Do If I've Become a Victim of Identity Theft?

Where Can I Find Out More About Identity Theft?

Student George Abukar chose the topic of identity theft because of a friend's experience with it. He began his research for a proposal essay by finding informative websites on the topic. On the website for the Department of Public Safety and Emergency Preparedness Canada, he found information on the ways in which identity theft is committed and on its impact. George was interested in the reasons why identity theft is such a difficult crime to stop and in the future repercussions of it. George came up with a list of reasons why identity theft is such a difficult crime to stop:

- *Technical weak spots in Internet transactions and storage of personal data*
- *Vast scope of problem — so many people have information in electronic form and Internet makes it all accessible*
- *Lack of comprehensive and co-ordinated public education and awareness to reduce it.*
- *Government legislation not strong enough until recently*

The last reason intrigued George. He was interested in the national discussion about identity theft in relation to the banking industry. After talking to his friend about the specifics of her identity theft experience, he decided to look more closely at the way identity theft is handled by banks and credit-reporting agencies. The question he used to guide his search was

- *Will government legislation help the banking industry prevent identity theft?*

After further research, George came to the conclusion that identity theft is a complex issue not easily solved by one institution. Even though recent legislation allows law enforcement agencies to charge criminals for possessing the personal information of others even before it is used for fraud or theft, he felt that a solution required both legislation and consumer education from a variety of sectors of society to prevent it. This led him to frame the following working thesis for his paper:

- *The growing, complex problem of identity theft encompasses all types of crime in which a person's identifying information is wrongfully used for the purpose of fraud. Law enforcement, government agencies, and the private sector all need to strengthen and co-ordinate their efforts through tough legislation and education in order to fully protect consumers and businesses in Canada.*

18

Finding and Evaluating Sources

Your library is the best place to begin any research assignment because it contains credible materials that are not available anywhere else. Moreover, professional librarians will help you locate sources quickly so you get the most out of your research time.

Determine the print sources you need

You will have a hard time finding the information you need if you don't know what you're looking for. To guide you in your library research, think about these questions:

Who are the parties involved in the issue?	• Who are the experts? • Who else is talking about it? • Who is affected by the issue?
What is at stake?	• How or why does this issue matter? • What stands to be gained or lost? • Who is likely to benefit or suffer?
What kinds of arguments are being made about the issue?	• Are people making proposals? • Are they trying to define terms? • What kinds of reasons do they offer? • What kind of evidence is provided? • What arguments are people not making that they could be making?
Who is the audience for this debate?	• Do people already have strong opinions? • Are they still trying to make up their minds? • How well informed are people about the issue?
Where is the issue being discussed?	• Is the issue being discussed in newspapers and on television? • Are experts writing about the issue in scholarly journals? • Has the issue been around long enough for books to be published about it?
What is your role?	• What is your position? • What else do you need to know? • What do you think should be done?

Your answers to these questions will provide you with keywords and phrases to use as you begin your search for information. Locating print, electronic, and Web sources begins with the development of keyword searches.

Search using keywords

In most cases, you will begin your research with a keyword search or a subject search. A keyword search looks for words anywhere in the record of a book or article. Subject searches use only the subject headings in the record.

Single keyword searches

The simplest keyword searches will return the most results, but often they are not the results you need.

> **EXAMPLE:**
> Type the word **capitalism** into the subject search window on your library's online catalogue, and you likely will find more than a thousand items.

Multiple keyword searches

If you start with only one keyword, chances are the search will give you too many items to be useful. To narrow your search, you can combine search terms. Some library catalogues, databases, and search engines require you to use AND to combine terms, but others do not.

> **EXAMPLE:**
> You may have read or heard that post-traumatic stress disorder is linked to visual memory.
>
> Type **post-traumatic stress disorder** AND **visual memory** (or leave out the AND, if your system permits) to narrow the topic. The combination of terms will yield more focused articles.

Find keywords

Entries for subjects in your library's online catalogue and in article databases will help you find keywords. If you find a book or article that is exactly on your topic, use the subject headings for this item to locate other similar items.

> **EXAMPLE:**
> AUTHOR:
> Ismael, Shereen T.
> TITLE:
> Child poverty and the Canadian welfare state: from entitlement to charity.
> PUBLISHED:
> Edmonton: University of Alberta Press, c2006.
> SUBJECTS:
> Children–Canada–Social Conditions
> Children–Services for–Canada
> Poverty–Canada
> Welfare state–Canada
> Canada–Social policy

Subject searches

When you use the exact subject headings for what you are looking for, they will focus and limit the number of items a search retrieves.

> **EXAMPLE:**
> See the subject headings at the bottom of the left column. They will all retrieve Shereen T. Ismael's *Child poverty and the Canadian welfare state: from entitlement to charity.*

Find books

Nearly all college and university libraries now organize books according to the Library of Congress Classification System, which uses a combination of letters and numbers to give you the book's unique location in the library. The Library of Congress call number begins with a letter or letters that represent the broad subject area into which the book is classified.

The Library of Congress classification scheme groups books by subject, and you can often find other items relevant to your search shelved close to the particular one you are looking for. You can search the extensive Library of Congress online catalogue (catalog.loc.gov) to find out how your subject might be indexed, or you can go straight to your own library's catalogue and conduct a subject search. The call number will enable you to find the item in the stacks. You will need to consult the locations guide for your library to find the book on the shelves.

When you find a book in your library catalogue, take time to notice the subject headings under which it is indexed. For example, if you locate Jeff Hawkins's *On Intelligence*, you will probably find it cross-listed under several subject headings including

```
Brain
Intellect
Artificial intelligence
Neural networks (Computer science)
```

Browsing within these categories, or using some of the keywords provided in a new search, may lead you to more useful sources.

LIBRARY OF CONGRESS

TS 171

through

Z

50B

Find journal articles

Searching for print or electronic articles in scholarly journals and magazines can be done using online indexes known as databases. Databases are fully searchable by author, title, subject, or keywords. Most databases contain the full text of articles, allowing you to email the contents onto your computer. Others give you a citation, which you then have to find in your library. Follow these steps to find articles:

1 Select a database appropriate to your subject.

2 Search the database using relevant subject headings or keywords.

3 Print or copy the complete citation to the article(s).

4 Print or copy the full text if it is available.

5 If the full text is not available, check the periodicals holdings to see if your library has the journal or magazine.

Many specialized databases list citations to journal articles in various fields. For example, *Medline* indexes articles in medical journals. If unsure of which database(s) to use, ask a librarian who works at the reference or information desk to help you.

Knowing what kinds of articles you want to look for—scholarly, trade, or popular—will help you select the right database. Many databases include more than one type of periodical. Although the difference among periodicals is not always obvious, you should be able to judge whether a journal is scholarly, trade, or popular by its characteristics. Some instructors frown on using popular magazines as sources in a research paper, but these journals can be valuable for researching current opinion on a particular topic. They cannot, however, be substituted for serious research articles written by accredited scholars.

Scholarly journals

- Contain long in-depth articles typically written by scholars in the field, usually affiliated with a university or research centre
- Usually include articles that report original research and have footnotes or a list of works cited at the end
- Are reviewed by other scholars in the field
- Assume that readers are also experts in the field
- Display few advertisements or illustrations
- Often are published quarterly or biannually

Examples of scholarly journals include *Journal of Advanced Nursing, British Journal of Sociology, Behavioral Science,* and *College English.*

Trade magazines

- Publish articles related to particular fields, occupations, and interests
- Often give practical information
- Usually include articles that do not report original research and have few or no footnotes, and do not have a list of works cited at the end
- Contain advertisements aimed at people in specific fields
- Are published weekly, monthly, or quarterly

Examples of trade journals include *Advertising Age, Byte, PC Computing,* and *Canadian Grocer.*

Popular magazines

- Publish short articles aimed at the general public
- Contain many advertisements and photos
- Seldom include footnotes or the source of information in detail
- Are published weekly or monthly

Examples of popular journals include *Cosmopolitan, GQ, Rolling Stone, Sports Illustrated,* and *Chatelaine.*

Evaluate print sources

Whether you use print or online sources, a successful search will turn up many more items than you can expect to use in your final product. You have to make a series of decisions about what is important and relevant. Return to your research question and working thesis (see Chapter 17) to determine which items are relevant.

How reliable are your sources? Books provide in-depth and sometimes valuable historical information. Print sources in libraries have an additional layer of selection because a professional has decided that they are worth purchasing and cataloguing. Websites, in contrast, can be posted and changed quickly by anyone, so information can be—and often is—unreliable.

But print sources can contain their share of biased, inaccurate, and misleading information. Over the years librarians have developed a set of criteria for evaluating print sources.

Source	Who published the book or article? Scholarly books and articles in scholarly journals are reviewed by experts in the field before they are published. They are generally more reliable than popular magazines and books, which tend to emphasize what is entertaining at the expense of comprehensiveness.
Author	Who wrote the book or article? What are the author's qualifications?
Timeliness	How current is the source? If you are researching a fast-developing subject such as vaccines for a new virus, then currency is very important. Currency might not be as important for a historical subject, but even historical figures and events are often reinterpreted.
Evidence	Where does the evidence come from: facts, interviews, observations, surveys, or experiments? Is the evidence adequate to support the author's claims?
Biases	Can you detect particular biases of the author? How do the author's biases affect the interpretation offered?
Advertising	Is advertising a prominent part of the magazine or newspaper? How might the ads affect what gets printed?

WRITE NOW

Evaluate information

Think of three or four different types of sources you have read recently: a novel, textbook, blog, letter, flyer, comic book, or online review. Evaluate each source according to the criteria above. Which item is the most reliable? For what purpose? Which is the least reliable?

Start a working bibliography

As you begin to collect your sources, make sure you get full bibliographic information for everything you might want to use in your assignment. This will save you a great deal of time and trouble later. Determine which documentation style you will use. If your instructor does not tell you which style is appropriate, ask. (Two major documentation styles—MLA and APA—are explained in detail in Chapters 20 and 21.) You can compile this information in a computer file, a notebook, or on note cards.

For books

You will need, at minimum, the following information. This information can typically be found on the front and back of the title page:

- Author's name
- Title of the book
- Place of publication
- Name of publisher
- Date of publication

You will also need

- page numbers if you are quoting directly or referring to a specific passage
- title, author, and page numbers of the individual chapter if your source is an edited book with contributions by several people.
- call numbers for the book or journal so you can find it easily in the future.

> JL
> 65
> .J318
> 2006
>
> Jackson, Robert J. _Canadian Government in Transition_. Toronto: Pearson Prentice Hall, 2006. Print.

For journals, magazines, and newspapers

You will need

- Author's name
- Title of the article
- Title of the journal
- Volume and issue of the journal
- Date of the issue
- Page numbers of the article

> Barlow, Andrew. "The Student Movement of the 1960s and the Politics of Race." _Journal of Ethnic Studies_ 19.3 (2003): 22–30. Print.

How to explore libraries

You may have heard people say that you can find any information you want on the Web. In fact, many books, journals. magazines, newspapers, and DVDs that you can find in a large library are not available full-text on the Web.

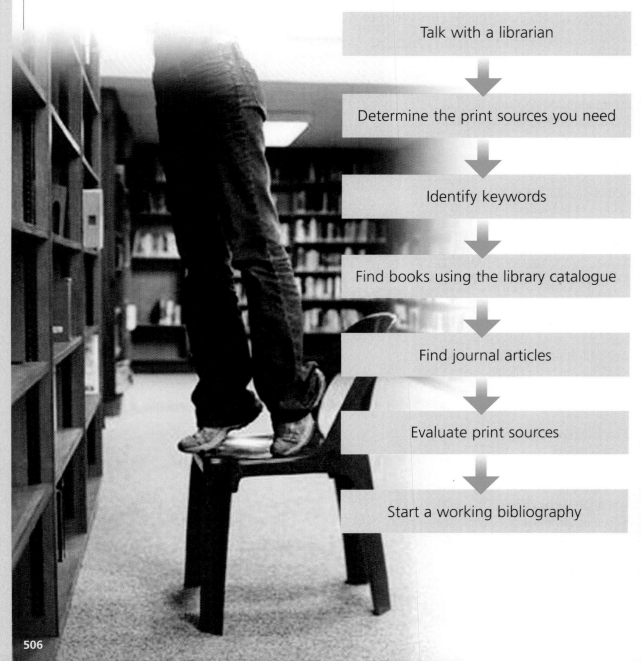

Talk with a librarian

Determine the print sources you need

Identify keywords

Find books using the library catalogue

Find journal articles

Evaluate print sources

Start a working bibliography

Researcher at work

Student Julia Lipton chose the topic of multiculturalism in Canada for a research assignment in one of her general education courses. She decided to search for books in order to get an in-depth, historical overview of the topic. She used Quick Search (keyword) to look for books on the topic in the library's online catalogue. She typed in "multiculturalism Canada" (AND is assumed).

Keyword search

It yielded the results shown here. Julia knew that she had to narrow the broad topic she had picked to a more specific topic within multiculturalism for her assignment. She browsed the titles that came up (see below). The first title was of interest because it was fairly current and, judging by the subject headings assigned to it, would deal with an overview of ethnic relations in Canada that would hopefully give a history of ethnic relations and possibly address the development of Canada into a multicultural society.

Julia noted the call number of the book in order to locate it on the library shelves. She also knew that she could browse in the call number area to find similar books of interest.

Subject headings assigned to book. Also links to additional books on the topic.

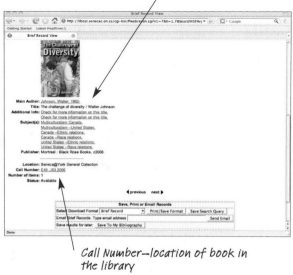

Title of book   Year book published

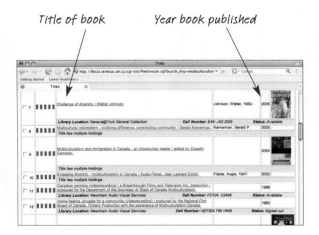

Call Number—location of book in the library

Find information in databases

You can learn how to use databases in your library with the help of a reference librarian. Your library may also have tutorials on how to use databases. Once you know how to access the databases you need, you can work from computers in other locations.

Most databases are by subscription only and must be accessed through your library's website. The following is a sample of some databases available to library users:

Academic Search Premier	Provides access to a large multi-disciplinary database of more than 3900 magazines, journals, newspapers, and trade publications. The publications cover social sciences, humanities, education, computer sciences, engineering, language and linguistics, literature, medical sciences, ethnic studies, and more.
ArticleFirst	Indexes journals in business, the humanities, medicine, science, and social sciences.
CBCA Reference	Provides access to a diversity of Canadian periodicals ranging from academic journals to special interest publications to general magazines.
Canadian Newsstand	Provides full-text access to 18 Canadian news sources.
CPI.Q (Canadian Periodical Index Quarterly)	Provides access to a comprehensive list of Canadian and international journals and magazines.
Expanded Academic ASAP	Provides access to a large multi-disciplinary collection of more than 2100 journals and magazines.
Factiva	Provides global news and business information from over 8000 international magazines, journals, and newspapers.
General OneFile	Provides access to articles in more than 11 000 magazines, journals, and newspapers dealing with a wide range of academic and general interest topics.
JSTOR	Provides access to over 8500 journals in the arts, humanities, and social sciences.
LexisNexis Academic	Provides access to a wide range of newspapers, magazines, government, and legal documents, as well as company profiles from around the world.
MasterFILE Premier	Provides access to many business, consumer health, general science, and multicultural magazines and journals.

Construct effective searches

To use databases effectively, make a list of keywords in advance (see page 500). For example, if you are researching the effects of hunting on deer populations, you could begin with the words *deer*, *hunting*, and *population*. If you are researching obesity in children, you might begin with *obesity*, *children*, and one more word such as *trend* or *Europe* or *fast food*, depending on your focus.

Select a database

Your next decision is to choose a database to begin your research. Newspapers might include stories on local deer populations and changes in hunting policy. Popular magazines such as *Field and Stream* might have articles on national trends in deer hunting, and might also summarize scholarly research on the subject. Scholarly journals, perhaps in the field of wildlife biology, would contain articles about formal research into the effects of deer hunting on population density, average size and weight of animals, range, and other specific factors.

To find newspaper stories, you can begin with LexisNexis Academic or Canadian Newsstand. To find popular and scholarly journal articles, go to Academic Search Premier, CBA Reference, Expanded Academic ASAP, or General OneFile.

Evaluate database sources

Databases collect print sources and put them in digital formats. Evaluate database sources the same way you evaluate print sources.

1. **Source:** Is the source a scholarly journal or popular magazine?
2. **Author:** What are the author's qualifications?
3. **Timeliness:** How current is the source?
4. **Evidence:** Where does the evidence come from?
5. **Biases:** Can you detect particular biases?
6. **Advertising:** Is advertising prominent?

Evaluate for relevance

Even reliable sources may not pertain to your topic. Consider the relevance of each source for your subject.

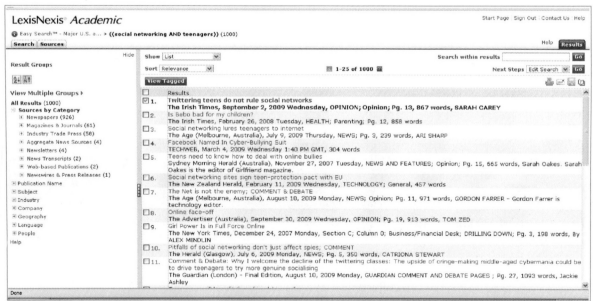

Results of a search on LexisNexis for social networking AND teenagers. If your topic is the effect of social networking on teenagers you may want to examine articles 1, 2, and 8.

Locate elements of a citation

To cite a source from a database, you will need the

- Author if listed
- Title of article
- Name of periodical
- Date of publication (and edition for newspapers)
- Section and page number

- Name of database
- Date of access (the day you found the article in the database)

A sample article from the CBCA Reference database search for "piracy" and "music industry."

The confusing part of citing this example is distinguishing between the database and the vendor. The vendor's name often appears at the top of the screen, making the vendor's name look like the name of the database. In this case, ProQuest is the vendor—the company that sells your library access to CBCA Reference and many other databases.

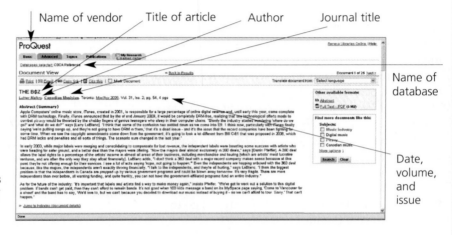

A citation for an article that you find on a database looks like this in MLA style:

Mallory, Luther. "THE B$Z." *Canadian Musician* 31.2 (2009): 54. *CBCA Reference*. Web. 12 Oct. 2009.

WORKING TOGETHER

Compare databases

In a group of three or four students

Identify keywords for your research topic, and use the same keywords for searches on three or more databases. If the search yields too many articles, use AND to connect the terms or add another keyword plus AND. Copy the results from each search and paste it into a file. Which database turned up more items? Which turned up more scholarly articles? Which turned up more articles in popular magazines? Which will be most helpful for your research topic?

How to explore online libraries

Libraries are increasingly becoming digital archives. Ebooks and articles in journals, magazines, and newspapers are read more and more onscreen. You can access a mountain of information through your library databases, but to get to the top of the mountain, you must know how to search efficiently.

Choose keywords for searching

Select appropriate databases for topic

Execute search

Evaluate search results

Locate elements of citation

Researcher at work

Student Larry Frankel is studying nutrition at college. One of his assignments required him to research how well-informed Canadian doctors are in the field of nutrition. Larry decided he would review current articles in Canadian magazines, newspapers, and journals. He planned to begin his search for articles by looking in some of the general Canadian databases and then, if necessary, move on to medical databases available in his college library.

He began his search with the CBCA Reference database, which covers a wide range of magazines and journals. Larry focused his search by narrowing it to how well-instructed students were in nutrition at medical school. He used the keywords "nutrition" and "medical students" in the advanced search screen of CBCA Reference.

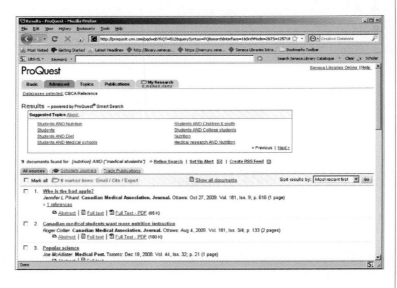

He found several articles and read their abstracts to see if they were appropriate for his research. One article in particular was of interest because it concentrated on the fact that Canadian medical students were lacking adequate education in nutrition and were not happy about it. Larry skimmed the article and then decided to email it to himself so he could print it out from his home computer. This was a good start for Larry's research focus.

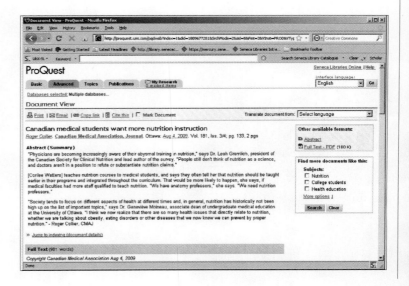

Find information on the Web

Because anyone can publish on the Web, there is no overall quality control and there is no system of organization as there are in a library. Nevertheless, the Web offers you some resources for current topics that would be difficult to find in a library. The keys to success are knowing where you are most likely to find current and accurate information about the particular question you are researching, and knowing how to access that information.

Search engines

Search engines designed for the Web work in a similar way to library databases and your library's online catalogue, but with one major difference. Databases typically do some screening of the items they list, but search engines potentially take you to every website that isn't password protected—millions of pages in all. Consequently, you have to work harder to limit searches on the Web or you can be deluged with tens of thousands of items.

Kinds of search engines

A search engine is a set of programs that sort through millions of items at incredible speed. There are four basic kinds of search engines.

1. Keyword search engines (e.g., Ask.com, Answers.com, Google)	Keyword search engines give different results because they assign different weights to the information they find. Google, for example, ranks websites according to how many other sites link to them and the quality of the linking sites.
2. Web directories (e.g., Best of the Web, Yahoo!, Librarians' Internet Index sites)	Web directories classify websites into categories and are the closest equivalent to the cataloguing system used by libraries. On most directories professional editors decide how to index a particular website. Web directories also allow keyword searches.
3. Metasearch sites (e.g., Dogpile, Metacrawler, WebCrawler)	Metasearch sites allow you to use several search engines simultaneously. While the concept is sound, metasearch sites are limited by the number of hits they can return and their inability to handle advanced searches.
4. Specialized search engines (e.g., Froogle [shopping], Google Scholar [academic], Monster.com [jobs], Pubmed [medicine], Thomasnet [business], WebMD [medicine])	Specialized search engines have been developed for specific subjects.

Advanced searches

Search engines often produce too many hits and are therefore not always useful. If you look only at the first few items, you may miss what is most valuable. The alternative is to refine your search. Most search engines offer you the option of an advanced search, which gives you the opportunity to limit numbers.

The advanced searches on Google and Yahoo! give you the options of using a string of words to search for sites that contain (1) all the words, (2) the exact phrase, (3) any of the words, or (4) that exclude certain words. They also allow you to specify the language of the site, the date range, the file format, and the domain. For example, government statistics on crime are considered the most reliable. So if you want to find statistics on murder rates, you can specify the domain as .gc.ca (for national statistics); .gov.on.ca, .gov.bc.ca, etc. (for provincial statistics); or .gov (for U.S. statistics).

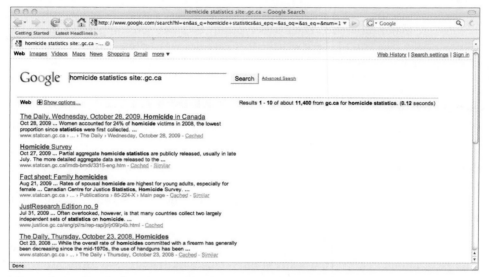

An advanced search on Google for government sites in Canada only (.gc.ca).

Discussion forums, groups, and blogs

The Internet allows you to access other people's opinions on thousands of topics. The Groups section of Google (groups.google.com) has an archive of several hundred million messages that can be searched. Much of the conversation on these sites is undocumented and highly opinionated, but you can still gather important information about people's attitudes and get tips about other sources, which you can verify later.

Web logs, better known as blogs, also are sources of public opinion. Several tools have been developed recently to search blogs: BlogDigger, Bloglines, Feedster, Google Blog Search, Technorati, and IceRocket. Blogs are not screened and are not considered authoritative sources, but blogs can sometimes lead you to quality sources.

Evaluate Web sources

All electronic search tools share a common problem: They often give you too many sources. Web search engines not only pull up thousands of hits, but these hits may vary dramatically in quality. No one regulates or checks information put on the Web, and it's no surprise that much information on the Web is highly opinionated or false.

Misleading websites

Some websites are put up as jokes. Other websites are deliberately misleading. Many prominent websites draw imitators who want to cash in on the commercial visibility. The website for the Campaign for Tobacco-Free Kids (www.tobaccofreekids.org), for example, has an imitator (www.smokefreekids.com) that sells software for antismoking education. The .com URL is often a tip-off that a site has a profit motive.

Biased websites

Always approach websites with an eye toward evaluating content. For example, websites with .com URLs that offer medical information often contain strong biases in addition to the motive to make money. The website Thinktwice.com, sponsored by the Global Vaccine Institute, opposes vaccination for H1N1. On the site you can find such claims as the new Canadian study that has found people vaccinated against seasonal flu are twice as likely to catch H1N1. Always look for other sources for verification. The website of the U.S. Centers for Disease Control, for example, publishes fact sheets on the latest information about diseases and their prevention, including one on H1N1.

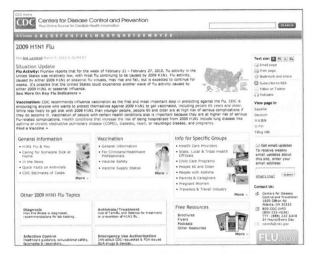

Fact sheet on H1N1 from the Centers for Disease Control (www.cdc.gov/h1n1flu).

Locate elements of a citation

To cite a website you will need
- Author if listed
- Title and URL of the Web page
- Date the site was last modified or copyright date
- Sponsoring organization if listed
- Date you visited

Canada. Aboriginal Canada Portal. Government of Canada, 2009. Web. 12 Oct. 2009.

A citation for a Web page looks like this in MLA style.

Criteria for evaluating Web sources

The criteria for evaluating print sources can be applied to Web sources if the special circumstances of the Web are acknowledged. For example, when you find a Web page by using a search engine, often you go deep into a complex site without having any sense of the context for that page. To evaluate the credibility of the site, you would need to examine the home page, not just the specific page you saw first.

Source	Look for the site's ownership in the Web address. If a website doesn't indicate ownership, then you have to make judgments about who put it up and why. The suffix can offer clues. For example, .gc.ca is used by federal government bodies, and .ca by Canadian organizations. In the United States, .gov is used by government agencies, and .edu by universities and colleges.
Author	Often websites give no information about their authors other than an email address, if that. In such cases it is difficult or impossible to determine the author's qualifications. Look up the author on Google. If qualifications are listed, is the author an expert in the field? Some sites, such as Wikipedia, a popular online encyclopedia, allow anyone to add or delete information.
Timeliness	Many Web pages do not list when they were last updated; thus you cannot determine their currency.
Evidence	The accuracy of any evidence found on the Web is often hard to verify. The most reliable information on the Web stands up to the test of print evaluation, with clear indication of the sponsoring organization and the source of any factual information.
Biases	Many websites announce their viewpoint on controversial issues, but others conceal their attitude with a reasonable tone and seemingly factual evidence such as statistics. Citations and bibliographies do not ensure that a site is reliable. Look carefully at the links and sources cited.
Advertising	Many websites are infomercials aimed at getting you to buy a product or service. While they might contain useful information, they are no more trustworthy than other forms of advertising.

Other Internet sources

Other Internet sources, such as online newsgroups, can give you useful ideas but are generally not considered authoritative. Email communication from an expert in the field might be considered an authoritative source, but personal emails are generally not considered worthy of inclusion in a research paper. Remember that a key reason to cite sources is so other researchers can read and evaluate the sources you used.

Find visual sources online

You can find images published on the Web using Google and other search engines that allow you to specify searches for images. For example, if you are writing a research paper on invasive plant species, you might want to include an image of kudzu, an invasive vine common in the American South. In Google, choose Images and type *kudzu* in the search box. You'll find a selection of images of plant, including several from the National Park Service.

Some search engines such as Ditto (www.ditto.com) are designed specifically to find images. Yahoo! Picture Gallery has over 400 000 images that can be searched by subject (gallery.yahoo.com). In addition to images, you can find statistical data represented in charts and graphs on government websites. Especially useful is the Statistics Canada site (www.statcan.gc.ca) for finding charts and graphs of population statistics. You can also find thousands of maps on the Web. (See Serge A. Sauer's map library at the University of Western Ontario, at www.geography.uwo.ca/maplibrary/weblinks.htm.)

Kudzu

Pueraria montana var. *lobata* (Willd.) Maesen & S. Almeida
Pea family (Fabaceae)

NATIVE RANGE: Asia

DESCRIPTION: Kudzu ia a climbing, semi-woody, perennial vine in the pea family. Deciduous leaves are alternate and compound, with three broad leaflets up to 4 inches across. Leaflets may be entire or deeply 2-3 lobed with hairy margins. Individual flowers, about 1/2 inch long, are purple, highly fragrant and borne in long hanging clusters. Flowering occurs in late summer and is soon followed by production of brown, hairy, flattened, seed pods, each of which contains three to ten hard seeds.

Kudzu was planted widely in the U.S. South to reduce soil erosion but has itself become a major pest, smothering native trees and plants.

Follow copyright requirements

Just because images are easy to download from the Web does not mean that you are free to use every image you find. Look for the image creator's copyright notice and suggested credit line. This notice will tell you if you can reproduce the image. You should acknowledge the source of any image you use.

In many cases you will find a copyright notice that reads something like this: "Any use or re-transmission of text or images in this website without written consent of the copyright owner constitutes copyright infringement and is prohibited." You must write to the creator to ask permission to use an image from a site that is not in the public domain, even if you cannot find a copyright notice.

WRITE NOW

Evaluate websites

Hoaxbusters (http://hoaxbusters.org/) provides an index of Internet hoaxes sorted into categories. Read several of the hoaxes, and select one to explore further. Use the criteria for evaluating Web sources on page 515 to evaluate your site. On which criteria does it fail to be reliable?

Next do a Google search for Ritalin, a commonly prescribed drug for attention deficit disorder (ADD) and attention deficit hyperactivity disorder (ADHD). You will find that the drug is quite controversial. Look at five different websites. Which sites do you find most reliable and the least reliable according to the criteria on page 515?

How to explore the Web

The Web offers a staggering amount of information about nearly any topic you can think of, but the Web also has two major drawbacks. Much of the information on the Web is unreliable because no one independently verifies information for accuracy, and much of the information is unstable because websites appear and disappear overnight. Doing research on the Web will test your skills in evaluating and recording information.

Find information on the Web

Evaluate Web sources

Find visual sources online

Researcher at work

Student Carol Berk chose the topic of Alzheimer's disease for a research paper she was writing for her sociology class. Her family experience with the disease was a motivating factor in deciding on the topic. She began by doing a comprehensive search of various resources. She searched the book catalogue for books, the databases for articles in magazines, journals, and newspapers, and then decided to look at websites to enhance the information she had. Carol discovered that using "Alzheimer's disease Canada" as her keywords brought up many results, some useful, but many that were not. She knew that she had to refine her search in order to develop a good thesis for her paper and to get the best results when searching the Web. Carol decided that she wanted to focus her research on programs, organizations, and associations in Canada that develop educational tools to support people with Alzheimer's disease and their respective families. She felt that individuals with the disease as well as the general public needed to be better educated and prepared, especially noting the statistics on Canada's aging population, and projected numbers that may be affected.

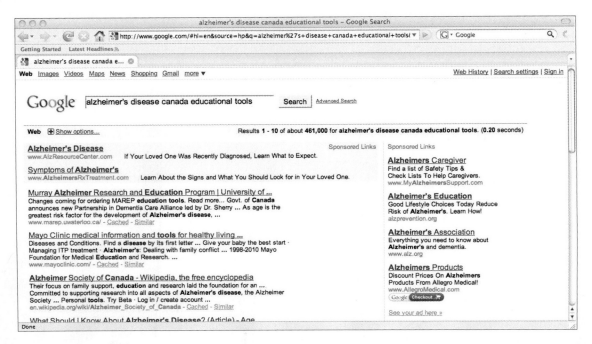

Carol added the keywords "educational tools" to her search on Alzheimer's disease in Canada. The results of the search provided a number of excellent sites for her research. One in particular, the Murray Alzheimer Research and Education Program at the University of Waterloo, provided a number of examples of educational tools. She also found the Public Health Agency of Canada provided excellent information in its article "What Should I Know About Alzheimer's Disease." Carol printed a copy of the article to work from as she drafted her paper.

19
Writing the Research Paper

If you have chosen a subject you're interested in, asked questions about it, and researched it thoroughly, you will have a wealth of ideas and information to communicate to your audience.

Plan your organization

Review your goals and thesis

Before you begin writing your paper, review the assignment and its requirements (see Chapter 17). Your review of the assignment will remind you of your purpose, your potential readers, your stance on your subject, and the length and scope you should aim for.

By now you should have formulated a working thesis, which will be the focus of your paper. You should also have located, read, evaluated, and taken notes on enough source material to write your paper. At this stage in the writing process, your working thesis may be rough and may change as you write your draft, but having a working thesis will help keep your paper focused.

Determine your contribution

A convincing and compelling research paper does not make claims based solely on the word of the writer. It draws on the expertise and reputations of others as well. Thus it is critical to show your readers which elements of your paper represent your original thinking.

Determine exactly what you are adding to the larger conversation about your subject.

- Whom do you agree with?
- Whom do you disagree with?
- What can you add to points you agree with?
- What original analysis or theorizing do you have to offer?
- What original findings from field research do you have to offer?

Determine your main points and group your findings

Look back over your notes and determine how to group the ideas you researched. Decide what your major points will be and how those points support your thesis. Group your research findings so that they match up with your major points.

Now it is time to create a working outline. Always include your thesis at the top of your outline as a guiding light. Some writers create formal outlines with roman numerals and the like; others compose the headings for the paragraphs of their paper and use them to guide their draft; still others may start writing and then determine how they will organize their draft when they have a few paragraphs written. Experiment and decide which method works best for you.

521

Avoid plagiarism

You know that copying someone else's paper word for word or taking an article off the Internet and turning it in as yours is plagiarism. That's plain stealing, and people who take that risk should know that the punishment can be severe. But plagiarism also means using the ideas, melodies, or images of someone else without acknowledging them, and it is important to understand exactly what defines plagiarism.

What you don't have to document

Fortunately, common sense governs issues of academic plagiarism. The standards of documentation are not so strict that the source of every fact you cite must be acknowledged. Suppose you are writing about the causes of maritime disasters and you want to know how many people drowned when the *Titanic* sank on the early morning of April 15, 1912. You check the *Britannica Online* website and find that the death toll was around 1500. Since this fact is available in many other reference works, you would not need to cite *Britannica Online* as the source.

But let's say you want to challenge the version of the sinking offered in the 1998 movie *Titanic*, which repeats the usual explanation that the *Titanic* side-swiped an iceberg, ripping a long gash along the hull that caused the ship to go down. Suppose that in your reading, you discover that a September 1985 exploration of the wreck by an unmanned submersible did not find the long gash previously thought to have sunk the ship. The evidence instead suggested that the force of the collision with the iceberg broke the seams in the hull, allowing water to flood the ship's watertight compartments. You would need to cite the source of your information for this alternative version of the *Titanic's* demise.

What you do have to document

For facts that are not easily found in general reference works, statements of opinion, and arguable claims, you should cite the source. You should also cite the sources of statistics, research findings, examples, graphs, charts, and illustrations. For example, if you state that the percentage of obese children aged 2 to 17 in Canada rose from 3% in 1978 to 8% in 2004, you need to cite the source.

As a reader you should be skeptical about statistics and research findings when the source is not mentioned. When a writer does not cite the sources of statistics and research findings, there is no way of knowing how reliable the sources are or whether the writer is making them up.

From the writer's perspective, careful citing of sources lends credibility. If you take your statistics from a generally trusted source, your readers are more likely to trust whatever conclusions or arguments you are presenting. When in doubt, always document the source.

Be careful when taking notes and copying material online

The best way to avoid unintentional plagiarism is to take care to distinguish source words from your own words.

- Don't mix words from the source with your own words. If you copy anything from a source when taking notes, place those words in quotation marks and note the page number(s) where those words appear.

- Write down all the information you need for each source for a list of works cited or a list of references (see Chapters 20 and 21).

- If you copy words from an online source, take special care to note the source. You could easily copy online material and later not be able to find where it came from.

- Photocopy printed sources and print out online sources. Having printed copies of sources allows you to double-check later that you haven't used words from the source by mistake and that any words you quote are accurate.

Quote sources without plagiarizing

Effective research writing builds on the work of others. You can summarize or paraphrase the work of others, but often it is best to let the authors speak in your text by quoting their exact words. Indicate the words of others by placing them inside quotation marks.

Most people who get into plagiarism trouble lift words from a source and use them without quotation marks. Where to draw the line is best illustrated with an example. In the following passage, Marcel Danesi takes a critical look at modern culture's desire to create a "teen-aging" of adult life:

The Greek myth of Narcissus holds a special warning today for those of us who live in a forever young society. It can be paraphrased as follows. One day in the woods, the nymph Echo met a handsome youth with whom she fell deeply in love. Echo stretched out her arms imploringly to him. But the conceited youth cruelly rebuffed her amorous gesture. Humiliated, Echo went to hide in a cave, where she wasted away until nothing was left of her but her voice. The goddess Nemesis witnessed the youth's heartless act of shunning and, to punish him, made him fall in love with his own face as he saw it reflected in a pool. Unable to remove himself from his image, the youth gradually withered away, changing into the narcissus plant.

Having the financial capability and leisure time to spoil and pamper oneself with the latest fashions and cosmetics was once the exclusive privilege of aristocrats—who (as a consequence) were considered to be too self-indulgent and narcissistic to be able to withstand any hardships that life presented to them. Now, self-indulgence and narcissism are the privilege of virtually everyone. Today's collective narcissism impels common folk to sculpt and maintain an ageless look. It is a phenomenon that goes largely unnoticed. The wearer of a particular clothing style, in fact, could be eight or fifty-eight and no one would make anything of it. But the warning built into the myth of Narcissus cannot be ignored—we risk falling in love with our own image to the detriment of everything else. In traditional cultures, separate dress and grooming codes for males and females, young and old, aristocrats and peasants were always (and continue to be) strictly enforced to signal critical differences in social role, age, and status. In modern societies, many of these distinctions have disappeared. But their disappearance is hardly the result of some well-meaning democratic movement. Rather, it is arguably the outcome of an obsessive narcissism that has been engendered by affluence. And this has had consequences for virtually everyone. Today, even those who cannot really afford to "look the look" will often go deeply into debt in order to keep up with the fashions perpetrated by the images of young Narcissuses (male and female) in movies, TV programs, and advertisements. Virtually no one wants to dress "like an old person." In fact, the latter phrase has virtually no meaning any longer.

Looking fashionably young has become an implicit norm, and only frail health or economic destitution seem to keep people from striving to do so.

Marcel Danesi. *Forever Young: The "Teen-Aging" of Modern Culture.* Toronto: U of Toronto P, 2003. 30-31. Print.

If you were writing a paper on the change in our society's view of youth and its desire to prolong it, you might want to mention Danesi's view of how society's dress and grooming codes amongst social roles has changed.

Use quotation marks for direct quotations

If you quote directly, you must place quotation marks around all words you take from the original:

> One observer notices a worrisome change in our culture: "Looking fashionably young has become an implicit norm, and only frail health or economic destitution seem to keep people from striving to do so" (Danesi 31).

Notice that the quotation is introduced and not just dropped in. This example follows Modern Language Association (MLA) style, where the citation–(Danesi 31)–goes outside the quotation marks but before the final period. In MLA style, source references are made according to the author's last name, which refers you to the full citation in the list of works cited at the end. Following the author's name is the page number where the quotation can be located. (Notice also that there is no comma after the name.)

Attribute every quotation

If the author's name appears in the sentence, cite only the page number, in parentheses:

> According to Marcel Danesi, "Looking fashionably young has become an implicit norm, and only frail health or economic destitution seem to keep people from striving to do so" (31).

Quoting words that are quoted in your source

If you want to quote material that is already quoted in your source, use single quotes for that material:

> Marcel Danesi discusses the use of teen slang throughout society: "Hardly ever can a youth transferred to the society of his betters unlearn 'the nasality and other vices of speech bred in him by the associations of his growing years.' In a phrase, adults tend to speak as they once did as adolescents" (73).

Summarize and paraphrase sources without plagiarizing

Summarizing

When you summarize, you state the major ideas of an entire source or part of a source in a paragraph or perhaps even a sentence. The key is to put the summary in your own words. If you use words from the source, you have to put those words within quotation marks.

PLAGIARIZED

Marcel Danesi argues in *Forever Young* that having the financial capability and leisure time to spoil and pamper oneself leads many adults to sculpt and maintain an ageless look (31).

[Most of the words are lifted directly from the original; see page 523.]

ACCEPTABLE SUMMARY

Marcel Danesi argues in *Forever Young* that due to rising incomes, many adults now have the means to buy themselves the image of a young person (31).

Paraphrasing

When you paraphrase, you represent the idea of the source in your own words at about the same length as the original. You still need to include the reference to the source of the idea. The following example illustrates what is not an acceptable paraphrase.

PLAGIARIZED

Marcel Danasi argues that narcissism used to be the exclusive privilege of rich people. But now, people everywhere can afford an ageless look. Yet people risk falling in love with their own image (31).

Even though the source is listed, this paraphrase is unacceptable. Too many of the words in the original are used directly here, including much or all of entire sentences.

When a string of words is lifted from a source and inserted without quotation marks, the passage is plagiarized. Changing a few words in a sentence is not a paraphrase. Compare these two sentences:

SOURCE

"Fashion models are contemporary icons of beauty. Hordes of people aspire to look and dress exactly like them. Fashion shows are part of the everyday scene" (Danesi 39).

UNACCEPTABLE PARAPHRASE

Fashion models are modern symbols of beauty. Many people aspire to look and dress similar to them. Fashion shows are part of the regular scene.

The paraphrase takes the structure of the original sentences and substitutes a few words. It is much too similar to the original.

A true paraphrase represents an entire rewriting of the idea from the source

ACCEPTABLE PARAPHRASE

Marcel Danesi argues that fashion models are yet another example of our current society's narcissistic and insatiable desire for youth and beauty. He believes that many people aspire to look and act like models, and that fashion shows provide a voyeuristic opportunity to emulate these icons of beauty (39).

Even though there are a few words from the original in this paraphrase, such as *aspire* and *icons of beauty*, these sentences are original in structure and wording while accurately conveying the meaning of the source.

Frame each paraphrase
Each paraphrase should begin by introducing the author and conclude with a page reference to the material that is paraphrased.

Incorporate quotations

Quotations are a frequent problem area in research papers. Review every quotation to ensure that each is used effectively and correctly.

- Limit the use of long quotations. If you have more than one block quotation on a page, look closely to see if one or more can be paraphrased or summarized.

- Check that each quotation supports your major points rather than making major points for you. If the ideas rather than the original wording are what's important, paraphrase the quotation and cite the source.

- Check that each quotation is introduced and attributed. Each quotation should be introduced and the author or title named. Check for verbs that signal a quotation: Smith *claims*, Jones *argues*, Brown *states*.

- Check that you cite the source for each quotation. You are required to cite the sources of all direct quotations, paraphrases, and summaries.

- Check the accuracy of each quotation. It's easy to leave out words or mistype a quotation. Compare what is in your paper to the original source. If you need to add words to make the quotation grammatical, make sure the added words are in brackets.

- Read your paper aloud to a classmate or a friend. Each quotation should flow smoothly when you read your paper aloud. Put a check beside rough spots as you read aloud so you can revise later.

When to quote directly and when to paraphrase

Use direct quotations when the original wording is important.

DIRECT QUOTATION

Smith notes that

> Although the public grew to accept film as a teaching tool, it was not always aware of all it was being taught. That was because a second type of film was also being produced during these years, the "attitude-building" film, whose primary purpose was to motivate, not instruct. Carefully chosen visuals were combined with dramatic story lines, music, editing, and sharply drawn characters to create powerful instruments of mass manipulation. (21)

Prose quotations longer than four lines (MLA) or forty words (APA) should be indented 2.5 cm from the left margin in MLA style or 1 cm in APA style. Shorter quotations should be enclosed within quotation marks.

PARAPHRASE

Smith points out that a second kind of mental hygiene film, the attitude-building film, was introduced during the 1940s. It attempted to motivate viewers, whereas earlier films explicitly tried to teach something. The attitude-building films were intended to manipulate their audiences to feel a certain way (21).

PARAPHRASE COMBINED WITH QUOTATION

In his analysis of the rise of fascism in twentieth-century Europe, George Mosse notes that the fascist movement was built on pre-existing ideas like individualism and sacrifice. It "scavenged" other ideologies and made use of them. "Fascism was a new political movement but not a movement which invented anything new," Mosse explains (xvii).

In the second example, the original wording provides stronger description of the attitude-building films. The direct quotation is a better choice.

Often, you can paraphrase the main idea of a lengthy passage and quote only the most striking phrase or sentence.

Verbs that introduce quotations and paraphrases

acknowledge	claim	emphasize	offer
add	comment	explain	point out
admit	compare	express	refute
advise	complain	find	reject
agree	concede	grant	remark
allow	conclude	illustrate	reply
analyze	contend	imply	report
answer	criticize	insist	respond
argue	declare	interpret	show
ask	describe	maintain	state
assert	disagree	note	suggest
believe	discuss	object	think
charge	dispute	observe	write

Quotations don't speak for themselves

Off track

Don't rely on long quotations to do the work of writing for you.

Richard Lanham writes:

> Economics . . . studies the allocation of scarce resources. Normally we would think that the phrase "information economy," which we hear everywhere nowadays, makes some sense. It is no longer physical stuff that is in short supply, we are told, but information about it. So, we live in an "information economy." But information is not in short supply in the new information economy. We're drowning in it. What we lack is the human attention needed to make sense of it all. (xi)

Lanham goes on to say:

> "Rhetoric" has not always been a synonym for humbug. For most of Western history, it has meant the body of doctrine that teaches people how to speak and write and, thus, act effectively in public life. Usually defined as "the art of persuasion," it might has well have been called "the economics of attention." It tells us how to allocate our central scarce resource, to invite people to attend to what we would like them to attend to. (xii–xiii)

These quotations are picked up out of context and dropped into the paper. Readers have no clue about why they are relevant to the writer's text.

On track

When sources are used effectively, they are woven into the fabric of a research project but still maintain their identity.

Most of the source is paraphrased, allowing the discussion to be integrated into the writer's text. The writer centres on how two key concepts, the "information economy" and "rhetoric," are reinterpreted by Richard Lanham. Only those words critical to representing Lanham's position are quoted directly.

In *The Economics of Attention*, Richard Lanham begins by pointing out that the "information economy" stands traditional economics on its head because there is no shortage of information today. Instead Lanham argues that attention is what is in short supply and that the discipline of rhetoric can help us to understand how attention is allocated. Rhetoric historically has meant the art and study of speaking and writing well, especially for participating in public life. Lanham maintains that what rhetoric has really been about is what he calls "the economics of attention" (xii). The central goal of rhetoric, according to Lanham, is "to invite people to attend to what we would like them to attend to" (xii–xiii).

Incorporate visuals

Here are a few guidelines to keep in mind for incorporating visual sources into your research paper.

• Use visuals for examples and supporting evidence, not for decoration. For example, if the subject of your research is Internet crime in Toronto, including a picture of the CN Tower is irrelevant and will detract from your paper.

• Refer to images and other graphics in the body of your research paper. Explain the significance of any images or graphics in the body of your paper.

• Respect the copyright of visual sources. You may need to request permission to use a visual from the Web.

• Get complete citation information. You are required to cite visual sources in your list of works cited just as you are for other sources.

• Describe the content of the image or graphic in the caption.

Façade of the Last Judgment, *Orvieto, Italy, c. 1310–1330. Medieval churches frequently depicted Christ as a judge, damning sinners to hell.*

WRITE NOW

Summarize, paraphrase, and quote directly

Read this quotation and then
• Write a summary of it;
• Write a paraphrase of it;
• Incorporate a direct quotation from it into a sentence.

There is no strife, no prejudice, no national conflict in outer space as yet. Its hazards are hostile to us all. Its conquest deserves the best of all mankind, and its opportunity for peaceful cooperation many never come again. But why, some say, the moon? Why choose this as our goal? And they may well ask why climb the highest mountain? Why, 35 years ago, fly the Atlantic? Why does Rice play Texas?

We choose to go to the moon. We choose to go to the moon in this decade and do the other things, not because they are easy, but because they are hard, because that goal will serve to organize and measure the best of our energies and skills, because that challenge is one that we are willing to accept, one we are unwilling to postpone, and one which we intend to win, and the others, too. (President John F. Kennedy, September 12, 1962)

Review your research project

Read your project aloud and put checks in the margin in places where you think it sounds rough or might need more development. When you finish, try to imagine yourself as a reader who doesn't know much about your subject or has a different viewpoint. What could you add to benefit that reader?

Reviewing another student's research project

Read through a paper twice. The first time you read through a paper, concentrate on comprehension and overall impressions. On your second reading show the writer where you got confused or highlight parts that were especially good by adding comments in the margins.

Questions for reviewing a research project

- Does the title describe the subject of the paper? Does it create interest in the subject?

- Are the introductory paragraphs effective and relevant to the paper that follows?

- Is the thesis clearly stated in the beginning paragraphs of the paper?

- Does the writer offer support for the thesis from a variety of valid and reliable sources?

- Does the paper go into enough detail to support the thesis, and are the details relevant to the thesis?

- Do the arguments presented in the paper flow logically? Is the paper well organized?

- Is the tone of the paper consistent throughout? Is the word choice varied and appropriate throughout?

- Did you have to read some parts more than once to fully understand them?

- Are quotations properly introduced and integrated into the text?

- Are all facts and quotations that are not common knowledge documented?

- Is the documentation in the correct form?

- Is the paper free of errors of grammar and punctuation?

Revise you research project

From your review and possibly reviews of other students, make a list of changes you might make. Start with the large concerns—reorganizing paragraphs, cutting unnecessary parts, and adding new sections. When you have finished revising, edit and proofread carefully.

How to write a research paper

Many people have described writing a research paper as entering a conversation. To create a conversation with those who have written about your subject, you must distinguish your words from the words of others. Paraphrasing, summarizing, and quoting directly are the key moves for bringing other voices into your paper.

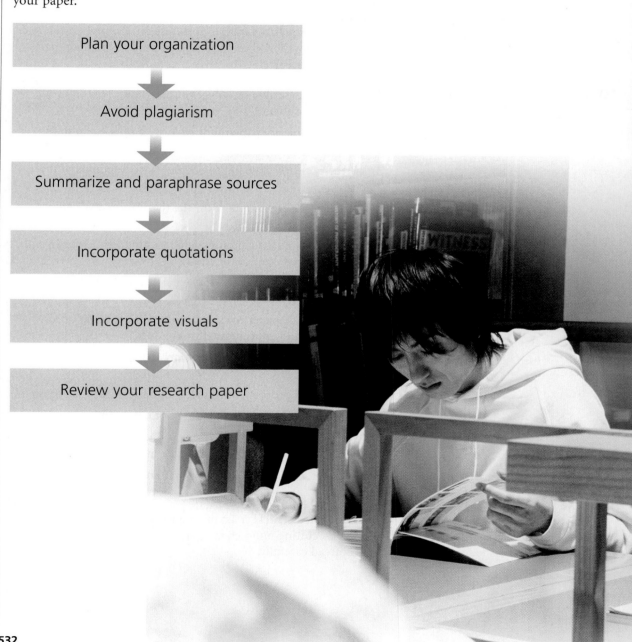

Plan your organization

Avoid plagiarism

Summarize and paraphrase sources

Incorporate quotations

Incorporate visuals

Review your research paper

Researcher at work

Student Paul Waller's research essay on the limits of free speech on social media such as Twitter, Facebook, and blogs proved to be a fascinating and complex issue. Paul found a variety of resources to use because of the great interest by the media on the topic of free speech and the potential for defamation. He located articles, websites, blogs, and videos that he knew he could use to develop his thesis and support the paper he was writing. Paul decided that he would focus his assignment on the future problem of controlling free speech and potential defamation on social media as it becomes more pervasive and powerful. Paul selected a number of quotations from an informative article in the *Toronto Star* by Tony S. K. Wong to weave into his assignment; but because he felt that Wong did not stress how potentially enormous a problem it could be in the future, he added his own commentary about it.

> According to Tony S.K. Wong, Canadian law will rarely "intervene to restrict or sanction users who post material that is shocking, offensive, and distasteful. At some point, however, a user's postings can cross a line and give rise to liability for libel" (25). Judging by the number of cases—some quite notable—involving defamation litigation, the potential for libel appears to be an ever-growing problem. As more people make use of social media to do everything from build relationships to support their run for public office, the opportunities for defamation would presumably increase substantially. According to Wong, defamation "is any communication about a person or company that injures the reputation of that person or company" (26). Wong also points out that liability for defamation can come from a "video, picture, cartoon or song" (26). There seems to be endless possibilities for defamation cases that could overwhelm our court system.

Paul found several writers, particularly on online publications, that cautioned users about how they advertize their opinions on social networking tools. He summarized their opinions in his paper rather than quoting them directly:

> In her article, "A World of Trouble in 140 Characters," an article on canada.com, Gillian Shaw of the Vancouver Sun points out the problems created by people using social networking tools incautiously, most especially in the U.S. Several celebrities have made the news by airing their views about others on Twitter and paying the consequences for it. Another well-known case is a non-celebrity who commented about her mouldy apartment and was sued for $50 000 by her landlord. Some lawyers are recommending that people use these public tools more carefully than they normally would. Until quite recently, only blogs and Internet postings have been a cause for concern in Canada, but sites such as Twitter and Facebook are now very popular. It is important to stress to users of social networking tools that once you put something online it is in the public domain and you can't bring it back.

20

MLA Documentation

The two styles of documentation used most frequently are the American Psychological Association (APA) style and the Modern Language Association (MLA) style. The APA style is followed in the social sciences and education (see Chapter 21), while the MLA style is the norm for the humanities and fine arts disciplines. If you have questions that this chapter does not address, consult the *MLA Handbook for Writers of Research Papers*, seventh edition (2009), and the *MLA Style Manual and Guide to Scholarly Publishing*, third edition (2008).

Works Cited

Campbell, Joseph. *The Hero with A Thousand Faces.* 2nd ed. Princeton: Princeton UP, 1968. Print.

---. *Myths to Live By.* New York: Penguin, 1972. Print.

Damrosch, David. "Epic Hero." *Smithsonian* 38.2 (2007): 94–103. *Academic Search Premier.* Web. 14 Nov. 2007.

"Darmok." *Star Trek: The Next Generation.* 30 Sept. 1991. CD-ROM.

Leeming, David A. *Mythology: The Voyage of the Hero.* New York: Lippincott, 1973. Print.

---. *The World of Myth.* New York: Oxford UP, 1990. Print.

Pringle, David, ed. *The Ultimate Encyclopedia of Fantasy.* London: ...ton, 1998. Print.

Chapter contents

Elements of MLA documentation

In MLA style, quotations, summaries, and paraphrases from outside sources are indicated by in-text citations in parentheses. When readers find a parenthetical reference in the body of a paper, they can turn to the list of works cited at the end of the paper to find complete publication information for the cited source.

Walker 3

. . . But how important is face-to-face interaction to maintaining good "social" behaviour in a group?

Describing humans as "innate mind readers," one observer argues that "our skill at imagining other people's mental states ranks up there with our knack for language and our opposable thumbs" (Johnson 196). The frequency of "flame wars" on Internet message boards and list serves, however, indicates that our innate skill at reading minds isn't always accurate. Some crucial information must be lacking in these forums that causes people to

The writer quotes a passage from page 196 of Johnson's book.

' mental states. for language and
Walker 5   thumbs"

Works Cited

Agre, Phil. "The Internet and Public Discourse."
    First Monday 3.3 (1998): n. pag. Web. 14 July
    2001.

**Johnson, Steven. *Emergence: The Connected
    Lives of Ants, Brains, Cities, and Software.*
    New York: Scribner, 2001. Print.**

Kleiner, Kurt. "Calling All Geeks." *New Scientist*
    15 May 1999: 10. Print.

Mallia, Joseph. "Authorities React to Abuse of
    Tax-funded Internet." *Boston Herald* 13 May
    1999: 6. Print.

Murphy, Dervla. *Full Tilt: Ireland to India with
    a Bicycle.* London: Murray, 1965. Print.

--- . *Through the Embers of Chaos: Balkan
    Journeys.* London: Murray, 2002. Print.

The reader can find the source by looking up Johnson's name in the list of works cited. The information there can be used to locate the book, to check whether the writer accurately represents Johnson, and to see how the point quoted fits into Johnson's larger argument.

Entries in the works-cited list

The list of works cited is organized alphabetically by authors or, if no author is listed, the first word in the title other than *a*, *an*, or *the* (see page 544). MLA style uses three basic forms for entries in the list of works cited: books, periodicals in print (scholarly journals, newspapers, magazines), and electronically available database and Web sources.

1. WORKS-CITED ENTRIES FOR BOOKS

Entries for books have three main elements:

1. Author's name.

2. *Title of book*.

3. Publication information.

Sterling, Bruce. *Shaping Things*. Cambridge: MIT P, 2005. Print.

1. Author's name.
- List the author's name with the last name first, followed by a period.

2. *Title of book*.
- Find the exact title on the title page, not the cover.
- Separate the title and subtitle with a colon.
- Print the title in italics and put a period at the end.

3. Publication information.
Publication information for books includes
- The place (usually the city) of publication,
- The name of the publisher,
- The date of publication.
- Format of publication.

Use a colon between the place of publication and the publisher's name (using accepted abbreviations), followed by a comma and then the publication date.

2. WORKS-CITED ENTRIES FOR PRINT PERIODICALS

Entries for periodicals have three main elements:

1. Author's name.

2. "Title of article."

3. *Publication information*.

Swearingen, C. Jan. "Feminisms and Composition." *College Composition and Communication* 57.3 (2006): 543-51. Print.

1. Author's name.
- List the author's name with the last name first, followed by a period.

2. "Title of article."
- Place the title of the article inside quotation marks.
- Insert a period before the closing quotation mark.

3. *Publication information*.
- Underline or italicize the title of the journal.
- Follow immediately with the volume number and issue number, separated by a period.
- List the date of publication, in parentheses, followed by a colon.
- List the page numbers, followed by a period.
- Include the format of publication.

3. WORKS-CITED ENTRIES FOR ELECTRONIC SOURCES (websites, images, email)

Basic entries for online sources have five main elements:

1. Author's name.

2. "Title of document" and/or title of website (in italics).

3. Publisher or sponsor of site.

4. Date of publication.

5. Format of source.

6. Date of access.

There are many formats for the different kinds of electronic publications. Here is the format of an entry for an online article.

Smith, Sonia. "Biting the Hand That Doesn't Feed Me: Internships for College Credit Are a Scam." *Slate*. WPN1, 8 June. 2006. Web. 24 July 2006.

4. WORKS-CITED ENTRIES FOR DATABASE SOURCES (magazine, journal, or newspaper articles)

Basic entries for database sources have six main elements:

1. Author's name.

2. Publication information.

3. Name of the database (in italics).

4. Format of the source.

5. Date of access.

Bayly, Christopher A. "Moral Judgment: Empire, Nation, and History." *European Review* 14.3 (2006): 385-91. *Academic Search Premier*. Web. 3 Aug. 2006.

---

1. Author's name.
- List the author's name with the last name first, followed by a period.

2. Title of document and/or title of website.
- Place the title of the article on the Web page inside quotation marks.
- Insert a period before the closing quotation mark.
- Put the title of the entire site or the online journal in italics, followed by a period.

3. Publication information.
- List the name of the publisher or sponsor of the website.
- Give the date of electronic publication.
- Provide the format.
- List the date of access.

1. Author's name.
- List the author's name with the last name first, followed by a period.

2. Publication information.
- Give the print publication information in standard format, in this case for an article found in a database.

3. Name of database.
- Put the name of the database in italics.

4. Format of the source.

5. Date of access.
- List the date you looked at the source, followed by a period.

In-text citations in MLA style

1. Author named in your text	Put the author's name in a signal phrase in your sentence. Business Professor Rosabeth Moss Kanter claims that "men and women employed in similar jobs in an organization will react in similar ways to their job conditions" (202).
2. Author not named in your text	In 2006, females in Canada had a longer life expectancy than males. Female children born in 2001 could expect to live an average of 82 years. Male children born the same year were expected to live just 77 years (Statistics Canada 12).
3. Work by one author	The author's last name comes first, followed by the page number. There is no comma. (Bell 3)
4. Work by two or three authors	The authors' last names follow the order of the title page. If there are two authors, join the names with *and.* If there are three, use commas between the first two names and a comma with *and* before the last name. (Francisco, Vaughn, and Lynn 7)
5. Work by four or more authors	You may use the phrase *et al.* (meaning "and others") for all names but the first, or you may write out all the names. Make sure you use the same method for both the in-text citations and the works-cited list. (Abrams et al. 1653)
6. Work by no named author	Use a shortened version of the title that includes at least the first important word. Your reader will use the shortened title to find the full title in the works-cited list. A review in *The New Yorker* of Ryan Adams's new album focuses on the artist's age ("Pure" 25). Notice that "Pure" is in quotation marks because it refers to the title of an article. If it were a book, the short title would be in italics.

7. Work by a group or organization	Treat the group or organization as the author. Try to identify the group author in the text and place only the page number in the parentheses.

> According to the *Irish Free State Handbook*, published by the Ministry for Industry and Finance, the population of Ireland in 1929 was approximately 4 192 000 (23).

8. Quotations longer than four lines	NOTE: When using indented (block) quotations of longer than four lines, the period appears *before* the parentheses enclosing the page number.

> In her article "Art for Everybody," Susan Orlean attempts to explain the popularity of painter Thomas Kinkade:
>> People like to own things they think are valuable. . . .The high price of limited editions is part of their appeal: it implies that they are choice and exclusive, and that only a certain class of people will be able to afford them. (128)
>
> This same statement could possibly also explain the popularity of phenomena like PBS's *Antiques Road Show*.

If the source is longer than one page, provide the page number for each quotation, paraphrase, and summary.

9. Online sources	If an online source includes paragraph numbers rather than page numbers, use *par.* with the number.

> (Cello, par. 4)

If the source does not include page numbers, consider citing the work and the author in the text rather than in parentheses.

> In a hypertext version of James Joyce's *Ulysses*, . . .

10. Work in an anthology	Cite the name of the author of the work within an anthology, not the name of the editor of the collection. Alphabetize the entry in the list of works cited by the author, not the editor. For example, Melissa Jane Hardie published the chapter "Beard" in *Rhetorical Bodies*, a book edited by Jack Selzer and Sharon Crowley.

> In "Beard," Melissa Jane Hardie explores the role assumed by Elizabeth Taylor as the celebrity companion of gay actors including Rock Hudson and Montgomery Cliff (278-79).

Note that Hardie, not Selzer and Crowley, is named in parenthetical citations.

> (Hardie 278-79)

11. Two or more works by the same author	Use the author's last name and then a shortened version of the title of each source.
	The majority of books written about coauthorship focus on partners of the same sex (Laird, *Women* 351).
	Note that *Women* is in italics because it is the name of a book.
12. Different authors with the same last name	If your list of works cited contains items by two or more different authors with the same last name, include the initial of the first name in the parenthetical reference. Note that a period follows the initial.
	Web surfing requires more mental involvement than channel surfing (S. Johnson 107).
13. Two or more sources within the same sentence	Place each citation directly after the statement it supports.
	Many sweeping pronouncements were made in the 1990s that the Internet is the best opportunity to improve education since the printing press (Ellsworth xxii) or even in the history of the world (Dyrli and Kinnaman 79).
14. Two or more sources within the same citation	If two sources support a single point, separate them with a semicolon.
	(McKibbin 39; Gore 92)
15. Work quoted in another source	When you do not have access to the original source of the material you wish to use, put the abbreviation *qtd. in* (quoted in) before the information about the indirect source.
	National governments have become increasingly what Ulrich Beck, in a 1999 interview, calls "zombie institutions"—institutions which are "dead and still alive" (qtd. in Bauman 6).
16. Literary works	To supply a reference to literary works, you sometimes need more than a page number from a specific edition. Readers should be able to locate a quotation in any edition of the book. Give the page number from the edition that you are using, then a semicolon and other identifying information.
	"Marriage is a house" is one of the most memorable lines in *Don Quixote* (546; pt. 2, bk. 3, ch. 19).

Books in MLA-style works cited

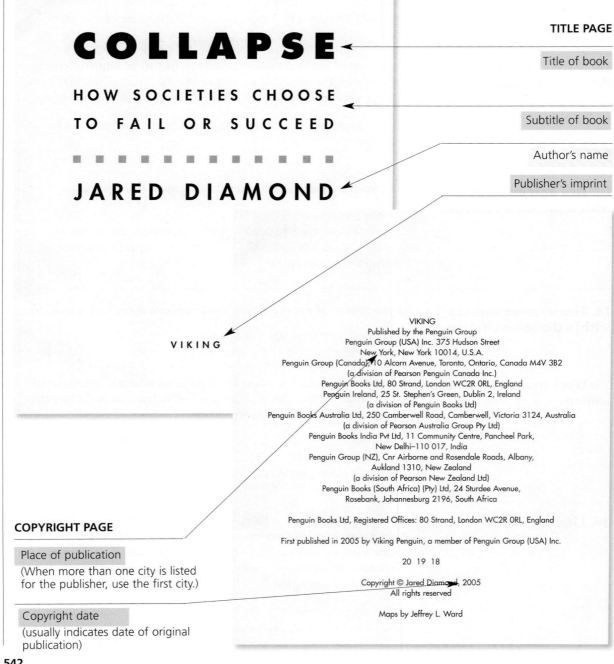

COLLAPSE ←

TITLE PAGE

Title of book

HOW SOCIETIES CHOOSE ←
TO FAIL OR SUCCEED

Subtitle of book

Author's name

JARED DIAMOND ←

Publisher's imprint

VIKING ←

VIKING
Published by the Penguin Group
Penguin Group (USA) Inc. 375 Hudson Street
New York, New York 10014, U.S.A.
Penguin Group (Canada), 10 Alcorn Avenue, Toronto, Ontario, Canada M4V 3B2
(a division of Pearson Penguin Canada Inc.)
Penguin Books Ltd, 80 Strand, London WC2R 0RL, England
Penguin Ireland, 25 St. Stephen's Green, Dublin 2, Ireland
(a division of Penguin Books Ltd)
Penguin Books Australia Ltd, 250 Camberwell Road, Camberwell, Victoria 3124, Australia
(a division of Pearson Australia Group Pty Ltd)
Penguin Books India Pvt Ltd, 11 Community Centre, Pancheel Park,
New Delhi–110 017, India
Penguin Group (NZ), Cnr Airborne and Rosendale Roads, Albany,
Aukland 1310, New Zealand
(a division of Pearson New Zealand Ltd)
Penguin Books (South Africa) (Pty) Ltd, 24 Sturdee Avenue,
Rosebank, Johannesburg 2196, South Africa

Penguin Books Ltd, Registered Offices: 80 Strand, London WC2R 0RL, England

First published in 2005 by Viking Penguin, a member of Penguin Group (USA) Inc.

20 19 18

Copyright © Jared Diamond, 2005
All rights reserved

Maps by Jeffrey L. Ward

COPYRIGHT PAGE

Place of publication
(When more than one city is listed
for the publisher, use the first city.)

Copyright date
(usually indicates date of original
publication)

Diamond, Jared. *Collapse: How Societies Choose to Fail or Succeed.*
New York: Viking, 2005. Print.

1. Author's or editor's name
- The author's last name comes first, followed by a comma and the first name.
- For edited books, put the abbreviation *ed.* after the name, preceded by a comma:

Kavanaugh, Peter, ed.

2. Book title
- Use the exact title, as it appears on the title page (not the cover).
- Put the title in italics.
- All nouns, verbs, pronouns, adjectives, and subordinating conjunctions, and the first and last words of the title are capitalized. Do not capitalize articles, prepositions, coordinating conjunctions, or *to* in an infinitive, unless they are the first or last word of the title.

3. Publication information

Place of publication
- If more than one city is given, use the first.

Publisher
- Omit words such as Press, Publisher, and Inc.
- For university presses, use UP: U of Toronto P
- Shorten the name. For example, shorten W.W. Norton & Co. to Norton and shorten McClelland & Stewart to McClelland.

Date of publication
- Give the year as it appears on the copyright page.
- If no year is given, but can be approximated, put a *c.* ("circa") and the approximate date in brackets: [c. 1999].
- Otherwise, put *n.d.* ("no date"):

Toronto: Oxford University Press, n.d.

Format of publication
- Include the format of publication: *Print.*

Sample works-cited entries for books

ONE AUTHOR

17. Book by one author

The author's last name comes first, followed by a comma, the first name, and a period.

> Mitic, Trudy Duivenvoorden. *People in Transition: Reflections on Becoming Canadian.* Toronto: Fitzhenry, 2001. Print.

18. Two or more books by the same author

In the entry for the first book, include the author's name. In the second entry, substitute three hyphens and a period for the author's name. List the titles of books by the same author in alphabetical order.

> Grimsley, Jim. *Boulevard.* Chapel Hill: Algonquin, 2002.
> ---. *Dream Boy.* New York: Simon, 1995. Print.

MULTIPLE AUTHORS

19. Book by two or three authors

The second and subsequent authors' names appear first name first. A comma separates the authors' names. If all are editors, use eds. after the names.

> Cruz, Arnaldo, and Martin Manalansan, eds. *Queer Globalizations: Citizenship and the Afterlife of Colonialism.* New York: New York UP, 2002. Print.

20. Book by four or more authors

You may use the phrase *et al.* (meaning "and others") for all authors but the first, or you may write out all the names. You need to use the same method in the in-text citation as you do in the works-cited list.

> Britton, Jane, et al. *The Broadview Anthology of Expository Prose.* New York: Broadview, 2001.

ANONYMOUS AND GROUP AUTHORS

21. Book by an unknown author

Begin the entry with the title.

> *The Baseball Encyclopedia.* 10th ed. New York: MacMillan, 1996. Print.

22. Book by a group or organization

Treat the group as the author of the work.

> Canadian Standards Association. *CE Code Handbook: An Explanation of Rules of the Canadian Electrical Code, Part 1.* Toronto: Canadian Standards Association. 2009. Print.

23. Religious texts

> *Holy Bible.* King James Text: Modern Phrased Version. New York: Oxford UP, 1980. Print.

EDITIONS, REPRINTS, AND UNDATED BOOKS

24. Book with an editor

List an edited book under the editor's name if your focus is on the editor. Otherwise, cite an edited book under the author's name.

> Lewis, Gifford, ed. *The Big House of Inver.* By Edith Somerville and Martin Ross. Dublin: Farmar, 2000. Print.

25. Book with no publication date

If no year of publication is given, but can be approximated, put a c. ("circa") and the approximate date in brackets: [c. 1999]. Otherwise, put n.d. ("no date").

> O'Sullivan, Colin. *Traditions and Novelties of the Irish Country Folk.* Dublin [c. 1793]. Print.
> James, Franklin. *In the Valley of the King.* Cambridge: Harvard UP, n.d. Print.

26. Reprinted works

For works of fiction that have been printed in many different editions or reprints, give the original publication date after the title.

> Wilde, Oscar. *The Picture of Dorian Gray.* 1890. New York: Norton, 2001. Print.

PARTS OF BOOKS

27. Introduction, Foreword, Preface, or Afterword

Give the author and then the name of the specific part being cited. Next, name the book. Then, if the author for the whole work is different, put that author's name after the word *By*. Place inclusive page numbers at the end.

> Jones, Spider. Foreword. *A Sporting Chance: Achievements of African Canadian Athletes.* By William Humber. Toronto: Natural Heritage, 2004. Print.

28. Single chapter written by same author as the book

> Ardis, Ann. "Mapping the Middlebrow in Edwardian England." *Modernism and Cultural Conflict: 1880-1922.* Cambridge: Cambridge UP, 2002. 114-42. Print.

29. Selection from an anthology or edited collection

> Lai, Larissa. "Two Houses and an Airplane." *Strike the Wok: An Anthology of Contemporary Chinese Canadian Fiction.* Ed. Lien Chao and Jim Wong-Chu. Toronto: TSAR, 2003. 1-18. Print.

Periodicals in MLA-style works cited

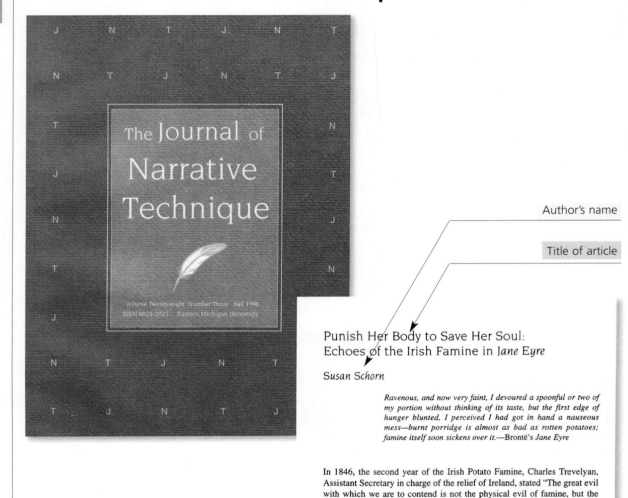

Author's name

Title of article

Punish Her Body to Save Her Soul:
Echoes of the Irish Famine in *Jane Eyre*

Susan Schorn

> *Ravenous, and now very faint, I devoured a spoonful or two of*
> *my portion without thinking of its taste, but the first edge of*
> *hunger blunted, I perceived I had got in hand a nauseous*
> *mess—burnt porridge is almost as bad as rotten potatoes;*
> *famine itself soon sickens over it.*—Brontë's *Jane Eyre*

In 1846, the second year of the Irish Potato Famine, Charles Trevelyan, Assistant Secretary in charge of the relief of Ireland, stated "The great evil with which we are to contend is not the physical evil of famine, but the moral evil of the selfish, perverse and turbulent character of the people" (Clarity). That same year, Charlotte Brontë penned the following speech for the character of Mr. Brocklehurst in her novel *Jane Eyre*: "Oh, madam, when you put bread and cheese, instead of burnt porridge, into these children's mouths, you may indeed feed their vile bodies, but you little think how you starve their immortal souls!" The similarity between the sentiment and policy of these two men, one fictional, one very real indeed, is no coincidence. Both express ideas that were then common currency with regard to "the Irish Problem." The connections between starvation, moral improvement, discipline, and nationality were familiar ones in Victorian England, and Brontë's use of this public, political sentiment in her novel—and of numerous other images borrowed from accounts of the

Name of journal, volume number, issue number, date of publication, page number

The Journal of Narrative Technique 28.3 (Fall 1998): 350–365. Copyright © 1998 by *The Journal of Narrative Technique.*

Schorn, Susan. "'Punish Her Body to Save Her Soul': Echoes of the Irish
Famine in *Jane Eyre*." *The Journal of Narrative Technique* 28.3 (1998):
350–65. Print.

1. Author's or editor's name
- The author's last name comes first, followed by a comma and the first name.

2. Title of Article
- Use the exact title, which appears at the top of the article.
- Put the title in quotation marks. If a book title is part of the article's title, put the title in italics. If a title requiring quotation marks is part of the article's title, use single quotation marks around it.
- All nouns, verbs, pronouns, adjectives, and subordinating conjunctions, and the first and last words of the title are capitalized. Do not capitalize articles, prepositions, coordinating conjunctions, or *to* in an infinitive, unless they are the first or last word of the title.

3. Publication information

Name of journal
- Put the title of the journal in italics.
- Abbreviate the title of the journal if it commonly appears that way.

Volume, issue, and page numbers
- List the volume number, a period, and then the issue number before the year and page numbers.
- For journals that use only issue numbers, include the issue number before the year.

Date of publication
- For magazines and journals identified by the month or season of publication, use the month (or season) and year in place of the volume.
- For weekly or biweekly magazines, give both the day and month of publication, as listed on the issue. Note that the day precedes the month and no comma is used.

Format of publication
- Include the format of publication: *Print*.

Sample works-cited entries for print periodicals

JOURNAL ARTICLES

30. Article by one author

Mallory, Anne. "Burke, Boredom, and the Theater of Counterrevolution." *PMLA* 118.2 (2003): 224–38. Print.

31. Article by two or three authors

Higgins, Lorraine D., and Lisa D. Brush. "Personal Experience Narrative and Public Debate: Writing the Wrongs of Welfare." *College Composition and Communication* 57.4. (2006): 694-729. Print.

32. Article by four or more authors

You may use the phrase *et al.* (meaning "and others") for all authors but the first, or you may write out all the names.

Malhi, R. S., et al. "Patterns of mtDNA Diversity in Northwestern North America." *Human Biology* 76.1 (2004): 33-54. Print.

33. Article in a journal that uses only issue numbers

Include the issue number alone.

Robinson, Laura. "Remodeling an Old-Fashioned Girl: Troubling Girlhood in Ann-Marie MacDonald's *Fall on Your Knees.*" *Canadian Literature* 186 (2005): 30-45. Print.

MAGAZINES

34. Monthly or seasonal magazines

Use the month (or season) and year in place of the volume. Abbreviate the names of all months except May, June, and July.

Barlow, John Perry. "Africa Rising: Everything You Know about Africa Is Wrong." *Wired* Jan. 1998: 142-58. Print.

35. Weekly or biweekly magazines

Give both the day and month of publication, as listed on the issue.

Toobin, Jeffrey. "Crackdown." *New Yorker* 5 Nov. 2001: 56-61. Print.

NEWSPAPERS

36. Newspaper article by one author

The author's last name comes first, followed by a comma and the first name.

> Hope, Marty. "Buyers Advised to Do Research; Expert Offers Tips for Purchasers." *Calgary Herald.* 24 Oct. 2009: J6. Print.

37. Newspaper article by two or three authors

The second and subsequent authors' names are printed in regular order, first name first:

> Walton, Dawn, and Katherine O'Neill. "Ontario to Use Amber Alerts More Broadly." *Globe and Mail.* [Toronto]. 27 Oct. 2009: A15. Print.

38. Newspaper article by an unknown author

Begin the entry with the title.

> "The Dotted Line." *Washington Post* 8 June 2006, final ed.: E2. Print.

REVIEWS, EDITORIALS, LETTERS TO THE EDITOR

39. Review

If there is no title, just name the work reviewed.

> Mendelsohn, Daniel. "The Two Oscar Wildes." Rev. of *The Importance of Being Earnest,* dir. Oliver Parker. *New York Review of Books* 10 Oct. 2002: 23–24. Print.

40. Editorial

> "Stop Stonewalling on Reform." Editorial. *Business Week* 17 June 2002: 108. Print.

41. Letter to the editor

> Patai, Daphne. Letter. *Harper's Magazine* Dec. 2001: 4. Print.

Electronic sources in MLA-style works cited

Title of online journal

Title of article

Author's name

Date of publication

Source: http://www.slate.com/id/2220878/

Levi, Michael A. "Living on Canada's Oil." *Slate*. WPNI, 19 June 2009.

Web. 28 Oct. 2009.

1. Author's name
- Authorship is sometimes difficult to discern for electronic sources. If you know the author or editor, follow the rules for books and journals.

2. Title of work and title of website
- Italicize the title of the work if independent; put in roman type and quotation marks if work is part of a larger work.
- List the title of overall website in italics.

3. Publication information
- Note the version or edition used.
- Note the publisher or sponsor of the site (if not available, use N.p.), followed by a comma.
- Note the date of publication (if not available, use n.d.).
- Note format of source (Web).
- Note the date you accessed the site.

Common questions about citing electronic sources

What if you cannot find publication or author information?
- Cite what is available.
- If the author's name is unknown, begin with the article title or website name

When do you include URLs (website addresses)?
- Do not include the URL unless requested by instructor or when the source cannot be easily located without it. When a URL is required, provide it at the end of the citation within angle brackets followed by a period <http://....>.

Sample works-cited entries for electronic sources

ELECTRONIC PUBLICATIONS

42. Article/document (in online magazine) from a professional or business website

"Corporate E-Mail Is Not All Business." *eMarketer.* eMarketer Inc., 5 Dec. 2005. Web. 6 Jan. 2009.

43. Newspaper article (in online newspaper) from a professional or business website

Stewart, Sinclair. "Flashy Bay St. Trader Faces Probe." *Globe and Mail.* CTVglobemedia, 29 June 2005. Web. 30 June 2009.

44. Article/document from a group/organization/ society

National Audubon Society. "State of the Birds." *Audubon.* Natl. Audubon Soc., 2009. Web. 28 Oct. 2009.

45. Article/document with an author and group/organization affiliation

Edwards, Rebecca. "Socialism." *1896.* Vassar College, 2000. Web. 29 Oct. 2009.

46. Article/document from a government website

Canada. Competition Bureau. "Competition Bureau Challenges Weight Loss Claims Made by Quebec Companies." Govt. of Canada, 28 June 2005. Web. 11 Apr. 2009.

ELECTRONIC SOURCES: DATABASES

47. Newspaper article from a database (unknown author)

"Canada's Public Schools Attract Foreign Families Willing to Pay Dearly." *Globe and Mail* [Toronto] 7 Sept. 2004: A1. *CPI.Q.* Web. 21 Sept. 2009.

48. Magazine article from a database

Newman, Peter C. "Our Policy: Made in America." *Maclean's* 14 Mar. 2005: 42-43. *Academic Search Premier.* Web. 30 June 2009.

49. Journal article from a database

Basok, Tanya, and Marshall Bastable. "'Knock, Knock, Knockin' on Heaven's Door': Immigrants and the Guardians of Privilege in Canada." *Labour* 63 (2009): 207–20. *CBCA Reference.* Web. 29 Oct. 2009.

50. Online book (ebook) from a database

West, Ray, and Tom Muck. *Dreamweaver MX: A Beginner's Guide.* Berkeley: McGraw, 2003. *Netlibrary.* Web. 11 Apr. 2009.

51. Reference/resource material from a database

"Art Deco." *Encyclopedia Britannica Online.* Encyclopedia Britannica Online. Web. 29 Oct. 2009.

Other sources in MLA-style works cited

52. Email communication

Give the name of the writer, the subject line, and the name of the email recipient. If written to you, type *Message to the author,* the date, and the medium.

> Anderson, Robert. "Re: Collecting Marketing Data." Message to the author. 20 Apr. 2009. Email.

53. Course web page/ instructor's notes online

Begin with the instructor's name, the name of the course, the title, the words *Course Notes,* the date the notes were created, the department, the institution, the publisher, the format (Web), and the date of access.

> Paulson, Marianne. "HUM 100: Week 5: Rome and the Rise of Empire." Course notes. 31 Mar. 2008. The Development of Western Thought. School of General Arts. Seneca College. *My Seneca Blackboard.* Web. 5 Apr. 2009.

54. Personal website

If there is no title for the website, list it by author or creator. If it is a personal website, place the words Home page after the name of the owner of the page.

> Stallman, Richard. Home page. Richard Stallman 21 Mar. 2004. Web. 8 Apr. 2004.

55. Sound recording

> Ochs, Phil. *There But for Fortune.* Elektra Records, 1989. CD.

56. Video/DVD

> *House of Flying Daggers.* Dir. Yimou Zhang. Perf. Takeshi Kaneshiro and Ziyi Zhang. Columbia Tristar, 2005. DVD.

57. Television or radio program

Provide the title of the episode, followed by the title of the program. After the title, list any performers, narrators, and directors who may be pertinent. Then give the name of the network, broadcast date, and format.

> "Kaisha." *The Sopranos.* Perf. James Gandolfini, Lorraine Bracco, and Edie Falco. HBO. 4 June 2006. Television.

58. Computer game

> Sims 2. Redwood City: Electronic Arts, 2004. CD-ROM.

Visual sources in MLA-style works cited

59. Cartoon

Chast, Roz. "Are You in Your Goddess Years?" Cartoon. *New Yorker* 10 Mar. 2004: 113. Print.

60. Advertisement

Air Canada. Advertisement. CNN. 15 May 1998. Television.

61. Map, graph, or chart

Montreal Street Map. Map. Montreal: Rand McNally, 2000. Print.

62. Work of visual art

Provide the artist's name, italicized title of the work, date of composition (if unknown write *N.d.*), the medium of composition, the name of the institution or individual who houses the work, and the city where it is housed.

Cloar, Carroll. *Odie Maude.* 1990. Drawing. David Lusk Gallery, Memphis.

Cite a photograph in a museum or collection as you would a painting or sculpture.

63. Map on a website

"Physical Map of Alberta, Canada." Map. *Canada Maps.* Tourizmmaps, 2006. Web. 20 Oct. 2009.

64. Art on a website

Seurat, Georges-Pierre. *Port-en-Bessin, Entrance to the Harbor.* 1888. Oil on canvas. Museum of Modern Art, New York. *MOMA.* Web. 30 Oct. 2009.

65. Online video

"Balloon Bowl." *YouTube.* YouTube, 8 June 2007. Web. 29 June 2009.

Sample MLA paper

Include your last name and page 1 cm from the top.

Holmes 1

Amanda Holmes
Professor Williams
SES 285BA
22, November 2007

All left justified
- Your name,
- Instructor's name
- Course number
- Date submitted

Have I Met You Before?

Centre title

It is telling that the television show *Star Trek: the Next Generation* would turn to the oldest written story for inspiration:

> Gilgamesh, a king. Gilgamesh, a king. At Uruk. He tormented his subjects. He made them angry. They cried out aloud, "Send our king a companion! Spare us from his madness!" Enkidu, a wild man from the forest, entered the city. They fought in the temple. They fought in the street. Gilgamesh defeated Enkidu. They became great friends. Gilgamesh and Enkidu, at Uruk. The new friends went out into the desert together where the Great Bull of Heaven was killing men by the hundreds. Enkidu caught the Bull by the tail; Gilgamesh struck him with his sword. Killed him. They were victorious. But Enkidu fell to the ground, struck down by the gods. And Gilgamesh wept bitter tears, saying, "He who was my companion through adventure and hardship, is gone forever … ("Darmok")

Introduce block quotations. Do not place block quotations within quotation marks

If quotation is longer than four lines, indent 2.5 cm.

In the 21st century heroes are everywhere. Bookstore shelves are filled with an abundance of fantasy literature; movie theatres show mainstream blockbuster quest films; classic tales are being made into musicals, operas and ballets; and anyone can create their own heroic alter-ego in an online game and become part of an adventure. But what is it that is so alluring about being a hero? Why has the fantasy genre become so popular in our culture? Is it merely an escape from the routine existence of daily life? Or is there something more vital, more deeply embedded in our human genetic makeup that attracts us? There seems to be an intimate connection between mythology and present day fantasy as the plots, themes and

2.5 cm margins on all sides, double-space all text, no extra spaces between paragraphs.

Holmes 2

heroic qualities that make today's stories so appealing can be
traced back in time, even to what has been called the very first
literary masterpiece: *The Epic of Gilgamesh.*

It is thought by scholars that Gilgamesh was a real person
who ruled as the Sumerian king in the city of Uruk sometime
between 2700-2500 BCE. It is believed that his story was passed
down orally for centuries before finally being written down in
cuneiform on clay tablets. In the mid 19th century two
archeologists, Austin Henry Layard and Hormuzd Rassam,
uncovered the library of the Assyrian king Ashurbanipal who
reigned from 668 to 627 BCE. From these ruins of Nineveh came
more than 100,000 clay tablets and fragments of tablets which
were sent to the British Museum. But it was not until 1872 that
the twelve Gilgamesh tablets in the collection were identified and
translated by a curator of the museum, George Smith, leaving
modern society with an ancient story of epic proportions that
had been lost to human knowledge for almost two millennia
(Damrosch 98).

In his book, *The Hero With A Thousand Faces,* Joseph
Campbell explores the idea of what he calls the monomyth, the
idea that no matter what time or place it comes from,
mythology is always the same: "For the symbols of mythology
are not manufactured; they cannot be ordered, invented or
permanently suppressed. They are spontaneous productions of
the psyche, and each bears within it, undamaged, the germ
power of its source" (4). What Campbell is saying here is that
similarities in mythology occur because the essence of the
stories comes from the unconscious mind. This explains why
heroes all have similar characteristics and quest stories follow
the same patterns, no matter how much the external detail may
vary. The character of Gilgamesh, then, could be called a
prototype for the ideal hero of modern day entertainment. At
the beginning of the epic, he is spoilt, rude, oppressive and
chauvinistic, almost childlike in his voraciousness for satisfying
his own desires. But Gilgamesh undergoes profound changes
during his adventures and his search for immortality is
bittersweet as he finds, and then carelessly loses, his chance of
everlasting life. It does not matter that his quest is a failure,
however; it is the psychological changes he undergoes that are

If author's name
mentioned in sentence
not necessary to put in
in-text citation

Holmes 3

important. According to Campbell, "The standard path of the mythological adventure of the hero is a magnification of the formula represented in the rites of passage: separation— initiation—return: which might be named the nuclear unit of the monomyth" (30). The hero must leave his everyday life, battle with the unknown monsters of the supernatural, and return with new abilities that benefit his society. David A. Leeming agrees:

> The psychological basis for all [these stories] is every human's need to define or "prove" himself—to suffer the agony of adult life, to gain its rewards, and to "make a name." The hero—our representative has established his origins, found divine destiny within himself, and now must act on that destiny. To leave the cave of meditation and embark on the quest is to move from the inner sufferings of adolescence to the active pursuits of the prime of life. (184–85)

The purpose of the hero's quest is not to slay actual monsters, but to journey inwards into the subconscious and transform the way he or she perceives the world. By slaying the monsters of the mind, the hero can realize his own full potential and, like Gilgamesh, develop into a mature and wise leader.

Today's fantasy owes its popularity to several events. A revival of interest in traditions and folk stories in 19th-century Europe; the legends and myths that have been rediscovered, or survived, into the 20th century; the American pulp magazines that saw the creation of "Sword and Sorcery" (*Science Fiction Citations*); and the awe-inspiring success of *The Hobbit* and *The Lord of the Rings* by J.R.R. Tolkien in the 1950s and 1960s. In his forward for the *Ultimate Encyclopedia of Fantasy*, Terry Pratchett, renowned author of the Discworld fantasy novels, suggests that: "Imagination, not intelligence, made us human. Squirrels are quite intelligent when it comes to nuts, but as far as we can tell they have never told stories about a hero who stole nuts from the gods. That ability has given us all our fiction and our mythology" (6). This genre, it seems, has the same purpose as mythology:

Do not include a page number for items without pagination, such as websites.

Introduce block quotations rather than just dropping them into the text.

Do not place blocked quotations within quotation marks.

> Pure fantasy, or what the critic John Clute calls "full
> fantasy", seems to deal in the fulfillment of desire . . .
> in the sense of the yearning of the human heart for a
> kinder world, a better self, a wholer experience, a sense
> of truly belonging. To use the ancient metaphor (but
> then most things about this genre are ancient, going
> back to the beginnings of our humanity), fantasy seeks
> to heal the waste land. (*Ultimate Encyclopedia* 8)

Like the knight Perceval who by healing the wounded Fisher
King would also heal the King's barren land, fantasy tries to
appeal to modern society and subsequently attempts to heal the
"waste land" of imagination that is symptomatic of a busy world.

With all the recent advances in multi-media technology and
special effects, fantasy and science fiction films have become
mainstream blockbusters. Films such as the *Star Wars* trilogies,
The Princess Bride, and *The Matrix,* to name but a few, perfectly fit
the pattern of the hero-quest. Today this genre of film is thrilling
millions of viewers and the popularity of the hero-quest story was
fully realized when Tolkien's epic trilogy *The Lord of the Rings*
came to life on the big screen, and completely legitimized when
the 3rd part, *The Return of the King,* won eleven academy awards,
including Best Picture, in 2003. In 2006 the musical version of
Tolkien's masterpiece hit the live stage complete with a moving
set and a very large and realistic looking Balrog (320). And as
Paramount has just released the film version of the epic myth
Beowulf, which uses state-of-the-art 3D technology, it is probably
only a matter of time until a major motion picture is made of the
Gilgamesh story. Already there are countless literary and
theatrical productions based on the epic and even an opera by
the Danish composer Per Nørgård.

But perhaps the closest thing to actually being a hero, is
playing one in a game. Since the original role-playing game,
Dungeons and Dragons, became popular in the 1970's the gaming
industry has taken off. The old style of gathering a small group of
people and having one player designated as the "Game Master"
(GM), or controller, of the story while the other players act out
their characters in whatever scenario the GM has in store for
them, has rapidly transformed into the now popular MMORPG

Holmes 5

(Massive Multi-Player Online Role Playing Game) where one can play online with others all over the world. Each player creates their own hero character, who can interact with other players' characters, team up to go on quests, develop experience, skills and knowledge, kill monsters and rescue princesses (or princes). The player is in control of how to shape the character and these choices influence how all the other player and non-player characters react. Anyone with an internet connection can now become a hero in these virtual worlds, and the possibilities are endless. And a familiar hero keeps popping up in all kinds of computer games. We have met him before. Gilgamesh is featured in SquareEnix's *Final Fantasy* series, Sid Meier's *Civilization III* and *Civilization IV,* and the online role-playing game *Adventure Quest.*

I was seventeen when I first read *The Hobbit* and *The Lord of the Rings.* In spite of being an enthusiastic science fiction reader since the age of nine or ten, I was completely unaware of the fantasy genre. I consumed these books with a passion, for they spoke to me in a way that I had never experienced before. While I was reading them I felt as if I actually existed in Tolkien's world. What I was experiencing was the powerful effect that mythology has in our lives. Whether told in a movie or a book, or acted out in a game, these adventures become important to us because they are symbolic of an inner quest, an attempt to understand one's own soul by fighting our inner demons and fears, and emerging as a better person. Campbell describes this process quite beautifully:

> [W]e have not even to risk the adventure alone; for the heroes of all time have gone before us; the labyrinth is thoroughly known; we have only to follow the thread of the hero-path. And where we had thought to find an abomination, we shall find a god; where we had thought to slay another, we shall slay ourselves; where we had thought to travel outward, we shall come to the center of our own existence; where we had thought to be alone, we shall be with all the world. (25)

After all, as Bilbo reminds us in *The Hobbit* the actual adventure is very uncomfortable. And so we read and we watch and we play.

Cite publications by the name of the author (or authors).

Holmes 6

Works Cited ◄

Campbell, Joseph. *The Hero with A Thousand Faces*. 2nd ed. Princeton: Princeton UP, 1968. Print.

---. *Myths to Live By.* New York: Penguin, 1972. Print. ◄

Damrosch, David. "Epic Hero." *Smithsonian* 38.2 (2007): 94–103. *Academic Search Premier.* Web. 14 Nov. 2007.

"Darmok." *Star Trek: The Next Generation.* 30 Sept. 1991. CD-ROM.

Leeming, David A. *Mythology: The Voyage of the Hero.* New York: Lippincott, 1973. Print.

---. *The World of Myth.* New York: Oxford UP, 1990. Print.

Pringle, David, ed. *The Ultimate Encyclopedia of Fantasy.* London: Carlton, 1998. Print.

Tolkien, J.R.R. *The Fellowship of the Ring: Being the First Part of the Lord of the Rings.* New York: Ballentine, 1994. Print.

Ziolkowski, Eric. "An Ancient Newcomer to Modern Culture." *World Literature Today* 81.5 (2007): 55–57. *Academic Search Premier.* Web. 17 Nov. 2007.

Centre "Works Cited" on a new page.

If an author has more than one entry, list the entries in alphabetical order by title. Use three hyphens in place of the author's name for the second and subsequent entries.

Double-space all entries. Indent all but the first line in each entry five spaces.

Alphabetize entries by the last names of the authors or by the first important word in the title if no author is listed.

Italicize titles of books and periodicals

Go through your text and make sure all the sources you have used are in the list of works cited.

21

APA Documentation

Social sciences disciplines—including government, linguistics, psychology, sociology, and education—frequently use the American Psychological Association (APA) documentation style. For a detailed treatment of APA style, consult the *Publication Manual of the American Psychological Association*, sixth edition (2010).

BODY OBJECTIFICATION

13

References

Akan, G. E. & Grilo, C. M. (1995). Sociocultural influences on eating attitudes and behaviors, body image, and psychological functioning: A comparison of African-American, Asian-American, and Caucasian college women. *International Journal of Eating Disorders, 18*(2), 181–87. Retrieved from http://www3. interscience.wiley.com/journal/34698/home

Altabe, M. N. (1998). Ethnicity and body image: Quantitative and qualitative analysis. *International Journal of Eating Disorders, 23*(2), 153–159. doi:10.1002/(SICI)1098-108X(199803)23 :2<153::AID-EAT5>3.0.CO;2-J

Chapter contents

APA citations

APA style emphasizes the date of publication. When you cite an author's name in the body of your paper, always include the date of publication. Notice, too, that APA style includes the abbreviation for page (p.) in front of the page number. When multiple pages are cited, give the full page range (Zukin, 2004, pp. 151–153). A comma separates each element of the citation.

Zukin (2004) observes that teens today begin to shop for themselves at age 13 or 14, "the same age when lower-class children, in the past, became apprentices or went to work in factories" **(p. 50).**

When you cite an author's name in the body of your paper, always include the date of publication.

APA style includes the abbreviation for page (p.) in front of the page number.

One sociologist notes that teens today begin to shop for themselves at age 13 or 14, "the same age when lower-class children, in the past, became apprentices or went to work in factories" **(Zukin, 2004, p. 50).**

If the author's name is not mentioned in the sentence, the reference looks like this.

References

The corresponding entry in the references list would be this.

Zukin, S. (2004). *Point of purchase: How shopping changed American culture.* New York: Routledge.

Where do you put the date?

You have two choices. You can put the date in your text in parentheses

   Zhang, Liu, and Cao (2006) specify . . .

or between the author's name and the page number in the citation note.

   . . . visual languages (Zhang, Liu, & Cao, 2006, p. 192).

When do you need to give a page number?

- Give the page number for all direct quotations.

- For electronic sources that do not provide page numbers, give the paragraph number when available. Use the abbreviation para.

- If the source does not include page numbers, it is preferable to reference the work and the author in the text.

   In Wes Anderson's 1998 film *Rushmore,* . . .

In-text citations in APA style

1. Author named in your text	Business Professor Rosabeth Moss Kanter (2002) claims "men and women employed in similar jobs in an organization will react in similar ways to their job conditions" (p. 202).
2. Author not named in your text	Women in Canada have a longer life expectancy than men (Statistics Canada, 2006, p. 12). Female children born in 2001 could expect to live an average of 82 years. Male children born the same year were expected to live just 77 years.
3. Work by a single author	(Moss Kanter, 2002, p. 202)
4. Work by two authors	Notice that APA uses an ampersand (&) with multiple authors' names rather than *and*. (Suzuki & Irabu, 2002, p. 404).
5. Work by three to five authors	The authors' last names follow the order of the title page. The first in-text citation includes all the authors' names. (Francisco, Vaughn, & Romano, 2001, p. 7) Subsequent references can use the last name of the first author and *et al.* (Francisco et al., 2001, p. 49)
6. Work by six or more authors	Use the first author's last name and *et al.* for all in-text references. (Swallit et al., 2004, p. 49)
7. Work by a group or organization	If the group author is in the text, place the date and page number in parentheses. The National Organization for Women (2001) observed that this "generational shift in attitudes towards marriage and childrearing" will have profound consequences (p. 325).
8. Work by an unknown author	Use a shortened version of the title (or the full title if it is short) in place of the author's name. Capitalize all key words in the title. If it is an article title, place it in quotation marks. ("Derailing the Peace Process," 2003, p. 44)

9. Quotations 40 words or longer

Indent long quotations 1.25 cm and omit quotation marks. Note that the period appears before the parentheses in an indented "block" quote.

> Orlean (2001) has attempted to explain the popularity of the painter Thomas Kinkade:
>> People like to own things they think are valuable. . . . The high price of limited editions is part of their appeal; it implies that they are choice and exclusive, and that only a certain class of people will be able to afford them. (p. 128)

10. Two works by one author with the same copyright date

Assign the dates letters (a, b, etc.) according to their alphabetical arrangement in the references list.

> The majority of books written about coauthorship focus on partners of the same sex (Laird, 2001a, p. 351).

11. Two or more sources within the same sentence

Place each citation directly after the statement it supports.

> Some surveys report an increase in homelessness rates (Alford, 2004) while others chart a slight decrease (Rice, 2003a) . . .

If you need to cite two or more works within the same parentheses, list them in the order they appear in the references list and separate them with a semicolon.

> (Alford, 2004; Rice, 2003a)

12. Work quoted in another source

Name the work and give a citation for the secondary source.

> Saunders and Kellman's study (as cited in McAtee, Luhan, Stiles, & Buell, 1994) . . .

Books in APA-style references list

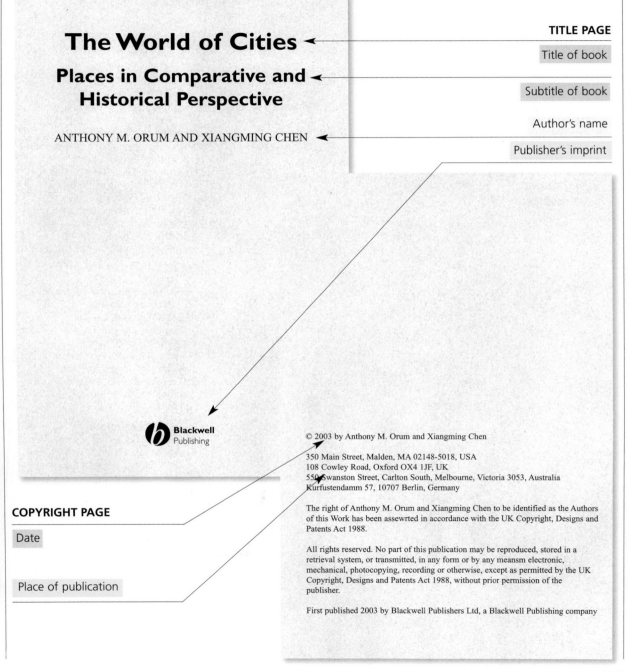

The World of Cities

Places in Comparative and Historical Perspective

ANTHONY M. ORUM AND XIANGMING CHEN

TITLE PAGE

Title of book

Subtitle of book

Author's name

Publisher's imprint

Blackwell Publishing

© 2003 by Anthony M. Orum and Xiangming Chen

350 Main Street, Malden, MA 02148-5018, USA
108 Cowley Road, Oxford OX4 1JF, UK
550 Swanston Street, Carlton South, Melbourne, Victoria 3053, Australia
Kurfustendamm 57, 10707 Berlin, Germany

The right of Anthony M. Orum and Xiangming Chen to be identified as the Authors of this Work has been assewrted in accordance with the UK Copyright, Designs and Patents Act 1988.

All rights reserved. No part of this publication may be reproduced, stored in a retrieval system, or transmitted, in any form or by any meansm electronic, mechanical, photocopying, recording or otherwise, except as permitted by the UK Copyright, Designs and Patents Act 1988, without prior permission of the publisher.

First published 2003 by Blackwell Publishers Ltd, a Blackwell Publishing company

COPYRIGHT PAGE

Date

Place of publication

Orum, A. M., & Chen, X. (2003). *The world of cities: Places in comparative and historical perspective*. Malden, MA: Blackwell.

1. Author's or editor's name
- The author's last name comes first, followed by a comma and the author's initials.
- Join two authors' names with an ampersand.
- If an editor, put the abbreviation *Ed.* in parentheses after the name:

Kavanaugh, P. (Ed.).

2. Year of publication
- Give the year the work was copyrighted in parentheses. If no year of publication is given, write *n.d.* ("no date") in parentheses:

Smith, S. (n.d.).

- If it is a multivolume edited work published over a period of more than one year, put the span in parentheses:

Smith, S. (1999–2001).

3. Book title
- Italicize the title.
- Capitalize only the first word, proper nouns, and the first word after a colon.
- If the book is part of a series, list the series name immediately after the title. Do not italicize or underline it.
- Use the same rules for capitalization as for the title.
- Close with a period.
- If the title is in a foreign language, copy it exactly as it appears on the title page.

4. Publication information
Place of publication
- For Canadian locations, give the city and province (e.g. Toronto, ON).
- For U.S. locations give the city and state (e.g. New York, NY).
- For all other locations, give the city and country (e.g. Paris, France).

Publisher's name
- Do not shorten or abbreviate words like *University* or *Press*.
- Omit words such as *Co., Inc.,* and *Publishers*.

Sample references for books

13. Book by one author

The author's last name comes first, followed by a comma and the author's initials.

Ball, E. (2000). *Slaves in the family*. New York, NY: Ballantine Books.

If an editor, put the abbreviation *Ed.* in parentheses after the name.

Kavanagh, P. (Ed.). (1969). *Lapped furrows*. New York, NY: Hand Press.

14. Book by two authors

Join two authors' names with a comma and ampersand.

Hardt, M., & Negri, A. (2000). *Empire*. Cambridge, MA: Harvard University Press.

If editors, use (*Eds.*) after the names.

McClelland, D., & Eismann, K. (Eds.).

15. Book by three or more authors

Write out all of the authors' names up to seven. For works with eight or more authors, write out the first six names, add an ellipsis mark (. . .), and give the last author's name.

Konishi, C., Hymel, S., Zumbo, B. D., Li, Z., Taki, M., Slee, P., . . . Kwak, K.

16. Chapter in an edited collection

Add the word *In* after the selection title and before the names of the editor(s).

Howard, A. (1997). Labor, history, and sweatshops in the new global economy. In A. Ross (Ed.), *No sweat: Fashion, free trade, and the rights of garment workers* (pp. 151–172). New York, NY: Verso.

17. Government document

Advisory Committee on Radiological Protection. (2001). *Guidelines on hospital emergency plans*. Ottawa, ON: Canadian Nuclear Safety Commission.

Periodicals in APA-style references list

JOURNAL COVER

Name of journal

Date

Issue number

Volume

Social Science Quarterly

December 1993
Volume 74, Number 4

OF GENERAL INTEREST

Foreign Debt and Economic Growth in the World System	GLASBERG/WARD
Household Out-of-Pocket Health Expenditures	RUBIN/KOELLN
Imprisonment in the American States	TAGGART/WINN
Political Opportunity and Peace and Justice Advocacy	IMIG/MEYER
Offshore Assembly in Developing and Developed Countries	CLARK/SAWYER/SPRINKLE
Alcohol Prohibition and Motor Vehicle Accidents	WINN/GIACOPASSI
Saturn Comes to Tennessee: Citizen Perceptions of Impacts	FOLZ/GADDIS/LYONS/SCHEB
Reciprocity and South Africa's Foreign Policy Behavior	VAN WYK/RADLOFF

CURRENT RESEAR
ETHNICITY

American Women Who W

Policy Effects of Suffrage E

Health and Pension Benef

Labor Supply of Puerto Ric

Black-White Differences i

Accent Penalties and the E

Effects of County-Level Alcohol Prohibition on Motor Vehicle Accidents*

Russell G. WINN, *New Mexico State University*

David GIACOPASSI, *Memphis State University*

All motor vehicle accidents in Kentucky were analyzed over a four-year period to determine if counties that prohibit the sale of alcohol have lower crash rates. The data reveal that dry counties have a lower rate of alcohol-related fatalities and significantly lower rates of alcohol-related nonfatal and property accidents. The authors caution that the results should not be taken as a general prescription for alcohol regulation since the counties studied are dry by choice.

Over the past 90 years more than 2.5 million Americans have died in automobile crashes, many of them alcohol-related (Jacobs, 1989). Based on the commonly assumed relationship between alcohol availability and a wide range of social problems, both state and local governments have sought to reduce the number of alcohol-related accidents by enacting regulations to limit alcohol use. These policy changes have included increasing legal drinking age and taxes; restrictions on hours of sale, type, and density of outlets; and changing criminal justice enforcement practices. Researchers have evaluated the effects of the restrictive policies in terms of alcohol-related behavior, principally driving under the influence (DUI), public drunkenness, and various health conditions such as cirrhosis. These studies have yielded inconsistent results (Moskowitz, 1989; Smith, 1988).

While numerous studies have analyzed the effects that tightened alcohol regulations have on deleterious conditions, few studies have looked at the impact of modern alcohol prohibition on alcohol-related behaviors and conditions. Currently, 15 states have local jurisdictions that prohibit the public sale of beverage alcohol. The proportion of dry population in these 15 states ranges from less than 1 percent of the population of Nebraska to over 40 percent of the population in Arkansas and Kentucky (Distilled Spirits Industry, 1983).

*Direct all correspondence to Russell Winn, Department of Government, Box 3BN, New Mexico State University, Las Cruces, NM 88003.

SOCIAL SCIENCE QUARTERLY, Volume 74, Number 4, December 1993
© 1993 by the University of Texas Press

FIRST PAGE OF ARTICLE

Title of article

Author's name

Abstract

Publication information

Boggs, A. M. (2009). Ontario's university tuition framework: A history and current policy issues. *Canadian Journal of Higher Education, 39,* 73–87.

1. Author's name
- The author's last name comes first, followed by the author's initials.
- Join two authors' names with a comma and an ampersand.

2. Date of publication
- Give the year the work was published in parentheses.
- Most popular magazines are paginated per issue. They might have a volume number, but are more often referenced by the season or date of publication.

3. Title of article
- Do not use quotation marks.
- If there is a book title in the article title, italicize it.
- The first word of the title, the first word of the subtitle, and any proper nouns in the title are capitalized.

4. Publication information
Name of journal
- Italicize the journal name.
- All nouns, verbs, and pronouns, and the first word of the title are capitalized.
- Do not capitalize any article, preposition, or coordinating conjunction unless it is the first word of the title or subtitle.
- Put a comma after the journal name.
- Italicize the volume number and follow it with a comma.

Volume, issue, and page numbers
- See sample references 21 and 22 on p. 572 for more on different types of pagination.

Sample references for print periodical sources

18. Article by one author	Kellogg, R. T. (2001). Competition for working memory among writing processes. *American Journal of Psychology, 114,* 175–192.
19. Article by multiple authors	Write out all of the authors' names, up to seven authors. For eight or more authors, write out the first six names, insert an ellipsis mark, and finish with the final author's name.
	Blades, J., & Rowe-Finkbeiner, K. (2006). The motherhood manifesto. *The Nation, 282*(20), 11–16.
20. Article by a group or organization	National Organization for Women. (2002). Where to find feminists in Austin. *The NOW guide for Austin women.* Austin, TX: Chapter Press.
21. Article in a journal with continuous pagination	Include only the volume number and the year, not the issue number.
	Engen, R., & Steen, S. (2000). The power to punish: Discretion and sentencing reform in the war on drugs. *American Journal of Sociology, 105,* 1357–1395.
22. Article in a journal paginated by issue	List the issue number in parentheses (not italicized) after the volume number. For a popular magazine that does not commonly use volume numbers, use the season or date of publication.
	McGinn, D. (2006, June 5). Marriage by the numbers. *Newsweek,* 40–48.
23. Monthly publications	Barlow, J. P. (1998, January). Africa rising: Everything you know about Africa is wrong. *Wired,* 142–158.
24. Newspaper article	Hagenbaugh, B. (2005, April 25). Grads welcome an uptick in hiring. *USA Today,* p. A1.

Electronic sources in APA-style references list

Title of Web page

Author's name

Websites are often made up of many separate pages or articles. Each page or article on a website may or may not have a title. If you are citing a page or article that has a title, treat the title like an article in a periodical. No retrieval date is needed unless the material may change over time.

> Fidler, D. P. (2004, April). *World Health Organization's international health regulations.* Retrieved from the American Society of International Law website: http://www.asil.org/insights/insigh132.htm

When no author is given, begin the citation with the title of the document first. Use (n.d.) If a publication date is not given.

> *Webcasting for rookies.* (n.d.). Retrieved http://www.tvworldwide/globe_show/iwa/040305

If there is no title for the website, list it by author or creator. If it is an informally published or self-archived work, cite it as follows:

> McDermott, John. (n.d.). *John McDermott tenor.* Retrieved from http://wwwjohnmcdermott.com/?m=3

De Leon-Gan, O. (2008–2010). *The cheap girl.* Retrieved November 11, 2009, from http://www.thecheapgirl.com/

1. Author's name, associated institution, or organization

- Authorship is sometimes hard to determine for online sources. If you do have an author or creator to cite, follow the rules for periodicals and books.
- If the only authority you find is a group or organization, list its name as the author.
- If the author or organization is not identified, begin the reference with the title of the document.

2. Dates

- List the date the site was produced or last revised (sometimes this is the copyright date) after the author. This date might be simply a year.
- If the information is likely to change (such as a wiki), list the date you accessed the site. Place this second date just before the URL, preceded by the word *Retrieved* and followed by a comma and the word *from*. Note that the month comes before the day and year. The day and year are separated by a comma.

3. Name of site and title of page or article

- Websites are often made up of many separate pages or articles. Each page or article on a website may or may not have a title. If you are citing a page or article that has a title, treat the title like an article in a periodical. Otherwise, treat the name of the website itself as you would a book.
- The name of a website will usually be found on its index or home page. If you cannot find a link back to the home page, look at the address for clues. You can work your way backward through the URL, deleting sections (separated by slashes) until you come to a home or index page.
- If there is no title for the website, list it by author or creator.

4. URL

- Copy the address exactly as it appears in your browser window. You can even copy and paste the address into your text for greater accuracy.
- Note that there are no angle brackets around the URL and no period after it.

Sample references for electronic sources

25. Journal article with Digital Object Identifier (DOI)

Some electronic content is assigned a unique number called a Digital Object Identifier (DOI). If a DOI is provided for an article, include it after the page number(s) of the article as **doi:doi number** (no spaces, and no period after it).

> Baruch, J. J. (2008). Combating global warming while enhancing the future. *Technology in Society, 30*(2), 111–121. doi: 10 .1016/j.techsoc.2007.12.008

26. Online journal article without Digital Object Identifier.

If no DOI number is assigned and the article was retrieved online, give the URL of the journal home page, even if the article was retrieved from a database.

> Elliot, A. (2003). Government faces pressure to tackle obesity. *British Medical Journal, 327*(7424), 1125. Retrieved from http://www.bmj.com

27. Online newspaper article

> Mitchell, A. (2007, August 16). A precautionary charge. *The Globe and Mail*, p. A14. Retrieved from http://theglobeandmail.com

28. Online magazine article

> Nicklen, P. (2007, June). Vanishing sea ice: Life at the edge. *National Geographic, 211*, 32–55. Retrieved from http://ngm.nationalgeographic.com/2007/06/vanishing-sea-ice/sea-ice-text.html

29. Article or document from an online reference work

> Lennox, J. (2010). Darwinism. In E. N. Zalta (Ed.), *The Stanford encyclopedia of philosophy* (Spring 2010 ed.) Retrieved from http://plato.stanford.edu/archive/spr2010/entries/darwinism

30. Online book (ebook)

> Immon, W. H., Imhoff, C., & Sousa, R. (2001). *Corporate information factory.* New York, NY: Wiley. Retrieved from http://www.ebooks.com/ebooks/book_display.asp?IID=117479

Other sources in APA-style references list

31. Television broadcast

Miller, W. (Producer/Director). (2006, January 4). *Encounters with Jack: Life and times of Jack Turner* [Television broadcast]. Toronto: CBC.

32. Videos and DVDs

Kaurismaki, A. (Director). (1999). *Leningrad cowboys go America* [Motion picture]. United States: MGM.

33. Presentation slides (PowerPoint)

Kunka, J. L. (n.d.). *Conquering the comma* [PowerPoint slides]. Retrieved from Purdue University Writing Lab website: http://owl.english.purdue.edu/Workshops/pp/index.html# presentations

APA reports of research

Reports of experimental research follow a specific organization in APA style, with a title page and an abstract that gives a brief summary of the contents and four distinct sections—introduction, method, results, and discussion—followed by the list of references. This organization allows other researchers to identify information quickly.

- **The introduction** identifies the problem, reviews previous research, and states the hypothesis that was tested.

- The **methods** section describes how the experiment was conducted and how the participants were selected.

- The **results** section reports the findings of the study. This section often includes tables and figures that provide statistical results and tests of statistical significance. Tests of statistical significance are critical for experimental research because they give the probability that the results could have occurred by chance.

- The **discussion** section interprets the findings and often refers to previous research.

Sample APA paper

A common type of APA paper is the review of research. Research reports in APA style have abstracts; reviews of research often do not have abstracts. This review of research, commissioned by the Women's Sports Foundation (www.WomensSportsFoundation.org), is an executive summary of a long report that examines physical activity and sport as solutions for many of the serious health and social problems faced by American girls.

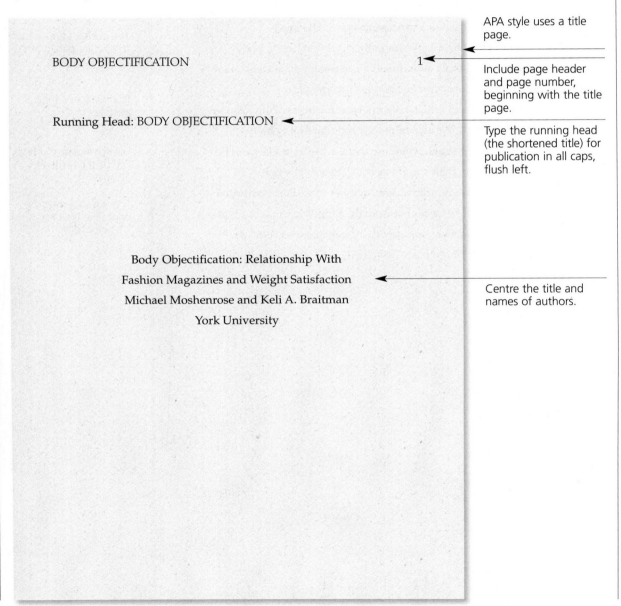

BODY OBJECTIFICATION   1

Running Head: BODY OBJECTIFICATION

Body Objectification: Relationship With
Fashion Magazines and Weight Satisfaction
Michael Moshenrose and Keli A. Braitman
York University

APA style uses a title page.

Include page header and page number, beginning with the title page.

Type the running head (the shortened title) for publication in all caps, flush left.

Centre the title and names of authors.

BODY OBJECTIFICATION 2

Abstract

This study examined the relationship between objectified body consciousness and the utilization of fashion magazines for information about fashion and beauty, comparison to models, and weight satisfaction. Participants were 180 female undergraduate students. We hypothesized that highly body-conscious individuals would read more fashion magazines than low body-conscious women and also rate magazine advertisements and articles as important for influencing fashion and beauty ideals. We also hypothesized that highly body-conscious women would compare themselves to models and be less satisfied with their weight as compared to low body-conscious women. A multivariate analysis of variance indicated that significant differences between the groups existed, but that group differences were opposite to hypotheses. Possible explanations for findings are discussed.

Use the running head at the top of the page on the left-hand side in capital letters. The page number goes at the top right.

The abstract appears on a separate page with the title *Abstract*.

Double-space the abstract.

Do not indent the first line of the abstract.

The abstract must be brief. The limit is 120 words.

Body Objectification: Relationship with Fashion
Magazines and Weight Satisfaction

Introduction

The cultural preoccupation with physical beauty has generated much research regarding how a woman's perception of her body contributes to negative body esteem. Feminist theorists argue that the female body is often treated as an object to be looked at. This objectification causes women to perceive their bodies as detached observers, which means they are attempting to see themselves as others see them. An internalization of the cultural body standards results in women believing that they created these standards and can achieve them. Therefore, objectified body consciousness (OBC) refers to perceiving the body as an object and the beliefs that sustain this perception (McKinley, 1995). McKinley and Hyde (1996) developed the 24-item instrument to assess OBC, and the three scale facets are body surveillance, control beliefs, and body shame. In order to conform to cultural body standards, women engage in self-surveillance to avoid negative evaluations (McKinley & Hyde, 1996). Thus, women are constantly seeing themselves as others see them, and this act of mental disassociation can have negative consequences for women.

The next aspect of OBC is that internalizing cultural body standards can cause women to experience intense shame (McKinley & Hyde, 1996). Because the cultural ideal of a "perfect" body is excessively thin, most women are unable to achieve that standard. Consequently, many women experience a discrepancy between their actual bodies and their ideal bodies (Noll & Fredrickson, 1998). Any comparisons that women make

Give the full title at the beginning of the body of the report.

Centre the heading *Introduction*.

Specify 2.5 cm margins.

Include the date in parentheses when you mention authors in the text.

Include authors and date in parentheses when you do not mention authors in the text.

between the ultra-thin standard and their bodies will produce body shame.

The final component of OBC is control beliefs, which assert that women are responsible for their physical characteristics and can alter their appearance to conform to cultural standards (McKinley & Hyde, 1996). However, women must first be convinced that they are responsible for how they look in order to accept attractiveness as a reasonable standard by which to judge themselves. When women perceive the attainment of the cultural body standards as a choice, they are more likely to believe that appearance can be controlled (McKinley & Hyde, 1996).

Related to the concept of self-objectification is exposure to appearance-related information via fashion and beauty magazines. Levine, Smolak, and Hayden (1994), for example, found that fashion magazines were instrumental in providing motivation and guidance for women striving to mirror the thin-ideal. Further, nearly half of the respondents in a sample of middle school girls indicated that they read fashion magazines frequently, and that the magazines were moderately important sources of information about beauty (Levine et al., 1994).

Given that fashion magazines are seen as sources of information about beauty ideals, it seems likely that women scoring high on objectified body consciousness would be more likely to utilize fashion magazines for these purposes. The objective of this study was to examine the relationship between objectified body consciousness and attitudes and behaviours regarding fashion magazines. Specifically, we hypothesized that women scoring high on the OBC scale were more likely to read fashion magazines and to rate both magazine articles and

Indent each paragraph five to seven spaces (1.25 cm] on the ruler in the word processing program).

advertisements as important in influencing their fashion and beauty ideals. Further, we hypothesized that highly body-conscious individuals would compare themselves to fashion models and be less satisfied with their bodies in comparison to women who were low on body consciousness.

Methods

Participants

Participants were 180 Caucasian females from undergraduate psychology classes. However, only the data from participants scoring above the median on all three OBC scales or below the median on all OBC scales were analyzed. Thus, data from only 56 participants were analyzed. The mean age of the participants was 19.0 (SD = 1.33). Participants were recruited through general psychology classes and received partial course credit for participation.

Instruments

Instruments were administered to measure (1) the extent to which an individual reads or is exposed to fashion magazines, (2) the importance of magazine *advertisements* in influencing fashion and beauty ideals, (3) the importance of magazine *articles* in influencing fashion and beauty ideals, (4) the extent to which an individual compares herself to fashion magazines on a variety of domains such as happiness and physical appearance, and (5) weight satisfaction.

To measure the magazine-related factors, a media questionnaire was created through a synthesis and modification of Levine et al.'s (1994) Media Questionnaire and Strowman's (1996) Media Exposure and Comparison to Models survey. The first 15 items of the instrument comprised the Exposure subscale. Participants were asked to rate how often they view a variety of listed magazines. Although the focus of the study explored exposure to fashion magazines, non-fashion magazines were also included in the list to make the focus of the study less apparent. A subscale score indicating exposure to fashion magazines was obtained by summing responses to each fashion magazine item, with a high score indicating higher exposure to fashion magazines.

The next 16 items of the instrument comprised the magazine information subscales. The first six of these items assessed the importance of magazine advertisements for providing information about beauty and fashion, and the remaining 10 items assessed the importance of magazine articles for the same purpose. Eight additional items comprised the Comparison to Models subscale, which assessed the extent to which participants compare themselves to models.

To assess weight satisfaction, we employed the Weight Satisfaction subscale of the Body Esteem Scale (Franzoi & Shields, 1984). The entire instrument was administered, but only scores for weight satisfaction were included in the analysis. Subscale scores were obtained by summing items for the weight satisfaction scale.

A demographics survey was included at the end of the questionnaire. This survey contained items assessing such characteristics as age, race, height, weight, and exercise habits. Based on self-reported height and weight, the body mass of each participant was calculated using the following formula: Weight $(kg)/Height^2$ (m^2).

Procedure

Participants were solicited from general psychology courses and were tested in small groups ranging in size from 1 to 10. The participants were provided with a packet marked only with an identification number. They were instructed to remove the informed consent form from the packet and read along with the experimenter as she read the informed consent aloud. The participants were told that the project was examining the effects of marketing on post-secondary school students. Participants agreeing to participate then removed the scantrons and seven-page questionnaire from the packets and began working. Without a time limit being imposed, participants completed the questionnaire and were then presented with a debriefing form describing the true nature of the experiment. Participants were encouraged to contact the researcher if they had any additional questions about the research project.

To identify participants who were either high or low scorers on objectified body consciousness, a median split was conducted for all OBC scales. Participants scoring above the median on all three scales were identified as high on objectified body consciousness, and those scoring below the median on all three OBC scales were identified as low on objectified body consciousness. We then conducted both multivariate and univariate analyses of variance.

Results

Table 1 presents the mean exposure score for each fashion magazine, and Table 2 presents the means, standard deviations, and F-values of the dependent variables for the high and low objectified body consciousness groups.

BODY OBJECTIFICATION   8

Table 1

Means and Standard Deviations for Magazines Included in the Media Exposure Scale

Magazine	Mean	SD
Seventeen	2.93	1.35
Cosmopolitan	2.93	1.17
Glamour	2.79	1.17
YM	2.57	1.26
Vogue	2.55	1.06
Mademoiselle	2.45	1.22
Newsweek	2.32	1.25
National Geographic	2.27	1.05
Reader's Digest	2.13	1.13
Marie Claire	1.93	1.25
Self	1.84	1.04
Better Homes and Gardens	1.80	0.88
In Style	1.80	1.00
Elle	1.67	0.97
Redbook	1.64	0.97
Shape	1.63	0.97
Fitness Magazine	1.54	0.97
US News & World Report	1.52	0.83
Model	1.39	0.78
Vanity Fair	1.23	0.66
Playboy	1.18	0.51

Note. 5-point scale: 1 = never look at it; 2 = look through it rarely; 3 = glance through it sometimes; 4 = look through it often; 5 = look through every new issue

Number tables and figures. Give each table and figure a descriptive title. Begin the title flush left and italicize it.

Double-space notes to tables.

Table 2

Means and Standard Deviations for the Objectified Body Consciousness Groups

| | Objectified Body Consciousness | | | | |
| | Low (n 5 25) | | High (n 5 31) | | |
Dependent Variable	M	SD	M	SD	F (1, 53)
Fashion Magazines	30.12	15.40	20.65	13.67	5.26
Magazine Advertisements	18.16	4.67	12.84	4.06	19.59***
Magazine Articles	3.24	7.37	21.90	6.14	37.55***
Comparison to Models	21.72	4.84	14.13	5.85	25.82**
Weight Satisfaction	19.36	5.82	26.16	7.65	12.08**

Asterisks are normally used for notes of statistical probability.

Note. **$p < .01$, ***$p < .001$.

Multivariate analyses of variance indicated that the two groups differed significantly on their mean profiles based on the five fashion magazine and weight satisfaction measures (Wilks' Lambda = .45, F [5, 49] = 12.01, $p < .001$; effect size = .55). Follow-up univariate tests indicated that these groups differed significantly with respect to the importance placed on both magazine advertisements and articles for obtaining information about beauty and fashion, with low objectifiers placing more importance on these items. Low objectifiers were also more likely to compare themselves to fashion models and were less satisfied with their weight than were high objectifiers. Furthermore, low objectifiers also looked at fashion magazines more frequently than did high objectifiers, but this difference was not statistically significant despite the relatively large mean difference between the groups.

Discussion

In contrast to our hypotheses, low objectifiers (1) were more influenced by magazine advertisements and articles than were high objectifiers, (2) were more likely to compare themselves to models, and (3) were less satisfied with their weight. Because our findings counter certain aspects of what the objectification theory predicts, there may be several reasons why this theory was not supported. First, it is assumed that women compare themselves to a cultural beauty ideal when they engage in self-objectification. The question then becomes: How are women exposed to the cultural ideal? In our study, we assumed that women obtain information about the cultural ideal from fashion magazines. The difficulty with this proposition is that the women in our study were not frequently exposed to fashion magazines. Table 1 shows that the highest mean frequency of exposure to any magazine was 2.93, for both *Seventeen* and *Cosmopolitan*. This frequency approached the level of women "glancing through it sometimes." Because of a lack of exposure to fashion magazines, women may not be influenced by the cultural ideals of beauty presented within their pages. Consequently, women may be procuring information regarding cultural standards from alternative media sources, such as television, films, and the internet. Future research may address the influence of these media sources in regard to their impact on women's self-perception.

Another possibility is that women may be making lateral comparisons to members of their peer group as opposed to making upward comparisons to models. According to the social comparison theory, individuals can make upward, lateral, or downward comparisons. It may be that women may accept the fact that they can never achieve the standard of beauty portrayed by the media. Hence, they may decide that the only salient standard for them to achieve is to look as good as their peers. In addition, women may experience intense stress by believing they must conform to a certain standard of appearance; thus, they may make downward social comparisons to regain self-esteem. These women may compare themselves to others whom they consider to be unattractive in order to feel better about themselves.

Although some women may make downward social comparisons, other women who rate highly on body consciousness may decide to invest more resources in their appearance. Because they are concerned with and aware of their appearance, these women may actively engage in activities that help to improve their appearance. According to the preceding logic, high objectifiers would then be more satisfied with their weight than low objectifiers. In support of this idea, Smith, Thompson, Raczynski, and Hilner (1999) found that physical appearance is more important to African-American women and men than to Caucasian women and men, but also that African Americans are more satisfied with their appearance compared to their Caucasian counterparts. Thus, these results support the idea that the more individuals value and invest in their physical characteristics, the more satisfied they will be with their appearance.

The generality of our study is limited by the use of a Caucasian, female, post-secondary school-age sample. However, this sample is appropriate to study because research examining the influence of ethnicity on body satisfaction has found that Caucasian women tend to be less satisfied with their appearance compared to Black and Asian-Canadian women (Akan & Grilo, 1995; Altabe, 1998; Cash & Henry, 1995). In addition to ethnicity, men and women also tend to differ in body image, with women

BODY OBJECTIFICATION 12

being less satisfied with their appearance than men (Mintz & Betz, 1986; Serdula et al., 1993). Thus, both sex and race differences exist in regard to body image, and these factors should therefore be considered when conducting body-image studies. For this reason, the findings of the present study should be generalized only to Caucasian females. Future studies may explore whether the findings from this study are replicated in samples of individuals of different ethnicity and sex. However, the questions in the instruments may need to be slightly modified to be appropriate with a male sample. For example, the fashion magazines included in the exposure subscale may not be the same magazines that would be appropriate for males. In particular, magazines such as *Seventeen* and *Glamour* may need to be replaced by magazines marketed to men and focusing on the male physique, such as weight-lifting or fitness magazines.

BODY OBJECTIFICATION 13

References

Akan, G. E. & Grilo, C. M. (1995). Sociocultural influences on eating attitudes and behaviors, body image, and psychological functioning: A comparison of African-American, Asian-American, and Caucasian college women. *International Journal of Eating Disorders, 18*(2), 181–87. Retrieved from http://www3. interscience.wiley.com/journal/34698/home

Altabe, M. N. (1998). Ethnicity and body image: Quantitative and qualitative analysis. *International Journal of Eating Disorders, 23*(2), 153–159. doi:10.1002/(SICI)1098-108X(199803)23:2<153::AID-EAT5>3.0.CO;2-J

Centre "References" heading.

Alphabetize entries by last name of the author.

When DOI is not available, find and include the homepage URL of the journal (or newspaper, magazine, etc.) or of the publisher.

BODY OBJECTIFICATION   14

Cash, T. F., & Henry, P. E. (1995). Women's body images: The
    results of a national survey in the U.S.A. *Sex Roles, 33*(1–2),
    19–28. doi:10.1007/BF01547933

Franzoi, S. L., & Shields, S. A. (1984). The Body Esteem Scale:
    Multidimensional structure and sex differences in a college
    population. *Journal of Personality Assessment, 48*(2), 173–178.

Levine, M. P., Smolak, L., & Hayden, H. (1994). The relation of
    sociocultural factors to eating attitudes and behaviors
    among middle school girls. *Journal of Early Adolescence, 14,*
    471–490. doi:10.1177/0272431694014004004

McKinley, N. M. (1995). Women and objectified body
    consciousness: A feminist psychological analysis.
    Dissertation Abstracts International, 56, 05B.
    (UMI No. 9527111)

Mintz, L. B., & Betz, N. E. (1986). Sex differences in the nature,
    realism, and correlates of body image. *Sex Roles, 15*(3/4),
    185–195. doi:10/1007/BF00287483

Noll, S. M., & Fredrickson, B. L. (1998). A mediational model
    linking self-objectification, body shame, and disordered
    eating. *Psychology of Women Quarterly, 22*(4), 623–636.
    doi:10.1111/j.1471-6402.1998.tb00181.x

Serdula, M. K., Collins, M. E., Williamson, D. F., Anda, R. F.,
    Pamuk, E., & Byers, T. E. (1993). Weight control practices of
    U.S. adolescents and adults. *Annals of Internal Medicine,*
    119(7), 667–671.

Smith, D. E., Thompson, J. K., Raczynski, J. M., & Hilner, J. (1999).
    Body image among men and women in a biracial cohort: The
    CARDIA Study. *International Journal of Eating Disorders, 25*(1),
    71–82.

Strowman, S. R. (1996). *Media exposure survey.* Unpublished
    manuscript, University of New Hampshire, Durham.

Double-space all entries.

Indent all but the first line of each entry five spaces.

Go through your text and make sure that everything you have cited, except for personal communication, is in the list of references.

Part 4

The Writer as Editor

22

Writing Effective Paragraphs

Paragraphs serve to order and develop a writer's ideas. Well-organized paragraphs follow a pattern similar to that of a well-organized paper, but in miniature.

Develop paragraphs

Readers expect paragraphs in essays to be developed.

This paragraph gives the main ideas but with no examples. The writing is abstract and limp.

THIN

> We now live in a global economy where all countries are connected. When something happens to the economy in one country, it affects others. Many factories have moved to developing nations, and the economic activity in advanced nations focuses more on concept development and marketing.

Developed paragraphs often include examples that illustrate main points. Key ideas are emphasized in vivid sentences.

DEVELOPED

> We now live in a global economy, where over a trillion dollars is exchanged in currency markets daily and where a burp in Malaysia can tumble stock exchanges in the West. The creation of wealth has moved from production in fortress-like factories to global networks of management and distribution, where, when you buy a product at your local WalMart or Costco, the purchase data is sent not only to the corporation but also to the manufacturer of that product. Tomorrow's production in distant developing nations is determined by what is purchased today in Canada and other affluent nations. In the fast and light capitalism of the new economy, how and where goods are produced has become relatively unimportant compared to creating new concepts and marketing those concepts.

CHECKLIST

In revising, focus on each paragraph—one at a time. For each one, ask yourself what your reader will notice and remember.

- Is the main point fully developed?
- Does the paragraph include examples?
- Are key ideas emphasized in vivid sentences?

Pay attention to paragraph length

Paragraphs in brochures, narrow columns, and on the screen

DENSE

Long paragraphs are often hard to read in narrow-column formats or on the screen. Look for ways to divide long paragraphs in these formats.

The well-developed paragraph suited for essays does not work as well in a narrow-column format. Often you can make a dense paragraph more readable by inserting paragraph breaks.

If music is a universal language, Venezuelan children and teenagers speak with rare fluency, thanks to an amazingly successful training program that deserves emulation in Canada. More than one million young people, many from poverty-stricken and violence-wracked barrios, have received free musical instruction since 1975 under what's called simply El Sistema (The System). The result has been an extraordinary flowering of exceptional musicians. Even more important, it has also given thousands of vulnerable young people an alternative to a life of gangs, guns, and crime. Today in our city, José Antonio Abreu, the economist and amateur musician who founded El Sistema more than 30 years ago, will receive an award from the Toronto-based Glenn Gould Foundation. Sometimes called "the Nobel Prize of music," the Glenn Gould Prize comes with $50 000. But instead of taking the cash, Abreu has parlayed it into $150 000 worth of musical instruments for his program. Canadians will benefit, too. Gustavo Dudamel, a product of El Sistema who is considered one of the world's great conductors, is to conduct the 200-member Simon Bolivar Youth Orchestra in a gala concert here tonight. There will also be a series of smaller performances at local schools and community centres, finishing with a massive concert of school bands at the Rogers Centre. The goal of these appearances, and an accompanying symposium on El Sistema, is to spark interest in setting up a similar program here. Musical training is already being used to help turn around young lives in Toronto, notably at the Regent Park School of Music. But the breadth, scale, and success of El Sistema is unmatched anywhere in the world. It is a model well-worth studying.

LIGHT

Essays rarely contain one-sentence paragraphs, but newspapers and websites often format long sentences as paragraphs.

If music is a universal language, Venezuelan children and teenagers speak with rare fluency, thanks to an amazingly successful training program that deserves emulation in Canada. More than one million young people, many from poverty-stricken and violence-wracked barrios, have received free musical instruction since 1975 under what's called simply El Sistema (The System).

The result has been an extraordinary flowering of exceptional musicians. Even more important, it has also given thousands of vulnerable young people an alternative to a life of gangs, guns, and crime.

Today in our city, José Antonio Abreu, the economist and amateur musician who founded El Sistema more than 30 years ago, will receive an award from the Toronto-based Glenn Gould Foundation. Sometimes called "the Nobel Prize of music," the Glenn Gould Prize comes with $50 000. But instead of taking the cash, Abreu has parlayed it into $150 000 worth of musical instruments for his program.

Canadians will benefit, too. Gustavo Dudamel, a product of El Sistema who is considered one of the world's great conductors, is to conduct the 200-member Simon Bolivar Youth Orchestra in a gala concert here tonight. There will also be a series of smaller performances at local schools and community centres, finishing with a massive concert of school bands at the Rogers Centre. The goal of these appearances, and an accompanying symposium on El Sistema, is to spark interest in setting up a similar program here.

Musical training is already being used to help turn around young lives in Toronto, notably at the Regent Park School of Music. But the breadth, scale, and success of El Sistema is unmatched anywhere in the world. It is a model well-worth studying.

CHECKLIST

Evaluate your paragraphs from a reader's perspective, with your purpose and format in mind.

- Divide paragraphs if you find long stretches of text without breaks.
- If you find too many short paragraphs, develop or combine them.

Link within and across paragraphs

Paragraphs that don't flow make readers struggle to understand how sentences relate to one another. Flow is achieved by making your sentences fit together and by using transitions to guide readers.

Repeat key terms and phrases

Repeated key terms and phrases within a paragraph help readers to trace major ideas. In this paragraph, the writer refers back to two central terms, *grass roots activism* and *battleground.*

The Web has become the primary medium for **grass roots activism**. Among thousands of websites created by individuals are many pages devoted to media criticism and parodies of advertising. **This activism** has come at a time when the Internet has become the **battleground** for the deregulated corporate giants. On **this battleground,** control of the coaxial cable and fibre optic conduits represents only a small part of the potential fortunes to be made from an array of services carried through the pipe.

Write strong transitions

Transitions at the beginnings and ends of paragraphs guide readers. They explain why a paragraph follows from the previous one. They offer writers the opportunity to highlight the turns in their thinking.

The first paragraph introduces the metaphor of the "Information Superhighway" and connects the metaphor to the American myth of the frontier.

The second paragraph begins with the frontier and examines how roads are also tied to ideas of a free-market economy.

The third paragraph repeats the "Information Superhighway" metaphor and shows how it embodies a vision of a new economy on the Internet.

The metaphor of the "Information Superhighway," popularized by Albert Gore in the 1990s, sprang from a long-standing American myth about the freedom of **the open road**. Throughout the twentieth century, the automobile represented freedom of action—not just the pleasures of driving around aimlessly for recreation but the possibility of exploring new territories and reaching **the frontier**. When talking about the Internet, both Republicans and Democrats in the 1990s invoked the idealized highway in the American imagination—**the highway** that leads to **the frontier.**

Exploration of the **frontier** is linked to democracy in this rhetoric. From Thomas Jefferson onward, American leaders have maintained that **good roads** are a prerequisite to democracy. By the end of the last century, **good roads** were the people's answer to the hated railroad monopolies depicted by Frank Norris in *The Octopus*. With **good roads** farmers could transport their crops directly to local markets and competitive railheads. When the Interstate system was proposed, it was advanced as a means of connecting the nation, stimulating the economy, and eliminating poverty in Appalachia and other regions that lacked **good roads**.

The "Information Superhighway" metaphor thus associated the economic prosperity of the 1950s and 1960s facilitated by new highways with the potential for vast amounts of commerce to be conducted over the Internet.

CHECKLIST

Be aware of transitions in your writing. Ask yourself why one main idea leads into the next. The answer to these questions can become your transition.

- What step or shift takes place between paragraphs?
- How does this step or shift fit into the overall development of the piece?

Start fast

Often you have but a few seconds to convince a reader to keep reading what you've written. Make those few seconds count.

Titles

Vague titles give no motivation for wanting to read.

VAGUE

Good and Bad Fats

Specific titles are like a tasty appetizer; if you like the appetizer, you'll probably like the main course.

SPECIFIC

The Secret Killer: Hydrogenated Fats

Opening paragraphs

The topic has potential and the paragraph is informative, but the writer gives no reason for starting with the molecular content of fatty acids.

BLAND

Essential fatty acids are the foundation of most functions of our bodies. They allow brain cells to function, hormones to act, cell walls to absorb nutrients, the digestive track to operate, and blood to transmit oxygen. A fatty acid molecule consists of a chain of double-bonded carbon atoms with hydrogen atoms attached. In natural unsaturated fatty acids, hydrogen atoms are on the same side of the carbon bond. In trans fatty acids the two hydrogen atoms are on opposite sides of the double bond. Food manufacturers create trans fatty acids by hydrogenating oils to improve the taste of food. Clinical tests have shown that trans fatty acids increase the level of LDL "bad" cholesterol and lower HDL "good" cholesterol.

Cut to the chase. If you want to alert readers to the dangers of partially hydrogenated oils, start with the threat, then move on to the technical explanation.

ENGAGING

Canadians today are more health conscious than ever before, yet most are unaware that they may be ingesting high levels of dangerous fat in the form of partially hydrogenated oils. Hydrogenation is the process of passing hydrogen bubbles through heated oil, which makes the oil taste like butter. Nearly all processed food contains some level of hydrogenated oils. The food tastes good, but the oil it contains will make you fat and can eventually kill you.

Cut out empty phrases and sentences

Writers often start a draft with empty phrases and sentences, much as speakers clear their throats before starting.

~~In our modern world of today,~~ the potent combination of digital and satellite technologies has brought a deluge of information to affluent people in affluent nations.

~~Canadians have seen many new digital technologies in just a few years. These technologies are capable of delivering massive amounts of information almost instantly.~~ Unlike the past two centuries, when each new communication technology was celebrated as the means to a glorious future, few but advertisers now claim that more information will lead to a better life. The glut of information that is readily accessible has not led to broader global understanding but instead in the view of many observers has led to increased fragmentation, confusion, and exhaustion.

CHECKLIST

Grab your reader's attention quickly by perfecting your title and opening paragraph. Be sure you provide strong reasons to keep reading.
- Be sure your title is specific enough to indicate both your topic and approach.
- Cut out any empty phrases and sentences that clutter up your opening paragraph.

Conclude with strength

The challenge in ending paragraphs is to leave the reader with something provocative, something beyond pure summary of the previous paragraphs.

Issue a call to action

Although ecological problems in Russia seem distant, students like you and me can help protect the snow leopard by joining the World Wildlife Fund campaign.

Make a recommendation

Russia's creditors would be wise to sign on to the World Wildlife Fund's proposal to relieve some of the country's debt in order to protect snow leopard habitat. After all, if Russia is going to be economically viable, it needs to be ecologically healthy.

Speculate about the future

Unless Nepali and Chinese officials devote more resources to snow leopard preservation, these beautiful animals will be gone in a few years.

Ask rhetorical questions

Generally the larger and more majestic (or better yet, cute) an endangered animal is, the better its chances of being saved. Bumper stickers don't implore us to save blind cave insects; they ask us to save the whales, elephants, and tigers. But snow leopards aren't cave bugs; they are beautiful, impressive animals that should be the easiest of all to protect. If we can't save them, do any endangered species stand a chance?

CHECKLIST

- Be sure that your ending paragraph is more than a summary of your main points.
- Use a strong concluding image or question to leave your readers with something to remember and think about.

Summary for editing paragraphs

Develop paragraphs	In revising, focus on each paragraph one at a time. For each one, ask yourself what your reader will notice and remember. • Is the main point fully developed? • Does the paragraph include examples? • Are key ideas emphasized in vivid sentences?
Pay attention to paragraph length	Evaluate your paragraphs from a reader's perspective, with your purpose and format in mind. • Divide paragraphs if you find long stretches of text without breaks. • If you find too many short paragraphs, develop or combine them.
Link within and across paragraphs	Be aware of transitions in your writing. Ask yourself why one main idea leads into the next. The answer to these questions can become your transition. • What step or shift takes place between paragraphs? • How does this step or shift fit into the overall development of the piece?
Start fast	Grab your reader's attention quickly by perfecting your title and opening paragraph. Be sure you provide strong reasons to keep reading. • Be sure your title is specific enough to indicate both your topic and approach. • Cut out any empty phrases and sentences that clutter up your opening paragraph.
Conclude with strength	• Be sure that your ending paragraph is more than a summary of your main points. • Use a strong concluding image or question to leave your readers with something to remember and think about.

23

Writing Effective Sentences

Sentences are the basic units in writing. Effective sentences bring
energy, clarity, and shape to a writer's ideas.

Understand sentence basics

Subjects and verbs

Except for a class of sentences called imperatives (*Be quiet*), all sentences have a subject (usually a noun or a pronoun) and a verb.

SUBJECT   **VERB**
Antoine **ran** the 4 x 100 relay.

Clauses

Clauses are the grammatical structures that underlie sentences. Each clause has a subject and a predicate, but not all clauses are sentences.

Subject-Verb-Object

On the predicate side of a clause is a main verb and often a direct object that is affected by the action of the verb.

S   V   O
Angela **kicked the ball.**

This basic pattern—called **subject-verb-object**, or **S-V-O**— is one of the most common in English. Verbs that take objects *(kick, revise)* are called **transitive** verbs.

Clauses without Objects

Not all clauses have objects.

S   V
Marshavet **rested**.

This clause pattern is **subject-verb** or **S-V**. Verbs that do not require objects are called intransitive verbs. Many verbs can be both transitive and intransitive.

INTRANSITIVE:
Ginny **runs** fast.

TRANSITIVE:
Ginny **runs** the company.

Linking-Verb Clauses

A third major pattern links the subject to what follows the verb. Most commonly used for this pattern are forms of the verb *to be*.

Tracy Riley **is** the new coach.
The results of the MRI **were** negative.

What follows the verb is either the subject complement *(coach)* or an adjective describing the subject *(negative)*.

Main versus subordinate clauses

Clauses that can stand by themselves as sentences are called **main** or **independent clauses**. Other clauses have the necessary ingredients to count as clauses—a subject and a main verb—yet they are incomplete as sentences.

Where you choose to go to college

Which was the first to be considered

As fast as my legs could pedal

These clauses are examples of **subordinate** or **dependent** clauses. They do not stand by themselves, but rather they must be attached to another clause: *I rode my bike as fast as my legs could pedal.*

Pay attention to verbs

The importance of verbs

A teacher may have once told you that verbs are "action words." Where are the action words in the following paragraph?

Yadda, yadda, yadda. Reading much of prose like this would put you to sleep quickly.

Last week, there was an installation of explosive detonators at the bottom of Lake Loch Ness for the purpose of the removal of Nessie. An appeal was made to local wizards of Scotland by Sir Godfrey of the Nessie Alliance for their assistance in the casting of a spell for the protection of the lake.

The above paragraph is adapted from the movie *Napoleon Dynamite*. When asked for his current event, Napoleon Dynamite responded:

Last week, Japanese scientists **placed** explosive detonators at the bottom of Lake Loch Ness to **blow** Nessie out of the water. Sir Godfrey of the Nessie Alliance **summoned** the help of Scotland's local wizards to **cast** a protective spell over the lake.

Even if Napoleon's current event might not be the one the teacher wants, his reply is lively because he uses verbs that express action: *place, blow, summon, cast.*

Use action verbs

Sentences that rely on forms of *be* verbs (*is, was, were*) often lack energy and direction.

Prime Minister Pierre Elliott Trudeau was in a tough position during the FLQ Crisis.

Think about what the actions in the sentence are and choose powerful verbs that express those actions.

Confronting the controversy, Prime Minister Pierre Elliott Trudeau **invoked** the War Measures Act during the FLQ Crisis.

CHECKLIST

Circle every *is, are, was,* and *were*. Think about the action. Does the verb express the action? Can you think of a better verb?

Jack Black **is** considerably skilled in physical comedy, and his overblown mannerisms **are** wisely downplayed.

Jack Black **excels** in physical comedy, and he wisely **downplays** his overblown mannerisms.

Stay active

Active versus passive

The **passive voice** reverses the order of a sentence, allowing whoever or whatever did the action expressed in the verb to be deleted.

Who misplaced the laptop? It's a mystery.

The laptop containing personal data on 38 000 employees was misplaced. (passive)

Revise passive sentences

Most of the time your goal is not to conceal but to communicate.

Watch for passive sentences and convert them to active voice whenever possible. Listen to the difference:

The pear tree in the front yard **was demolished** by the storm. (passive)

The storm **demolished** the pear tree in the front yard. (active)

Uses of the passive

In some situations, passive voice can be used in academic and workplace writing. Passive sentences are useful when

- you want to keep the focus on the person or thing being acted on,
- you don't know the actor, or
- you and your readers know the actor's identity.

Our January sales **were increased** substantially by our deep discounts.

The focus is on *increased January sales*, not *deep discounts*.

Analog and digital data **are simulated** together before the company commits to the expense of manufacturing.

The process of simulation is the focus, not the unknown people who perform the simulations.

CHECKLIST

Ask who or what is doing the action. If the doer is not the subject, consider rewriting so the doer is the subject.

A request on your part **will be reviewed** by the admissions committee. (passive)

The graduate admissions committee **will review** your request. (active)

Find characters

Focus on people

The **agent** is the person or thing that does the action. Powerful writing puts the agents in sentences.

The use of a MIDI keyboard for playing the song will facilitate capturing it in digital form on our laptop for the subsequent purpose of uploading it to our website.

It sounds dead, doesn't it? Putting people into the sentence makes it come alive:

By playing the song on a MIDI keyboard, **we** can record the digitized sound on our laptop and then upload it to our website.

Including people makes your writing more emphatic. Most readers relate better to people than to abstractions. Putting people in your sentences also introduces active verbs because people do things.

Identifying characters

Even when you are not writing about people, keep the focus on your agents. Read this passage from a report written by an engineer who was asked to recommend which of two types of valves an oil company should purchase for one of its refineries.

Farval valves have two distinct advantages. First, Farval grease valves include a pin indicator that shows whether the valve is working. Alemite valves must be checked by taking them apart. Second, Farval valves have metal seals, while Alemite valves have rubber grommet seals. If an Alemite valve fails, the pressure will force grease past the rubber grommet seals, creating a grease puddle on the floor. By contrast, Farval's metal seals contain the grease if the valve fails.

This engineer not only makes a definite recommendation supported by reasons, she also makes her report easy to read by keeping the focus on the two types of valves she is comparing.

CHECKLIST

Use characters as the subjects of sentences.

Mayoral approval of the recommended zoning change for a strip mall will have a negative impact on the traffic and noise levels of the residential environment.

If the **mayor** approves the recommended zoning change to allow a strip mall, **people who live on Walnut Street** will have to endure much more noise and traffic.

Write concise sentences

Revise wordy sentences

Unnecessary words creep into writing in the form of clutter and wordy phrases. Writers who are unsure of themselves overuse phrases like "in my opinion" or "I think" to qualify their points. Stock phrases plague writing in the media and workplace, where some writers may think that "at this point in time" sounds more impressive than "now." If you find wordy phrases in your own prose, cut them.

The words in **bold** are unnecessary. You can say the same thing with half the words and gain more impact as a result.

In regards to the website, the content is **pretty** successful **in consideration of** the topic. The site is **fairly** good **writing-wise** and is **very** unique in telling you how to adjust the rear derailleur one step at a time.

Writers who impress us most are those who use words efficiently.

The well-written website on bicycle repair provides step-by-step instructions on adjusting your rear derailleur.

Eliminate redundancy

Some words act as modifiers, but when you look closely at them, they repeat the meaning of the word they pretend to modify. Have you heard someone refer to a *personal friend*? Aren't all friends personal? Likewise, you may have heard expressions such as *red in colour, small in size, round in shape*, or *honest truth*. Imagine *red* not referring to colour or *round* not referring to shape.

Intensifiers modify verbs, adjectives, and other adverbs, and they often are overused. *Very* and *totally* are but two of a list of empty intensifiers that usually can be eliminated with no loss of meaning. Other empty intensifiers include *absolutely, awfully, definitely, incredibly, particularly*, and *really*. When you use *very, totally*, or another intensifier before an adjective or adverb, always ask yourself whether there is a more accurate adjective or adverb you could use to express the same thought.

CHECKLIST

Eliminate wordy phrases, redundant modifiers, and empty intensifiers from your sentences.

After much deliberation about Smith's future in football **with regard to** possible permanent injuries, I **came to the conclusion that** it would be **in his best interest** not to continue **his pursuit of** playing football again.

Because Smith risks permanent injury if he plays football again, I decided to release him from the team.

Write ethical sentences

Avoid stereotypes

A stereotype makes an assumption about a group of people by applying a characteristic to all of them based on knowledge of only a few of them. Of course you want to avoid harmful and inaccurate stereotypes, such as *People on welfare are lazy*, or *All Canadians are beer-drinking hockey fanatics*.

More subtle stereotypes, however, may be harder to identify and eliminate. If you want to offer an engineer as an example, will you make the engineer a man? Try to choose examples that go against stereotypes.

Avoid bias

The best way to avoid bias is to write inclusively. Pay attention to the way your language characterizes individuals and groups of people based on their gender, race, ethnicity, sexual orientation, or age. While the conventions of inclusiveness change continually, three guidelines for inclusive language toward all groups remain constant:

- Do not point out people's differences unless those differences are relevant to your argument.
- Call people whatever they prefer to be called.
- When given a choice of terms, choose the more accurate one. (*Vietnamese*, for example, is preferable to *Asian*.)

Don't use masculine nouns and pronouns to refer to both men and women. Eliminate gender bias by using the following tips:

- Don't say *boy* when you mean *child*.
- Use *men and women* or *people* instead of *man*.
- Use *humanity* or *humankind* in place of *mankind*.

CHECKLIST

Avoid stereotypes and biased language by using inclusive and accurate language instead.

Canadian census data examine both **poor, uneducated Blacks** and **rich Orientals**.

Canadian census data examine **the diverse ethnic and socioeconomic groups living in Canada**.

Match structure with ideas

Use parallel structure with parallel ideas

When writers neglect to use parallel structure, the result can be jarring. Reading your writing aloud will help you catch problems in parallelism. Read this sentence aloud:

> At our club meeting we identified problems in **finding** new members, **publicizing** our activities, and **maintenance** of our website.

> The end of the sentence does not sound right because the parallel structure is broken. We expect to find another verb + *ing* following *finding* and *publicizing*. Instead, we run into *maintenance*, a noun. The problem is easy to fix: Change the noun to the *-ing* verb form.

> At our club meeting we identified problems in finding new members, publicizing our activities, and **maintaining** our website.

Use parallel structure with lists

Lists are an effective way of presenting a series of items at the same level of importance. The effectiveness of a list is lost, however, if the items are not in parallel form. For example, in a bullet list of action items, such as a list of goals, beginning each item with a verb emphasizes the action.

> **Sailing Club goals**
> - **Increase** membership by 50% this year
> - **Offer** beginning and advanced classes
> - **Organize** spring banquet
> - **Publicize** all major events

CHECKLIST

Match grammatical elements to provide strong parallelism in sentences with parallel ideas or lists.

Purchasing the undeveloped land **not only** gives us a new park **but also** is something that our children will benefit from in the future. (awkward)

Purchasing the undeveloped land **not only** will give our city a new park **but also** will leave our children a lasting inheritance. (parallel)

Summary for editing sentences

Pay attention to verbs	Circle every *is, are, was,* and *were*. Think about the action. Does the verb express the action? Can you think of a better verb?
Stay active	Ask who or what is doing the action. If the doer is not the subject, consider rewriting so the doer is the subject.
Find characters	Use characters as the subjects of sentences.
Write concise sentences	Eliminate wordy phrases, redundant modifiers, and empty intensifiers from your sentences.
Write ethical sentences	Avoid stereotypes and biased language by using inclusive and accurate language instead.
Match structure with ideas	Match grammatical elements to provide strong parallelism in sentences with parallel ideas or lists.

24
Avoiding Errors

Most common errors in writing can easily be corrected once they are spotted. Learning to recognize and identify these errors is the key to avoiding them.

Fix fragments

Fragments are incomplete sentences. They are punctuated to look like sentences, but they lack a key element—often a subject or a verb—or else are a subordinate clause or phrase. Remember that every sentence must have a subject and a complete verb, and that a subordinate clause cannot stand alone as a sentence. Ask these questions when you are checking for sentence fragments.

Does the sentence have a subject? Except for commands, sentences need subjects.

Jane spent every cent of credit she had available. **And then applied for more cards.**

Does the sentence have a complete verb? Sentences require complete verbs. Verbs that end in *-ing* must have an auxiliary verb to be complete.

Ralph keeps changing majors. **He trying to figure out what he really wants to do after college.**

If the sentence begins with a subordinate clause, is there a main clause in the same sentence?

Even though Vancouver is known for its rainy climate, many people consider it one of Canada's most beautiful cities. **Which is one reason people continue to move there.**

CHECKLIST

When revising, use these basic strategies for turning fragments into sentences.

- **Incorporate the fragment into an adjoining sentence**

  INCORRECT
  I was hooked on the **game. Playing** day and night.

  CORRECT
  I was hooked on the **game, playing** day and night.

- **Add the missing element.** If you cannot incorporate a fragment into another sentence, add the missing element.

  INCORRECT
  When aiming for the highest returns, **and** also **thinking** about the possible losses.

  CORRECT
  When aiming for the highest returns, **investors** also **should think** about possible losses.

Fix run-on sentences

Run-ons jam together two or more sentences, failing to separate them with appropriate punctuation.

The problem is that the two main clauses are not separated by punctuation. The reader must look carefully to determine where one main clause stops and the next one begins.

A period should be placed after *was*, and the next sentence should begin with a capital letter.

I do not recall what kind of printer it was all I remember is that it could sort, staple, and print a packet at the same time.

I do not recall what kind of printer it was all I remember is that it could sort, staple, and print a packet at the same time.

I do not recall what kind of printer it was**. A**ll I remember is that it could sort, staple, and print a packet at the same time.

CHECKLIST

Use a three-step strategy to correct run-on sentences.

1. Identify the problem.

If you find two main clauses with no punctuation separating them, you have a run-on sentence.

(**bold black** = subject   green type = verb)

Internet businesses are not **bound** to specific locations or old ways of running a business **they** are more flexible in allowing employees to telecommute and to determine the hours they work.

2. Determine where the run-on sentence needs to be divided.

Internet businesses are not bound to specific locations or old ways of running a business they are more flexible in allowing employees to telecommute and to determine the hours they work.

3. Choose the punctuation that indicates the relationship between the main clauses.

- **Insert a period.**

Internet businesses are not bound to specific locations or old ways of running a business. They are more flexible in allowing employees to telecommute and to determine the hours they work.

- **Insert a semicolon (and possibly a transitional word).**

Internet businesses are not bound to specific locations or old ways of running a business; **therefore**, they are more flexible in allowing employees to telecommute and to determine the hours they work.

- **Insert a comma and a coordinating conjunction** (*and, but, or, nor, for, so, yet*).

Internet businesses are not bound to specific locations or old ways of running a business, **so** they are more flexible in allowing employees to telecommute and to determine the hours they work.

Fix comma splices

Comma splices occur when two or more sentences are incorrectly joined by a comma: a comma links two clauses that could stand on their own.

Most of us were taking the same classes, if someone had a question, we would all help out.

Such sentences include a punctuation mark—a comma—separating two main clauses. However, a comma is not a strong enough punctuation mark to separate two main clauses.

CHECKLIST

Fix comma splices by using one of these strategies.

- **Change the comma to a period.**

It didn't matter that I worked in a windowless room for 40 hours a ~~week, on~~ the Web I was exploring and learning more about distant people and places than I ever had before. [CORRECTION: **week. On**]

- **Change the comma to a semicolon.**

A semicolon indicates the close connection between the two main clauses.

It didn't matter that I worked in a windowless room for 40 hours a ~~week,~~ on the Web I was exploring and learning more about distant people and places than I ever had before. [CORRECTION: **week;**]

- **Insert a coordinating conjunction.**

Some comma splices can be repaired by inserting a coordinating conjunction (*and, but, or, nor, so, yet, for*) to indicate the relationship of the two main clauses. The coordinating conjunction must be preceded by a comma.

Digital technologies have intensified a global culture that affects us daily in large and small ways**, yet** their impact remains poorly understood.

- **Make one of the main clauses a subordinate clause.**

~~Community~~ is the vision of a great society trimmed down to the size of a small town, it is a powerful metaphor for real estate developers who sell a mini-utopia along with a house or condo.
[CORRECTION: **Because community**]

- **Make one of the main clauses a phrase.**

Community—**the vision of a great society trimmed down to the size of a small town**—is a powerful metaphor for real estate developers who sell a mini-utopia along with a house or condo.

Make verbs agree with subjects

A verb must match its subject. If the subject is singular (*I, you, he, she,* or *it*), the verb must take a singular form. If the subject is plural (*we, you, they*), the verb must take a plural form. Therefore, verbs are said to *agree in number* with their subjects. This single rule determines subject–verb agreement.

When two subjects are joined by *and*, treat them as a compound (plural) subject.

The teacher and the lawyer are headed west to start a commune.

When two nouns linked by *and* are modified by *every* or *each*, these two nouns are likewise treated as one singular subject.

Each night and day brings no news of you.

An exception to this rule arises when the word *each* follows a compound subject. In these cases, usage varies depending on the number of the direct object.

The army and the navy each have their own air forces.

The owl and the pussycat each has a personal claim to fame.

If a subject is joined by *or, either... or,* or *neither...nor,* make sure the verb agrees with the subject closest to the verb.

Is it **the sky or the mountains** that **are** blue?

Is it **the mountains or the sky** that **surrounds** us?

CHECKLIST

When you check for subject–verb agreement, identify the subject and the verb. Ignore any words that come between them.

INCORRECT

↓ *Ignore this phrase*

Students who live in the residence **gets** to sleep in later than students who live off campus.

CORRECT

Students who live in the residence **get** to sleep in later than students who live off campus.

Students is plural and *get* is plural; subject and verb agree.

INCORRECT

↓ *Ignore this phrase*

The whale shark, the largest of all sharks, **feed** on plankton.

CORRECT

The whale shark, the largest of all sharks, **feeds** on plankton.

The plural noun *sharks* that appears between the subject *the whale shark* and the verb *feeds* does not change the number of the subject. The subject is singular and the verb is singular. Subject and verb agree.

Make pronouns agree

Because pronouns usually replace or refer to other nouns, they must match those nouns in number and gender. The noun that the pronoun replaces is called its **antecedent**. If pronoun and antecedent match, they are in **agreement**. When a pronoun is close to the antecedent, usually there is no problem.

Maria forgot **her** coat.

The band **members** collected **their** uniforms.

Pronoun agreement errors often happen when pronouns and the nouns they replace are separated by several words.

INCORRECT
The players, exhausted from the double-overtime game, picked up **his** sweats and walked toward the locker rooms.

CORRECT
The **players,** exhausted from the double-overtime game, picked up **their** sweats and walked toward the locker rooms.

Careful writers make sure that pronouns match their antecedents.

CHECKLIST

Words that begin with *any, some,* and *every* are usually singular.

INCORRECT
Everybody can choose **their** roommates.

CORRECT
Everybody can choose **his or her** roommate.

Use plural pronouns for antecedents joined by *and.*

CORRECT
Moncef and Driss practised **their** music.

Use singular pronouns for antecedents preceded by *each* or *every.*

CORRECT
Every male cardinal and warbler arrives before the female to define **its** territory.

Use a pronoun that agrees with the nearest antecedent when compound antecedents are joined by *or* or *nor.*

INCORRECT
Either the Ross twins or Angela should bring **their** CDs.

CORRECT
Either the Ross twins or Angela should bring **her** CDs.

BETTER
Either Angela or the Ross twins should bring **their** CDs.

When you put the plural *twins* last, the correct choice becomes the plural pronoun *their.*

Fix shifts

Unintentional shifts in tense, voice, person, or number often distract readers.

Shifts in tense

The shift from present tense (*looks*) to past tense (*relied*) is confusing. Correct the mistake by putting both verbs in the present tense.

INCORRECT

While Brazil **looks** to ecotourism to fund rain forest preservation, other South American nations **relied** on foreign aid.

CORRECT

While Brazil **looks** to ecotourism to fund rain forest preservation, other South American nations **rely** on foreign aid.

Shifts in voice

Watch for unintended shifts from active (*I ate the cookies*) to passive voice (*the cookies were eaten*).

The unexpected shift from active voice (*toppled*) to passive (*were broken*) forces readers to wonder whether it was the sudden storm, or something else, that broke the windows.

INCORRECT

The sudden storm **toppled** several trees and numerous windows **were shattered**.

CORRECT

The sudden storm **toppled** several trees and **shattered** numerous windows.

Shifts in person and number

Sudden shifts from third person (*he, she, it, one*) to first (*I, we*) or second (*you*) are confusing to readers and often indicate a writer's uncertainty about how to address a reader.

INCORRECT

When **one** is reading a magazine, **you** often see several different type fonts used on a single page

CORRECT

When reading a magazine, **you** often see several different type fonts used on a single page.

CHECKLIST

Watch for sudden shifts in tense, voice, person, or number and edit them out of your writing unless you are certain that their purpose is clear and evident to your readers.

Use modifiers correctly

Modifiers come in two varieties: adjectives and adverbs. Adjectives answer the questions *Which one? How many?* and *What kind?* Adverbs answer the questions *How often? To what extent? When? Where? How?* and *Why?*

Comparative modifiers weigh one thing against another. They either end in *er* or are preceded by *more.*

Road bikes are **faster** on pavement than mountain bikes.

The **more courageous** juggler tossed flaming torches.

Superlative modifiers compare three or more items. They either end in *est* or are preceded by *most.*

April is the **hottest** month in New Delhi.

Wounded animals are the **most ferocious.**

Absolute modifiers are words that represent an unvarying condition and thus aren't subject to the degrees that comparative and superlative constructions convey. Common absolute modifiers include *complete, ultimate,* and *unique.* Absolute modifiers should not be modified by comparatives (*more + modifier* or *modifier + er*) or superlatives (*most + modifier* or *modifier + est*).

CHECKLIST

Do not use both a suffix (*er* or *est*) and *more* or *most.*

INCORRECT
The service at Jane's Restaurant is **more slower** than the service at Alphonso's.

CORRECT
The service at Jane's Restaurant is **slower** than the service at Alphonso's.

Be sure to name the elements being compared if they are not clear from the context.

UNCLEAR COMPARATIVE
Mice are **cuter**.

CLEAR
Mice are **cuter than rats.**

UNCLEAR COMPARATIVE
Nutria are the **creepiest.**

CLEAR
Nutria are the **creepiest rodents.**

Place modifiers carefully

Words such as *almost, even, hardly, just, merely, nearly, not, only*, and *simply* are called **limiting modifiers.** Although people often play fast and loose with their placement in everyday speech, limiting modifiers should always go immediately before the word or words they modify in your writing.

Many writers have difficulty with the placement of *only*. Like other limiting modifiers, *only* should be placed immediately before the word it modifies.

The word *only* modifies *one* in this sentence, not *gives*.

INCORRECT
The Gross Domestic Product **only** gives one indicator of economic growth.

CORRECT
The Gross Domestic Product gives **only** one indicator of economic growth.

A **dangling modifier** does not seem to modify anything in a sentence; it dangles, unconnected to the word or words it presumably is intended to modify.

When still a girl, my father joined the army.

It sounds like *father* was once a girl. The problem is that the subject, *I*, is missing.

When I was still a girl, my father joined the army.

Dangling modifiers usually occur at the head of a sentence when a subject is implied but never stated.

INCORRECT
After lifting the heavy piano up the stairs, the apartment door was too small to get it through.

CORRECT
After lifting the heavy piano up the stairs, **we discovered** the apartment door was too small to get it through.

CHECKLIST

- Place limiting modifiers immediately before the word(s) they modify.
- Modifiers should be clearly connected to the words they modify, especially at the beginning of sentences.

Summary for editing for errors

Fix fragments
- Incorporate the fragment into an adjoining sentence.
- Add the missing element.

Fix run-on sentences
1. Identify the problem. If you find two main clauses with no punctuation separating them, you have a run-on sentence.
2. Determine where the run-on sentence needs to be divided.
3. Choose the punctuation that indicates the relationship between the main clauses.

Fix comma splices
- Change the comma to a period.
- Change the comma to a semicolon.
- Insert a coordinating conjunction.
- Make one of the main clauses a subordinate clause.
- Make one of the main clauses a phrase.

Make verbs agree with subjects
When you check for subject–verb agreement, identify the subject and the verb. Ignore any words that come between them.

Make pronouns agree
- Words that begin with *any, some*, and *every* are usually singular.
- Use plural pronouns for antecedents joined by *and*.
- Use singular pronouns for antecedents preceded by *each* or *every*.
- Use a pronoun that agrees with the nearest antecedent when compound antecedents are joined by *or* or *nor*.

Fix shifts
Watch for sudden shifts in tense, voice, person, or number and edit them out of your writing unless you are certain that their purpose is clear and evident to your readers.

Use modifiers correctly
- Do not use both a suffix (*er* or *est*) and *more* or *most*.
- Be sure to name the elements being compared if they are not clear from the context.

Place modifiers carefully
- Place limiting modifiers immediately before the word(s) they modify.
- Modifiers should be clearly connected to the words they modify, especially at the beginning of sentences.

25

Understanding Punctuation and Conventions

Punctuation and other conventions give readers vital clues about how to read. They tell readers when to pause and how ideas relate to each other.

Identify where commas are needed

Use commas with introductory words and phrases

Introductory words like *also, however, instead, likewise, therefore,* and *thus* are conjunctive adverbs. Conjunctive adverbs and introductory phrases that signal a shift in ideas usually need to be set off by commas.

Commas allow the reader to pause and take notice of these pivotal elements.

Therefore, Graceland will remain open despite rumours of Lisa putting it up for sale.

Above all, remember to order your Pearl Jam tickets as soon as they go on sale.

When a conjunctive adverb comes in the middle of a sentence, set it off with commas before and after.

If you really want great seats, however, plan to get in line with your sleeping bag a day early.

Occasionally the conjunctive adverb or phrase blends into a sentence so smoothly that a pause would sound awkward.

AWKWARD

Even though Pearl Jam began a gruelling concert tour of twenty countries on four continents in November 2005, they play each show as if it was their last, nevertheless.

BETTER

Even though Pearl Jam began a gruelling concert tour of twenty countries on four continents in November 2005, they play each show as if it was their last nevertheless.

Use commas to separate main clauses joined by a conjunction

Main clauses carry enough grammatical weight to be punctuated as sentences. When two main clauses are joined by a coordinating conjunction (*and, but, or, yet, so, for*), place a comma before the coordinating conjunction in order to distinguish them.

Sandy borrowed my iPod on Tuesday, and she returned it on Friday.

CHECKLIST

Place commas after introductory elements and between main clauses joined by *and, but, or, yet, so* and *for*.

Also, Tori Amos covered Neil Young's "Heart of Gold," and Oasis sang Young's "Hey Hey, My My."

Place commas correctly with modifiers

Use commas with free modifiers

Free or nonrestrictive modifiers add information without changing the meaning of the base sentence. You can identify free modifiers by deleting the modifier and then deciding if the remaining sentence has changed.

For example, delete *a Canadian rock band from Kingston, Ontario* in this sentence.

The Tragically Hip, a Canadian rock band from Kingston, Ontario, has received many honours and awards.

The result leaves the meaning of the base sentence unchanged. Thus, the modifier should be set off with commas.

The Tragically Hip has received many honours and awards.

Use commas with coordinate adjectives

Coordinate adjectives modifiy the same noun independently and require a comma.

Coldplay is an introspective, alternative band from London, England.

Use commas with items in a series

In a series of three or more items, place a comma after each item except the last one.

Ellen DeGeneres has succeeded as a stand-up comedian, a television and film actress, a producer, a television host, and an author.

CHECKLIST

Use commas with free modifiers, coordinate adjectives, and items in a series.

Innovative, outspoken rapper Kanye West, who attended Chicago State University, uses production techniques of sped-up samples, string compositions, and layered sounds.

Place commas correctly with clauses and phrases

Use commas after introductory clauses and long introductory phrases

Introductory clauses and long introductory modifiers should be followed by a comma.

Because Ang Lee's first Hollywood films were not as successful at the box office as his earlier Chinese-language films, he went to China to direct *Crouching Tiger, Hidden Dragon*.

After directing the award-winning and commercially successful *Crouching Tiger, Hidden Dragon,* Ang Lee won the Academy Award for Best Director for *Brokeback Mountain*.

Avoid unnecessary commas

Do not use a comma to separate two verbs with the same subject.

Ang Lee completed his mandatory military service in Taiwan and went to the U.S. to study theatre at the University of Illinois at Urbana-Champaign.

Do not use a comma before a list.

Ang Lee's films have some common themes such as the interaction of tradition and modernity, deep secrets that come to the surface, and internal torment.

Do not use a comma before *because* and similar subordinate conjunctions (*although, if, since, unless, until, when, where, while*) that follow the main clause.

Many viewers in China objected to *Crouching Tiger, Hidden Dragon* because some actors spoke Mandarin with unfamiliar accents.

CHECKLIST

Use a comma after an introductory clause or a long introductory phrase but not to set off a *because* clause at the end.

Although *Crouching Tiger, Hidden Dragon* became a surprise hit throughout the world, it was not as popular in China because the audience was saturated with martial arts films.

Use semicolons and colons correctly

Use semicolons with closely related ideas

Deepa Mehta is an Indian-born Canadian screenwriter and director; she is known for addressing elements of the Indian community in her films.

Use semicolons with conjunctive adverbs that join main clauses

Deepa Mehta's *Water* faced much hostility and protest from some members of the Hindu community; nevertheless, the film was nominated for many awards.

Use colons to link a main clause that expands another main clause

Colons, like semicolons, join closely related ideas. A colon signals that the second idea expands the first one.

Deepa Mehta is most renowned for her trilogy of the elements: *Water* was the third and final installment of the series.

Use colons correctly with lists

Colons are used correctly to introduce lists only when a complete sentence is before the colon.

INCORRECT
The three films in Mehta's elemental series are: *Fire, Earth,* and *Water.*
BETTER
There are three films in Mehta's elemental series: *Fire, Earth,* and *Water.*

Use colons correctly with quotations

Colons are used correctly to introduce quotations only when a complete sentence is before the colon.

Despite all the upset around the film *Water,* Deepa Mehta kept a positive view: "All these were hard blows. But as they say, all's well that ends well."

CHECKLIST

Pay close attention to semicolons and colons that join main clauses.

This sentence pattern is frequently used; therefore, it pays to learn how to punctuate it correctly.

Use hyphens, dashes, and parentheses correctly

When to hyphenate

Hyphenate a compound modifier that precedes a noun.	middle-class values	self-fulfilling prophecy
Hyphenate a phrase when it is used as a modifier that precedes a noun.	out-of-body experience	step-by-step instructions
Hyphenate the prefixes *pro-*, *anti-*, *post-*, *pre-*, *neo-*, and *mid-* before capitalized nouns.	mid-Atlantic states	pre-Columbian art
Hyphenate a compound modifier with a number when it precedes a noun.	eighteenth-century drama	tenth-grade class

Use dashes and parentheses to set off additional information

Joni Mitchell's third album featured "Woodstock"—a song that helped increase her fame. "Woodstock" (a song about the legendary festival) has been covered by many artists.

Don't use dashes as periods

INCORRECT
Avril Lavigne's debut album reached number one in Canada, Australia, and the United Kingdom—this is an achievement that she was fortunate enough to experience as the youngest female soloist yet in the United Kingdom.

BETTER
Avril Lavigne's debut album reached number one in Canada, Australia, and the United Kingdom—an achievement that she was fortunate enough to experience as the youngest female soloist yet in the United Kingdom.

CHECKLIST

Know the difference in how hyphens and dashes are used, and don't use dashes as periods.
The Dixie Chicks—an all-female country music trio—gained large-scale popularity when Natalie Maines (a native of Lubbock, Texas) joined the group.

Use quotation marks correctly

Use quotation marks with direct quotations

Put other people's verbatim words inside quotation marks and cite the source.

Quotations of more than four lines are blocked and do not require quotation marks (see page 527).	Julius Henry Marx, known to the world as Groucho, never used profanity in a performance but got his laughs instead from one-liners like "I was married by a judge; I should have asked for a jury" (Kanfer 45).
Use single quotation marks for quotations within quotations	Groucho recalled his early years in comedy: "Because we were a kid act, we travelled at half-fare, despite the fact that we were all around twenty. Minnie insisted we were thirteen. 'That kid of yours is in the dining car smoking a cigar,' the conductor told her. 'And another one is in the washroom shaving.'" "Minnie shook her head sadly. 'They grow so fast.'"
Use quotation marks with periods, commas, and question marks inside them Place periods and commas inside closing quotation marks. Place question marks inside unless the entire sentence is a question.	"Those are my principles," Groucho announced. "If you don't like them, I have others." "Why should I care about posterity? What's posterity ever done for me?" is a typical Groucho quip.
Place the titles of essays, short stories, short poems, articles, and other short works inside quotation marks	**"Light Is like Water,"** by Gabriel Garcia Márquez

CHECKLIST

Check that all direct quotations are within quotations marks and that periods and commas are inside the closing quotation mark.

One of Groucho's most famous lines, "I never forget a face, but in your case I'll make an exception," actually was delivered by his brother Chico in *Duck Soup*.

Use other punctuation correctly

Use periods with abbreviations

Many abbreviations require periods; however, there are few set rules. Use the dictionary to check how to punctuate abbreviations on a case-by-case basis. The rules for punctuating two types of abbreviations do remain consistent: postal abbreviations for provinces and most abbreviations for organizations do not require periods. When an abbreviation with a period falls at the end of a sentence, do not add a second period to conclude the sentence.

Use question marks with direct questions

A direct question is one that the questioner puts to someone outright. In contrast, an indirect question merely reports the asking of a question.

INDIRECT QUESTION
Desirée asked whether Dan rides his motorcycle without a helmet.

DIRECT QUESTION
Desirée asked, "Does Dan ride his motorcycle without a helmet?"

Use exclamation points to convey strong emotion

Exclamation points conclude sentences and, like question marks, tell the reader how a sentence should sound. Use exclamation points sparingly in formal writing; they are rarely appropriate in academic and professional prose.

Use exclamation points correctly with quotation marks

In quotations, exclamation points follow the same rules as question marks. If a quotation falls at the end of an exclamatory statement, place the exclamation point outside the closing quotation mark.

The singer forgot the words to "O Canada"!

Use ellipses to indicate an omission from a quotation

When you quote only a phrase or short clause from a sentence, you usually do not need to use ellipses. When you omit words from the middle of a passage from a source, use an ellipsis.

"The female praying mantis . . . tears off her male partner's head during mating."

CHECKLIST

Check all periods, question marks, exclamation points, and ellipses.
When asked in 1975 if he had seen any recent movies, Groucho replied, "*Jaws* . . . would have been funnier if a guppy had swallowed the boat instead of the shark!"

Understand print conventions

Capitalize the initial letters of proper nouns (nouns that name particular people, places, and things)

Do not capitalize the names of seasons, academic disciplines (unless they are languages), or job titles used without a proper noun.

African-**A**merican bookstore

Avogadro's number

Irish music

Italicize the titles of entire works (books, magazines, newspapers, films)

Also italicize the names of ships and aircraft.

I am fond of reading ***The Globe and Mail*** in the morning.

Italicize unfamiliar foreign words

Italicize foreign words that are not part of common English usage. How do you decide which words are common? If a word appears in a standard English dictionary, it can be considered as adopted into English.

Abbreviate titles before and degrees after full names

Ms. Ella Fitzgerald

San-qí Li, **MD**

Use conventions for using abbreviations with years and times

BCE (before the common era) and CE (common era) are now preferred for indicating years, replacing BC (before Christ) and AD (*anno Domini* ["the year of our Lord"]). Note that all are now used without periods.

479 **BCE** (or **BC**)

The preferred written conventions for times are a.m. (*ante meridiem*) and p.m. (*post meridiem*).

9:03 **a.m.**   3:30 **p.m.**

Use conventions for using abbreviations in college and university writing

Most abbreviations are inappropriate in formal writing except when the reader would be more familiar with the abbreviation than with the words it represents. When your reader is unlikely to be familiar with an abbreviation, spell out the term the first time you use it in a paper, followed by the abbreviation in parentheses.

The Royal Canadian Mounted Police (RCMP) is the national police service of Canada.

Spell out any number that can be expressed in one or two words

Hyphenate two-word numbers from twenty-one to ninety-nine. In scientific reports and some business writing that requires the frequent use of numbers, using numerals more often is appropriate. Most styles do not write out in words a year, a date, an address, a page number, the time of day, decimals, sums of money, phone numbers, rates of speed, or the scene and act of a play. Use numerals instead.

> In 2001 only 33% of respondents said they were satisfied with the City Council's proposals to help the homeless.

CHECKLIST

Check all capitalization, italics, abbreviations, and numbers.

In 1970 *Let It Be* had the largest initial sales in U.S. record history up to that time with 3.7 million advance orders.

Summary for punctuation and conventions

Commas	• Place commas after introductory elements and between main clauses joined by *and, but, or, nor, yet, so*, and *for*. • Use commas with nonrestrictive modifiers, coordinate adjectives, and items in a series. • Use a comma after an introductory clause or a long introductory phrase but not to set off a *because* clause at the end.
Semicolons and colons	• Pay close attention to semicolons and colons that join main clauses.
Hyphens, dashes, and parentheses	• Know the difference in how hyphens and dashes are used, and don't use dashes as periods.
Quotation marks	• Check that all direct quotations are within quotations marks and that periods and commas are inside the closing quotation mark.
Other punctuation	• Check all periods, question marks, exclamation points, and ellipses.
Print conventions	• Check all capitalization, italics, abbreviations, and numbers.

Appendix A: Delivering Presentations

The best speakers draw their inspiration from their audience, and they maintain contact with their audience, communicating with body language and presentation style in addition to the content. Audience members leave feeling like they've had a conversation with the speaker even if they have been silent through the presentation.

Plan a presentation

A successful presentation, like successful writing, requires careful planning. Look closely at what you are being asked to present and how long you will have. Decide early on what kind of presentation you will give and what visuals you will incorporate.

Select your topic

Choosing and researching a topic for a presentation is similar to choosing and researching a topic for a written assignment. Ask these questions:

- Will you enjoy speaking on this topic?
- Does the topic fit the assignment?
- Do you know enough to speak on this topic?
- If you do not know enough, are you willing to do research to learn more about the topic?

Remember that if your presentation requires you to do any research, then you will need to develop a written bibliography as you would for a research assignment. You will need to document the sources of your information and provide those sources in your presentation.

Think about your audience

Unlike writing, when you give a speech you have your audience directly before you. They will give you concrete feedback during your presentation by smiling or frowning, by paying attention or losing interest, by asking questions or sitting passively. Ask these questions:

- Will your audience likely be interested in your topic?
- Are there ways you can get them more interested?
- What is your audience likely to know or believe about your topic?
- What does your audience probably not know about your topic?
- What key terms will you have to define or explain?
- Where is your audience most likely to disagree with you?
- What questions are they likely to ask?

Organize your presentation

Make a list of your key points	Think of the best way to order your key points.
Plan your introduction	You have to get the audience's attention, introduce your topic, convince the audience that it is important to them, present your thesis, and give your audience either an overview of your presentation or a sense of your direction.
Plan your conclusion	End on a strong note. Simply summarizing is a dull way to close. Think of an example or an idea that your audience can take away with them.

Design effective visuals

Visual elements can both support and reinforce your major points. They give you another means of reaching your audience and keeping them stimulated. Visuals should communicate content and not just be eye candy. Some of the easier visuals to create are outlines, statistical charts, flow charts, photographs, and maps.

At a minimum, consider putting an outline of your talk on a transparency or on a PowerPoint slide. An outline allows an audience to keep track of where you are in your talk and when you are moving to your next point.

Create visuals

Follow these guidelines to create better visuals.

Keep the text short	You don't want your audience straining to read long passages on the screen and neglecting what you have to say. Except for quotations, use short words and phrases on transparencies and slides.
Always proofread	Typos and misspelled words make you look careless and can distract the audience from your point.
Use dark text on a white or light-coloured background	Light text on a dark background is hard to read.
Use graphics that reproduce well	Some graphics do not show up well on the screen, often because there isn't enough contrast.
Plan your timing when using visuals	Usually you can leave a slide on the screen for one to two minutes, which allows your audience time to read the slide and connect its points to what you are saying.

Know the advantages and disadvantages of presentation software

Presentation software allows you to combine text, images, sounds, animations, and even video clips on *computer-generated* slides, which can be projected onto a large screen. Presentation software, such as Microsoft PowerPoint, allows you to import charts and other graphics that you have created in other programs, and it gives you several options for presentation, including printed handouts and Web pages.

The major drawback of presentation software is perhaps that it is too easy to use. An attractive presentation can be empty of content. You can quickly get carried away with all the special effects possible—such as fade-ins, fade-outs, and sound effects. Presentations with many special effects often come off as heavy on style and light on substance. They also can be time-consuming to produce.

Give a memorable presentation

What makes an effective presentation?

Usually more effective	Usually less effective
Talk	Read
Stand	Sit
Make eye contact	Look down
Move around	Stand still
Speak loudly	Mumble
Use visual elements	Lack visual elements
Focus on main points	Get lost in details
Give an overview of what you are going to say in the introduction	Start your talk without indicating where you are headed
Give a conclusion that summarizes your main points and ends with a key idea or example	Stop abruptly
Finish on time	Run overtime

Appendix B: Working as a Team

Much writing in the workplace and in organizations—especially important writing tasks like reports, analyses, and proposals—is done by teams of people. The better you understand how to write effectively with others, the more enjoyable and more productive the process will be for you.

Organize a team

Unlike sports teams where a coach is in charge, writing team members often have to organize themselves.

Analyze the assignment	• Identify what exactly you are being asked to do. • Write down the goals as specifically as you can and discuss them as a team. • Determine which tasks are required to meet those goals. Be as detailed as you can. Write down the tasks and arrange them in the order they need to be completed.
Make a work plan	• Make a time line. List the dates when specific tasks need to be completed and distribute it to all team members. Charts are useful tools for keeping track of progress. • Assign tasks to all team members. Find out if anyone possesses additional skills that could be helpful to the team.
Keep goals in mind	• Revisit the team's goals often. To succeed, each team member must keep in mind what the team aims to accomplish. • Communicate often. Most writing teams will not have an assigned leader. Each team member shares responsibility.

What makes a good team?

In sports, in the workplace, and in everyday life, successful teams have well-defined goals and work together to achieve these goals. Successful teams communicate well, make good decisions together, act quickly on their decisions, and continuously evaluate their progress. Successful teams achieve the right balance so that each team member can contribute.

Understand the team process

Analyze
Take time to analyze the writing assignment with your team members. Discuss the goals of the assignment as a group.

Question
Ask as many questions as you can think of about the assignment and about how the team will work together.

Listen
Listen carefully to each team member's ideas and how they can contribute to achieving the goals.

Decide
Write down the team's goals. Make a work plan that lists dates when each task needs to be completed. Assign tasks to team members.

Create
Work closely together in creating content. It's more fun to work with other people, and you'll have help when you get stuck.

Evaluate
Evaluate often if you are meeting the goals on your time line. If something isn't getting done, find out why. When you complete a draft, each member of the team should evaluate it.

Revise
Compare your evaluations and decide as a group what revisions and additions need to be made. Decide who will revise each section.

Review
Arrange for one or more people outside your group to review your work. Meet to decide what additional changes need to be made in light of the external review.

Work as a team

Work closely together in creating and revising content. You'll enjoy writing more and you'll have the benefit of more ideas.

Carry out the plan

- Decide on a process for monitoring progress. Set up specific dates for review and assign team members to be responsible for reviewing work that has been done.
- When you have a complete draft, each team member should evaluate it by providing written comments.
- Meet to compare evaluations and decide on a plan for revising and adding content.
- After revising, arrange for one or more people to review the project. Meet again to determine if additional changes are needed.

Be aware of team dynamics

Teamwork requires some flexibility. Different people have different styles and contribute in different ways. Keep talking to each other along the way.

- Deal with problems when they come up.
- If a team member is not participating, find out why.
- If team members have different ideas about what needs to be done, find time to meet so that the team can reach an agreement.
- Get the team together if you are not meeting the deadlines you established in the work plan and, if necessary, devise a new plan.

Appendix C: Creating Portfolios

Your instructor may ask you to submit a portfolio of written work for part of your grade. Some schools also require a writing portfolio in the third or fourth year. A portfolio includes a range of documents, giving readers a broader, more detailed picture of your writing than a single document could.

Portfolios have different purposes and different requirements. For some portfolios, you might assemble a notebook of printed writing, while for others you might submit documents online into an electronic portfolio system. For any kind of portfolio, your goal is to provide tangible evidence of your learning. You may be asked to submit earlier drafts of your submitted papers and projects to show the revisions you made to them. Your instructor should give you instructions about the purpose of your portfolio, what it should contain, and how you should arrange and submit it.

Types of portfolios

What you choose to include will depend on your portfolio guidelines. Here are some common portfolio types, their purposes, and documents they might contain.

Developmental

A developmental writing portfolio demonstrates a writer's developing skills over a given period of time—perhaps a semester, a year, or several years. Developmental portfolios may focus on skills like critical thinking, research, argument, style, collaboration, and mechanical competence. A developmental portfolio will usually include examples of revised work, providing evidence to readers that you have learned to evaluate and improve your own work. Often, writing in a developmental portfolio ranges from simple, short pieces to longer, more complex work. Your selections may demonstrate how you built upon or combined earlier ideas to produce a more substantial project.

Disciplinary

A disciplinary or professional writing portfolio demonstrates the writer's mastery of important writing forms in a field or discipline. An engineering writing portfolio might include examples of a survey, an accident report, an email to clients, a competitive bid, and similar documents. A business writing portfolio might include examples of a complaint resolution letter, an interoffice memo, a prospectus, an executive summary, and a PowerPoint presentation. A portfolio for a creative writing class might include examples of different genres, such as personal essays, short fiction, poetry, drama, and criticism.

Like a developmental portfolio, a disciplinary portfolio may also reflect how your knowledge about a subject progressed over a period of time. To show how you learned, you might provide examples of informal writing where you wrestle with new concepts; short papers where you research, expand, or connect your growing knowledge; and drafts or sections of longer analytical papers that demonstrate how you have learned to manipulate complex ideas.

Stylistic

Some portfolios are used to give readers a sense of the various styles and genres a writer can employ. Such a portfolio might include humorous writing, formal oratory, descriptive writing, and other types of writing that aim to produce different effects for the reader.

The reflective letter or summary

Usually, a portfolio includes a reflective letter, a summary statement, or some other written document in which you provide an overview of the material and your experience in the course. You may be asked to explain why you chose the pieces you did, or to discuss what you feel you have accomplished. The reflective letter is your opportunity to frame the different documents in the portfolio and explain how they add up to a single, comprehensive picture of your performance as a writer.

The letter does not simply make a claim that you performed well; it tracks your experience in the course, using the writing samples as a step-by-step guide to your learning. You will get the most out of your reflective letter if you perform an honest, impartial examination of your challenges, setbacks, and successes in the course.

Sample portfolio

Here is a sample portfolio assignment for a rhetoric class, including the Table of Contents and reflective letter submitted by Grace Bernhardt.

End of Semester Portfolio Requirements
Rhetoric 309: 20th Century Rhetoric—Professor Morrison

Your grade for the semester will be based upon a portfolio of your writing, chosen by you, and submitted the final week of class. I will meet individually with each of you at least twice during the semester to talk about your portfolios and answer any questions you have about them. I will also make periodic suggestions about work that you should include in your portfolio.

I will evaluate your portfolio for evidence of the following:

- Awareness of rhetorical terms and techniques.
- Comprehension of the ways rhetoric was used in the 20th century, and ability to discuss individual examples.
- A growing ability to use and to discuss the use of rhetorical techniques in your own writing and in that of your peers.
- Steady improvement in the power and readability of your own prose, including mechanical facility and vocabulary.

Of course, I do not expect you to know all the course material the minute you walk through the door. Nor do I expect you to be a perfect writer on the first day of class. That is what this class is for: to teach you about rhetoric and to help you improve your writing. Therefore, your portfolio should demonstrate to me how you have approached each element of the class—the readings, the class discussions, the writing process, and the research—and what you have learned from it. You should begin your portfolio with a reflective letter that sums up your experience in the class. In particular, I am interested in how the class experience might be useful to you in the future.

Please follow the letter with a list of your portfolio contents. Arrange your materials in whatever order you like, and place them in a three-ring binder with your name on the outside. The portfolio is due at the beginning of class on Monday, May 1.

Grace Bernhardt's reflective letter:

Dear Professor Morrison,

I learned a great deal about writing, speaking, and thinking this semester. When I first started this class I had only done freewriting in a creative writing workshop. The exercises we did almost every day showed me how writing can get me started thinking and can help get me out of feeling stuck when I am not sure where to go next. I have included two examples of my freewriting from the beginning and the end of semester so you can see how much more useful they became to me.

I also learned how to take criticism. I was proud of my first draft of the paper on Tommy Douglas, and was shocked to get it back with many comments and suggestions from you. But when I sat down and read your comments, I realized how much better the paper could be. Your help, along with our peer review and a session with a consultant in the writing centre, helped me improve the paper. The experience taught me that I can improve any paper and that I should always try to do so. My final research paper is probably the best writing I've done so far in my life, but I hope to get even better.

I discovered how helpful my peers could be to my learning. Writing peer reviews taught me how to look closely at someone else's words and consider how they could be stronger. The discussions were the best part of class, and it was on the online class discussion forum that I worked out the focus for my final research project. I have included a transcript of this forum discussion.

The research we did for our final project was difficult and time consuming, but I learned much about the resources in our library. You can see from my annotated bibliography that I finally figured out the difference between primary and secondary sources!

Finally, this class taught me so much about history and the power of words. I feel like I know more about why North America is the way it is. I am considering majoring in Radio, Television, and Film, and this class helped me understand the impact of words on audiences.

Thanks for a great class!
Sincerely,
Grace Bernhardt

Portfolio Contents

1. First informal writing assignment: What do I know about rhetoric?

2. Last informal writing assignment: What would you do with your final research project if you had another semester to work on it?

3. First draft (with instructor comments): Selling Health: An Analysis of Tommy Douglas's Speech "The Future of Medicare"

4. Peer review of Selling Medicare

5. Final draft of Selling Medicare

6. Peer review for Kevin Gi

7. Discussion forum transcript: "Special Elements of Oratory"

8. Proposal and annotated bibliography for final research paper

9. Final draft of research paper: "Powerful Speeches That Changed Canadian History"

Image Credits

Page 2–3: © Philippe Renault/Hemis/Corbis; **3 (left):** © North Wind Picture Archives/Alamy; **3 (right):** © Megapress/Alamy; **4 (left):** Toronto Star/GetStock.com; **4 (bottom right):** CP PHOTO/Steve White; **5 (centre):** © Dorling Kindersley; **10 (bottom):** Used with permission of Google Inc.; **23:** © John T. Fowler/Alamy; **34:** © Witold Skrypczak/GetStock.com; **38 (top left):** © Arcticphoto/Alamy; **38 (top right):** Darwin Wiggett/AllCanadaPhotos.com; **38 (centre):** CP Photo/Andrew Vaughan; **38 (bottom):** Rolf Hicker/AllCanadaPhotos.com; **41 (all photos):** Paul Bolland; **42 (bottom left):** © Kevin Ebi/Alamy; **42 (bottom right):** CP PHOTO/Jonathan Hayward; **44 (bottom):** © Dorling Kindersley; **54:** © Janine Wiedel Photography/Alamy; **81–85 (all photos):** Material reprinted with the express permission of: "Windsor Star Group Inc.", a CanWest Partnership; **120:** CP PHOTO/Fred Chartrand; **121 (top):** © Philip Scalia/Alamy; **157 (left):** Jupiter Unlimited; **174:** Shutterstock; **197 (left):** © Mika/Corbis; **237 and 286:** AP Images; **253 (top):** Hoffmann/Getty Images; **253 (bottom left):** Gaslight Ad Archives; **253 (bottom right):** Volkswagen AG; **254 (top left):** PhotoFest; **254 (bottom):** © 2006 Volkswagen of America, Inc.; **255:** Keith Beford/Reuters/Corbis; **346 (left):** Toronto Star/GetStock.com; **353:** David Byrne; **356:** Inge Druckrey; **388 (main):** CP PHOTO/The Halifax Chronicle-Herald - Ingrid Bulmer; **388 (inlay):** CP PHOTO/Peterborough Examiner - Clifford Skarstedt; **389 (centre):** CP PHOTO/Toronto Sun - Dave Abel; **389 (bottom):** © IFAW International Fund for Animal Welfare/P. Doyle; **432:** Don Denton; **433:** CP PHOTO/Ian Barrett; **437 (top):** Licensed under Health Canada copyright; **461 (top):** Janni Chavakis/Zefa/Corbis; **461 (bottom):** Tim Pannell/Corbis; **464 (left):** Ausloeser/Zefa/Corbis; **464 (right):** © Royalty Free/Corbis; **465 (left):** © Royalty Free/ Corbis; **502–503:** © Dorling Kindersley; **506:** Getty Images; **532:** Getty Images; **535:** JLP/Deimos/Zefa/Corbis; **563:** Getty Images; **590–591:** Sean Burges/Mundo Sport Images; **592:** CP PHOTO/Robert Dall; **594:** Geoff Robins/Mundo Sport Images; **596:** Sean Burges/Mundo Sport Images; **602:** Sean Burges/Mundo Sport Images; **611:** Sean Burges/Mundo Sport Images.

Unless otherwise credited, all photos © Lester Faigley Photos.

Text Credits

Page 10: Screenshot © 2010 Google; **59 (left):** Chung, Amy. "'Coming Out' not easy for gay kids; Religious and cultural values cause fear, anger - and backlash," *Toronto Sun*, June 25, 2008:10; **59 (right):** Courtesy of www.sexetc.org; **74–78:** "A Homeless Past Stirs Pain" copyright © 2009 by Evelyn Lau. First published in *Canada by the Georgia Straight* on February 19, 2009. Reprinted by permission of the author; **81–85:** Material reprinted with the express permission of: "Windsor Star Group Inc.", a CanWest Partnership; **86–90:** Jamaica Kincaid. "A Small Place." From *A Small Place.* Copyright © 1988 by Jamaica Kincaid. Reprinted by permission of Farrar, Straus and Giroux, LLC; **92–99:** Tom Meagher and Suzanne Travers. "Low Wages, Strong Backs." As published in the *Herald News*, October 16, 2005. Copyright © 2005. Reprinted by permission of the North Jersey Media Group; **124–135:** Courtesy of Eva Kende; **138–139:** Courtesy Canadian Healthcare Association; **140–146:** Pam Houston. "A Blizzard Under Blue Sky." From *Cowboys Are My Weakness.* Copyright © 1992 by Pam Houston. Used by permission of W.W. Norton & Company, Inc.; **147–149:** David Sedaris. "Let it Snow." From *Dress Your Family in Corduroy and Denim.* Copyright © 2004 by David Sedaris. By permission of Little, Brown and Co., Inc.; **150–155:** Material reprinted with the express permission of: "Windsor Star Group Inc.", a CanWest Partnership; **179–182:** Joseph Berger & Andrew Parkin, The Price of Knowledge: Access and Student Finance in Canada, in Part III, Chapter 1; **185–187:** Lynn Greiner, Hacking Social Networks, *netWorker*, Volume 13, Issue 1, March 2009; **188–190:** *Sustainability within a Generation: A New Vision for Canada*, David R. Bold, David Suzuki Foundation; **192–195:** © Heike Verster/Ocean Sounds; **234–238:** Tim Collins. "Straight from the Heart." From *The Guardian*, July 13, 2005. Copyright Guardian Newspapers Limited 2005. Reprinted by permission; **241–245:** "Dude, where's my job?" By Lianne George. *Maclean's*, January 19, 2009; **247–249:** Reproduced with permission of author Zebedee Nungak; **256–263:** Alice Walker. "Everyday Use." From *In Love & Trouble: Stories of Black Women*, copyright © 1973 and renewed 2001 by Alice Walker, reprinted by permission of Harcourt, Inc.; **294–297:** Stentor Danielson. "Pesticides, Parasite May Cause Frog Deformities." From *National Geographic News*, July 9, 2002. Copyright © 2002. Reprinted by permission of The National Geographic Society; **300–301:** Canadian women on their own are the poorest of the poor by Monica Townson, Canadian Centre for Policy Alternatives, www.policyalternatives.ca; **303–307:** Jay Walljasper. "If You Build It They Will Come—On Foot." First published in the *New Statesman* on August 15, 2005. Copyright © 2005. Reprinted by permission; **308–316:** Emily Raine. "Why Should I Be Nice to You? Coffee Shops and the Politics of Good Service." From *Bad Subjects*, issue 74, December 2005. Copyright © 2005. Reprinted by permission of the author; **318–319:** Catherine Pratt, www.Life-with-Confidence.com; **347–350:** Courtesy Bob Kull; **356–358:** Edward Tufte. "PowerPoint is Evil." Reprinted by permission from Edward R. Tufte, *The Cognitive Style of PowerPoint* (Chesire, Connecticut, Graphics Press, 2003), as appeared in *Wired* magazine, September 2003; **360–361:** "Junk food that's good for you?" by Cathy Gulli. Macleans.ca, May 15, 2009; **363–365:** Stephanie Rosenbloom. "The Nitpicking Nation." From *The New York Times*, May 7, 2006. Copyright © 2006 by The New York Times Co. Reprinted with permission; **394–396:** "Enhanced Driver's Licenses too Smart for Their Own Good" by Roch Tassé and Stuart Trew; **399–401:** Michel Marriot. "The Color of Mayhem." From *The New York Times*, August 12, 2004. Copyright © 2004 by The New York Times Co. Reprinted by permission; **403–404:** Courtesy Norm Bolen, President and CEO, CFTPA; **406–407:** "The Death of English (LOL)" by Lily Huang. *Newsweek*, August 2, 2008; **438–446:** The Universal Declaration of Human Rights. © United Nations 2010. Reproduced with permission; **449–451:** Paul Saffo. "A Trail of DNA and Data." From the *Washington Post*, April 3, 2005. Copyright © 2005 by Paul Saffo. Reprinted by permission of the author; **453–455:** Canadian Federation of Students; **457–459:** Courtesy of NEDIC; **460–463:** Nancy Clark. "Mirror, Mirror on the Wall, Are Muscular Men the Best of All?" From *American Fitness*, Jan/Feb 2004. Copyright © 2004 American Fitness. Reprinted by permission; **480–485:** Courtesy of Tanvir Taghezidian; **491:** YAHOO! Inc.

Index

A